America at Century's End

America at Century's End

—

EDITED BY

Alan Wolfe

UNIVERSITY OF CALIFORNIA PRESS
Berkeley   Los Angeles   Oxford

University of California Press
Berkeley and Los Angeles, California
University of California Press, Ltd.
Oxford, England
© 1991 by
The Regents of the University of California

Library of Congress Cataloging-in-Publication Data

America at century's end / edited by Alan Wolfe.
  p.   cm.
  Includes bibliographical references and index.
  ISBN 0-520-07476-9 (cloth)
  1. United States—Social conditions—1980–   2. Social change.
  3. Social institutions—United States.   4. Social problems.
  I. Wolfe, Alan, 1942–
  HN52.2.A44   1991
  306'.0973—dc20   91-14455
                                                          CIP

Printed in the United States of America

1 2 3 4 5 6 7 8 9

CONTENTS

v

PART V · EMERGING AMERICA

ACKNOWLEDGMENTS

Although he may not know it, Ulf Himmelstrand is responsible for this book. When I was in Scandinavia doing research for *Whose Keeper?* Ulf invited me to be a consultant on a project he was conducting at the University of Uppsala on changes in Swedish life. His notion of asking a number of leading Swedish sociologists to write chapters on different aspects of everyday life struck me as a wonderful way to try to come to grips with social change. (The book was eventually published as *Sverige— Vardag och Struktur: Sociologer Beskriver det Svenska Samhallet,* or *Sweden— Everyday Life and Structure: Sociologists Describe Swedish Society,* edited by Ulf Himmelstrand and Goran Svensson and published by Norstedt's in 1988). I immediately saw the idea for an American book.

When I described Ulf's project to Naomi Schneider at the University of California Press, her first reaction was that they were unlikely to publish a book on Sweden. "No," I said, "I mean a book on America." Naomi was quickly taken by the idea and has been an enthusiastic supporter ever since. She has also been a first-rate editor. I am delighted to acknowledge my gratitude to her.

It was Katherine Newman who first suggested that Herb Gans would be delighted to know about this book and could be encouraged to write a preface. My thanks to her for the suggestion and to Herb for carrying it out. And, it goes without saying, I am grateful to all those who contributed chapters to the book, for, in nearly all cases, they not only wrote what I had hoped they would but they also read the work of others, provided suggestions, and participated actively in shaping the final form of the book. Even while recognizing how inappropriate it is to single one of them out for special mention, I feel I must acknowledge Judith Stacey's wise help as consultant and sounding-board.

The contributors to the volume met twice while the project was underway, once on the West Coast and once on the East Coast. I was fortunate enough to receive funds from the American Sociological Association/National Science Foundation Fund for the Advancement of the Discipline, funds that were matched by Steven Cahn, Provost of the City University of New York Graduate Center. I am grateful to both for their help in strengthening this volume. Thanks also to Dan Poor, who demonstrated superb administrative and intellectual skills in numerous ways. Jonathan Imber generously helped with the proofreading, as did Autumn Ward, Susan Guglielmetti, and Lisbeth Summ. This book was edited during a year in which it was my wife's turn to write a book. I promised her that I would refrain from writing to give her more time. (I said nothing about editing.) I want to thank her for her encouragement and support during a time when she was wrestling with conundrums of her own. And the kids were terrific.

Alan Wolfe
New York, August 1990

PREFACE

Although I have not contributed a chapter to this book, I have been involved in it nearly from the start, albeit marginally, and am therefore not the stranger who is invited to write the foreword once a book is finished.

I participated in this venture principally because its purpose—to produce an empirically reasonable but also evaluative portrait of some of America toward the end of the twentieth century—is vitally important. No one can picture all of America in a single book, but the editor and the authors have covered an amazingly wide area, from the family, community, and workplace as well as the political, educational, health, leisure and other major institutions central to everyday life, all the way to the world economy—without which neither America's institutions nor everyday life can be understood anymore.

Trying to make sense of America is, and ought to be, a never-ending process, which I think can best be done by sociologists and social or cultural anthropologists, or by like-minded members of other disciplines. Journalists are also trying to make sense of America, to be sure, but unlike sociologists, who look for recurring patterns and their contexts, journalists usually have to focus on the atypical and deviant. For example, as I write this their picture of America stars street-, Wall Street-, and inside-the-Beltway criminals and features the underclass, yuppies, and the allegedly indifferent and confused generation now in its twenties, or what the *Washington Post* has called the "doofus generation."

This book is also important because many of its chapters are based on data gathered with "ethnographic" methods. Once a word used solely by anthropologists to describe their research method for studying small preindustrial cultures, ethnography is now becoming an umbrella term to cover fieldwork, participant-observation, and informal interviewing. To me, it means being with and talking to people, especially those whose activities are not newsworthy, asking them thoughtful and empathic questions, and analyzing the resulting data without the need to prove prior ideological points.

This method, which I consider the most scientific for understanding social life, has been used in sociology nearly since its beginning, but in the last half century or so the discipline has been overwhelmed by quantitative researchers, who rarely talk to people or do so only to count and correlate them. Quantitative sociologists learn something about America, too, but they are forever limited by their methods and the numbers available to them.

The book is noteworthy as well because it is sociology and social anthropology sans jargon, written for the general reader as well as the specialist. It is an example of what sociology should be most of the time (except when it has to be written solely for the specialist), and one way in which sociology can discharge its public responsibilities.

Finally, I think the book is important because it deals not only with America toward the end of the twentieth century but also with social change. As such, it raises or revives some questions about the study of social change that go beyond the book itself, but that make it particularly stimulating reading.

These questions take off from editor Alan Wolfe's description of the authors as a third generation of post–World War II sociologists, and of me, by implication, as a member of the first generation, since I was trained right after the end of that war. However, I studied sociology at the University of Chicago in the late 1940s, when it was the center and virtually the sole practitioner of ethnographic research—and, incidentally, of a reflexive kind that is now, like almost everything else, called postmodern. In addition, the people I worked with, notably David Riesman, Earl Johnson, and Everett Hughes, emphasized the study of institutions. Consequently, I am not very different in background from many of the contributors to this book, except in age, and my questions are therefore mainly temporal.

Since studying a whole society, especially a continent-sized and highly diverse one like America, is immensely difficult, researchers have had to make a number of limiting assumptions, one of which is usually chronological. Thus, a number of the chapters of this book make explicit or implicit comparisons of the present with the past—for example, the 1950s and/or the 1960s—and for some authors some aspects of these periods are treated as good old days.[1]

This is a perfectly reasonable way of studying social change, but one question it raises is why sociologists are joining journalists in looking at social change by decades, even though decades do not seem to make major differences in how institutions work or people behave. (The exceptions are institutions and organizations which operate on the basis of fiscal years, and some of their activities are affected, among other things, by the frequent need to spend all budgeted money quickly at the end of a fiscal year.) This question is especially relevant now that the end of a millennium is near, when all kinds of people will make all kinds of observations, most of them likely to be proven wrong, about the changes that will take place because an old millennium is ending and a new one is beginning. Still, whether and how perceptions of the new millennium will affect social life is a relevant research topic when the time comes, and therefore a possible chapter topic for a future edition of this book.

Whether the past was better than the present has always been a fascinating issue, because all periods are good old days for some but not for others, which evokes the question of which past periods are good for whom and why. We all remember specific social and economic phenomena that were central to our lives, and while most white Americans may remember the 1950s as what is now described as the era of postwar affluence, poor whites, blacks, and other racial minorities surely feel differently.[2]

Obviously, even nonpoor whites will not be unanimous about the 1950s, if only because different populations have different collective memories of every decade, assuming they can structure their memory by decades. I wonder for whom the 1950s were dominated by dark days, and assume that the victims of the McCarthy witchhunts and the Korean War were in that category.[3] Many sociologists of my age are also apt to remember the 1950s as a time when there were virtually no jobs in sociology, and when sociology was still regularly being confused with social work and socialism. In any case, what people, even sociologists, remember from the past, is a social construction of the present, which must be studied alongside that present.

Another question the book raises for me has to do with the speed of change. While comparisons with the past make the present, and change sui generis, come alive in print, in the so-called real world of the people whom sociologists study, change is often gradual. In fact, most people are less likely to see change than the consequences, good or bad, of change: not when the family is changing but when parental rules of family life are no longer obeyed by the young. Even sociologists do not always see change as easily as they write about it. Many new social phenomena have to grow for a while before they become sufficiently widespread and anchored to become visible—and to be trusted as raw material for generalizations about change.

Furthermore, reading these chapters made me wonder whether the age of the researcher could affect how he or she constructs descriptions of various social changes. Perhaps some of the changes emphasized in this book that look new today to young researchers look more venerable to older ones. For example, the corporate speculation and greed that marked the 1980s may look very different to a young researcher than say, to a very old one who recalls the speculation and scandals that preceded the Great Depression in the late 1920s, or to a historian specializing in the late nineteenth century, when the original robber barons still stalked the earth. Likewise, the negative political advertising in recent elections appears fairly tame (although still abhorrent) to this writer, who grew up in Chicago in the 1940s when the Democratic machine of Edward Kelly (and later Richard Daley) used dirty tricks which no politician today could get away with. But those political tricks were tame when compared with some of the negative political advertising in nineteenth-century America.

Curiously enough, in some respects the greatest changes since the 1950s, and earlier, have taken place in America's self-knowledge—thanks to the increase in the number of years of schooling, the expansion of feature and analytic journalism, the growth of interest in history and even the more modest growth of sociology. (For example, in 1955, the American Sociological Association had 4450 members, virtually all invisible to the general public, whereas in 1990 it had nearly 13,000.)

As a result, the sociologists who wrote this book know far more about America's institutions and America than my colleagues and I did in the 1950s. Consequently, I wonder whether contemporary sociologists—of any era—see their era's complexity and assume the past to have been simpler and more integrated, without taking into account that what is known about the past—any past—is always simpler than what is known about the present.

This leads also to the questions Alan Wolfe raises in the last chapter about today's lack of integration and consensus, which he calls decentering, as well as the search for various kinds of recentering. These questions are significant in part because they address old issues about the need for community in new ways and from a different angle. So far, however, not much research has been done to determine how much of what kinds of integration or consensus people want and how much they and society need to function. Furthermore, politicians and other organizational leaders often call for integration and consensus but do so largely to create or obtain support for their own policies.

I think, for example, that the White House has worked hard for a number of years and over several administrations at its own kind of recentering project: to become the country's symbolic center and power center, although whether it has succeeded is worth debating. Whether it should succeed is even more important to debate, however.

Indeed, I am nervous about the general notion of society having a center, whether that center is conceptual, symbolic, or instrumental. Even if the sole purpose of the center is to help social integration, a societal center of any kind, and perhaps the metaphor itself, always seems to carry with it inegalitarian consequences for those who are not at, or associated with, the center. Whether the center is the carrier and protector of the society's dominant values, or of its sacred symbols and institutions, or of the economic core, those at the periphery are usually treated as being of a lower status or otherwise inferior. Consequently, I would suggest that, paraphrasing Bertolt Brecht, blessed is the society that needs no center!

Herbert J. Gans
Columbia University

INTRODUCTION

Change from the Bottom Up

Alan Wolfe

CONSERVATIVE POLITICS, UNSTABLE SOCIETY

Someone who visited the United States in the first decade after World War II and then came back in the last decade of the twentieth century would have seen two entirely different countries.[1] From the relations between husbands and wives and parents and children, to patterns of home ownership and living space, to the relative power of the two political parties, to the role of the United States in the international economic and political order, to the racial and ethnic composition of the population, to the ways in which people understand such social institutions as schools, churches, and medical offices—the texture of American life bears little resemblance to the way things once existed, at least in the American imagination. No wonder so many Americans, politicians as well as ordinary citizens, seem bewildered by what is emerging around them.

The transition to a new century marks the culmination of a major generational shift in the American social, economic, and political landscape. To the degree that any order can be imposed on a society as diverse as that of the United States, there did emerge, after the twin traumas of the Great Depression and World War II, patterns of social life that many would, with some mistaken nostalgia, later come to call "normal." It was assumed that economic growth and moderate government intervention led by centrists of both parties would ensure enough stability in the political economy to make possible generalized home ownership, moves to the suburbs, secure futures for offspring, intergenerational upward mobility, and global peace guaranteed by American military strength. Obviously there were dissenters, first on the right during the McCarthy period, and later, in the 1960s, on the left. Ultimately, moreover, the dissenters would make their critiques stick, and both political parties would be reshaped by them. Nonetheless a significant number of Americans came to believe that the America of the late

1

1950s and early 1960s was the "real" America, a feeling that surely contributed to the election to the presidency of someone whose television
and movie career had helped to define the culture of that earlier era.

The election of conservative presidents, however, is a symptom of,
not a solution to, radical change in the society. Despite efforts to punish
flag-burning, to go back to basics in education, or to reverse gains won by
racial minorities, a world in which people "know their place" simply cannot be brought back into existence. The twenty-five-year period between
the end of World War II and the end of the 1960s will surely come to be
viewed by future historians as the exception, not the rule. An affluent
society in which families were supported by the husband's income and in
which ever-increasing economic growth seemed to offer the solution to
any problems—private or public, domestic or foreign—that might appear, no longer accords with reality, no matter how many people wish it
would. Conservatism is helpless in the face of that fact, not only because
talk of order at the top is a frustrated reaction to disorder at the bottom,
but also because the particular conservatism that came to power in America in the 1980s was also powered by a vision of change. There is no party
of order in America.

Although politicians like to give the impression that they are in control of events, it seems clear that events are in control of them. No one
planned an outcome in which children born in the 1970s would face a
radically different set of life choices than those born in the 1950s. That
contemporary family life would take on a completely different colora-
tion from what some had proclaimed as the "natural" nuclear family of
the 1950 television sit-com was as much a surprise as the decline of
American power in the world, let alone the arrival on these shores of a
new generation of immigrants from parts of the world that Americans—
never the strongest in geography—had previously known little about.
The changes that have affected the United States over the past four decades are taking place behind our backs, appearing with their results already in place before we even have a chance to register that something
has been going on. Because the reshaping of the contours of American
life is not the product of any particular political agenda, or even the result of any social planner's vision, its consequences are that much more
likely to be unsettling.

Caught between expectations formed in an earlier period and the realities of new political and economic forces, Americans are unsure how
to respond, sometimes giving vent to populist anger, sometimes retreat-
ing into private life, at still other times voting for the most conservative
candidates they can find. It is time to begin to take stock of what has been
happening in this country since the days when people thought they
knew what was normal. This book is an effort to do so, not so much by

focusing on the changes at the top, but by trying to understand them as the product of forces unleashed at the bottom. Every contributor to this book save one is a sociologist, and the one who is not is a social anthropologist. The assumption that guides our efforts is that changes of great magnitude and rapidity can only be grasped by understanding how those affected by such changes perceive them. The authors were charged to go out and listen. The chapters that follow are their reports of what they heard.

SEVENTEEN CHANGES IN AMERICAN LIFE

Before turning to concrete studies of how people understand their families, communities, jobs, and social institutions in a time of transition, it is worthwhile to try to set the scene by cataloging the changes that have made American society so unsettled. There are, after all, large forces at work, and their impact on people's lives will be significant. Any attempt to catalog such forces is bound to be somewhat selective; here, nonetheless, is mine.

1. Population shifts have produced a new demographic profile of the country. Newer regions of the United States, such as the South and West, have achieved economic and political prominence over the older cities of the Eastern Seaboard and Midwest. (Some Brooklynites know exactly the day when America changed for good—and for the worst.) Moreover immigration, especially from Latin America and Asia, has also changed the literal image of what it means to be an American.[2] Since Washington's Farewell Address, Americans have always been somewhat reluctant to engage themselves in the affairs of the world. Now the world, perhaps tired of waiting, has decided to engage itself in the affairs of the United States.

2. Concomitant with demographic changes are political ones. The New Deal coalition, linking working-class and ethnic votes in the North with the solid South, can no longer automatically win presidential elections.[3] Yet the fact that the presidency has been dominated by Republicans, while Congress has remained under control of the Democrats, suggests that there is no one political mood in the country at all but rather many moods, often contradictory, and in any case localized and privatized. Indeed, the important point may be that it is not the content of politics that has shifted so rapidly, but more the form, as expensive campaigns, media simplifications, and "sound bite" politics dominate the campaign strategies of both parties.[4]

3. No longer are the fundamental values and culture of the society shaped by a Yankee consciousness inherited from Great Britain. A book like *The Lonely Crowd,* with its Weber-inspired discussion of inner-

directedness, might as well have been written about a foreign country. A Protestant ethic stressing thrift, honesty, hard work, sacrifice, and community service has less currency for a country that, with each passing year, is decreasingly Protestant. While some segments of America have become "more" religious, as witnessed by the rise of fundamentalism in many forms, others have become "less" so that preachers, academics, and others charge that hedonistic utilitarianism has become America's only compelling source of ethical values.[5] Morality in America has more to do with the subcommunities to which one belongs than to the national community to which all belong.

4. Both upward and downward mobility seem to have increased, at least in the consciousness of most Americans. On the one hand, energy crises and inflation have raised the specter of a world without endless growth, transforming middle-classness from a "natural" condition to a matter of positional struggle.[6] Downward mobility, moreover, has even begun to reach into the heights of the upper middle class, and, as it does, basic assumptions about progress and the good life are undergoing significant alteration.[7] Yet even as they face the prospect that their children might not achieve the same level in life as they did, Americans also are treated to stories of exceptionally rapid upward mobility, as new capitalists, many from "marginal" ethnic backgrounds, assume prominent places in the American consciousness. A once-existing link between status and wealth seems broken: there are as many who have the latter without the former as there are who have the former without the latter.

5. Conditions at work have been almost completely transformed. In part this is due to radical changes in the nature of American industrial relations, such as the decline of large manufacturing firms, the reorganization of industries, and the rise of such financing techniques as leveraged buy-outs.[8] For the average American worker, especially the unionized worker, the resulting changes are dramatic. The stereotypical situation twenty-five years ago was one in which trade-union-conscious men left each morning for high-paying factory jobs while their wives stayed home and raised the children. Now the men no longer belong to a union, no longer work in factories, and no longer receive high pay, while their wives, who also work (probably in the service sector), earn enough to bring the family income barely up to what it was, in real dollars, a quarter century ago. (America's "working man" is no longer necessarily a man.) When union density was high, worker solidarity strong (or at least stronger than now), and competition held at bay through monopolies and protectionism, the world of work could to some degree be shielded from the rest of society.[9] Now, for more and more Americans, everything about work is negotiated constantly—between husbands and wives and between employees and employers.

6. The reality of two-career families has changed both family ideology and family practice since the 1950s.[10] What Arlie Hochschild has called "the second shift" alters everyday life, as women come home from work only to go to work.[11] Child care arrangements all but inconceivable a generation ago are being invented from scratch, for not only are mothers working but grandparents have moved away and extended kin networks are harder to maintain given geographic mobility and higher housing prices.[12] Women and men have been forced to negotiate their ways around these changes, discovering for themselves patterns that work rather than following textbook formulas that explain what the family is (or ought to be). For some writers such changes signify family decline, while for others they represent new possibilities for the empowerment of women.[13] It is, however, clear from both that if there is a postmodern family, it is something to which we are moving back, something from a period before the one in which the "natural" nuclear family was constructed.

7. Children have become contested terrain as well. On the one hand, as part of the nostalgia characteristic of the 1980s, we seem to want to reassert the innocence of childhood.[14] On the other hand, as phenomena from illegal drugs to quite legal commercials make clear, we deprive children of the time to just be children. Meanwhile, young people themselves go their own way, as, of course, they always have, developing their own subcultures, markets, institutions, and rituals.[15] Americans have long thought of themselves as a child-oriented culture, but hair-raising stories of latchkey kids, sexual abuse, poor schools, and a failure to recognize the need for adequate child care have forced a reevaluation. Nonetheless, at least at the level of public policy, Americans seem surprised that new generations of children somehow keep making their appearance in the world.

8. Housing for most families has also changed radically. There may have been no more important piece of domestic legislation in postwar America than the Housing Act of 1949, which symbolically linked home ownership with democratic ideology. Now there are more renters, more homeless, more foreclosures, more young people unable to accumulate a down payment, and more speculative profits for some. No one knows what the future implications of these changes will be; markets have their downswings as well as their upswings, and a very recent crisis in real estate has begun to make homes affordable once more. Yet a house in America has never been merely an investment but, instead, the center of a richly textured symbolic world.[16] Even "affordable" houses take so much of the typical young family's income that the home can no longer be viewed as a protection against the market, but has come to symbolize one's largest investment in the market.

9. Housing is just one factor in a transformation of the American economy and its relationship to the world economy. Most Americans now understand that these two economies are no longer synonymous, which forces them to confront unprecedented questions, such as whether local communities should welcome foreign investment, put controls on growth, or attempt to regulate the quality of life in their regions. When American-based corporations are multinational while foreign-based corporations create jobs for Americans, whose economic success should Americans be cheering? The experience of the state of New Jersey—which, in its efforts to supply its troopers with cars made in America, had to reject Fords only to accept Volkswagens—will become increasingly common. Just as Europe is increasingly being integrated economically and politically, the United States may be breaking into two economies: one inward looking and protectionist, the other global and expansionist. It is a sign of the times that neither political party can tell which economy is preferable.

10. Americans are in a postimperial mood, without ever quite having admitted to themselves that they have given up the empire.[17] The collapse of communism, America's ideological enemy in the postwar years, coming alongside a major weakening of the Eastern bloc, America's geopolitical enemy during the same period, was not enough to arouse an American president to eloquence or even the American people to a greater concern with the rest of the world. All this changed, and rather dramatically, with the American victory over Iraq in 1991, yet the consequences over the long run may not be that great. To be sure the victory over Iraq was in part the result of stunning diplomacy, especially the ability to keep the allied forces together despite repeated attempts to split them. And it clearly represented an overcoming of the "Vietnam syndrome," putting to rest the notion that Americans had become reluctant to use military power. In the short run, the war in the Middle East would seem to suggest a turn back toward globalism. Yet the very success of the Bush administration in Iraq may also wind up contributing to an American withdrawal from the world. The war in some ways solidified the uniquely American belief that it is possible to obtain diplomatic objectives through violence without substantial loss of life. The brilliance of the diplomacy was matched by a lack of political objectives, not only for the Middle East but also for America's role in the post–Cold War world. As America approaches century's end, there is a clear sense that a new world order is necessary, but the fact that the first step in the new world order was the deployment of massive firepower reminiscent of the old world order does not suggest new breakthroughs. Whatever else happens in world politics—a topic far too broad to be broached here—there is little question that, despite the victory in Iraq, Americans will be living with foreign policy uncertainty for some time.

11. It is possible to debate whether Americans have or have not withdrawn their attention from the world, but on the question of whether they have withdrawn their attention from social problems at home, there can be no dispute: they have. The notion that a national problem can be identified, that funds can be mobilized to address it, and that a solution for the problem would be available—the atmosphere characteristic of the Kennedy-Johnson years—no longer exists in American domestic life. This change is deeper than a shift from reform to conservatism, from Democrats to Republicans. It represents a retreat from a spirit of can-do optimism that has characterized American life since the early nineteenth century. On the one hand, crack cocaine, AIDS, and homelessness seem to present problems of such depth and social cost as to be beyond anything ever experienced in American memory. On the other hand, the willingness to tackle such problems—indeed, any problems—is hamstrung by a reluctance to raise taxes that would make policies possible. To the degree that these concerns overlap with race, and they do in public perception, if not always in reality, they point to a mood that has emerged among some Americans that raises questions about whether racial harmony is possible in the United States at all, and, consequently, whether it remains possible to speak of one American experience.[18] In such areas as schooling, residence, and opportunity, the realities facing racial minorities are so different from those facing middle-class whites as to make progress toward equality seem all but inconceivable.

12. It is often the case that social change and technological change do *not* necessarily reinforce each other. The "traditional" American family and suburban home, for example, were reinforced at a time when quite untraditional new technologies, such as television and modern appliances, were altering how Americans used their time.[19] But in the past decade, social changes have been accompanied by very noticeable technological changes, each strengthening the other.[20] As a result of computer technology, for example, working at home is made possible by the modem and the fax machine. Cottage industries are therefore returning, as highway congestion makes going to work increasingly unthinkable. Flexible working patterns, in turn, will have consequences for families and communities. Between them, new technologies and new patterns of allocating time will combine to change how people work, how they spend their leisure time, and how they travel from one to the other.

13. In the absence of traditional understandings of community, Americans are creating new experiments with subcommunities. The elderly, living longer than ever before, symbolize this development, concentrating, if they have the means, in specific regions and supporting specific industries that cater to their needs.[21] But retirement communities are only one example of the general trend: urban gentrification, increasing segregation by class, and the development of "high-tech" subecono-

mies—Silicon Valley and all its spin-offs—all represent living patterns that come closer to Durkheim's definition of traditional society based on likeness than toward his understanding of modern society based on a complex division of labor. The protection of the local environment against change is the theme of political and social movements often characterized as NIMBY ("not in my backyard") groups. Some new communities regulate the architectural details of the homes within them down to the color and shape of doors. Other communities have become adept at protesting the encroachment of undesirable change. The tremendous diversity of America at the national level, it would seem, is being matched by an emphasis, often futile, on homogeneity at the local level.

14. In part because they live and act in new ways, Americans are no longer sure how to represent reality to themselves, let alone to others. For the first time in our history, the media have become nationalized, creating the possibility of a richer national community. But with the success of chain bookstores, national newspapers, and twenty-four-hour-a-day cable news has also come a "thinning" of the reality that is represented, as if Americans had more and more information and less and less understanding. The general pattern seems to be one characterized by an explosion of the outlets that make communication possible combined with an increasing inability to find much that is original and interesting to communicate. One can now watch the same news program anywhere in the United States—indeed, anywhere in the world—and yet still not have the context and historical understanding to make sense of the events being reported.

15. How Americans understand their relationships to each other has been changing as well. Although they like to think of themselves as neighborly, Americans increasingly resort to ways of resolving their disputes with each other that are more formal than a chat over a fence. The increasing litigiousness of American society, the new role of insurance companies as makers of public policy, the formalization of trust, the increasing use of binding arbitration, the rise (and now fall) of an interventionist judiciary, the increasing privatization of government services all represent steps away from *Gemeinschaft* to *Gesellschaft*. Yet it would be foolish to lament these changes: Even as they wax nostalgic for a world they believe to be lost, Americans take steps to ensure their rights, realize their self-interests, and protect themselves against what they perceive to be the intrusive claims of community. The net result is a change in the texture of everyday life, one bound to be felt at places as diverse as the physician's waiting room, the court room, the local prison, and the suburban shopping mall.

16. No one, in a sense, seems to obey the rules any more. This is not meant to be part of a conservative lament that always accompanies social

change, bemoaning the fact that people no longer know their place, but instead as a reflection of the fact that new issues have arisen for which traditional rules can no longer guide conduct: surrogate mothering, computer hacking, organ transplants, the prolongation of life, corporate crime, abortion, and AIDS are only some of the examples. It is as if the United States is caught between two moral codes, one of which no longer applies and the other of which has not yet been developed.

17. Although they are not among the most important of American institutions, the social sciences have also been caught up in transformations that question their very existence. There are prominent exceptions—I hope this book demonstrates that—but most work in social science seems increasingly unable to deal with changing economic, social, and political realities. The premise that the social sciences could be modeled on the value-free nature of the physical sciences has been undermined by an epistemological revolution in the "hard" sciences themselves. No longer is it possible to believe in the liberal optimism that led social scientists to accumulate inventories of findings about human behavior, in the belief that this would make for a better society. Yet unsure of how to respond to its own crisis of meaning, the social sciences either retreat into an ever-greater empiricism or develop models of rational choice or refinements of structuralism that explain everything except how real people act. The crisis of meaning in American society exists as well among those who make the study of meaning their business.

We are, it seems, no longer the society we once were, but neither are we the society we had hoped to be. As we approach century's end, something new is emerging, helter-skelter, in our midst that bears little resemblance to any existing political, theological, or sociological model of how the world is supposed to work. These emerging patterns may constitute the prelude to a new order that we will eventually come to view as normal or it may be a period of disorder that will usher in ever greater disorder; at this point, no one knows. But if we cannot know where these changes will take us, we can at least take pictures of American life in transition. Sociology, with its focus on real people living real lives, ought to make it possible to do so.

THE REDISCOVERY OF INSTITUTIONS

The assumption that links the chapters of this book is that a sociological approach to American society offers a way to get a grip on a process that is undergoing rapid change. But what kind of sociological approach should it be? When America was understood to be stable, the sociological study of America was also relatively straightforward. The 1950s were not only self-proclaimed "golden years" for such cherished—if both short-lived and somewhat illusory—institutions as the nuclear family and the well-disciplined school; they were also celebratory years for the social sciences.[22] The notion prevailed that one could start out on a five- or ten-year project to study some American institution with the expectation—all the more powerful because simply assumed rather than examined—that the institution under study would still be much the same when the study was published. In textbooks dealing with American society at that time, chapters seem to write themselves: marriage and the family, religion, voluntary associations, business, the welfare state, and, for the not-so-self-congratulatory, social problems.

At the present time, by contrast, it would be nearly impossible to imagine any one sociologist or journalist capable of analyzing all the many ways in which American society has been transformed. That is why I wanted to edit this book rather than write it myself. To capture the fluidity of American society in recent years, it seemed preferable to have many authors, diverse points of view, multiple methodologies, and tentative conclusions. There was a time when sociologists believed that if we did not know it all, we at least knew most of it. It would hardly do to go to the opposite extreme, as some postmodernists do, and argue that we do not, and cannot, know anything—that there is no reality out there for social science to represent. It is enough to suggest that the realities of American life are far more complex than we once imagined and to be as humble in assuming that we have discovered the truth of those realities as we are aggressive in using our tools to discover what the truth, or truths, may be.

The transformations in American society described in this book, therefore, invoke what could be called a "third generation" of sociologists. The first generation of postwar sociologists, under the influence of Talcott Parsons, tended to stress the stability of American institutions and their contribution to the overall functioning of the society.[23] This relatively complacent view was shaken to pieces during the 1960s when a second generation, the "New Left," made its mark on American sociology. Institutions were then seen as oppressive, their replacement by newer forms necessary as a first step toward greater liberation.[24] The view now emerging demands that we pay attention to and understand the institutions of American society, not because they fulfill some grand design and not because they are inherently oppressive. They are, simply put, understood as interesting, as changing, as constantly running away from the analytic models we develop to understand them.

The third generation of sociologists can be called "the new institutionalists," after the movement in economics of the 1920s and 1930s that wanted to look behind abstractions at the realities of economic activity in the real world. Clearly because of the changes taking place in American society, there seems to be something of a cross-disciplinary *zeitgeist* emphasizing the role of institutions. In political science, Johan Olson and James March have called for an explicit return to the focus on institutions that characterized the study of public administration a generation ago.[25] Economists—who tend, with Jon Elster, to believe that "there are no societies, only individuals who interact with each other"[26]—are less likely to focus on institutions, but even among those most committed to rational-choice assumptions, the role of large organizations such as corporations has come under scrutiny.[27] Even literary criticism, including the deconstruction tendency, has begun to ask questions about institutions and the role they play in interpretation.[28]

Not surprisingly, this concern with institutions has also affected sociology: the study of the welfare state, for example, a traditional sociological concern, is inevitably a preoccupation, not only with government, but with a variety of other social institutions as well.[29] Sociologists, indeed, are increasingly concerning themselves with how institutions actually work, despite how received opinion suggests they do; what impact they have on the people whose lives are affected by them; how they are created and recreated by social practices; what relations exist between them; and whether, how, and why they change.[30] But it is not just through a revival of the sociology of organizations that sociology will come to understand the changing nature of American institutions.[31] It is also by a return to the post–World War II roots of contemporary sociology, to a time when sociologists pooled their efforts to write for a general audience about the relevance of their discipline to the problems of the day.[32] Already efforts are emerging to bring back to sociology its concern with real social issues. Besides the contributors to this book, one can point to a broad group of sociological investigators looking, nontechnically, at the institutions of American society with a curious eye.[33]

What these scholars have in common is not age—though most, but not all, of the contributors to this book were born between 1949 and 1955—but three other commitments. First, neo-institutionalism shows respect for the nitty-gritty empirical realities of social life. All these sociologists are in touch with the lived reality of America. They are neither, to use C. Wright Mills's famous terms, abstract empiricists nor grand theorists. Ethnographic approaches, to be sure, predominate, because ethnography—with its emphasis on understanding how people themselves understand the world around them—is the unique contribution that sociology (and anthropology) can give to the world. But there is an important place for other forms of empirical investigation as well. Much of the new institutional scholarship, for example, is inspired by historical methods, which provide a way to get a grounding in the lived realities of institutions and how they change. Others are not averse to statistics;

good number crunching is often essential to complete a picture of what is going on in the world, as, I hope, some of the essays in this book demonstrate.

Second, each of these writers shows open-mindedness toward political issues. While each of them has taken strong positions on issues involving class, race, and gender, there is a lack of dogmatism of any form in their work, an appreciation of the unexpected. Again, to be sure, this pluralism has its bias: sociologists generally find themselves to the left of, say, nuclear engineers, and this book certainly reflects that trend. But each author was charged to let the data speak. Not all of them found what their political perspectives suggested they ought to find. We sought a combination of commitment and openness rather than dogmatic certainty, apolitical cynicism, and artfully contrived compromises between conflicting positions.

Finally, all of these contributors were selected because they could write. Some write with genuine literary skill and others with marked social science training, but all of them are committed to writing as clearly as possible. We hope to harken back to the days when a career in social science did not necessarily mean that one wrote as many obscure articles in technical journals as possible, but also involved an obligation to comment for general readers on important trends in society. I asked the contributors to think of David Riesman as they wrote, to try and keep alive the spirit—if not always the politics—of C. Wright Mills.[34] The spirit that motivated this book is the sense that the inward turn taken by the social sciences in the 1970s and 1980s was not a permanent development but a moment of introspection preparing the way for a return to larger themes—and larger audiences to read them. Understanding that sociology is not a discipline that stands outside American society looking in, we recognize ourselves to be part of the transformations for which we are trying to account. We hope this sense of involvement gives our chapters less certainty but, because it is tentative, greater authenticity.

FROM THE BOTTOM TO THE TOP

There is no going back—all the authors assembled here would agree. The transformations in American practices and institutions being analyzed in this volume have, as all transformations do, both positive and negative sides, but it seems a fair generalization that our experience with the nuclear family is typical: what has emerged in place of the family of the 1950s is beset with difficulties, but it is clearly preferable to an institution that stifled the human potential of so many women. The same could be said for the schools, for the doctor-patient relationship, the community, and all the rest. In all cases, the transition to newly emerging patterns is rocky, unstable, and fraught with contradiction, yet also exciting for the new possibilities that are opened up. Although no one can know what shape emerging America will ultimately take, it is likely to be different, and for those who find in difference rewards as well as problems—as do most of us writing here—that change alone will be one to welcome.

It was not part of the charge to these authors to outline their own political hopes and policy suggestions (although some of them did so). Their collected observations, however, paint a picture of America that may be helpful to those who think more explicitly about public policy. What we offer is, in the jargon of Washington, D.C., an "outside the Beltway" perspective. There are real people out there in America. They are neither the secular-humanist, pornography-loving decadents imagined by the right-wing fundamentalist nor the deeply reactionary, racist, and ignorant know-nothings that the left invokes to explain the right. They are trying to live as best they can, and any public policy ought to begin with that.

When I first began to practice social science, there was a clear link between what social scientists wrote and what policymakers thought. It was not always a beneficial relationship; the war in Vietnam was intellectually inspired by social scientists, let alone some of the more dubious ideas about poverty and how to fight it. Still, what took place then is preferable, in my opinion, to what takes place now, which is that policy decisions are based on tomorrow's public opinion poll, demands made by this or that interest group, or assessments of how to "win" by playing on emotions and fears—as if the best efforts of social scientists trying to understand the world were of no consequence whatsoever for the country and its future.

My hope is that a chastened social science and a chastened policy elite may someday meet again and learn from each other. I cannot speak for the policy elites. But social scientists have learned a good deal over the past few decades: There is less arrogance and more willingness to listen in what many of them do. If policymakers are going to respond adequately to the transformations America has been experiencing, they ought first to consult, not quick and shallow public opinion polls nor the well-financed views of those with an immediate stake in whatever policy is being debated, but instead those whose lives constitute and are constituted by the policies they make. It is a long way from the "bottom up" to the "top down"—longer than from the "top down" to the "bottom up"—but like many longer journeys, the rewards at the end of the trip are more lasting.

PART ONE

———

Intimacy and Community

ONE

Backward toward
the Postmodern Family
Reflections on Gender, Kinship,
and Class in the Silicon Valley

Judith Stacey

> *The extended family is in our lives again. This should make all the people*
> *happy who were complaining back in the sixties and seventies that the reason*
> *family life was so hard, especially on mothers, was that the nuclear family had*
> *replaced the extended family. . . . Your basic extended family today includes*
> *your ex-husband or -wife, your ex's new mate, your new mate, possibly your new*
> *mate's ex, and any new mate that your new mate's ex has acquired. It consists*
> *entirely of people who are not related by blood, many of whom can't stand each*
> *other. This return of the extended family reminds me of the favorite saying*
> *of my friend's extremely pessimistic mother: Be careful what you wish for,*
> *you might get it.*
> —DELIA EPHRON, *Funny Sauce*

In the summer of 1986 I attended a wedding ceremony in a small pente-costal church in the Silicon Valley. The service celebrated the same "tra-ditional" family patterns and values that two years earlier had inspired a "profamily" movement to assist Ronald Reagan's landslide reelection to the presidency of the United States. At the same time, however, the pas-tor's rhetoric displayed substantial sympathy with feminist criticisms of patriarchal marriage. "A ring is not a shackle, and marriage is not a rela-tionship of domination," he instructed the groom. Moreover, complex patterns of divorce, remarriage, and stepkinship linked the members of the wedding party and their guests—patterns that resembled the New Age extended family satirized by Delia Ephron far more than the "tradi-tional" family that arouses the nostalgic fantasies so widespread among religious and other social critics of contemporary family practices.

This chapter summarizes and excerpts from my ethnographic book *Brave New Families: Stories of Domestic Upheaval in Late Twentieth-Century America* (New York: Basic Books, 1990). For constructive responses to an earlier draft, I am grateful to Alan Wolfe, Aihwa Ong, Ruth Rosen, Evelyn Fox Keller, and Naomi Schneider.

In the final decades before the twenty-first century, passionate con-
tests over changing family life in the United States have polarized vast
numbers of citizens. Outside the Supreme Court of the United States,
righteous, placard-carrying Right-to-Lifers square off against feminists
and civil libertarians demonstrating their anguish over the steady dismantling of women's reproductive freedom. On the same day in July
1989, New York's highest court expanded the legal definition of "family"
in order to extend rent control protection to gay couples and a coalition
of conservative clergymen in San Francisco blocked implementation of
their city's new "domestic partners" ordinance. "It is the totality of the
relationship," proclaimed the New York judge, "as evidenced by the dedication, caring, and self-sacrifice of the parties which should, in the final
analysis, control," the definition of family.[1] But just this concept of family is anathema to "profamily" activists. Declaring that the attempt by the
San Francisco Board of Supervisors to grant legal status to unmarried
heterosexual and homosexual couples "arbitrarily redefined the time-
honored and hallowed nature of the family," the clergymen's petition
was signed by sufficient citizens to force the ordinance into a referendum battle.[2] When the reckoning came in November 1989, the electorate
of the city many consider to be the national capital of family change had
narrowly defeated the domestic partners law. One year later, a similar
referendum won a narrow victory.

Betraying a good deal of conceptual and historical confusion, most
popular, as well as many scholarly, assessments of family change anxiously and misguidedly debate whether or not "the family" will survive
the twentieth century at all.[3] Anxieties like these are far from new. "For
at least 150 years," historian Linda Gordon writes, "there have been periods of fear that 'the family'—meaning a popular image of what families
were supposed to be like, by no means a correct recollection of any actual
'traditional' family—was in decline; and these fears have tended to escalate in periods of social stress."[4] The actual subject of this recurring, fret-
ful discourse is a historically specific form and concept of family life, one
that most historians identify as the "modern family." No doubt, many of
us who write and teach about American family life have not abetted public understanding of family change with our counter-intuitive use of the
concept of the modern family. The "modern family" of sociological theory and historical convention designates a family form no longer prevalent in the United States—an intact nuclear household unit composed of
a male breadwinner, his full-time homemaker wife, and their dependent
children—precisely the form of family life that many mistake for an ancient, essential, and now endangered institution.

The past three decades of postindustrial social transformations in the
United States have rung the historic curtain on the "modern family"

regime. In 1950 three-fifths of American households contained male breadwinners and full-time female homemakers, whether children were present or not.[5] By 1986, in contrast, more than three-fifths of married women with children under the age of eighteen were in the labor force, and only 7 percent of households conformed to the "modern" pattern of breadwinning father, homemaking mother, and one to four children under the age of eighteen.[6] By the middle of the 1970s, moreover, divorce outstripped death as the source of marital dissolutions, generating in its wake a complex array of family arrangements caricatured by Delia Ephron in the epigraph.[7] The diversity of contemporary gender and kinship relationships undermines Tolstoy's famous contrast between happy and unhappy families: even happy families no longer are all alike![8] No longer is there a single culturally dominant family pattern, like the modern one, to which the majority of Americans conform and most of the rest aspire. Instead, Americans today have crafted a multiplicity of family and household arrangements that we inhabit uneasily and reconstitute frequently in response to changing personal and occupational circumstances.

RECOMBINANT FAMILY LIFE

We are living, I believe, through a tumultuous and contested period of family history, a period following that of the modern family order but preceding what, we cannot foretell. Precisely because it is not possible to characterize with a coherent descriptive term the competing sets of family cultures that coexist at present, I identify this family regime as postmodern. I do this, despite my reservations about employing such a controversial and elusive cultural concept, to signal the contested, ambivalent, and undecided character of contemporary gender and kinship arrangements. "What is the post-modern?" Clive Dilnot asks rhetorically in the title of a detailed discussion of literature on postmodern culture, and his answers apply readily to the domain of present family conditions in the United States.[9] The postmodern, Dilnot maintains, "is first, an uncertainty, an insecurity, a doubt." Most of the "post-" words provoke uneasiness because they imply simultaneously "both the end, or at least the radical transformation of, a familiar pattern of activity or group of ideas," and the emergence of "new fields of cultural activity whose contours are still unclear and whose meanings and implications . . . cannot yet be fathomed." The postmodern, moreover, is "characterized by the process of the linking up of areas and the crossing of the boundaries of what are conventionally considered to be disparate realms of practice."[10]

Like postmodern culture, contemporary family arrangements in the United States are diverse, fluid, and unresolved. *The* "postmodern family" is not a new model of family life equivalent to that of the "modern family"; it is not the next stage in an orderly progression of family history, but the stage in that history when the belief in a logical progression of stages breaks down.[11] Rupturing the teleology of modernization narratives that depict an evolutionary history of the family, and incorporating both experimental and nostalgic elements, the postmodern family lurches forward and backward into an uncertain future.

FAMILY REVOLUTIONS AND VANGUARD CLASSES

Two centuries ago leading white middle-class families in the newly united American states spearheaded a family revolution that gradually replaced the diversity and fluidity of the premodern domestic order with a more uniform and hegemonic modern family system.[12] But "modern family" was an oxymoronic label for this peculiar institution, which dispensed modernity to white middle-class men only by withholding it from women. The former could enter the public sphere as breadwinners and citizens because their wives were confined to the newly privatized family realm. Ruled by an increasingly absent patriarchal landlord, the modern middle-class family, a woman's domain, soon was sentimentalized as "traditional."

It took most of the subsequent two centuries for substantial numbers of white working-class men to achieve the rudimentary economic passbook to "modern" family life—a male breadwinner family wage.[13] By the time they had done so, however, a second family revolution was well underway. Once again, middle-class white families appeared to be in the vanguard. This time women like myself were claiming the benefits and burdens of modernity, a status we could achieve only at the expense of the "modern family" itself. Reviving a long-dormant feminist movement, frustrated middle-class homemakers and their more militant daughters subjected modern domesticity to a sustained critique, at times with little sensitivity to the effects that our anti-modern-family ideology might have on women for whom full-time domesticity had rarely been feasible. Thus, feminist family reform came to be regarded widely as a white middle-class agenda, and white working-class families were thought to be its most resistant adversaries.

I shared these presumptions before I conducted fieldwork among families in Santa Clara County, California. My work in the "Silicon Valley" radically altered my understanding of the class basis of the postmodern family revolution. Once a bucolic agribusiness orchard region, during the 1960s and 1970s this county became the global headquarters of the electronics industry, the world's vanguard postindustrial region. While economic restructuring commanded global attention, most outside observers overlooked concurrent gender and family changes that preoccupied many residents. During the late 1970s, before the conservative shift in the national political climate made "feminism" seem a derogatory term, local public officials proudly described San Jose, the county seat, as a feminist capital. The city elected a feminist mayor and hosted the statewide convention of the National Organization for Women (NOW) in 1974. Santa Clara County soon became one of the few counties in the nation to elect a female majority to its board of supervisors. And in 1981, high levels of feminist activism made San Jose the site of the nation's first successful strike for a comparable worth standard of pay for city employees.[14]

During its postindustrial makeover, the Silicon Valley also became a vanguard region for family change, a region whose family and household data represented an exaggeration of national trends. For example, although the national divorce rate doubled after 1960, in Santa Clara County it nearly tripled; "nonfamily households" and single-parent households grew faster than in the nation, and abortion rates were one and one-half the national figures.[15] The high casualty rate for marriages of workaholic engineers was dubbed "the silicon syndrome."[16] Many residents shared an alarmist view of the fate of family life in their locale, captured in the opening lines of an article in a local university magazine: "There is an endangered species in Silicon Valley, one so precious that when it disappears Silicon Valley will die with it. This endangered species is the family. And sometimes it seems as if every institution in this valley—political, corporate, and social—is hellbent on driving it into extinction."[17]

The coincidence of epochal changes in occupational, gender, and family patterns make the Silicon Valley a propitious site for exploring ways in which "ordinary" working people have been remaking their families in the wake of postindustrial and feminist challenges. The Silicon Valley is by no means a typical or "representative" U.S. location, but precisely because national postindustrial work and family transformations were more condensed, rapid, and exaggerated there than elsewhere, they are easier to perceive. In contrast to the vanguard image of the Silicon Valley, most of the popular and scholarly literature about white working-class people portrays them as the most traditional group—indeed, as the last bastion of the modern family. Relatively privileged members of the white working class, especially, are widely regarded as the bulwark of the Reagan revolution and the constituency least sympathetic to feminism and family reforms. Those whose hold on the accoutrements of the American dream is so recent and tenuous, it is thought, have the strongest incentives to defend it.[18]

For nearly three years, therefore, between the summer of 1984 and the spring of 1987, I conducted a commuter fieldwork study of two extended kin networks composed primarily of white working people who had resided in Santa Clara County throughout the period of its startling transformation. My research among them convinced me that white middle-class families are less the innovators than the propagandists and principal beneficiaries of contemporary family change. To illustrate the innovative and courageous character of family reconstitution among pink- and blue-collar people, I present radically condensed stories from my book-length ethnographic treatment of their lives.[19]

REMAKING FAMILY LIFE IN THE SILICON VALLEY

Two challenges to my class and gender prejudices provoked my turn to ethnographic research and my selection of the two kin groups who became its focus. Pamela Gama,* an administrator of social services for women at a Silicon Valley antipoverty agency when I met her in July of 1984, provided the first of these when she challenged my secular feminist preconceptions by "coming out" to me as a recent born-again Christian convert. Pamela was the forty-seven-year-old bride at the Christian wedding ceremony I attended two years later. There she exchanged Christian vows with her second husband, Albert Gama, a construction worker to whom she was already legally wed and with whom she had previously cohabited. Pamela's first marriage (in 1960 to Don Franklin, the father of her three children) lasted fifteen years, spanning the headiest days of Silicon Valley development and the period of Don's successful rise from telephone repairman to electronics packaging engineer.

In contrast, Dotty Lewison, my central contact in the second kin network I came to study, secured that status by challenging my class prejudices. The physical appearance and appurtenances of the worn and modest Lewison abode, Dotty's polyester attire and bawdy speech, her husband's heavily tattooed body, and the demographic and occupational details of her family's history that Dotty supplied satisfied all of my stereotypic notions of an authentic "working-class" family. But the history of feminist activism Dotty recounted proudly, as she unpacked a newly purchased Bible, demonstrated the serious limitations of my tacit understandings. When I met Dotty in October of 1984, she was the veteran of an intact and reformed marriage of thirty years duration to her disabled husband Lou, formerly an electronics maintenance mechanic and supervisor, and also, I would later learn, formerly a wife and child abuser.

Pamela, Dotty, and several of their friends whom I came to know during my study, were members of Betty Friedan's "feminine mystique"

*I employ pseudonyms and change identifying details when describing participants in my study.

generation, but were not members of Friedan's social class. Unlike the more affluent members of Friedan's intended audience, Pam and Dotty were "beneficiaries" of the late, ephemeral achievement of a male family wage and home ownership won by privileged sectors of the working class. This was a pyrrhic victory, as it turned out, that had allowed this population a brief period of access to the modern family system just as it was decomposing. Pam and Dotty, like most white women of their generation, were young when they married in the 1950s and early 1960s. They entered their first marriages with conventional "Parsonsian" gender expectations about family and work "roles." For a significant period of time, they and their husbands conformed, as best they could, to the then culturally prescribed patterns of "instrumental" male breadwinners and "expressive" female homemakers. Assuming primary responsibility for rearing the children they had begun to bear immediately after marriage, Pam and Dotty supported their husbands' successful efforts to progress from working-class to middle- and upper-middle-class careers in the electronics industry. Their experiences with the modern family, however, were always more tenuous and less pure than were those of women to whom, and for whom, Betty Friedan spoke.

Insecurities and inadequacies of their husbands' earnings made itinerant labor force participation by Dotty and Pam necessary and resented by their husbands before feminism made female employment a badge of pride. Dotty alternated frequent childbearing with multiple forays into the labor force in a wide array of low-paying jobs. In fact, Dotty assembled semiconductors before her husband Lou entered the electronics industry, but she did not perceive or desire significant opportunities for her own occupational mobility at that point. Pamela's husband began his career ascent earlier than Dotty's, but Pamela still found his earnings insufficient and his spending habits too profligate to balance the household budget. To make ends meet in their beyond-their-means middle-class life-style without undermining her husband's pride, Pam shared child care and a clandestine housecleaning occupation with her African-American neighbor and friend, Lorraine. Thus Pam and Dotty managed not to suffer the full effects of the "problem without a name" until feminism had begun to name it, and in terms both women found compelling.

In the early 1970s, while their workaholic husbands were increasingly absent from their families, Pam and Dotty joined friends taking reentry courses in local community colleges. There they encountered feminism, and their lives and their modern families were never to be the same. Feminism provided an analysis and rhetoric for their discontent, and it helped each woman develop the self-esteem she needed to exit or reform her unhappy modern marriage. Both women left their husbands, became welfare mothers, and experimented with the single life. Pam obtained a divorce, pursued a college degree, and developed a social service career. Dotty, with lesser educational credentials and employment options, took her husband back, but on her own terms, after his disabling heart attack (and after a lover left her). Disabled Lou ceased his physical abuse and performed most of the housework, while Dotty had control over her time, some of which she devoted to feminist activism in antibattering work.

By the time I met Pamela and Dotty a decade later, at a time when my own feminist-inspired joint household of the prior eight years was failing, national and local feminist ardor had cooled. Pam was then a recent convert to born-again Christianity, receiving Christian marriage counseling to buttress and enhance her second marriage to construction worker Al. Certainly this represented a retreat from feminist family ideology, but, as Pamela gradually taught me, and as Susan Gerard and I have elaborated elsewhere, it was a far less dramatic retreat than I at first imagined.[20] Like other women active in the contemporary evangelical Christian revival, Pam was making creative use of its surprisingly flexible patriarchal ideology to reform her husband in her own image. She judged it "not so bad a deal" to cede Al nominal family headship in exchange for substantive improvements in his conjugal behavior. Indeed, few contemporary feminists would find fault with the Christian marital principles that Al identified to me as his goals: "I just hope that we can come closer together and be more honest with each other. Try to use God as a guideline. The goals are more openness, a closer relationship, be more loving both verbally and physically, have more concern for the other person's feelings." Nor did Pamela's conversion return her to a modern family pattern. Instead she collaborated with her first husband's live-in Jewish lover, Shirley Moskowitz, to build a remarkably harmonious and inclusive divorce-extended kin network whose constituent households swapped resources, labor, and lodgers in response to shifting family circumstances and needs.

Dotty Lewison was also no longer a political activist when we met in 1984. Instead she was supplementing Lou's disability pension with part-time paid work in a small insurance office and pursuing spiritual exploration more overtly postmodern in form than Pam's in a metaphysical Christian church. During the course of my fieldwork, however, an overwhelming series of tragedies claimed the lives of Dotty's husband and two of the Lewisons' five adult children. Dotty successfully contested her negligent son-in-law for custody of her four motherless grandchildren. Struggling to support them, she formed a matrilocal joint household with her only occupationally successful child, Kristina, an electronics drafter-designer and a single mother of one child. While Dotty and Pamela both had moved "part way back" from feminist fervor, at the same time both had migrated ever further away from the (no-longer) modern family.

Between them, Pamela and Dotty had eight children—five daughters and three sons—children of modern families disrupted by postindustrial developments and feminist challenges. All were in their twenties when I met them in 1984 and 1985, members of the quintessential postfeminist generation. Although all five daughters distanced themselves from feminist identity and ideology, all too had semiconsciously incorporated feminist principles into their gender and kin expectations and practices. They took for granted, and at times eschewed, the gains in women's work opportunities, sexual autonomy, and male participation in child-rearing and domestic work for which feminists of their mothers' generation had struggled. Ignorant or disdainful of the political efforts feminists expended to secure such gains, they were instead preoccupied, coping with the expanded opportunities and burdens women now encounter. They came of age at a time when a successful woman was expected to combine marriage to a communicative, egalitarian man with motherhood and an engaging, rewarding career. All but one of these daughters of successful white working-class fathers absorbed these post-feminist expectations, the firstborns most fully. Yet none has found such a pattern attainable. Only Pam's younger daughter, Katie, the original source of the evangelical conversions in her own marriage and her mother's, explicitly rejected such a vision. At fourteen, Katie joined the Christian revival, where, I believe, she found an effective refuge from the disruptions of parental divorce and adolescent drug culture that threatened her more rebellious siblings. Ironically, however, Katie's total involvement in a pentecostal ministry led her to practice the most alternative family arrangement of all. Katie, with her husband and young children, has lived "in community" in various joint households (occasionally interracial households) whose accordion structures and shared child-rearing, ministry labors, and expenses have enabled her to achieve an exceptional degree of sociospatial integration of her family, work, and spiritual life.

At the outset of my fieldwork, none of Pam's or Dotty's daughters inhabited a modern family. However, over the next few years, discouraging experiences with the work available to them led three to retreat from the world of paid work and to attempt a modified version of the modern family strategy their mothers had practiced earlier. All demanded, and two received, substantially greater male involvement in child care and domestic work than had their mothers (or mine) in the prefeminist past. Only one, however, had reasonable prospects of succeeding in her "modern" gender strategy, and these she secured through unacknowledged benefits feminism helped her to enjoy. Dotty's second daughter, Polly, had left the Silicon Valley when the electronics company she worked for opened a branch in a state with lower labor and housing costs. Legalized abortion and liberalized sexual norms for women allowed Polly to experiment sexually and defer marriage and childbearing until she was able to negotiate a marriage whose domestic labor arrangements represented a distinct improvement over that of the prefeminist modern family.

I have less to say, and less confidence in what I do have to say, about postmodern family strategies among the men in Pam's and Dotty's kin groups. Despite my concerted efforts to study gender relationally by defining my study in gender-inclusive terms, the men in the families I studied remained comparatively marginal to my research. In part, this is an unavoidable outcome for any one individual who attempts to study gender in a gendered world. Being a woman inhibited my access to, and likely my empathy with, as full a range of the men's family experiences as that which I enjoyed among their female kin. Still, the relative marginality of men in my research is not due simply to methodological deficiencies. It also accurately reflects their more marginal participation in contemporary family life. Most of the men in Pam's and Dotty's networks narrated gender and kinship stories that were relatively inarticulate and undeveloped, I believe, because they had less experience, investment, and interest in the work of sustaining kin ties.[21]

While economic pressures have always encouraged expansionary kin work among working-class women, these have often weakened men's family ties. Men's muted family voices in my study whisper of a masculinity crisis among blue-collar men. As working-class men's access to breadwinner status recedes, so too does confidence in their masculinity.[22] The decline of the family wage and the escalation of women's involvement in paid work seems to generate profound ambivalence about the eroding breadwinner ethic. Pam's and Dotty's male kin appeared uncertain as to whether a man who provides sole support to his family is a hero or a chump. Two of these men avoided domestic commitments entirely, while several embraced them wholeheartedly. Two vacillated between romantic engagements and the unencumbered single life. Too many of the men I met expressed their masculinity in antisocial, self-destructive, and violent forms.

Women strive, meanwhile, as they always have, to buttress and reform their male kin. Responding to the extraordinary diffusion of feminist ideology as well as to sheer overwork, working-class women, like middle-class women, have struggled to transfer some of their domestic burdens to men. My fieldwork leads me to believe that they have achieved more success in the daily trenches than much of the research on the "politics of housework" yet indicates—more success, I suspect, than have most middle-class women.[23] While only a few of the women in my study expected or desired men to perform an equal share of housework and child care, none was willing to exempt men from domestic labor. Almost all of the men I observed or heard about routinely performed domestic tasks that my own blue-collar father and his friends never deigned to contemplate. Some did so with reluctance and resentment, but most did so willingly. Although the division of household labor remains profoundly inequitable, I am convinced that a major gender norm has shifted here.[24]

FAREWELL TO ARCHIE BUNKER

If this chapter serves no other purpose, I hope it will shatter the image of the white working class as the last repository of old-fashioned "modern" American family life. The postmodern family arrangements I found among blue-collar people in the Silicon Valley are at least as diverse and innovative as those found within the middle class. Pundits of postmodern family arrangements, like Delia Ephron, satirize the hostility and competition of the contemporary divorce-extended family. But working women like Pamela and Dotty have found ways to transform divorce from a rupture into a kinship resource, and they are not unique. A recent study of middle-class divorced couples and their parents in the suburbs of San Francisco found one-third sustaining kinship ties with former spouses and their relatives.[25] It seems likely that cooperative ex familial relationships are even more prevalent among lower-income groups, where divorce rates are higher and where women have far greater experience with, and need for, sustaining cooperative kin ties.[26]

Certainly, the dismantling of welfare state protections and the reprivatizing policies of the Reagan-Bush era have given lower-income women renewed incentives to continue their traditions of active, expansionary kin work. The accordion households and kin ties crafted by Dotty Lewison, by Katie's Christian ministry, and by Pam and Shirley draw more on the "domestic network" traditions of poor, urban African-Americans described by Carole Stack and on the matrifocal strategies of poor and working-class whites than they do on family reform innovations by the white middle class.[27] Ironically, sociologists are now identifying as a new middle-class "social problem," those "crowded," rather than empty, nests filled with "incompletely launched young adults," long familiar to the less privileged, like the Lewisons.[28] Postindustrial conditions have reversed the supply-side, "trickle-down" trajectory of family change predicted by modernization theorists. The diversity and complexity of postmodern family patterns rivals that characteristic of premodern kinship forms.[29]

One glimpses the ironies of class and gender history here. For decades industrial unions struggled heroically for a socially recognized male breadwinner wage that would allow the working class to participate in the modern gender order. These struggles, however, contributed to the cheapening of female labor that helped gradually to undermine the modern family regime.[30] Then escalating consumption standards, the expansion of mass collegiate coeducation, and the persistence of high divorce rates gave more and more women ample cause to invest a portion of their identities in the "instrumental" sphere of paid labor.[31] Thus middle-class women began to abandon their confinement in the modern family just as working-class women were approaching its access ramps. The former did so, however, only after the wives of working-class men had pioneered the twentieth-century revolution in women's paid work. Entering employment in mid-life during the catastrophic 1930s, participating in defense industries in the 1940s, and raising their family incomes to middle-class standards by returning to the labor force soon after child-rearing in the 1950s, wives of working-class men quietly modeled and normalized the postmodern family standard of employment for married mothers. Whereas in 1950 the less a man earned, the more likely his wife was employed, by 1968 wives of middle-income men were the most likely to be in the labor force.[32]

African-American women and white working-class women have been the genuine postmodern family pioneers, even though they also suffer most from its most negative effects. Long denied the mixed benefits that the modern family order offered middle-class women, less privileged women quietly forged alternative models of femininity to that of full-time domesticity and mother-intensive childrearing. Struggling creatively, often heroically, to sustain oppressed families and to escape the most oppressive ones, they drew on "traditional," premodern kinship resources and crafted untraditional ones, creating in the process the postmodern family.

Rising divorce and cohabitation rates, working mothers, two-earner households, single and unwed parenthood, and matrilineal, extended, and fictive kin support networks appeared earlier and more extensively among poor and working-class people.[33] Economic pressures, more than political principles, governed these departures from domesticity, but working women soon found additional reasons to appreciate paid employment.[34] Eventually white middle-class women, sated and even sickened by our modern family privileges, began to emulate, elaborate, and celebrate many of these alternative family practices.[35] How ironic and unfortunate it seems, therefore, that feminism's anti-modern-family ideology should then offend many women from the social groups whose gender and kinship strategies helped to foster it.

If, as my research suggests, postindustrial transformations encouraged modern working-class families to reorganize and diversify themselves even more than middle-class families, it seems time to inter the very concept of "*the* working-class family." This deeply androcentric and class-biased construct distorts the history and current reality of wage-working people's intimate relationships. Popular images of working-class family life, like the Archie Bunker family, rest upon the iconography of industrial blue-collar male breadwinners and the history of their lengthy struggle for a family wage. But the male family wage was a late and ephemeral achievement of only the most fortunate sections of the modern industrial working-class. It is doubtful that most working-class men ever secured its patriarchal domestic privileges.

Postmodern conditions expose the gendered character of this social-class category, and they render it atavistic. As feminists have argued, only by disregarding women's labor and learning was it ever plausible to designate a family unit as working class.[36] In an era when most married mothers are employed, when women perform most "working-class" jobs,[37] when most productive labor is unorganized and fails to pay a family wage, when marriage links are tenuous and transitory, and when more single women than married homemakers are rearing children, conventional notions of a normative working-class family fracture into incoherence. The life circumstances and mobility patterns of the members of Pamela's kin set and of the Lewisons, for example, are so diverse and fluid that no single social-class category can adequately describe any of the family units among them.

If the white working-class family stereotype is inaccurate, it is also consequential. Stereotypes are moral (alas, more often, immoral) stories people tell to organize the complexity of social experience. Narrating the working-class people as profamily reactionaries suppresses the diversity and the innovative character of a great proportion of working-class kin relationships. Because it contains socially divisive and conservative political effects, the Archie Bunker stereotype may have helped to contain feminism by estranging middle-class women from working-class women. Barbara Ehrenreich argues that caricatures that portray the working class as racist and reactionary are recent, self-serving inventions of professional, middle-class people eager "to seek legitimation for their own more conservative impulses."[38] In the early 1970s, ignoring rising labor militancy as well as racial, ethnic, and gender diversity among working-class people, the media effectively imaged them as the new conservative bedrock of "middle America." "All in the Family," the early 1970s television sit-com series that immortalized racist, chauvinist, working-class hero-buffoon Archie Bunker, can best be read, Ehrenreich suggests, as "the longest-running Polish joke," a projection of middle-class bad faith.[39] Yet, if this bad faith served professional middle-class interests, it did so at the expense of feminism. The inverse logic of class prejudice construed the constituency of that enormously popular social movement as exclusively middle-class. By convincing middle-class feminists of our isolation, perhaps the last laugh of that "Polish joke" was on us. Even Ehrenreich, who sensitively debunks the Bunker myth, labels "startling" the findings of a 1986 Gallup poll that "56 percent of American women considered themselves to be 'feminists,' and the degree of feminist identification was, if anything, slightly higher as one descended the socioeconomic scale."[40] Feminists must be attuned to the polyphony of family stories authored by working-class as well as middle-class people if we are ever to transform poll data like these into effective political alliances.

While my ethnographic research demonstrates the demise of "*the* working-class family," in no way does it document the emergence of the classless society once anticipated by postindustrial theorists.[41] On the contrary, recent studies of postindustrial occupation and income distribution indicate that the middle classes are shrinking and the economic circumstances of Americans are polarizing.[42] African-Americans have borne the most devastating impact of economic restructuring and the subsequent decline of industrial and unionized occupations.[43] But formerly privileged white working-class men, those like Pam's two husbands and Lou Lewison, who achieved access to the American Dream in the 1960s and 1970s, now find their gains threatened and difficult to pass on to their children.

While high-wage blue-collar jobs decline, the window of postindustrial opportunity that admitted undereducated men and women, like Lou and Kristina Lewison and Don Franklin, to middle-class status is slamming shut. "During the 1980s, the educated got richer and the uneducated got poorer. And it looks like more of the same in the 1990s," declared a recent summary of occupational statistics from the Census Bureau and the Labor Department.[44] Young white families earned 20 percent less in 1986 than did comparable families in 1979, and their prospects for home ownership plummeted.[45] Real earnings for young men between the ages of twenty and twenty-four dropped by 26 percent between 1973 and 1986, while the military route to upward mobility that many of their fathers traveled constricted.[46] In the 1950s men like Lou Lewison, equipped with Veterans Administration loans, could buy homes with token down payments and budget just 14 percent of their monthly wages for housing costs. By 1984, however, those veterans' children, looking for a median-priced home as first-time would-be home owners, could expect their housing costs to be 44 percent of an average male's monthly earnings.[47] Few could manage this, and in 1986 the U.S. government reported "the first sustained drop in home ownership since the modern collection of data began in 1940."[48]

Postindustrial shifts have reduced blue-collar job opportunities for the undereducated sons of working-class fathers I interviewed. And technological developments like Computer-Aided Design have escalated the entry criteria and reduced the numbers of those middle-level occupations that recently employed uncredentialled young people like Kristina Lewison and Pam's oldest child, Lanny.[49] Thus the proportion of American families in the middle-income range fell from 46 percent in 1970 to 39 percent in 1985. Two earners in a household now are necessary just to keep from losing ground.[50] Data like these led social analysts to anxiously track "the disappearing middle class," a phrase which, Barbara Ehrenreich now believes, "in some ways missed the point. It was the blue-collar working class that was 'disappearing,' at least from the middle range of comfort."[51]

Postindustrial restructuring has had contradictory effects on the employment opportunities of former working-class women. Driven by declines in real family income, by desires for social achievement and independence, and by an awareness that committed male breadwinners are in scarce supply, such women have flocked to expanding jobs in service, clerical, and new industrial occupations. These provide the means of family subsidy or self-support and self-respect gained by many women, like Pam and Dotty; but few of these women enjoy earnings or prospects equivalent to those of their former husbands or fathers. Recent economic restructuring has replaced white male workers with women and minority men, but at less well paid, more vulnerable jobs.[52]

WHOSE FAMILY CRISIS?

This massive reordering of work, class, and gender relationships during the past several decades is what has turned family life into a contested terrain. It seems ironic, therefore, to observe that at the very same time that women are becoming the new proletariat, the postmodern family, even more than the modern family it is replacing, is proving to be a woman-tended domain. To be sure, as Kathleen Gerson reports in the chapter that follows this one, there is some empirical basis for the enlightened father imagery celebrated by films like *Kramer versus Kramer*. Indeed my fieldwork corroborates emerging evidence that the determined efforts by many working women and feminists to reintegrate men into family life have not been entirely without effect. There are data, for example, indicating that increasing numbers of men would sacrifice occupational gains in order to have more time with their families, just as there are data documenting actual increases in male involvement in child care.[53] The excessive media attention that the faintest signs of this "new paternity" enjoy, however, may be a symptom of a deeper, far less comforting reality. We are experiencing, as Andrew Cherlin aptly puts it, "the feminization of kinship."[54] Demographers report a drastic decline in the average number of years that men live in households with young children.[55] Few of the women who assume responsibility for their children in 90 percent of divorce cases in the United States today had to wage a custody battle for this privilege.[56] We hear few proposals for a "daddy track" in the workplace. And few of the adults providing care to sick and elderly relatives are male.[57] Yet ironically, most of the alarmist and nostalgic literature about contemporary family decline impugns women's abandonment of domesticity, the flipside of our tardy entry into modernity. Rarely do the anxious public outcries over the destructive effects on families of working mothers, high divorce rates, institutionalized child care, or sexual liberalization scrutinize the family behaviors of men.[58] Anguished voices emanating from all bands on the political spectrum lament state and market interventions that are weakening "the family."[59] But whose family bonds are fraying? Women have amply demonstrated a continuing commitment to sustaining kin ties. If there is a family crisis, it is a male's crisis.

The crisis cannot be resolved by reviving the modern family system. While nostalgia for an idealized world of "Ozzie and Harriet" and "Archie Bunker" families abounds, little evidence suggests that most Americans genuinely wish to return to the gender order these symbolize. On the contrary, the vast majority, like the people in my study, are actively remaking family life. Indeed, a 1989 survey conducted by the *New York Times* found more than two-thirds of women—including a substantial majority even of those living in "traditional," that is to say "modern," households, as well as a majority of men—agree that "the United States continues to need a strong women's movement to push for changes that benefit women."[60] Yet many people seem reluctant to affirm their family preferences. They cling, like Shirley Moskowitz, to images of themselves as "back from the old days," while venturing ambivalently, but courageously, into the new.[61]

Responding to new economic and social insecurities as well as to feminism, higher percentages of families in almost all income groups have adopted a multiple-earner strategy.[62] Thus, the household form that has come closer than any other to replacing the modern family with a new cultural and statistical norm consists of a two-earner, heterosexual married couple with children.[63] It is not likely, however, that any type of household will soon achieve the measure of normalcy that the modern family long enjoyed. Indeed, the postmodern success of the voluntary principle of the modern family system precludes this, assuring a fluid, recombinant familial culture. The routinization of divorce and remarriage generates a diversity of family patterns even greater than was characteristic of the premodern period, when death prevented family stability or household homogeneity. Even cautious demographers judge the new family diversity to be "an intrinsic feature . . . rather than a temporary aberration" of contemporary family life.[64]

"The family" is *not* "here to stay." Nor should we wish it were. The ideological concept of "the family" imposes mythical homogeneity on the diverse means by which people organize their intimate relationships, and consequently distorts and devalues this rich variety of kinship stories. And, along with the class, racial, and heterosexual prejudices it promulgates, this sentimental, fictional plot authorizes gender hierarchy. Because the postmodern family crisis ruptures this seamless modern family "script," it provides a democratic opportunity. Feminists', gay liberation activists', and many minority rights organizations' efforts to expand and redefine the notion of family are responses to this opportunity. These groups are seeking to extend social legitimacy and institutional support for the diverse patterns of intimacy that Americans have already forged.

If feminism threatens many people and seems out of fashion, struggles to reconstitute gender and kinship on a just and democratic basis are more popular than ever.[65] If only a minority of citizens are willing to grant family legitimacy to gay domestic partners, an overwhelming majority subscribe to the postmodern definition of a family by which the New York Supreme Court validated a gay man's right to retain his deceased lover's apartment. "By a ratio of 3 to 1," people surveyed in a Yale University study defined the family as "a group of people who love and care for each other." And while a majority of those surveyed gave negative ratings to the quality of American family life in general, 71 percent declared themselves "at least very satisfied" with their own family lives.[66]

I find an element of bad faith in the popular lament over the decline of the family. Nostalgia for "the family" deflects criticism from the social sources of most "personal troubles." Supply-side economics, governmental deregulation, and the right-wing assault on social welfare programs have intensified the destabilizing effects of recent occupational upheavals on flagging modern families and emergent postmodern ones alike. Indeed, the ability to provide financial security was the chief family concern of most of the people surveyed in the Yale study. If the postmodern family crisis represents a democratic opportunity, contemporary economic and political conditions enable only a minority to realize its tantalizing potential.

The discrepant data reported in the Yale study indicate how reluctant most Americans are to fully acknowledge the genuine ambivalence we feel about family and social change. Yet ambivalence, as Alan Wolfe suggests, is an underappreciated but responsible moral stance, and one well suited for democratic citizenship: "Given the paradoxes of modernity, there is little wrong, and perhaps a great deal right, with being ambivalent—especially when there is so much to be ambivalent about."[67]

Certainly, as my experiences among Pamela's and Dotty's kin—and my own—have taught me, there are good grounds for ambivalence about contemporary postmodern family conditions. Nor do I imagine that even a successful feminist family revolution could eliminate all family distress. At best, it would foster a social order that could invert Tolstoy's aphorism by granting happy families the freedom to differ, and even to suffer. Truly postfeminist families, however, would suffer only the "common unhappiness" endemic to intimate human relationships; they would be liberated from the "hysterical misery" generated by social injustice.[68] No nostalgic movement to restore the modern family can offer as much. For better and/or worse, the postmodern family revolution is here to stay.

TWO

Coping with Commitment
Dilemmas and Conflicts of Family Life

Kathleen Gerson

Since 1950, when the breadwinner-homemaker household accounted for almost two-thirds of all American households, widespread changes have occurred in the structure of American family life. Rising rates of divorce, separation, and cohabitation outside of marriage have created a growing percentage of single-parent and single-adult households. The explosion in the percentage of employed women, and especially employed mothers, has produced a rising tide of dual-earner couples whose patterns of child rearing differ substantially from the 1950s' norm of the stay-at-home mother. As Judy Stacey also shows in this volume, the breadwinner-homemaker model of family life has become only one of an array of alternatives that confront men and women as they build (and often change) their lives over the course of an expanded adulthood.[1]

As changes in family structure have become apparent to intellectuals, politicians, and ordinary citizens, a national debate has arisen over their nature and significance. The most widely embraced interpretation of family change is one of alarm and condemnation. Analysts and social critics across the political spectrum routinely blame "the breakdown of the family" for a host of modern social ills, extending from the drug epidemic and increases in violent crime to teenage pregnancy, child abuse and neglect, the decline of educational standards, and even the birth dearth.[2] But a competing and less pessimistic perspective emphasizes the resilience of families, which are adapting rather than disintegrating in the face of social change, and the resourcefulness of individuals, who are able to build meaningful interpersonal bonds amid the uncertainty and fragility of modern relationships.[3] By arguing that changes in family structure represent a necessary adaptation to structural change, this perspective refuses to hold "nontraditional" families responsible for circumstances they did not create or social trends that accompany, but are not caused by, family change.[4] It also calls attention to the positive side of social change by taking into account the benefits of women's increasing opportunities outside the home.

The "stability within change" perspective provides an important rebuttal to the gloomy and accusatory picture presented by the "family breakdown" thesis. It upholds the validity of women's struggle for gender equality and freedom of choice regarding sexuality, marriage, and childbearing. However, its relatively benign view tends to understate some of the costs of social change. In the context of persistent gender inequality, these costs have fallen most heavily on the women and children who can no longer count on a man's economic support and have not gained access to other economic bases. The growing percentage of women and children who live in poverty is, for example, an unfortunate consequence of the loosening of the bonds of permanent marriage and the erosion of male breadwinning.[5]

Posing the situation as one of family breakdown versus family stability and adaptive resilience oversimplifies the nature of the change process. This chapter argues, instead, that both the current debate on the family and the difficulties most families now face result less from the fact of fundamental social change than from the inconsistent and contradictory nature of change.[6] Incomplete and unequal social change has created new personal dilemmas over how to balance parental and employment commitments and new social conflicts between those who have developed "traditional" and "nontraditional" resolutions to the intransigent conflicts between family and workplace demands.[7] These dilemmas and conflicts pose the central challenges to which new generations of women, men, and children must respond.[8]

PERSONAL DILEMMAS AND FAMILY DIVERSITY: THE CONSEQUENCES OF UNEQUAL SOCIAL CHANGE

Social change in family structure remains inconsistent in two consequential ways. First, some social arrangements have changed significantly, but others have not. Even though an increasing percentage of families depend on the earnings of wives and mothers, women continue to face discrimination at the workplace and still retain responsibility for the lion's share of household labor.[9] Similarly, despite the growth of dual-earner and single-parent households, the structural conflicts between family and work continue to make it difficult for either women or men to combine child rearing with sustained employment commitment.[10] The combination of dramatic change in some social arrangements (for example, women's influx into the labor force) and relatively little change in others (for example, employers' continuing expectation that job responsibilities should take precedence over family needs) has created new forms of

gender inequality and new dilemmas for both women and men who confront the dual demands of employment and parenthood.

Second, social change is inconsistent because social groups differ
greatly in how and to what degree they have been exposed to change.
Not only are the alternatives that women and men face structured differently, but within each gender group, the alternatives vary significantly. A growing group of women, for example, have gained access to
highly rewarded professional and managerial careers, but most women
remain segregated in relatively ill-rewarded, female-dominated occupations. Similarly, the stagnation of real wages has eroded many men's ability to support wives and children on their paycheck alone, but most men
still enjoy significant economic advantages. This variation in opportunities and constraints has, in turn, promoted contrasting orientations
toward family change among differently situated groups of women
and men.

This chapter draws on two studies of how differently situated groups
of women and men are responding to the dilemmas posed by unequal
social change.[11] These studies have examined, first, how women are responding to the structural conflicts between family and employment
commitments and, second, how men are responding to the conflict between preserving their historic privileges and confronting their growing
need to share breadwinning responsibilities with women. It analyzes the
similarities and differences between women's and men's responses, how
their family situations affect their personal and political strategies, and,
finally, the short-term and long-term implications of men's and women's
attempts to resolve these dilemmas and conflicts.

Women and men have developed a range of strategic responses to
cope with the contrasting dilemmas they confront. We can compare the
"coping strategies" of those who developed a "traditional orientation"
with the strategies that grew out of two alternative orientations—an orientation that stresses the avoidance of parental commitments and, finally, an orientation based on seeking a balance between work and family commitments. Since the conflicts and dilemmas inherent in each
family pattern vary according to gender, women's and men's strategic responses are analyzed separately. Women and men confront a different
set of opportunities and constraints, but each group must respond to the
dilemmas posed by unequal and uneven social change. Their contend-
ing resolutions to these family dilemmas shape the terms of political conflict as well as the contours of social change.

CHOOSING BETWEEN EMPLOYMENT AND MOTHERHOOD

Although most women, including most mothers, now participate in the
paid labor force, this apparent similarity masks important differences in

women's responses to the conflicts between employment and mother-hood. Not only do some mothers continue to stay home to rear children, but many employed women work part time or intermittently and continue to emphasize family over employment commitments.[12] These "do-mestically oriented" women stand in contrast to a growing group of "nondomestic" women, who have developed employment ties that rival, and for some surpass, family commitments. Women develop "domestic" or "nondomestic" orientations in response to specific sets of occupational and interpersonal experiences. These contrasting orientations to family life are not only rooted in different social circumstances; they also represent opposing responses to the conflicts between motherhood and employment.[13]

All women face an altered social context, but they differ in how and to what extent they have been exposed to structural change. This uneven exposure to new opportunities and constraints has produced contrasting orientations toward employment and motherhood. In my research on how women make family and work decisions, I found that regardless of class position or early childhood experiences and expectations, those women who were exposed to change in marital and work institutions were more likely to develop nondomestic orientations as adults, whereas those who were sheltered from these changes tended to develop a do-mestic orientation in adulthood. About two-thirds of the respondents who held domestic orientations as children ultimately became work-committed. Similarly, over 60 percent of those who were ambivalent about childbearing or who held career aspirations as children became committed to domesticity in adulthood.

Unanticipated encounters with changing structures of marriage and employment led some women to veer away from domesticity and others to veer toward it. Those who experienced instability in their relation-ships with men, who encountered often unanticipated chances for advancement at the workplace, who were disillusioned with the experience of motherhood, and who met severe economic squeezes in their house-holds tended to develop strong work commitments. These women found full-time mothering and homemaking relatively isolating, devalued, and unfulfilling compared to the rewards of paid jobs. Exposure to unantici-pated opportunities outside the home combined with unexpected dis-appointment in domestic pursuits to encourage a nondomestic orienta-tion even among those who had initially planned for a life of domesticity.

In contrast, women who encountered blocked mobility at work and became disillusioned by dead-end jobs decided that motherhood pro-vided a more satisfying alternative to stifling work conditions. They were, furthermore, able to establish stable marital partnerships in which they could depend on economic support from husbands with secure careers. When the experience of blocked mobility at the workplace was combined with unexpected marital commitment to a securely employed spouse, even women who once held career aspirations were encouraged to loosen their employment ties and turn toward domestic pursuits. Over 60 percent of those who initially planned to have a work career ultimately opted for domesticity in response to constraints at the workplace and opportunities for domestic involvement. Amid the currents of social change, exposure to a traditional package of opportunities and constraints led these women to conclude that their best hope for a satisfying life depended on subordinating their employment goals to motherhood and family pursuits.

In sum, exposure to expanded opportunities outside the home (for example, upward employment mobility) and unanticipated insecurities within it (for example, marital instability or economic squeezes in the household) tends to promote a nondomestic orientation, even among women who once planned for full-time motherhood. Exposure to a more traditional package of opportunities and constraints (such as constricted employment options and stable marriage) tends, in contrast, to promote a domestic orientation even among those who felt ambivalent toward motherhood and domesticity as children. Both orientations reflect contextually sensible, if unexpected and largely unconscious, responses to the structural conflicts between employment and motherhood.

Uneven exposure to structural change, like the partial nature of change, promotes contrasting family orientations among women. Some women remain dependent on a traditional family structure that emphasizes sharp social differences between the sexes along with male economic support for women's mothering. Others increasingly depend on social and economic supports outside the home—which can be guaranteed only if women are accorded the same rights, responsibilities, and privileges as men. Rising marital instability and stagnant male wages have eroded the structural supports for female domesticity, but persistent gender inequality at the workplace and in the home also make domesticity an inviting alternative to those who still face limited options in the paid labor force. In the context of this ambiguous mix of expanded options and new insecurities, the choices of both domestically oriented and work-committed women remain problematic, however personally fulfilling they may be.

Strategies of Domestically Oriented Women

Despite the forces leading other women out of the home, domestically oriented women confront ample reasons to avoid such a fate. Blocked occupational opportunities leave these women poorly positioned to enjoy the benefits of work outside the home. They have concluded that domestic pursuits offer significant advantages over workplace commitment. A homemaker and mother of two declared:

I never plan to go back [to work]. I'm too spoiled now. I'm my own boss.
I have independence; I have control; I have as much freedom as anyone is
going to have in our society. No [paid] job can offer me those things.

Since their "freedom" depends on someone else's paycheck, domestically oriented women are willing to accept responsibility for the care of
home and children in exchange for male economic support. As this disillusioned ex-schoolteacher and full-time mother of two pointed out, they
have little desire to change places with their breadwinning husbands:

> I have met guys who were housepersons, but I can't see any reason [for it].
> It would turn it all crazy for me to come home around five thirty, and he'd
> have to have things ready for me. I think if I thought that [bringing in a
> paycheck] was my role for the rest of my life, I would hate it. I don't want
> to be [my husband]; then I would have to go and fight the world. I don't
> want the pressures that he has to bear—supporting a family, a mortgage,
> putting in all those hours at the office. Ugh!

Whether or not they work, domestically oriented women put their
family commitments first. When employed, they carefully define their
work attachments as a discretionary choice that can be curtailed if necessary and that always comes second to their children's needs. A part-time
clerk and mother of two defined paid work as a "job," not a career:

> I would never want to get us in a situation where I would *have* to work,
> because then I would really hate it. I don't work to have a career. Without a
> career, I can quit a job whenever I want. To have a career, you have to stick
> with it, and it takes a lot. I'd have to give up a lot of things my kids need,
> and it's not worth it to me. A job, I don't have to give up anything.

Although relatively insulated from the pushes and pulls that lead
other women toward strong labor force attachment, domestically oriented women are nevertheless affected by the social changes taking place
around them. The erosion of structural and ideological supports for a
traditional arrangement has made their commitment to a family form
based on a strict sexual division of labor problematic. The increased fragility of marriage, for example, poses an abiding, if unspoken, threat to
domestic women's security. In the context of high divorce rates, homemaking women cannot assume that the relationships they depend on will
last. This ex-clerk and mother of a young daughter complained:

> [Having a child] has made me more dependent on my husband. I think he
> was attracted to me because I was very independent, and now I'm very de-
> pendent. I don't know what I would do if things didn't work out between
> [us] and we had to separate and I had to go to work to support my child.
> I think I'd be going bananas. It's scary to me.

Even when their marriages are secure, domestically oriented women
face other incursions on their social position. The rise of work-commit-

ment among other women has not only provided an alternative to domesticity, it has also eroded the ideological hegemony that homemakers once enjoyed. Domestically oriented women feel unfairly devalued by others, as these ex-clerical workers explained:

> There are times when I have some trouble with my identity; that has to do with being a mother. Because of society, sometimes the recognition or lack of it bothers me.

> People put no value on a housewife. If you have a job, you're interesting. If you don't, you're really not very interesting, and sometimes I think people turn you off.

This ex-nurse added that even when economic pressures are weak, the social pressures to seek employment make domesticity a difficult choice:

> I have been feeling a lot of pressure . . . there's a lot of pressure on women now that you should feel like you want to work. Sometimes it's hard to know what you feel, because I really don't feel like I want to [work], but I think I *should* feel like I want to.

The erosion of the structural and ideological supports for domesticity has left domestically oriented women feeling embattled. They are now forced to defend a personal choice and family arrangement that was once considered sacrosanct.[14] For these reasons, domestically oriented women cannot afford to take a neutral stance toward social change, and many have developed ideologies of opposition to other people's choices. Domestically oriented women tend to view employed mothers as either selfish and dangerous to children or overburdened and miserable, as these two homemakers suggested:

> I have a neighbor with young children who works just because she wants to. I get sort of angry . . . I think I resent the unfairness to the child. I don't know how to answer the argument that men can have families and work, but women can't. Maybe it's not fair, but that's the way it is.

> Most of the time all I hear from them is griping, and they're tired, and they're frantic to get everything done. It's a shame. I hate hurrying like that.

They viewed career-committed women as selfish, unattractive, and, at least in the case of childless women, unfulfilled:

> Women can [take on men's jobs], but it's a blood-and-guts type of thing. Those who make it are witches because they found out what they had to do to get there. [ex-saleswoman planning first child]

> I feel like they're missing out on something. If they're going to make a long-term thing of it and never have children, I think they're missing something.

Finally, domestically oriented women support men's right and duty to be primary breadwinners. They frown on men who shirk their duties to support women and children. This homemaker and mother of two could not understand why "undependable" men were considered glamorous:

> There's this mystique about the charismatic, not decent and dependable, sort of man. They're movie types. . . . My husband goes to work at eight and comes home at five, and [people] say, "Isn't that boring?" And I say, "No. Not at all," because it gives me time to do what I want.

Although their strategies have unfolded against the tide of social change, domestically oriented women illustrate the forces that not only limit the change but provide a powerful opposition to it. Their personal circumstances give them ample reason to view change as a dangerous threat to their own and their children's well-being, even when it leads in the direction of greater gender equality.

Strategies of Work-Committed Women
Work-committed women lack the option of domesticity, or the desire to opt for it, but they nevertheless face significant obstacles. Persistent wage inequality and occupational sex segregation continue to deny most employed women an equal opportunity to succeed at the workplace. In addition, limited change in the organization of work, especially in male-dominated occupations, combines with the "stalled revolution" in the sexual division of domestic work to make it difficult for employed women to integrate career-commitment with motherhood. Work-committed women have responded in several ways to this predicament. A small but significant proportion have decided to forgo childbearing altogether, but the majority of work-committed women are attempting to balance child rearing with strong labor force attachment.[15]

Childless women have concluded that childbearing is an unacceptably dangerous choice in a world where marriage is fragile and motherhood threatens to undermine employment prospects. A strong skepticism regarding the viability of marriage led a divorced executive to reject childbearing:

> [Having children] probably would set back my career . . . irretrievably. The real thing that fits in here is my doubts about men and marriage, because if I had real faith that the marriage would go on, and that this would be a family unit and be providing for these children, being set back in my career wouldn't be that big a deal. But I have a tremendous skepticism about the permanency of relationships, which makes me want to say, "Don't give anything up, because you're going to lose something that you're going to need later on, because [the man] won't be there.

Childless women also have considerable skepticism about men's willingness to assume the sacrifices and burdens of parenthood. Since gender equality in parenting seems out of reach, so does motherhood. For this childless physician, even avowedly egalitarian men appeared untrustworthy:

> I would *never* curtail my career goals for a [child] . . . I would not subjugate my career any more than a man would subjugate his career. . . . [And] I don't know anybody who says he wants an egalitarian relationship. Among the married ones with children, everybody says, "Sure, we'll share with children equally." But nobody does.

Given the lack of structural supports for combining career commitment and childbearing, these women are convinced they must choose between the two. They have decided that the continuing obstacles to integrating employment and child rearing leave women facing a curiously "old-fashioned" choice between mutually exclusive alternatives:

> I think you either do one or the other. . . . You could have children and work, but you wouldn't really be a very senior sort of involved person. Although men can be presidents of companies and have children, women can't. [single interior designer]

> I just think that [children] are a responsibility, and you have to be willing to devote all your time to them. If you can't do that, I don't think you should have them. I know that's really old-fashioned, but I tend to believe it. [high school–educated secretary]

Most work-committed women, however, do eventually have children. Many hold the beliefs this lawyer voiced:

> I don't think it's fair that [working] women can't have kids. They make things fuller, more complete. I think it rounds out your life.

Work-committed mothers must create strategies to meet the competing demands of child rearing and employment. However, their strategic choices are severely limited by intransigence in the workplace. This aspiring banker lamented:

> [My bosses] figure that I'm to have my career, and what I do at home is my own business, but it better not interrupt the job. I've been pushed as far forward as I have because I was a maniac and I never went home.

Since most employers continue to penalize workers, regardless of gender, for parental involvement that interferes with the job, employed mothers have had to look elsewhere for relief from the competing demands of employment and child rearing. Three strategies, in particular, offer hope of easing their plight. First, employed mothers limit their demands by limiting family size. Although the two-child family remains the preferred alternative, the one-child family is gaining acceptance.[16] This upwardly mobile office worker concluded:

> I know one child won't drive me crazy, and two might. I know I couldn't work and have two. . . . I don't think [one child] would affect [my work plans] at all. More than one would. That's one of the reasons I only want one.

Employed mothers must also reevaluate and alter the beliefs about child rearing they inherited from earlier generations, who frowned on working mothers. One work-committed office worker rejected the idea that children suffer when mothers work, despite having been raised by a full-time mother:

> I liked my mother being home, but I think it's okay for a mother to work. As long as she doesn't make her children give things up, and I don't think I'd make my children give anything up by me working.

Finally, work-committed mothers have engaged in a protracted struggle to bring men into the process of parenting. Their male partners' support of their independence gives them leverage to demand sharing, even if it doesn't guarantee that such sharing will be equal. A professor acknowledged:

> [My husband] respects my accomplishments. He wants me to keep doing something I enjoy. He wants me to be fairly independent, and he also wants his own independence . . . as long as he can support himself and half a child.

Some have decided that male parental involvement is a precondition to childbearing, as these upwardly mobile workers explained:

> I want [equal] participation, and without it I don't want children. I want it for the children, for myself. Without two people doing it, I think it would be a burden on one person. It's no longer a positive experience. [lawyer engaged to be married, in her early thirties]

> I think it's going to come to the point that if we're willing to have children, we work things out pretty much [equally] between ourselves. And I think he would rather help out than to not have [children] at all. It's a two-way thing. [office manager in her late twenties]

In rejecting childlessness, most work-committed women have developed strategies to cope with the dual burdens of employment and motherhood. In addition to having smaller families, developing new ideologies about child rearing and mothering, and pressuring men to become involved fathers, work-committed mothers are challenging traditional work and family arrangements based on the assumption of a male worker with a wife at home or, at most, loosely tied to paid employment. Like their domestically oriented counterparts, the need to defend their choices against other people's disapproval encourages them to denigrate different resolutions to the conflict between employment and motherhood. From this perspective, it becomes tempting to define domestically oriented women as:

> . . . kind of mentally underdeveloped and not too interesting. Let's face it, it's kind of boring. I guess I don't consider just having children as doing something.

Inconsistent and unequal social change has promoted differing strategic reactions among women that leave them socially divided and politically opposed. The contours of change, however, also depend on men's reactions to the emerging conflicts and dilemmas of family life.[17]

CHOOSING BETWEEN PRIVILEGE AND SHARING: MEN'S RESPONSES TO GENDER AND FAMILY CHANGE

While the transformation in women's lives has garnered the most attention, significant changes have also occurred in men's family patterns. The primary breadwinner who emphasizes economic support and constricted participation in child rearing persists, but this model—like its female counterpart, the homemaker—no longer predominates. Alongside this pattern, several alternatives have gained adherents. An increasing proportion of men have moved away from family commitments—among them single and childless men who have chosen to forgo parenthood and divorced fathers who maintain weak ties to their offspring.[18] Another group of men, however, has become more involved in the nurturing activities of family life. Although these "involved fathers" rarely assume equal responsibility for child rearing, they are nevertheless significantly more involved with their children than are primary breadwinners, past or present.[19] Change in men's lives, while limited and contradictory, is nonetheless part of overall family change.

As with women's choices, men's family patterns reflect uneven exposure to structural change in family and work arrangements. In my research on men's changing patterns of parental involvement, I found that men who established employment stability in highly rewarded but demanding jobs, and who experienced unexpected marital stability with a domestically oriented spouse, were pushed and pulled toward primary breadwinning even when they had originally hoped to avoid such a fate. In contrast, men who experienced employment instability and dissatisfaction with the "rat race" of high-pressure, bureaucratically controlled jobs tended to turn away from primary breadwinning. When these experiences were coupled with instability in heterosexual relationships and dissatisfying experiences with children, many rejected parental involvement altogether—opting instead for personal independence and freedom from children. When declining work commitments were coupled with unexpected pleasure in committed, egalitarian heterosexual relationships and unexpected fulfillment through involvement with children, men tended to become oriented toward involved fatherhood. Thus, while about 36 percent of the respondents developed a primary breadwinning orientation, the remaining men did not. Unanticipated encounters in relationships with women and at the workplace encouraged these men to establish either greater distance from family life (about 30 percent of the sample) or, alternatively, to become more involved in parenthood than did primary breadwinners (about 34 percent of the sample).

As with women, these contrasting orientations among men represent reasonable, if often unexpected and typically unconscious, reactions to encounters with contrasting packages of constraints and opportunities in adulthood. They also reflect different responses to the trade-offs men face in their family choices. Although men do not typically have to choose between workplace participation and childbearing, they do confront conflicts and dilemmas. As women's lives have been transformed, men, too, are increasingly caught on the horns of a dilemma between preserving their historic privileges and taking advantage of expanded opportunities to share or reject the economic and social burdens of breadwinning.[20] Among men (as among women), different experiences and orientations promote contrasting strategies to cope with the tensions between maintaining male privilege and easing traditional male burdens.

Strategies of Primary Breadwinning Men

Just as domestically oriented women interpret the meaning of work through the lens of their family commitments, whether or not they are employed, so primary breadwinning men define their parental involvement in terms of income, whether or not their wives work. First, these men emphasize money, not time, in calculating their contributions to the household. For this surveyor, "good fathering" means being a good provider—that is providing financial support, not participating in child rearing:

> What is a good father? It's really hard to say. I always supported my children, fed them, gave them clothes, a certain amount of love when I had time. There was always the time factor. Maybe giving them money doesn't make you a good father, but not giving it probably makes you a bad father. I guess I could have done maybe a little more with them if financially I wasn't working all the time, but I've never hit my kids. I paid my daughter's tuition. I take them on vacation every year. Am I a good father? Yes, I would say so.

Even when their wives are employed, primary breadwinning men devalue the importance of wives' earnings. They define this income as "extra" and nonessential and thus also define a woman's job as secondary to her domestic responsibilities. Even though his wife worked hard as a waitress, this architect did not believe that she shared the duties of breadwinning:

> She took care of [our son], and I did all the breadwinning. When we got the house, she started working for extra money. She worked weekends, but her job doesn't affect us at all. Financially, my job takes care of everything plus. Her income is gravy, I guess you'd call it.

By defining fatherhood in terms of financial support and wives' income as supplementary and nonessential, primary breadwinners relieve themselves of the responsibility for domestic chores and of a sense of guilt that such an arrangement might generate. A park worker was proud to announce:

> I do nothing with the cooking or cleaning. I do no household, domestic anything. I could, but I won't, because I feel I shouldn't have to. If my wife's not sick, I see no reason why I should do it. I feel my responsibility is to bring home the money and her responsibility is to cook and clean.

And like the domestically oriented women who felt fortunate not to *have* to work, primary breadwinners see their wives as the fortunate recipients of personal freedom and material largesse. The park worker continued:

> My wife's got it made. The cat's got it made, too. I'm very good to my wife. She drives a new car, has great clothes, no responsibilities. She's very happy to be just around the house, do what she wants. She's got her freedom; what more could you want?

Although primary breadwinning men, like domestically oriented women, have been relatively insulated from the social-structural incentives that promote nontraditional choices among others, they, too, are affected by changes in others' lives. Despite stable employment and marriages, these men fear the erosion of the material and ideological supports for male privilege that their fathers could take for granted. As women have fought for equal rights at the workplace and other men have moved away from family patterns that emphasize separate spheres, those who remain committed to the "good provider" ethic feel embattled and threatened. Even the small gains made by women at the workplace are perceived as unfair as the historic labor market advantages of men undergo reconsideration, if not drastic alteration. A plumber and father of five resented the incursions some women are making into his field of expertise:

> Women have it a little easier as far as job-related [matters] is concerned [*sic*]. The tests are getting easier, classifications are going down [to let

women in]. From what I hear in plants with women, they *can't* do the job. This isn't chauvinistic guys talking; this is guys talking in general. We pick up a 250-pound motor, but there's no way a young lady will pick it up unless she's a gorilla, a brute. But when she's got to do the job, two other guys have got to come along to help. I'm not saying women can't handle the job, [but] a woman comes to work for us, and they [the bosses] have got five men covering for her. Usually it's a hardship, but the guys bend over backwards for her. If she can't handle her job, why should she be there?

Similarly, primary breadwinners make a distinction between their situation and that of other men—especially childless, single men who, presumably, do not share their heavy economic responsibilities. They define their interests not just in terms of being a man, but a particular type of man who sacrifices for the good of his family and therefore needs to protect his interests in a hostile, changing world. The park worker explained:

Being a father is a responsibility. If you don't have a wife, don't have children—you get fired, who cares? When you have someone who's depending on your salary, you protect your interest on the job more. You become more afraid, and you become more practical. You realize you're out in the ocean, and nobody's going to help you. You're on your own, and you grow up real quick and start behaving like an adult.

In response to this perceived need to protect their interests, primary breadwinning men, like domestically oriented women, hold tightly to a set of social and political beliefs that emphasize the natural basis and moral superiority of gender differences and inequalities. Primary breadwinners argue that their own sexual division of labor is both natural and normal, as the plumber maintained:

As far as bread and butter is concerned, the man should have a little more [of] the responsibility than the woman. I'm not chauvinistic or anything, but it's basic, normal [that] it's a man. There aren't many men where the wife works full-time.

Who should take care of the children?

Again, you go back to whoever's home and whoever's working. Primary would be the mother. It's natural; it comes natural. In my house, it's *my* wife. She's doing it all.

If their own choices are viewed as natural and normal, then other patterns appear abnormal, unhealthy, and dangerous. Men who are unable or unwilling to meet the demands of breadwinning are judged to be moral and social failures, as the park worker pointed out.

The husband may not be able to provide. Just because he's a man, doesn't mean he can provide. There's a lot of losers out there, a lot of guys have a thirty-dollar-an-hour drug habit. How are they going to work? The wife might have to. Considering both people are normal, the breadwinner in my opinion should be the man.

Primary breadwinners hold similar beliefs about nondomestic patterns for women. Along with domestically oriented women, they tend to argue that career and motherhood are mutually exclusive alternatives for women and that responsible mothering requires forgoing a career. With five children and his own wife a homemaker, the plumber had little sympathy for mothers who feel the need for a life outside the home:

> A career is a career; a family is a family. When you have a career, you donate your whole self to your career. If you have a family, you donate yourself to your family. [If a woman] has a career and no children, that's different. If she's a mother, her place should be at home. If she doesn't need the money, she has to have an ulterior motive for going to work. She's either tired of the kids or she's tired of being around the kids. If she's trying to keep her sanity, if she's unhappy at home, then she's got nobody to blame but herself, because she created that.

If a strict sexual division of caretaking and breadwinning is morally correct, it follows that current social changes are dangerous. Primary breadwinners tend to view these changes as hazardous for women as well as for men and children. Like their domestically oriented female counterparts, they argue, according to the park worker, that the decline of inequality threatens the historic protections women have enjoyed:

> The woman should be protected, have a higher place. A mother is the most cherished thing you could be on this earth, and the woman should be respected and cared for. Equality would reduce that. A woman should be put on a pedestal above the man, and equality would put them on the same level. Why would they want to be equal with men who are dying earlier, under stress, who are really in the firing position? They already got it all. Equality for a woman would be the worst thing, because she already has the advantage. Women would lose from equality. Why would they want it? What is the need for it?

Despite their contrasting commitments, primary breadwinning men and domestically oriented women are interdependent in ways that lead their world views and political ideologies to converge. Their outlooks contrast not only with those of nondomestic women, but with those developed by nontraditional men as well.

ALTERNATIVES TO PRIMARY BREADWINNING AMONG MEN

Men who eschew primary breadwinning have concluded that the privileges afforded "good providers" are not worth the price that privilege entails. They view breadwinning responsibilities as burdensome and constricting, but their rejection of breadwinning poses its own dilemmas. The loosening bonds of marriage allow these men greater latitude to avoid parental responsibilities, both economic and social. On the other hand, the increasing number of work-committed women encourages and, indeed, pressures some nontraditional men to become more involved in the noneconomic aspects of family life than was typical of men a generation ago. These two patterns—forgoing parental commitments and becoming involved in caretaking—represent increasingly popular, if quite different, responses to the search for an alternative to traditional masculinity amid a contradictory and ambiguous set of options.

Forgoing Parental Commitments

Like permanently childless women, some men have opted to forgo parental responsibilities. This group includes childless men who do not wish or plan to become fathers and divorced fathers who have significantly curtailed their economic and social ties to their offspring in the wake of marital disruption. These men have come to value autonomy over commitment and to view children as a threat to their freedom of choice. A social service director, for example, was convinced that childlessness opened vocational options he would not have enjoyed as a breadwinning father:

What do you think things would be like if you did have kids?

Vocationally, I would have had to make other choices because the field I'm in just doesn't pay a terrific amount of money, and with children, you have expenses, and you have to look forward to a lot more future planning than I have to do with my current situation. So I've been able to sort of play with my career, and really just have a lot of fun in doing what I do, without having that responsibility.

Permanently childless men have decided that the potential benefits of fatherhood are not worth its risks. A childless psychologist admitted with some discomfort:

Does seeing other men with young children bring out any response in you?

Relief! [laughs] I don't just see the good parts; I see it all. I see the shit they have to wade through literally and figuratively, and very often I say to myself, "There but for the grace of God go I." It's a very ambivalent position I have about it.

This ambivalence toward fatherhood is not necessarily confined to childless men. Some divorced fathers also develop a relatively weak emotional and social attachment to their children. Whether their reaction is a defense against the pain of loss or an extension of their lack of involvement in child rearing prior to divorce, divorced fathers who become distant from their children tend to discount the importance of parenthood. A truck driver and divorced father of two, who sees his children and pays their child support sporadically, explained:

> *How would you feel if you had never had kids?*
>
> I don't think that would bother me. Being that I do have them, it's okay. I enjoy them when I see them. But if I never had them, I don't think I'd really miss them. I don't think it would be that important if they weren't there.

And even though this divorced dentist spent little time with his school-age daughter, who resided with her mother in another city, he envied his childless counterparts:

> Men who don't have any children just seem to have more time to do the things they want to do and don't have to deal with the trials and tribulations of raising a child.

In contrast to traditional women and men, these men agree with work-committed women that traditional arrangements are neither inherently superior nor more natural family forms. Instead, they argue that primary breadwinning is oppressive to men and harmful to society. Though more vociferous than most, the psychologist, who at age 43 had never married, painted a vivid picture of the personal and social costs these men attach to male breadwinning:

> At this particular period in history, the woman is getting all the sympathy for her desperate position in the home by herself, lonely and isolated, taking care of these kids. I also have sympathy for the guy who has to be out getting his ass kicked by industrial tyrants and corporate assholes and the whole competitive complex. I think it's a tough life, and very often the man is tremendously underestimated, underrated.

Another confirmed bachelor, a childless free-lance writer, equated the woes of materialism with the "trap" of primary breadwinning:

> I just see these people, and they seem so closed and so materialistic, and it makes me sad for them. Because all this free spirit seems to go down the drain and they're trapped. I wrote a song called "When You're My Age, You'll Be Selling Insurance." It makes me happy that I managed to avoid it, that I haven't been trapped by that.

Although permanently childless men and uninvolved fathers have rejected the "good provider" ethos, they are less certain about what to put in its place. They reject traditional beliefs about gender, but they are also ambivalent about what gender equality should mean.

In contrast to primary breadwinners and domestically oriented

women, these men argue that gender differences are smaller, more malleable, and less desirable than traditional views suggest. A single, childless physician argued that perceived gender differences are socially constructed and reflect social evaluations of behavior rather than essential,
sex-related characteristics:

> To me, the key to being a man, the same thing as being a woman, is being
> a good human being. For me, there's nothing that really defines being a
> man. It doesn't mean you can't cry. I could stay at home and be happy and
> have a lot of what would be quote feminine characteristics. In some situa-
> tions, it helps to be macho, but a lot of that just reflects stereotypes. If it's a
> guy, he's aggressive; if it's a woman, she's a ball buster. One's negative; one's
> positive. And it can be the same behavior. Sometimes I wish it was a little
> clearer, but basically you've got to say, "What are you as an individual?"

If gender is socially constructed and thus malleable, it follows that it
can be reconstructed in a different way. He believed that a change in the
social definitions of gender is desirable:

> I look at the grief and anxiety my father had by being the sole provider. So
> if being a man is being the rock and support of your family, let's change
> that definition of being a man. Because that doesn't look very good to me.

Although men who have opted for freedom from parental commitments argue that gender differences are neither natural nor necessarily
desirable, they remain ambivalent about what gender does or should
mean. They believe that gender equality is a desirable goal, but equality
defined in a specific and limited way. They emphasize women's equal responsibilities in the context of equal rights. For these men, equality
means exactly what domestically oriented women fear it will mean—that
women should relinquish the economic and legal "protections" that have
accompanied their second-class status.[21] As the divorced truck driver,
quoted earlier, argued:

> [If] women want equal rights, let them pay child support, alimony. Let
> them get drafted. You want to be equal, you do everything equal not just
> certain things. They got girls now in the sanitation department. God bless
> them if that's what [they] want to do, but when it comes down to it, you've
> got to pick up that pail and dump it in the truck. I'm not going to go over
> and help you. You want the job, you do what I do and that's it.

Similarly, these men support women's economic self-sufficiency, for
their own ability to remain autonomous is closely linked to women's independence. A systems analyst who had never married declared:

> I'm not really big on women who stay at home and just raise kids. I think
> everybody should be a fully functioning, self-supporting adult, and cer-

tainly economically that's a necessity now. I believe, in terms of women's issues, that if they prepared themselves for the idea that they have to assume their financial burdens and responsibilities, they won't have to be emotional hostages to toxic relationships. And men won't either.

This vision of economic and social equality does not, however, easily extend to the domestic sphere. Because these men place a high value on their freedom, they resist applying the principle of equality to child rearing. Indeed, the paradox of espousing the equal right to be free while resisting the equal responsibility for parenthood leads them to avoid parental commitments. The systems analyst feared he would be drawn into what he deemed the least attractive aspects of parenting:

> [If I had a child,] I could see that I would want to take a role in playing with the child, overseeing its training and schooling, providing that type of thing. I don't really see me wanting to do a lot in the way of getting up in the middle of the night, formulas, changing diapers. I'm not at all into that.

And so, these men are able to resolve the dilemma between their support of some aspects of gender equality and their resistance to its more threatening implications only by forgoing both the burdens and the joys of raising a child.

Caretaking Fathers

A more equal sharing of both earning income and rearing children provides another alternative to primary breadwinning. While complete equality remains rare even among dual-earner couples, male participation in caretaking is nevertheless on the rise.[22] Men who are married to work-committed women and divorced fathers who have retained either joint or sole custody of their children are particularly likely to participate in child rearing.[23] In contrast to childless men, these men have placed family at the center of their lives. In contrast to primary breadwinners, they value spending time with their families as much as contributing money to them. A utility worker with a young daughter and a wife employed as a marketing manager insisted:

> For me, being with my family is the major, the ultimate in my life—to be with them and share things with them. Money is secondary, but time with them is the important thing in life. That's why I put up with this job— because I can get home early. To me, spending time with [my daughter] makes up for it. I'm home at 3:40 and spend a lot of time with her, just like the long days when she was young and I was on unemployment.

Some involved fathers view the time spent in child care not as simply helping out, but as an incomparably pleasurable activity and an essential component of good parenting. This thirty-seven-year-old construction

worker chose to work the night shift so that he could spend his days with
his newborn daughter while his wife pursued a dancing career:

> I take care of [my daughter] during the morning and the day. [My wife]
> takes care [of her] in the evenings. I work from three to eleven P.M. and
> wake up with the morning ahead of me, and that's important with a little
> one. Even if I'm pretty tired when I get up, all I have to do is look at that
> little face, and I feel good. It's not just a case of doing extra things. I'm not
> doing extra things. This is what has to be done when you have a baby. . . .
> You learn so much too. It's a thrill to watch the various senses start to come
> into play. She'll make a gurgling noise that's close to a vowel sound or an
> actual syllable, and I'll repeat it. I love the communication. The baby smiles
> more around me than she does around [her mother].

Unlike primary breadwinners or childless men, these "involved fathers" do not draw distinct boundaries between the tasks of mothers and
fathers. The time constraints on their wives combine with their own
need and preference for economic sharing to promote financial and social interdependence. Neither breadwinning nor nurturing is defined as
one person's domain. As the utility worker pointed out:

> It's not like, "Give me your money, and I hold it; or you take my money
> and hold it." We put it in one pot and take care of whatever we need. . . .
> We pull the same weight. . . . As far as time and being around the house is
> concerned, I can stay home more than [my wife] can stay home. I come
> home in the afternoon, and I'm here with [my daughter] after school. [My
> wife] can come home at night to be with her. She likes her job, and she likes
> the sharing. She's got both worlds. So it has worked out good.

Like employed mothers, involved fathers must juggle the dual demands of employment and parenthood. While men do not generally
jeopardize their chances for workplace success by becoming fathers,
those men who wish to spend time with their children must trade off between work and family in much the same kinds of ways that employed
mothers do. A bank vice-president, married to a woman with a career
in public relations, began to relax his obsessive work habits when his
daughter was born:

> They changed immediately, which is exactly what I expected would hap-
> pen, and I've never really gone back to my old habits of working all the
> time. I still work long days in the office, but I get home every night to re-
> lieve the babysitter by six. I hardly ever work on weekends, and I don't
> work at home. So, yes, my habits have changed.

These involved fathers come closest to embracing the "interdependent" vision of gender equality upheld by work-committed mothers.
They see moral and practical advantages to shared caretaking. Accord-

ing to the construction worker quoted earlier, domestic as well as work-place equality is not only the most practical response to changed economic conditions but also the best way to avoid the resentment and conflict that too often occur between husbands and wives:

> With the baby, we do everything even-steven. What other way can you go nowadays, the whole economy being what it is? But that's also the way it should be. Even if I had the money to take care of things [myself], [my wife] has a calling, a vocation, that she needs to fulfill and I want her to fulfill. We're in this together; we both want to be an influence on the child. The next logical step is for both of us to spend time with her. . . . I feel there won't be any of this women-against-men in our marriage.

If work-committed women face numerous obstacles in their search for ways to combine career and motherhood, then nurturing fathers also face deeply rooted structural barriers to full equality in parenting. Even when the desire to participate in parenting is strong, these men encounter significant constraints on implementing their preferences. Role reversal, for example, is rarely a realistic option, since men's wages remain essential to the survival of the vast majority of households and few couples are comfortable with an arrangement in which a woman supports a man. The utility worker found being a "househusband" unacceptable, despite his preference for not working:

> *Is there an ideal job for you?*
>
> Staying home. But, it's just not possible. I couldn't just quit and say, "You work, and I'll stay home." But if we were put into the situation where we didn't have to work, I could tell her we could both quit. When I hit the Lotto . . . but right now, I'm stuck.

Were it not for the economic and psychological need to earn a steady income through paid employment, these men might be far more involved in child rearing than is currently possible. Yet, as the supports for homemaking mothers erode, supports for homemaking fathers have not arisen to offset the growing imbalance between children's needs and families' resources. Like domestically oriented women, a rehabilitation counselor defined paid work in terms of a "job," not a "career." Unlike such women, however, he lacked the option to trade his paid but tiresome job for the more personally fulfilling work of parenting:

> I don't like to work. I work because I need the money, and I want to give my family the best I could [*sic*], but work's not that important to me. I'm not the type that has career aspirations and [is] very goal-oriented. To tell you the truth, if I won the lottery, and I didn't have to work, I wouldn't. But I would volunteer. I would work in a nursery school. I would do a lot more volunteer work with my daughter's school. I would love to go on trips

that the mothers who don't work get a chance go to on. I would like to be more active in the PTA, get my hands into a lot of different volunteer organizations. I would *love* that. But I can't.

In sum, while women grapple with the choice between motherhood and committed employment, men are generally denied such a choice. Even when a man wishes to be an involved father, rarely is he able to trade full-time employment for parental involvement. The primary breadwinning surveyor noted, with some envy, that although women remain disadvantaged, many still retain the option not to work—an option few men enjoy:

> Women can have the best of both worlds, whereas men can only have one choice. A woman has a choice of which way she wants to go. If she wants to be a successful lawyer, she has that choice. If she wants to stay home, she also has that choice most of the time. Women have doors opened for them and their meals paid for. They have the best of both worlds; men are just stuck with one.

Structural and ideological barriers to men's participation in child rearing inhibit the prospects for genuine equality in parental and employment options. Limits on men's options constrain even the most feminist men's ability and willingness to embrace genuine symmetry in gender relations. The truncated range of choices available to men restricts the options open to women as well.

BEYOND THE DEBATE ON THE FAMILY

Social change in family arrangements has expanded the range of options adult women and men encounter, but the inconsistent nature of change has also created new personal dilemmas, more complex forms of gender inequality, and a growing social and ideological cleavage between more traditional family forms and the emerging alternatives. Since people have different exposure to changes in the structure of marriage, the economy, and the workplace, they have developed contrasting responses. Some have developed new patterns of family life that emphasize either greater freedom from family commitments (for example, childless women and men and uninvolved divorced fathers) or more equal sharing of breadwinning responsibilities (for example, work-committed women and involved fathers). Others have endeavored to re-create a more traditional model of gender exchange in spite of the social forces promoting change (for example, women who are domestically oriented and men who are primary breadwinners). The growth of alternative patterns of family life amid the persistence of more traditional forms has not produced a new consensus to replace the old, but rather an increasing competition among a diverse range of family types. This range cuts across gender, as different groups of women and of men find themselves in opposing positions. The complex landscape of emerging family patterns defies generalizations about either the decline or persistence of American families. Instead, men and women are developing multiple "family strategies" and contradictory directions of change to cope with the contrasting dilemmas they confront.

If the uneven and inconsistent nature of change has produced social division and political conflict in the short run, then the long-run fate of American family life depends on finding genuine resolutions to the dilemmas and conflicts that make all family choices problematic.[24] Such an approach would move beyond a "zero-sum" politics of the family to acceptance of and support for diversity in family life; it would reduce the barriers to integrating work and family for employed parents of either sex; and it would promote gender equality in rights, responsibilities, and options regarding parenting and employment. The conflicts and dilemmas spawned by uneven social change can only be resolved by striving to make change itself more equal and consistent.

The structural changes that have produced the diversification of family forms and the emergence of new family dilemmas are deeply rooted, mutually reinforcing, and far beyond the capacities of either individuals or governments to reverse. The loosening of the bonds of permanent marriage, the erosion of the male "family-breadwinner wage," the expansion of workplace opportunities for women, and the decline in the incentives and supports for childbearing and full-time mothering, are not to be reversed. The foreseeable future is unlikely to provide a return to a period of hegemony for the breadwinner-homemaker family (often mislabeled "traditional") or to any one family type, no matter what its form. But clear-cut and fully satisfying resolutions to the dilemmas and conflicts of unequal and uneven change have yet to emerge. In this context, the central political challenge should not be defined as how to halt the so-called decline of the family. Instead, we need to find a way to transcend the conflicts among the emerging array of "family groups." Surely, the first step is to abandon the search for one, and only one, correct family form in favor of addressing the full range of dilemmas and needs spawned by inevitable but unequal change. Only then will citizens and policymakers be able to forge a humane and just set of opportunities for all parents and their children.

THREE

Minor Difficulties

Changing Children in the Late Twentieth Century

Gary Alan Fine and Jay Mechling

Our children, as Peter Berger once put it, serve as "our hostages to history," by which he meant that the human imperative for continuity—the projecting into the future for one's own children, whatever good things one has in one's own life—has an essentially conservative influence on the institutional order. To love one's children is to have "a stake in the continuity of the social order," and to love one's parents is to want to preserve at least something of their world.[1] Children are not merely reproductions of our individual selves; they bear our communities' values and meanings. They are the guardians of the twenty-first century.

The way that we view the future is linked to our images of our offspring and to our hopes and fears for them. Likewise, these images influence how our children respond to us, and our response influences their behaviors. If we look at the history of childhood, as described in Philippe Ariès's *Centuries of Childhood,* we see that images of children have varied considerably over time.[2] Similarly, children's images of themselves are in dynamic tension because their cultures are based in the adult cultures that surround them and are shaped through material circumstances.

Unlike some apocalyptic writers, we avoid the claim that change in the role of children in the late twentieth century has been *particularly* radical. The gloomy view seems more moral or ideological than empirical. We may be too close to the changes to assess their dimensions and effects with confidence, or to understand latent effects that are tethered to manifest ones. Still, we do accept that as this century ends, we have witnessed substantial changes in the lives of children. While we have not reached the "end of childhood" in a society that hates children, children's lives and cultures are responsive to shifts in the ways adults lead their lives. Since the lives of adults have changed, the conditions of children have clearly been transformed as well.

Children's dependency poses special problems for adult historians and social scientists wishing to understand childhood.[3] Identifying changes in the lives of children since World War II entails our sorting out the changing images of the child from the changing practices of child rearing, and this is not an easy distinction. Our goal is to understand the interplay between the environment that children inhabit, the forms of control used by adults, and the responses of children to this environment and control.

First, we explore the effects of the choices and control of adults on children—how the physical and material bases of society channel children's responses and how adult beliefs and actions affect children and adult behaviors toward children. The world as it is given to children is formulated by adults; the social problems that children face are determined by the adult social order. Adults set the material bases of childhood (both the physical and the economic aspects) and they also largely dominate the arrangements of social structure. We explore the way adults channel children into such social institutions as schools, social service agencies, religious establishments, and, of course, the family. The world children inhabit depends on how adults understand their children, how adults think they should interact with their children, and how they understand the ways other adults interact with children.

We also explore the ways children manage to sustain their own culture within the hegemonic structure imposed by adults. Adult practices are not so determining that children are not able to create their own meanings. Children find realms in which they can "be themselves" and share a social structure and folk structure. Whether children's cultures are "oppositional cultures" that eventually fall to the socializing power of the adult cultures is a question worth asking.[4] Our examination of adults' practices, of children's responses, and the complex negotiations between the two groups, moves toward identifying *paradoxes* in the lives of American children in the last half century. We are not the first to observe the "biformities," "dualisms," or contradictions within patterns of American culture.[5] We shall leave it to historians and other readers to decide whether the paradoxes in children's lives in late twentieth-century America are simply local versions of enduring dualisms or indicate something new.

THE PARADOX OF ADULT CHOICES

The contemporary realities of American life seem remarkably different from the realities that were current a half century ago. Some of the trappings of today, such as computers and televisions, were barely ideas fifty years ago. Other currently important trends existed prior to World War II, but did not have the impact that they now have, such as divorce, drug use, the existence of an urban underclass, federal welfare programs, suburbs, automobiles, sexually transmitted diseases, and the rise of consumer culture. Children are born into a world not of their own making. The world they confront is one created and sustained by adults in institutions ranging from families and neighborhoods to schools, youth organizations, churches, and more. This world was created over generations and a physical and social structure was established.

The physical and material reality of American society has been altered in the past forty-five years in both subtle and dramatic ways. The suburbanization of America has been particularly dramatic (from 23 percent of the population in 1950 to 45 percent in 1980).[6] Less dramatic, but still significant is the decline of the farm population (from 23 percent to 2 percent during the period 1940–87).[7] On the one hand, fewer children now reside outside of hailing distance of other children. On the other hand, in most areas of our cities, dense street culture has diminished. The faded images of New York City's Lower East Side at the turn of the century—the stoop culture—have largely vanished, except for enclaves in the poorest areas of large, urban, Eastern conglomerations, such as New York or Washington, D.C.[8] We have witnessed a "suburbanization of the city," not necessarily in terms of housing types, but in the disappearance of formerly "public" activities into protected spheres indoors.

These effects are filled with paradox. We argue that children have been both incorporated into adult society and set apart from it, to be given their own special, marginalized treatment. Children have been treated, sometimes simultaneously, as adults and as nonadults. We find this paradox in both adult attitudes toward children and in adult behavior.

On the "incorporated" side of the paradox are those critics of culture who argue some version of the "disappearance of childhood" thesis, namely, that television and other adult institutions have erased the boundary between childhood and adulthood, exposing children to every ugly secret of adulthood.[9] They say that childhood is no more, that children have been too integrated into knowledge of the stresses of adult society from which they should be protected for a while longer.

At the same time, children are increasingly isolated from contact with adults and adult worlds. Outside of formal, adult-sanctioned institutions, such as school or organized play, children are often left alone by adults. Brian Sutton-Smith, for example, demonstrates how toys contribute to what he sees as a main function of modern child rearing—"to turn the child into a person capable of functioning in isolation by itself."[10] The modern middle-class parent first buys the child a toy as a symbol of affection and bonding, then sends the child off to his or her own room to play alone with it. Careful analysis of toys and the ways in which children play with them confirms for Sutton-Smith that toys tend to decrease the sociability of play, modeling for children "the solitariness on which modern civilization relies." [11] Adult use of the television as a babysitter further models solitary activity, and the home video game means that the child no longer needs to go to a video game arcade (the 1970s equivalent of the pool hall) to bring at least some sociability into video play.

This is not to say that children only play alone. Children do play in peer groups, but the circumstances of group play have changed considerably. The children's peer groups of an earlier time were more *public,* operating in public spaces they shared with adults who had the right and moral authority to intervene in the activities of children. [12] The neighborhood was an extended family and, on some level, all adults had the right to intervene in the activities of all children. In a perverse way the drug dealer who hires children to hawk his wares and to warn him of trouble is harkening back to our "romantic" notions of the relationships between adults and children, in which the children were truly a part of the community. The relationship between the child and the adult criminal gang is by no means a "new" problem, even though these connections speak more to economic transactions than to moral education. [13]

Although children are being exposed to the themes of adult life, through television and through contact with adult deviance, they are receiving little guidance as to how they should respond. This leads to the greater sophistication of children—a sophistication that can both be a positive and a negative consequence of their access to adult information and their independence. The rise of computer literacy among some groups of children and their skills in the arts and sciences is deeply satisfying to their adult mentors. However, while there are these successes, there are children who are driven to obtain material objects at any cost, who become bored and alienated, and who make choices that adult society deems improper (pregnancy, alcohol, drug use, or gang activity). In the connection between informational access and lack of supervision the suburb and the inner city have more in common with each other than either has with our images of the small town.

Physical and Material Considerations

As we indicated earlier, adult practices have tended to separate the public spaces of children from those of adults, pushing the children to the margins. Urban folklore portrays an adult world filled with danger for children and teaches the lesson that children must behave in that sphere with adult-defined decorum. The children's public spaces (parks, corners, and some businesses) are continually subject to appropriation by adults.

The single area that is "supposed" to be a child's domain is the school, but adults are rarely content to let children be children within school boundaries. For instance, well-meaning supervisors rigidly prevent children from participating in school-yard fights.[14] What had once been a central feature of childhood jurisprudence, important for maintaining the status system of childhood, has been marginalized and transformed into deviance.[15] Recess has been eliminated in many school districts because educators could not easily define its benefits, and injuries were seen as outweighing the pleasure given to children. Case law holding cities and schools liable for injury, coupled with increasing insurance costs, have led to the closing of school yards and playgrounds outside of school hours, when they cannot be supervised.[16] So those elements that gave children control of their social world have been limited or eliminated entirely. Our concern for the welfare of our children has resulted in denying them responsibility for making mistakes, and for learning from those mistakes.

Another locale in which children (especially adolescents) bump into adults—often quite literally—is the shopping mall. Mall managers recognize that junior-high- and high-school-aged kids like to "hang out" at the mall, sometimes creating a "nuisance." Case law pertaining to malls tends to define malls as public spaces, so it is not easy to evict teenagers. Besides, teens do bring money to the malls and are tomorrow's affluent shoppers. Children have the privilege of consumption within the limits of their budgets, and consequently share these adult spaces so long as they behave according to the rules established by adults, rules often enforced differentially upon adults and minors. (Adolescents are often sanctioned for actions that are tolerated when performed by adults.)[17] For adolescents the mall is a place to "hang out," an expressive locale that is supposed to be devoted to adult, instrumental activities (though adult shopping can be just as expressive as the adolescent behavior). Some mall managers have decided on the solution of creating special places in the malls, such as video game arcades, and put those places down the "side streets" of the mall, away from the main thoroughfares. Thus, even "malling" by America's kids is structured to preserve both the social control that adults have over children and to minimize informal social contacts between the groups.

On the other hand, the suburbanization of American neighborhoods, the continuing geographical mobility of nuclear families, and the pervasive view of the private home as a "haven" from the public world combine to give children more control over their unsupervised free play. Parks with their large, unpatrolled expanses, backyards, homes lacking adult presence, and, especially, bedrooms provide arenas for relatively autonomous action. Children often acquire creative control over their own rooms. It is not uncommon for adults to have to ask permission to enter these spaces; the child's room serves as a haven from the family.

Changes in public technology affect the relationships between adults and children. The availability of transportation, coupled with American affluence since World War II, has increased children's mobility, thereby widening the geography of their experiences. It sometimes has been said that the geographical range of a preadolescent's bicycle represents the limits of his or her community.[18] Bicycles are, of course, a primitive technology, primarily suitable for younger children. Adolescents adore automobiles. The last few decades have witnessed unprecedented numbers of adolescents who can drive and who have access to automobiles. The proportion of fifteen- to nineteen-year-old licensed drivers increased from 46.9 percent in 1963 to 54.4 percent in 1987.[19] With the growth and sophistication of the used car market in the decades since World War II, it has become easier for adolescents to acquire moderately priced automobiles, affordable by adolescents or their parents. The automobile combines the opportunity for an expansion of mobility with a private domain, much like the adolescent's bedroom. The reality that the same sort of activities occur in both spaces (drinking, smoking, joking, and sexual expression) indicates how connected the two locations are. Further, adolescents' automobiles can invade and interfere with adults' spaces and, as a consequence, need to be controlled. Adults have attempted—with mixed success—to prevent cruising, partly by establishing curfews that eliminate late-night driving and by bearing down on adolescent drinking and driving. All of these actions, while grounded in a concern for the adolescent, are equally based in the belief that driving is a privilege that can be suspended at the whim of adult society.

Social Environment

During the past several decades American social relations have changed enormously with significant effects on children. It was only in 1954 that the Supreme Court determined that it was unconstitutional for black and white children to attend segregated schools, and it took several decades for this ruling to be implemented even partially. Along with desegregation, the United States significantly liberalized its immigration policy in 1965 with the passage of the Immigration and Nationality Act. Today the immigrants from Southeast Asia, Eastern Europe, the Soviet Union, Mexico, Africa, and Latin America bring to school classrooms and to neighborhoods a new multicultural texture. Add to this the mainstreaming of mentally and physically handicapped (differently abled) children, and one finds the range of peers for children in the 1990s dramatically wider than for children in the 1950s. These changing social conditions will di-

versify children's cultures, since those cultures depend on a transformation of known cultural elements.[20] To the extent that the store of known
information increases, the diversity of children's culture will increase, although this depends on the assumption that children from diverse backgrounds will mix informally, as well as in adult-controlled settings.

Consequently one must be careful not to expect a grand melding of
the cultures of childhood. To date it has been easier for Asian-American
children to be integrated into the culture of "majority" children than for
blacks or Hispanics to be so integrated. We see plenty of evidence of the
influence of the forms of African-American expressive cultures upon
the cultures of white Americans, but white children can appropriate these
cultural elements (slang, dress, music, dance, gesture, and so on) without
accepting black children as equals and without acknowledging the worth
of the values that led to the creation of these expressive elements.

The revolution in gender roles during the past quarter century, although slow, has had some impact on children's cultures. The women's
movement and related demographic changes affect the circumstances of
children. Girls are no longer fitted with occupational and avocational
"girdles," at least in the overt fashion that was so evident a few years ago.
Women's employment outside the home has altered children's lives. With
many women working at full-time jobs, children are either placed in
after-school cultures that permit them to interact with peers, often with
only occasional oversight by adults, or, if they are older, they are permitted to live their lives separate from the oversight of their adult supervisors. Latchkey children are not a new phenomenon, but they have a
special importance in today's communities, in which few neighbors, if
any, will serve as surrogate parents or feel responsibility for doing so.

The increased numbers of women working outside the home also
affects younger children. Perhaps the most significant change in child
rearing has been the dramatic growth in the number of full-time day
care providers. Day care providers include corporate entities ("McKids,"
as they are sometimes called) as well as individuals who care for children
in private homes. Much debate has ensued over whether day care has
deleterious effects on the health of children who are put into it and
whether these children are more aggressive.[21] Whatever the case, these
venues permit children to form their own group cultures at an earlier
age than had been customary before collective child-rearing systems became common. American child-rearing practices can be conceptualized
as a blend of the nuclear family structure (on evenings and weekends)
and a kibbutz nursery (during weekdays). The long-term effects of this
type of system are uncertain, and, because of the many cross-cutting factors that prevent causal certainty, may never be known definitively. Atti-

tudes toward these changes depend to a great degree on our ideological beliefs about these changes in family life.

Family structure also influences the culture of childhood. As the two previous chapters have documented, the number of family forms in the United States has multiplied, perhaps exponentially. In many schools, fewer than half the members of a high school class live with both biological parents. Many children pass through several family transformations during their maturation. While neither single parents, step-parents, nor blended families constitutes "the norm," all are normal. Contacts among children from a variety of family types and life experiences increase the range of family group cultures that children can draw upon in creating their own group cultures. Some family types may broaden the networking of children, particularly when the mother and father reside apart; a modern child may belong to two radically different social networks. This mobility also increases the knitting together of the youth subculture, tightening the network of small groups.[22]

The Professionalization of Parenting

An important feature of American culture in the years since World War II has been the greater willingness of citizens to rely on experts to tell them how to think, feel, and act.[23] Child rearing is an activity adults feel increasingly unprepared for and anxious about performing, so it is little wonder that expert advice so quickly came to dominate this aspect of life. Dr. Benjamin Spock's *The Common Sense Book of Baby and Child Care*, first published in 1945, is only the most famous of a stream of postwar volumes providing advice to parents—and not merely the nuts and bolts of physical child care but also guidance in forming the emotional life of the child.

As Stearns and Stearns demonstrate, expert advice to parents, to married couples, to school teachers, and to office managers has increasingly stressed the domestication of anger and of other unpleasant emotions.[24] Parents have attempted to control their physical aggression and anger toward their children, and children are expected to do likewise. Temper tantrums are seen as social problems that must be dealt with by emphasizing rational discussion and the value of controlling one's emotions. Experts stress the importance of emotional stability and tranquility for healthy family life. This has a dual effect. Anger has been given a "magical" power, power that separates it from the mundane realm of everyday life. Now, a patina of guilt overlays the expression of anger, previously considered a natural emotion.

Parents and other adults are inevitably powerful influencers of children's lives. Adults read children stories, sing them songs, give them books to read, tell them proverbs, teach them games, buy them toys, take them to movies, and control the televised narratives, including commercials, that consume so much time. (The average American preschool child watches twenty-five hours of television every week.) It seems obvious that as parents face new social realities, so will their children. What we have witnessed in the past half century, sped up, no doubt, in the past twenty-five years, is a change in the relationship between American parents and their children so that children are both more and less autonomous, more and less dependent, than ever before.

THE EXPANSION OF CHILDREN'S RIGHTS

To take one important example of the changing relationship between parents and children, consider the issue of "children's rights" as a variant of the incorporation/separation paradox.[25] The notion of "rights" emerged relatively recently in Western history, and debates over competing rights occur in specific times and places in response to social strains.[26] Children's rights movements in America go back at least to nineteenth-century worries about child labor, but the establishment of the modern welfare state in this century has led to children's rights battles, revealing the paradoxical status of minors.[27] During the past few decades adults have both given additional rights to children and taken significant privileges from them. The individual child is given increased rights of access to institutions and state-guaranteed protection from harm, while, simultaneously, the behaviors that children and adolescents are permitted to enact have been limited.

The proper role of children in our society, particularly in relationship to adult society, is a matter of vehement debate. Some advocates for children claim that we are a society that does not much care for our children.[28] Others claim that we need to give children additional freedoms, while still others say that we should restrict those freedoms. Some call for additional protections, and others say that these protections have costs. When we speak of the expansion of children's rights, we tend to speak about "rights" that are institutionally protected. Each child is guaranteed the right to be protected and to have equal access to resources. These guarantees typically come from the state in one of its various manifestations—schools, courts, social welfare agencies, and the like: these are sponsored rights. Children are less likely than they once were to be harmed or discriminated against because of their special conditions or their helplessness vis-à-vis adults. The expansion of children's rights, therefore, comes by virtue of defining them as relatively powerless. Consider two examples.

Most school districts prevent teachers from physically disciplining or restraining children except under unusual circumstances. This policy, while protecting the child from abuse and pain, reduces the social power of teachers, and consequently reduces the range of informal options that teachers have to deal with unruly children. Through current arrangements, discipline in the classroom is only possible if the children accept it. Disruptive children and their parents are not always willing to be party to the discipline. As a consequence, other, more formal and bureaucratic systems of disciplining children need to be established, and these have the effect of turning the school into a kind of court.[29] The child who resists informal understandings may become enmeshed with psychologists, counselors, and psychiatrists, ostensibly to protect the rights of the child, but equally to protect the system from claims that those rights have been violated.

A second contest between the rights of individual children and the rights of the collectivity or institution arises in the issue of "mainstreaming" difficult children in the schools. For example, in the small, rural community of Cannon Falls, Minnesota, a dispute has erupted over the right of a first-grade girl to attend a regular classroom.[30] The girl had a behavior disorder involving a lack of impulse control and low social intuition. She regularly assaulted the other children in her classroom, kicking, punching, and biting them, dozens of times each week. What is to be done for this girl and her classmates? The school district, lacking a special education class, determined that she had a right to remain in the class and that she would benefit from being mainstreamed, despite advice of doctors that she be institutionalized. The school considered the child handicapped and, consequently, entitled to education in a regular classroom under the Education of All Handicapped Children Act of 1975. The child and her parents wanted her to remain in the regular classroom.

Yet, what about the other children? Our education system once routinely segregated handicapped, difficult, and disruptive children, and poor students were given little incentive to continue schooling. Today a "normal" education is seen as a right, but this right is not without social costs. The children in this girl's class, one is led to believe, cannot fully devote themselves to learning because of her actions. Many are frightened, and perhaps some will even suffer psychological trauma as a consequence of her behavior. They feel that they are being sacrificed on the altar of mainstreaming, a choice adults make that affects the children. As this case demonstrates, the balancing point between the individual rights of the child and the collective good have shifted over the past two decades to provide more access for the individual child at the expense of other children. A similar issue concerns the rights of children with AIDS to attend public schools. While AIDS is not per se a children's issue, the presence of infected children in school raises the question of whether the individual child has rights that transcend the desires of other classmates and their parents? Even if some children are made anxious and parents band together to object, the consensus now seems to be that a child with AIDS should be treated similarly to children who are not infected.

RESTRICTION OF PRIVILEGES

As suggested above, the expansion of rights in some areas has been met by a restriction of privileges in others. Children's rights to equal access to institutions and protection have been expanded at the same time that their behavioral freedoms have been curtailed. Adolescents seem the most notable targets of efforts to curtail freedoms. During the late 1960s and early 1970s a greater variety of behavioral options were available for teens, options not always legally permitted, but winked at by adults. During the past decade the government has felt increasingly secure in limiting choices for minors. This is evident in adults' attempts to control adolescents' sexual behavior and access to alcohol, tobacco, and other drugs. Consider changes in the drinking laws. Whereas between 1970 and 1975 twenty-nine states lowered the age at which young people could legally purchase alcoholic beverages, between 1975 and 1984 twenty-seven states raised their drinking ages. By 1986 the federal government demanded that the minimum legal drinking age be raised to twenty-one, and threatened states that did not comply with the loss of federal highway funds.[31] High schools were eliminating smoking rooms and declaring their campuses "smoke-free zones." Simultaneously, a drug panic gripped the nation, particularly with regard to teenage usage. With the increase of teenage pregnancy (or "promiscuity") and sexually transmitted diseases, baby-boomer adults demanded that adolescents refrain from behaviors that they had enjoyed as teens.

What sustains these paradoxes about the rights and privileges accorded to children is late-twentieth-century ideas about *the innocent child.* Children and even adolescents are increasingly seen as being in need of protection from themselves and from others. If we consider the dramatic social problems of the 1980s, we find that a large number deal with threats to children. Those social problems that do not specifically center on children—such as the homeless, AIDS, and cocaine addiction—are often framed in terms of their effects upon children: homeless families, pediatric AIDS, and cocaine babies. This trend shows no sign of abating; indeed, each morning newspaper brings new examples. As Joel Best notes, the image of the "threatened innocent" became common in the 1980s.[32]

One can see these ideas played out early in the decade in parents' efforts to transform Halloween from a child's folk festival of liminal disorder and inversion to an orderly, "safe" event, closely supervised by adults. The Tylenol product tampering incident of October 1982 sparked the adult move to protect the innocent child from the ravages of Halloween mass murderers, even though the two events seemed on the surface to have little in common. For decades, American adults and children alike had dealt casually with cautionary legends about razor blades in apples, poisoned candy, and heated pennies. But adults responded to the Tylenol tampering by virtually eliminating Halloween altogether that year. As Best and Horiuchi observe, Halloween crystalizes the fears that parents have for their children.[33] The world, even the suburban neighborhood, is a dangerous place for children, a place where even most neighbors are more or less strangers. Halloween epitomizes this concern because it is the only night when children seek routine contact with adult strangers to demand "treats." Despite the absence of children being poisoned by strangers on Halloween, fear runs deep. Hospitals now routinely x-ray children's treats, but in the 1980s adults preferred to organize community Halloween parties and tried to eliminate trick-or-treating altogether.[34] The taming of Halloween that Gregory Stone noted near mid-century has continued, as it has been taken away from the control of children.[35]

The recent social problem of "missing children" dramatically reflects adult fears for innocent children. The number of children abducted by strangers remains very small, certainly under a hundred each year.[36] Most children who "vanish" are either runaways or are snatched by non-custodial parents. While these may be important problems, our interest is in the cultural implications of the unrealistic, widespread adult panic over missing children. A child's vanishing galvanizes a neighborhood and community. In Minnesota, the apparent adbuction of an eleven-year-old from rural Stearns county set off numerous community activities—billboards, rewards, rallies, arm-bands, vigils, and the like. The missing boy, Jacob Wetterling, brought Minnesota together as a community of care and fear.

The "epidemic" of physical and sexual abuse of children in the 1980s taps the same adult anxieties as do Halloween and missing children. There can be no doubt that children are abused, physically and sexually; the nature of abuse and the circumstances of the victims make child abuse a difficult phenomenon to study for large cultural trends. Is child abuse increasing, or have the conditions for uncovering abuse changed? Again, the cultural response to abuse is the "text" that concerns us here. Stories about alleged "sex rings," pornographic filming in day care centers, and satanic rituals circulate far out of proportion to the actual instances. The horror and anger experienced by adult audiences hearing these stories show us the symbolic potency and centrality of our adult view of children as innocent victims.

In 1984, for example, Minnesota was shocked by a county prose-cutor's claim of a child sex ring operating in a small exurban community of Minneapolis. The prosecutor accused two dozen adults of sexually abusing twenty children. Eventually she dropped all of the charges (one man pleaded guilty), claiming that further prosecutions might jeopardize a case involving child murder and pornography. State investigators found that the sexual abuse case was mismanaged from the start, and, aside from the single conviction, most of the other people who were charged were almost certainly innocent. The McMartin preschool case, in which the directors of a preschool in Manhattan Beach, California, were tried on fifty-two counts of child molestation, ended in January 1990 with an acquittal. The jury was unable to arrive at a guilty verdict in the longest-running (two and a half years) and most expensive criminal trial in the nation's history. The public was outraged; some callers to a San Francisco Bay Area radio talk show were almost sputtering in their anger. The prosecutors, bowing to public pressure, decided to refile the charges on which the jury could not reach a verdict, but the second jury was also unable to reach agreement and the case was finally dropped.

Parents' concerns that their children could be harmed, or even driven to suicide, by fantasy role-playing games or rock music lyrics are part of this fear of the corruption of innocent children. In many cases, adults envision a vast, hidden conspiracy of satanists who are pied pipers to the young. While not all of those who campaign against fantasy games and rock music share these apocalyptic visions, the concern they do share stems from the image of children being corrupted by evil strangers. Such cultural products can destroy the child's, or even the adolescent's, free will. Several notorious cases, including a case involving Judas Priest, involve the deaths of teenagers who allegedly listened to heavy metal rock songs advocating suicide.[37] However, these cases have not led to conviction of the musicians. Some adult groups, such as the Parents' Music Resource Center, cofounded by Tipper Gore and other political figures, advocate warning labels on rock music packaging or, in some cases, bans on certain offensive lyrics.

Certainly a few abductions by strangers occur each year; certainly children are abused by parents, relatives, trusted caretakers, and some strangers; and certainly some adolescents commit suicide. But the scale, intensity, and rhetoric of the public reaction to these cases suggest that even a few instances raise powerful alarms. Children remain a screen upon which adults tend, in many cases, to project their own fears about the larger social world.

THE AGE OF THE INNOCENT CHILD

Why have the 1980s seemed to adults such a dangerous time for children? What is there about our culture and the social location of the people worrying about these matters that these should be seen as serious social problems at the present time?

The most straightforward explanation is that we are more concerned about these issues because dangers to children actually have increased. Unfortunately, this approach does not get us very far. For one thing, we do not have reliable data for drawing comparisons across time. Changes in reporting practices and changing definitions of behaviors such as child abuse erode our confidence in the data.[38] Even if we could trust the data, figures on injuries, deaths, and kidnappings suggest that the last decade has been no more dangerous for children than past decades; indeed, one could argue that children were much more at risk before World War II than since.

More persuasive, we believe, is an approach stressing the construction of social problems. Those issues that the public turns its attention to are symbolic constructions, and this symbolization mediates reality. We do not claim that parents are misguided or wrong in their choice of social concerns, but rather that circumstances selected and defined as major public concerns are chosen out of social and psychological pressures. As Kessen has argued, the very notion of the *child* is a social construction.[39] What becomes a salient issue depends on factors that transcend statistics. Statistics can be massaged in numerous, rhetorically sophisticated ways.

Children are subject to a particular form of *symbolic demography*. Symbolic demography refers to cultural beliefs that result from the intersection of demographic trends with the ideologies of the populations experiencing the trends. Zelizer, for example, argues that over the past century, American children have increasingly been defined as "priceless."[40] With the decline in family size, each child is less replaceable; yet, paradoxically, because of restrictions on child labor and increased affluence, the child has no intrinsic economic value. Since World War II, parents have decided to raise small families, to give extensive attention and resources to each child. Children, it is said, should be works of art. The modern child becomes priceless not only because of his or her replacement value but also because of the child's investment value, both in material and emotional terms. Our point is that many demographic trends are currently filtered through popular perception with cultural consequences.

Consider the symbolic demography of the American baby-boom cohort. During the 1970s and 1980s the baby-boom generation became parents, producing the "echo boom." If parents in the 1950s and 1960s had anxieties peculiar to their social arrangements, so did the baby-boomers when they became parents.[41] Postwar families established patterns of suburban life relatively isolated from the extended family and the world of work. Children growing up in suburban families in the 1960s experienced a dramatic, gender-based division of labor—the existence of relatively clear, if not always fully functional, roles. Cultural images of the family reflected and reinforced these demographic patterns. The baby-boom generation followed the television lives of the Anderson family ("Father Knows Best"), Ozzie and Harriet Nelson, and "Beaver" Cleaver.

The demographic realities of family life changed in the 1970s and 1980s, though the public images of the family were slow to catch up. Economic trends, divorce rates, the women's movement, and other forces undermined the gender-based organization of the family. Memories and images of growing up in the 1950s could no longer serve as useful guides for behaving in the 1970s and 1980s. Eventually, popular culture images began to catch up with the demographic realities; "The Brady Bunch" depicted a blended family, and several popular television series (for example, "One Day at a Time" and "Kate and Allie") featured single mothers struggling to make a living and to be good parents—and succeeding.

Still, television sit-coms provide little real guidance for a generation of parents experiencing a radical discontinuity between the family lives they knew as children and the family lives they were attempting to create for their own children. These discontinuities help to create the fears and anxieties motivating the adult choices we described earlier. People project personal and social uncertainties onto external dangers.[42] Uncertainty and stress are transformed into external threats, making them psychologically tolerable. Fears of kidnappers and Halloween sadists reflect fears of being an inadequate parent.

Perhaps a more dramatic fear is the physical abuse of children. All parents get angry with their children and the vast majority use physical force or psychological pressure.[43] At one time, these behaviors were considered normal for child rearing.[44] Today this "normal" parenting is fraught with guilt in the face of the ideological domestication of anger. Worse, wrongly or publicly labeled actions can lead to an official investigation and the possibility of having one's own child—that most valuable of possessions—snatched away by agents of the state. Every yell, each slap, has a nascent terror for the parent, as well as for the child. The conflation of missing children with unhappy runaways simply adds to parental fears and mistrust. The public narratives of missing children embroider real events with the power of real anxieties.

Parents of the 1970s and 1980s suffer complex reactions to their own insecurities about raising children. They project their own fears and concerns about their potential inadequacies. The threats must not come from inside the family, but from outside, because imagining the threats from inside the family are too painful and too psychologically possible. Guilt feelings about latchkey children and about putting children in day care centers—both necessities, given the demographic and economic realities of the 1970s and 1980s—find expression in the outrage over "missing" children. In a sense, it is the parents who are "missing," both in the sense that they are absent from their children's worlds and in the sense that they are "missing" their children's growing up.

Similarly, the meanings of paradoxical messages to 1980s children about drugs, alcohol, and sex may lie as much in the life experience of the baby-boomer parents as in the objective conditions of the lives of children in the 1980s and 1990s. There is strong evidence of alcohol abuse and drug abuse in children, rates of teenage pregnancies and abortions are startling, and sexually transmitted diseases increase the risks of sexual behavior; thus there is a real basis for the fears that parents have about their children. At the same time, however, one cannot deny that parents' experiences also condition their responses to what they perceive as the world in which their children are coming of age.

Baby-boomers grew up in the relatively repressed 1950s and early 1960s. The "cult of domesticity" of the 1950s demanded control of sexuality. Elaborate dating rituals delayed sexuality, marriage, and childbirth. Alcohol continued to be the intoxicant of choice for the middle class, and recreational drugs were out on the dark edges of society, supposedly used by people of color and other marginal folk, such as artists and musicians. In general, public discourse of the 1950s favored the clean, cool, and controlled, over the dirty, hot, and wild. As a result, many baby-boomers coming of age in the 1960s began experimenting with sexuality and drugs, often simultaneously. The availability of the birth control pill changed things in ways historians and social scientists are still sorting out. The women's movement, the Civil Rights Movement, and the anti-war movement changed the conditions of childhood and adolescence in many ways. Marginal cultures of the 1950s moved into the center of attention in the 1960s, as African-American, Far Eastern, and other cultures produced the multivocal music, dress, dance, and philosophies of the 1960s. In contrast with the cool, controlled 1950s, the 1960s and early 1970s reveled in ecstasy, abandon, and sometimes reckless experimentation.

We can read the late 1970s and 1980s as a cultural commentary on the 1960s. Baby-boomers who smoked marijuana, ingested drugs, and experimented sexually in their youth now scorn cigaret smokers and white sugar.[45] Middle age blunts the edges of experimentation. If this interpretation is correct, then parents of the 1980s come to "read" the alcohol use, drug abuse, and sexual behavior of their children. The child's body again has become a potent symbol, and the treatment of that body— including abduction, physical abuse, sexual abuse, sexual behavior, drug use, alcohol use, suicide, and abortion—has become a powerful cultural text dominating public discourse. The centrality of these images, grounded in the experiences of the baby-boom generation, is a function of that generation's real and symbolic importance in the nation's demographic profile. In a crucial sense, the concerns of the baby-boom generation are the concerns of public discourse.[46] Because so many in the baby-boom cohort are parents, that group's agenda is the agenda for the nation.

Of course, we must not overextend our argument for the centrality of symbolic demography for understanding the effects of adult decisions on children over the past four decades. Class and race differences in this period are dramatic, and attitudes about female children probably have changed a great deal more than attitudes about male children. In all instances, however, the social scientist must look at how the demographic conditions of a social group interact with the symbolic framing of their lives. Parents attempt to socialize their children according to their own subjective and symbolic understandings of the conditions of their lives.

THE RESPONSES OF CHILDREN

We have thus far painted a one-sided portrait of the lives of American children. As we have aimed to show, adults have been particularly confused and ambivalent in their treatment of children over the past few decades, in part because adults have been facing a bewildering array of social transformations. Amidst certain kinds of neglect of children, and perhaps in response to this neglect, adults have moved to exert increasing control over children, from the domestication of anger to the domestication of play.

Yet, children have their own resources for resisting adult control. Children have always maintained their cultures—both authentic and derivative—separate from the cultures of adults. This chapter will conclude by looking at changes in the ways children create their social worlds.

Developmental and sociohistorical forces collide in the creation of the child's world. Our common sense tells us that biological and psychological development must be significant elements in children's cultures; yet we also know that theories about the biology and psychology of child development in any historical period are not immune from ideological pressures. It is therefore impossible to present a true and complete picture of children's culture. The social psychoanalytic approach of Harry Stack Sullivan, for example, led him to emphasize the separateness of the preadolescent's chumship, wherein "one finds oneself more and more able to talk about things which one had learned, during the juvenile era, not to talk about."[47] Others downplay the importance of the chum for social development. These disagreements should not stymie us, but we do need to recognize that our models of the child's development bear social meanings that affect the child we "find" in our inquiries and, further, we need to recognize that there are numerous children's cultures grounded in groupings that may be quite different from each other.

The first thing we can say about children's cultures is that despite differences in content, most research has indicated that children maintain folk traditions that are remarkably resilient. Although children's cultures draw on a wide range of adult cultural materials, they remain indigenous social forms. Folklorists of childhood recognize that many elements in the cultural life of children are nearly unchanging, lasting for centuries, transmitted from older to younger cohorts.[48] This transmission is remarkable in that it is grounded in oral communication. Unlike adult culture (in many respects a written, material, or electronic culture), children rely on their memories. Children remember and share what is important to them. These materials are malleable and alter according to children's changing interests and needs. Here we find what one of us has called "Newell's Paradox," which means the paradox that children's folk cultures are distinctive in being both conservative and innovative.[49] On the thematic level, children's cultures are remarkably stable, but on the level of a local group, traditions are continually being developed.

A distinctive feature of children's expressive cultures are their antithetical stances toward official (adult) cultures.[50] The 1988 presidential election provided an instructive example of the antithetical nature of children's cultures. George Bush had raised as a campaign issue the fact that Michael Dukakis had vetoed, as governor of Massachusetts, a bill requiring teachers to lead students in the Pledge of Allegiance. Bush made it clear that children would pledge allegiance to the flag in the America he meant to lead. The scholar of children's expressive cultures, however, knows the foolishness of this debate. Art Linkletter built a 1950s television career around the fact that when young children learn such things by rote, they garble the text into nonsense words. When children finally are old enough to understand the words, they then invent and pass on parodies of the adults' sacred texts. Thus, the hallowed Pledge of Allegiance becomes, in the mouth of an eleven-year-old, "I pledge allegiance to the flag / Michael Jackson is a fag / Pepsi Cola burned him up / Now he's drinking 7 Up."

The antithetical stance of children's cultures sometimes requires secrecy or esoteric encoding in order for the lore to exist alongside adult cultures. Many antithetical strategies (for example, parody and non-sense) are built into children's lore, but one of the most prominent is "dirty play."[51] Children may be personally wonderful, kind, and good and still engage in play deemed highly undesirable by adult moral standards. Given the ideological suppression of disagreeable emotions, children may have good reasons to keep traditions that involve aggression, vandalism, obscenity, and racism hidden from sensitive adult guardians. Although children, if asked, would admit to behaving in ways adults find disagreeable because such "misbehaving" is fun, we can see such playful subversion as involving children's needs for control, status, social differentiation, and socialization to perceived adult norms.

Control

Dirty play constitutes a claim-making behavior. It proposes that children have the right to engage in activities and have opinions that contradict adult pressures. Children demand for themselves the right to make judgments about race, sex, and authority—precisely those areas of social structure that adults wish to preserve for themselves. Although the content of this play is troubling to adults, it is equally troubling that children should feel competent to make these judgments. Perhaps we can speak of children's culture that undermines the adult authority structures as "playful terrorism," a kind of mock guerrilla warfare. Such terrorism is politically impotent because of the disorganization of the "terrorist group," their lack of commitment and uniformity of beliefs, the tight control that adults have over them, and the rewards that can be offered to those who conform. Still, there are potential threats in the testing of boundaries and legitimacy, and so such actions, when they become known, may provoke harsh retribution.

Status

Children's cultures shape relationships within the group as well as outside. Behavior that is unacceptable to adults may gain a child status with peers. Children are engaged in a continual and consequential contest for status. Within any particular children's community resources are spread relatively equally, so status becomes crucial for distinguishing individuals. A premium exists for being willing to do things that other boys and girls want to do but are afraid to do. If consensus exists that a prank is desirable, the boy or girl who performs it or leads the group gains status for breaking the barrier of fear. The social rewards of "deviant" play suggest why it is so rare for children to engage in these behaviors while alone. It is not that children have destructive impulses, but rather that they want to show off in the presence of friends.

Social Differentiation

One important task for children is to define themselves in contrast to other groups that share characteristics with them. Whites are not blacks, boys are not girls; race and gender make a difference, and society reinforces these differences. Public norms of tolerance and civility find such judgments heretical and morally repugnant. Yet, from the standpoint of the child, these beliefs, like so much ethnocentrism, seem natural. Casting racial or gender insults on others provides a group with some measure of collective self-worth, admittedly at the expense of another group. While this need to put down another to gain self-esteem is unfortunate, the process is common at all ages. In childhood, when questions of identity-formation are crucial, it has a particular weight.

Socialization to Perceived Adult Norms

Hidden culture is not created *de novo;* rather, it is a transformation of what children see enacted by older peers and adults and in the various media to which they are exposed. It is transformed to meet their developmental imperatives and their level of understanding. The content of adult discourse and media to which children are exposed has impact, though often it is content that many adults sincerely wish they had not communicated because of its sexual, aggressive, and anti-social themes. To the extent that children are exposed to large segments of adult life, their cultures will represent transformations of these adult themes. Adults cannot shield preadolescents from what they do not wish them to learn. Aggression, sexism, and racism exist in adult activities and discourse, even when the adults are trying to discourage those behaviors. The exasperated parent's warning, "Listen to what I mean, not what I say," acknowledges the adult's impotence in the face of children's interpretation of messages.

CONCLUSION

Children reside in a world that they do not create. Dealing with this reality is complicated by the fact that it is constantly changing. It is not the world that children—and adults—faced in the past. The world changes, we change the world, and our responses to that new world change. One should be skeptical of the view that society today is especially at risk. Writers earn their keep by convincing gullible parents, educators, and care providers that some new, unique threat to children exists, but the truth is that the state of the world can always be pictured as a crisis by those with a mind and a motivation to do so.

Children and adults reside in a world that is delicately balanced; it always has been so. Yet, it is a moving equilibrium. The social drama, despite the obvious power difference between adults and children, is not entirely one-sided. As we approach the end of the century and embark on the inevitable self-reflection that such milestones always provoke, it is well to recognize that adults and children do not necessarily have the same cultural or social agendas. Children can, in some measure, resist the control of adults. While we, as adults, have some responsibility to help shape the worlds of children, we should also come to respect their natural response to our aid—a mix of gratitude and an understandable human desire to be left at peace.

If, as Berger suggests, children are hostages to history, socialization inevitably will be proactive. Through our children, we attempt to shape a future vision of society. We plant seeds that we hope others will harvest. Our collective concern about child rearing suggests that we care about more than ourselves: our children do matter, the communities in which they will reside count, and both can be shaped from a distance. How the twenty-first century will unfold is being determined in homes and schools in the twentieth.

FOUR

Ambivalent Communities
How Americans Understand Their Localities

Claude S. Fischer

Americans of the Left and of the Right esteem the local community. It rests in the pantheon of American civil religion paradoxically close to that supreme value, individualism. In our ideology, the locality is, following the family, the premier locus for "community," in the fullest sense of solidarity, commitment, and intimacy. Thus, activists of all political hues seek to restore, empower, and mobilize the locality.[1]

This chapter reviews, in broad strokes, the complex changes that have shaped the American locality and Americans' attachments to it in this century. Over the years, Americans have become more committed, in practical ways, to their localities, even while enjoying access to ever-widening social horizons. This localism has served most individual American families well, but the political role of the locality exacts severe costs to the national community.

CONTRASTING VISIONS OF COMMUNITY

Americans' affections for "community" are ironic, for much of American history and ideology undercut traditional local solidarity. Unlike Europe, the United States lacks the feudal experience of closed, corporate communities; its founders resisted hierarchy; marketplace liberalism undergirds its economics and politics; its settlers were linguistically, religiously, and culturally diverse; its people have always been mobile; its once-dominant farmers usually lived in isolated homesteads; and in all, unlike Europe, Americans have been, consensus has it, intensely individualistic.[2]

Paul Burstein and David Hummon, as well as Alan Wolfe, provided comments that helped improve this chapter, but I remain responsible for any errors it may contain.

79

In spite—or perhaps because—of these conditions, Americans have glorified and sought the local community.[3] From before Tocqueville to beyond Riesman, observers have described us as inveterate joiners, people in quest of fellowship. The quest has been for the locally based association as much or more than any other. Although American culture esteems the wilderness as an escape from society, as for Thoreau, it simultaneously values the small, rural community as the locus of intimate society, as in Brook Farm. Most Americans believe that small communities preserve morality.[4] Politicians' rhetoric celebrates the virtues of the small, local community. (Recall Geraldine Ferraro's claim in 1984 that her corner of Queens, New York City, was *really* just a small town—like Mondale's Elmore, Minnesota, and Reagan's Dixon, Illinois—and by being that, entitled her to the same halo of grassroots innocence that the others claimed.) And local political autonomy has long been entrenched in strong home rule, dispersed authority, and checks against central government. Americans continue to subscribe to "community ideologies," beliefs about the inherent connection between place and *persona,* theories that where we live partly determines who we are, and most often that the best people are to be found in the smallest, most localized places.[5]

This contradiction between individualism and the pursuit of fellowship has yielded paradoxical forms of "voluntary community" in the United States. The classic old-world village, nowadays viewed through pastel prisms, was a place of constraint. Confined together by barriers of geography, poverty, illness, ignorance, law, prejudice, and custom, most old-world people lived out their lives in a small group, shared a common fate, and knew one another intimately.[6] This familiarity, by the way, did not necessarily mean affection.[7] In contrast, Americans have more typically found their fellowship in voluntary associations, be it clubs, churches, or neighborhoods. They have also joined or left those associations as each individual deemed appropriate.[8] We can see this voluntarism in the American approach to caring for the unfortunate, well expressed in George Bush's "thousand points of light" rhetoric. And so with our neighborhoods. They are, as Morris Janowitz termed them, "communities of limited liability," associations in which we invest our families, wealth, and concern—but we guiltlessly leave them for larger houses, more rewarding jobs, or finer amenities.[9]

With minor exceptions, Americans founded their towns as business ventures.[10] Developers platted the land and advertised its bountiful future. Settlers came and then left in search of a higher standard of living.[11] Indeed, they left in vast numbers, making for a great churning of population in nineteenth-century America, through big cities and small towns alike. Despite sentiment, then, we have for the most part long treated our residential communities as "easy come, easy go," rather than as social worlds that envelop us.[12]

IS OURS A "ROOTLESS" SOCIETY?

How has the connection of Americans to their localities changed over the years? Many believe that ours has become an ever more "rootless" society; sage commentators diagnose "placelessness" as the source of modern America's ills.[13] The facts are more complex. In several ways, Americans have become more "rooted" to their localities, and in several ways, less rooted. To simplify these complexities, I will argue that, in net, several historical changes have *increased* Americans' commitments to their localities, *decreased* their dependence on the locality for sociability, but *increased* their political—and thus, social—significance.

We cannot directly judge how people of earlier periods felt about their localities and compare them to people of today, but we can examine several changes that, logically, should have affected Americans' attachments to place.[14] Several historical changes probably increased how much Americans care about and invest themselves in their localities.

Reduced residential mobility is one such change. Americans are more mobile than other Western peoples, and they have always been highly mobile. But this mobility has been declining. Historians, by comparing lists of town residents from one year to another, have found that Americans in the nineteenth century were at least as geographically mobile and perhaps twice as much so as contemporary Americans.[15] Since World War II, Census Bureau evidence shows, the total rate of moving from one house to another generally dropped (see figure 4.1). Among those who moved, proportionately more crossed county lines recently, a change attributable to suburbanization and thus implying that these movers remained in the same urban area. The year-to-year fluctuations can be tied to oscillations in the job and housing markets. But the general picture is one of modestly increasing residential *stability*.[16]

In cross-national perspective, however, Americans remain notably more footloose than Europeans, although only a little more so than the other continental Anglophone countries, Canada and Australia.[17] The reasons are probably structural (our many dispersed metropolises), historical (our open-door immigration until 1924), and cultural (our famed individualism). What has probably changed over the years is a modest shift from "push" to "pull" mobility. Some pushes on nineteenth-century Americans to move—such as land shortages, job losses, disasters, and poverty—weakened in the twentieth century, while pulls—such as retirement communities, climate, college, and job opportunities—expanded.

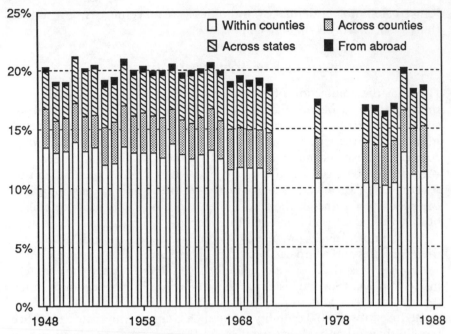

4.1 Percentage of U.S. Population Changing Residence in Previous Year.

SOURCES: Larry H. Long, *Migration and Residential Mobility in the United States* (New York: Russel Sage Foundation, 1988), 51; U.S. Bureau of the Census, *Geographic Mobility: March 1986 to March 1987*, Current Population Reports, Series P-20, No. 430 (Washington, D.C.: Government Printing Office, 1989), 2.

NOTE: *Year* refers to the twelve months prior to the spring of the indicated year.

Americans' greater residential stability has probably increased their attachment to their localities. Studies have repeatedly shown that the longer people live in a place the stronger their emotional and social commitments to it.[18]

Another secular change that, in net, probably increased local commitment is the dispersal of the urban population. Despite the popular image of the ever more crowded city, over the last century, American metropolises have been spreading and thinning out. As a result, proportionally more Americans live in suburban single-family houses, located in small, autonomous, suburban municipalities. For about a generation now, more Americans have lived in suburbs than in either center cities or non-metropolitan areas. These, low-density housing, and suburban governments, in turn, tend to encourage local commitments.[19]

(What about the great migration from farm to city in this century? In that area, one of rural Americans' chronic problems was their difficulty in forming communities—in organizing associations, mobilizing politically, or seeing one another socially.[20] For former homesteaders, the move to town probably increased local involvement.)

A third change, one connected to the growth of urban sprawl, has been the evolution of class-homogenous neighborhoods. At least until the early streetcar era in the 1880s, all but the affluent lived close to their jobs. The elite had their suburban enclaves, but different classes mixed in city neighborhoods, although residents were sometimes well separated by ethnicity. Today, neighborhoods are less segregated by ethnicity— greatly excepting black ghettos—but more finely differentiated by income level.[21] Greater local homogeneity also reinforces neighboring and attachment to the neighborhood.[22]

The great exception of the black ghettos in fact gives emphasis to the general increase in local homogeneity. During the twentieth century, blacks, at least those in the North, became more segregated from whites, even as white ethnic groups, and for that matter Asians and Hispanics, became less segregated from one another. This racial divide has provided to whites neighborhoods devoid of what many find to be the unsettling presence of blacks. It has largely confined blacks, including many in the middle class, to districts with other blacks, including the very poor. Analyses by Douglas Massey and his colleagues suggest that there may have been some small breaches in racial walls recently, but for poor blacks, geographic isolation increased through the 1970s.[23]

A fourth trend is increasing home ownership. Over the century, most American families came to own their homes, with the fastest increase occurring between 1940 and 1960, as figure 4.2 illustrates. The most dramatic change was among the young. In the 1940s the median age of male homeowners was forty-one, but in 1970 it was 28.[24] Home ownership has stagnated in the last fifteen to twenty years of housing inflation and economic doldrums, but remained historically high. (These data do not consider any increase in homelessness.)

Although Americans have long vested their dwellings with important moral qualities—a proper house both reflects and nurtures noble values[25]—in the nineteenth century, Americans did not esteem ownership as they do now. Many middle-class families were content to be renters. The connection between property and propriety apparently arose around the turn of the century, when increasing affordability, suburbanization, and ideologies of domesticity combined to make ownership easier and socially correct. Then, in the twentieth century, rising affluence, new mortgage instruments, government subsidies, tax breaks, and in the 1950s the family boom spurred home ownership to its current levels.[26]

Today, home ownership, preferably of a single, detached house, is the American ideal, despite the financial hurdles involved. In a 1985 poll, for example, 76 percent of respondents agreed that people who do not

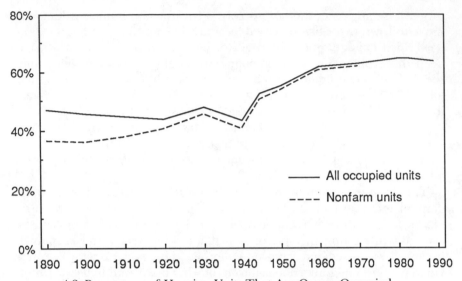

4.2 Percentage of Housing Units That Are Owner-Occupied.

SOURCES: U.S. Bureau of the Census, *Historical Statistics of the United States, Colonial Times to 1970* (Washington, D.C.: Government Printing Office, 1975), 646; U.S. Bureau of the Census, *Statistical Abstract of the United States 1988* (Washington, D.C.: Government Printing Office, 1987), 688; U.S. Bureau of the Census, *Census and You* 25 (December 1990), 5.

own their homes are "missing out on an important part of the American dream."[27] Being a renter is stigmatizing unless the person is in a transitional stage, a young single, or elderly.[28]

Growth in home ownership has slowed and even declined slightly in the late 1980s.[29] A sense of crisis about middle-class housing arose, a sense that Michael Dukakis tried to exploit in his presidential campaign in 1988. In historical perspective, still, the decline has been mild. Demographic changes in the last thirty years—aging of the baby-boomers, more divorce, delayed marriage and child rearing—should have led to home ownership sagging much more than it did. The big drop in ownership during the 1980s was precisely among Americans under thirty, who were increasingly putting off marriage and childbearing. Still, income losses, housing speculation, and financing changes strained many families, forcing some to rely on two incomes when they would have preferred one, and pushing some home-seekers out of the market.[30] Other would-be owners turned to condominiums or, in rural areas, mobile homes.[31] The proportion of available housing that is single detached units has dropped since the 1960s.[32] This shift to condos or trailers also contributes to a sense of crisis, since the American dream is so closely tied to the single-family house. Altogether, much of the concern arises from a comparison to the late 1960s, when, with boom times, owning a detached house was easier than now and seemed so normal.

Despite fluctuations owing to changes in demographics and economics, the great increase in home ownership during the twentieth century is unlikely to be soon reversed.

These conditions—urban sprawl, segregation, and home ownership—distinguish America from most European societies. David Popenoe credits them for creating a higher level of neighborhood involvement in the United States than he observed in either Sweden or the United Kingdom.[33] Changes in these conditions over the last few generations, along with declining mobility, would all seem to have helped Americans further attach themselves to their neighborhoods and towns. Besides, most Americans have enjoyed increasing freedom of choice in where they live. Freedom can mean lack of commitment and transiency; but it seems here to have made it easier for most people to find and stay in places they most prefer.[34]

Yet, other changes in the twentieth century may have reduced commitment to the locality. One such change has been the increasing separation of home and workplace. Although some commentators have exaggerated the extent to which home and work were entwined in the past—most people in days gone by were *not* independent craftsmen working in their homes—the distance between where people live and where they work expanded, particularly with the coming of streetcars in the 1880s.[35] Working outside one's home area probably detracts not only from the time people spend in the neighborhood but also from their subjective feeling of commitment to it.

A second such change is the increasing participation of married women in the labor force. In 1900, 6 percent of married women worked for pay; by 1987, 56 percent did. (The rates for divorced women, a growing fraction of all women, were much higher.)[36] Though married women's employment has typically been part-time, it does mean that fewer American households have a "traditional" homemaker at home all day, the same homemaker who critically connected the family to the neighborhood.[37]

Third, households shrank. With the virtual disappearance of servants, boarders, and lodgers, with later marriage, more divorce, and fewer children, the size of the median American household shrank from 4.8 people in 1900 to 2.7 in 1987.[38] We can assume that, generally, the fewer people at home, the less attached the household is to the locality.

Thus, in the complex weave of twentieth-century social changes, some drew Americans closer to and some pulled them from their neighborhoods and towns. Could we assess past people's identifications, sentiments, and actions more directly, we would not need to so indirectly esti-mate the change in local attachment. As it stands, the changes that more tightly bound people to places probably outweighed those that weak-ened the bonds, and the best estimate is that, contrary to convention, Americans are more "rooted," practically and sentimentally, to their communities than ever before.

THE FATE OF LOCAL TIES

On another dimension, however, Americans have probably become less rooted to their residential communities: social ties. Although this evi-dence is also indirect, probably fewer of Americans' relatives, friends, and associates live near them than was true in earlier generations. (I am not referring here to "neighboring," defined as casual interaction with people living nearby. Americans are often "neighborly" but rarely so-cially close to their neighbors.) In one study, fewer than a third of re-spondents' important relations were with people living within a five-minute drive. This dispersion was even greater for the middle class. The neighborhood provides proportionately few of middle-class Americans' important ties.[39]

How much recent generations differ from earlier ones in this regard is uncertain. On the one hand, Avery Guest and his co-workers found that neighborhood associations in Seattle in 1979 hosted fewer social activities than they did in 1929.[40] On the other hand, a few researchers have asked whether marrying couples are coming from increasingly dis-tant homes—an index of dispersing social contacts—and the answers are mixed.[41] So far, the evidence for a historical dispersion of social ties is largely indirect: Those people who seem most "modern"—the educated, affluent, young, and urban—tend to have more spread-out networks than those who seem less so. By (a perhaps unwarranted) historical trans-lation, then, we should have seen an increase in the dispersal of social relations.

We can also infer a decline in local ties from other social changes. Those changes that presumably uprooted Americans from their com-munities also should have scattered their networks: separation of home and work, mothers working, and smaller families. On the other hand, the changes that seemingly rooted Americans also should have con-tained their social ties: residential stability, suburbanization, neighbor-hood homogenization, more home ownership. Yet an additional con-sideration is changing communications and transportation. As early as 1891, an observer claimed that the newly developed telephone had intro-duced an "epoch of neighborship without propinquity." With the addition of cheap automobiles, analysts often claimed, space was "annihilated" and relations transcended distance.[42] It stands to reason (although reason is sometimes wrong), that with affordable telephones and automobiles, not to mention airplane tickets, people *can* sustain social ties at farther distances than their great-grandparents could have. We can enjoy an evening with friends who live twenty miles away or celebrate Thanksgiving with kin in another state. Whether, or to what extent, Americans' ties are in fact more dispersed today than previously is still unproven.[43]

The best guess is that there has been a historical change, that Americans' social lives are today less localized than they were a century ago. The more striking conclusion, however, is that the change may not have been as great as we imagine.

THE PERSISTENCE OF LOCAL AUTONOMY

Localities are more than where we live and the people with whom we dwell. They are also polities. It is especially in "home rule" that the American affection for the locality is problematic. Although tested through the twentieth century, local autonomy continues to shape crucial aspects of daily life, perhaps satisfying most Americans, but undermining the collective good.

Spurred by economic growth and economic crises, technology, and war, state and federal governments undertook vast new responsibilities in the twentieth century, dwarfing the localities in scale and public attention.[44] Also, local governments increasingly depended on cash infusions from the outside, the major shift occurring during the Depression.[45] Higher levels of government usurped some authority from the localities. Early, state governments took over, for example, regulation of utilities and road management. In later years, federal authorities intervened in voting, schools, and zoning to protect civil rights and the environment. These changes probably also shifted media and citizen attention toward higher levels of government.[46]

But the fundamental principle of local autonomy, long distinctive of the American system, has not been breached. Although dwarfed by the growth of state and federal authorities, local governments also increased their financial role in this century.[47] Other changes also strengthened the autonomy of small—especially suburban—municipalities. States granted small cities greater financial independence, including the right to incur debts. Town control over land use, notably through zoning, expanded.[48] In recent years, some authorities, especially the courts, have been able to intervene in local decision making,[49] but the basic independence of the locality remains. One sign is that since World War II the number of municipal employees has grown twice as fast as the number of federal employees.[50]

Most urban Americans now live in the small towns surrounding the center city,[51] and these are the better-educated, more affluent, and whiter urban Americans. They live in distinct, albeit neighboring, communities that differ from one another and surely from the center city in population profile, finances, and land use.[52] Suburban residents, although usually content to leave politics to caretaker governments, do mobilize to protect the legal, fiscal, and social boundaries of their towns.[53] By moving across a municipal line, usually by doing little more than crossing a street, some Americans can obtain better civic services at lower tax rates; choose among different housing styles, prices, and taxes; enroll their children in schools unburdened by poor students; and otherwise "purchase" by their relocation a better "basket" of social goods.[54]

Even within large cities, localities' clout seems to have grown through neighborhood movements. Neighborhood ideology arose at the end of the nineteenth century, was encouraged by Progressive reformers and planners, and then was renewed by "community power" militancy in the 1960s and 1970s.[55] Neighborhood movements have defended local communities from intrusions, resisted growth, and contested with downtown business interests. Critics, however, charge them with creating urban paralysis by NIMBY (not in my backyard) vetoes of citywide endeavors. Although new politics and new laws, such as required "impact" assessments, empowered many low-income neighborhoods—it is hard to imagine that Robert Moses could bulldoze the Bronx today—neighborhood power is still more easily and more often exercised by the same sorts of advantaged people who protect their exclusive suburbs, some of whom now live in gentrified city quarters.

THE PLACE OF PLACE

Peter Rossi has pointed out that "the world has become increasingly cosmopolitan, but the daily lives of most people are contained within local communities."[56] Place still matters. The variations in house prices between and within regions, for example, mock economists' models and futurists' projections that the nation is leveling out into a uniform, placeless realm.[57] How important place will be in the future we can only speculate. Will "cocooning," a media buzzword of the 1980s, typify the next decades, or will there be increasing cosmopolitanism? Much will depend on economic changes and demographic shifts. Unless the economy fails, American wealth should help sustain residential stability and home ownership. As baby-boomers move beyond child rearing and then retire, they will increase geographical mobility, but they will also release more single-family housing for their grandchildren. Spots of inner-city gentrification notwithstanding, the sprawling of the metropolises continues, augmenting suburbanization and "exurbanization" beyond the suburbs. That trend suggests yet more homogeneity, low-density housing, and autonomous political localities.

Most Americans would, in all likelihood, applaud those trends. Raising a family in a detached house, in a homogeneously middle-class, suburban locality, governed by people much like oneself, seems almost ideal. As with other equity issues, even Americans who lack this privilege would preserve it. Experts may criticize localism for its "collective irrationalities" costly to residents themselves—traffic congestion, governmental paralysis, unbalanced growth, domination by business interests, and so on—and for its "externalities" costly to the wider community—ghettoization of the poor, abandonment of the great cities, unjust tax burdens, and so on. No matter. In America, the free pursuit of the private good *is* the public good. Localism is, as much as ever, an instrument to that good.

Herein lies a seeming contradiction: an inconsistency between the locality's communal role and its role as a vehicle for individual interest.[58] American ideologies of community paint the locality, especially the small one, as a site for fellowship, in contrast to the atomism of the wider, especially the urban, world. Many Americans value and enjoy the congeniality of a local community. They often resist that same local community, yet, when it constrains their interests, be the constraint in taxes, behavioral codes, or infringements of private property. Neighborhood organizations, for example, typically awaken when outsiders threaten residents' safety or wealth. Otherwise, the energy that drives them usually rests dormant. Neighborhood groups rarely act as local governments. Other evidence of the priority of the individual comes in negotiations within condominium complexes, where collective needs and rules run up against assertions of home owners' rights.[59] While Americans value the locality as solidarity, it takes second place to individual freedom.

Another seeming contradiction appears between the persistence of home-rule politics and the dramatic growth of the national government.[60] How can locally oriented Americans tolerate the Washington behemoth? One answer is that the national government has not grown as much as we think.[61] More important, growth in the federal government's role and in its income was a response to seemingly unavoidable crises. The Depression justified social engineering and costly programs. The world wars and the Cold War justified other national initiatives. Officials invoked the Cold War, for example, to rationalize the interstate highway system and subsidies to higher education. And still, the United States is, by Western standards, an incomplete welfare state. The reality is that

Americans generally resist government at all levels, but give more grudg-
ing preference to local rule by like-minded neighbors as the lesser evil.

National action, piecemeal as it is, also occurs in response to translocal
coalitions. That was one lesson, for example, of the Civil Rights struggle,
which as movement and as legislation ran roughshod over local autonomy. The environmental movement is a more complex example. In
some ways, it too imposed national concerns over local ones, for example, threatening local jobs for old trees or peculiar fish. (In other
ways, though, it reinforced the NIMBY pattern of localism, legitimat-
ing a "draw up the drawbridge" style of conservatism.) Although local
events—Love Canal, for one—dramatized the environmental agenda,
the movement's power still appears to rest on coalitions of interests that
are translocal.

A strategy to move the nation in a progressive direction would in a
similar way involve rethinking the ideology of locality, an ideology really
more attuned to privilege than to reform. Thomas Bender has pointed
out the dangers of confusing values attached to "community" with the
needs of the public, political sphere. To insist, for example, on personal
knowledge of political candidates may mean selecting the lesser rather
than the better candidate. Or, to cry for "local control" for a community
wealthier in needs than in resources may end by perpetuating disadvantage.[62] It is important to look clear-eyed at the consequences of America's
localism, not with romanticized nostalgia.

PART TWO

Economics and Politics: Global and National

FIVE

Mirrors and Metaphors
The United States and Its Trade Rivals

Fred Block

THE DECLINE OF AMERICAN COMPETITIVENESS

In the winter of 1990, the Chrysler Corporation ran a television commercial that featured its chairman, Lee Iacocca, complaining about an American inferiority complex toward the Japanese. He was referring to the perception that Japanese manufactured goods, including automobiles, were generally of higher quality than those made in the United States. This unusual advertising strategy was symptomatic of a radical reversal that occurred over less than forty years. In the 1950s, the label "Made in Japan" was an object of derision; it was synonymous with cheap goods of poor quality. By the 1980s, Japan had established itself as the world's most successful exporter of highly sophisticated manufactured goods.

While Japan's shift is the most dramatic instance, it is symptomatic of a broader transformation of the United States' position in international trade. Immediately after World War II, the United States was the only industrialized country whose manufacturing base had actually been strengthened during the war. U.S. industrial capacity had expanded significantly, while the economies of England, France, Germany, and Japan were all severely damaged. The enormous international appetite for U.S. manufactured goods in the post–World War II years made it possible for the United States to export far more than it imported. The only constraint on this appetite was the difficulty that other nations had in obtaining the dollars with which to purchase U.S. goods. The United States tried to overcome this "dollar gap" through aid programs that were designed to hasten the reconstruction of the economies of Western Europe and Japan. By every possible indicator, the United States dominated the world economy from 1945 through 1965.[1]

By the end of the 1960s, though, it was apparent that U.S. efforts to bolster the economies of its industrialized trading partners had been too

TABLE 5.1 U.S. Foreign Trade Surplus
or Deficit for Various Years
(in millions of current dollars)

1947	$10,124
1950	1,122
1960	4,892
1970	2,603
1980	−25,480
1988	−127,215

SOURCE: *Economic Report of the President* (Washington, D.C.: U.S. Government Printing Office, 1990), table C-9, 410–11.
NOTE: These figures are for merchandise trade, exclusive of military shipments.

successful. The U.S. trade position went from surplus to deficit as Western Europe and Japan sold increasing volumes of manufactured goods to the United States (see table 5.1). During the 1970s, however, the inflows were largely of consumer goods; the United States still enjoyed a healthy surplus in the export of capital goods, such as computers, machine tools, and airplanes. But in the 1980s, this last remaining advantage weakened as the U.S. economy was overwhelmed both with high-tech manufactured imports from Japan and Western Europe and low-tech imports from Newly Industrializing Countries such as Taiwan and South Korea.[2]

These dramatic shifts in the U.S. trade balance are linked to changes in national self-confidence. The trade surplus after 1945, combined with U.S. military superiority, encouraged talk of the "American Century"— a period of U.S. international dominance comparable to the *Pax* Britannica of the nineteenth century. However, it was to be a very short century; by the 1980s, the growing trade deficit catapulted Paul Kennedy's *The Rise and Fall of the Great Powers* onto the national best-seller list. Kennedy argued that the growing U.S. trade deficit meant that the United States was following a long-established pattern of imperial decline.

The United States' competitive decline has become a central issue in the country's politics. Debate focuses on the question of what can be done to improve our international trade position. The AFL-CIO and some of its allies in the Democratic party have consistently argued that the major problem is the unfair trading practices of some of our competitors, but this has been a minority position. Thus far, no clear majority position has emerged, but politicians in both parties increasingly argue that their pet proposals—from cuts in the capital gains tax to educational reform—are necessary to solve the trade problem.

Since 1980, it has been increasingly common for domestic commentators to compare the United States with its leading trade rivals to gain perspective on what should be done. This use of other countries as a kind of mirror—to better assess one's own society—has been a common practice in the history of other countries. Russian history, for example, has been marked by episodes in which invidious comparisons with foreign nations have been used to stimulate domestic reform. The Gorbachev era is only the most recent example. Yet this type of comparative national introspection has been rare in modern U.S. history; for most of this century, national confidence has been so great that the only comparative question was why other nations had been so slow to adopt American institutions and practices.

But faced with trade deficits and a perception of competitive decline, U.S. analysts have increasingly looked to Japan and West Germany for insight into what is wrong in the United States. The intention, of course, is to spark national renewal by recognizing and eliminating those national characteristics that are holding the United States back. Unfortunately, the perceptions from these comparisons that have entered the public debate have been like the images in fun house mirrors. Some of the features of those societies that are most important in explaining their economic successes have been almost completely ignored, while others of marginal or questionable importance have loomed far too large as explanations for economic success. Most sadly, the comparisons—like distorted reflections—have served to obscure rather than to enlighten; they have made it more difficult for this society to understand how to handle its economic and social problems.

COMPARING THE UNITED STATES, JAPAN, AND WEST GERMANY

In pursuing comparisons among the United States, Japan, and West Germany, it is important to distinguish between the scholarly literature—books and articles that are very rarely read outside of university settings—and the popular literature of newspapers and magazines read by millions of people. In scholarly literature, there are five important areas of contrast between Japan and West Germany and the United States, but in the popular arena, only one—or possibly two—of these factors are emphasized.

Before beginning the comparison, it is important to emphasize that neither Japan nor West Germany is an unequivocal economic success story. West Germany has gone through the 1980s with unemployment rates higher than those in the United States. Large parts of the Japanese economy, particularly the service sector, remain relatively underdeveloped. And both Japan and West Germany have provided far fewer economic opportunities for women than has the United States. Different economies have succeeded with certain parts of the puzzle of how to organize an advanced, postindustrial economy, but no single nation has been able to put the whole puzzle together. Hence, the main economic achievement in both Japan and West Germany has been quite specific— to reorganize manufacturing to produce high-quality goods that are particularly attractive in international trade. In a period in which a number of Newly Industrializing Countries have greatly increased their international market share for such simpler manufactured goods as apparel and steel, Japan and West Germany have run large surpluses in manufacturing trade by specializing in more complex goods, such as automobiles, machine tools, and consumer electronics.

Also, the West German and Japanese economies are very different from each other in their specific institutional arrangements. It is not a simple matter to create a single composite "successful competitor country" out of these quite different national experiences. Nevertheless, there are a number of dimensions on which these two countries are both similar to each other and different from the United States that might account for the variation in the three countries' recent experiences with sophisticated manufacturing. On some of these dimensions, the specific institutional arrangements through which a given set of ends are achieved might be quite different, but the ultimate outcome appears similar. All of these dimensions have been discussed in the scholarly literature, but only a few of them have played a part in more popular discussions.

Marginality of Military Production

One obvious point of comparison between West Germany and Japan is that both were defeated in World War II. As a consequence of that defeat, both nations were constrained to limit their military expenditures. The result has been that defense spending and military production have played far more marginal roles in their economies than in that of the United States.[3] This has contributed substantially to Japan's and West Germany's successes in civilian manufacturing.[4]

In the United States, a large percentage of scientists and engineers have been employed in defense and defense-related industries.[5] Moreover, the proportion of "the best and the brightest" from these technical fields who end up working in the military rather than the civilian side of the economy is even greater. Firms doing military research and development are able to pass their costs along to the government, so they are able to pay higher wages than civilian firms. Also, the needs of the arms industry have profoundly shaped engineering education in the United States, so that the definition of what is exciting and interesting work has been shaped by military demands. The consequence is that the use of scientific and engineering talent in civilian manufacturing in America has been far more limited and far less effective than in Japan and West Germany.

The different use of technical labor is only part of a larger contrast. High levels of U.S. defense spending have fostered a business style that is particularly unsuited to success in highly competitive civilian markets. It is a style that involves mastery of the bureaucratic complexities of the procurement process, in which cost of production considerations are relatively unimportant, and where there are few rewards for high levels of flexibility in the production process. This style contrasts sharply with the sensitivity to consumer preferences, the sustained effort to reduce production costs, and the emphasis on flexibility that are characteristic of the firms that have been most successful in competitive civilian industries.[6]

Cooperative Work Arrangements

In both Japan and West Germany, a relatively high level of trust exists between employees and managers in manufacturing. While there are significant differences in the industrial relations patterns of the two countries, with West German unions being far stronger than unions in Japan, both countries have been able to mobilize high levels of employee motivation and initiative. In particular, both countries have evolved practices that protect core employees from displacement as a result of technological change. The consequence has been greater employee receptivity to technological innovation and, thus, quicker and more effective utilization of new productive technologies.[7]

Similar practices have evolved in some of the most important U.S. firms in the computer and electronic industries where no-layoff policies and commitments to retraining have created an openness to continual technological innovation.[8] However, the industrial relations in most U.S. manufacturing firms continue to be characterized by low trust and continued worker fears of displacement resulting from technological innovation. While many Fortune 500 firms have experimented with quality-of-work-life and employee involvement programs in the hope of emulating foreign competitors' high-trust manufacturing environments, the results have been uneven.[9] In many cases, U.S. firms have been unable or unwilling to provide the increased employee job security that is an indispensable part of a more cooperative system of industrial relations.

Supportive Financial Institutions

In both Japan and West Germany, banks have historically played a central role in providing finance for manufacturing firms; the sale of corporate stock to nonbank purchasers—the chief mechanism by which firms raise money in the United States—has played a distinctly secondary role. This greater role of banks in the manufacturing sector has several positive consequences. First, banks tend to have a longer-term time horizon than stock markets. When bankers invest heavily in a firm, the advice that they give and the pressures they exert tend to be oriented to the long term. In contrast, corporate stock prices are heavily influenced by quarterly earnings reports, and concern about the stock price forces firms to emphasize profits in the next quarter over longer-term considerations. At the extreme, the emphasis on next quarter's bottom line can lead firms to sacrifice spending for preventive maintenance, research and development, and good employee relations—all factors that play a large role in the firm's long-term prospects.[10]

Similarly, banks with substantial stakes in manufacturing firms can play an active role in coordinating relations across firms. They can facilitate joint ventures between firms that might have complementary strengths, and they can use their influence to dampen destructive competition in a particular industry. Perhaps, most significantly, neither Japanese nor West German manufacturing has seen anything like the takeover wars that the United States experienced in the 1980s. In those countries, the banks can use their influence to get rid of ineffective management teams without the huge costs that have been incurred in U.S. corporate takeovers.

Social Inclusion

Both West Germany and Japan have dramatically reduced poverty in their societies, although they have accomplished this through different means. In Japan, there has been a very strong political commitment to maintaining high levels of employment, so there are relatively few adult males who are marginal to the economy. Full employment combined with a reasonable minimum wage and a low divorce rate has made it possible to pull most people above the poverty level with comparatively low levels of social welfare spending. In West Germany, where unemployment has been relatively high, the elimination of poverty has required—in addition to a high minimum wage—fairly extensive state welfare spending in support of the unemployed and single-parent families. The results are that in West Germany only 4.9 percent of children live in poverty; in Japan, 8.1 percent of children aged ten to fourteen live in poverty; while in the United States, the comparable figure is 22.4 percent.[11]

The contrast between a large population of poor children in the United States and much smaller populations in Japan and West Germany has direct implications for education. The reduction of poverty goes along with substantially higher levels of educational achievement by young people. There is considerable evidence that the average high school graduate in Japan has substantially higher levels of mathematics and science skills than the average American high school graduate, but the most striking contrast is in the percentage of students who complete high school.[12] In the United States only 71.5 percent of students graduate in contrast to 88 percent in Japan.[13] In West Germany, rates of high school completion are lower, but most of those who leave school at age sixteen enter highly structured three-year apprenticeship programs that combine on-the-job training with formal learning.[14]

The proportion of eighteen-year-olds in the United States who are unqualified for skilled employment is probably as high as 40 percent if one includes both dropouts and students who graduate from high school with only minimal skills. This puts U.S. firms at a distinct disadvantage compared to Japanese and West German firms, who have a much deeper pool of young people who can easily be trained for skilled employment. In some sectors of the economy, the United States can partially make up for this disadvantage by making greater use of female employees than do Japan and West Germany, but this compensating mechanism does not work for skilled manufacturing jobs, where women still only make up about 6 percent of the labor force. Hence policies of social inclusion that result in the general reduction of poverty contribute to Japanese and West German industrial competitiveness by raising the level of educational attainment of the bottom half of the population. This advantage over the United States in the quality of the human input into the production process makes it easier for Japan and West Germany to develop more cooperative employment relations and to place more emphasis on the improvements in worker skill that facilitate the use of advanced production technologies.

Higher Rates of Personal Savings

It is widely believed that in Japan and West Germany households save a much higher proportion of their income than do those in the United States. Official data show that Japanese and West German household savings rates were at least twice as high as those for the United States in the 1980s.[15] This greater frugality means that there is a relatively larger pool of savings available for productive investment by firms at a lower interest rate. The lower interest rate means that firms can justify productive investments that could not be pursued if the cost of capital was higher.[16]

It follows, in turn, that Japan and West Germany use this savings advantage to invest more heavily in manufacturing, with the consequence that their manufacturing productivity has grown substantially faster than that of the United States. The faster rate of productivity growth makes it possible for them to control costs and compete successfully against the United States in manufacturing markets.

Of these five possible explanations for Japanese and West German economic success, it is clear that the fifth explanation—the difference in household savings rates—has completely overshadowed all of the others in popular discussions. By 1989 concern about the low rate of personal savings in the United States had become such a national preoccupation that both major political parties advanced proposals designed to stimulate higher rates of savings. The popular press was filled with laments about the decline of personal savings. Peter Peterson, a former secretary of commerce, wrote a typical column in the *New York Times* (July 16, 1989), in which he reminisced lovingly about the frugality of his immigrant parents before he made this argument:

> Up until about two decades ago, Americans would have considered it unthinkable that they could not save enough as a nation to afford a better future for their children, and that each generation would not "do better" and that the resources we invest into the beginning of life might be dwarfed by the resources we consume at the end of life. Yet, today the unthinkable is happening.
>
> Our net national savings rate is now the lowest in the industrial world, forcing us to borrow abroad massively just to keep our economy functioning.

Later in this chapter I will show how Peterson's argument is based on problematic data and mistaken assumptions about how the economy works. The point to be emphasized here, however, is that of all of the important institutional contrasts between the United States and its major competitors, the difference in the savings rates of households has received disproportionate attention.

Some of the other contrasts have also been part of broader public discussions, but in each case, one element has been emphasized in a very telling fashion. For example, there has been considerable public concern about the shortcomings of U.S. public education, and a number of prominent corporate executives have argued that the failings of our schools have put them at a disadvantage relative to our major international competitors. George Bush promised to be the "Education President" precisely to address these problems. However, the problem of education in the United States is almost never related to the larger issue of social inclusion; it is rarely argued that the best way to improve our schools is to eliminate poverty. On the contrary, discussions of school failure tend to emphasize the personal shortcomings of those who drop out. This constant emphasis on individual characteristics helps give plausibility to the otherwise implausible arguments of those educational reformers who want to "get back to basics" and place renewed emphasis on discipline.

There has also been some broader discussion of the more cooperative employment relations that Japan and West Germany enjoy. Here again, the discussion moves quickly away from the specific institutional arrangements, such as strong unions or employment guarantees, that undergird that cooperation. Instead, the focus shifts to the cultural values of individual workers. Japanese and West German workers are seen as embodying the values of the work ethic: they are disciplined and they take pride in their work, and they contrast sharply with American workers, who are depicted as selfish, lazy, or both.

In short, in the mirror that the United States has held up to itself, only differences in the characteristics of individuals are revealed; the Japanese and West Germans are seen to do better because they are more frugal, more hardworking, and their children are more disciplined. Differences in institutional arrangements disappear from view completely. This kind of selective reflection has important political implications. The focus on individual qualities assures that blame will always be distributed according to Pogo's famous phrase, "We have met the enemy, and he is us." Failures of the U.S. economy thus appear to result from the personal failings of ordinary Americans, above all the failure to save.

ECONOMICS AND METAPHOR

Why is it that in public debate and discussion about declining U.S. competitiveness, comparisons of the United States to its trading partners have focused almost exclusively on differences in personal savings practices? The other institutional contrasts certainly raise all kinds of interesting questions about what the United States is doing wrong as a nation and how it could do better, but these issues are never explored. In my view, the explanation for this strange selectivity lies in the importance of metaphors in economic thinking.

While economists make great claims about the scientific nature of their discipline, economic discourse is dominated by metaphors.[17] From Adam Smith's "invisible hand" to recent discussions of economic "soft landings," economic activity is frequently understood in reference to something else. Even some of the most basic economic concepts, such as the ideas of inflation and deflation, rest on analogies to physical processes.

This is hardly surprising; metaphors are powerful and indispensable tools for understanding complex and abstract processes. Difficulties arise only when we forget that we are thinking metaphorically. A particular metaphor can be taken so much for granted in our intellectual framework that it structures our perception of reality in subtle and hidden ways. Such hidden metaphors can make our theories totally impervious to any kind of disconfirmation. No matter how much evidence a critic might amass, there is simply no way to persuade someone who has organized his or her thinking around one of these taken-for-granted metaphors.

There are three metaphors that loom particularly large in contemporary understandings of the economy in the United States. The first of these is so familiar that it is not worth discussing at length; it is the metaphor of government as spendthrift. The idea is simply that the public sector will invariably use its resources in ways that are inferior to their use by the private sector.[18] The other two metaphors are more hidden, but they have a profound impact on both the thinking of economists and the more popular economics of journalists and politicians.

Capital as Blood

In one metaphor, the economy is seen as a hospital patient and money for capital investment is likened to the blood that runs through the veins of the endangered individual. When the supply of money capital diminishes, the patient's heartbeat slows and the vital signs deteriorate. But when the patient's supply of blood is replenished by an intravenous transfusion, there is virtually an instantaneous improvement. Not only does the patient look better, but he or she is suddenly able to move about and do things that were previously unthinkable.

This metaphor establishes money capital as the indispensable element for economic health. Nothing else—not the cooperation of labor nor the ways in which economic institutions are structured—can compare in importance to the availability of money capital. Moreover, virtually any economic problem can ultimately be traced back to an insufficient supply of money capital.

For relatively underdeveloped economies, this metaphor holds an indisputable element of truth; such economies suffer a chronic shortage of resources available for productive investment. However, for economies like those of the United States and its major trading partners, the metaphor is deeply misleading. For one thing, the relationship between the dollar amount of new investment and economic outcomes such as the rate of economic growth is unclear. Frequent attempts have been made to prove that lagging rates of U.S. productivity growth were caused by insufficient rates of new investment, but these attempts have failed. Even the White House Conference on Productivity, convened by Ronald Reagan in 1983, was unable to provide unequivocal evidence of inadequate rates of investment in the United States.[19] The difficulty, of course, is that throwing money at any problem—whether it is lagging productivity or widespread drug abuse—never guarantees success. There are too many other variables that intervene to determine the effectiveness or ineffectiveness of particular expenditures. The picture has become even more clouded recently because computerization has created a pervasive process of capital savings in the economy; a million dollars of capital investment in 1990 bought capital goods that were far more powerful and effective than what the equivalent dollars would have bought five or ten years before. Capital savings is most obvious with computers themselves; the costs of computing power have been falling by 15 to 20 percent a year. But a parallel albeit slower change is occurring with a whole range of other capital goods. This pattern of capital savings means that each year less money capital is necessary to buy the same amount of new plant and equipment.[20]

There are also a number of other contenders for the most indispensable element for an advanced economy. First, it is increasingly obvious that even when there is enough money capital, it cannot be taken for granted that it will be used productively or effectively. When financiers and firms engage in "paper entrepreneurialism," they can spend vast sums of money in corporate raids and leveraged buy-outs that do nothing to enhance the society's productive capacity. Unlike the infusion of blood, there is nothing automatic about the effect of money capital on the economy. One could argue instead that institutional arrangements that effectively channel money capital to productive use are the most indispensable element for a modern economy.

Another crucial element is the flow of new ideas that results from research and development. Without the capacity to innovate effectively in both products and production processes, a modern economy will quickly fall behind competitors who are better at anticipating consumer needs or reducing the costs of production. Still another element to consider is the flow of educated employees who are capable of developing and implementing these innovations. This is not just a question of scientists and engineers, since there is mounting evidence that advanced production processes in both manufacturing and services require workers with significant intellectual skills to use computer-based technologies effectively.[21]

It is, of course, a silly exercise to argue over which is the most indispensable element for a modern economy; one would expect a number of different factors to be extremely important. The point, however, is that the capital-as-blood metaphor is simply wrong in its insistence that one element of economic life can be elevated in importance over all of the others.

Redemption through Sacrifice

The second metaphor, redemption through sacrifice, is Christian rather than medical, but it also rests on the comparison of the economy to an individual. In this case, however, the economy is an individual who has succumbed to temptation. Instead of following the path of righteousness, hard work, and self-discipline, the individual has become either lazy or preoccupied with the pursuit of sensual pleasures. If the individual remains on this path, the future will bring complete moral decay and probable impoverishment. The alternative is to seek redemption through sacrifice; this means not only rejecting all temptations, but even forgoing some of the innocent pleasures that the person previously enjoyed. Only a sustained period of asceticism will atone for past sin and allow the person to return to the path of righteousness.

Economic maladies such as inflation or deflation are seen as evidence that the economy has veered from the correct path, either as a result of insufficient effort or of excessive emphasis on consumption. The remedy is always a sustained period of austerity—of collective belt-tightening. Austerity simultaneously demonstrates that people have remembered the correct priorities and it frees resources for new investment to make the economy more productive. If sustained for an adequate length of time, the pursuit of austerity is almost guaranteed to restore the strength of the economy, no matter how serious the original transgression.

The two metaphors clearly intersect in that austerity is seen as a means to guarantee that the flow of money capital will once again be swift enough to restore the health of the economic patient. Health in one framework is the same as righteousness in the other. Moreover, it is also important that both metaphors equate the economy to an individual. The classic justification of the free market was that the pursuit of greed by individuals was transformed by the invisible hand into a benevolent outcome. However, the disjunction in that argument between individual and collective morality is troubling for those who see the world in purely individualistic terms. They experience some discomfort with the idea that individual greed should produce a positive outcome. These metaphors eliminate that discomfort by restoring the notion that individual virtue is necessary for the collective good and that collective failures can be traced to individual weaknesses. With these metaphors as guides, the path to a more prosperous economy is seen as being reached by persuading individuals to act virtuously.

In actual economies, however, the relationship between individual orientations and collective outcomes is far more uncertain. Nice guys often finish last, while those who lack all virtue might well live happily and prosperously ever after. Virtuous farmers can work diligently to produce a bumper crop that results in a disastrous fall in prices for their products. Similarly, an abstemious nation can find itself in the midst of severe depression when consumption fails to keep pace with production.

For this reason, austerity is often an imperfect route to economic improvement. The Great Depression of the 1930s was a classic illustration; individuals were promised that a period of belt-tightening would inevitably generate a spontaneous recovery. But what actually happened was that the restricted purchasing power of consumers meant that there was insufficient demand to justify new investments and the economy remained stagnant until the government intervened to bolster demand. More recently, the theorists of supply-side economics promised that if people accepted a period of austerity as income was shifted to the rich, there would be a dramatic economic expansion that would raise everyone's standard of living. While the economy did expand in the Reagan years, the consequences were far more uneven than the supply-siders had promised. The rich prospered on an unprecedented scale, but the promised acceleration of productive investment did not occur, and large sectors of the population found themselves worse off than they had been before. Many of the defects of the expansion can be directly traced to the consequences of austerity, such as the cutbacks in nondefense federal spending and the weakness of consumer demand among households whose incomes are below the median.

Nevertheless, the belief in redemption through sacrifice taps deep cultural themes. Even beyond the obvious parallel with Christian notions of individual salvation, there is a close fit with the cultural anxieties of the middle class. Barbara Ehrenreich has written persuasively of the profound fear of affluence that haunts the American middle class.[22] Those who have achieved a comfortable existence through their own efforts as doctors, lawyers, or corporate managers cannot usually guarantee their children a comparable existence unless the children enter a middle-class occupation. While the truly wealthy can usually find sinecures for untalented children or even provide for shiftless children through trust funds, those options are not available to the middle class. The danger for the middle class is that children who grow up in economic comfort will lack the drive and discipline to surmount the hurdles that block entry to middle-class occupations for most children of the poor and working classes. Hence, a periodic invocation of the virtues of austerity fits well with the middle class's own efforts to persuade their children of the necessity of self-discipline and hard work.

These two powerful metaphors act as filters through which the United States' perceptions of its major economic competitors have been refracted. While there are many significant differences between the U.S. economy and those of Japan and West Germany, the preoccupation with differences in personal savings can now be understood. The idea that people in the United States do not save enough fits perfectly with both of these hidden metaphors.

THE SAVINGS MYTHOLOGY

Is it really true that people in the United States are far less frugal than people in Japan and West Germany? Discovering the answer requires examining the way in which Commerce Department economists measure personal savings. The problem is that personal savings is not an item that government statisticians find out directly; there is no question on the IRS form that asks "how much have you put aside this year for savings?" Some of the most important economic measures are derived by asking people; for example, the monthly unemployment figure is based on a survey in which thousands of people are questioned about their work experience in the previous month. However, there is no regular large-scale survey in which people are asked about their savings behavior. The government economists are forced to calculate personal savings indirectly; the frequently cited figures on personal savings are derived by subtracting all consumer purchases from the total disposable income that individuals have. In short, personal savings is simply what is left over from income after individuals have paid taxes and purchased all of their consumption items. Here are the formulas:

1. Personal income − Taxes = Disposable personal income
2. Disposable personal income − Personal consumption expenditures =
   Personal savings

3. Personal savings rate =
   Personal savings *divided by* Disposable personal income

This makes sense because individuals can only save income that they have not spent on other items. However, the accuracy of the personal savings figure rests entirely on the accuracy of the estimates of personal income and personal consumption expenditures. But there are three problems here. First, since the personal savings figure is derived by subtracting one very large number from another very large number, it is extremely sensitive to small changes in those large numbers. For example, if the personal income figure for 1987 were 5 percent higher than the official data indicated, the personal savings figure would increase by 54 percent. Second, there are items where data are highly problematic. In calculating personal income, for example, the government economists make use of a fairly solid source—reports by firms of how much they have paid their employees. But this has to be supplemented with data on the income of self-employed individuals, which is based on their own self-reports to the Internal Revenue Service. Such reports are obviously problematic because individuals have an interest in understating their income to save on taxes.[23]

The third problem is that these estimates of personal income and personal consumption expenditures are made within an elaborate accounting framework that was structured to provide a coherent picture of the economy as a whole. This accounting framework involves a series of detailed decisions about how certain kinds of income flows or expenditures will be handled, and quite often, these decisions are not made to improve the accuracy of the personal savings figure but for the sake of consistency or to improve some other part of the accounts. However, these detailed accounting conventions can have a very significant impact on the estimates of personal income and personal consumption expenditures and indirectly on personal savings.

One of these accounting conventions concerns the treatment of public pension funds. There are public pension funds that work in exactly the same way as private pension funds. Both employers and employees put money aside in a trust fund whose earnings are used to pay pension benefits. However, in the national income accounts, it is assumed that all public pension funds pay benefits directly out of state revenues. One recent study showed that when funded public pension funds are treated in the same way as private pension funds, the personal savings figure for 1985 increased by 37.3 percent.[24]

Another convention that is important concerns the treatment of owner-occupied housing. In figuring out personal consumption expenditures, government statisticians use a strange procedure. They treat people who own their own housing as though they are renters paying rent to themselves. Hence, one of the largest items in personal consumption expenditure is the estimate of the total amount of rent that owner-occupiers pay. While this procedure makes sense for other parts of the accounts, it wreaks havoc on the personal savings figure since the estimate of owner-occupied rent might be quite different from the actual current expenditures that home owners incur. In fact, one consequence of this convention is that the personal savings figure largely excludes one of the main forms of household savings in the United States—the accumulation of equity in homes.

These detailed conventions are particularly important in international comparisons of savings rates. While the basic accounting framework used in Japan and West Germany is quite similar to the American system, there are numerous differences in the detailed conventions and the way that specific estimates are constructed. For example, one recent study of the Japanese savings rate noted differences in the ways capital transfers and depreciation are treated in the two countries. When adjustments are made for these differences for 1984, the Japanese savings rate declines from 16.2 percent to 13.7 percent.[25]

Another important part of the discrepancy between Japanese and U.S. savings rates is related not to accounting conventions, but to geography. The high population density in Japan makes land extremely valuable in that country; in 1987, land constituted two-thirds of all Japanese wealth, but only 25 percent of U.S. wealth.[26] This means that the acquisition of land is a much larger component of total personal savings in

Japan than in the United States. However, the money that is being put aside for acquiring land for owner-occupied homes is not money that is available for investment by the business sector.[27] Hence, a significant part of the discrepancy between U.S. and Japanese savings rates is irrelevant to the question of international competitiveness.

In short, it is necessary to be extremely skeptical of cross-national comparisons of savings rates because the accounting conventions and the economic institutions differ. Moreover, the differences in institutions can magnify the importance of relatively minor differences in accounting conventions. Instead of pursuing these international comparisons of savings rates further, it is more useful to look at another data source that provides information on personal savings in the United States. The statistical offices of the Federal Reserve Board have developed a number of measures of savings as part of their effort to develop a comprehensive accounting of financial flows in the economy. This data source includes estimates of the annual changes in holdings of financial assets and liabilities (debts) of households. These estimates are based in part on very solid data, such as official reports by pension funds and insurance companies of their holdings, and some less solid data that depend on the indirect calculations of the holdings of households. (See figure 5.1.)

According to the Federal Reserve data, personal savings was quite strong in the United States in the 1980s, and the savings rate actually increased. Since the mid-1970s, the two different government series on personal savings have moved in the opposite direction. While the Commerce Department's figures have slid down, the Federal Reserve figures have gone up. Commerce Department analysts have argued that their data are more accurate because the Federal Reserve figures have been thrown off by unrecorded flows of foreign capital into the United States. However, the Federal Reserve figures are actually more reliable because they are based on an analysis of actual financial flows rather than the indirect methodology of the Commerce Department.

The Federal Reserve data include the annual increase in the assets of pension funds and life insurance reserves. This is a figure that is reported directly and involves a minimum of guesswork. It also represents a form of personal savings that is extremely important because it is directly available for productive investment in other parts of the economy. In 1988, the increase in pension fund and insurance reserves (exclusive of capital gains) was $224.4 billion. This is an enormous sum; it was 50 percent higher than the Commerce Department estimate of *all* personal savings—$144.7 billion. It was also enough to finance by itself 94.8 percent of all net private domestic investment—in capital goods, plants, and housing—in that year. Of course, increases in pension and insurance re-

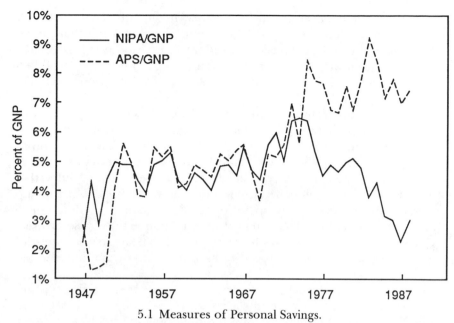

5.1 Measures of Personal Savings.

SOURCES: *Economic Report of the President* (Washington, D.C.: U.S. Government Printing Office, 1990), table C-29, 327. The Alternative Personal Savings is calculated from the table "Savings by Individuals." Net increases in debt, exclusive of mortgage debt, are subtracted from increases in financial assets. Some additional adjustments are made for 1986–90 to compensate for the substitution of home equity loans for other forms of consumer credit. For a fuller description of data and methods, see Fred Block, "Bad Data Drive Out Good: The Decline of Personal Savings Reexamined," *Journal of Post Keynesian Economics*, 13 (1) (Fall 1990): 3–19.

serves do not exhaust the supply of personal savings; there are also substantial accumulations of assets in bank accounts, stocks, and bonds.

The Federal Reserve data also make intuitive sense. It is well known that rich people are responsible for the bulk of household savings because they have far more discretionary income than everybody else. It is also known that the Reagan administration's policies significantly increased the percentage of income going to the richest families. For the Commerce Department figures to be true, the rich would have had to consume their increased income on a scale even more lavish than Leona Helmsley's home remodeling and the late Malcolm Forbes's famous Moroccan birthday party.[28]

Furthermore, personal savings as measured with the Federal Reserve data exceeded net private investment in the economy in every year of the 1980s, sometimes by more than $100 billion. When one adds undistributed corporate profits that are also available to finance investment, the surfeit is even greater. Michael Milken—the convicted junk bond king—was fond of saying, "The common perception is that capital is scarce . . . but in fact capital is abundant; it is vision that is scarce."[29] An examination of the data on personal savings indicates that Milken is correct; the United States does not suffer from a chronic inability to save.

Finally, it is important to emphasize that all of this preoccupation with personal frugality ignores *the* single most important way in which individuals contribute to economic prosperity—through what can be called "productive consumption."[30] When individuals or the society spends to educate young people or to retrain or deepen the skills of adults, that is productive consumption because it enhances the capacity of people to produce efficiently. Similarly, spending to rehabilitate drug addicts or to improve the physical and mental health of the population is also productive consumption. It is now widely recognized that the development of the capacities of the labor force is an extremely important determinant of a society's wealth.

Yet all of the standard calculations of savings ignore spending on productive consumption. The results are bizarre; a family that deprives its child of a college education in order to put more money in the stock market is seen as contributing to national savings, while the family that does the opposite could appear recklessly spendthrift. This backwards logic makes it harder to identify types of spending and social policies—such as the policies of social inclusion in Japan and West Germany—that could have an important impact on U.S. competitiveness in manufacturing.

CONCLUSION

The metaphors of "capital as blood" and "redemption through sacrifice" have dominated economic thinking in the United States. The international trade successes of Japan and West Germany have been refracted through these metaphors with the result that people in the United States have learned nothing from the comparisons. On the contrary, the comparisons combined with problematic data have served only to reinforce traditional—but now largely irrelevant—concerns with the quantity of available capital for investment. In the process, institutional issues have been totally forgotten, so that few serious reform proposals have emerged.

And yet, if we return to the neglected institutional dimensions on which Japan and West Germany are similar to each other and different from the United States—the marginality of military production, cooperative work arrangements, supportive financial institutions, and social inclusion—we already have the main elements of a serious program of national economic renewal. Moreover, the passing of the Cold War creates a unique historical opportunity for such a program, since for the first time in forty years a significant reduction in defense spending and a shift of resources to civilian purposes are imaginable.

But this is not the place to flesh out such a program of reform.[31] The point is rather that comparisons with other countries can be the source of real insight into the weaknesses of our own institutions, provided that people are not blinded by obsolete and irrelevant metaphors. As I write this, it is far too early to tell whether the United States will have its own experience of *perestroika*—the restructuring of economic institutions—in the 1990s. However, several points seem clear. Without an American *perestroika,* the U.S. economy will continue to weaken and our domestic social problems will only deepen. Furthermore, the most important precondition for a period of domestic reform is what Gorbachev has termed "new thinking"—a willingness to discard outdated metaphors and ideological preconceptions and to examine the world as it actually is.

SIX

Uncertain Seas
Cultural Turmoil and the Domestic Economy

Katherine S. Newman

One kid . . . I don't even know if we can afford having one child. . . . There were two in my family, three in Jane's, and that would be the range [we'd like]. I wouldn't want to have any more than that, but certainly let's say two. But two is going to be a tremendous, tremendous financial burden and drain. Not that you want to think of it in those terms, but right now I can't afford one child, no less two children. Especially when you think about the expenses, maternity expenses and child rearing expenses and all those expenses . . . and then you combine that with the loss of the second income, right? Because you can't have Jane working. Well, you're gonna lose, I figure, a year or two [of her income]. And it's just a double whammy that cannot be overcome.

Dan and Jane Edelman live in a small two-bedroom townhouse on an estate crammed with identical dwellings in northern New Jersey. The houses are stacked cheek by jowl, there is no yard to speak of, and the commute from home to work consumes two hours of their time every day. But the Edelmans count themselves lucky to own a home at all, since many of their friends have found themselves priced out of the market by skyrocketing real estate costs. Thus far they have been able to hold on to their corner of the American dream, but the issue of children looms large in their lives, and as Dan explained it, they cannot easily see past the "double whammy."

Their dilemma is symptomatic of a widespread disease generated by long-term structural changes in the domestic economy. After decades of postwar prosperity and seemingly unlimited opportunity, the American job machine seems to be running down. Wages have stagnated, income inequality is growing, unemployment—though down from its catastrophic levels in the early 1980s—remains troublesome, especially in the Rust Belt cities, and the cost of living continues to rise. Where the Edelman's parents were able to raise a family on the strength of a single

This research was supported by the Social/Cultural Anthropology Program of the National Science Foundation (grant number BNS 89-11266).

income and the assistance of a GI Bill mortgage, Dan and Jane are having to make tough, unpleasant choices between a standard of living they consider barely acceptable and the pleasures of family life.

The end of the postwar boom has spelled a slowdown, and in many cases a reversal, in the life chances of young families for career advancement, economic stability, and secure membership in the middle class. For many, downward mobility has become a reality: they will never see the occupational trajectory or lifestyle that their parents took for granted. Baby-boomers will not be able to raise their own children in the fashion they themselves took for granted. Remaining in the middle class mandates that husbands and wives will both have to work, coping as best they can with the task of raising children (and the scramble to find day care).

How did this situation come to pass? What happened to the American economy such that college graduates like Dan and Jane Edelman must struggle to provide a middle-class standard of living for their children-to-be? Our domestic economy has undergone profound changes since the end of World War II, changes that have seen American manufacturing industries yield to foreign competition and then disappear at an alarming rate, and our labor force shift into service jobs that do not pay as well as the unionized blue-collar jobs of the past. Variously termed the "deindustrialization of America"[1] or the emergence of a postindustrial economy,[2] this economic transformation has brought with it profound rearrangements in the way Americans earn their keep, in the way wealth is distributed within the country, and in the prospects for racial, gender, and generational groups to claim a "fair share" of the economic pie.

Evidence of long-term structural change in the economy of the United States abounds, and one purpose of this chapter will be to examine it briefly. Inspecting the facts of industrial decline or income inequality is, however, a starting point for a sociological analysis that must dig beneath the language of labor economics to the lived reality these changes impose upon American families. The domestic economy organizes how and where we spend our time, whether we can afford to marry and raise families, the consequences of divorce for an adult's life-style and a child's well-being, the quality of an individual's life in retirement, one's access to child care or health care. Virtually all aspects of our everyday lives and our long-term dreams are shaped by the economic constraints that have emerged during the latter half of the century.

Beyond the practical concerns of organizing work and family life, the undercurrents of economic transformation also reach deep into our cultural universe. Expectations for individual prosperity and upward mobility are deeply engrained in the generations descended from the survivors of the Great Depression. The post–World War II economic boom fueled this tremendous optimism, creating a baby-boom generation steeped in the belief that home ownership was a birthright and a good white-collar job as normal as a "chicken in every pot."

Economic stagnation and rising inequality brought on by deindustrialization have produced frustration and confusion as people discover that the "normal" future they envisioned, and feel entitled to by virtue of being American, may not materialize. Rates of home ownership among young people (twenty-five to thirty-four) have dropped dramatically, with little prospect for reversal. Men and women raised in suburban comfort now find that they cannot provide the same kind of security for their children. In the 1950s and early 1960s, when most of the babyboomers were born and raised, Ozzie could expect to support Harriet and the kids in a middle-class fashion solely on the strength of his income. Today that life-style has become ever more difficult to sustain, even though the vast majority of Harriets work full time.[3]

If life is proving less affluent than expected among the white middle class, the picture has become far more grim for America's poor, rural and urban. In the past twenty years, family farms collapsed at the highest rate since the Great Depression. Rural poverty, a phenomenon Americans associate with the dark days of the 1930s, has re-emerged as a major social problem in the midwestern states. Some 17 percent of rural dwellers—nearly ten million people—live in poverty, a figure comparable to the poverty rates in inner cities.[4] Inner cities are plagued by abandoned buildings, larger numbers of school dropouts than ever before, the spectre of homelessness amidst the splendor of gentrification, and rising crime as the underground economy (primarily the crack cocaine trade) engulfs neighborhoods in which prospects for legitimate employment have dried up. The problems of the poor spill out of ghetto enclaves and onto middle-class byways in the form of homeless beggars.

How are these social facts connected to the macroeconomic phenomenon of deindustrialization? Even more important, how has the social experience of economic stagnation and increasing inequality shaped a new view, however confused and ambiguous, of the American experience? The meaning of "being American" has been inextricably embedded in expectations for upward mobility and domination of international trade. The 1970s and 1980s have reshaped this self-perception in ways that we have yet to fully articulate. The change is evident in our fears for the country's economic future and our frustrations over the impact of change on our standard of living, a resurgent conservatism over the responsibilities of the fortunate toward the fate of the poor, a heightened sense of competition between and within generations for the resources needed to raise a family or retire in comfort, and increasing worries over the long-term impact of inner-city decay and minority poverty.

The dimensions of change are best understood by looking first at the macroeconomic facts of industrial decline. Thereafter, I explore the impact of this transformation in the realm that matters most to American families: income and employment. Finally, I will consider how deindustrialization has influenced the expectations and experiences of the different generations of Americans who must find their way through the new economy. My quest is to consider the cultural meaning of the country's economic decline.

THE PARAMETERS OF DEINDUSTRIALIZATION

The unprecedented wave of industrial plant shutdowns in the 1970s and 1980s attracted the attention of a wide variety of labor economists and industrial sociologists. Conservatives among them argued that the downturn was simply another "swing" in the business cycle, a term used to describe the episodic ups and downs considered natural, normal features of capitalist systems. If anything else was to blame for America's economic doldrums, conservatives suggested that unproductive and "overpriced" labor was primarily at fault. Union demands were understood to be the root cause of the flight of manufacturing overseas, where wages are lower.

Liberal economists took issue with this view and began to look for new paradigms to describe the postwar development of the U.S. economy. Two well-known scholars on the political left, Barry Bluestone and Bennett Harrison, argued that a fundamental change in the country's economic structure was underway. Their much-debated book, *The Deindustrialization of America*, united the demise of the country's manufacturing sector with the movement of industry overseas and the spectacular increase in corporate mergers, and in so doing articulated a new and darker vision of the country's economic predicament:

> Underlying the high rates of unemployment, the sluggish growth in the domestic economy, and the failure to successfully compete in the international market is the deindustrialization of America. By deindustrialization is meant a widespread, systematic disinvestment in the nation's basic productive capacity. . . . Capital . . . has been diverted from productive investment in our basic national industries into unproductive speculation, mergers and acquisitions, and foreign investment. Left behind are shuttered factories, displaced workers, and a newly emerging group of ghost towns.[5]

Bluestone and Harrison accused American corporations of dismantling even profitable plants to provide revenue for diversified investment, and the relocation of manufacturing facilities to low-wage, nonunionized communities, often at the taxpayers' expense, since these shutdowns could be written off corporate tax bills.

Deindustrialization has been most pronounced in the Rust Belt zones of the Northeast and Midwest, yet Bluestone and Harrison showed that nearly half the jobs lost to plant shutdowns during the 1970s were located in the Sun Belt states of the South and West. Hence the trend cannot be dismissed as a regional problem; it is a nationwide migraine headache. Overall, the 1970s saw the loss of nearly thirty-eight million jobs to runaway shops, plant shutdowns, and cutbacks.[6]

The vulnerability of labor in the face of rising unemployment quickly lead to declining average wages, even for those who were still on the job. Downward pressure on wages was exerted through "freezes and cuts in wages, the introduction of two-tiered wage systems, the proliferation of part-time and "home" work, and the shifting of work previously performed by regular (often unionized) employees to independent, typically nonunion subcontractors."[7] Estimates of overall wage losses in the durable goods sector—which includes automobiles, steel, machinery, and electrical equipment—amount to nearly 18 percent between 1973 and 1986. This translates into a loss of more than $16 million dollars per hour of work, deducted from American paychecks.[8]

Communities suffer collective punishment when faced with local economic contraction. Towns plagued by plant shutdowns usually see sharp declines in the health of industries that supplied parts or raw materials to the now-vacant factory. Taverns and grocery stores feel the pinch not long thereafter, as workers laid off from major employers cut back on their spending. Unemployment benefits cushion the impact for a time, but eventually long-term joblessness translates into mortgage defaults, higher welfare expenditures, and outmigration. When workers are no longer on the payroll, their home towns must weather the loss of income and sales tax revenues. This in turn forces unwelcomed cuts in the quality and quantity of public services (schools, hospitals, roads, etc.), which makes an economically depressed area even less attractive for new investment. As if this weren't enough, the gloom and doom of deindustrialization generates rising demand for social and medical services that can address stress disorders: psychological problems, alcoholism, and high blood pressure, among them.[9]

Enterprising officials, hoping to find ways to reverse the downhill slide, search high and low for new industries to fill the gap in the local economy. With their backs against the wall, communities compete against each other to attract new corporations by providing tax breaks or promises to construct new sewer lines in the hopes of beating out others offering less. Apart from the fiscal burden this places on local residents, the very vulnerability of deindustrializing communities provides them little leverage in bargaining with new companies. They dare not ask much in return for the tax breaks lest they risk the loss of a new business to another town that has proven to be less demanding. Hence, despite the public investment involved they cannot insist that a company return the favor and stay put (or even necessarily exact the promise of a warning if a plant shutdown happens again).

The spectre of industrial decline does not tell the whole story of deindustrialization. There is a growth side to the saga as well, represented by an employment boom in the service sector. Conservatives often point to the remarkable record the United States enjoys in job creation when compared to its relatively stagnant European counterparts. What is often missed in this laudatory portrait is the low-wage character of the American "job machine." Services ranging from fast food to banking, from child care to nursing home attendants, have burgeoned. In most of these growth areas, however, the wage structure has been unfavorable. A small number of professional jobs that pay well has been swamped by minimum wage positions. About 85 percent of the new jobs created in the 1980s were in the lowest paying industries—retail trade and personal, business, and health services.[10] More than half of the eight million (net) new jobs created in the United States between 1979 and 1984 paid less than $7,000 per year (in 1984 dollars). While many of these were part-time jobs (another growth area of dubious value), more than 20 percent of the year-round, full-time jobs created during this period paid no more than $7,000.[11] The economic expansion of the 1980s, much heralded by Presidents Reagan and Bush, failed to improve the standard of living of many Americans because the jobs it generated were disproportionately to be found at the low-wage end of the spectrum.[12]

Hence workers displaced by deindustrialization, new entrants to the labor market (young people and women), and the increasing number of elderly returning to the employment scene to supplement retirement, find their options limited. Moreover, the improvement experienced by black, Hispanic, and Asian workers in the 1960s and early 1970s was all but wiped out in the 1980s as they flooded into low-wage jobs. Younger workers were also disadvantaged: one-fifth of the net new year-round, full-time jobs held by workers under thirty-five years old paid under $11,000.[13] Workers unlucky enough to find themselves in the industrial heartland faced the most hostile climate of all since the region exceeds all other areas of the country in the "ability" to generate bad jobs: 96 percent of the new employment in the Rust Belt Midwest is in the low-income category.

These "replacement" jobs are even more problematic because they generally fail to offer the benefits routinely attached to "good" jobs. As of 1987, roughly 17 percent of American employees had no health insurance and 40 percent were not covered by a pension plan.[14] This is partially attributable to the low levels of unionization in the growing service sector industries: workers who are not organized have no collective bargaining power and hence suffer from relatively low wages and poor benefits.

Employers' increasing reliance on temporary workers hardly helps matters. These "marginal" workers—for example, "Kelly Girls" and "Accountemps"—are often employed full-time, but lack yearly contracts and can be let go with virtually no notice. Temporary jobs are notorious for denying workers insurance and pension coverage as well as prospects for advancement. When compared to the growth rates of permanent employment, temporary work has skyrocketed, growing nine times faster than total employment since 1979. By 1987, Kelly Girls and organizations like it could claim nearly 1.2 million workers.[15]

Moonlighting is also on the increase, with large numbers of men and women working two jobs, either in order to make ends meet or to squirrel away some savings. The practice was not unknown in the past for men, particularly those attempting to support families without the assistance of working wives. Now, however, with divorce increasing (and the prospects for supporting a family on a single income growing ever more problematic), women are moonlighting in record numbers. In 1970 only 636,000 women held down two jobs; by 1989 the numbers had jumped to 3.1 million.[16] If low-wage job growth persists and divorce remains a fixture of the social landscape, we can look forward to more of the same.

The imagery of deindustrialization—ghost towns and empty parking lots—can easily lead one to imagine that the old single-industry cities have gone the way of the dinosaurs. Although it is true that many a company town has disappeared and that urban economies appear to be more diverse in their industrial base than they were in the days of the robber barons, narrowly based local economies are not entirely of the past. The growth of white-collar industries has introduced a new form of dependence into the domestic economy. Stripped of their manufacturing giants, cities like New York, Boston, Los Angeles, Houston, and Chicago have increasingly come to rely on the white-collar businesses—particularly in financial services and information technology—as the engine of their economic development.

The consequences of such a dependence are twofold. On the one hand, we see an increasing divide among city dwellers between those who have high wages, fancy apartments, and affluent life-styles, and those who were turned out of the old manufacturing industries that once dominated city life.[17] Fur-clad brokers are confronted by homeless men, women, and children in the subways and on the streets. Poor people's housing (for example, single-room occupancy hotels, flophouses, and the like) has evaporated in the face of demand for luxury buildings, and the results of this wholesale eviction of the dispossessed is visible to everyone.[18] In the cities and the suburbs, Americans are relentlessly exposed to the growing gap between the haves and the have-nots.

But those in the fur coats are not so secure either. In February of 1990, the pages of the *Wall Street Journal*—the self-proclaimed "daily diary of the American dream"—were filled with stunned accounts of the bankruptcy of Drexel, Burnham, Lambert, one of the country's premier brokerage firms. After a decade of astronomical profits, Drexel filed for Chapter 11 and stranded 5,000 fast-track traders. Two weeks later, Shearson/Lehman announced a 4 percent reduction in its workforce—another 2,000 well-paid workers were let go, with more to follow. Nineteen ninety was not a particularly opportune year to be an unemployed stockbroker, for Wall Street was still reeling from the impact of the massive downturn of October 1987; thirty thousand employees received pink slips in the aftermath of Black Monday, when the worst stock market crash since 1929 sent millions of dollars in investment capital up in smoke. Wall Street salaries have plummeted as overqualified movers and shakers flood the market. The volatile nature of financial services, which is sensitive to fluctuating interest rates, plus the whims of foreign and domestic investors, and the feverish takeover activity of the past decade have combined to make life a bit precarious at the top. Once filled with unstoppable optimism and a degree of arrogance over their successes, the denizens of these high-level firms have joined the ranks of fellow white-collar workers who have learned to watch their backs and duck—if possible—when the pink slips cascade out of the boardroom.[19]

The consequences of this volatility for a city's employment and tax base are considerable. Ray Brady, the CBS News reporter for economic affairs, reported the downsizing at Shearson/Lehman with an ominous tone in his voice.[20] Brady pointed out that every job on Wall Street generated two "support" positions elsewhere in the Big Apple. The corollary seems obvious: the loss of those big salaries translates into higher unemployment for the "little guys." Indeed, Brady noted, the impact of the 1987 Black Monday crash has already translated into a local downturn of no small proportions: in the two years after the Wall Street disaster, retail sales in New York were down 6 percent, restaurant business fell by 10 percent, and the real estate market dropped by about 9 percent, with sales sluggish and prices falling. A variety of factors may have influenced these "secondary" losses, but it is fairly clear that cities like the Big Apple have developed an unhealthy dependency on financial and information service industries. In the postindustrial city, when the brokerage business contracts pneumonia, the rest of the town may be in for a bad bout of the flu, at the very least.

City Hall in the postindustrial urban center is no less vulnerable to the fluctuating health of white-collar industries than the political leadership of the older Rust Belt centers was on heavy manufacturing. When service industries fire their workers, or transfer their operations out of expensive city centers to remote "back room" facilities in faraway suburbs, or threaten to leave altogether unless they are given tax breaks for staying, tax coffers begin to empty. Caught between the twin demands of declining revenues and rising demands for services in the wake of human displacement (homelessness, unemployment, ghetto deterioration), the Gotham cities of the United States are in trouble. Politicians hint at the inevitable need for new taxes to balance the books and refurbish urban infrastructures, only to find resistance strong from industries already straining to compete with overseas counterparts and urban families trying to keep their heads above water.

WHO OWNS THE AMERICAN DREAM?

As the concentration of the work force shifts from manufacturing cars to flipping hamburgers or processing insurance claims, communities are thrown into upheaval. The industries that once provided continuity for generation after generation of blue-collar workers disappear, leaving behind empty parking lots and empty souls. People who have spent their entire working lives in one factory find they must accept premature, and comparatively meagre, retirement, bereft of all the entitlements they expected: health insurance, pension funds, and the peace of mind that comes with knowing that your efforts were part of a larger enterprise that will go on after you.[21]

Young men, particularly minority men, experience rising unemployment as the industries that traditionally provided jobs for unskilled newcomers to the labor market (urban manufacturing) dry up.[22] Meanwhile, job growth in service industries is most pronounced in suburban areas, far from the inner-city ghettos most in need of entry-level employment. The "mismatch" between those in need of jobs and employers in need of employees has become a major logistical and social problem.[23] At all levels of the social structure, economic upheaval leads to social disorganization.

The chaos of deindustrialization brings with it a particularly unfortunate departure from post–World War II trends toward greater equality in the distribution of resources. During the twenty-five years that followed the war, average income in the United States grew at a healthy pace. But even more important (at least from the standpoint of fairness), the distribution of these gains benefited Americans who fell into middle and lower income groups. The country still had its rich and its poor, to be sure, but the gap between them closed to a greater degree than had been the case before 1945. But beginning in 1973, economic growth came sputtering to a halt.[24] Family incomes stopped growing, even though a record number of families had multiple earners. Workers lucky enough to be in high-wage industries fared comparatively well during the post-1973 period, but those in low-wage sectors took the brunt of the slowdown. The real income of the bottom 40 percent of the population fell by about 11 percent between 1979 and 1986. At the same time, income growth for the richest segments of the country grew at rates far exceeding the average. The top 1 percent gained by 20 percent.[25] It will surprise no one to learn that these differential growth rates led to a stunning 18 percent jump in the inequality of income distribution. Virtually all the progress made toward equality in America during the 1950s and 1960s was wiped out by the rising income inequality of the fifteen years that followed.[26]

Some scholars argue that the erosion of equality threatens to put the American middle class on the endangered species list.[27] For as the fortunate few ascend from the middle income level to the upper middle class, and the unfortunate many experience downward mobility and land in lower income groups, it is the middle that seems to be disappearing. Definitions of the middle class are notoriously slippery since they sometimes refer to income, while at other times revolve around occupational prestige. But if we examine the income measure for a start, there is evidence to suggest that the percentage of American families who earn what might be termed a middle income ($20,000 to $50,000 per year) is declining. Katherine Bradbury, a senior economist at the Federal Reserve Bank of Boston, calculated that the size of the middle class shrank by about 5 percent between 1973 and 1984, with the lion's share of these ex-middles dropping down the income charts and less than 1 percent moving up.[28] These kinds of findings have caused Harrison and Bluestone to dub our time the epoch of the "Great U-Turn," since the evidence points to a historic watershed, a reversal of the trends we had come to see as quintessentially true of the American economic experience.

Downward mobility in terms of income is bad enough, but when one considers the difficulty of using what remains to secure a middle-class standard of living, the real social significance of postindustrial wage structures becomes even clearer. Frank Levy, professor of economics at the University of Maryland and author of the influential volume *Dollars and Dreams,* has shown that up until the 1970s being in the middle income range virtually guaranteed home ownership and most of the other perquisites of the American Dream. After 1973 even remaining in the middle (much less dropping down into the low end of the income spectrum) no longer did the trick. Housing prices rose faster in the 1970s than other goods, owing in part to the unprecedented demand created by the baby-boom generation's desires for real estate. This coupled with wage stagnation combined to place home ownership out of bounds for a growing number of American families—even though more and more of those families were dual-income households. Owning a house is an indispensable benchmark of middle-class status.[29] Men and women who discover that this goal is out of their reach have effectively been written out of the American Dream.

When we look at aggregate statistics on income or housing, we often miss what is sociologically most significant about the changes that postindustrialism creates. The impact of declining average wages on life-style, for example, was experienced most profoundly by younger families. When the slowdown in income growth started in 1973, families that were already secure in their homes, with fixed-rate mortgages, savings accounts, and the like, were "over the hump" and had relatively little to fear. They saw the value of their assets skyrocket and were able to trade up the real estate market, exchanging a two-bedroom starter house for a larger, more elegant one, using the exploding value of their original home to finance the move. But young families, particularly those in the baby-boom generation, were caught on the other side of the divide. They came of age in a sick economy and, owing in part to the pressure of their sheer numbers, never fully recovered.

Climbing out of the Great Depression, each succeeding generation has expected to do better than their parents. The gospel of upward mobility received tremendous reinforcement in the two decades after World War II because economic expansion, coupled with generous government intervention in the form of the GI Bill and other middle-class entitlements, did make it possible for adults of the 1950s to fulfill their material ambitions. But after 1973, this great "American assumption" ran into the wall of economic stagnation and high inflation. The generation gap is no longer simply a matter of musical tastes or the length of one's hair: it now describes a material chasm.[30] Baby-boomers who grew up in suburbia, with Mom at home and Dad at the office, are finding the gates to the suburbs locked and the pressure to keep Mom and Dad in the workplace unrelenting.

THE CULTURAL COSTS OF DOWNWARD MOBILITY

American culture has always celebrated forward motion, progress, upward mobility. We are true optimists, always assuming that the world—or at least our corner of it—will continue to provide more for us than it did for our parents, and more for our children than we have today. This central expectation dies hard. When reality fails to provide what we think we are owed, we seldom readjust our expectations. Instead, we stew in frustration or search for a target for our anger, pointing fingers at more fortunate generations, incompetent presidents, disloyal corporations. When this fails to satisfy, Americans are often inclined to look within, to personalize wide-scale economic disasters in the form of individual moral failings.

Downward mobility, both within and between generations, is an experience particularly ripe for this kind of morality play. Managers who lost their jobs in the last decade's merger mania often find that they cannot hold on to a systemic, structural vision of their loss. Even when they know, at some level, that forces larger than any individual have left them pounding the pavement in search of new jobs that will pay less, be less secure, and symbolize their descent down the class ladder, they cannot hold on to the notion that they are not to blame. Instead, managerial culture in its American form leads them to internalize their occupational troubles and pushes them to comb through their personalities for the hidden flaws that justify their fate.

The culture of meritocracy they embrace teaches that a person's occupational standing is an accurate barometer of his or her intrinsic moral worth. When that barometer fails, it can only mean that the person is a less than fully respectable human being. Meritocratic individualism is so potent a theme in American culture that it can thoroughly undermine decades of evidence to the contrary. John Kowalski, a denizen of the Forty Plus Club, an organization for unemployed executives in Manhattan, devoted thirty years of his working life to a trade association representing the chemical industries. He rose steadily up the ladder of responsibility, graduating over time from assistant secretary to vice-president. John was proud of his work, and had every reason to think he had done a good job, when the board of directors suddenly announced he was to be passed over for the vacant presidency. They let it be known that John was no longer really welcome in his job and that "for his own sake" he ought to be looking elsewhere.

One might think that someone like John, who has dedicated virtually his entire adult life to this organization, would be furious, indeed, filled with righteous indignation. Yet his belief in the truth of meritocracy leads him instead to point the finger back at himself: "I'm beginning to wonder about my abilities to run an association, to manage and motivate people. . . . Having been demoted . . . has to make you think. I have to accept my firing. I have to learn that that's the way it is. The people who were involved in it are people I respect for the most part. . . . They are successful executives. . . . So I can't blame them for doing what they think is right. I have to say where have I gone wrong."[31] I interviewed dozens of men and women cast out from the heartland of corporate America, and rarely did anyone fail to reach the same conclusion John expresses here: "There must be something wrong with me." The cost of intragenerational (within an adult's lifetime) downward mobility has been a massive loss of confidence among some of America's most experienced white-collar managers. As the economic disruptions described earlier in this chapter spread, so too does this culturally defined uneasiness and depression. It engulfs workers and surrounds their children, who look at their parents and think, "If this could happen to them, it could happen to me."

The psychic pain caused by unemployment is an enduring problem for those on the receiving end. During depressions and recessions, the number of people who must survive this relentless destruction of their self-esteem grows. But even in good times there are always thousands of American men and women who find themselves falling out of the social structure, struggling to regain a place and an identity they can live with. Some manage to succeed, but many do not: they live for years with their identities in limbo. This is particularly true when the only jobs they can find pay a fraction of what they earned before they found themselves on the unemployment line. For American culture accepts the meritocratic argument that your job defines your worth as a person and subjects those who have moved down the ladder to a devastating critique of their value.

Even after they have recovered, the experience of downward mobility leaves most people insecure and shaken. They never quite trust their new employers or themselves. They cannot leave the past behind, but worry instead that they may plunge down again and join the legions of the lost for a second time. And many do have just that experience, for in their new jobs they are last hired, and when shake-ups occur, as they routinely do, they are often first fired once again.

When downward mobility occurs in one person's adult lifetime, the tragedy sticks in the craw and afflicts the generations to come in the form of nagging insecurity and self-doubt: will this awful descent down the occupational ladder happen to me, the son or daughter of the dispossessed? Am I carrying a gene for disaster? Children of the dispossessed, downwardly mobile can never be entirely sure that the security they once considered a middle-class birthright will be theirs to claim in adulthood.

In fact, there are reasons to suspect that downward mobility of another kind will describe the fate of many in the future. This "other kind" involves a comparison between the standard of living enjoyed by the baby-boom generation (and younger groups coming behind it) with the good fortunes of the generation that graduated to adulthood in the immediate aftermath of World War II. For as I noted earlier, the economic slowdown that began in 1973 caught different generations at different points in the life cycle and bifurcated their experience vis-à-vis the American dream. Where the older generation could expect to own their own homes, the younger group is finding this increasingly beyond reach. Where postwar adults were party to the creation of a "new middle class" of engineers, doctors, psychologists, corporate managers, and the like, their children found the professions crowded and competitive.[32] If all went well, the adult generation of the 1950s could expect to see their careers rocket upward, only to "plateau" (in terms of advancement up the corporate hierarchy) some time in their mid-fifties. Today's corporate managers are finding that the pressure of their numbers, combined with a slowing economy, will force the "plateau" to come earlier in their lives: in their forties. They will have to contend with salaries that are slower to increase, and the psychic consequences of an artificially shortened horizon for professional development. They will "top out" and be unable to go any higher in the organizational structure in which they work at a much younger age than was true for their fathers (or mothers).

Intergenerational downward mobility is causing broadbased cultural confusion. It is a byproduct of economic stagnation and demographic pressure, but these sociological facts are of little comfort to average people who cannot understand why they cannot fulfill the promise of bettering their parents' standard of living. It has been part of the American belief system to assume that each generation outdoes the last, and that the parents' sacrifices (taking a sweatshop job at the turn of the century) will be repaid by childrens' successes.[33] Increasingly, it would appear that with or without parental sacrifice, the baby-boom generation and those coming behind it are likely to experience a significant drop in their standard of living compared to that of their parents.

If human beings were able to adjust their expectations every time the consumer price index came out, this would be of little concern. But our sense of what is normal, of what the average person is entitled to have in life, does not change so easily. Men and women raised in suburban comfort do not simply say to themselves, "This is beyond my reach now; my children will have to settle for less; so be it." Instead, their expectations remain and their frustration grows to epidemic proportions.

For the past two years, I have been collecting life histories from two generations of Americans who graduated from one ordinary high school in a small town near New York City. The community they grew up in was a typical middle-income suburb of Manhattan. It is a bucolic, quiet enclave of commuter homes for people who earn a living in the Big Apple or in the larger cities of northern New Jersey. Developed in the 1950s, "Doeville"[34] attracted growing families out of the congested city. Mothers stayed home in those days, and the fathers of this town went out to work as skilled blue-collar labor, midlevel managers, and young professionals at the beginning of their careers in medicine or law. Many fathers established their own businesses, as contractors or freight haulers, and made a good living off the booming housing industry of the 1950s and 1960s.

There are homes in Doeville that are genuine mansions, with white pillars and circular driveways. But most of the houses are modest three-bedroom New England–style places or fake colonials, with comfortable yards and two-car garages. Their first owners, those who moved into Doeville in the early 1950s, could purchase a home fairly easily on a single income, financed by the GI Bill. Doeville's children (of the 1950s and 1960s), who are now in their late twenties and late thirties, remember their early years building treehouses in the backyard, playing in the woods and the creeks near by, going swimming in the local pool, and gradually moving through the normal ups and downs of adolescence. They had a "perfectly average," not particularly privileged, way of life, as they see it now.[35]

Today Doeville homes cost a fortune. Modest houses that were easily within reach when my "informants" were kids, now routinely sell for a third of a million dollars. The houses haven't changed and the people who grew up in the town haven't changed their view that living in Doeville is an entitlement of middle-class life. But almost none of the people who graduated from high school in this town could possibly afford to live there now. They have been evicted from their own little corner of the world—or anywhere similar to it—by the declining value of their paychecks and the exponential increase in the cost of those ordinary houses.

Fred Bollard is verging on thirty, a 1980 graduate of Doeville High School, who lived at home while he finished a night school accounting degree at a local private college. Fred's parents still live in Doeville, but this is out of the question for Fred or anyone else he grew up with:

> People who grew up—myself, my friends, my brothers and sisters and their friends—they don't stay in the area. Probably first and foremost, they can't afford it. The housing is literally ridiculous. My parents purchased their house for $25,000. Now the house on that little piece of property is appraised at $280,000. So now you have to make $70,000 a year to afford it. On two incomes you could do it, but one person? So that's why I think the major change is that the people who grew up there can't stay there. They have to leave and live elsewhere.

The progeny of Doeville who are now in their late twenties and thirties are finding that even when they give up the hope of living in a community like the one they grew up in, they cannot really satisfy their desires for a comfortable standard of living and the pleasures of family life. Jane and Dan Edelman, whom we encountered at the beginning of this chapter, would like to live in a place like Doeville, but can see that this is impossible, even on their combined incomes. Now that they would like to start a family, even their ability to support their modest home may be compromised.

The Edelman's are caught in a squeeze that makes them squirm. Raising a family is supposed to be a personal decision, an expression of love between parents, and a dramatic confirmation of the solidarity that binds their own relationship together. It is meant to be the antithesis of the calculating, rational decision that, for example, buying a car might represent. American culture separates emotional and pragmatic domains. But the purity of this distinction cannot always be maintained, and wasn't during the Great Depression, when sheer necessity forced men and women to calculate carefully over the most personal of decisions. But absent catastrophic conditions, American culture regards pragmatism as a separate orientation from the affairs of the heart. Adhering to this cultural blueprint now seems something of a luxury. Young adults who grew up in Doeville feel compelled to choose between maintaining a standard of living they feel is essential, though hardly equivalent to what they grew up with, and establishing a family. It is a dilemma not easily resolved, for owning a home and having a family are fundamentally intertwined. Men and women who grew up in private homes feel that they must provide the same for their own children and that it would be irresponsible of them to plan a family absent that critical resource.

One might argue that previous generations managed on the strength of rented apartments and a much-reduced standard of living. This is beside the point. The expectations fueled by the postwar boom period of the 1950s and 1960s have become benchmarks against which descendants measure what is reasonable to expect in life. The comparison they naturally make between generations that are chronologically contiguous makes the wound run even deeper. For Dan and Jane ask, "Why are we in this predicament when it seemed so easy only twenty years before our time?"

One disturbing consequence of this intergenerational squeeze is the need baby-boomers and their younger siblings feel to calculate every move they make. Spontaneity appears to be a luxury; planning a necessity. Hypercalculation rears its head where family planning is concerned. It is also omnipresent when career decisions are at stake. For one cannot afford to make a mistake, or to be too much of a risk taker. The consequences could be disastrous: you could fall off the fast track and never recover. The workplace becomes an arena of relentless competition, as Anthony Sandsome (another Doeville graduate of the class of 1980) puts it:

> Brokerage is the kind of thing where I get up in the morning and I'm in a boxing ring—not even in a boxing ring—I'm in a jungle. I'm armed with guns, knives, fists, you know, I am fighting for my money each day. I'm knocking the hell out of someone and someone is knocking the hell out of me.

Anthony can't get out of the ring, even though it sometimes exhausts him. He might never get back in. One might be inclined to expect this attitude from a broker, since the field is well known for its cutthroat tendencies. But sentiments of this sort are commonly expressed by Anthony's classmates who are accountants, teachers, secretaries, and the like. Work is not the place where one finds personal fulfillment or fellowship; it is the place where survival of the fittest is the goal and the consequence of being less than the best is likely to be a serious drop in one's standard of living.

To a degree this has always been an aspect of the American workplace. It is viewed by many as an arena for the Darwinian struggle. But for this generation, making a mistake may have draconian consequences. For the treadmill begins when a young woman or man must choose a college degree course that will lead to practical payoffs in the workplace and a job that has the advancement potential needed to purchase a lifestyle consistent with middle-class expectations. That this has become increasingly difficult to pull off is met not with abject resignation, but by winching up the demands an individual places on him- or herself to calculate life decisions more carefully, and by building frustration over the knowledge that despite this increased self-surveillance, life may not turn out to be what was expected.

Who is to blame if this happens? Doeville residents are not entirely sure. But when they reflect on the apparent permanence of their economic exile, the dismay of both generations in Doeville is layers deep. Doeville parents believe their children are entitled to live in their hometown or somewhere just like it. That is what they worked for, to ensure that their children would be as well off, if not better off, than they have been. What they are witnessing is the opposite trend: their children are falling farther and farther behind. Doeville's refugee youth couldn't agree more. Anyone who has been able to escape this pressure is perceived as having benefitted from some unfair advantage. There are such people moving into Doeville now, and most of them are of Asian origin. New York City is a magnet for overseas placement of Asian executives, posted stateside by Japanese and Korean firms with American subsidiaries. Doeville is an attractive place for these newcomers to live since it is close to the City, yet is cloistered from the perceived dangers of urban living. The strength of Asian currencies against the American dollar puts Doeville homes well within reach of overseas executives, even as it recedes from the grasp of "native" Americans. As Maureen Oberlin, a life-long Doeville resident who cannot afford to buy into the community as an adult, sees it, this is a cause for alarm:

> This area particularly has had a heavy Asian [influx]. If you go into some of the schools, Doeville is a perfect example, the high school . . . is getting to the point that it's almost 50-50, the percentage of Asians as opposed to Caucasians. The elementary schools are even higher [in percentages of

Asian students]. It's frustrating that they can afford it and we can't. We've lived here all our lives. We're working for it and they can just come up with the cash.

We are accustomed to the idea that blue-collar auto workers in Detroit will take a sledge hammer to a stray Toyota parked in the factory parking lot. The expression of frustration in the face of growing Japanese dominance of the American automobile market is understandable. Blue-collar labor faces a direct economic threat in the form of a competition we are losing. This is hardly news.

That the displacement has reached the quiet streets of America's middle and upper middle classes may come as something of a surprise. Nativism, a xenophobic reaction to the threat of "invasion" by alien peoples, is rearing its head behind the white picket fences of suburbia. Residents of Doeville, parents and exiled grown children, question whether the American melting pot is big enough for these newcomers, who seem to be starting at the top rather than working their way up through the ranks.

CONCLUSION

Deindustrialization is a macroeconomic phenomenon with profound consequences for our daily lives and our long-term ideals. The great American assumption of prosperity dies hard. When our experience falls short of expectations, as it does when downward mobility strikes a business executive, we are inclined to blame ourselves. Here the system appears to function perfectly well; we simply see ourselves as defective parts that need to be cast out or repositioned at a lower rank, more in keeping with our "natural" abilities.

When downward mobility distances the experience of one generation from that of another (adjacent) generation, the blame may also fall on the shoulders of the hapless individual who failed to calculate properly, who allowed an interest in music to overwhelm his or her better judgment (to pursue accounting). Or it may surface in scapegoating. Doeville families look at their new Asian neighbors and ask: why are they able to waltz in here and buy up homes in the neighborhoods we cultivated when we can no longer do so? The sentiment is not a pretty one, for it reflects an underlying sense of entitlement: only certain kinds of people—real Americans who speak English and want to assimilate—should be allowed the fruits of Doeville life. But it is an understandable reaction to the frustration of an intergenerational trajectory that is headed downhill in a culture that only has room for the good news of ever increasing prosperity.

Nativism is but one potential response. One hears as well the faint beat of intergenerational warfare: why should a thirty-year-old woman pay hefty Social Security taxes to pay for the retirement of elder Doevillians, when they no longer pass school bond issues to support the education of young children in a neighboring part of the county? Should the generation that saw the postwar boom and reaped the benefits be entitled to a comfortable retirement, when the baby-boomers pushing up from below may see neither? America's social contract is fraying at the edges. We are no longer certain what we owe each other in the form of mutual support, or how open we can "afford" to be in enfolding immigrants into our society. We first calculate the costs and often fail to see any benefits.

Awareness of the fragility of the bonds holding us together is dim at best. Doeville residents look upon the country as an anthropomorphic being that once had a secure identity and is now adrift. They are confused by the apparent weakness of the economy and by the sense of directionless motion we encounter at every turn. We seize upon high technology as the solution, only to find that we have lost our markets to foreign competition. We indulge in a frenzy of hostile takeovers and mergers, only to find that unemployment and burdensome debt follows in its wake. We send our sons and daughters to Wall Street in search of a financial holy grail, and discover instead that they are nearly as vulnerable to downward mobility as the steel mill worker on Chicago's South Side.

The turmoil we have seen in the domestic economy since the postwar period has brought us tremendous prosperity at times, and a roller coaster of insecurity at others. Most of all, it has created a "postmodern" sense of unpredictability: we no longer have a firm grip on where the domestic economy is headed, on where the end point of change is to be found. This is not a particularly easy moment for Americans, who look toward the twenty-first century with clouded vision. We have not given up on our identity as a dominant force in the international world, but we see the limits of our power in the faltering economy. There are times when reality is at dramatic odds with our cultural expectations, and this is one of those times.

SEVEN

Labor and Management
in Uncertain Times
Renegotiating the Social Contract

Ruth Milkman

*The U.A.W. . . . is the largest labor union on earth. Its membership of
1,300,000 embraces most of the production workers in three major American
industries. . . . The U.A.W. itself is diverse and discordant, both in its leaders
and its members, among whom are represented every race and shape of political
opinion. . . . The union's sharp insistence on democratic expression permits
bloc to battle bloc and both to rebel at higher-ups' orders. They often do.
But U.A.W. is a smart, aggressive, ambitious outfit with young, skillful
leaders. . . . It has improved the working conditions in the sometimes frantically
paced production lines. And it has firmly established the union shop in an
industry which was once firmly open shop. . . . It is not a rich union. Its dues
are one dollar a month, which is low. . . . U.A.W. makes its money go a long
way. It sets up social, medical, and educational benefits. . . . In its high
ranks are men like Reuther, who believes labor must more and more be given
a voice in long-range economic planning of the country.*[1]

Curious as it may seem to a late-twentieth-century sensibility, this hom-
age to the United Auto Workers is not from a union publication or some
obscure left-wing tract. It appeared in *Life* magazine in 1945, a month
after V-J Day and not long before the century's largest wave of industrial
strikes, led by the auto workers, rocked the nation. The cover photo featured a 1940s Everyman: an unnamed auto worker in his work clothes,
with factory smokestacks in the background. Blue-collar men in heavy
industry, with powerful democratic unions and, at least implicitly, a
strong class consciousness—only forty-five years ago this was standard
iconography in the mass media and in the popular thinking that it both
reflected and helped shape. Organized labor, then embracing over a
third of the nation's nonfarm workers and 67 percent of those in man-

Thanks to Miriam Golden, Naomi Schneider, Judith Stacey, and Alan Wolfe for their helpful comments on an earlier version of this chapter.

ufacturing, was a central force in the Democratic party and a vital influence in public debate on a wide range of social questions. The industrial unions founded in the New Deal era were leaders in opposing race discrimination (and to some extent even sex discrimination) in this period, and their political agenda went far beyond the narrow, sectional interests of their members. Indeed, as historian Nelson Lichtenstein has written, in the 1940s "the union movement defined the left wing of what was possible in the political affairs of the day."[2]

Today, this history is all but forgotten. Blue-collar workers and labor unions are conspicuous by their absence from the mainstream of public discourse. Across the political spectrum, the conventional wisdom is that both industrial work and the forms of unionism it generated are fading relics of a bygone age, obsolete and irrelevant in today's postindustrial society. As everybody knows, while the unionized male factory worker was prototypical in 1945, today the labor force includes nearly as many women as men, and workers of both genders are more likely to sit behind a desk or perform a service than to toil on an assembly line. Union density has fallen dramatically, and organized labor is so isolated from the larger society that the right-wing characterization of it as a "special interest" prevails unchallenged. Public approval ratings of unions are at a postwar low, and such new social movements as environmentalism and feminism are as likely to define themselves in opposition to as in alliance with organized labor (if they take any notice of it at all).[3]

What has happened in the postwar decades to produce this change? Part of the story involves structural economic shifts. Most obviously, the manufacturing sector has decreased drastically in importance, accounting for only 20 percent of civilian wage and salary employment in the United States in 1987, compared to 34 percent in 1948.[4] And for complex political as well as economic reasons, unionization has declined even more sharply, especially in manufacturing, its historical stronghold. Although numbers fail to capture the qualitative aspects of this decline, they do indicate its massive scale: in 1989, only 16 percent of all U.S. workers, and 22 percent of those in manufacturing, were union members—half and one-third, respectively, of the 1945 density levels.[5] Alongside these massive processes of deindustrialization and deunionization, the widespread introduction of new technologies and the growing diffusion of the "new" industrial relations, with its emphasis on worker participation, have in recent years dramatically transformed both work and unionism in the manufacturing sector itself.

Few workplaces have been affected by these changes as dramatically as those in the automobile industry, the historical prototype of mass production manufacturing and the core of the U.S. economy for most of this century. Since the mid-1970s, hundreds of thousands of auto workers have been thrown out of work as some factories have closed and others have been modernized.[6] And although the U.A.W. still represents the vast bulk of workers employed by the "Big Three" auto firms (General Motors, Ford, and Chrysler), in recent years the non-union sector of the industry has grown dramatically. Union coverage in the auto parts industry has fallen sharply since the mid-1970s, and the establishment of new Japanese-owned "transplants" in the 1980s has created a non-union beachhead in the otherwise solidly organized assembly sector.[7] Profoundly weakened by these developments, the U.A.W. has gingerly entered a new era of "cooperation" with management, jettisoning many of its time-honored traditions in hopes of securing a place for itself in the future configuration of the industry. Meanwhile, the Big Three have invested vast sums of money in such new technologies as robotics and programmable automation. They have also experimented extensively with worker participation schemes and other organizational changes.

The current situation of auto workers graphically illustrates both the historical legacy of the glory days of American industrial unionism and the consequences of the recent unravelling of the social contract between labor and management that crystallized in the aftermath of World War II. This chapter explores current changes in the nature of work and unionism in the auto industry, drawing on historical evidence and on fieldwork in a recently modernized General Motors (GM) assembly plant in Linden, New Jersey. The analysis focuses particularly on the effects of new technology and the new, participatory forms of management. While it is always hazardous to generalize from any one industry to "the" workplace, the recent history of labor relations in the auto industry is nonetheless suggestive of broader patterns. The auto industry case is also of special interest because it figures so prominently in current theoretical debates about workplace change, which are briefly considered in the concluding section.

The story I will recount here is largely a story of failure—on the part of both management and labor—to respond effectively to rapidly changing circumstances. On the management side, the Big Three auto firms (and especially GM) have experienced enormous difficulty in overcoming bureaucratic inertia, particularly in regard to changing the behavior of middle management and first-line supervisors. As a result, their internal organizational structures and traditional corporate cultures have remained largely intact, despite strenuous efforts to institute changes. The auto firms have been unable to reap the potential advantages of the new technologies or to make a successful transition to a more participatory system of workplace management, even though they have invested considerable resources in both areas. Management's own inertia has been reinforced, tragically, by the weakening of the U.A.W. in this critical period. Long habituated to a reactive stance toward management initiatives, in recent years the union has concentrated its energies on the crisis of job security, leaving the challenge of reorganizing the workplace itself largely to management while warily embracing "cooperation" in hopes of slowing the hemorrhaging of jobs in the industry. The net result has been an increasingly uncompetitive domestic auto industry, which in turn has further weakened the union, creating a vicious circle of decline.

Because so much of the recent behavior of automobile manufacturing managers and of the U.A.W. and its members is rooted in the past, the first step in understanding the current situation is to look back to the early days of the auto industry, when the system of mass production and the accompanying pattern of labor-management relations that is now unravelling first took shape.

FORDISM AND THE HISTORY OF LABOR RELATIONS IN THE U.S. AUTO INDUSTRY

The earliest car manufacturers depended heavily on skilled craftsmen to make small production runs of luxury vehicles for the rich. But the industry's transformation into a model of mass production efficiency, led by the Ford Motor Company in the 1910s, was predicated on the systematic removal of skill from the industry's labor process through scientific management, or Taylorism (named for its premier theorist, Frederick Winslow Taylor). Ford perfected a system involving not only deskilling but also product standardization, the use of interchangeable parts, mechanization, a moving assembly line, and high wages. These were the elements of what has since come to be known as "Fordism," and they defined not only the organization of the automobile industry but that of modern mass production generally.[8]

As rationalization and deskilling proceeded through the auto industry in the 1910s and 1920s, the proportion of highly skilled jobs fell dramatically. The introduction of Ford's famous Five Dollar Day in 1914 (then twice the going rate for factory workers) both secured labor's consent to the horrendous working conditions these innovations produced and helped promote the mass consumption that mass production required for its success. Managerial paternalism, symbolized by Ford's "Sociological Department," supplemented high wages in this regime of labor control. Early Ford management also developed job classification systems, ranking jobs by skill levels and so establishing an internal labor market within which workers could hope to advance.[9]

Deskilling was never complete, and some skill differentials persisted among production workers. Even in the 1980s, auto body painters and welders had more skill than workers who simply assembled parts, for example. But these were insignificant gradations compared to the gap between production workers and the privileged stratum of craft workers known in the auto industry as the "skilled trades"—tool and die makers, machinists, electricians, and various other maintenance workers. Nevertheless, the mass of the industry's semiskilled operatives united with the skilled trades elite in the great industrial union drives of the 1930s, and in the U.A.W. both groups were integrated into the same local unions.

The triumph of unionism left the industry's internal division of jobs and skills intact, but the U.A.W. did succeed in narrowing wage differentials among production workers and in institutionalizing seniority (a principle originally introduced by management but enforced erratically in the pre-union era) as the basic criterion for layoffs and job transfers for production workers. For the first decade of the union era, much labor-management conflict focused on the definition of seniority groups. Workers wanted plantwide or departmentwide seniority to maximize employment security, while management sought the narrowest possible seniority classifications to minimize the disruptions associated with workers' movement from job to job. But once the U.A.W. won plantwide seniority for layoffs, it welcomed management's efforts to increase the number of job classifications for transfers, since this maximized opportunities for workers with high seniority to choose the jobs they preferred. By the 1950s, this system of narrowly defined jobs, supported by union and management alike, was firmly entrenched.[10]

Management and labor reached an accommodation on many other issues as well in the immediate aftermath of World War II. But at the same time, the U.A.W. began to retreat from the broad, progressive agenda it had championed in the 1930s and during the war. The failure of the 1945–46 "open the books" strike, in which the union demanded that GM raise workers' wages without increasing car prices, and the national resurgence of conservatism in the late 1940s and 1950s led the U.A.W. into its famous postwar "accord" with management. Under its terms, the union increasingly restricted its goals to improving wages and working conditions for its members, while ceding to management all the prerogatives involved in the production process and in economic planning. The shop steward system in the plants was weakened in the postwar period as well, and in the decades that followed, the U.A.W. was gradually transformed from the highly democratic social movement that *Life* magazine had profiled in 1945 into a more staid, bureaucratic institution that concentrated its energies on the increasingly complex technical issues involved in enforcing its contracts and improving wages, fringe benefits, and job security for its members.[11]

The grueling nature of production work in the auto industry changed

relatively little over the postwar decades, even as the U.A.W. continued
to extract improvements in the economic terms under which workers
agreed to perform it. High wages and excellent benefits made auto workers into the blue-collar aristocrats of the age. It was an overwhelmingly
male aristocracy, since women had been largely excluded from auto assembly jobs after World War II; blacks, on the other hand, made up a
more substantial part of the auto production work force than of the nation's population. In 1987, at the Linden GM assembly plant where I did
my fieldwork, for example, women were 12 percent of the production
work force and less than 1 percent of the skilled trades. Linden production workers were a racially diverse group: 61 percent were white, 28 percent were black, and 12 percent were Hispanic; the skilled trades work
force, however, was 90 percent white.[12]

While the union did little to ameliorate the actual experience of work
in the postwar period, with the job classification system solidified, those
committed to a long-term career in the industry could build up enough
seniority to bid on the better jobs within their plants. Although the early,
management-imposed job classification systems had been based on skill
and wage differentials, the union eliminated most of the variation along
these dimensions. Indeed, the payment system the U.A.W. won, which
persists to this day, is extremely egalitarian. Regardless of seniority or
individual merit, assembly workers are paid a fixed hourly rate negotiated for their job classification, and the rate spread across classifications
is very narrow. Formal education, which is in any case relatively low (both
production workers and skilled trades at Linden GM averaged twelve
years of schooling), is virtually irrelevant to earnings. At Linden GM, production workers' rates in 1987 ranged from a low of $13.51 per hour for
sweepers and janitors to a high of $14.69 for metal repair work in the body
shop. Skilled trades workers' hourly rates were only slightly higher, ranging from $15.90 to $16.80 (with a twenty-cent-an-hour "merit spread"),
although their annual earnings are much higher than those of production workers because of their extensive overtime.[13]

Since wage differentials are so small, the informal *de facto* hierarchy
among production jobs is based instead on what workers themselves perceive as desirable job characteristics. While individual preferences always
vary somewhat, the consensus is reflected in the seniority required to secure any given position. One testament to the intensely alienating nature
of work on the assembly line is that among the jobs auto workers prefer
most are those of sweeper and janitor, even though these jobs have the
lowest hourly wage rates. Subassembly, inspection, and other jobs where
workers could pace themselves rather than be governed by the assembly
line are also much sought after. At Linden in 1987, the median seniority of unskilled workers in the material and maintenance departments,

which include all the sweepers and janitors and where all jobs are "off the line," was 24 years—twice the median seniority of workers in the assembly departments![14] By contrast, jobs in particularly hot or dirty parts of the plant, or those in areas where supervision is especially hostile, are shunned by workers whose seniority gives them any choice. Such concerns are far more important to production workers than what have become marginal skill or wage differentials, although there is a group that longs to cross the almost insurmountable barrier between production work and the skilled trades.[15]

Such was the system that emerged from the post–World War II accord between the U.A.W. and management. It functioned reasonably well for the first three postwar decades. The auto companies generated huge profits in these years, and for auto workers, too, the period was one of unprecedented prosperity. Even recessions in this cyclically sensitive industry were cushioned by the supplementary unemployment benefits the union won in 1955. However, in the 1970s, fundamental shifts in the international economy began to undermine the domestic auto makers. As skyrocketing oil prices sent shock waves through the U.S. economy, more and more cars were imported from the economically resurgent nations of Western Europe and, most significantly, Japan. For the first time in their history, the domestic producers faced a serious challenge in their home market.[16]

After initially ignoring these developments, in the 1980s the Big Three began to confront their international competition seriously. They invested heavily in computerization and robotization, building a few new high-tech plants and modernizing most of their existing facilities. GM alone spent more than $40 billion during the 1980s on renovating old plants and building new ones.[17] At the same time, inspired by their Japanese competitors, the auto firms sought to change the terms of their postwar accord with labor, seeking wage concessions from the union, reducing the number of job classifications and related work rules in many plants, and experimenting with new forms of "employee involvement" and worker participation, from quality circles to flexible work teams.[18]

The U.A.W., faced with unprecedented job losses and the threat of more to come, accepted most of these changes in the name of labor-management cooperation. To the union's national leadership, this appeared to be the only viable alternative. They justified it to an often skeptical rank and file membership by arguing that resistance to change would only serve to prevent the domestic industry from becoming internationally competitive, which in turn would mean further job losses. Once it won job security provisions protecting those members affected by technological change, the union welcomed management's investments in technological modernization, which both parties saw as a means of meeting the challenge of foreign competition. Classification mergers and worker participation schemes were more controversial within the union, but the leadership accepted these, too, in the name of enhancing the domestic industry's competitiveness.

Most popular and academic commentators view the innovations in technology and industrial relations that the auto industry (among others) undertook in the 1980s in very positive terms. Some go so far as to suggest that they constitute a fundamental break with the old Fordist system. New production technologies in particular, it is widely argued, hold forth the promise of eliminating the most boring and dangerous jobs while upgrading the skill levels of those that remain. In this view, new technology potentially offers workers something the U.A.W. was never able to provide, namely, an end to the deadening monotony of repetitive, deskilled work. Similarly, many commentators applaud the introduction of Japanese-style quality circles and other forms of participative management, which they see as a form of work humanization complementing the new technology. By building on workers' own knowledge of the production process, it is argued, participation enhances both efficiency and the quality of work experience. The realities of work in the auto industry, however, have changed far less than this optimistic scenario suggests.

NEW TECHNOLOGY AND THE SKILL QUESTION

Computer-based technologies are fundamentally different from earlier waves of industrial innovation. Whereas in the past automation involved the use of special-purpose, or "dedicated," machinery to perform specific functions previously done manually, the new information-based technologies are flexible, allowing a single machine to be adapted to a variety of specific tasks. As Shoshana Zuboff points out, these new technologies often require workers to use "intellective" skills. Workers no longer simply manipulate tools and other tangible objects, but also must respond to abstract, electronically presented information. For this reason, Zuboff suggests, computer technology offers the possibility of a radical break with the Taylorist tradition of work organization that industries like auto manufacturing long ago perfected, moving instead toward more skilled and rewarding jobs, and toward workplaces where learning is encouraged and rewarded. "Learning is the new form of labor," she declares.[19] Larry Hirschhorn, another influential commentator on computer technology, makes a similar argument. As he puts it, in the computerized factory "the deskilling process is reversed. Machines extend workers' skill rather than replace it." [20]

As computer technology has transformed more and more workplaces, claims like these have won widespread public acceptance. They are, in fact, the basis for labor market projections that suggest a declining need for unskilled labor and the need for educational upgrading to produce future generations of workers capable of working in the factory and office of the computer age. Yet it is far from certain that workplaces are actually changing in the ways that Zuboff and Hirschhorn suggest.

The Linden GM plant is a useful case for examining this issue, since it recently underwent dramatic technological change. In 1985–86, GM spent $300 million modernizing the plant, which emerged from this process as one of the nation's most technologically advanced auto assembly facilities and as the most efficient GM plant in the United States. There are now 219 robots in the plant, and 113 automated guided vehicles (AGVs), which carry the car bodies from station to station as they are assembled. Other new technology includes 186 programmable logic controllers (PLCs), used to program the robots. (Before the plant modernization there was only one robot, no AGVs, and eight PLCs.)[21]

Despite this radical technological overhaul, the long-standing division of labor between skilled trades and production workers has been preserved intact. Today, as they did when the plant used traditional technology, Linden's skilled trades workers maintain the plant's machinery and equipment, while production workers perform the unskilled and semi-skilled manual work involved in assembling the cars. However, the number of production workers has been drastically reduced (by over 1,100 people, or 26 percent), while the much smaller population of skilled trades workers has risen sharply (by 190 people, or 81 percent). Thus the overall proportion of skilled workers increased—from 5 percent to 11.5 percent—with the introduction of robotics and other computer-based production technologies. In this sense, the plant's modernization did lead to an overall upgrading in skill levels.[22]

However, a closer look at the impact of the technological change on GM-Linden reveals that pre-existing skill differentials among workers have been magnified, leading to skill *polarization* within the plant rather than across-the-board upgrading.[23] After the plant modernization, the skilled trades workers enjoyed massive skill upgrading and gained higher levels of responsibility, just as Zuboff and Hirschhorn would predict. In contrast, however, the much larger group of production workers, whose jobs were already extremely routinized, typically experienced still further deskilling and found themselves subordinated to and controlled by the new technology to an even greater extent than before.

The skilled trades workers had to learn how to maintain and repair the robots, AGVs, and other new equipment, and since the new technology is far more complex than what it replaced, they acquired many new skills. Most skilled trades workers received extensive retraining, especially in robotics and in the use of computers. Linden's skilled trades workers reported an average (median) of forty-eight full days of technical training in connection with the plant modernization, and some received much more.[24] Most of them were enthusiastic about the situation. "They were anxiously awaiting the new technology," one electrician recalled. "It was like a kid with a new toy. Everyone wanted to know what was going to happen."[25] After the "changeover" (the term Linden workers used for the plant modernization), the skilled trades workers described their work as challenging and intellectually demanding:

> We're responsible for programming the robots, troubleshooting the robots, wiping their noses, cleaning them, whatever. . . . It's interesting work. We're doing something that very few people in the world are doing, troubleshooting and repairing robots. It's terrific! I don't think this can be boring because there are so many things involved. There are things happening right now that we haven't ever seen before. Every day there's something different. We're always learning about the program, always changing things to make them better—every single day. [an electrician]

> With high technology, skilled trades people are being forced to learn other people's trades in order to do their trade better. Like with me, I have to understand that controller and how it works in order to make sure the robot will work the way it's supposed to. You have to know the whole system. You can't just say, "I work on that one little gear box, I don't give a damn about what the rest of the machine does." You have to have a knowledge of everything you work with and everything that is related to it, whether you want to or not. You got to know pneumatics, hydraulics— all the trades. Everything is so interrelated and connected. You can't be narrow-minded anymore. [a machine repairman]

However, the situation was quite different for production workers. Their jobs, as had always been the case in the auto industry, continued to involve extremely repetitive, machine-paced, unskilled or semiskilled work. Far from being required to learn new skills, many found their jobs were simplified or further deskilled by the new technology:

> It does make it easier to an extent, but also at the same time they figure, "Well, I'm giving you a computer and it's going to make your job faster, so instead of you doing this, this, and this, I'm going to have you do this and eight other things, because the time I'm saving you on the first three you're going to make it up on the last." Right now I'm doing more work in less time, the company's benefiting, and I am bored to death—more bored than before! [a trim department worker with nineteen years seniority]

> I'm working in assembly. I'm feeding the line, the right side panel, the whole right side of the car. Myself and a fellow worker, in the same spot. Now all we do, actually, is put pieces in, push the buttons, and what they

call a shuttle picks up whatever we put on and takes it down the line to be welded. Before the changeover my job was completely different. I was a torch solderer. And I had to solder the roof, you know, the joint of the roof with the side panel. I could use my head more. I liked it more. Because, you know, when you have your mind in it also, it's more interesting. And not too many fellow workers could do the job. You had to be precise, because you had to put only so much material, lead, on the job. [a body shop worker with sixteen years seniority]

Not only were some of the more demanding and relatively skilled traditional production jobs—like soldering, welding, and painting car bodies—automated out of existence, but also many of the relatively desirable off-the-line jobs were eliminated. "Before there were more people working subassembly, assembling parts," one worker recalled. "You have some of the old-timers working on the line right now. Before, if you had more seniority, you were, let's say, off the line, in subassembly."

Even when they operate computers—a rarity for production workers—they typically do so in a highly routinized way. "There is nothing that really takes any skill to operate a computer," one production worker in the final inspection area said. "You just punch in the numbers, the screen will tell you what to do, it will tell you when to race the engine and when to turn the air conditioner off, when to do everything. Everything comes right up on the screen. It's very simple."

The pattern of skill polarization between the skilled trades and production workers that these comments suggest is verified by the findings of an in-plant survey. Skilled trades workers at Linden, asked about the importance of twelve specific on-the-job skills (including "problem solving," "accuracy/precision," "memory," and "reading/spelling") to their jobs before and after the plant was modernized, reported that all but one ("physical strength") increased in importance. In contrast, a survey of the plant's production workers asking about the importance of a similar list of skills found that all twelve declined in importance after the introduction of the new technology.[26] The survey also suggested that boredom levels had increased for production workers; 45 percent stated that their work after the changeover was boring and monotonous "often" or "all the time," compared to 35 percent who had found it boring and monotonous before the changeover. Similarly, 96 percent of production workers said that they now do the same task over and over again "often" or "all the time," up from 79 percent who did so before the changeover.

In the Linden case, the plant modernization had opposite effects on skilled trades and production workers, primarily because no significant job redesign was attempted. The boundary between the two groups and the kinds of work each had traditionally done was maintained, despite the radical technological change. While management might have chosen (and the union might have agreed) to try to transfer some tasks from the skilled trades to production workers, such as minor machine maintenance, or to redesign jobs more extensively in keeping with the potential of the new technology, this was not seriously attempted. Engineers limited their efforts to conventional "line balancing," which simply involves packaging tasks among individual production jobs so as to minimize the idle time of any given worker. In this respect they treated the new technology very much like older forms of machinery. The fundamental division of labor between production workers and the skilled trades persisted despite the massive infusion of new technology, and this organizational continuity led to the intensification of the already existing skill polarization within the plant.

GM-Linden appears to be typical of U.S. auto assembly plants in that new technology has been introduced without jobs having been fundamentally redesigned or the basic division of labor altered between production workers and the skilled trades. Even where significant changes in the division of labor—such as flexible teams—have been introduced, as in the new Japanese transplants, they typically involve rotating workers over a series of conventionally deskilled production jobs, rather than changing the basic nature of the work. While being able to perform eight or ten unskilled jobs rather than only one might be considered skill upgrading in some narrow technical sense, it hardly fits the glowing accounts of commentators who claim that with new technology "the deskilling process is reversed." Rather, it might be characterized best as "flexible Taylorism" or "Toyotism."[27]

Perhaps work in the auto industry *could* be reorganized along the lines Zuboff and Hirschhorn suggest, now that new technology has been introduced so widely. However, a major obstacle to this is bureaucratic inertia on the management side, for which GM in particular is legendary. As many auto industry analysts have pointed out, the firm's investments in new technology were typically seen by management as a "quick fix," throwing vast sums of money at the accelerating crisis of international competitiveness without seriously revamping the firm's organizational structure or its management strategies to make the most efficient possible use of the new equipment. As MaryAnn Keller put it, for GM "the goal of all the technology push has been to get rid of hourly workers. GM thought in terms of automation rather than replacing the current system with a better system."[28] The technology was meant to replace workers, not to transform work.

Reinforcing management's inertia, ironically, was the weakness of the U.A.W. The union has an old, deeply ingrained habit of ceding to management all prerogatives on such matters as job design. And in the 1980s, faced with unprecedented job losses, union concerns about employment security were in the forefront. The U.A.W. concentrated its efforts on minimizing the pain of "downsizing," generally accepting the notion that new technology and other strategies adopted by management were the best way to meet the challenge of increased competition in the industry. After all, if the domestic firms failed to become competitive, U.A.W. members would have no jobs at all. This kind of reasoning, most prominently associated with the U.A.W.'s GM Department director Donald Ephlin, until his retirement in 1989, also smoothed the path for management's efforts to transform the industrial relations system in the direction of increased "employee involvement" and teamwork, to which we now turn.

WORKER PARTICIPATION AND THE "NEW INDUSTRIAL RELATIONS"

Inspired by both the non-union manufacturing sector in the U.S. and by the Japanese system of work organization, the Big Three began to experiment with various worker participation schemes in the 1970s. By the end of the 1980s, virtually every auto assembly plant in the United States had institutionalized some form of participation. Like the new technologies that were introduced in the same period, these organizational innovations—the "new industrial relations"—were a response to the pressure of international competition. And even more than the new technologies, they signaled a historic break with previous industrial practices. For both the Taylorist organization of work in the auto industry and the system of labor relations that developed around it had presumed that the interests of management and those of workers were fundamentally in conflict. In embracing worker participation, however, management abandoned this worldview and redefined its interests as best served by cooperation with labor, its old adversary.[29]

For management, the goal of worker participation is to increase productivity and quality by drawing on workers' own knowledge of the labor process and by increasing their motivation and thus their commitment to the firm. Participation takes many different forms, ranging from suggestion programs, quality circles, and quality-of-work-life (QWL) programs, which actively solicit workers' ideas about how to improve production processes, to "team concept" systems, which organize workers into small groups that rotate jobs and work together to improve productivity and quality on an ongoing basis. All these initiatives promote communication and trust between management and labor, in the name of efficiency and enhanced international competitiveness. Like the new technologies with which they are often associated, the various forms of worker participation have been widely applauded by many commentators who see them as potentially opening up a new era of work humanization and industrial democracy.[30]

In the early 1970s, some U.A.W. officials (most notably Irving Bluestone, then head of the union's GM department) actively supported experimental QWL programs, which they saw as a means for improving the actual experience of work in the auto industry, a long-neglected part of the union's original agenda. But many unionists were more skeptical about participation in the 1980s, when QWL programs and the team concept became increasingly associated with union "give-backs," or concessions. In a dramatic reversal of the logic of the postwar labor-management accord, under which economic benefits were exchanged for unilateral management control over the production process, now economic concessions went hand-in-hand with the promise of worker participation in decision making. However, QWL and the team concept were introduced largely on management's terms in the 1980s, for in sharp contrast to the period immediately after World War II, now the U.A.W. was in a position of unprecedented weakness. In many Big Three plants, participation schemes were forced on workers (often in the face of organized opposition) through what auto industry analysts call "whip-sawing," a process whereby management pits local unions against one another by threatening to close the least "cooperative" plants. Partly for this reason, QWL and the team concept have precipitated serious divisions within the union, with Ephlin and other national union leaders who endorse participation facing opposition from a new generation of union dissidents who view it as a betrayal of the union's membership.[31]

The New United Motor Manufacturing, Inc., plant (NUMMI) in Fremont, California, a joint venture of Toyota and GM, is the focus of much of the recent controversy over worker participation. The plant is run by Toyota, using the team concept and various Japanese management techniques. (GM's responsibility is limited to the marketing side of the operation.) But unlike Toyota's Kentucky plant and the other wholly Japanese-owned transplants, at NUMMI the workers are U.A.W. members. Most of them worked for GM in the same plant before it was closed in 1982. Under GM, the Fremont plant had a reputation for low productivity and frequent wildcat strikes, but when it reopened as NUMMI two years later, with the same work force and even the same local union officers, it became an overnight success story. NUMMI's productivity and quality ratings are comparable to those of Toyota plants in Japan, and higher than any other U.S. auto plant.[32] Efforts to emulate its success further accelerated the push to establish teams in auto plants around the nation.

Many commentators have praised the NUMMI system of work organization as a model of worker participation; yet others have severely criticized it. The system's detractors argue that despite the rhetoric of worker control, the team concept and other participatory schemes are basically strategies to enhance *management* control. Thus Mike Parker and Jane Slaughter suggest that, far from offering a humane alternative to Taylorism, at NUMMI, and at plants that imitate it, workers mainly "participate" in the intensification of their own exploitation, mobilizing their detailed firsthand knowledge of the labor process to help management speed up production and eliminate wasteful work practices. More generally, "whether through team meetings, quality circles, or suggestion plans," Parker and Slaughter argue, "the little influence workers do have over their jobs is that in effect they are organized to time-study themselves in a kind of super-Taylorism."[33] They see the team concept as extremely treacherous, undermining unionism in the name of a dubious form of participation in management decisions.

Workers themselves, however, seem to find intrinsically appealing the idea of participating in what historically have been exclusively managerial decision-making processes, especially in comparison to traditional American managerial methods. This is the case even though participation typically is limited to an extremely restricted arena, such as helping to streamline the production process or otherwise raise productivity. Even Parker and Slaughter acknowledge that at NUMMI, "nobody says they want to return to the days when GM ran the plant."[34] Unless one wants to believe that auto workers are simply dupes of managerial manipulation, NUMMI's enormous popularity with the work force suggests that the new industrial relations have some positive features and cannot simply be dismissed as the latest form of labor control.

Evidence from the GM-Linden case confirms the appeal of participation to workers, although reforms in labor relations there were much more limited than at NUMMI. Linden still has over eighty populated job classifications, and although 72 percent of the production workers are concentrated in only eight of them, this is quite different from NUMMI, where there is only one job classification for production workers and seniority plays a very limited role. Nor has Linden adopted the team system. However, when the plant reopened after its 1985–86 modernization, among its official goals was to improve communications between labor and management, and both parties embraced "jointness" as a principle of decision making. At the same time, "employee involvement groups" (EIGs) were established. Production workers were welcomed back to the plant after the changeover with a jointly (union-management) developed two-week (eighty-hour) training program, in the course of which they were promised that the "new Linden" would be totally different from the plant they had known before. In particular, workers were led to expect an improved relationship with management, and a larger role in decision making and problem solving on the shop floor.[35]

Most workers were extremely enthusiastic about these ideas—at least initially. The problem was that after the eight-hour training program was over, when everyone was back at work, the daily reality of plant life failed to live up to the promises about the "new Linden." "It's sort of like going to college," one worker commented about the training program. "You learn one thing, and then you go into the real world. . . ." Another agreed:

> It sounded good at the time, but it turned out to be a big joke. Management's attitude is still the same. It hasn't changed at all. Foremen who treated you like a fellow human being are still the same—no problems with them. The ones who were arrogant bastards are still the same, with the exception of a few who are a little bit scared, a little bit afraid that it might go to the top man, and, you know, make some trouble. Everyone has pretty much the same attitude.

Indeed, the biggest problem was at the level of first-line supervision. While upper management may have been convinced that workers should have more input into decision making, middle and lower management (who also went through a training program) did not always share this view. Indeed, after the training raised workers' expectations, foremen in the plant, faced with the usual pressures to get production out, seemed to quickly fall back into their old habits. The much-touted "new Linden" thus turned out to be all too familiar. As the workers pointed out:

> You still have the management that has the mentality of the top-down, like they're right, they don't listen to the exchange from the workers, like the old school. So that's why when you ask about the "new Linden," people say it's a farce, because you still . . . do not feel mutual respect, you feel the big thing is to get the jobs out. This is a manufacturing plant; they do have to produce. But you can't just tell this worker, you know, take me upstairs [where the training classes were held], give me this big hype, and then bring me downstairs and then have the same kind of attitude.

> With management, they don't have the security that we have. Because if a foreman doesn't do his job, he can be replaced tomorrow, and he's got nobody to back him up. So everybody's a little afraid of their jobs. So if you have a problem, you complain to your foreman, he tries to take care of it without bringing it to his general foreman; or the general foreman, he don't want to bring it to his superintendent, because neither of them can control it. So they all try to keep it down, low level, and under the rug, and "Don't bother me about it—just fix it and led it slide." And that is not the teachings that we went through in that eighty-hour [training] course!

Many Linden workers expressed similar cynicism about the EIGs. "A lot of people feel very little comes out of the meetings. It's just to pacify you so you don't write up grievances," one paint department worker said, articulating a widespread sentiment. "It's a half-hour's pay for sitting there and eating your lunch," he added.

Research on other U.S. auto assembly plants suggests that Linden, where the rhetoric of participation was introduced without much substantive change in the quality of the labor-management relationship, is a more representative case than NUMMI, where participation (whatever its limits) is by all accounts more genuine. Reports from Big Three plants around the nation suggest that typical complaints concern not the *concept* of participation—which workers generally endorse—but management's failure to live up to its own stated principles. Gerald Horton, a worker at GM's Wentzville, Missouri, plant "thinks the team concept is a good idea if only management would abide by it." Similarly, Dan Maurin of GM's Shreveport, Louisiana, plant observes, "it makes people resentful when they preach participative management and then come in and say, 'this is how we do it.'"[36] Betty Foote, who works at a Ford truck plant outside Detroit, expressed the sentiments of many auto workers about Employee Involvement (EI): "The supposed concern for workers' happiness now with the EI program is a real joke. It looks good on paper, but it is not effective. . . . Relations between workers and management haven't changed."[37]

At NUMMI, workers view participation far more positively. Critics of the team concept suggest that this is because workers there experienced a "significant emotional event" and suffered economically after GM closed the plant, so that when they were recalled to NUMMI a few years later they gratefully accepted the new system without complaint. But, given the uncertainty of employment and the history of chronic layoffs throughout the auto industry, that this would sharply distinguish NUMMI's workers from those in other plants seems unlikely. Such an explanation for the positive reception of the team concept by NUMMI workers is also dubious in light of the fact that even the opposition caucus in the local union, which criticizes the local U.A.W. officials for being insufficiently militant in representing the rank and file, explicitly supports the team concept.[38]

Instead, the key difference between NUMMI and the Big Three assembly plants may be that workers have *more* job security at NUMMI, where the Japanese management has evidently succeeded in building a high-trust relationship with workers. When the plant reopened, NUMMI workers were guaranteed no layoffs unless management first took a pay cut; this promise and many others have (so far) been kept, despite slow sales. In contrast, the Big Three (and especially GM) routinely enrage workers by announcing layoffs and then announcing executive pay raises a few days later; while at the plant level, as we have seen, management frequently fails to live up to its rhetorical commitments to participation.[39] On the one hand, this explains why NUMMI workers are so much more enthusiastic about participation than their counterparts in other plants. On the other hand, where teamwork and other participatory schemes have been forced on workers through "whipsawing," the result has been a dismal failure on its own terms. Indeed, one study found a negative correlation between the existence of participation programs and productivity.[40]

Insofar as the U.A.W. has associated itself with such arrangements, it loses legitimacy with the rank and file when management's promises are not fulfilled. Successful participation systems, however, can help strengthen unionism. It is striking that at NUMMI, with its sterling productivity and quality record, high management credibility, and relatively strong job security provisions, the U.A.W. is stronger than in most Big Three plants. For that matter, the local union at NUMMI has more influence than do enterprise unions in Japanese auto plants, where teamwork systems are long-standing.[41] But here, as in so many other ways, NUMMI is the exceptional case. In most U.S. auto plants, the weakness of the U.A.W.—in the face of industry overcapacity and capital's enhanced ability to shift production around the globe—has combined with management's inability to transform its own ranks to undermine the promise of participation.

CONCLUSION

In recent literature, the introduction of new technologies and worker participation in industries like auto manufacturing are often cited as evidence of a radical break from the traditional Fordist logic of mass production.[42] Owing to changed economic conditions, the argument goes, Fordism is becoming less and less viable, so that advanced capitalist countries are now moving toward a more flexible "post-Fordist" production regime. In most such accounts, including the influential "flexible specialization" model of Michael Piore and Charles Sabel, this transformation is driven primarily by the growth of increasingly specialized markets and by the new information-based technologies. Theorists of post-Fordism generally agree with analysts like Zuboff and Hirschhorn that new technologies should lead to skill upgrading and thus reverse the logic of Taylorism. Thus Piore and Sabel write that the computer is "a machine that meets Marx's definition of an artisan's tool; it is an instrument that responds to and extends the productive capacities of the user," and that, together with changes in product markets, computer technology is contributing to "the resurgence of craft principles." Post-Fordist theorists also view QWL programs, the team concept, and other forms of worker participation as changes that will help to humanize and democratize the workplace. Thus Piore and Sabel urge organized labor to "shake its attachment to increasingly indefensible forms of shop floor control" so as not to impede progress toward flexible specialization, and they explicitly applaud the U.A.W. for its willingness to experiment with classification reductions and worker participation.[43]

Opposing this type of interpretation of recent events is another perspective, inspired by the labor process theory of Harry Braverman and associated with such writers as Harley Shaiken and David Noble.[44] While the post-Fordists emphasize the contrast between the historical logic of deskilling in mass production industries and contemporary developments, the labor process theorists instead stress the continuities. The key force shaping work experience in both the past and present, in this alternative view, is the systematic removal of skill from the labor process by Taylorist managers. While accepting the idea that new technologies can potentially increase skill levels, labor process theorists argue that this potential is often impossible to realize in the organizational context of the capitalist firm. In their view, management uses computerization in the same way that it used earlier forms of technology: to appropriate knowledge from workers and tighten control over labor—even when skill upgrading might be a more efficient strategy. As Shaiken puts it, "Unfortunately, the possibility exists for introducing authoritarian principles in flexible as well as more traditional mass-production technologies. Under these circumstances, the extraordinary economic potential of these systems is not realized."[45] Commentators in this tradition are also skeptical about worker participation schemes, which they view, not as authentic efforts to enhance the experience of work, but rather as new tools of managerial control. They are especially troubled by the fact that management-initiated participation schemes are often coupled with anti-unionism and concession bargaining.[46]

Although they have contributed many valuable insights into recent workplace changes, both these perspectives are one-sided. The post-Fordists fail to take seriously the firm-level organizational obstacles to the kind of macroeconomic transition they envision. They tend to romanticize the emergent new order, and especially its implications for workers, often ignoring the persistent determination of employers to maintain control over labor—as if this fundamental feature of capitalism were disappearing along with the Fordist system of mass production. At the other extreme, labor process theorists tend to reduce all the recent innovations in work organization to new forms of managerial manipulation, and to see capital's desire for control over labor as an insuperable obstacle to any meaningful improvements in the workplace.

Both schools of thought claim to reject technological determinism, but they consistently posit opposite outcomes of the introduction of new technology. The post-Fordists have devoted a great deal of energy to highlighting instances of skill upgrading associated with new technology.

When confronted with examples of deskilling, they retreat to the argument that the post-Fordist perspective is merely an account of emergent tendencies whose full realization is contingent and contested. For their part, labor process theorists also disclaim technological determinism, arguing that the abstract potential of new technology to increase skill levels cannot be realized within the concrete social structure of the capitalist firm. Numerous case studies (including several from the auto industry) have appeared supporting each side of the skill debate.[47] The contradictory evidence suggests that attempts to generalize about overall deskilling or upgrading trends are fruitless. As Kenneth Spenner has persuasively argued on the basis of an extensive literature review, the effects of new technology on skill "are *not* simple, *not* necessarily direct, *not* constant across settings and firms, and *cannot* be considered in isolation."[48] Rather, as the evidence from GM-Linden also indicates, skill effects are conditioned by a variety of social factors, among them organizational culture and managerial discretion—factors that both the post-Fordists and the labor process theorists ultimately ignore or trivialize.

Like the effect of new technology on skills, the impact of worker participation is impossible to analyze in general terms. Here again, much depends on the organizational context in which participation is introduced, and especially on the relationship between labor and management. The specific characteristics of a firm's management and the relative strength and influence of unions (where they exist) can be crucial determinants of the outcome of workplace reform efforts. Yet neither labor process theory nor post-Fordism takes adequate account of these factors. This is not especially surprising for labor process theory, since as critics of Braverman have frequently complained, he neglected workers' resistance entirely. But the result is that commentators in this tradition tend to view all changes in labor relations as management schemes to enhance its control over the work force, and they can barely even contemplate the possibility that worker participation programs or other innovations could benefit workers in any way. The post-Fordist school, in sharp contrast, tends to romanticize the recent experiments in labor-management cooperation, despite the fact that, in the United States at least, most of them have been forced on unions decimated by increased capital mobility and economic globalization.

Although it is impossible to generalize from any one case, the automobile industry is an especially important test of these competing theoretical perspectives on workplace change if only because it figures so prominently in both of them. Indeed, the very concept of Fordism derives from the history of this industry. Yet organizational inertia seems more compelling an explanation for the recent history of automobile manufacturing than either theory. In recent years, automotive management's reluctance or inability to abandon its longstanding system of work organization or its tradition of authoritarianism vis-à-vis labor has meant that both technological change and experimentation with participation have produced only a superficial transformation in the workplace. Both were introduced in response to a crisis of international competition, and in both cases management undertook the changes with a limited understanding of their potential impact. Consequently, they have neither resolved the continuing problem of foreign competition, nor have they produced the kinds of benefits for workers—skill upgrading and increased job satisfaction—that the optimistic projections of post-Fordist theorists promised. Yet the existence of more positive examples, such as the NUMMI plant, suggests that the alternative view of the labor process theorists, which constructs capitalist control imperatives as inherently incompatible with the possibility of changes that can offer real benefits to workers, is also problematic.

If management's ineptitude and bureaucratic inertia is the main reason for the limited impact of new technology and the new industrial relations in the U.S. auto industry, the weakness of the U.A.W. has also played a role. Following the habits it developed over the decades following World War II, the U.A.W. continued to cede to management all decisions about technology and its applications. It has yet to demand that jobs be redesigned in tandem with new technology so as to maximize the benefits to its members. The union has been more engaged in the issue of worker participation, but because in most cases QWL and teams were introduced in the context of massive job losses and industry overcapacity, the terms of labor-management "cooperation" were largely dictated by management. The U.A.W. necessarily shares the domestic industry's concern about restoring international competitiveness, but rather than serve as a basis for genuine cooperation, this has all too often become a whip for management to use in extracting concessions on wages and work rules, sending the union into a spiral of declining power and legitimacy and severely weakening the plant seniority system that had been its historical hallmark. In exchange, the U.A.W. has sought enhanced job security provisions, but it has won only modest improvements in this area, while plant closings and job losses continue. Contrary to the popular belief that union strength is an obstacle to restoring American industry to an internationally competitive position, the weakness of unionism in this period of potentially momentous changes in the workplace may be the real problem, along with the organizational ineptitude of management. The sad truth is that both labor and management in this critical industry are ill-prepared to face the future.

EIGHT

The Blue-Collar Working Class
Continuity and Change

David Halle and Frank Romo

The blue-collar working class in America (and elsewhere) has always evoked extreme pronouncements about its political and social attitudes. Observers have long been drawn to one of two polar positions: either the working class is a conservative force that is integrated into the class structure or the working class is a radical force at odds with the middle class and with capitalists.[1]

In the depression years of the 1930s and in the context of the burgeoning of radical new labor unions affiliated with the CIO, many observers saw a radical and even revolutionary American working class. After World War II, by contrast, in the context of a sustained period of economic growth in the West, the model of a working class integrated into the mainstream of society (and often dubbed "affluent"), gained ground. The American working class was, at that time, usually seen as the extreme case among the Western working classes (just as America was the economically and politically dominant capitalist society), and the phrase "the American worker" became, for some, a shorthand term for a working class that was politically quiescent and socially integrated.[2] In the 1960s and 1970s, a model of the radical working class regained popularity, as a series of studies disputed the idea that the working class was integrated into society or especially content with its position.[3] Now the pendulum has swung again, and the model of the quiescent (if not content) American working class has returned to dominance.[4]

The reason for the oscillation between these extreme models in part has to do with actual changes in the position and attitudes of the working class itself. Blue-collar Americans were, for example, surely more dis-

The names of the coauthors of this chapter appear in alphabetical order. The authors wish to thank James Bardwell for his help with computer programming.

content and more inclined to political radicalism in the 1930s than in the 1950s. But in part the pendulum swings between the two models because neither is fully adequate to capture the situation of blue-collar workers in advanced capitalism in the United States (and elsewhere). A convincing model has to take account of three separate, though related, spheres that influence blue-collar lives and beliefs. There is, first of all, life at the workplace—in the mode of production. It is on this crucial sphere that many classic studies of blue-collar workers have concentrated. Second, there is life outside the workplace—the neighborhood of residence, family, and leisure life. With suburbanization and the widespread possession of automobiles, life outside the workplace is often located at a considerable geographic distance from the plant or other work site. Finally, there is life vis-à-vis the government, especially the federal government. This involves the critical act of voting—above all in presidential elections—as well as basic attitudes toward the federal government and the political system, and attitudes toward a whole range of national policy issues. These three areas are somewhat distinct. What is often done, though it should not be, is to focus on just one aspect of workers' lives and from it infer the character of behavior and attitudes in either of the other two spheres.

Here we will use a combination of case studies and national survey data to demonstrate the inadequacies of extreme models of the blue-collar working class that do not take account of each sphere of blue-collar life or of changes that have taken place in those spheres over time. Most of the survey data have been drawn from the National Election Study (NES) carried out by the Survey Research Center of the University of Michigan, which represent the best continuous data series on political attitudes in America. This multidimensional account of working-class attitudes also sheds light on some of the main transformations in American life that have occurred over the past twenty-five or thirty years.

The first question to be addressed is the actual size of the blue-collar working class today, and its relative size compared with the other main occupational groups. In view of prevailing notions of the demise of blue-collar labor in America, it is important to note that the *number* of blue-collar workers reached its highest level ever in 1989—31.8 million (see figure 8.1).[5] (The blue-collar working class is here defined as consisting of skilled workers, such as electricians and plumbers; factory workers; transportation workers, such as truck and bus drivers; and nonfarm laborers. Men constitute about three-quarters of all blue-collar workers and over 90 percent of skilled blue-collar workers.[6])

Moreover, blue-collar workers were still a larger proportion of the labor force than either of the two main white-collar groups (see figure 8.2). Thus in 1989 blue-collar workers constituted 27.1 percent of the labor

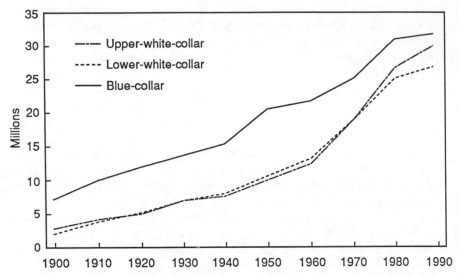

8.1 Composition of the Civilian Labor Force, Major Occupational Groups,
1900–1989: Number of Workers by Year.

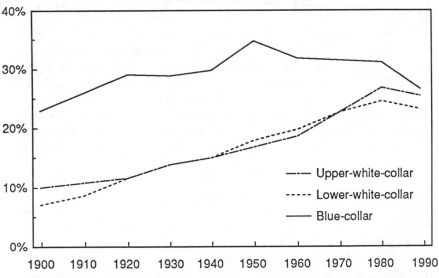

8.2 Composition of the Civilian Labor Force, Major Occupational Groups,
1900–1989: Percent Composition by Year.

force. Compare this with the upper-white-collar sector, defined as managers and professionals, who composed 25.9 percent of the labor force; and compare this with the lower-white-collar sector—defined as clerical, secretarial, and sales workers—who composed 24.2 percent of the labor force.

What is true is that the proportion of blue-collar workers in the labor force has declined, from a peak of 34.5 percent in 1950, and is now declining faster than before. Still, it should be noted, especially given the talk about "postindustrial" or "deindustrial" society, that the proportion of blue-collar workers in the labor force is now either higher than or about the same as it was in the period 1900–1940, when America was unarguably an "industrial society."[7]

BLUE-COLLAR WORKERS AND THE FEDERAL GOVERNMENT

Presidential Elections and Political Party Identification

Blue-collar workers were a crucial part of the electoral coalition that Franklin Delano Roosevelt put together for the Democratic party. The current disaffection of blue-collar workers, especially of the skilled and better-paid blue-collar workers, from the Democratic party represents one of the major changes in American politics.

Skilled blue-collar workers voted, by a clear majority, for the Democratic candidate in five of the seven presidential elections that took place between 1952 and 1976 (1952, 1960, 1964, 1968, and 1976); they voted by a clear majority for the Republican candidate only once, in 1972 (see figure 8.3). Less-skilled blue-collar workers (defined here as all blue-collar workers except the skilled ones) also voted, by a clear majority, for the Democratic candidate in five of these seven elections, as shown in figure 8.4.[8] They too voted, by a clear majority, for the Republican candidate only once, in 1960. However in the three presidential elections since 1976, the picture is far less clear-cut. Skilled blue-collar workers voted Republican more heavily than Democrat in 1988, while splitting their vote about evenly between Democrats and Republicans in 1980 and 1984. Less-skilled blue-collar workers split their vote about evenly between Republicans and Democrats in 1988, voted more heavily Democrat in 1984, and more heavily Republican in 1980. By contrast, upper-white-collar workers have voted, by large majorities, for the Republican candidate in every election from 1952 to 1988, except for 1964, when they were clearly presented with an intolerable candidate in Barry Goldwater (see figure 8.5).

Figures 8.6 through 8.14 give a detailed analysis of the determinants of the blue-collar vote in the 1988 presidential election, showing that

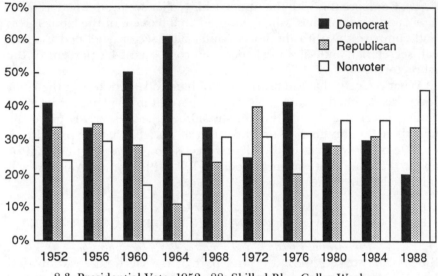

8.3 Presidential Vote, 1952–88: Skilled Blue-Collar Workers.

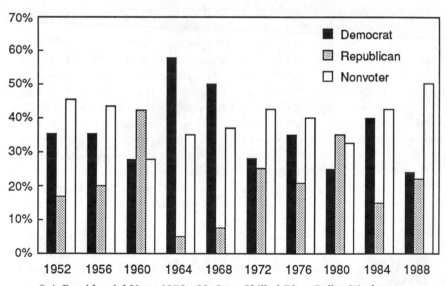

8.4 Presidential Vote, 1952–88: Less-Skilled Blue-Collar Workers.

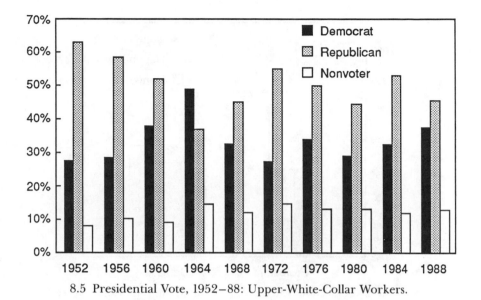

8.5 Presidential Vote, 1952–88: Upper-White-Collar Workers.

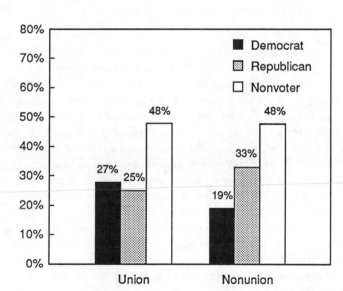

8.6 The 1988 Election: Effects of Union Membership on the Blue-Collar Vote.

SOURCE: Based on figures from the logistic regression model presented in the appendix to this chapter.

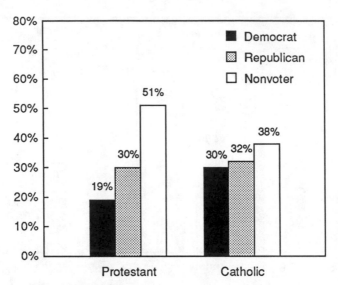

8.7 The 1988 Election: Effects of Religion on the Blue-Collar Vote.

SOURCE: Based on figures from the logistic regression model presented in the appendix to this chapter.

several of the traditional factors associated with voting Democratic still hold for blue-collar Americans. (These figures and figure 8.15 are based on a multivariate logistic analysis of the vote; see the appendix to this chapter for details.) Union members were more likely than non-union members to vote Democrat (figure 8.6). Blue-collar Catholics were more likely to vote Democratic than were blue-collar Protestants (figure 8.7).[9] Blue-collar blacks were more likely to vote Democrat than whites (figure 8.8). And as their income rises, the proportion of blue-collar workers voting Republican increases (figure 8.13). Notice, however, that the effect of region is now complex. Ironically, the voting profile of blue-collar workers in the East (controlling for such factors as religious differences) is now rather similar to that of blue-collar workers in the South (figure 8.10). Notice also that gender—not one of the factors traditionally associated with voting Democratic or Republican—still makes no difference. Male and female blue-collar workers are alike in their voting preferences (figure 8.9).

The movement of blue-collar workers away from Democratic presidential candidates in recent elections is paralleled by, and partly the result of, a tendency that is at least as striking—that of blue-collar workers not to vote at all in presidential elections.[10] Thus in 1980, 1984, and 1988, a larger percentage of skilled blue-collar workers did not vote than voted for either the Republican or Democratic candidate; and among

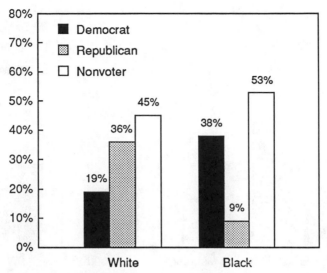

8.8 The 1988 Election: Effects of Race on the Blue-Collar Vote.

SOURCE: Based on figures from the logistic regression model presented in the appendix to this chapter.

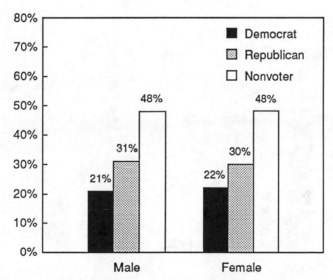

8.9 The 1988 Election: Effects of Gender on the Blue-Collar Vote.

SOURCE: Based on figures from the logistic regression model presented in the appendix to this chapter.

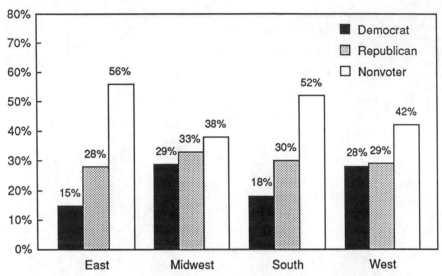

8.10 The 1988 Election: Effects of Region on the Blue-Collar Vote.

SOURCE: Based on figures from the logistic regression model presented in the appendix to this chapter.

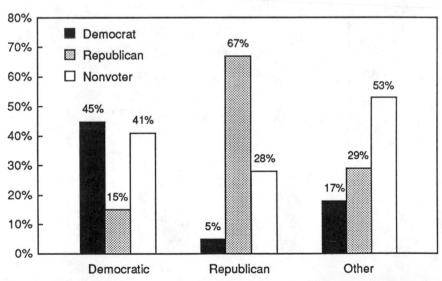

8.11 The 1988 Election: Effects of Party Identification on the Blue-Collar Vote.

SOURCE: Based on figures from the logistic regression model presented in the appendix to this chapter.

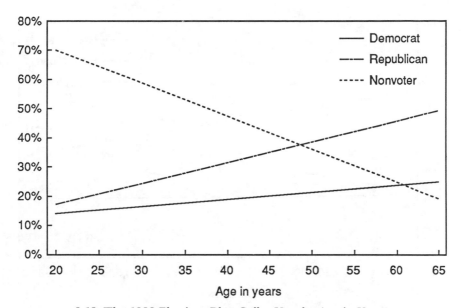

8.12 The 1988 Election: Blue-Collar Vote by Age in Years.

SOURCE: Based on figures from the logistic regression model presented in the appendix to this chapter.

less-skilled blue-collar workers in four of the five elections from 1972 to 1988, a larger number did not vote than voted for either the Republican or Democratic candidate (see figures 8.3 and 8.4). Further, the proportion of blue-collar workers not voting in the 1988 presidential election was especially high (51 percent of less-skilled and 45 percent of skilled workers). More detailed analysis shows that age, income, and education are the most important determinants of whether blue-collar workers vote (see figures 8.12, 8.13, and 8.14). The younger they are, and the lower their income and level of education, the less likely they are to vote.

Figure 8.15 sums up this tendency of blue-collar workers not to vote. It shows the affect of occupation on the 1988 vote, controlling for race, union membership, religion, age, family income, region and gender. Blue-collar workers were about as likely as either of the white-collar groups to vote Republican, but much less likely than the upper-white-collar sector to vote Democratic, mostly because they were less likely than the upper-white-collar sector to vote at all.

The upper-white-collar sector is in sharp contrast to the blue-collar sector in the matter of voting. The percentage of upper-white-collar workers who did not vote was low in 1988 (only 14.1 percent)[11] and at no time in the period 1952–1988 was it higher than 15.3 percent (see figure 8.18).[12]

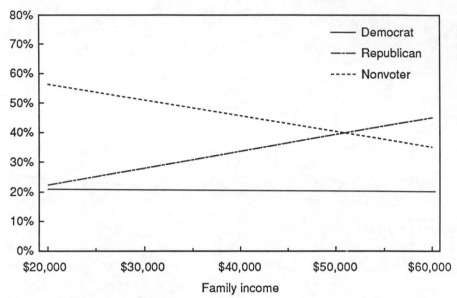

8.13 The 1988 Election: Blue-Collar Vote by Family Income.

SOURCE: Based on figures from the logistic regression model presented in the appendix to this chapter.

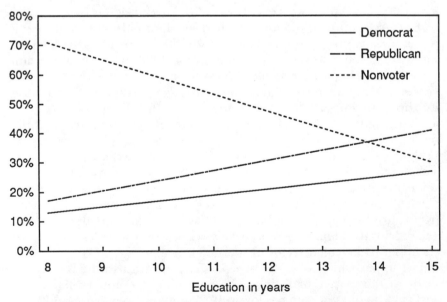

8.14 The 1988 Election: Effects of Education on the Blue-Collar Vote.

SOURCE: Based on figures from the logistic regression model presented in the appendix to this chapter.

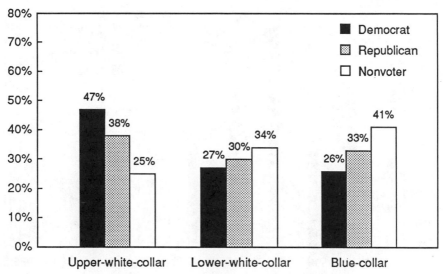

8.15 The 1988 Election: Effects of Occupational Status on the
Presidential Vote.

SOURCE: Based on figures from the logistic regression model presented in the appendix to
this chapter.

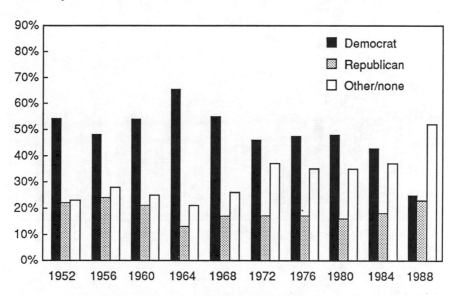

8.16 Party Identification, 1952–88: Skilled Blue-Collar Workers.

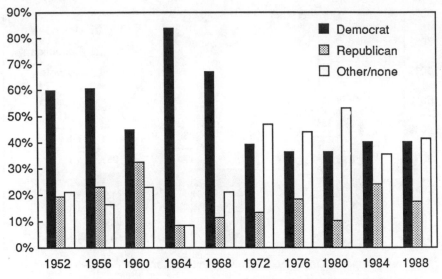

8.17 Party Identification, 1952–88: Less-Skilled Blue-Collar Workers.

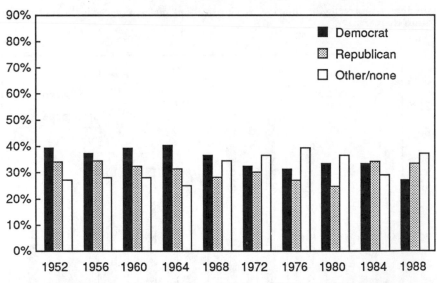

8.18 Party Identification, 1952–88: Upper-White-Collar Workers.

Changes in the political party identification of blue-collar workers
since 1952 are also central. Blue-collar workers once identified in large
numbers with the Democratic Party. For most of the time from 1952 to
1968, 60 percent or more of less-skilled blue-collar workers saw themselves as Democrats (the exception is 1960 for less-skilled blue-collar

workers), while only 20 percent or less saw themselves as Republicans (see figure 8.17). During most of the same period, 50 percent or more of skilled blue-collar workers saw themselves as Democrats, while only 25 percent or less saw themselves as Republicans (see figure 8.16). There have been two clear changes since 1972. First, a decline in the proportion of blue-collar workers identifying as Democrats (among the less-skilled, the proportion has hovered around 35 percent since 1972; among the skilled, it stabilized in the mid-forties until 1988, when it dropped sharply to 23 percent). The second change is a large increase in the proportion of blue-collar workers reporting no party identification (among less-skilled workers it is now about 40 percent; among skilled workers, it rose to about 38 percent in the period 1972 to 1984, and then climbed sharply in 1988). Interestingly, there has been no major shift of party identification toward the Republicans.

Attitude toward the Political System and Power Structure

The belief that government, including the federal government, is in the hands of a small number of organized groups who have unofficially usurped power is widespread and striking. This belief is common among blue-collar workers, though also among other occupational groups. When asked whether they thought the government was run for the benefit of everybody or for the benefit of a few big interests, 59 percent of blue-collar workers in 1984 answered that the government was run for the benefit of a few big interests. About the same percentage of Americans in upper-white-collar, lower-white-collar, and service-sector occupations agreed, as did 51 percent of housewives.[13]

Survey data going back to 1964 (when the question was first asked) suggest that this belief has been a fairly stable part of the political outlook of most Americans, including blue-collar workers. Thus in every election year except 1964, at least 40 percent of the entire population has believed that the government is run for a few big interests, and in five of the seven election years in this period more than 50 percent of the population has believed this. As in 1988, variation by occupation is not especially pronounced; blue-collar and upper-white-collar Americans both followed this trend from 1964 onward (see figures 8.19 and 8.20). The survey studies do not explore these beliefs further. For example, they do not ask the obvious follow-up question, namely, which are the "few big interests" for whose benefit so many blue-collar workers (and other Americans) believe the government is run. However, data from detailed case studies give an indication of an answer. A study of employees (almost all truck drivers) of a California company that delivers packages, a study of blue-collar and lower-white-collar Italians in Brooklyn, and a study of blue-collar chemical workers in New Jersey, all came to similar conclusions.[14] The vast majority of blue-collar workers believe that Big

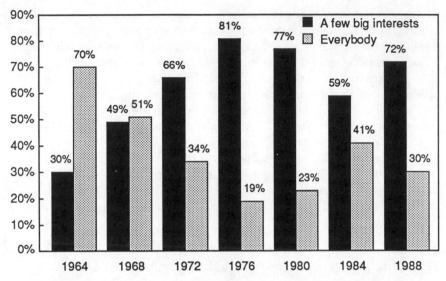

8.19 Who Benefits from Government, 1964–88: Blue-Collar Workers.

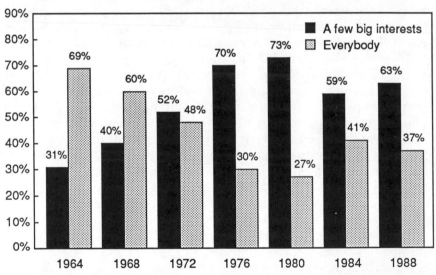

8.20 Who Benefits from Government, 1964–88: Upper-White-Collar Workers.

Business really runs America. The dominant view is that corrupt politicians are a venal facade behind which major corporations, "Big Business," prevails, in politics and economics. Remarks like "it's business that runs the country," "big corporations are behind everything," "the [political] power is in the hands of the people with money," and "oil, steel.

insurance, and the banks run this country" are commonplace. These were typical comments: "Politics? It's all money! Big Business pays out money to get what it wants." "Who runs the country? Well, I suppose the president does. He makes the decisions. Of course, business is behind him. They make the real decisions. Politicians are all on the take."

That this attitude toward Big Business is widespread is also suggested by Erik Olin Wright's survey data, which found that over 74 percent of blue-collar workers believe that "big corporations have too much power" in America. It is noteworthy that, in terms of their beliefs about the power of corporations in society, American blue-collar workers are just as class conscious as workers in Sweden (presented in Wright's analysis as far more class conscious than American workers). For in both societies, between 75 percent and 82 percent of blue-collar workers believe that "big corporations have too much power" in their respective countries.[15] This underlines the importance of considering separately the three spheres: attitude toward the political regime, attitude toward the work setting, and attitude toward life outside the workplace.

Despite these critical and sceptical beliefs that American blue-collar workers have about who runs the country, the lack of approval for alternatives to the current political system is notable. The general acceptance of the American Constitution ranges from enthusiasm ("it's the best in the world") to lukewarm ("I complain a lot, but it isn't any better anywhere else"). This phenomenon needs explaining. In part it is based on a distinction between the system and those who operate it, between politicians and the Constitution: the political system is sound, but it is in the hands of scoundrels. In part, lack of support for alternative political systems results from a perception that radical change in the United States is impractical: the country is too large, and potential leaders are too prone to sell out. But in part the widespread acceptance of the Constitution and the political system is based on a key distinction most workers make, either explicitly or implicitly, between freedom and democracy. The United States does offer freedom and liberties, which are very valuable. Consider these typical comments, all made by workers who believe venal politicians subvert the electoral process: "In America you have freedom. That's important. I can say Reagan is a jerk and no one is going to put me in jail." Another worker: "You know what I like about America? You're free. No one bothers you. If I want to take a piss over there [points to a corner of the tavern], I can." Socialism and communism are ruled out in almost everyone's eyes, for they are seen as synonymous with dictatorship. They are political systems that permit neither popular control of government (democracy) nor individual freedom and liberties.[16] Survey data suggest that, like mistrust of government, this attitude toward freedom is widespread among blue- and white-collar Americans.

The vast majority both value freedom and consider it an important feature of contemporary America.[17]

LIFE OUTSIDE THE WORKPLACE

Home Ownership and Suburbia

The combination of home ownership and suburbia is of considerable importance for understanding the American working class. Together they provide the material context for American blue-collar workers to live, or to hope to live, a residential, leisure, and social life in which the barrier between blue- and upper-white-collar is considerably muted (at least, as compared with the typical workplace situation of blue-collar workers).

The high rate of home ownership among Americans, including blue-collar Americans, has for a long time been striking. Back in 1906, Werner Sombart contrasted the United States with his native Germany: "A well-known fact . . . is the way in which the American worker in large cities and industrial areas meets his housing requirements: this has essential differences from that found among continental-European workers, particularly German ones. The German worker in such places usually lives in rented tenements, while his American peer lives correspondingly frequently in single-family or two-family dwellings."[18] By 1975, three-quarters of all AFL-CIO members owned houses.[19] Home ownership not only offers blue-collar workers the possibility of economic gain but also provides a site where they can control their physical and social surroundings—not, of course, completely, but far more than in the work setting where they are typically subordinate to the authority of a direct supervisor, as well as of management and the owners.[20]

Suburbanization, in combination with home ownership, has played a crucial role in undermining working class residential communities, especially after World War II. Suburbanization can be defined as a process involving two crucial factors. First, there is the systematic growth of fringe areas at a pace more rapid than that of the core cities; second, there is a life-style involving a daily commute to jobs in the urban center.[21] The regular commute to a workplace a considerable distance from the work site is an important factor in the fading of working-class residential communities. Many classic labor movements established their strongholds in the nineteenth century in towns and urban areas that were not especially large (by later standards), or especially spread out. Paterson, New Jersey, for example, had only 33,000 inhabitants in 1870. These places were typically urban villages, where, as Eric Hobsbawm put it, "people could walk to and fro from work, and sometimes go home in the dinner-hour . . . places where work, home, leisure, industrial relations, local government and home-town consciousness were inextricably mixed together."[22]

In fact, suburbanization involving the commute to work by public transport started before many of these working-class communities were formed. It began in 1814, with the first steam ferry, and continued with newer modes of public transport (the omnibus in 1829, the steam railroad in the 1830s and 1840s, the electric streetcar in the late 1880s).[23] Each of these developments doubtless somewhat undermined working-class occupational communities. But so long as workers were dependent on public transport to get to the workplace, there were limits to where they could live (nowhere too far from public transport).[24] After World War II, as automobiles became widely owned by blue-collar workers, a qualitative change occurred. Workers could live anywhere they could afford that was within commuting range. And since the incomes of better-paid blue-collar workers often approached, equalled, or exceeded those of several upper-white-collar groups (such as teachers and social workers), there developed many occupationally mixed suburbs, where the proportion of blue-collar workers ranged from about 20 percent to about 45 percent, as did the proportion of upper-white-collar workers.[25] For example, when the vast new suburb Levittown, New Jersey, opened in 1958, these two groups bought houses there in roughly equal proportions. By 1960, 26 percent of the employed males there were in blue-collar occupations, while 31 percent were in upper-white-collar occupations.[26]

This residential context provides the framework for the marital and leisure lives of many blue-collar Americans. Several other factors that are also important influences on the leisure lives of blue-collar workers cut across occupational or educational lines. These include gender, age, position in the marital cycle, and income level. For example, many blue-collar workers are enormously interested in sports, as participants and spectators. Among the sports in which they participate are hunting, fishing, and softball; golf, traditionally an upper-white-collar activity, has grown in popularity among blue-collar workers. And, like other American males, many blue-collar workers spend considerable time watching sports on television. Clearly, this interest in sports, shared in many ways by upper-white-collar males and other Americans, has as much to do with gender as with class.

It is true that certain factors add a flavor to the lives of blue-collar workers. In particular, they typically have modest levels of education (an average of twelve years) as compared with upper-white-collar workers (an average of fifteen years of education).[27] Partly as a result, blue-collar workers are less likely than upper-white-collar workers to be interested in high culture (opera, ballet, classical music, serious theater). However, these differences should not be exaggerated, for the level of interest in high culture among upper-white-collar workers is not great. For example, a survey conducted in the early 1970s on exposure to the arts in twelve major American cities showed that no more than 18 percent of managers and professionals had been to a symphony concert in the past year, no more than 9 percent had been to the ballet, and no more than 6 percent had attended the opera.[28]

Finally, there is the issue of marital life. There are certain features of working-class life that may add a distinct flavor to the marriages of blue-collar workers. For example, blue-collar jobs can carry somewhat low status as compared with upper-white-collar jobs and even as compared with some lower-white-collar jobs. Some couples' comments suggest that wives of blue-collar men sometimes resent their husbands' low status occupations. And the modest level of education that blue-collar workers typically possess may affect the character of their marriages; for example, some studies suggest that the level and quality of "communication" between spouses increase with their amount of education.

Still, as with leisure life, there are a variety of forces that affect the marital lives of blue-collar workers but that are by no means confined to them. These include the conflicting demands of home life and work life, the difficulties (and benefits) that arise when both spouses work, and the host of questions associated with raising children (all of which are discussed in other chapters of this book).[29] The best studies of the marital lives of blue-collar Americans suggest that there are as many similarities as differences between their marital lives and those of upper-white-collar people.[30] One explanation is that, as with leisure lives, gender differences are at least as important as class differences. For example, whatever their class, many American wives face the likelihood of being able to find jobs only in poorly paid, lower-white-collar occupations and, at home, of having the major responsibility for child care and housework.[31]

LIFE AT THE WORKPLACE

It is in the workplace that differences between blue-collar and white, especially upper-white-collar, are most pronounced. Blue-collar jobs are often dirty and sometimes dangerous, and usually require some degree of physical labor (hence the need to wear special protective clothes—the "blue collar").[32] In addition, such jobs usually involve the following features: (1) work that is repetitive and therefore dull; (2) work that is clearly connected to the creation of a tangible product; (3) work that offers little chance of upward mobility (workers may rise to first-line supervision, but above that level, lack of educational qualifications poses a serious barrier); and (4) work that is supervised, in an obtrusive or unobtrusive manner (there is human supervision, and there is the mechanical supervision of a time clock). These features provide enough real basis for distinguishing blue-collar from upper-white-collar jobs and, to a lesser extent, from lower-white-collar jobs.[33] In occupational settings with a variety of work levels, management usually has little difficulty deciding which workers should be classified as blue-collar and therefore be assigned to distinct work areas and required to wear special work clothes, though some groups on the margin may be hard to classify.

CLASS CONSCIOUSNESS

Last, but definitely not least, there is the question of class consciousness. How do blue-collar workers see their position in the class structure, with whom do they identify, and whom do they oppose? These questions have always been, and remain, central in the debates over the blue-collar working class. In a recent article dramatically titled "Farewell to the Labor Movement?" Eric Hobsbawm, one of the foremost socialist historians, stressed the question of class consciousness:

> It is class consciousness, the condition on which our parties [mass socialist or workers parties] were originally built, that is facing the most serious crisis. The problem is not so much objective de-proletarianization, but is rather the subjective decline of class solidarity. . . . What we find today is not that there is no longer any working class consciousness, but that class consciousness no longer has the power to unite.[34]

Hobsbawm cites the fact that in 1987 almost 60 percent of British trade union members voted for parties other than the Labor party. Clearly this is comparable to the tendency for blue-collar Americans nowadays to be at least as likely to vote Republican as Democratic in presidential elections.

Much of the debate over class consciousness has revolved around, or at least begun with, the issue of whether blue-collar workers tend to see themselves as "working class" (and therefore more class conscious) or "middle class" (and therefore less class conscious). It is, then, surprising to discover that in 1988, asked if they saw themselves as "working class" or "middle class," 75 percent of American blue-collar workers said working class. Further, this is only a little less than in 1952, when 80 percent of blue-collar workers categorized themselves as working class in response to the same question (see figure 8.21). Indeed, the proportion of blue-collar workers categorizing themselves as working class has never fallen below 64 percent in the period between 1952 and 1988. Clearly a certain kind of working-class identity can coexist with a declining tendency for blue-collar workers to vote for Democratic presidential candidates and to identify with the Democratic party. This suggests a problem with the debate over class consciousness, which, as we have pointed out, has long pervaded the general debate over the blue-collar working class, namely, the tendency to infer from one area of blue-collar life the nature of behaviors and beliefs that prevail in other areas of those lives. In the

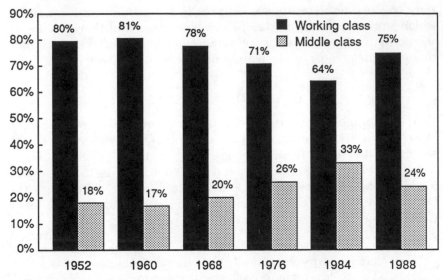

8.21 Social Class Identification by Major Occupational Group, 1952–88:
Blue-Collar Workers.

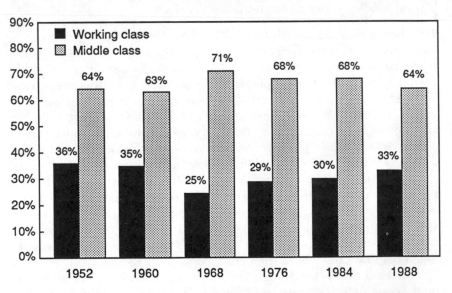

8.22 Social Class Identification by Major Occupational Group, 1952–88:
Upper-White-Collar Workers.

case of class consciousness and class identity, this amounts to assuming that blue-collar workers have a single image of their position in the class structure.

A central theme of this chapter has been that the lives of blue-collar workers revolve around three separate, though related, spheres—life at the workplace (in the mode of production), life outside the workplace (residential, marital, and leisure), and life vis-à-vis the federal government. Indeed, there is reason to think that many American blue-collar workers have three social identities, each relating to one of these spheres. These identities are that of the "working man," (or "working woman" for female blue-collar workers); that of being "middle class" or "lower middle class" or "poor," with reference to life outside the workplace; and that of being part of "the people" or "the American people," with reference to the notion of the individual citizen vis-à-vis the federal government and the related power structure. If these spheres have not emerged clearly in much previous research, it is because the main methods used to study class consciousness have tended to encourage, explicitly or implicitly, only one of these identities.

The analysis that follows is based on David Halle's study of class identity among blue-collar chemical workers in New Jersey. These workers were, in several ways, among the better-off blue collar workers. They were comparatively well paid and unionized; about one-quarter of them were skilled; 69 percent were homeowners. They were all men, reflecting the dominance of men in more desirable blue-collar jobs.

Consider, first, the concept of "the working man." A close reading of formal and informal interviews reported by a variety of researchers suggests that male blue-collar workers in America commonly refer to themselves as "working men," but rarely as "working class." This can be seen in interviews with voters during the 1968 and 1972 presidential election campaigns; in the views working-class residents of a new suburban township expressed about their preferred political candidate; from the comments of a group of skilled workers in Providence, Rhode Island; from comments of a group of white working-class males in an East Coast city; from comments of workers in Milwaukee, Chicago, and Pennsylvania; from comments of auto workers in Detroit; and from comments of Italian construction workers in Brooklyn.[35] The concept of the "working man" has also been central in the history of the American labor movement. For example, when trade and craft workers before the Civil War founded political parties, they called them "Workingmen's Political Parties," and the *Workingman's Advocate* was the name of one of the most important newspapers of the nineteenth century.

The concept of the working man, among the chemical workers studied by Halle, has as its central idea the notion that blue-collar work takes a distinctive form and is productive in a way that the work of other classes is not. This notion has two central components. One involves the features of the job. Being a working man involves one or more of the following clusters of related ideas: (a) physical work ("It's hard physical work," "It's working with your hands"); (b) dangerous or dirty work ("We get our hands dirty"); (c) boring and routine work ("We do the same thing over and again"); (d) factory work (as opposed to office work); (e) closely supervised work ("We have to punch in and out," "We're told what to do").

The other central component of the concept of the "working" man links it to a moral and empirical theory about who really works in America. It implies, in one or more of the following ways, that those who are not working men are not really productive, do not really work. Those who are not "working" (a) literally do not work ("Big business don't work, they just hire people who do," "People on welfare aren't working men, they don't want to work"); (b) perform no productive work ("Teachers aren't teaching the kids anything," White-collar office workers "just sit on their butts all day"); (c) are overpaid ("Doctors earn huge fees," "Lawyers charge whatever they want").

The combination of the "job features" and the "productive labor" aspects of the concept logically entails the idea that only those whose labor involves such job features are productive. As a result, blue-collar work is generally seen as productive. But those whose work lacks many or all such job features, definitely big business and the white-collar sectors in general, are not.

A central point about the concept of the working man is that the term expresses both class and gender consciousness. It expresses class consciousness in implying that blue-collar work is especially productive. But it also implies that blue-collar work is for men (working *man*) rather than women, which is a form of gender consciousness. This reflects the history of American labor. In the early stages of industrial growth, women (and children) were the first factory workers, for at that time such jobs were seen as less desirable than agricultural work. As the status and pay of factory and other blue-collar work rose, women were pushed out of almost all except the least desirable jobs. The blue-collar working class is now composed primarily of men, and this is especially true for the better paid and more highly skilled blue-collar jobs.

Among the chemical workers Halle interviewed, the idea that blue-collar work was for men was a form of sexism that most workers were prepared to explicitly support in discussing their *own* jobs. For example, they would maintain, sometimes in arguments with those of their wives who are feminists, that women cannot be chemical workers because they are too weak to move heavy chemical drums. But such sex stereotyping of occupations is under increasing attack in the United States. As a result, few workers were prepared to explicitly defend this sort of view for the entire spectrum of blue-collar jobs.

This discussion also raises the question of how female blue-collar workers see their position in the class structure at work. Naturally, they see themselves as working women rather than working men. How they use the concept of the "working woman," and how its meaning compares with the concept of the working man, is a question that scarcely has been investigated.[36]

The blue-collar workers that Halle interviewed also place themselves in the class structure, in part according to their life away from work rather than on the job. In this second image, they assume a class structure composed of a hierarchy of groups that are distinguished, above all, by income level but also by standard of living and residential situation. Income level, life-style, consumer goods, and neighborhood constitute the material framework of their lives outside work. (It is true that income originates from their employment, but its effect on their lives is outside, where almost all income is spent.) These criteria for determining position in the class structure increase the range of persons with whom workers consider they have common interests (as compared with the concept of the working man). Thus, though most see clear gaps between their situation and those of the upper and lower extremes (for instance, "the rich" and "the poor"), the categories in between are almost all ones to which they consider they do or could belong. As a result, according to this perspective, the class structure has a sizeable middle range that displays some fluidity, permits individual movement, and takes no account of a person's occupation. This reflects the actual ability of workers, in their life outside the factory, to enjoy a certain mobility through their choice of house, neighborhood, possessions, and life-style.

Income level is the most important of the factors underlying this second image of class. Almost everyone has at least a rough idea of the income distribution in America and his place within it. Workers read government statistics in newspapers and magazines on the average income of an American family, and they are aware of estimates of the income level needed to maintain a minimum, a comfortable, and an affluent standard of living. The federal and state income tax systems both entail a picture of the class structure based on income, and most workers follow with keen interest the relation between their weekly earnings and the taxes deducted from their paychecks. Income level is not the only criterion underlying class distinction based on the setting outside work. Life-style, material possessions, and the quality of residence and neighborhood are other criteria that people often use.

Most, but not all, workers place themselves in the middle of the hierarchy (below the "rich" and above the "poor"). But some identify with a category between the poor and the middle class. This view is most common among younger workers. They may have a mortgage, young children, and a spouse who stays at home to look after the children. But for these workers, being middle class implies being able to maintain that life-style without economic pressure. They deem their own situation below that of the middle class because they cannot live such a life-style without a strain—perhaps a serious strain—on their resources. Their income level, material possessions, and life-style make them better off than the poor, but not comfortable or free from major economic worries (as they believe the middle class to be).

The chemical workers studied by Halle were comparatively well paid for blue-collar workers, so it is likely that numerous less well paid blue-collar workers, in thinking of themselves outside the workplace, would classify themselves as below middle class.[37] The coexistence of these two identities—that of being a "working" man, with reference to life at work, and that of being middle class or less, with reference to life outside the workplace—would explain the large number of blue-collar workers who categorize themselves as "working class" rather than "middle class" in response to a survey question on that topic (see figure 8.21). Some workers categorize themselves as working class because they think of themselves as "working" men. Others place themselves in the working class because they are thinking of their position in the class structure outside work and believe their income level or life-style is not high enough to place them in the middle class. Either way, the forced choice of "working class" or "middle class" conceals the coexistence of two images of position in the class structure.

Almost all the blue-collar chemical workers have what amounts to a third image of their position in the class structure. They routinely use the concepts of "the American people" and "the people" in a populist sense. This concept involves the idea of a clear opposition between the power structure, especially big business and politicians, and the rest of the population. According to this view, "the American people" means all those excluded from the heights of political and economic power. Consider this worker, discussing corruption in politics: "Take Johnson for example. When he entered the White House he had $20,000 and then he bought all those estates with the American people's money."

This populist current is the third major aspect of the class consciousness of these workers. The concept of the working man refers to a position in the system of production. The concept of being middle class or lower middle class refers to a position outside work—to a life-style and standard of living. The concept of the people, or the American people, in the populist sense, refers to the division between all ordinary citizens and those with political and economic power.

CONCLUSION

The situation of blue-collar workers is complex and cannot be summed up by approaches that assume that the three main areas of blue-collar life are changing in concert. On the federal level, there is a movement away from voting for Democratic presidential candidates and away from voting at all, which is especially pronounced among younger workers. This has been accompanied by a diminished identification with the Democratic party (though identification with the Republican party has not taken its place). It is this fading of party loyalty and, perhaps, the declining tendency of blue-collar workers to vote at all, that is probably the most distinctive feature of the later decades of the twentieth century. If class solidarity for blue-collar Americans means voting for Democratic presidential candidates and identifying with the Democratic party, then class solidarity is definitely on the wane.

However, a majority of blue-collar workers (and other Americans) be-lieves that the country is "run by a few big interests," particularly by large corporations. And there is reason to think that many blue-collar work-ers, like many other Americans, will at times subscribe to a version of populism that contrasts "the people" (as those excluded from the heights of political and economic power) with the power structure (above all, big business and politicians). This entire perspective has probably long been a central component of the belief system of many ordinary Americans. (It was, for example, surely prominent during the "trust-busting" move-ment of the early 1900s.) It is likely to remain so as long as large corpora-tions (American or foreign) play a central role in American life.

Further, the vast majority of blue-collar Americans appear to see themselves, in the workplace, as "working men" (or "working women"), with an implicit solidarity at least with other blue-collar Americans (and probably, in varying degrees, with lower-white-collar Americans, too). This reflects a kind of class consciousness and identity that has long been important and is unlikely to fade, so long as the distinctions in the work-place between blue-collar workers on the one hand and white-collar workers (especially upper-white-collar workers) on the other hand, are pronounced. The current weakness of the union movement is significant in its own right, but may not diminish this class identity. Indeed, to the extent that blue- and lower-white-collar workers are less protected by unions than they once were, their feelings of vulnerability in the face of, and hostility toward, the corporations that employ them are as likely to increase as to wane.

Outside of the workplace, class identity is somewhat more fluid, re-flecting the greater degree of penetration and intermingling of blue- and white-collar people outside the workplace—in places of residence, in leisure, and in marital lives.

Some of these trends in the attitudes and behavior of blue-collar workers have been present for a long time. Others are more recent. Examining a number of arenas of working-class experience at once, and allowing each to express its own internal dynamics, shows the inadequacies of the two prevailing models of the working class—the radical working class and the integrated working class—each of which focuses on one or two areas of experience to the exclusion of the others. Social life is complex, and the fact that blue-collar workers have several bases for their attitudes and behavior reflects this complexity, which must be incorporated into any model of the American working class.

Appendix to Chapter Eight

Several data sets were used to construct the figures presented in this chapter. The source of the employment data in figures 8.1 and 8.2 is explained in note 5. Figures 8.3, 8.4, 8.16, 8.17, and 8.18, which chart presidential vote and political party identification by year and major occupational groupings, are based on the National Election Study (NES) combined file, 1952 to 1986, produced by the Survey Research Center at the University of Michigan. Figures 8.19, 8.20, 8.21, and 8.22, which chart beliefs about who benefits from government and social class identification, for selected years from 1952 to 1988, are based on the specific NES studies for years reported. Figures 8.6–8.15, which take a detailed look at the blue-color vote in 1988, are based on a multinomial logistic regression equation calculated on the NES data for 1988.

The 1988 Logit Model can be clarified as follows. A multinomial logistic regression model was calculated (using maximum likelihood estimation) on the 1988 National Election Study data to assess the impact of demographic variables on the presidential vote.[38] The model is a simple linear regression when the dependent variable is converted to the log of the odds ratios. The dependent variable in this analysis comprises three categories: Voted Republican; Voted Democrat; and Did Not Vote. The odds ratios are (Voted Republican)/(Did Not Vote) and (Voted Democrat)/(Did Not Vote). These two odds ratios (resulting in the estimation of two simultaneous equations) are sufficient to calculate every combination or odds comparison implied by a three-category dependent variable. Independent variables include family income in thousands of dollars (direct effect); age in years (direct effect); education in years (direct effect); region (categorical effect: East, Midwest, South, West); union membership (categorical effect: yes, no); religion (categorical effect: Protestant, Catholic, Jewish); race (categorical effect: white, black); gen-

TABLE 8.1a   The 1988 Presidential Election:
Analysis of Variance

Effect	Direct Effect	Chi-Square	Alpha
Intercept	2	68.72	0.0001
Family Income	2	22.32	0.0001
Age in Years	2	51.19	0.0001
Education in Years	2	30.25	0.0001
Region	6	17.76	0.0069
Union Membership	2	6.86	0.0324
Religion	4	16.39	0.0025
Race	2	17.68	0.0001
Gender	2	0.04	0.9815
Occupational Group	8	15.39	0.0520
Party Identification	4	190.73	0.0001
Likelihood Ratio	1970	1553.69	1.0000

der (categorical effect: male, female); occupation (categorical effect: homemaker, upper-white-collar, lower-white-collar, service, blue-collar); and party identification (Republican, Democrat, other). Variables identified as "direct effects" are quantitative insofar as their interval values are entered directly into the design matrix. Categorical effects are qualitative, and each category forms a variable in the model, with the exception of the last category, which is estimated by the intercepts. In this model, categorical variables are estimated using an "effect coded" design matrix.[39]

The results of the logistic regression model are given in tables 8.1a and 8.1b. Table 8.1a (analysis of variance) assesses the fit of the overall model and the significance of each set of independent estimators. It reveals that, with the exception of gender, all estimators have obtained a chi-square large enough to be significant at an alpha-level less than 0.05. At the bottom of table 8.1a is the "likelihood ratio," which permits an assessment of the fit of the model to the underlying data. This statistic is distributed as chi-square with degrees of freedom equal to that listed at the bottom of table 8.1a. If the chi-square is large relative to the degrees of freedom, the model demonstrates a poor fit, but if it is small relative to the degrees of freedom, then the model exhibits a close fit to the original data. Traditionally, a chi-square that cannot obtain an alpha-level greater than 0.05 is considered a strong indicator that the model does not fit the data. In the case of the model assessed in table 8.1a, the chi-square is such that the alpha-level is at its maximum of 1.0, indicating a very good fit between the model and the data. It should be noted that the linear design matrix used in this model is an extreme simplification of

TABLE 8.1b The 1988 Presidential Election Vote: Analysis of Individual Parameters

Effect	Equation[a]	Estimate	Standard Error	Chi-Square	Alpha
Intercept[b]	Ln(P1/P3)	−7.04	0.87	64.94	0.0001
	Ln(P2/P3)	−4.60	0.82	31.22	0.0001
Family Income Direct Effect	Ln(P1/P3)	0.03	0.01	20.52	0.0001
	Ln(P2/P3)	0.01	0.01	2.88	0.0896
Age in Years Direct Effect	Ln(P1/P3)	0.05	0.01	44.56	0.0001
	Ln(P2/P3)	0.05	0.01	32.85	0.0001
Education in Years Direct Effect	Ln(P1/P3)	0.25	0.05	25.32	0.0001
	Ln(P2/P3)	0.22	0.05	19.61	0.0001
Region East	Ln(P1/P3)	−0.25	0.19	1.74	0.1875
	Ln(P2/P3)	−0.55	0.20	7.49	0.0062
Midwest	Ln(P1/P3)	0.31	0.17	3.40	0.0652
	Ln(P2/P3)	0.48	0.17	7.93	0.0049
South	Ln(P1/P3)	−0.12	0.16	0.60	0.4379
	Ln(P2/P3)	−0.29	0.16	3.24	0.0720
Union Membership Member	Ln(P1/P3)	−0.14	0.12	1.36	0.2435
	Ln(P2/P3)	0.16	0.12	1.91	0.1668
Religion Protestant	Ln(P1/P3)	0.41	0.28	2.16	0.1413
	Ln(P2/P3)	−0.29	0.24	1.50	0.2209
Catholic	Ln(P1/P3)	0.77	0.29	7.01	0.0081
	Ln(P2/P3)	0.47	0.25	3.56	0.0591

TABLE 8.1b *(continued)*

Effect		Equation[a]	Estimate	Standard Error	Chi-Square	Alpha
Race	White	Ln(P1/P3)	0.78	0.26	9.43	0.0021
		Ln(P2/P3)	−0.26	0.14	3.66	0.0557
Gender	Male	Ln(P1/P3)	0.02	0.12	0.03	0.8611
		Ln(P2/P3)	0.00	0.12	0.00	0.9815
Occupational Group	Homemaker	Ln(P1/P3)	−0.08	0.25	0.11	0.7358
		Ln(P2/P3)	0.11	0.23	0.21	0.6505
	Upper White	Ln(P1/P3)	0.23	0.21	1.20	0.2734
		Ln(P2/P3)	0.63	0.22	8.17	0.0042
	Lower White	Ln(P1/P3)	0.08	0.18	0.19	0.6636
		Ln(P2/P3)	0.18	0.18	1.02	0.3133
	Service	Ln(P1/P3)	−0.24	0.25	0.96	0.3280
		Ln(P2/P3)	−0.48	0.24	3.98	0.0462
Party Identification	Republican	Ln(P1/P3)	1.14	0.15	56.26	0.0001
		Ln(P2/P3)	−0.74	0.20	13.22	0.0003
	Democrat	Ln(P1/P3)	−0.77	0.16	23.63	0.0001
		Ln(P2/P3)	0.98	0.15	41.95	0.0001

[a] P1 indicates the probability of voting Republican, P2 indicates the probability of voting Democrat, and P3 indicates the probability of not voting at all.

[b] The Intercept estimates the following omitted categories: Region = South; Union = No; Religion = Jewish; Race = Black; Gender = Female; Occupation = Blue-Collar; and Party = Other.

TABLE 8.2 1988 Sample Means for Major Occupational Groups

Variable		Blue-Collar	Service	Lower-White-Collar	Upper-White-Collar
Family Income	Direct Effect	$28,252.00	$20,936.17	$34,271.21	$42,639.45
Age in Years	Direct Effect	37.44	39.24	37.62	40.16
Education in Years	Direct Effect	11.66	11.84	13.26	14.99
Region	East	16.1%	22.4%	18.5%	21.3%
	Midwest	23.0%	32.2%	31.3%	26.2%
	South	44.0%	30.9%	31.3%	28.7%
	West	17.0%	14.5%	18.8%	23.8%
Union Membership	Member	30.0%	20.0%	20.9%	18.9%
	Nonmember	70.0%	80.0%	79.1%	81.1%
Religion	Protestant	76.3%	71.8%	68.9%	65.8%
	Catholic	22.7%	28.2%	28.2%	30.1%
	Jew	1.0%	0.0%	3.0%	4.1%
Race	White	86.4%	77.0%	82.1%	52.8%
	Black	13.6%	23.0%	17.9%	47.2%
Gender	Male	75.6%	18.4%	31.3%	90.8%
	Female	24.4%	81.6%	68.7%	9.2%
Party Identification	Republican	20.2%	21.7%	29.9%	34.5%
	Democrat	34.4%	40.8%	31.0%	27.7%
	Other	45.4%	37.5%	39.1%	37.8%

the possible interactions among categories of the independent variables and the possible nonlinear direct effects implied by such a complex set of variables. Hence, the fit of this very simple logit model is indeed a significant finding.

Table 8.1b (analysis of individual parameters) gives the logit estimates, their individual standard errors, the associated chi-squares and alpha-levels. The estimates are linear with respects to the log of the odds ratios. This makes direct interpretation of the estimates nonintuitive. As a result, we have interpreted the estimates in figures 8.5 through 8.15 for the blue-collar vote. That is, we held the effect of occupation constant at "blue-collar" and calculated the ceteris paribus effects of each independent variable on the probability of voting in one of the three ways (Republican, Democrat, No Vote). For each calculation, the effects of all other independent variables included in the model were held at their "blue-collar" mean effects. These means are presented in table 8.2.

NINE

The Enduring Dilemma of Race in America

Bart Landry

When future historians look back at the late 1960s, the period will appear in many respects as the golden age of American history. Prosperity was at an unprecedented high, while the economy offered the promise of unlimited growth. A cultural revolution, furthermore, was in the making, and Americans had committed themselves, for the first time in their history, to eliminating what Gunnar Myrdal had called the "American dilemma"—the racism and discrimination that had kept millions of Americans in the position of second class citizens. With the passage of the Civil Rights Act in 1964, discrimination was redefined as racism. No longer was the discriminator a "good old boy" and the fair-minded white person a "nigger lover." Lester Maddox, standing in the doorway of his store, ax handle in hand, was not seen any more as a folk hero, but as a national shame. The first steps in the path toward racial equality had been taken.

How long ago it all seems now. Rather than a fruition of the dreams of those golden days, the past two decades have brought confusion and even retrogression. The cultural revolution of the 1960s and early 1970s was overwhelmed by the economic reality of recessions and a declining economy. Though American society would never be quite the same again, it stopped far short of the goals of the reforms of the 1960s. In less than ten years, the nation was tiring of the effort to extend full opportunity to blacks. A new term entered the lexicon of race relations, "reverse discrimination"—elbowing for room with "equal employment opportunity," "discrimination," and "racism."

The turning point, it seems in retrospect, was a suit by Allan Bakke in 1974 accusing the University of California Medical School at Davis, of "reverse discrimination." The decision handed down by the Supreme Court was ambiguous, a victory neither for Bakke nor for those opposed to his position. At the heart of the issue was the nation's commitment not only to provide equal opportunities to all its citizens today, regardless of color, but also to redress the injustices of the past—injustices that have placed blacks at a considerable disadvantage in the competition for desirable jobs. Since *Bakke,* the courts have been called upon again and again to decide whether the nation can legally redress the market effects of past injustices of slavery and discrimination against blacks. Quotas, timetables, and set-asides have all been challenged. For the time being, the tide has shifted against the struggle of blacks for equality, as a conservative judiciary, including the Supreme Court, has returned numerous decisions that have chipped away at the very foundations of the fight against persistent racial discrimination.

The recent study by the National Academy of Science, *A Common Destiny: Blacks and American Society,* concludes that "race still matters greatly in the United States."[1] Reminders of the truth of this conclusion are numerous in the United States as we approach a new century. They range from racially motivated incidents and attacks on blacks at predominantly white college campuses to racial attacks in several northeastern communities. While surveys have found that the commitment of whites to the *principle* of equality for blacks has grown steadily over the decades, the authors of the National Academy of Science report conclude:

> Principles of equality are endorsed less when they would result in close, frequent, or prolonged social contact, and whites are much less prone to endorse policies meant to implement equal participation of blacks in important social institutions. In practice, many whites refuse or are reluctant to participate in social settings (e.g., neighborhoods and schools) in which significant numbers of blacks are present.[2]

Today, whites are more likely to say that "blacks have gone far enough" than that there remains an "unfinished agenda" to be completed. This sentiment exists in spite of the studies of black progress by the National Academy of Sciences, as well as others, that have provided ample evidence of the negative effects of discrimination among blacks.[3] These negative effects, moreover, have continued well after the Civil Rights era and the emergence of a black middle class.[4] A review of the record since 1940 prompted the authors of the National Academy of Science study to comment: "The status of black Americans today can be characterized as a glass that is half full—if measured by progress since 1939—or as a glass that is half empty—if measured by the persisting disparities between black and white Americans since the early 1970s."[5] Among the signs of the "half empty" glass is a large economic disparity between blacks and whites that has been traced directly to the discrimination blacks encounter in the employment and housing markets.[6] Caught in this economic disparity are the almost one-third of all blacks who live in poverty, compared to only 11 percent of whites; a growing black under-class incorporating about 13.2 percent of employable black adults in the late 1980s, compared to 3.7 percent of whites; an unemployment rate twice that of whites; continued lower life expectancy than whites; and a serious lag in the proportions of high school graduates who attend college. Though many observers point to the negative impact of a changing economy characterized by a shrinking manufacturing sector and expanding service sector, the authors of the National Academy of Science study unambiguously conclude that "a considerable amount of remaining black/white inequality is due to continuing discriminatory treatment against blacks."[7]

How is it that more than 100 years after emancipation, race is still a salient issue in the United States and blacks continue to lag significantly behind whites on every meaningful economic indicator? Most studies addressing this issue provide descriptions of the remaining black/white gap in indices of economic progress and social well-being. While these studies often offer detailed and invaluable documentation needed by policy makers, they generally fail to offer explanations that might help us understand the persistence of racial inequality. If we are to understand why a movement that began with such promise thirty years ago has, toward the end of the twentieth century, stalled and even gone backward, we need to dig deep below the surface.

In this chapter, therefore, I will not add to already ample descriptions of racial inequality in contemporary America. Because the roots of racism and discrimination are so deep, it is best to rely on a historical approach in analyzing the dynamics by which the present state of black/white relations came into being.

THEORIES OF RACIAL INEQUALITY

When one sifts through the books and articles on race relations that have appeared over the past fifty years, one finds that the overwhelming majority of scholars have focused in some fashion on the role of individual attitudes. Two of the best examples of this approach can be found in the writings of Gordan Allport and Lloyd Warner. To Allport we owe the emphasis on *prejudice* as the motivator of discriminatory behavior. Lloyd Warner, for his part, argued that the negative evaluation of all blacks by whites in the South had produced a southern society characterized by a *caste* division between blacks and whites.[8]

These studies led to a preoccupation among social scientists with racial attitudes and an interest in measuring changes in white attitudes toward blacks over time. The best known of these studies were surveys conducted by the National Opinion Research Center (NORC) and published in a series of articles in *Scientific American* over many years, beginning in 1956. Subsequently, both Gallup and the Institute for Social Research at the University of Michigan took periodic pulses of the racial attitudes of whites. At the heart of these studies was an attempt to measure the extent and depth of prejudicial attitudes held by whites against blacks, and the degree to which these attitudes might be changing over time. From this perspective, white attitudes was the key to black progress. If whites abandoned, or at least softened, their racist attitudes toward blacks, social scientists reasoned, the "race problem" would be solved. At the same time, a kind of social Darwinism informed their thinking, suggesting that white attitudes had to change *before* discriminatory behavior would cease.[9]

Within this framework, the *social distance scale*—a measure of the extent to which whites were willing to associate with blacks in various settings characterized by ever greater closeness, from the workplace to interracial marriages—became a major tool. Any sign of a decline in racist attitudes was greeted with enthusiasm, as an indicator of racial progress. While these studies have documented a liberalization of white attitudes toward blacks over the decades, however, other researchers have continued to discover extensive discriminatory *behavior* in schools, housing, and the workplace.[10]

Recently, several scholars have turned away from the "individual prejudice" approach in favor of some type of "structural" explanation for the limited progress of blacks, as compared to whites, in American society. One version, advanced by Nathan Glazer, attributes the difference to the allegedly more recent arrival of blacks to urban America.[11] Another, proposed by Thomas Sowell, argues that, coming from a rural background, blacks have been hampered by the absence of a work ethic.[12] Both of these approaches fall under what has been called a "blacks-as-the-last-of-the-immigrants" theory, a theory suggesting that blacks lag behind white ethnics primarily because the latter settled in the urban Northeast and Midwest earlier than southern blacks. Their greater progress, therefore, is simply a matter of opportunities that come with time. Two other explanations differing from the prejudice approach are offered by Bonacich and Wilson. Bonacich blames inequality on the manipulation of black workers by capitalists in their struggle with the white working class.[13] Wilson argues that an increasingly impoverished underclass today is the result of structural shifts in the economy that have resulted in the relocation of jobs from the inner city to the suburbs.[14]

The individual prejudice approach attributes the continuing inequality of blacks to racist attitudes held by whites; the structural approach more or less blames impersonal market forces. The first sees a black/white polarization in America. The second tends to focus on the varied experiences of numerous ethnic and ethnic minority groups and to minimize a black/white polarization. Taken alone, each of these two explanations has serious shortcomings.

Though Gordon Allport argued for a universal tendency among all societies toward prejudice and stereotyping, it is one thing to hold negative attitudes toward individuals and quite another to *dehumanize* them. It is an even greater leap to predict behaviors such as lynching from negative attitudes or stereotyping. Some scholars even challenge the one-to-one correspondence between prejudice and discrimination that is generally presumed. Earl Raab and Seymour Martin Lipset, for instance, have argued that black stereotypes, such as the Sambo image, are neither direct outcomes of negative attitudes toward a group nor predictors of the actions that might result from stereotypically held beliefs.[15] Other scholars have shown that discrimination can occur in the absence of prejudicial attitudes when the practices of institutions are inherently biased.[16]

In spite of its limitations, however, the structural approach broadens the search for an understanding of racial inequality by requiring an explanation for the variability in economic progress among white ethnics as well as between whites and blacks. In his book *Ethnic America,* Sowell presents a rank ordering of ethnics using a family income index that shows a variation from 103 for Irish-Americans to 172 for Jewish-Americans; and from 60 for Native Americans to 99 for Filipino-Americans (table 9.1). Such data force us to examine more closely the factors relevant to upward mobility and the degree to which these factors have been available to various groups—including blacks. They also prompt questions about the environment and circumstances encountered by immigrants upon their arrival. The structural approach encourages an analysis of the factors relevant to upward mobility in American society, while the individualistic approach emphasizes a black/white polarization that overshadows the variability among white ethnics and among ethnic minorities. The tendency to view structural forces as the impersonal workings of the market, however, has been called into serious question.

Both Stanley Liberson and Stephen Thernstrom present carefully analyzed historical data on the experiences of blacks and white ethnics that discredit the theory of "blacks-as-the-last-of-the-immigrants," and point instead to persistent discrimination against blacks by whites.[17] Even in data assembled to demonstrate ethnic variability, such as Sowell's family income index, an economic polarization along white/nonwhite lines is apparent. For although Sowell's index makes it clear that ethnic groups have experienced different degrees of success in scaling the economic ladder, it is also evident that, with the exception of Japanese- and Chinese-Americans, all groups with a family income index above the mean are white.

TABLE 9.1   Family Income Average
(U.S. average = 100)

Jewish	172
Japanese	132
Polish	115
Chinese	112
Italian	112
German	107
Anglo-Saxon	107
Irish	103
TOTAL U.S.	100
Filipino	99
West Indian	94
Mexican	76
Puerto Rican	63
Black	62
Indian	60

SOURCE: Thomas Sowell, *Ethnic America: A History*
(New York: Basic Books, 1981), 5.

Bonacich's theory of a "split labor market" is similarly limited. While there is no doubt that white employers have at times used blacks as strikebreakers in their struggle with white labor, Bonacich's theory does not account for discrimination in the North that occurred before the influx of black migrants or in periods when the struggle between capital and labor was not intense. Nor does it help us understand why blacks, rather than some other group, were used as strikebreakers, or why all white ethnics united in their opposition to black workers.

This is not to deny that both individual prejudice and structural conditions have had an impact on black progress. However, either explanation taken alone is inadequate. Missing, therefore, is a link between individual prejudice and structural impediments to black achievement. Rather than view prejudice and structural conditions as factors operating independently of each other, it may be more accurate to see them as connected in some systematic fashion. In the remainder of this chapter I will argue that racism and prejudice are not simply the attitudes of malevolent individuals, but are *cultural norms* into which whites have been socialized and that have found expression in both systemic institutional and individual discriminatory behavior. From this point of view, structural conditions can no longer be viewed as the impersonal forces some have suggested, and racism is raised from the level of individual "quirks" to that of a *societal phenomenon* requiring analysis and solutions on the societal level.

The following discussion will therefore focus on the societal level and will be placed within the general framework of economic progress through upward mobility. From this point of view, there are three issues to investigate: (1) the factors that promote upward mobility in American society and the process through which mobility occurs, (2) the reasons for different degrees of ethnic success, and (3) the reasons for the more limited success of most ethnic minorities. The first two issues will be discussed briefly, while primary attention is directed toward answering the third question.

GETTING A PIECE OF THE PIE

Since the publication of the classic work by Peter Blau and Otis Dudley Duncan, scholars have tried to identify the factors that affect an individual's movement up the class ladder. According to the Blau-Duncan model, an individual's movement up the class ladder involves three stages, beginning with family background, moving on through a period during which education and training are attained, and ending in a particular occupation upon entry into the job market.[18] From the family, the individual receives economic support, encouragement, and the social skills needed to negotiate the next two stages—acquiring an education and entering the work force. An individual's educational achievement is greatly affected by the family's economic resources. As one moves up the class ladder, a family's ability to control the environment within which its children will grow and develop increases. A neighborhood in which all or most families belong to the middle class will not only provide more resources for the local school system but also will place children in schools with other students who arrive equally well prepared. Much of their preparation results from the enriching experiences middle-class children are routinely exposed to in families with college-educated parents, experiences such as visits to museums and puppet shows, and possession of children's books and a variety of educational toys.

Working-class parents above and below the poverty line live in progressively less affluent neighborhoods, depending on income. Their children attend schools with children who often are poorly prepared to begin the educational journey. Because the tax bases upon which the schools' economic structures rely are smaller than in middle-class communities, the resources of such schools are typically inadequate. Differences in the education of working- and middle-class children intensify beyond the elementary level. Children from working-class families—particularly minority children—are more likely to be placed in lower tracks that do not provide preparation for college.[19] Teachers hold lower expectations for them and give them less encouragement to excel.

Middle-class children, by virtue of both their educational experiences and their families' greater financial resources, are more likely than working-class children to continue on to college, a must for entry into an upper-middle-class occupation and a chance at the American dream. That the economic success of college-educated individuals far surpasses that of those with only a high school degree has been documented time and time again. In 1989, the median net worth of black college graduates was four times greater than that of college dropouts and six times that of those with only a high school diploma.[20]

As Jencks has pointed out, there is, of course, an element of chance involved in an individual's progress up the class ladder.[21] It is also true that personal or family contacts—"who you know"—can also affect the outcome. Nevertheless, the model proves that the class position of the family into which we are born greatly affects our future success. Although this country prides itself in being a "land of opportunity," opportunity is not uniformly distributed throughout all classes. Different degrees of individual economic success are not accidental, therefore. They are built into our society's structure by variations in the economic resources of the families upon which we all depend to get started along the road to success. Thus some people begin with high-tech running shoes, others with yesterday's models, and some without any shoes at all.

Governmental programs to "equalize" starting opportunities, or at least minimize differential advantages, have had mixed results. Project Head Start has been a real success, but suffers from underfunding and lack of follow-through at the elementary school level. Efforts to eliminate other educational disadvantages through school desegregation have met with massive resistance. At bottom is the failure of political leaders and white citizens to fully commit the nation to institutionalizing equality of opportunity. The goal seemed like a good idea during the late 1960s, when prosperity held the promise of eliminating the black/white economic gap without sacrifices by whites. In the economically insecure decades of the 1970s and 1980s, however, whites have been prone to argue that blacks have gone far enough, or that they lag behind economically through their own fault.

DIFFERENCES IN THE DEGREE OF ETHNIC SUCCESS

But if the Blau-Duncan attainment model identifies the factors and process through which individuals climb the class ladder, why are there differences in economic success on the aggregate level between ethnic groups? Why have more members of some ethnic groups moved into the middle class than others? Stephen Steinberg disputes the traditional view that different rates of ethnic success are due to differences in "their value systems" and that therefore the causes are "to be found within the groups themselves."[22] Rather, he argues, external factors *to which the entire group was exposed*—such as patterns of settlement, time of arrival, external obstacles, and opportunities in the immediate environment, as well as resources possessed, such as skills and education—have been far more important than internal values.

Some ethnic groups, for instance, tended to settle in rural areas, others in industrial cities. Arriving early in our history and coming from rural backgrounds in Europe, Germans and Swedes sought out the opportunities provided by rich inexpensive land in the Midwest. Other groups, like Jews, Italians, and Irish, seemed to find urban areas more suited to their previous experiences, or they arrived at times when land was no longer plentiful and cheap. On the whole, however, the *time* of their arrival alone seems to explain little of their eventual success. Poles and Jews who immigrated around the turn of the century have higher family income indices than Germans and Anglos who came decades earlier in the nineteenth century.

The early occupational experiences of ethnics sometimes had a serendipitous explanation. The far greater numbers of Irish—than either Jewish or Italian—girls in domestic work is a case in point. While many analysts have attributed this pattern to different cultural values with respect to domestic work, Steinberg notes that Irish girls often immigrated alone, while Jewish and Italian women accompanied their families. Since domestic work provided lodging as well as income, it was well suited to single girls in cities. Jewish and Italian girls had no such need and therefore concentrated more in the garment industry or factory work. As a result of these immigration patterns, 54 percent of employed Irish women were classified by the U.S. Census as engaged in "domestic and personal" work in 1900, compared to only 9 percent of Italian and 14 percent of Jewish female workers. In contrast, only 8 percent of Irish women worked in the needle trades, compared to 41 percent of Jewish and 38 percent of Italian women.[23]

It is along these lines that Steinberg also explains the rapid upward mobility of Jews to their position above all other ethnic groups in the United States. When Eastern European Jews arrived in the United States they found a particularly good fit between their urban background and skills and the employment needs of a burgeoning garment industry in New York City. Forbidden to own land in Russia, they nevertheless "worked in occupations that prepared them for roles in a modern industrial economy."[24] According to the 1897 Russian census, 38 percent of Jews worked as artisans or were employed in manufacturing, primarily in the production of clothing. Another 32 percent were in commerce. In commerce they were often middlemen, linking the urban and rural economies, a role that has been successfully played earlier by Korean immigrants on the West Coast of the United States and by Koreans today.[25]

Comparing Jews with six other ethnic groups that arrived in the United States between 1899 and 1910 (English, Germans, Scandinavians, Italians, Irish, and Poles), Steinberg found that the highest percentage of skilled workers was found among Jews: 67 percent.[26] The next highest percentage of skilled workers, 49 percent, was found among the English, a group no longer heavily represented among immigrants at that time. Among Germans, only 30 percent of immigrants were skilled; while the lowest percentage was found among Polish immigrants, only 6 percent of whom were skilled.

Skills are useless, however, without a demand for those skills in the area of settlement. By chance, Russian Jews found a demand for their extensive array of skills at the port of arrival, New York City, particularly in the clothing industry, which was primarily concentrated there. As a result of the fit between their extensive skills and the city's economy, Jews "ranked first in 26 of the 47 trades" tabulated by the U.S. Immigration Commission in 1911. The rapid upward mobility of Eastern European Jews, therefore, can be traced to the occupational fit they encountered at their point of entry into the United States. Their occupational success was then translated into sponsorship of their children in similar occupations and in educational attainment. Although, like every other immigrant group, Jews encountered discrimination, it was not sufficient to prevent them from entering skilled occupations or educating their children. They thus followed the classic pattern of each generation doing a little better than the previous one. While other ethnic groups also followed this same pattern, it is clear that the external factors encountered and the skills possessed differed from group to group. Thus some were more successful than others in moving up the class ladder.

THE PENALTY FOR BEING BLACK

In spite of their slave experience, blacks in many respects occupied an advantageous position in 1865 relative to most European immigrants who arrived after this date. They were, first of all, experienced farmers in the southern agricultural economy. They knew the land; they understood the crops and the means of cultivating them. Secondly, blacks constituted most of the skilled workers in the urban South, having learned and practiced numerous skills in the slave economy. Thirdly, though their illiteracy rate was high, they knew the language of the country and understood its customs. They were not strangers in a strange land. Finally, blacks lived in proximity to the growing number of industrial jobs in the North. As slaves, many had worked in tobacco factories and in the towns of the South.

Had blacks received the promised forty acres and a mule, or at least been allowed to acquire land, thousands would have become small independent farmers at a time when land was still the backbone of the southern economy. Thousands more—if given the chance—would have moved into the industrial economy of the North to work in the factories of Chicago, Pittsburgh, and Detroit. However, blacks were not viewed or treated as another ethnic group in a plural society. Rather, the issue became polarized in both the South and North along black/white lines. Instead of allowing freedmen to acquire land after emancipation, southern planters moved quickly to preserve their cheap labor pool of agricultural workers by denying freedmen access to land throughout the South. At a time when land provided millions of whites a means of achieving self-sufficiency and the possibility of capital accumulation, freedmen did not receive the forty acres and a mule promised them. As W. E. B. Du Bois points out, this was unique in the experience of western societies. When the serfs were freed in Europe, from Russia to England, they were given parcels of land for their livelihood. In the postbellum period, freedmen were not only denied the promised forty acres and a mule, but were effectively prevented from purchasing land throughout the South.[27] In New Orleans, a program by wealthy blacks to lease plantations seized from former owners of slaves and to rent this land to freed blacks was effectively thwarted by the return of plantations to their former owners by a Republican party tiring of reconstruction and eager to ensure a continued flow of cotton to northern textile mills. Faced with these obstacles, only 5 percent to 8 percent of blacks managed to either become or remain landowners.

After some experimentation, a system of sharecropping emerged that ensured plantation owners a cheap labor pool if not always an entirely tractable one. There were, first of all, conflicts over the definition of the labor pool itself. Both southern planters and northern reconstructionists defined black women as part of the new southern plantation labor force, while blacks attempted to redefine the role of their wives in conformity with the "cult of domesticity," newly emerged within the white middle class. "The women," one planter complained, "say that they never mean to do any more outdoor work, that white men support their wives, and they mean that their husbands shall support them."[28]

To enforce their own interpretation of the black work force, planters often used armed riders to go from cabin to cabin, forcing black women into the fields. In the end, the sharecropping system effectively kept most southern blacks in virtual peonage. On "settlement day" (the annual calculation of debits and credits between planter and sharecroppers), the typical black family found itself in debt to the planter, who used their dependency on the plantation store for provisions as a means of cheating them. Those black families "in debt" at the end of the year had to remain another year to work off their debt. Nor could blacks move into the newly found textile mills of the South. This was work reserved for poor whites by a southern planter class, determined to prevent a political alliance between poor blacks and whites. The few blacks admitted to the mills were confined to the most menial tasks.[29]

Those blacks who moved into the urban economy of the South found their labor as exploited there as in rural areas. The dominant position held by black males among the urban crafts workers at the end of the Civil War was lost over the next three decades, through unfair competition and the growing reluctance of whites to employ their skills. By 1900, the class of black artisans had been decimated, reduced from five out of six to only 5 percent in the urban South. There remained only menial, often sporadic, work for them, making it necessary for other family members to supplement their income. Summarizing the experience of black families in the urban South during the decades of the late nineteenth and early twentieth centuries, historian Jacqueline Jones writes: "Husbands were deprived of the satisfaction of providing their families with a reliable source of income, while wives found their duties enlarged as they added paid employment to their already considerable domestic responsibilities."[30]

The only work to which black women could aspire was domestic or laundry work, work of such low status that even poor white women avoided these jobs at all costs. Like white immigrant women in the North, black women in the South sought factory work in preference to domestic work whenever possible. Here, too, they found themselves relegated to the most menial of the available factory work. This included sorting, stripping, and stemming leaves in tobacco factories, work so difficult and unhealthy that white women could not be found to take these jobs. Those white women who did work in tobacco factories were given the more skilled tasks and worked in healthier surroundings, segregated from blacks.[31] When one employer hired a black woman to work in their area, white women walked off the job in protest, forcing the factory owner to fire the black worker. As a result of these kinds of restrictions, 90 percent of the servants in southern cities were black by 1900, as were the majority of laundresses.

In the North, employers showed a decided preference for white immigrant labor over the readily available pool of southern or northern blacks. Because of discrimination, there were no blacks in the brass and ship industries of Detroit in 1890, and only 21 blacks among the 5,839 male workers in the tobacco, stove, iron, machine, and shoe industries. By 1910, only 25 blacks could be found among the 10,000 primarily foreign workers in the burgeoning auto factories.[32] The discrimination black workers faced in northern cities could be felt in the lament of a

Detroit whitewasher in 1891: "First it was de Irish, den it was de Dutch, and now it's de Polacks as grinds us down. I s'pose when dey [the Poles] gets like de Irish and stands up for a fair price, some odder strangers'll come over de sea 'nd jine de faimily and cut us down again."[33]

Not until World War I cut off the flow of white immigrants did northern industrialists begin recruiting blacks from the South to work in the factories of Chicago, Philadelphia, Detroit, and other northern cities. Even then, black workers found a labor market in which white ethnics were firmly united in their opposition to competition from black labor, while employers reserved the better jobs for native whites and immigrants alike. When white workers turned to unionization, blacks were excluded.

Black women, forced to work in large numbers to supplement their husbands' and fathers' incomes, did not fare much better in the northern economy than they had in the South. As immigrant women abandoned domestic work for less odious factory jobs and native white women entered the new clerical occupations, black women alone found themselves overwhelmingly confined to domestic and laundry work. In Pittsburgh after World War I, 90 percent of all domestics were black women; in Philadelphia, over half. Those who found work in factories—only 5.5 percent in 1930, compared to 27.1 percent of the foreign born—were confined to the most dangerous and menial tasks. Nevertheless, domestic work represented such an undesirable alternative, the absolutely lowest status work in the economy, that black women sought factory work whenever possible. Their sentiments were unambiguously expressed by a black woman in a Chicago box factory in 1920: "I'll never work in nobody's kitchen but my own any more. No indeed! That's the one thing that makes me stick to this job."[34] These same black women had to watch helplessly as their own daughters were passed over by white employers who filled clerical and sales positions with native white and even immigrant girls, who had no more education than their children.

By 1940, only 5.7 percent of black males and 6.6 percent of black females had been able to enter middle-class occupations, the majority in predominantly black institutions, while 35.7 percent of whites held middle-class jobs.[35] In the ensuing decades, few blacks managed to climb the class ladder into the middle class. On the eve of the Civil Rights Movement, 1960, the effectiveness of discriminatory practices in the job market was apparent in the sizes of the black and white middle classes, which were now 13.4 and 44.1 percent of employed workers, respectively. The job ceiling remained almost as low for blacks in 1960 as it had been at the turn of the century.

How is it that of all ethnic groups, African-Americans still rank near the bottom on all economic indicators? Why have all European ethnics had more success than blacks in moving up the class ladder? As I pointed out earlier, if one considered only the objective characteristics and circumstances of blacks and of white immigrant groups from southeastern Europe, one would have predicted a far different outcome. Blacks' skills were at least equal to those of the new immigrants, and their motivation to succeed was as high. While the selectivity of immigrants is well known, African-Americans emerged from slavery with a tremendous motivation to begin new lives for themselves. Denied the right of an education during slavery, they possessed a strong desire for this forbidden fruit. Adults eagerly flocked to the schools established by northern philanthropists and missionaries, to learn to read, and they were eager to send their children to school. Those who eventually migrated to the North were more likely than many of the new ethnics to send their children to school rather than out into the labor force. Yet these same families had to stand by helplessly while their children were passed over for the better jobs the economy had to offer in factories and offices.

The answer is not simply to be found in the economic competition among ethnic groups. For that would not explain why white ethnics, who competed among themselves, united in competing against blacks. Nor is Bonacich's theory of a split labor market a sufficient explanation. To be sure, employers sometimes profited by using blacks as strikebreakers and as a reserve army of cheap labor, but not on a scale sufficient to suppress the aspirations of white labor. Blacks were never given sufficient access to semiskilled or skilled jobs to play that role. Rather, I would argue that both white employers and ethnics united in their opposition to blacks competing in the market on an equal footing with white workers. But why? It is at this point that we are forced to return to the black/white polarization in American society. But rather than view racism as simply operating on the individual level as prejudice, it has to be interpreted in structural terms—as part of the culture.

BLACK/WHITE POLARIZATION

My argument is that primarily *because of their racial attitudes,* whites of all classes have historically reserved the worst jobs in the economy for black workers. It is true that, with the exception of work in the slave economy, whites have at times performed these same tasks in the urban economy. Yet these menial jobs were always viewed as temporary positions in the class structure, stepping stones toward a better life for themselves or their children higher up the class ladder. These white workers, immigrant and native, did in fact move up to better jobs, or at least were able to see their sons and daughters securing better jobs than their own in the next generation. Each new generation of European immigrants competed for positions in the economy and moved a little further up the class ladder.

This competition for desirable work, however, was open to whites alone. The norms of the market dictated that throughout the economy black workers be denied opportunities to compete equally with whites for desirable positions. Rather, black workers—both male and female—were reserved for the most menial labor at the very bottom of the class structure: unskilled labor and domestic work. This was not a "reserve labor pool" to be drawn upon by employers to undercut the price of white labor in semiskilled and skilled work. It was a system that *defined* some jobs as "colored jobs" and others as "white jobs."

Unlike the situation for whites, progress for blacks was not a matter of working harder or acquiring more skills and education. Since blacks were denied opportunities to compete in the market on an equal footing, for the same jobs, as whites, their upward mobility was stymied at its very source: the opportunity for husbands and wives to gain good and secure employment to improve their own living standard and thus be able to sponsor their sons and daughters in the next two stages of their movement up the occupational ladder. For although black parents placed greater emphasis on educating their children than many immigrant groups, they were nevertheless forced to stand by helplessly as their sons and daughters remained shut out of the growing number of skilled and clerical jobs becoming available. While the children of immigrants only recently arrived in this country could aspire to move further up the class ladder than their parents, generation after generation of black youth could aspire to little more than the unskilled labor and domestic work at which their parents toiled. A survey by the Bureau of Jewish Employment Problems of Chicago in 1961 found this to be true in the North as well as the South. Their report concluded that "98 percent of the white-collar job orders received from over 5,000 companies were not available to qualified Negroes" in that year.[36] "No blacks need apply" was the common experience of blacks seeking to move up the class ladder. Those blacks who managed to escape these restrictions to some extent by acquiring an education in a black college found themselves confined to serving the black community, rather than being able to contribute their talents to the development of the entire society.[37] The brain power, creativity, and talents of millions of blacks were lost to both the black community and to the larger society.

Earlier I noted that an individual's movement up the class ladder has been modeled as a three-stage process, involving family background, educational attainment, and entry into the job market. At each of these points, blacks found themselves handicapped. Black families were denied opportunities to increase their economic resources, which then could be used to sponsor their children at the next stage. The education of black children was separate and unequal. When moving into the job market, blacks encountered a ceiling above which they could not aspire

to climb. Though immigrants from southeastern Europe frequently encountered discrimination, it was never as severe or prolonged as that
faced by blacks.[38] Furthermore, these same immigrants who were themselves discriminated against, united in their opposition to blacks. Thus,
their own upward mobility was facilitated at the expense of blacks, who
were kept at the very bottom of the occupational structure—all in spite
of the initially more favorable position of blacks.

White workers did gain economically from the subjugation of black
workers, just as they had profited from the elimination of Chinese workers in California during the late nineteenth century, and just as Anglos
profited from the seizure of Mexican-American land after the Mexican-
American War. White ethnics could have gained equally from the subjugation of another ethnic group, such as Poles, Jews, or Italians. These
latter groups did, in fact, experience discrimination from the older ethnics from northern and western Europe. But none of the new European
ethnic groups was confined to unskilled labor and domestic work. Each
quickly moved from unskilled labor and domestic work into factories,
the first springboard up the class ladder. There they secured the best
jobs, while blacks either could not gain access or found only the most
menial and dangerous work open to them.

Though discrimination has been part of American history from colonial times and has affected all groups other than Anglos to some degree,
it is ethnic minorities, those with *darker skins,* who have experienced the
severest discrimination and faced the most obstacles in their movement
up the class ladder. From the very beginning, the class system in America has been a color-conscious class system.[39] Within this color-conscious
class system, African-Americans have experienced earlier and more persistent discrimination than any other group except Native Americans.

CULTURAL RACISM AND THE ROLE OF BLACKS
IN THE U.S. CLASS SYSTEM

The role of blacks in the U.S. class system was first established with the
importation of Africans to labor as slaves on the plantations of the South.
This development followed the failure of southerners' attempts to use
the quasi-free labor of Indians and white indentured servants on plantations. With the failure of these attempts, planters turned to the use of
African slaves. Unlike Native Americans, Africans were accustomed to
agricultural work, and they could not blend into the population as did
white indentured servants if they escaped, making them an ideal inexpensive work force from the planters' viewpoint.

To justify the total subjugation of Africans through the slave system,
negative imaging and stereotyping of African-Americans was resorted

to. In time, blacks were portrayed as somewhat less than human, without a Christian soul and devoid of refined, civilized sentiments. During the abolitionist movement in the early nineteenth century, the propaganda of slaveholders intensified. According to Frederickson, a pamphlet published in New York in 1833, entitled *Evidence Against the Views of the Abolitionists, Consisting of Physical and Moral Proofs of the Natural Inferiority of the Negroes,* presented "the basic racist case against the abolitionist assertion of equality."[40] In this pamphlet the author, Richard Colfax, argued for the innate intellectual inferiority of blacks, based on their alleged physical differences. This theme would later be taken up again and given pseudoscientific support by racist white scholars.

Southern apologists for the system of slavery went beyond the inferiority thesis to argue the *benefits* slavery held for an inferior race. Such a position was made in the United States Senate in 1858 by Hammond, a planter-intellectual and senator for the State of South Carolina:

> In all social systems there must be a class to do the menial duties, to perform the drudgery of life. That is a class requiring but a low order of intellect and but little skill. Its requisites are vigor, docility, fidelity. Such a class you must have. . . . It constitutes the very mud-sill of society. . . . Fortunately for the South we have found a race adapted to that purpose to her hand. . . . We do not think that whites should be slaves either by law or necessity. Our slaves are black, of another, inferior race. The *status* in which we have placed them is an elevation. They are elevated from the condition in which God first created them by being made our slaves.[41]

Slavery, then, was portrayed as *beneficial* to blacks, so much so, as one writer asserted, that under slavery they became "the most cheerful and merry people we have among us."[42] Sambo, the grinning, happy-go-lucky, singing and dancing, simple-minded black was a natural product of this thinking and became an image of all blacks—free as well as slave. Nor did these negative images and stereotypes end with slavery. Rather, as Frederickson notes, they "engendered a cultural and psychosocial racism that after a certain point took on a life of [its] own and created a powerful irrational basis for white supremacist attitudes and actions."[43] These attitudes became part of white culture and belief systems well into the twentieth century.

Thus we find that in a serious dissertation, written for his doctoral degree at Columbia University in 1910, Howard Odum wrote:

> The Negro has little home conscience or love of home, no local attachments of the better sort. . . . He has no pride of ancestry, and he is not influenced by the lives of great men. . . . He has little conception of the meaning of virtue, truth, honor, manhood, integrity. . . . He does not know the value of his word or the meaning of words in general. . . . They sneer at the idea of work. . . . Their moral natures are miserably perverted.[44]

Odum's dissertation later became an influential book under the title *Social and Mental Traits of the Negro*. Odum's conception of blacks was no different in 1910 than that expressed almost immediately after emancipation in 1866 by George Fitzhugh, who wrote: "They [Negro orphans] lost nothing in losing their parents, but lost everything in losing their masters. Negroes possess much amiableness of feeling, but not the least steady, permanent affection. 'Out of sight, out of mind' is true for them all. They never grieve twenty-four hours for the death of parents, wives, husbands, or children."[45]

Because of the racist ideas about African-Americans before and after the Civil War, debates over their fate "never contemplated an integration of black workers into the nation's industrial labor force."[46] Rather than simply allow blacks to take their place in American society as another ethnic group attempting to struggle up the class ladder, they were viewed collectively as a "problem." One southerner expressed what was the view of many in 1867 when he wrote: "No permanent lodgment, no enduring part nor lot, must the black and baneful Negroes be permitted to acquire in our country. Already have they outlived their usefulness—if, indeed, they were ever useful at all."[47]

The idea of expelling African-Americans from the society altogether was, in fact, entertained by Lincoln himself, who persuaded Congress to pass legislation subsidizing the voluntary emigration of ex-slaves to the Caribbean.[48] A number of northern states, including Pennsylvania, Ohio, and Illinois, went so far as to pass laws to prevent migration of free blacks into their states. Everywhere, the issue was expressed as a competition between black and white labor, rather than as competition between workers, even though Irish and German workers, and later Polish, Italian, and Slav workers, would be in competition. Thus in 1862, as blacks who had been freed by the Union Army drifted northward, the *Boston Pilot*, an Irish-Catholic newspaper, remarked that "we have already upon us bloody contention between white and black labor. . . . The North is becoming black with refugee Negroes from the South. These wretches crowd our cities, and by overstocking the market of labor, do incalculable injury to white hands."[49] In a similar vein, the Democratic party of Pennsylvania inveighed against the Republican party in 1862 calling them "the party of fanaticism, or crime . . . that seeks to turn the slaves of the Southern states loose to overrun the North and enter into competition with the white laboring masses, thus degrading and insulting their manhood by placing them on an equality with Negroes in their occupations is insulting to our race, and merits our most emphatic and unqualified condemnation."[50]

In the late nineteenth century, whites in California and other far western states would become alarmed at the "yellow peril," and western states would pass discriminatory laws against the Chinese. Similarly, Nativists were instrumental in the passage of the first immigration quota system in 1921, which severely restricted access of eastern and southern Europeans to the United States. In both cases, however, the discrimination was not rooted so far in the past or so deep in the cultural psyche as that aimed against blacks. Eventually, fear of the "yellow peril" subsided, and Asians were able to develop businesses that were patronized by the general white public. And immigrants from southeastern Europe became just so many immigrant groups on the American landscape. Yet, the discriminatory structures and laws enacted against blacks in the South, and the discriminatory practices of the North, persisted for 100 years following the end of slavery. Only when confronted with a major threat to societal order posed by the upheaval of the Civil Rights Movement and the "long hot summers" of ghetto rebellion was American society persuaded to commit itself—for the first time in its history—to equal status for African-Americans. Coming after a century of oppression that left a disproportionate number of black citizens on the last rung of the class ladder, with little wealth, property, or educational resources, the Civil Rights Laws of 1964 could be nothing more than a beginning, a ticket to run in a race for which millions of blacks were ill prepared. The task of redressing the cumulative consequences of past discrimination remained, as well as that of providing truly equal opportunities to those blacks now entering the educational systems and job market.

THE PRESENT AND FUTURE OF RACIAL POLARIZATION

To some extent, the disadvantaged position in which blacks found themselves in 1964 was recognized. Lyndon Johnson launched the War on Poverty during the euphoria of the prosperous era of the late 1960s, a period in which all things seemed possible. Educational disadvantages were addressed through attempts to desegregate schools at all levels. The Head Start program was launched to help disadvantaged children overcome the educational deprivation associated with poverty. The Office of Civil Rights and the Equal Employment Opportunity Commission (EEOC) were established, the latter to oversee the implementation of Title VII, which outlawed discrimination in employment. An open-housing bill was passed, and the government moved to grant blacks access to the ballot box.

From hindsight, we now see that the federal government and the nation did not fully appreciate the magnitude of the task: to eradicate 100 years of deprivation and oppression, and to remove from the hearts and minds of whites the cultural baggage of racism. In time, discouragement over the slow pace of progress set in. Rather than fine-tune efforts begun during the War on Poverty with more sophisticated approaches and additional resources, the "War" was eventually abandoned.

In the atmosphere of economic insecurity that slowly gripped the nation during the downturn of the 1970s and 1980s, even the white middle class became preoccupied with bread-and-butter issues. A white society still imbued with a racist culture turned once more to a familiar tool in a new guise, discrimination. Concern about "equal opportunity" for blacks was replaced with concern over "reverse discrimination," a term symbolizing the growing unwillingness of present generations of whites to individually and collectively accept the challenge (and burden) of rectifying the evils created by past generations of whites. Well-meaning but naive policymakers had not anticipated the depth of white resistance to the full incorporation of blacks into American society or whites' unwillingness to pay the societal cost of achieving that task. Even today, as the National Academy of Science study notes, while whites are increasingly supportive of the "principles" of racial equality, they offer "substantially less support for policies intended to implement principles of racial equality" and continue to shun sustained and close contacts with blacks.[51] Granted that the unfinished agenda is challenging in the best of times, and even painful in periods of economic sluggishness, such as we faced in the 1970s and 1980s, the subjugation of blacks has been even more painful. Their continued economic inequality is not only debilitating to them, but costly to the nation in terms of both the expense of maintaining the dependent poor and the pool of productive talent lost. The financial loss to the nation associated with the lower earnings of blacks has been estimated by Billy J. Tidwell of the Urban League to equal almost 2 percent of our gross national product, or about $104 billion in 1989.[52]

The problem of fully incorporating blacks into the American mainstream is a societal problem that requires compensatory measures to rectify the disadvantages created by racism. Since this is a societal, rather than merely an individual problem, it is the task of government to mobilize resources and persuade white society to support this undertaking. Such a mobilization of resources and sentiment was begun under John F. Kennedy and continued by Lyndon Johnson. It included the passage of the Civil Rights Act and the launching of the War on Poverty. Many successes can be counted.

There are just as many failures as successes, however. The comprehensive study by the National Academy of Science makes this painfully clear. Efforts to desegregate schools have faltered at all levels, and they continue to fail to provide quality education to blacks generally. Head Start remains far below its full potential because of inadequate funding. As a result of the failure of schools to address the educational disadvantages many blacks face because their socioeconomic backgrounds are lower than those of whites, the National Academy's study concludes: "American students leave the schools with black/white achievement gaps not having been appreciably diminished."[53] A college education, the key to "an estimated 50 percent of new jobs created between [1989] and the year 2000," is becoming less and less accessible to blacks.[54] The proportion of black high school graduates entering college is now lower than in 1976, a victim of declining federal aid to education and the virtual abandonment of desegregation in higher education by the federal government during the Reagan administration.[55] Discrimination in housing remains little changed from the past, so much so that blacks remain today the most residentially segregated of all ethnic minorities. According to the findings of Douglas Massey, "a black person who makes more than $50,000 a year will be virtually as segregated as a black person who makes only $2,500 a year."[56]

While blacks have made tremendous strides in employment since 1964, they still lagged far behind whites in both occupational achievement and income by 1990. The optimism of the late 1960s has given way to caution or even pessimism, leading the authors of the National Academy of Sciences' study to conclude that "since the early 1970s, the economic status of blacks relative to whites has, on average, stagnated or deteriorated."[57]

Signs of this stagnation are evident in both income and occupational statistics. In 1989, the median income of two-earner black families was $36,709, only $8,751 higher than the figure for white families with one earner.[58] The wealth gap was even larger, with whites having a net worth more than three times that of blacks. Black upward mobility into the middle class has also slowed. My overall projections for the black middle class for the years 1990 and 2000, which were based on statistics for the years 1973 to 1981, have proven to be overly optimistic.[59] Rather than a black middle class that is 48.6 percent of employed blacks in 1990, the proportion was closer to 45 percent. At the same time, projections for a white middle class of 59.5 percent in 1990 was just about on target, evidence that whites have not suffered economically during this period as much as blacks. Blacks have had an especially difficult time penetrating the seats of power in the workplace. Although constituting 10.1 percent of all employed workers, they held only 6.1 percent of the managerial and professional jobs in 1989.[60] Dispelling the idea that discrimination is a thing of the past, the National Academy of Science study concludes that "a considerable amount of remaining black/white inequality is due to continuing discriminatory treatment of blacks."[61] The task of fully incorporating African-Americans into American society remains "unfinished business."

Much of this failure can be laid at the feet of the federal government, especially the two-term Reagan administration, which not only failed to provide the leadership needed to complete the task but was actively hostile to the only truly successful tools in this struggle: desegregation of the educational system and implementation of equal employment opportunity laws. The Reagan administration's hostility to quotas and timetables, the only meaningful means of forcing reluctant employers to implement affirmative action, has been especially devastating. It is at best naive to believe that employers who have discriminated against blacks in the past will suddenly have a change of heart and voluntarily afford the same opportunities to blacks as they do to whites. The study by the National Academy of Science should erase all doubts, even among the most skeptical. Rather than race declining in significance, as William Wilson suggested in 1978, it is now clear that race remains a deep, pervasive, and intractable characteristic of white society in the 1990s. The most recent indication of persistent racism comes from the finding of a 1990 national NORC survey that over half of all whites still hold the negative stereotype that blacks are lazy and less intelligent than whites.[62]

CONCLUSION

Simple justice and a commitment to equality demand that we free ourselves of racism and discrimination. Yet, as this historical review of race relations in the United States indicates, white resistance to black progress has been so deep, and has gone on for so long, that racism seems intractably built into the American experience. Despite such resistance, however, the problem must be addressed. Today it can be said that the future not only of blacks but the nation itself depends on the full incorporation of minorities into the American mainstream. Because of changing demographics, the economy will depend more on minority workers in the future.[63] By the year 2000, about one-third of all workers entering the labor force will be minorities. When combined with patterns of immigration described by Rubén Rumbaut in his chapter in this book, it is clear that perhaps the single biggest change facing the United States is the increasing racial and ethnic diversity of its population. By the year 2080, all minorities taken together may well constitute slightly over half of the U.S. population. Even the selfish self-interest of whites demands their strong support for affirmative action and the elimination of all forms of racism and discrimination. Yet millions of whites (perhaps the majority) do not understand this. The business community—always preoccupied with the present—is just beginning to glimpse this truth.

It should be clear that the problem of racism and discrimination will not resolve itself. Almost every day the news media report some new sign of racial tension in America. Blacks continue to have a difficult time buying homes because of bias by lenders and lower incomes than whites.[64] Discriminatory election laws in many states continue to hinder the election of blacks at the state level, leading the Justice Department to file suit against the state of Georgia.[65] The upper levels of management continue to elude blacks today as they did ten years ago. Even while the economic position of blacks in the 1980s is declining, as measured by falling incomes and rising unemployment, employment agencies continue to assign job interviews to whites more than to blacks, as CBS's "60 Minutes" documented in the summer of 1990.

I have argued throughout this chapter that racism and discrimination should be seen as societal problems, not simply the aberrations of malevolent individuals. Just as the most positive historical changes, such as emancipation and the Civil Rights Act, resulted from leadership at the highest levels of government, so today it is only the initiative and leadership from state and, especially, the federal government, that are up to the task. Without a massive effort, similar to the Civil Rights era of the 1960s, the racial problems of today will only become worse in the twenty-first century.

TEN

Passages to America

Perspectives on the New Immigration

Rubén G. Rumbaut

Once I thought to write a history of the immigrants in America. Then I discovered that the immigrants were American history.
—OSCAR HANDLIN, *The Uprooted* (1951)

Ironically, those opening lines of Handlin's famous portrait of immigrant America ring truer today than they did when he penned them at mid-century. As Handlin would add in a postscript to the second edition of *The Uprooted* two decades later, immigration was already "a dimly remote memory, generations away, which had influenced the past but appeared unlikely to count for much in the present or future"; and ethnicity, not a common word in 1950, seemed then "a fading phenomenon, a quaint part of the national heritage, but one likely to diminish steadily in practical importance."[1] After all, the passage of restrictive national-origins laws in the 1920s, the Great Depression and World War II had combined to reduce the flow of immigrants to America to its lowest point since the 1820s. But history is forever ambushed by the unexpected. Handlin might have been surprised, if not astonished, to find that in at least one sense the "American Century" seems to be ending much as it had begun: the United States has again become a nation of immigrants, and it is again being transformed in the process. To be sure, while the old may be a prologue to the new, history does not repeat itself, whether as tragedy or as farce. America is not the same society that processed the "huddled masses" through Castle Garden and Ellis Island, and the vast majority of today's immigrants and refugees hail not from Europe, but from the developing countries of the Third World, especially from Asia and Latin America. Not since the peak years of immigration before World War I have so many millions of strangers sought to make their way in America. They make their passages legally and illegally, aboard jumbo jets and in the trunks of cars, by boat and on foot; incredibly, in 1990 a Cuban refugee came across the Straits of Florida riding a windsurfer. Never before has the United States received such diverse

groups—immigrants who mirror in their motives and social class origins
the forces that have forged a new world order in the second half of this
century and who are, unevenly, engaged in the process of becoming the
newest members of American society.[2]

The American ethnic mosaic is being fundamentally altered; ethnicity
itself is being redefined, its new images reified in the popular media and
reflected in myriad and often surprising ways. Immigrants from a score
of nationalities are told that they are all "Hispanics," while far more diverse groups—from India and Laos, China and the Philippines—are
lumped together as "Asians." There are foreign-born mayors of large
American cities, first-generation millionaires who speak broken English,
a proliferation of sweatshops exploiting immigrant labor in an expanding informal economy, and new myths that purport to "explain" the success or failure of different ethnic groups. Along "Calle Ocho" in Miami's
Little Havana, shops post signs to reassure potential customers that
they'll find "English spoken here," while Koreatown retailers in Los Angeles display "Se habla español" signs next to their own Hangul script, a
businesslike acknowledgment that the largest Mexican and Salvadoran
communities in the world outside of Mexico and El Salvador are located
there. In Brooklyn, along Brighton Beach Avenue ("Little Odessa"),
signs written in Cyrillic letters by new Soviet immigrants have replaced
old English and Yiddish signs. In Houston, the auxiliary bishop is a
Cuban-born Jesuit who speaks fluent Vietnamese—an overflow of 6,000
faithful attended his recent ordination, and he addressed them in three
languages—and the best Cuban café is run by Koreans. In a Farsi-
language Iranian immigrant monthly in Los Angeles, *Rah-E-Zendegi*,
next to announcements for "Business English" classes, a classified ad
offers for sale a $20 million square block on Boston's Commonwealth
Avenue, and other ads deal with tax shelters, mergers, and acquisitions.
In Santa Barbara, a preliterate Hmong woman from the Laotian high-
lands, recently converted to Christianity, asked her pastor if she could
enter heaven without knowing how to read; while in Chattanooga, Ten-
nessee, a twelve-year-old Cambodian refugee, Linn Yann, placed second
in a regional spelling bee (she missed on "enchilada"). At the Massachusetts Institute of Technology, Tue Nguyen, a twenty-six-year-old Vietnamese boat refugee, set an MIT record in 1988 by earning his seventh
advanced degree, a doctorate in nuclear engineering, just nine years
after arriving in the United States—and landed a job at IBM designing
technology for the manufacture of semiconductors. In the San Jose telephone directory, the Nguyens outnumber the Joneses fourteen columns
to eight, while in Los Angeles, a Korean restaurant serves kosher bur-
ritos in a largely black neighborhood. And then there was this in the *New
York Times:* "At the annual Lower East Side Jewish Festival yesterday, a

Chinese woman ate a pizza slice in front of Ty Thuan Duc's Vietnamese grocery store. Beside her a Spanish-speaking family patronized a cart with two signs: 'Italian Ices' and 'Kosher by Rabbi Alper.' And after the pastrami ran out, everybody ate knishes."[3]

Immigration to the United States is a social process, patterned within particular structural and historical contexts. The contemporary world has shrunk even as the populations of developing countries have expanded. Societies have become increasingly linked in numerous ways—economically, politically, culturally—as states and markets have become global forms of social organization, and modern consumption standards (especially American life-styles) are diffused worldwide. Over time, social networks are created that serve as bridges of passage to America, linking places of origin with places of destination. Indeed, transnational population movements of workers, refugees, and their families are but one of many other exchanges of capital, commodities, and information across state borders, all facilitated by a postwar revolution in transportation and communication technologies. In general, the patterns reflect the nature of contemporary global inequality: a flow of capital from more developed countries (MDCs) to less developed countries (LDCs), a flow of labor from LDCs to MDCs, and—in an era of Cold War and global superpower confrontation, decolonization and the formation of new states, revolutions and counterrevolutions—continuing flows of refugees, primarily from one Third World country to another.[4]

Still, moving to a foreign country is not easy, even under the most propitious circumstances. In a world of 5 billion people, only a fraction—perhaps 2 percent—are immigrants or refugees residing permanently outside their country of birth. In absolute numbers, the United States remains by far the principal receiving country: by the late 1950s the United States had admitted half of all legal immigrants worldwide, and that proportion had grown to two-thirds by the 1980s. In relative terms, the picture is different: only 6.2 percent of the 1980 U.S. population was foreign-born, a percentage exceeded by many other countries. For example, recent censuses showed a foreign-born population of 20.9 percent in Australia, 16.1 percent in Canada, 8.2 percent in France, 7.6 percent in West Germany, 7.2 percent in Venezuela, 6.8 percent in Argentina, and 6.6 percent in Great Britain. Some smaller countries have much higher proportions, such as Israel (42 percent) and Saudi Arabia (36 percent). But the 14.1 million foreigners counted in the 1980 U.S. census formed the largest immigrant population in the world.[5]

The public image of today's new American immigration clashes with its complex realities. Because the sending countries are generally poor, many Americans believe that the immigrants themselves are poor and uneducated. Because the size of the new immigration is substantial and concentrated in a few states and metropolitan areas, concerns are raised that the newcomers are taking jobs away from the native-born and unfairly burdening taxpayers and public services. Because of the non-European origins of most new immigrants and the undocumented status of many, their prospects for assimilation are sometimes perceived as worse than those of previous flows. And as in the past—if without much of the vitriol and blatant racism of yesterday's nativists—alarms are sounded about the "Balkanization" of America, the feared loss of English as the national language and even of entire regions to potential secessionist movements. As this chapter will attempt to show, such concerns are fundamentally misplaced, even though immigration again plays a central role in an American society in transition. Within its limits, the essay has three objectives: (1) to sketch a portrait of the contours and diversity of recent immigration to the United States, (2) to examine the modes of incorporation of main types of immigrant groups, and (3) to consider some of the determinants of the new immigration and its consequences for the American economy and society.

IMMIGRATION TO THE UNITED STATES:
HISTORICAL TRENDS AND CHANGING POLICIES

Decennial trends in immigration to the United States are summarized in table 10.1 for the century from 1890 to 1989. Authorized immigration reached its highest levels (8.8 million) during 1901–10, more than doubling the number of immigrants admitted in the preceding decade. Much of this flow was initiated by active recruitment on the part of employers, and many immigrants (over one-third) returned home after a few years in the United States—"birds of passage," often young single men, whose movements tended to follow the ups and downs of the American business cycle.[6] In the post–World War II period, legal immigration flows have been much less clearly a function of economic cycles and deliberate recruitment, and much more apt to be sustained by social networks of kin and friends developed over time. Since 1930, moreover, some two-thirds of all legal immigrants to the United States have been women and children.[7] After the peak decade of 1901–10, immigration began a steady decline until the trend reversed itself immediately after World War II. Only 23,000—the smallest annual flow recorded since the early nineteenth century—entered in 1933 and again in 1943, in the midst of the Depression and then the world war. The number of legal immigrants doubled from the 1930s to the 1940s, more than doubled again in the 1950s (to 2.5 million), and more than doubled yet again by the 1980s. Indeed, if the 3 million people who recently qualified for legalization of their status under the amnesty provisions of the Immigration Reform

TABLE 10.1 Historical Trends in the U.S. Foreign-Born Population and Legal Immigration, 1890–1989, by Region of Origin, and Net Immigration Proportion of Total U.S. Population Growth

Census Year/ Decade Ending	Foreign-Born Population		Immigration by Intercensal Decade and Region of Last Residence						Population Growth Due to Net Immigration (%)
	N (1000s)	% Foreign-Born of Total Population	N (1000s)	North/West Europe and Canada (%)	South/East Europe (%)	Latin America (%)	Asia (%)		
1900	10,445	13.6	3,688	44.7	51.8	1.0	2.0		20.3
1910	13,360	14.7	8,795	23.8	69.9	2.1	3.7		39.6
1920	14,020	13.2	5,736	30.3	58.0	7.0	4.3		17.7
1930	14,283	11.6	4,107	53.8	28.7	14.4	2.7		15.0
1940	11,657	8.8	528	58.0	28.3	9.7	3.1		1.6
1950	10,431	6.9	1,035	63.8	12.8	14.9	3.6		8.8
1960	9,738	5.5	2,515	51.8	16.0	22.2	6.1		10.6
1970	9,619	4.7	3,322	30.0	16.3	38.6	12.9		16.1
1980	14,080	6.2	4,493	10.2	11.4	40.3	35.3		17.9
1981–89[a]	NA	NA	5,323	8.0	5.9	37.6	45.1		29.2

SOURCES: U.S. Bureau of the Census, *Statistical Abstracts of the United States*, 109th ed., (Washington, D.C.: Government Printing Office, 1989), tables 1, 5–6, 46; Leon F. Bouvier and Robert W. Gardner, "Immigration to the U.S.: The Unfinished Story," *Population Bulletin* 41 (November 1986), tables 1, 3, 6; U.S. Immigration and Naturalization Service, *Statistical Yearbooks* (Washington, D.C.: Government Printing Office, 1980–89); U.S. Bureau of the Census, *Current Population Reports*, Series P-25, no. 1018 (Washington, D.C.: Government Printing Office, 1989).

[a] Data do not include 478,814 immigrants who had resided in the United States since 1982 and whose status was legalized in fiscal year 1989 under the provisions of the Immigration Reform and Control Act (IRCA) of 1986. Beginning in 1990 an additional 2.6 million legalization applicants, including over one million special agricultural workers (SAW), became eligible to adjust their status to permanent resident.

and Control Act (IRCA) of 1986 were added to the regular admission totals for the 1980s, the decade ending in 1990 would exceed 8 million immigrants and rival the record numbers registered during the first decade of this century.[8] At that time, however, foreign-born persons constituted 14.7 percent of the total U.S. population, more than twice the relatively small 6.2 percent counted in the 1980 census. As table 10.1 also shows, net immigration accounted for nearly 40 percent of total population growth in the United States by 1910—a level not since approached, though net immigration today (adjusting for both emigration and illegal immigration) makes up an increasing proportion of total U.S. population growth. Given a declining national fertility rate, the demographic impact of immigration will continue to grow in importance.[9]

Until 1890 the overwhelming number of immigrants had come from northwest Europe—particularly from Ireland, Great Britain, Germany, and Scandinavia. From Asia, Chinese laborers were recruited, especially to California, after 1850, until their exclusion by federal law in 1882 (rescinded in 1943, when the United States and China were allies in World War II); their place was taken by Japanese immigrants, who were themselves restricted (though not entirely excluded) by the "Gentleman's Agreement" of 1907 between the U.S. and Japanese governments. After 1890, however, a much larger "new" immigration from southern and eastern Europe—particularly from Italy and the Russian and Austro-Hungarian empires—significantly changed the composition of the transatlantic flow. From 1890 to 1920, as shown in table 10.1, well over half of all immigrants to America arrived from these regions. In response, the most restrictive immigration laws in the nation's history were passed in 1921 and 1924 (fully implemented in 1929), limiting the annual flow to 150,000 for Eastern Hemisphere countries and setting national-origins quotas that barred Asians and allocated 82 percent of all visas to northwestern Europeans, 16 percent to southeastern Europeans, and 2 percent to all others. Largely at the urging of American growers, no limits were set on Western Hemisphere countries; it was understood that Mexican labor could be recruited when needed (as happened during World War I and the 1920s, and again during the Bracero Program of contract-labor importation, begun in 1942 to meet labor shortages during World War II but maintained until 1964), and that those laborers could be deported en masse when they were no longer needed (as happened during the 1930s and again during "Operation Wetback" in the mid-1950s).

The McCarran-Walter Act of 1952 retained the national-origins quota system, slightly increasing the annual ceilings for the Eastern Hemisphere to 159,000 and the allocation of visas to northwestern Europeans to 85 percent. It included—again at the urging of growers—a "Texas Proviso" that exempted employers from sanctions for hiring illegal aliens (a loophole, formally closed by IRCA in 1986, that in fact encouraged undocumented immigration, all the more after the Bracero Program was ended in 1964). And it set up a preference system to meet specified labor needs and family reunification priorities. Among numerically restricted immigrants, half of the visas were granted to highly skilled professional and technical workers, and half to immediate relatives of permanent residents and to the parents, siblings, and married children of U.S. citizens. Exempted from the numerical quotas were spouses and unmarried minor children of U.S. citizens. Many British, German, and other European scientists and professionals journeyed to America in the aftermath of the war to pursue opportunities not available in their countries, and the first "refugees" recognized as such by the U.S. government—European "displaced persons" in the late 1940s, Hungarian escapees after the 1956 revolt—were admitted under special legal provisions. In any case, as table 10.1 shows, from 1920 to 1960 the majority of all immigrants to the United States again came from northwest Europe and Canada. After 1960, however, the national composition of the flow changed dramatically, and by the close of the 1980s more than 80 percent of total legal immigration originated in Asia and Latin America.

The Hart-Celler Act of 1965 (fully implemented in 1969), which eliminated the national-origins quota system and basically remained in effect until 1990, has been frequently cited as the main reason for these changes. For a variety of reasons, however, this explanation is insufficient; entry policies do influence but do not determine immigrant flows. As in the past, rules governing immigration are ultimately defeasible and are accompanied by consequences never intended by policymakers. The 1965 Act—amended in 1976, again by the Refugee Act of 1980 and IRCA in 1986—is a case in point. Emmanuel Celler, Brooklyn congressman who cosponsored the 1965 law, had long sought to repeal the discriminatory quota system, but noted that "my efforts were about as useless as trying to make a tiger eat grass or a cow eat meat." He lobbied for the new law—in a political climate changed by the Civil Rights Movement at home and by the geopolitical interests of U.S. foreign policy abroad—by offering opponents family preferences as an alternative to national-origins quotas, confidently predicting that "there will not be, comparatively, many Asians or Africans entering this country . . . since [they] have very few relatives here."[10] Similar pronouncements were made by the Attorney General and other officials in testimony before the Congress; they expected instead that the number of southern and eastern European immigrants would grow. Historically, after all, Asian immigration to the United States had averaged only 2 percent to 4 percent of total admissions—until the 1950s, when 6 percent of legal immigrants came from Asian countries, most of them as brides of U.S. servicemen overseas—and (uncoerced) African immigration had never been a factor. But by the 1980s, Asian immigration accounted for 45 percent of total admissions, and African immigration—though still small in relative numbers—increased eightfold from the early 1960s to the late 1980s. European immigration, in turn, decreased significantly over the same period—precisely the opposite of what had been anticipated.

Immigrants who are legally admitted to the United States fall into two broad categories: those subject to a worldwide limitation and those who are exempt from it. With minor modifications until it was overhauled in late 1990, the 1965 law set a worldwide annual ceiling of 270,000 immigrants, with a maximum of 20,000 per country, under a preference system that greatly emphasized family reunification. The number of immigrants subject to this worldwide limitation remained relatively constant from year to year, since the demand for visas far exceeded the annual limit of 270,000. For example, as of January 1989, there were 2.3 million active registrants awaiting immigrant visas at consular offices abroad.[11] Among these numerically restricted immigrants, 20 percent of the visas were granted to persons certified by the Department of Labor to possess needed job skills (half of them professional, managerial, and technical workers) and their immediate families, and 80 percent to immediate relatives of permanent residents and to siblings and married children of U.S. citizens. But parents as well as spouses and unmarried minor children of American citizens are numerically unrestricted—opening "chain migration" channels for those with family connections—and in addition, refugees and asylees are admitted outside the worldwide limitation under separate ceilings determined each year by the Administration and the Congress (the 1990 refugee ceiling was raised to 125,000). The flow of immigrants thus exempt from numerical limits increased significantly over the past two decades, underscoring the progressive nature of network building processes: for example, 27 percent of the 1.9 million immigrants admitted during 1970–74 came outside the regular quota, as did 36 percent of the 2.4 million admitted during 1975–79, 50 percent of the 2.8 million admitted during 1980–84, and 56 percent of the 3 million admitted during 1985–89.[12] Of all nonquota immigrants legally admitted into the United States in recent years, two-thirds have been immediate relatives of American citizens, and one-third have been admitted as refugees.

Since 1960, the overwhelming majority of refugees have come from Cuba and, since the end of the Indochina War in 1975, primarily from Vietnam, Laos, and Cambodia. Indeed, the consolidation of communist revolutions in Cuba and Vietnam represent by far the worst defeats of American foreign policy in modern history. U.S. refugee policy, a product of the Cold War era, has always been guided by fundamentally political and not purely "humanitarian" objectives, and refugees fleeing from communist-controlled states to the "free world" have served as potent symbols of the legitimacy of American power and foreign policy. Even after the 1980 Refugee Act accepted the United Nations' ideologically neutral definition of a refugee, more than 90 percent of entrants granted refugee or asylee status by the United States during the 1980s continued to be from communist countries; most escapees from noncommunist regimes, such as Salvadorans and Guatemalans fleeing death squads and civil wars in their countries, have instead been generally labeled as "economic migrants"—and deported or driven underground along with other undocumented immigrants.[13] The conferral or denial of asylum or refugee status has significant consequences for immigrants' incorporation in the American economy and society, since persons so classified have the right to work (which illegal immigrants and temporary visitors do not) and to access public assistance programs on the same basis as U.S. citizens (which legal immigrants do not, at least during their first three years in the country).

The undocumented immigrant population has not only grown but diversified during the 1980s. As noted previously, over 3 million immigrants qualified for legalization of their status under IRCA's amnesty provisions by 1989—including residents who had entered the United States illegally prior to 1982, and Special Agricultural Workers (SAWs) who had been employed in seasonal work during the mid-1980s. Immigrants who entered illegally after 1981 (other than SAWs) were not eligible to qualify for legalization under IRCA, and thus reliable data on the size and composition of that population are unavailable. However, a majority of Central Americans in the country today are probably included—themselves in some measure an unintended consequence of U.S. policy and intervention in their home region—as well as an estimated 100,000 Irish immigrants who have, since 1982, overstayed their temporary visitor visas and clustered in historical areas of Irish settlement in Boston and New York.[14] Furthermore, again contrary to official predictions, IRCA has not stopped the flow of unauthorized migrants; in fact, the number of apprehensions along the Mexican border increased abruptly after 1989 and may again reach historically high levels.[15] In addition, the growing backlog and waiting periods faced by persons applying legally for numerically restricted immigrant visas—above all in Mexico and the Philippines—are likely to encourage further extralegal immigration. Former Immigration and Naturalization Service (INS) Commissioner Leonel Castillo estimated in 1990 that the waiting period for Mexicans applying under the second preference (spouses and children of permanent U.S. residents) could jump to 22 years, and to 10 to 17 years for Filipinos under various family preference categories.[16]

IMMIGRATION TO THE UNITED STATES:
CONTEMPORARY TRENDS AND THE CHANGING
ETHNIC MOSAIC

National Origins of the New Immigration

Quinquennial trends in U.S. immigration from 1960 to 1989 are summarized in table 10.2, broken down by the major sending countries. While today's immigrants come from over 100 different nation-states, some countries send many more than others, despite the egalitarian numerical quotas provided by U.S. law. The 21 countries listed in table 10.2 accounted for nearly three-fourths of all legal immigration since 1960. One pattern, a continuation of trends already under way in the 1950s, is quite clear: immigration from the more developed countries has declined over time and that from less developed countries has grown steadily. Among the MDCs, this pattern is clearest for Canada, Great Britain, Italy, and Germany, with the sharpest reductions occurring during the 1960s. Although traditional countries of immigration in the past, their prosperous postwar economies dampened the relative attraction of America, while many Italian "guest-workers" sought instead newly opened opportunities in Germany and Switzerland. The smaller flows of Polish and Soviet refugees have oscillated over time, reflecting changes in exit policies in those countries and in their bilateral relations with the United States. The flow from Japan, which as of the early 1960s was still the largest source of immigrants from Asia, has remained small and stable at about 4,000 per year, nearly half entering as spouses of U.S. citizens—in part reflecting labor shortages and exit restrictions at home. Among the LDCs, the major countries of immigration are located either in the Caribbean Basin—in the immediate periphery of the United States—or are certain Asian nations also characterized by significant historical, economic, political, and military ties to the United States. These historical relationships, and the particular social networks to which they give rise, are crucial to an understanding of the new immigration, both legal and illegal—and help explain why most LDCs are not similarly represented in contemporary flows, as might be predicted by orthodox "push-pull" or "supply-demand" theories of transnational labor movements.

In fact, just eight countries have accounted for more than half of all legal immigration since 1975: Mexico, the Philippines, Vietnam, South Korea, China, India, Cuba, and the Dominican Republic. Of these, Mexico and the Philippines alone have sent 20 percent of all legal immigrants to the United States over the past three decades, and Mexico also remains by far the source of most unauthorized immigration. Of the 3 million immigrants who qualified for legalization of their status under IRCA by 1989, about 2 million were Mexican nationals; and while most

TABLE 10.2 Trends in Legal Immigration to the United States, 1960–89, by Region and Principal Sending Countries

Region/Country of Birth	Period of Immigrant Admission to U.S. Permanent Resident Status						Total
	1960–64	1965–69	1970–74	1975–79	1980–84	1985–89[a]	
Worldwide:	1,419,013	1,794,736	1,923,413	2,412,588	2,825,036	3,028,368	13,403,154
Latin America	485,016	737,781	768,199	992,719	995,307	1,201,108	5,180,130
Asia	114,571	258,229	574,222	918,362	1,347,705	1,336,056	4,909,145
Europe and Canada	803,596	766,347	530,925	429,353	388,700	297,609	3,216,530
Africa	11,756	21,710	34,336	51,291	73,948	89,636	282,677
More Developed Countries:							
Canada	167,482	136,371	54,313	60,727	57,767	56,701	533,361
United Kingdom	123,573	117,364	56,371	65,848	73,800	66,682	503,638
Italy	86,860	109,750	106,572	43,066	20,128	14,672	381,048
Germany	138,530	83,534	36,971	32,110	33,086	34,464	358,695
Poland*	43,758	33,892	20,252	22,194	31,506	44,581	196,183
Japan	23,327	26,802	20,649	21,993	20,159	21,177	132,107
U.S.S.R.*	10,948	6,292	4,941	28,640	46,530	22,451	119,802

Less Developed Countries:

Mexico	217,827	213,689	300,341	324,611	330,690	361,445	1,749,603
Philippines	15,753	57,563	152,706	196,397	215,504	251,042	888,965
Cuba*	65,219	183,499	101,070	176,998	53,698	109,885	690,369
China^b	20,578	65,712	81,202	107,762	168,754	194,330	638,338
Korea	9,521	18,469	93,445	155,505	163,088	173,799	613,827
Vietnam*	603	2,564	14,661	122,987	246,463	149,480	536,758
Dominican Republic	26,624	57,441	63,792	77,786	98,121	127,631	451,395
India	3,164	18,327	67,283	96,982	116,282	134,841	436,879
Jamaica	7,838	49,480	65,402	72,656	100,607	104,623	400,606
Colombia	27,118	39,474	29,404	43,587	50,910	55,990	246,483
Haiti	7,211	24,325	28,917	30,180	40,265	82,156	213,054
Laos*	NA	NA	166	8,430	102,244	46,937	157,777
El Salvador	6,766	7,615	9,795	20,169	38,801	57,408	140,554
Cambodia*	NA	NA	166	5,459	58,964	54,918	119,507

SOURCES: U.S. Immigration and Naturalization Service, *Annual Reports* (Washington, D.C.: Government Printing Office, 1960–77); and U.S. Immigration and Naturalization Service, *Statistical Yearbooks* (Washington, D.C.: Government Printing Office, 1978–89).

^a Data do not include 478,814 persons whose status was legalized in fiscal year 1989 under the Immigration Reform and Control Act (IRCA).

^b Includes Mainland China and Taiwan.

* Denotes country from which the majority of immigrants to the United States have been admitted as refugees.

of the remaining amnesty applicants came from nearby Caribbean Basin countries, Filipinos ranked sixth (behind Salvadorans, Guatemalans, Haitians, and Colombians, but ahead of Dominicans, Jamaicans, and Nicaraguans).[17] Indeed, Mexicans and Filipinos comprise, respectively, the largest "Hispanic" and "Asian" populations in the United States today.[18]

Not surprisingly, Mexico and the Philippines share the deepest structural linkages with the United States, including a long history of dependency relationships, external intervention, and (in the case of the Philippines) colonization. In both countries, decades of active agricultural labor recruitment by the United States—of Mexicans to the Southwest, Filipinos to plantations in Hawaii and California—preceded the establishment of self-sustaining migratory social networks. In the case of Mexico, the process has evolved over several generations. From California to Texas, the largest Mexican-origin communities in the United States are still located in former Mexican territories that were annexed in the last century, and they are today linked to entire communities on the other side of the border.[19] In the Philippines—unlike Puerto Rico, which also came under U.S. hegemony as a result of the 1898 Spanish-American War—its formal independence from the United States after World War II has since led to different patterns of immigration. During the half-century of U.S. colonization, the Americanization of Filipino culture was pervasive, especially in the development of a U.S.-styled educational system and the adoption of English as an official language, and the United States today is not only the Philippines' major trading partner but also accounts for more than half of total foreign investment there.[20] Since the 1960s, as will be detailed below, the Philippines have sent the largest number of immigrant professionals to the United States, as well as a high proportion of the many international students enrolled in American colleges and universities. Moreover, the extensive U.S. military presence in the Philippines—including the largest American bases in the Asian-Pacific region—has fueled immigration through marriages with U.S. citizens stationed there, through unique arrangements granting U.S. citizenship to Filipinos who served in the armed forces during World War II, and through direct recruitment of Filipinos into the U.S. Navy. Remarkably, by 1970 there were more Filipinos in the U.S. Navy (14,000) than in the entire Filipino navy.[21] During 1978–85, more than 51 percent of the 12,500 Filipino babies born in the San Diego metropolitan area—site of the largest naval station in the United States and the third largest destination of Filipinio immigrants—were delivered at just one hospital: the U.S. Naval Hospital.[22]

Among the other six leading countries of recent immigration, linkages unwittingly structured by American foreign policy and military intervention since the 1950s are most salient in the exodus of the Koreans and Vietnamese. Indeed, an ironic consequence of the wars that took tens of thousands of Americans to Korea and Vietnam is that tens of thousands of Koreans and Vietnamese—including many Amerasians— have since come to America, albeit through quite different routes. Emigration connections variously shaped by U.S. intervention, foreign policies, and immigration policies are also a common denominator in the exodus of the Chinese after the 1949 revolution, the Cubans after the 1959 revolution, and the Dominicans after the U.S.-backed coup in 1965. In the case of India, South Korea, and Taiwan, large-scale U.S. foreign aid, technical assistance, trade, and direct investment (which in India surpassed that of the United Kingdom soon after decolonization) helped to forge the channels for many professionals and exchange students to come to America.[23] It has been estimated that since the early 1950s fewer than 10 percent of the many thousands of students from South Korea, Taiwan, China, and Hong Kong who have come to the United States for training on nonimmigrant visas ever returned home; instead, many adjusted their status and gained U.S. citizenship through occupational connections with American industry and business, thus becoming eligible to send for family members later on.[24] None of this is to suggest, of course, that the complex macrostructural determinants that shape migration flows—above all global market forces, which will be considered further on, and internal dynamics and crises in the sending countries—can be reduced to politico-military factors or state policies, but rather to focus attention on the importance of particular historical patterns of U.S. influence in the creation and consolidation of social networks that over time give the process of immigration its cumulative and seemingly spontaneous character.[25]

Social Class Origins of the New Immigration

There is no doubt that wage differentials between the United States and the LDCs act as a magnet to attract immigrants to America. This is especially the case along the 2,000-mile-long border between the United States and Mexico—the largest point of "North-South" contact in the world. During the 1980s, the minimum wage in the United States ($3.35 per hour) was six times the prevailing rate in Mexico, and higher still than most rates in Central America. But wage differentials alone do not explain why even in neighboring Mexico only a small fraction of the population ever undertakes the journey to "El Norte." What is more, 10 of the 15 poorest nations of the world (with sizable populations and national per capita incomes below U.S. $200)—Chad, Zaire, Mozambique, Mali, Burkina Faso, Nepal, Malawi, Bangladesh, Uganda, and Burma— are scarcely represented among immigrants to America, if at all. Significantly, the only sizable groups of recent immigrants who do hail from the world's 15 poorest countries—from Cambodia, Laos, and Vietnam, and (though to a much lesser extent) Ethiopia and Afghanistan—have been admitted as political refugees.[26]

Moreover, the fact that most newcomers to America come from comparatively poorer nations—such as the 14 LDCs listed above in table 10.2—does not mean that the immigrants themselves are drawn from the uneducated, unskilled, or unemployed sectors of their countries of origin. Available evidence from the INS, summarized in table 10.3, indicates just the opposite. Over the past two decades, an average of more than 60,000 immigrant engineers, scientists, university professors, physicians, nurses, and other professionals and executives have been admitted each year into the United States. From the 1960s through the early 1980s, about one-third of all legal immigrants to the United States (excluding dependents) were high-status professionals, executives, or managers in their countries of origin. The proportion of these so-called brain drain elites declined somewhat to 26.5 percent by the late 1980s—still a higher percentage than that of the native-born American population—despite the overwhelming majority of immigrants having been admitted under family preferences over the past two decades. In part, these data suggest that while many "pioneer" immigrants have entered with formal credentials under the occupational preferences of U.S. law, their close kin who join them later are drawn from the same social classes—accounting for both the relative stability and similarity of their flows over time, if with a gradually diminishing upper-crust occupational profile as family "chain migration" processes evolve and expand. But the dynamics of particular types of flows are much more complex than might seem at first glance.

Take, for example, the case of so-called foreign medical graduates (FMGs). Worldwide, about 5 percent of physicians have immigrated to foreign countries in recent decades, of whom about half have come to the United States—75,000 entered in the 1965–74 decade alone.[27] During the 1950s and 1960s, enrollments in U.S. medical schools remained virtually stationary, while the American health care system expanded greatly (all the more after the passage of Medicaid and Medicare in the early 1960s), creating many vacancies in the number of internship and residency positions in U.S. hospitals (especially in underserved areas such as inner cities, which did not attract U.S. medical graduates). The demand, reinforced by the new channels opened up by U.S. immigration law and the higher salaries offered by U.S. hospitals, enabled FMGs and nurses to flock to America, particularly from developing countries such as India and the Philippines, where English-language textbooks are used and where many more professionals were graduating than the economies could absorb. Few of these people were directly recruited by

TABLE 10.3 Trends in Occupational Backgrounds of Legal Immigrants, 1967–87, by Region and Main Sending Countries: Percentage of Immigrant Professionals, Executives, and Managers, in Regional Rank Order

Region/Country of Birth	Reported Occupation of Immigrants Prior to Admission to Permanent Resident Status[a] (Percentage Professional Specialty, Executives, and Managers)				
	1967	1972	1977	1982	1987
Worldwide:	32.4	36.0	33.0	31.9	26.5
Asia	59.3	67.3	53.2	39.9	39.5
Africa	53.7	67.3	60.7	45.8	39.4
Europe and Canada	29.7	26.6	41.5	44.4	40.7
Latin America	22.3	13.8	15.4	15.8	11.3
More Developed Countries:					
Japan	57.6	50.1	44.6	48.5	42.2
Canada	48.7	51.6	61.3	57.9	55.0
United Kingdom	43.3	51.5	58.3	60.8	52.9
U.S.S.R.*	40.9	41.0	42.0	39.1	47.0
Poland*	32.3	27.1	30.6	32.1	26.9
Germany	30.5	43.5	37.2	40.9	35.7
Italy	8.4	8.5	21.0	30.8	33.6
Less Developed Countries:					
India	90.6	91.6	79.1	73.7	61.7
Korea	80.5	72.9	49.6	42.9	44.0
Philippines	60.2	71.6	46.8	44.9	45.9
China[b]	48.6	52.5	53.9	47.3	34.3
Vietnam*	71.6	56.9	36.6	11.4	7.7
Cuba*	33.1	13.9	14.4	22.3	5.1
Colombia	32.5	27.5	17.4	20.2	20.6
Haiti	23.3	26.8	14.1	17.4	8.1
Jamaica	19.1	15.9	33.4	21.6	18.6
Dominican Republic	14.5	15.3	13.1	13.8	12.2
El Salvador	15.2	16.0	10.0	13.0	7.1
Mexico	8.5	5.1	6.6	7.0	5.9
Cambodia*	NA	NA	NA	7.1	2.0
Laos*	NA	NA	NA	4.7	2.1

SOURCES: U.S. Immigration and Naturalization Service, *Annual Reports* (Washington, D.C.: Government Printing Office, 1967, 1972, 1977); and U.S. Immigration and Naturalization Service, *Statistical Yearbooks* (Washington, D.C.: Government Printing Office, 1982, 1987).

[a] About two-thirds of immigrants admitted as permanent residents report no prior occupation to the INS; they are mainly homemakers, children, retired persons, and other dependents. Data above are based on 152,925 immigrants who reported an occupation in 1967; 157,241 in 1972; 189,378 in 1977; 203,440 in 1982; and 242,072 in 1987.

[b] Includes Mainland China and Taiwan.

*Denotes country from which the majority of immigrants to the United States have been admitted as refugees.

American hospitals; most made their own arrangements through professional networks of friends who were or had been in the United States, or by writing blind letters to hospitals listed in American Medical Association or state directories. By the mid-1970s there were about 9,500 Filipino and 7,000 Indian FMGs in the United States—more than the number of American black physicians—as well as some 3,000 FMGs each from Cuba and South Korea, and 2,000 each from Mexico and Iran. Perhaps the most extraordinary instance occurred in 1972, when practically the entire graduating class of the new medical school in Chiangmai, Thailand, chartered a plane to America. The effect of this kind of emigration on the sending countries' domestic stock of physicians has varied greatly: in 1972 the number of Mexican and Indian FMGs in the United States represented only 4 percent of Mexico's stock and 5 percent of India's, but the proportion was 18 percent of South Korea's, 22 percent of Iran's, 27 percent of Thailand's, 32 percent of the Dominican Republic's, 35 percent of Taiwan's, 43 percent of Cuba's, 63 percent of the Philippines', and—incredibly—95 percent of Haiti's. Since the late 1970s the flow of FMGs has declined, due to a constricting job market (as the supply of U.S.-trained physicians has increased) and the passage of more restrictive U.S. visa and medical licensing requirements, but by the late 1980s, FMGs still comprised 20 percent of the nation's physicians.[28]

The worldwide trends presented in table 10.3 conceal a wide range in the class character of contemporary immigration to the United States; among the principal sending countries there are considerable differences in the occupational backgrounds of immigrants. "Brain drain" immigrants have dominated the flows of Indians, Koreans, Filipinos, and Chinese (including Taiwanese) since the 1960s. High proportions are also in evidence among the Japanese, Canadian, and British groups—although their immigration flows are smaller, as seen earlier—as well as among some refugee groups, particularly Soviet Jews and Armenians and the more sizable first waves of refugees from Vietnam and Cuba. By contrast, immigration from Mexico, El Salvador, the Dominican Republic, and (until very recently) Italy has consisted predominantly of manual laborers and low-wage service workers, as has also been the case among refugees from Laos and Cambodia, and the more recent waves of Vietnamese, Cubans, and Haitians. Between these extremes in occupational profiles are Colombians, Jamaicans, Germans, and Poles.

Over time, the drop in the proportion of highly skilled immigrants within particular national groups is most apparent among non-European refugees, consistent with a general pattern that characterizes refugee flows: initial waves tend to come from the higher socioeconomic strata, followed later by heterogeneous working-class waves more representative of the society of origin. As table 10.3 shows, rapid declines are seen among refugees who come from poor countries, such as Vietnam, where only a small proportion of the population is well educated.

The information provided in table 10.3, while useful as a first step to sort out the diverse class origins of the new immigration, is limited in several ways. The INS does not collect data on the educational backgrounds of legal immigrants, nor on the occupations they enter once in the United States, nor, for that matter, on the characteristics of undocumented immigrants or of emigrants (those who leave the United States after a period of time, estimated at about 160,000 annually). A more precise picture can be drawn from the last available census, which counted a foreign-born population of 14.1 million persons in 1980 (including an estimated 2.1 million undocumented immigrants). Census data on several relevant indicators for the largest foreign-born groups in the United States as of 1980 are presented in table 10.4, rank-ordered by their proportions of college graduates. The picture that emerges shows clearly that the foreign-born are not a homogeneous population; instead, to borrow a term from Milton Gordon, the formation of different "ethclasses" is apparent. Less apparent is the fact that within particular nationalities there is often also considerable socioeconomic diversity.

An upper stratum is composed of foreign-born groups whose educational and occupational attainments significantly exceed the average for the native-born American population. Without exception, all of them are of Asian origin—Indians, Chinese (especially Taiwanese), Filipinos, Koreans, and Japanese—with the most recently immigrated groups reflecting the highest levels of attainment. It is precisely this stratum that accounts for the popularization of the recent myth of Asian-Americans as "model minorities," whose children are overrepresented among the nation's high school valedictorians and in admissions to elite universities from Berkeley to Harvard. For instance, foreign-born students collected 55 percent of all doctoral degrees in engineering awarded by American universities in 1985, with one-fifth of all engineering doctorates going to students from Taiwan, India, and South Korea alone. In 1988 the top two winners of the Westinghouse Science Talent Search, the nation's most prestigious high school competition, were immigrant students from India and Taiwan in New York City public schools; indeed, 22 of the top 40 finalists were children of immigrants. Moreover, the stories of competitive success are not limited to science and math-based fields (where Asian immigrant students tend to concentrate to reduce their English-language handicaps): the 1985 U.S. National Spelling Bee champ was Chicago schoolboy Balu Natarajan, who speaks Tamil at home, and the 1988 winner was a thirteen-year-old girl from a California public school, Indian-born Rageshree Ramachandran, who correctly spelled "elegiacal" to beat out runner-up Victor Wang, a Chinese-American.[29]

TABLE 10.4 Characteristics of the Largest Foreign-Born Groups in the United States in 1980, Ranked by Their Proportion of College Graduates, Compared to the Native-Born Groups

| Country of Birth | Persons (N) | Education[a] | | Occupation[b] | | Year of Immigration | | | Not a Citizen (%) |
		College Graduate (%)	High School Graduate (%)	Professional Specialty (%)	Service Occup. (%)	1970–80 (%)	1960–69 (%)	Pre-1960 (%)	
Above U.S. Average:									
India	206,087	66.2	88.9	42.8	5.3	76.8	19.3	3.9	76.0
China (Taiwan)	75,353	59.8	89.1	30.4	13.7	81.1	17.0	1.9	71.1
Philippines	501,440	41.8	74.0	20.1	16.2	63.6	22.6	13.8	55.3
Korea	289,885	34.2	77.8	14.7	17.0	83.9	13.0	3.1	65.4
China (Mainland)	286,120	29.5	60.0	16.8	24.4	47.5	27.3	25.2	49.7
Japan	221,794	24.4	78.0	13.6	20.8	45.2	22.7	32.1	56.7
Close to U.S. Average:									
England	442,499	16.4	74.6	17.4	12.2	21.9	22.0	56.1	42.0
Cuba	607,814	16.1	54.9	9.2	12.2	26.9	60.4	12.8	54.9
U.S.S.R.	406,022	15.7	47.2	15.9	13.2	24.3	5.3	70.4	27.4

Germany	849,384	14.9	67.3	13.4	14.1	10.6	20.6	68.8	21.4
Colombia	143,508	14.6	62.8	8.1	15.8	55.0	37.1	7.9	75.1
Canada	842,859	14.3	61.8	16.2	11.4	15.2	20.1	64.7	39.0
Vietnam	231,120	12.9	62.1	8.6	16.4	97.6	2.1	0.2	88.9
Jamaica	196,811	11.0	63.5	10.2	29.9	58.7	29.8	11.6	63.7
Below U.S. Average:									
Poland	418,128	10.0	40.5	10.8	13.5	11.0	14.5	74.5	22.2
Greece	210,998	9.5	40.4	8.0	25.0	32.0	27.7	40.3	35.0
Ireland	197,817	8.8	52.1	14.5	21.7	7.3	14.5	78.1	18.8
Italy	831,992	5.3	28.6	6.1	16.3	12.1	18.2	69.8	22.6
Dominican Republic	169,147	4.3	30.1	3.1	18.5	56.8	37.2	6.1	74.5
Portugal	211,614	3.3	22.3	2.3	10.0	45.0	34.0	21.0 –	61.6
Mexico	2,199,221	3.0	21.3	2.5	16.6	57.8	21.9	20.3	76.4
Σ Foreign-Born	14,079,906	15.8	53.1	12.0	16.1	39.5	22.3	38.2	49.5
Σ Native-Born	212,465,899	16.3	67.3	12.3	12.7	—	—	—	—

SOURCES: U.S. Bureau of the Census, *Statistical Abstracts of the United States*, 109th ed. (Washington, D.C.: Government Printing Office, 1989); table 47; and U.S. Bureau of the Census, *1980 Census of Population: Detailed Population Characteristics*, PC80-1-D1-A (Washington, D.C.: Government Printing Office, 1984), table 254.

[a] Years of school completed by persons aged twenty-five years or older.
[b] Present occupation of employed persons aged sixteen years or older.

Yet also during the 1980s, the highest rates of poverty and welfare dependency in the United States have been recorded among Asian-origin groups, particularly refugees from Indochina. One study found poverty rates ranging from over 50 percent for the Vietnamese to 75 percent for the Chinese-Vietnamese and the Lao, 80 percent for Cambodians, and nearly 90 percent for the Hmong. And Southeast Asian and, to a lesser extent, Korean workers are much in evidence, along with undocumented Mexican and Salvadoran immigrants, in a vast underground sweatshop economy that has expanded during the 1980s and into the 1990s in Southern California. Those findings debunk genetic and cultural stereotypes that have been propounded in the mass media as explanations of "Asian" success, and point instead to the diversity of recent Asian immigration and to the class advantages of particular Asian-origin groups.[30]

A middle stratum evident in table 10.4, composed of groups whose educational and occupational characteristics are close to the U.S. average, is more heterogeneous in terms of national origins. It includes older immigrants from England, the U.S.S.R., Germany, and Canada (the majority entering the United States prior to 1960), and more recent immigrants from Cuba, Colombia, Vietnam, and Jamaica. The post-1980 waves of Mariel refugees from Cuba and Vietnamese "boat people" from more modest social class backgrounds are not reflected in the data in table 10.4, since they arrived after the census was taken; the 1990 census will probably reflect much wider differences in the characteristics of these two refugee populations, underscoring the internal diversification of particular national groups over time.

Finally, as table 10.4 shows, a lower stratum is composed of working-class groups who fall substantially below native-born norms. It includes recent immigrants from Mexico and the Dominican Republic—of whom a substantial number entered without documents—but also includes less visible, older European immigrants from Poland, Greece, Ireland, Italy, and Portugal. The 1990 census most probably will add to this stratum several groups who have arrived in sizable numbers during the past decade, including Salvadorans, Guatemalans, Nicaraguans, Haitians, and Cambodian and Laotian refugees. Not included in this bottom stratum are Puerto Ricans, since they are not "foreign-born" but are U.S. citizens by birth; but their aggregate socioeconomic characteristics would place them here, and their large-scale post—World War II migration to the mainland resembles in many respects that of Mexican labor immigration. Mexicans and Puerto Ricans make up the overwhelming majority of the supranational "Hispanic" population of the United States, and their particular characteristics and circumstances have colored the construction of negative ethnic typifications.[31] In any case, these findings, too, debunk cultural stereotypes that have been propounded in the mass media as explanations for the lack of "Hispanic" success in contrast to that of "Asians" and white European ethnics, and point instead to the diversity of recent Latin American immigration and to the class disadvantages of particular groups.

Significantly, there is an imperfect correlation between educational and occupational attainment among these groups. For example, as table 10.4 shows, the percentage of longer-established Canadian and certain European immigrants employed in professional specialties actually exceeds the respective proportion of their groups who are college graduates. By contrast, the percentage of more recently arrived Asian and Latin American immigrants who are employed in the professions is generally far below their respective proportions of college graduates—and, for that matter, far below their respective proportions of those who held professional positions in their countries of origin prior to admission into the United States (as documented previously in table 10.3). These discrepancies offer a clue about barriers such as English proficiency and strict licensing requirements that regulate entry into the professions and that recent immigrants—most of them nonwhite, non-European, and non–English speakers—must confront as they seek to make their way in America. In response, some immigrants shift instead to entrepreneurship as an avenue of economic advancement—and as an alternative to employment in segmented labor markets. Indeed, the process of occupational and economic adaptation is complex and not simply a function of the "human capital" brought by the immigrants. Their varying social-class resources at the time of entry interact with other differences in the contexts of reception experienced by particular groups—such as government policies and programs, local labor markets, cultural prejudices and racial discrimination, and existing ethnic communities and networks—to mold their diverse modes of incorporation in the American economy and society.

In general, however, immigrants who come to the United States are positively selected groups, not only in terms of their above-average urban backgrounds and socioeconomic resources compared to homeland norms, but also in terms of their ambition, determination, and willingness to work and to take risks. Legally or illegally, most make their passages to America not so much to escape perennial unemployment or destitution, but to seek opportunities for advancement that are unavailable in their own countries. They are "innovators," in Robert Merton's sense of the term, who choose immigration as a feasible solution to a widening gap between life goals and actual means, between their own rising aspirations and the dim possibilities for fulfilling them at home. The lure of America is greatest for those who experience this gap at its widest and who have the requisite resources and connections to meet the costs of immigration to a foreign world—such as well-educated cosmopolitans in the less developed countries—and those groups have taken full advantage of the preferences available under U.S. law. Immigration requires both restlessness and resourcefulness, and on the whole, the main reason the richest of the rich and the poorest of the poor do not immigrate is because they are, respectively, unmoved or unable to move.

Even undocumented migrants must be able to cover the often considerable costs of transportation and surreptitious entry into the United States, as must refugees such as "boat people" be willing to take extraordinary risks and pay the costs of surreptitious exit from their countries. Although the socioeconomic origins of unauthorized immigrants are modest by U.S. standards, they consistently meet or surpass the average for their countries of origins. Recent studies report that "coyotes" (smugglers) charge U.S. $700 to get border-crossers from Mexico to Los Angeles, $500 to Houston, $250 to $450 to San Antonio—in large groups the fee may be lowered to $200—and that undocumented Mexican immigrants are on average more urban and literate than the general Mexican population. In the Dominican Republic, it may cost $1,000 to $2,000 to obtain papers and be smuggled out of the country, and undocumented Dominicans actually tend to be more educated than those who immigrate legally. Haitian "boat people" reportedly pay $500 to $1,000 per person to buy passage aboard barely seaworthy craft to South Florida. A decade ago in Vietnam, ethnic Chinese and Vietnamese refugees were paying five to ten gold pieces ($2,000 to $4,000) per adult to cross the South China Sea in flimsy fishing boats—a price well beyond the means of the average Vietnamese. To afford this often required ingenious exchange schemes through kinship networks. For example, a family in Vietnam planning to escape by boat contacted another that had decided to stay to obtain the necessary gold for the passage; they in turn arranged with family members of both already in the United States (usually "first wave" refugees) for the relatives of the escaping family to pay an equivalent amount in dollars to the second family's relatives.[32] Those who surmount such obstacles and succeed in reaching America are far from being representative of the population of their societies of origin. They, too, add to the vitality, energy, and innovativeness that immigrants contribute to American society.

THE NEW IMMIGRANTS IN AMERICA: IMPACTS ON ECONOMIC AND CULTURAL INSTITUTIONS

Patterns of Settlement and Incorporation

Although fewer than one in ten persons in the United States today is an immigrant, the impact of the new immigration on American communities is much more significant than might appear at first glance. The main reason is that immigrants tend to concentrate in urban areas where co-ethnic communities have been established by past immigration. Such spatial concentrations serve to provide newcomers with manifold sources of moral, social, cultural, and economic support that are unavailable to immigrants who are more dispersed. In general, patterns of concentration or dispersal vary for different classes of immigrants (professionals, entrepreneurs, manual laborers) with different types of legal status (regular immigrants, refugees, the undocumented). The likelihood of dispersal is greatest among immigrant professionals—who tend to rely more on their qualifications and job offers than on pre-existing ethnic communities—and, at least initially, among recent refugees who are sponsored and resettled through official government programs that have sought deliberately to minimize their numbers in particular localities. However, refugee groups, too, have shown a tendency to gravitate as "secondary migrants" to areas where their compatriots have clustered (for example, Cubans to South Florida, Southeast Asians to California). The likelihood of concentration is greatest among working-class immigrants—who tend to rely more on the assistance offered by pre-existing kinship networks—and among business-oriented groups, who tend to settle in large cities. Dense ethnic enclaves provide immigrant entrepreneurs with access to sources of cheap labor, working capital and credit, and dependable markets. Over time, as the immigrants become naturalized U.S. citizens, local strength in numbers also provides opportunities for political advancement and representation of ethnic minority group interests at the ballot box.[33] Social networks are thus crucial for an understanding not only of migration processes, as noted earlier, but also of adaptation processes and settlement patterns in areas of final immigrant destination.

Table 10.5 lists the states and metropolitan areas of principal immigrant settlement (SMSAs) in the United States as of 1980. In addition, table 10.5 provides comparative data on the places of settlement of recent legal immigrants (those admitted during 1987–89) as well as of the 3 million illegal immigrants who qualified for legalization of their status under IRCA in 1989. While there are immigrants today in every one of the fifty states, just six states (California, New York, Florida, Texas, Illinois, and New Jersey) accounted for two-thirds of the total 1980 foreign-born population, for nearly three-fourths of 1987–89 legal immigrants, and for almost nine-tenths of all IRCA applicants. A pattern of increasing spatial concentration is clear for the four states of greatest immigrant settlement (California, New York, Florida, and Texas). California alone, which in 1980 already accounted for 25 percent of all the foreign-born, drew 29 percent of 1987–89 immigrants and a whopping 54 percent of IRCA applicants. New York and Florida combined for another quarter of the foreign-born in 1980 and also of 1987–89 immigrants, but only 11 percent of IRCA applicants. Texas, whose share of immigrants increased

TABLE 10.5 States and Metropolitan Areas of Principal Immigrant Settlement in the United States: Location of the 1980 Foreign-Born Population, 1987–89 Immigrants, and 1989 Legalization Applicants

	Foreign-Born Population, 1980			Immigrants, 1987–89[a]		IRCA Applicants, 1989[b]	
	N	Percentage of Total Population	Percentage of U.S. Foreign-Born Population	N	Percentage of Total Immigrants Admitted	N	Percentage of Total Legalization Applicants
States:							
California	3,580,033	15.1	25.4	530,795	28.6	1,636,325	53.9
New York	2,388,938	13.6	17.0	336,845	18.1	170,601	5.6
Florida	1,058,732	10.9	7.5	155,108	8.4	160,262	5.3
Texas	856,213	6.0	6.1	123,446	6.6	440,989	14.5
Illinois	823,696	7.2	5.9	81,011	4.4	158,979	5.2
New Jersey	757,822	10.3	5.4	100,697	5.4	44,184	1.5
Metropolitan Areas:							
New York, N.Y.-N.J.	1,946,800	21.3	13.8	285,840	15.4	153,072	5.0

Los Angeles-Long Beach, Calif.	1,664,793	22.3	11.8	231,096	12.4	809,248	26.6
Chicago, Ill.	744,930	10.5	5.3	64,821	3.5	136,081	4.5
Miami-Hialeah, Fla.	578,055	35.6	4.1	93,776	5.1	66,792	2.2
San Francisco-Oakland, Calif.	551,769	15.4	3.9	81,780	4.4	64,111	2.1
Boston, Mass.	280,080	10.1	2.0	38,218	2.0	12,512	0.4
Anaheim-Santa Ana, Calif.	257,194	13.3	1.8	42,835	2.3	144,521	4.8
Washington, D.C.	249,994	8.2	1.8	56,676	3.1	31,182	1.0
San Diego, Calif.	235,593	12.7	1.7	38,332	2.1	98,875	3.3
Houston, Tex.	220,861	7.6	1.6	33,296	1.8	131,186	4.3
San Jose, Calif.	175,833	13.6	1.2	35,176	1.9	41,857	1.4
U.S. Totals	14,079,906	6.2	100.0	1,856,651	100.0	3,038,825	100.0

SOURCES: U.S. Bureau of the Census, *1980 Census of Population: General Social and Economic Characteristics*, PC80-1-C1, State and SMSA Summaries (Washington, D.C.: Government Printing Office, 1983); U.S. Bureau of the Census, *Detailed Population Characteristics*, PC80-1-D1-A (Washington, D.C.: Government Printing Office, 1984), table 253; U.S. Immigration and Naturalization Service *Statistical Yearbooks* (Washington, D.C.: Government Printing Office, 1987–89).

[a] Data indicate the "intended destination" of regular immigrants admitted to permanent resident status during 1987–89, as reported to the INS; data do not include the 478,814 immigrants whose status was legalized in fiscal year 1989 under the Immigration Reform and Control Act (IRCA).

[b] Persons who formally applied for legalization of their status by May 1990 under IRCA.

from 6.1 percent in 1980 to 6.6 percent in 1987–89, also accounted for 14.5 percent of IRCA applicants. In fact, over two-thirds of IRCA applicants resided in California and Texas alone—both states situated along the Mexican border. In Illinois, the proportion of immigrants decreased from 5.9 percent in 1980 to 4.4 percent in 1987–89—partly because Chicago has ceased to be a preferred destination for Mexican immigrants— while in New Jersey the levels for the two time periods remained unchanged at 5.4 percent.

Patterns of immigrant concentration are even more pronounced within particular metropolitan areas. As table 10.5 shows, just eleven SMSAs accounted for more than half of all legal and illegal immigrants in the United States during the 1980s, and five of these were California cities. As in the past, the New York metropolitan area remains the preferred destination of immigrants, accounting for 13.8 percent of the 1980 U.S. foreign-born population and another 15.4 percent of 1987–89 immigrants, though only 5 percent of IRCA applicants resided in New York. Los Angeles is not far behind, with 11.8 percent and 12.4 percent of 1980 and 1987–89 immigrants, respectively—but a huge 26.6 percent of all IRCA applicants nationally (more than 800,000 persons) were concentrated in Los Angeles, more than five times the number in any other urban area. Adjacent areas in Southern California (Santa Ana and San Diego) also show significant increases in both legal and especially illegal immigrant settlement. Of the leading SMSAs, only Chicago showed a drop in its relative proportion of immigrants, from 5.3 percent in 1980 to 3.5 percent in 1987–89 (although more IRCA applicants were recorded in Chicago than in Houston), while Boston's share remained at 2.0 percent during the decade (although only a tiny fraction of IRCA applicants lived in the Boston area). All other cities in table 10.5—Miami; San Francisco; Washington, D.C.; Houston; and San Jose—showed significant increases over time.

Moreover, different immigrant groups concentrate in different metropolitan areas and create distinct communities within each of these cities. For example, among the largest contingents of recent immigrants, Miami remains the premier destination of Cubans (they are already a majority of the city's total population), as is New York for Dominicans, Jamaicans, and Soviet Jews. Colombians and Haitians are also most concentrated in Miami and New York. The Los Angeles area is the main destination for Mexicans, Salvadorans, Filipinos, Koreans, Vietnamese, and Cambodians—their communities there are already the largest in the world outside their respective countries—and it is the third choice of Chinese and Indians. After Los Angeles, recent Mexican immigrants have settled in largest numbers in San Diego and El Paso; Filipinos in San Diego and San Francisco; Koreans in New York and Washington, D.C.; and

Vietnamese in Santa Ana and San Jose. More Chinese immigrants settle in New York than in any other city, followed by San Francisco; more Indians also settle in New York, followed by Chicago (although among all major immigrant groups Indians tend to be the most dispersed, reflecting their significantly greater proportion of professionals).[34]

Notwithstanding the relative dispersal of immigrant professionals, they have significant impacts in the sectors within which they are employed. Rather than compete with or take jobs away from the native-born, these groups fill significant national needs for skilled talent and in some respects also serve as a strategic reserve of scarce expertise. For example, we have already mentioned the disproportionate impact of immigrant engineers in U.S. universities. Given the continuing decline of enrollments in advanced engineering training among the native-born, the proportion of the foreign-born in these fields has grown rapidly. By 1987 over half of all assistant professors of engineering under thirty-five years of age in U.S. universities were foreign-born, and it is estimated that by 1992 over 75 percent of all engineering professors in the United States will be foreign-born. Already one out of every three engineers with a doctorate working in U.S. industry today is an immigrant.[35]

The impact of foreign medical graduates (FMGs) is almost as great: over the past two decades they have constituted about 20 percent of the nation's physicians and from about 33 percent (in the 1970s) to 18 percent (by the late 1980s) of its interns and residents. They are not, however, randomly dispersed throughout the country: in New York City in the mid-1970s, for instance, more than half of the interns in municipal hospitals and four-fifths of those at voluntary hospitals were Asian immigrant doctors. Their mode of incorporation into the American health care system is largely determined by the U.S. market for interns and residents. By the mid-1970s, for example, 35 percent of available internships and residency positions could not be filled by U.S. and Canadian medical graduates, and the geographical clustering of immigrant doctors in some northeastern and midwestern states is largely a function of job availability in certain types of hospitals that draw heavily on FMGs. In general, FMGs are concentrated in the less prestigious, non-university-affiliated hospitals in underserved areas that do not attract native-born physicians, and they are relatively few in hospitals with the greatest scientific emphasis and degrees of specialization located in the most desirable areas (such as California). Among FMGs, a further process of socio-cultural stratification is evident: FMGs from countries like Great Britain have exhibited patterns of entry most similar to those of U.S. and Canadian medical graduates; followed by a second stratum of FMGs from countries like Argentina, Colombia, and India; then a third stratum from countries like Taiwan, South Korea, Iran, and the Philippines; and lastly by Cuban refugee physicians (who entered the least prestigious and least scientifically oriented training hospitals). Despite substantial increases in the pool of U.S. medical graduates during the 1980s, many hospitals have been unable to attract even native-born nurse practitioners or physician assistants to replace FMGs who are willing to accept resident salaries and put in the typical 80-to-100-hour resident work week. A recent survey found that FMG-dependent teaching hospitals would each lose $2 to $5 million a year in Medicare training funds were they required to replace FMG residents, forcing cutbacks and affecting patient care. FMGs thus not only perform key functions in American medical care—especially in rural and inner-city hospitals serving Medicaid patients and the uninsured working poor—but they also give U.S. medical graduates more options in choosing jobs.[36]

Concerns about the economic impact of working-class immigrants more often focus on claims that they take jobs away from or depress the wages of native-born workers. Such claims, however, are made in the absence of any evidence that unemployment is caused by immigrants either in the United States as a whole or in areas of high immigrant concentration, or that immigration adversely affects the earnings of either domestic majority or minority groups. To the contrary, recent research studies of both legal and undocumented immigration point to significant net economic benefits accruing to U.S. natives. As a rule, the entry of immigrants into the labor market helps to increase native wages as well as productivity and investment, sustain the pace of economic growth, and revive declining sectors, such as light manufacturing, construction, and apparel (New York City, Los Angeles, and Miami offer recent examples). An influx of new immigrant labor also has the effect of pushing up domestic workers to better supervisory or administrative jobs that may otherwise disappear or go abroad in the absence of a supply of immigrant manual labor. Less-skilled immigrants, paralleling the pattern noted above for FMG professionals, typically move into manual labor markets deserted by native-born workers, who shift into preferred nonmanual jobs.[37] In addition, immigrants, on average, actually pay more taxes than natives, but use much smaller amounts of transfer payments and welfare services (such as aid to families with dependent children [AFDC], supplemental security income, state unemployment compensation, food stamps, Medicare, and Medicaid). It has been estimated that immigrants "catch up" with natives in their use of welfare services only after 16 to 25 years in the United States. Because of their vulnerable legal status, undocumented immigrants, in particular, are much less likely to use welfare services, and they receive no Social Security income, yet about three-fourths of them pay Social Security and federal income taxes. And because newly arrived immigrants are primarily younger workers rather than elderly persons, by the time they retire and are eligible to collect Social Security (the costliest government program of transfer payments), they have usually already raised children who are contributing to Social Security taxes and thus balancing their parents' receipts.[38]

Rather than take jobs away, entrepreneurial immigrants often create them. For example, among Koreans in Los Angeles in 1980, a recent study found that 22.5 percent were self-employed (compared to 8.5 percent of the local labor force), and they in turn employed another 40 percent of Korean workers in their businesses. The 4,266 Korean-owned firms thus accounted for two-thirds of all employed Koreans in the Los Angeles metropolitan area.[39] In Miami, Cuban-owned enterprises increased from about 900 to 25,000 between the late 1960s and the late 1980s; by 1985 the $2.2 billion in sales reported by Hispanic-owned firms in Dade County ranked that area first in gross receipts among all such firms in the country. A longitudinal survey of Cuban refugees who arrived in Miami in 1973 showed that by 1979, 21.2 percent were self-employed and another 36.3 percent were employed in businesses owned by Cubans. A subsequent survey of Mariel Cubans who arrived in Miami in 1980 found that by 1986 28.2 percent were self-employed and another 44.9 percent were employed by their co-nationals.[40] In Monterey Park ("Little Taipei"), east of Los Angeles, Chinese immigrants from Taiwan and Hong Kong—who in 1988 already comprised over half of its 61,000 residents—owned two-thirds of the property and businesses in the city. During 1985 an estimated $1.5 billion was deposited in Monterey Park financial institutions (equivalent to about $25,000 for each city resident), much of it the capital of Hong Kong investors nervous about the impending return of Hong Kong to Mainland China.[41] And, although not yet rivaling the scale of these ethnic enclaves, a burgeoning center of Vietnamese-owned enterprises has been developed over the past decade in the city of Westminster ("Little Saigon") in Orange County. In all of these cases, immigrants have built "institutionally complete" ethnic communities offering opportunities for advancement unavailable in the general economy. Already Miami and Monterey Park have mayors who are Cuban and Chinese immigrants, respectively.

To be sure, other newcomers in areas of immigrant concentration—especially the undocumented and unskilled immigrant women—are exploited as sources of cheap labor in a growing informal sector that is fueled by foreign competition and the demand for low-cost goods and services in the larger economy. They find employment in the garment industry (in Los Angeles, perhaps 90 percent of garment workers are undocumented immigrants), as well as in electronics assembly, construction, restaurants, domestic service, and a wide range of other informal activities—often at subminimum wages and under conditions that violate federal and state labor laws. In this context the presence of a large supply of cheap labor does keep wages down: the low wages paid to the immigrants themselves, who under their precarious circumstances are willing to accept whatever work is offered. In regions like Southern California there is the added irony that undocumented immigrants are attracted by an economic boom that their own labor has helped to create. IRCA did provide 3 million immigrants with an opportunity to emerge from the shadows of illegality, but at a cost: the new law has had the effect of driving those ineligible for legalization (virtually all post-1981 arrivals) further underground, but without stopping the flow of illegal immigration; it has also led—according to a 1990 report by the General Accounting Office—to increasing ethnic discrimination by employers against legal residents. The new post-IRCA underclass of undocumented (and sometimes homeless) Mexican and Central American workers is increasingly visible, not only in traditional agricultural and horticultural enterprises but especially in dozens of street corners of California cities, from Encinitas to North Hollywood, where groups huddle during the day waiting for job offers from homeowners and small contractors. The situation has bred a new upsurge of nativist intolerance in heavily impacted areas.[42]

Refugees differ from other categories of immigrants in that they are eligible to receive public assistance on the same means-tested basis as U.S. citizens, and the federal government has invested considerable resources since the early 1960s to facilitate the resettlement of selected refugee groups. Prior to that time, refugee assistance depended entirely on the private sector, particularly religious charities and voluntary agencies. The expansion of the state's role in refugee resettlement roughly parallels the expansion of the American welfare state in the 1960s and early 1970s. In the twelve years from 1963 (when federal outlays officially began) to 1974, domestic assistance to mostly Cuban refugees totaled $2.3 billion; and in the twelve years from 1975 to 1986, aid to mostly Indochinese refugees totaled $5.7 billion, peaking in 1982, when $1.5 billion were expended, and declining sharply thereafter (all figures are in constant 1985 dollars). The lion's share of those federal funds goes to reimburse states and localities for cash and medical assistance to refugees during their first three years in the United States. Public assistance to eligible refugees is conditioned upon their attendance in assigned English-as-a-second-language (ESL) or job training classes and acceptance of employment; it also formally allows these groups (at least during a transition period after arrival) an alternative mode of subsistence outside existing labor markets and ethnic enclaves. However, states have different "safety nets"—levels of benefits and eligibility rules vary widely from state to state—forming a segmented state welfare system in the

United States. For example, AFDC benefits for a family of four in California in the early 1980s were $591 a month (second highest in the country), compared to only $141 in Texas (second lowest); intact families (two unemployed parents with dependent children) were eligible for AFDC and Medicaid in California, but ineligible in Texas; and indigent adults without dependent children were eligible for general assistance in California localities, but not in Texas. Hence, the initial decision to resettle refugees in one state or another affects not only their destinations but their destinies as well. Welfare dependency rates vary widely among different refugee nationalities, and from state to state among refugees of the same nationality. Not surprisingly, the highest rates have been observed among recently arrived, less-skilled, "second-wave" Southeast Asian families with many dependent children in California; still, all research studies of Cambodian, Laotian, and Vietnamese refugees throughout the country have found that welfare dependency (which even in California keeps families below the federal poverty line) declines steadily over time in the United States.[43]

Language and the Second Generation

A more salient issue concerns the impact of the new immigration on public school systems and their rapidly changing ethnic composition. The issue itself is not new: at the turn of the century, the majority of pupils in many big-city schools from New York to Chicago were children of immigrants. Today, nowhere are immigrant students more visible—or more diverse—than in the public schools of California. By the end of the 1980s, almost a third of California's 4.6 million students in kindergarten through twelfth grade (K–12) in the public schools spoke a language other than English at home; while 70 percent of them spoke Spanish as their mother tongue, the rest spoke over 100 different languages. Yet of California's scarce pool of bilingual teachers, 94 percent spoke only Spanish as a second language, a few spoke various East Asian languages, and there was not a single certified bilingual teacher statewide for the tens of thousands of students who spoke scores of other mother tongues. Table 10.6 summarizes the trend over the past decade in the annual enrollments of language-minority students, who are classified by the schools as either fluent English proficient (FEP) or limited English proficient (LEP). In 1973 there were 168,000 students classified as LEP in the state, and that number doubled by 1980; from 1981 to 1989, as table 10.6 shows, the number of LEP students doubled again to about 743,000, and the number of FEP students increased by over 40 percent to 615,000. The FEP classification marks an arbitrary threshhold of English proficiency, which schools use to "mainstream" students from bilingual or ESL classrooms to regular classes. Indeed, bilingual education in Cali-

TABLE 10.6   Trends in California Public School Enrollments (K–12) of LEP and FEP Students Who Speak a Primary Language Other than English at Home, 1981–89

Year	Total Students N	Total LEP[a] Students N	%	Total FEP[a] Students N	%	Total LEP/FEP[a] N	%
1981	3,941,997	376,794	9.6	434,063	11.0	810,857	20.6
1982	3,976,676	431,443	10.8	437,578	11.0	869,021	21.9
1983	3,984,735	457,542	11.5	460,313	11.6	917,855	23.0
1984	4,014,003	487,835	12.2	475,203	11.8	963,038	24.0
1985	4,078,743	524,082	12.8	503,695	12.3	1,027,777	25.2
1986	4,255,554	567,564	13.3	542,362	12.7	1,109,926	26.1
1987	4,377,989	613,222	14.0	568,928	13.0	1,182,150	27.0
1988	4,488,398	652,439	14.6	598,302	13.3	1,250,741	27.9
1989	4,618,120	742,559	16.1	614,670	13.3	1,357,229	29.4

SOURCE: California State Department of Education, Bilingual Education Office, DATA BICAL series, 1981–89 (Sacramento, Calif.).

[a] LEP means Limited English Proficient; FEP means Fluent English Proficient. The overwhelming majority of LEP/FEP student are immigrants or children of immigrants. These students speak over 100 different primary languages, although Spanish is the language spoken by about 70 percent of total 1989 LEP/FEP enrollments in California public schools. The largest of the other ethnolinguistic groups, in rank order, include speakers of Vietnamese, Filipino (Tagalog, Ilocano, and other dialects), Chinese (Cantonese, Mandarin, and other dialects), Korean, Cambodian, Hmong, Lao, Japanese, Farsi, Portuguese, Indian (Hindi, Punjabi, and others), Armenian, Arabic, Hebrew, Mien, Thai, Samoan, Guamanian, and a wide range of European and other languages.

fornia largely consists of "transitional" programs whose aim is to place LEP students in the English-language curriculum as quickly as possible. While immigrant children gain proficiency in English at different rates— depending on such extracurricular factors as age at arrival, their parents' social class of origin, community contexts, and other characteristics—very few remain designated as LEP beyond five years, and most are reclassified as FEP within three years.[44]

In some smaller elementary school districts near the Mexican border, such as San Ysidro and Calexico, LEP students alone account for four-fifths of total enrollments. In large school districts in cities of high immigrant concentration, language minorities comprise the great majority of K–12 students. In 1989, LEP students accounted for 56 percent of total enrollments in Santa Ana schools, 31 percent in Los Angeles, 28 percent in San Francisco and Stockton, 25 percent in Long Beach, and close to 20 percent in Oakland, Fresno, San Diego, and San Jose; the number of FEP students nearly doubled those proportions, so that in districts like Santa Ana's over 90 percent of the students were of recent immigrant origin. These shifts, in turn, have generally been accompanied by so-called white flight from the public schools most affected, producing an extraordinary mix of new immigrants and native-born ethnic minorities. In the Los Angeles Unified School District, the nation's second largest, the proportion of native white students declined sharply from about 65 percent in 1980 to only 15 percent in 1990. To varying degrees, the creation of ethnic "minority majorities" is also visible in the school systems of large cities, including all of the SMSAs listed earlier in table 10.5. While a substantial body of research has accumulated recently on the experience of new first-generation immigrants, relatively little is yet known about the U.S.-born or U.S.-reared second generation of their children, although they will represent an even larger proportion of the American school-age population in years to come.

Until the 1960s, bilingualism in immigrant children had been seen as a cognitive handicap associated with "feeblemindedness" and inferior academic achievement. This popular nostrum was based in part on older studies that compared middle-class native-born English monolinguals with lower-class foreign-born bilinguals. Once social class and demographic variables are controlled, however, recent research has reached an opposite conclusion: bilingual groups perform consistently better than monolinguals on a wide range of verbal and nonverbal IQ tests.[45] Along these lines, a 1988 study of 38,820 high school students in San Diego—of whom a quarter were FEP or LEP immigrant children who spoke a diversity of languages other than English at home—found that FEP (or "true") bilinguals outperformed both LEP (or "limited") bilinguals and all native English monolinguals, including white Anglos, in various indicators of educational attainment: they had higher GPAs and standardized math test scores, and lower dropout rates. The pattern was most evident for Chinese, Filipino, German, Indian, Iranian, Israeli, Korean, Japanese, and Vietnamese students: in each of these groups of immigrant children, both FEPs and LEPs exhibited significantly higher GPAs and math (but not English) test scores than did white Anglos. These findings parallel the patterns of educational stratification noted earlier in table 10.4 among foreign-born and native-born adults in the United States. Remarkably, two groups of lower-class LEP refugees—the Cambodians and the Hmong—had higher GPAs than native whites, blacks, and Chicanos. White Anglos (but not blacks and Chicanos) did better than some other language minorities, whether they were classified as FEP or LEP—Italians, Portuguese, Guamanians, Samoans, and "Hispanics" (predominantly of Mexican origin)—almost certainly reflecting intergroup social class differences. And among students whose ethnicity was classified by the schools as black or Hispanic—with the lowest achievement profiles overall in the district—FEP bilinguals outperformed their co-ethnic English monolinguals.[46] Research elsewhere has reported similar findings among Central American, Southeast Asian, and Punjabi Sikh immigrant students, and separate studies have found that Mexican-born immigrant students do better in school and are less likely to drop out than U.S.-born students of Mexican descent.[47]

The idea that bilingualism in children is a "hardship" bound to cause emotional and educational maladjustment has been not only refuted but contradicted by every available evidence; and in a shrinking global village where there are thirty times more languages spoken as there are nation-states, the use of two languages is common to the experience of much of the world's people. But pressures against bilingualism in America—as reflected today by the "U.S. English" nativist movement and the passage of "English Only" measures in several states—are rooted in more fundamental social and political concerns that date back to the origins of the nation. As early as 1751, Benjamin Franklin had put the matter plainly: "Why should Pennsylvania, founded by the English, become a colony of aliens, who will shortly be so numerous as to Germanize us, instead of our Anglifying them?" The point was underscored by Theodore Roosevelt during the peak years of immigration at the turn of the century: "We have room but for one language here, and that is the English language; for we intend to see that the crucible turns our people out as Americans, and not as dwellers in a polyglot boardinghouse." It is ironic that, while the United States has probably incorporated more bilingual people than any other nation since the time of Franklin, American history is notable for its near mass-extinction of non-English languages. A generational pattern of progressive anglicization is clear: immigrants (the first generation) learned survival English but spoke their mother tongue to their children at home; the second generation, in turn, spoke accentless English at school and then at work, where its use was required and its social advantages were unmistakable; and with very few exceptions their children (the third generation) grew up as English monolinguals.

For all the alarm about Quebec-like linguistic separatism in the United States, the 1980 census suggests that this generational pattern remains as strong as in the past. It counted well over 200 million Americans speaking English only, including substantial proportions of the foreign-born. Among new immigrants who had arrived in the United States during 1970–80, 84 percent spoke a language other than English at home, but over half of them (adults as well as children) reported already being able to speak English well. Among pre-1970 immigrants, 62 percent still spoke a language other than English at home, but the overwhelming majority of them spoke English well: 77 percent of the adults and 95 percent of the children. Among the native-born, less than 7 percent spoke a language other than English at home, and over 90 percent of them (adults as well as children) spoke English well. More detailed studies have confirmed that for all American ethnic groups, without exception, children consistently prefer English to their mother tongue, and the shift toward English increases as a function of the proportion of the ethnic group that is U.S.-born. To be sure, immigrant groups vary significantly in their rates of English language ability, reflecting differences in their levels of education and occupation. But even among Spanish speakers, who are considered the most resistant to language shift, the trend toward anglicization is present; the appearance of language loyalty among them (especially Mexicans) is due largely to the effect of continuing high immigration to the United States. For example, a recent study of a large representative sample of Mexican-origin couples in Los Angeles found that among first-generation women, 84 percent used Spanish only at home, 14 percent used both languages, and 2 percent used English only; by the third generation there was a complete reversal, with 4 percent speaking Spanish only at home, 12 percent using both, and 84 percent shifting to English only. Among the men, the pattern was similar except that by the second generation their shift to English was even more marked.[48]

English proficiency has always been a key to socioeconomic mobility for immigrants, and to their full participation in their adoptive society. It is worth noting that in the same year that Proposition 63 (the initiative declaring English as the state's official language) passed in California, more than 40,000 immigrants were turned away from ESL classes in the Los Angeles Unified School District alone: the supply of services could not meet the vigorous demand for English training. Indeed, English language dominance is not threatened in the United States today—or for that matter in the world, where it has become already firmly established as the premier international language of commerce, diplomacy, education, journalism, aviation, technology, and mass culture. What is threatened instead is a more scarce resource: the survival of the foreign languages brought by immigrants themselves, which in the absence of social structural supports are, as in the past, destined to disappear.

Given the immense pressure for linguistic conformity on immigrant children from peers, schools, and the media, the preservation of fluent bilingualism in America beyond the first generation is an exceptional outcome. It is dependent on both the intellectual and economic resources of parents (such as immigrant professionals) and their efforts to transmit the mother tongue to their children, and on the presence of institutionally complete communities where a second language is taught in schools and valued in the labor market (such as those found in large ethnic enclaves). The combination of these factors is rare, since most immigrants do not belong to a privileged stratum, and immigrant professionals are most likely to be dispersed rather than concentrated in dense ethnic communities. Miami may provide the closest approximation in the United States, but even there the gradual anglicization of the Cuban second generation is evident. Still, the existence of pockets where foreign languages are fluently spoken enriches American culture and the lives of natives and immigrants alike.[49]

The United States has aptly been called a "permanently unfinished society," a global sponge remarkable in its capacity to absorb tens of millions of people from all over the world. Immigrants have made their passages to America a central theme of the country's history. In the process, America has been engaged in an endless passage of its own, and through immigration the country has been revitalized, diversified, strengthened, and transformed. Immigrant America today, however, is not the same as it was at the turn of the century; and while the stories of human drama remain as riveting, the cast of characters and their circumstances have changed in complex ways. In this chapter, I have touched on a few of the ways in which the "new" immigration differs from the "old." But a new phase in the history of American immigration is about to begin. New bills have been introduced in Congress once again to change immigration policies—to reduce or eliminate some of the legal channels for family reunification, to increase quotas for "brain drain" and "new seed" immigrants, to allocate special values for immigrant millionaires who will invest in job-producing businesses, to rescind the "employer sanctions" provisions of the last law, to grapple with the sustained flow of undocumented immigrants, to consider whether persons from newly noncommunist states in Eastern Europe and Nicaragua are eligible for refugee status—and the debate remains surrounded by characteristic ambivalence. The "new" immigration of the post–World War II period was never simply a matter of individual cost-benefit calculations or of the exit and entry policies of particular states, but is also a consequence of historically established social networks and U.S. economic and political hegemony in a world system. The world as the century ends is changing profoundly—from Yalta to Malta, from the Soviet Union to South Africa, from the European Economic Community to East Asia and the Arab world, from the East-West Cold War to perhaps new North-South economic realignments and Third World refugee movements—and new bridges of immigration will likely be formed in the process. For the future of immigration to America, as in the past, the unexpected lies waiting.[50]

ELEVEN

The Hollow Center
U.S. Cities in the Global Era

Sharon Zukin

Cities graphically represent the disappearing center of American society. Over the past twenty years, they have become both more visible and less important symbols of the economy. Paradoxically, despite enormous efforts at rebuilding, they are less different from each other than they were before. The problems of big cities—crime, drugs, high housing prices, unemployment—are just as familiar in Spokane or Tulsa as in New York City. Meanwhile, the provincial decay of smaller cities has been negated by the spread of television, computers, and imported consumer goods. We ordinarily describe America as an urban society, but most Americans no longer live in cities. They are as likely to find their "center" in the suburban shopping mall or office park as in the downtown financial district. To some degree, Americans have always had a love-hate relationship with cities. Throughout American history the major thinkers and many ordinary men and women have loved the countryside because it offers an escape from social pressures. Cities had their own compensation because they brought a varied population into a common public life. Today, however, the public middle ground that was previously identified with cities is dissolving into a collage of racial, ethnic, and other private communities. At the same time, even cities as commanding as Los Angeles and New York are being "globalized"; that is, they are becoming more dependent on political and economic decisions that are made at the global level.

In 1986, a list of urban trends drawn up for the U.S. Conference of Mayors described a sorry situation: population drain, increased poverty, an income gap between city and suburban residents, gaps among racial groups, long-term unemployment in places where manufacturing has declined and services grow slowly, homelessness, hunger, low education levels, high crime rates, and very high taxes.[1] Such conditions cannot be described as anything but structural. Disinvestment by industry and the middle class feeds—and in turn responds to—concentrations of the poor, the ill-educated, and the unemployable. Nonetheless, neither the federal government nor private markets give cities much encouragement. Since the early 1970s, no president of the United States has drawn up an explicit urban policy. Under the Reagan administration, the Department of Housing and Urban Development was used as a patronage arm of the Republican party. The conservative thrust of federalism over the past twenty years has consistently reduced both programs and grants. And during the 1980s, the cities' biggest demands—for social services, public housing, and jobs—were sacrificed to the rhetoric of fiscal purity.

Between the Gramm-Rudman Act of 1985 and the attacks on Big Government by two Reagan administrations, state and local governments were squeezed to only 10 percent of the federal budget. In New York City, the federal government contributed the same amount—$2.5 billion—to an $11 billion municipal budget in 1981 and one that had grown to $27 billion in 1989.

Businesses and households that can afford to move have been leaving cities for many years. Industrial decentralization to the suburbs began a century ago, closely followed by middle-class households seeking "bourgeois utopias." Land is both cheaper and more attractive outside cities. Labor is generally cheaper, too, more docile, less likely to be nonwhite. Restrictions on uses of suburban property also tend to benefit the "haves." Large companies can influence weak suburban governments for preferential zoning and tax laws, and wealthy home owners provide a pressure group for socially exclusive development. In recent years, however, cities have lost jobs and residents to areas farther away. Among households, suburbanization has grown less rapidly since the 1970s than moves to "exurban" locales. Businesses, for their part, have decentralized operations. Many have moved to, or set up branches in, low-wage regions of the country and overseas. To some degree this "footloose capital," as Bluestone and Harrison and others call it, is related to a desire to lower costs and escape the limits imposed by unionization. In part it also reflects a shift from local to nonlocal ownership of firms (as in Buffalo, New York, or Youngstown, Ohio), and an intensification of outsourcing strategies (especially devastating to Detroit). More important, footloose capital also applies to new business start-ups in growth sectors, such as electronics and telecommunications, where manufacturing is likely to be exurban. Once limited only to industrial plants, the outflow of economic activity from cities now includes a significant number of offices and corporate headquarters. The resulting "counter-urbanization" has further reduced most cities' claim to functional pre-eminence in American society.[2]

Not surprisingly, Americans have been attracted by alternatives to traditional cities. On the one hand, they increasingly live, work, and shop in exurbs, especially in the Sun Belt, in regions not previously known as centers of urban life. On the other hand, a small but growing middle-class population inhabits the gentrified centers of older cities. Like exurban residents, gentrifiers enjoy the amenities of personal consumption that are typical of a geographically mobile population. But they are tied to the city by a desire for access to its cultural markets as well as its historic symbols of power. In terms of numbers, gentrification has had a much smaller impact on cities than either suburbanization or exurban migration. It has great appeal, however, because like the exurbs, gentrified areas become great spaces of consumption.

Exurbs and gentrified downtowns are important not only because of visible spatial shifts. They are also significant "fictive spaces" in America's social geography. They convey a powerful image of the way many Americans want to live, an image of escape from the constraints of cities and a confirmation of the free movement of both people and investment capital. A simultaneous decentering to the exurbs and recentering of downtowns tear apart the old image of cities as engines of production. A more subtle picture, instead, differentiates among cities according to their position in both the service economy and a new organization of consumption. This new order alters the relation between urban space and economic and cultural power.

CITIES AND ECONOMIC POWER

The post-postwar economy has sharpened the effects on cities of global organization. Since the 1970s, the major area of growth—business services—has depended on linking local to multinational firms in expanding markets. While some services have been bought by or have merged with international companies, others seek clients and contracts overseas. This course of development imposes a dual dependence on American cities. The cities rely on the services to fuel further growth, employ residents, and expand the tax base; but the largest employers among local service institutions, as in mass-production manufacturing, are increasingly responsive to global rather than local trends.

These conditions are especially acute in cities whose financial institutions are major players in global markets. New York and Los Angeles, with their large concentrations of international bankers, stock market traders, and foreign investors, owe their growth since the 1970s to globalization. Just as these two cities have the largest number of corporate financial headquarters and other institutional resources, so they also have the tallest office buildings, the highest land values, and the most business expansion in their downtowns. In large part the economic value of doing business downtown reflects an infusion of foreign property investment. Foreign financial institutions, especially Japanese and other Asian banks, occupy a major portion of downtown office buildings. Not surprisingly, New York and Los Angeles, as major concentrations of the power that moves capital around the world, are considered "world cities." Whether this refers only to their pre-eminent position in global financial markets, or to some index of greater cultural sophistication as well, is unclear.

In some aggregate terms—new employment, for example, or business revenues—the financial, insurance, and real estate industries compensate for cities' losses in traditional manufacturing employment.[3] Yet aspects of the new economy suggest reasons for alarm. Most of the highly paid, prestigious downtown jobs are held by suburban rather than city residents. Men and women of color, who represent a growing portion of all cities' populations, have not made such inroads into the financial services area as they have into the public sector. Because of the layoffs that follow stock market downturns, all employment in this area is risky. The threat of global financial crisis also imposes risk on many property investments, from office construction to the ownership of "signature" or "trophy" buildings that are designed by famous architects and located in high-rent districts.

The technological revolution in computers and telecommunications that made office decentralization possible also creates the means for local financial institutions to move away. "Back offices" that house computer and routine clerical operations have easily been detached from money-center banks, while headquarters and other "front offices" remain in more central locations. The importance of face-to-face contact and the symbolic legitimacy of place may enhance the city's viability as the site of a world financial market. Yet even in New York, high land prices and high wages for clerical personnel create a potential for the city's being abandoned by financial institutions.[4]

In cases where banks, stock brokerages, and insurance companies have not moved away, they have destabilized the labor force by shifting from permanent to temporary employment. These arrangements are not limited to cities, of course. Since 1980, temporary employment of all kinds has been the largest growth sector in jobs around the country (as well as overseas). Some temporary positions may pay as well as permanent jobs and may also offer health insurance and other benefits. But by establishing a large number of temporary positions that are outside the normal career stream, financial services organizations create a tenuous base for urban economic development.

Neither do financial services firms recruit widely among the cities' populations. Jobs at the top are often filled through networks established in college and business school; these job holders live in gentrified areas downtown or in the suburbs. For the most part, high-level positions are also still restricted by race and gender. When it comes to entry-level jobs requiring lesser skills, urban residents confront another type of barrier. Financial and other business services firms do not find adequate personnel among the city's high school graduates. Lacking training in math, competence in standard interpersonal communication, and skills in dress, deference, and punctuality, young men and women from the city are passed over in favor of suburban youth. Growing opportunities for employment outside cities, however, as well as a shrinking labor pool, cause urban employers much concern. In some cities, notably Boston, the financial community has developed a training-and-recruitment partnership with local high schools. In others, such as New York, this degree of institutional interdependence has not yet grown.[5]

Some demographically minded researchers speak of these employment problems in terms of a job-skills mismatch, and the structural roots of this analysis also appeal to those who think in terms of a postindustrial economy. They consider that the decline in traditional manufacturing industries drastically reduces the number of entry-level jobs that are available to high school graduates of modest academic achievements. Further, if job requirements in business services emphasize math, interpersonal, and other job skills that urban high school graduates (and dropouts) lack, then the growth of such jobs takes place without benefiting the urban population. The concentration of ethnic and racial minorities in cities, however, introduces a disquieting series of bias questions. According to the job-skills mismatch analysis, urban minority residents are unemployed in the city's growth sector because they are intellectually and culturally unemployable. Their soaring unemployment rates first of all reflect the loss of a base in blue-collar jobs in plants that have moved out of the city or shut their doors. Second, this unemployment reflects the diminishing educational achievements of the urban minority population.[6]

But the job-skills mismatch explanation of urban unemployment ignores several important factors. At least since the 1950s, many men and women of color have been employed in the service industries. They have generally been steered toward certain areas—notably, personal rather than business services, and the public rather than the private sector—and discouraged from entering others. In recent years, as racial and ethnic minority students have made up greater proportions of urban high school and college graduates, these students have, presumably, gained the qualifications to get financial jobs. At graduation, however, they confront a decreasing number of entry-level jobs, many of which have been shifted overseas or eliminated by automation (for example, insurance claims processors and bank tellers in financial services, telephone opera-

tors in other fields). Further, the hiring process in the financial services
area is socially exclusive. It still segregates men from women and people
of color from the jobs traditionally held by whites.[7]

This exclusion of part of the urban population is heightened by their
absence, by and large, from another growth area in most cities, the sector of individually owned small businesses that are often identified with
ethnic or immigrant entrepreneurs. The ethnic concentrations in most
large cities enable businesses that cater to their special needs (such as
food and travel services) to succeed in an "enclave economy." Alternatively, the capital that many immigrants have access to by means of self-
help or mutual-aid associations often provides a base for those groups to
enter various niches in the urban economy (as owners of manicure par-
lors, greengrocers, restauranteurs, and newsstand proprietors). Many of
these businesses rely on family capitalism. Family members work long
hours at low wages, and defer their individual advancement in favor of
the family as a whole or the younger generation. But a preference for
recruitment among their own group reinforces other hiring practices in
the larger society. The garment industry has had a resurgence in the last
ten years, especially in the Chinatowns of New York and Los Angeles,
but Asian owners and foremen do not recruit Latinos and blacks.

Immigrants' entrepreneurialism has, at any rate, made a broader,
though not necessarily cheaper, array of goods and services available in
many urban areas. Child care day workers, street peddlers, and house-
keepers represent new or reborn segments of the ethnic division of labor, while their better-educated compatriots staff health care facilities
in both the public and private sectors. Despite the success of many immigrant groups—Chinese, Koreans, Indians, Filipinos, Cubans, West
Indians, and others—poverty still bears a racial edge. Many of the Latinos and U.S.-born blacks who live in cities are among the poorest urban
residents. Although statistical indices of racial segregation have steadily
declined, these men and women are more concentrated by race than
other groups. Race counts again in the tendency for middle- and low-
income African-Americans to live in the same neighborhood. Moreso
than in other ethnic and racial minorities, social class fails to separate urban blacks who have steady work from those who do not.[8]

Opportunities for entrepreneurialism and employment do not compensate for the low-wage jobs many urban immigrants hold. Some researchers describe these jobs as "sweatshop" labor, pointing to conditions in such growth areas as the garment and computer industries in
New York and Los Angeles. Child labor, piece rates, long hours, and
other types of exploitation have not been documented for these industries, but to the degree that they hire only non-union labor, perhaps paid
off the books and informally contracted, employers contribute to a para-

doxically cash-rich, mobility-poor urban population. The simultaneous proliferation of these jobs and high-level jobs in business services, as well as the absolute difference in incomes between them, has shaped a polarized social structure. Because the polarization of incomes in the city so clearly refers to the ability, or lack of ability, to consume, the urban class system is seen as even more divided between rich and poor than in the country as a whole.[9]

In New York City, where the average income of the poorest 10 percent of the population (including welfare payments) was $3,698 in 1986, there were 53,000 taxpayers with adjusted gross incomes of $100,000 or more; 2,840 with at least $500,000; and 1,764 with more than $1 million. Eighty-two people in New York are believed to have assets worth more than $275 million. The second-place city, Los Angeles, has only 32.[10]

Polarization also refers to divided spaces. Although a "dual city" image is much used by urban critics, the segmentation of incomes and separation of classes and races really require a more specific mapping. Peter Marcuse heuristically outlines a "quartered city," made up of the luxury city of the rich; the gentrified city of managers, professionals, and intellectuals; the "suburban" city of the lower middle class and well-paid blue-collar workers; the tenement city of the working poor; and the ghetto of outcasts, the unemployed, the homeless.[11] Significantly, the occupants of each quarter have more in common with their counterparts in other cities—in terms of jobs, mobility, and choices about what to consume—than they have either contact or common interests with residents of the other quarters. This is especially true for the luxury and gentrified areas, whose residents are likely to be foreign investors or at least consumers in an upscale global culture. The rich and upper middle class also tend to set themselves apart from other city residents by using private facilities (car phones, taxis, prep schools) instead of relying on public institutions.

Such images break the myth of the city as a middle ground between social groups. Both visually and metaphorically, the spaces occupied by more affluent groups are "islands of renewal in seas of decay."[12] Yet the area that attracts reinvestment has become larger and more visibly coherent in recent years. Like new office buildings, new upper-income housing in most older cities is mainly centered downtown. Downtown's expansion feeds on relatively undervalued property markets, the growth of business services, and investors' desire for centrally located projects that minimize risk. But in visual terms, it represents a new and broader landscape of power that grows by incorporating, eliminating, or drastically reducing the "vernacular" inner city inhabited by the city's powerless. These men and women are pushed toward less central areas and nearby suburbs that are relatively cheap and may be racially mixed. No longer geographically bound to the inner city, the less affluent and the poor carry the inner city with them as both a racial stigma and an inability to attract investment.

Public officials are not oblivious of trying to govern "the city of the poor masquerading as the city of the rich."[13] Neither luxury investment nor gentrification raises a city population's median income, which makes the city government that much more dependent on those who pay high taxes. The problem, however, is that city budget authorities are chasing mobile investors. Not only industrial firms but also real estate developers who used to operate only in local markets are now national and even international in scope. To compel them to stay in cities and build the business centers that seem to attract more growth, municipal authorities make concessions. Business influence has always been an important factor in local government, but the new element since 1980 is the formalization of these arrangements in public-private partnerships.

Private-sector organizations like the Chamber of Commerce or the local real estate trade association now initiate redevelopment projects. Their financing depends in part on city government's ability to float municipal bonds and take out short-term loans, as well as its willingness to offer tax reductions, zoning incentives, and aid in acquiring land. "Public" goals tend to converge with those of private developers. The common program is worked out in meetings among business leaders and public officials, and managed by public authorities dominated by business institutions. A focus on high-rent downtown land and new construction is supported by the city's commitment to block off streets, enhance cultural amenities, and, in general, facilitate the "privatization" of development. Under these conditions, urban planners in public employ have no creative work.

Pressure to counter new downtown development with housing that is "affordable," that is, slightly below market rate, reflects the strength of "neighborhoods" where middle-income voters live. The linkage mechanism that was developed (in Boston and San Francisco) in response to such pressure permits developers to have their downtown development—but requires more affordable housing as a quid pro quo. Developers are assessed a percentage of development costs for building such apartments, or agree to allocate a portion of their project to less affluent groups. In some cases, as in Battery Park City in New York, the below-market-rent housing is built elsewhere, outside the most expensive areas. This gains new low- or, more often, middle-income housing at the cost of strengthening social class segregation in the heart of the city. At any rate, such linkages are viable only where developers have a lot to gain by agreeing to them; in other words, in cities like Boston, San Francisco, and New York in the mid-1980s, when "market forces" buoyed the economy. Chicago suggests more a rigorous pressure to make developers respond to public goals (that is, racial integration, increasing the affordable housing stock, and letting neighborhoods share in downtown's prosperity). There, however, the opportunity has depended in large part on a new African-American mayor, the late Harold Washington. He attracted strong black support, dedicated staff members in city agencies, and white coalition partners—all at a time when the city attracted a new round of corporate investment downtown by nationally oriented business services.[14]

Public-private partnerships institutionalize the acknowledgment of dependence on the financial sector that followed the mid-1970s outbreak of fiscal crisis. At that time, commercial banks and other financial institutions threatened New York City, Yonkers, and Cleveland with bankruptcy, supposedly for the city government's profligate use of public finances. Calling in municipal debt served to discipline city agencies and remind them of the need to balance budgets. But fiscal crisis also fulfilled another end. It dramatized the death of the War on Poverty and ended the long New Deal era of social welfare at city—and federal government—expense. Most cities survived the fiscal crisis of the 1970s by concentrating layoffs and reductions on such "nonessential" services as schools and libraries, leaving police, fire, and sanitation agencies wounded but not completely cut down. In more drastic cases, such as New York, Yonkers, and Cleveland, bankers imposed a nonelected supercommission made up of leaders from the financial community and the state to oversee the spending of elected city officials. These supercommissions were given the right of approval on city budgets. Both formally and informally, they exercised control over mayors who were inclined toward populism.[15]

In the United States, linkages are usually limited to the developers' impact on the city's built environment. Provision of low-income housing units is only one possibility; developers may also provide "public areas," such as plazas or indoor galleries; they may preserve a landmark structure on the building site; or they may contribute funds to renovate publicly owned infrastructure, especially transportation facilities. The entire situation, however, is dominated by the private sector. A city's leverage depends on how marketable the project is and how much profit it can bring the developer. No linkage requires developers to extend their efforts to the sore area of employment. Often the indoor public spaces that developers provide are designed to be inhospitable to strangers, and after they are built, they are policed by private security guards. Most of them are entries or backdrops to shops. Even the outdoor spaces that are most praised for their use of public art and open landscaping (New York's Battery Park City being a prominent example) serve to advertise an image of the city as clean, safe, and almost classically cultural.[16]

Dependence on the private sector for creating new public spaces is only a visible means of privatization. Many cities have also tried to save money by privatizing essential public services, that is, by contracting out work, letting private, for-profit firms build and operate facilities, and selling publicly owned assets.[17] While hiring a privately owned towing or waste removal company may seem a reasonable way to reduce the public payroll, shifting other services strikes at government's reason for existence. Courtrooms and prisons may be leased, hospitals may be run by private chains, and forms may be processed outside the public sector. But the efficiency of private managers is based on skewing service to the ability to pay, not equity or universal service. Turning city services over to private firms also means losing control. It suggests that the last vestige of citizenship in the city is gone, that the bureaucracy of city government is just a functional arrangement with no pretense to mediating a moral order.

Though hardly new, the dominance of private organizations in redevelopment and the divorce between downtown and the neighborhoods have been accentuated during the recent growth in service economies. Cities face renewed problems of allocating scarce public resources among needy populations while attracting successful businesses that could easily move away. The irony of a city's success in enhancing its "business climate" is that the occupants of high-income jobs go elsewhere to live. Moreover, the expansion of corporate facilities displaces poor residents farther from the core. And the wide array of private consumption opportunities in the city is monopolized by a narrow band of the most literate, affluent, cosmopolitan men and women. Under these conditions, most public institutions are degraded. They are either ceded to the poor, like public schools, or harnessed to the private sector, like public building authorities. Economically, the sense of public life in the city is eroded.[18]

CITIES AND CULTURAL POWER

The shift from an industrial to a service economy is paralleled by visual as well as social changes. Just as the use of space shifts from "dirty" to "clean" work, so the visible legend of the city changes to reflect a new landscape of cultural power. To some degree this change is based on the consumption patterns of more affluent, highly educated residents—gentrifiers who graduated from college during the 1960s and 1970s. But it also represents change in the ideological meaning of the city, and as such it shapes the conscious production of city space.

Architecture and design are the intimate partners of redevelopment in this process. Downtown becomes a competitive arena of style, the real estate market's cutting edge. Whether they are in Pittsburgh's Golden Triangle, Renaissance Center in Detroit, or New York's Battery Park City, the buildings are both monumental and commercial. Indeed, they are monumental *because* they are commercial. They are meant to provide a new skyline for the city, a vertical perspective on the city's financial power. Not coincidentally, they are all important waterfront developments. Reusing this land wrenches it from the docks, the dives, the wholesale markets that for many years enclosed the commercial district and limited its expansion. The waterfront's reuse grows out of both the desire to capture a scarce amenity and a reconsideration of the cultural value of centrality.[19]

Cities never lose the moral aura of central places. This is the secret of their uniqueness that, in turn, explains the endless fascination with rebuilding and the deep nostalgia for structures that have been torn down. What common history there is in American cities is located in the center. This is the marketplace of ideas and commerce, the site of oldest buildings, the area of public ceremony and desire. Theaters coexist with peep shows, corporate headquarters with wholesalers and jobbers, city halls with video arcades. Despite its heterogeneous uses, this is the most attractive place for real estate investment. The irony is that more investment tends to destroy the center by eating away at its diversity.

The recent redevelopment of the center is partly a reaction by institutional investors to risk in alternative investments such as Third World loans, suburban shopping malls, and office buildings in economically troubled Houston or Denver. But it also reflects a quest by certain parts of the middle classes for access to the city's historic cultural power. Beginning in the 1960s, a reaction against publicly funded urban renewal among more culturally sophisticated middle-class men and women inspired them to advocate the preservation rather than the tearing down of old buildings with historic value. They were mainly attracted to buildings in the center—the public halls and private houses that once belonged to, or were designed by, a patrician elite. These were among the first structures to attract the aesthetic eye of gentrification.

During the 1970s, the number of gentrifiers who put down roots in center-city neighborhoods rose. Mostly single men and women or childless couples, they bought nineteenth-century houses that had become run down and restored their old-style beauty. The way they used these houses differed from previous residents. They preferred architectural

restoration to modernization (except for creature comforts like bath-
rooms, kitchens, and air-conditioning). If the houses had been converted to rentals or single-room-occupancy hotels, they returned them
to single-family use, usually the owner's, or converted them into pricey
condominiums. Gentrifiers also tended to empty the streets. They didn't
congregate on corners or in front of their homes, and they didn't mingle
with neighbors. Neither did they patronize some of the old neighborhood stores, which were soon replaced by the restaurants, bookshops,
and clothing stores that catered to gentrifiers. From one point of view,
gentrification created a middle-class neighborhood on the basis of
cultural consumption. From another, considering the relative costs of
housing downtown and in the suburbs, it represented a rational form
of middle-class housing investment.[20]

By the 1980s, a significant movement of investors into some downtowns created pressure on government to generalize the benefits of incremental, private-sector urban renewal. While local governments created historic landmark districts and enacted legislation to encourage
reuse of old buildings in the center, the federal government changed the
tax laws to make historic preservation and commercial reuse more de-
ductible. Every U.S. city now glories in its historic downtown as a magnet
for further private-market investment. Gentrification thus provided a
stepping-stone from the federally funded urban renewal that tore down
so many old buildings during the 1950s and 1960s to the speculative new
construction that augmented the central city during the 1980s. Today, no
downtown is considered complete without office towers, ethnic quarters,
cultural complexes, and gentrification.

As a cultural ensemble, downtown's selling point is that it contributes
to urban economic growth by attracting tourists. But the major tourists
are the city's own residents. Those at higher income levels seek out new
restaurants, shop for imports of finely wrought or singular goods, and
go to look at the places where art is produced, exhibited, and sold. These
spaces for cultural consumption are generally located in the center, or
in adjacent derelict districts, where rents are cheap, buildings are old
enough to provide an atmosphere, and a dense pattern of support services emerges. New York's SoHo provided an unplanned model for this
sort of urban revitalization. But during the 1970s, Boston's Faneuil Hall
Marketplace and Baltimore's Inner Harbor turned it into a planning
model. Faneuil Hall is particularly interesting because its developers
took a strong design concept from the existing use of the building and
used it to displace the fruit and vegetable vendors who rented stalls
there. They were replaced by stands selling arts and crafts products, imported foods, and other gift items that can be found elsewhere. The essence of the transformation, however, is that it opens Faneuil Hall to

middle-class use and signals to white residents and tourists that this is a place for them. By making a permanent commercial "festival" out of a grubby daily market, the developers of Faneuil Hall eliminated both the "periodic" use of the space and authentic, even functional, popular culture.[21]

In large part, redeveloping the downtown depends on the commercial re-creation of an urban middle-class culture. More sophisticated than suburbia, the newly interesting downtown is a realm of the senses. Its spatial organization and visual cues "open" the center to a highly selective consumption. In its conversion from small shops, industrial lofts, and working-class homes, downtown is caught up in—and spearheads—an "artistic mode of production." Artists are the primary consumers in this image of the city, and everyone in the more cerebral, or more pretentious, part of the middle class is interested in bridging art and life.[22]

The new downtown also bridges public and private spheres. Large mixed-use projects typically blend shops on the lower floors, offices in the middle, and apartments above. They allude to the density and vitality of older city streets without the hint of chaos, the expectation of the unexpected, that is part of an old city's fabric. New urban spaces give a clear sense of keeping the unruliness of the city out. To enter them, people come inside from the street: they are neither purely public nor private spaces. The State of Illinois Center in Chicago is perhaps the most perverse example of this "liminality." Built for government offices, the project has the atrium design of modern hotels, and the first few floors comprise a shopping center. Projects like these usually enclose an extremely large volume of space. They often include glass-sided elevators or high escalators, which are likely to be filled with moving crowds. But the grandeur of their scale conflicts with the triviality of their function. While shopping may have become a social experience that men and women value in itself, the stores in these mixed-use projects are usually branches of national chains that sell mass-produced goods.[23]

To some extent the quest for distinction in mixed-use spaces has come to rest on the notion of the city as festival. This suits the reorganization of the city as a consumption space, where shoppers are provided with a built environment that contextualizes the ephemeral while the buildings themselves are decontextualized from the city's past. The festival aspect of urban space fits a postmodern susceptibility to eccentricity and invention. Its "free-market populism" benefits the eclectic consumer while segregating those who can pay from those who live on the street. Much of the festival use of the city center relates to the "society of spectacle" that is described in the work of contemporary cultural critics. Born of the late-nineteenth-century burst of commercialism and urbanization, a city of spectacle features passive crowds floating among commercial dis-

tractions. But the city's adoption of a festival theme also reflects the influence of theme parks in the culture of contemporary spaces. Theme
parks, or their urban equivalents in either red-brick or atrium shopping
centers, organize varied bundles of consumption. Equally important,
they also organize how people experience the space of consumption: the
city becomes an imaginary stage-set for dream fulfillment.[24]

While the qualities of place can be abstracted in both historic preservation and new construction, the real downtown is formed by joining cir-
cuits of economic and cultural capital. Old buildings provide an object of
aesthetic interest; a site for relatively low-cost cultural production and
consumption, especially among more adventurous cultural consumers;
and a magnet for real estate investment. The physical infrastructure
generates markets for architectural restorations as well as avant-garde
art; together, they create a downtown "scene" that—with enough consumers—sparks a booming local service economy. This local economy,
however, is highly skewed toward high-class and international uses. It
has more art galleries than dry cleaners, more clothing boutiques than
supermarkets. The local real estate market grows in tandem with the sale
of historical replicas, from Victorian furniture to "French country an-
tiques." Recognizing these areas of the city as historic landmark districts
legitimizes property investment there and gives a certain cachet to local
business establishments. The areas become well known by means of articles in the daily newspapers and magazines. Target of an ever more
mediated middle-class consumption, the historic and cultural downtown
attracts more new investment to the central business district. In part because of the arrival of foreign investors, the old financial district sprouts
new office towers. What these buildings represent—their cultural power
in the world economy—contradicts the local or avant-garde spirit of
most initial gentrifiers.

If downtown spells fun for the more sophisticated middle class, it is
not so hospitable to the unemployed, the homeless, and lower-income
groups. Over the past twenty years revitalization has eliminated low-rent
housing from the center, especially the skid row flophouses and single-
room-occupancy hotels that catered to a transient, older, jobless group
of men that used to be labeled homeless. Revitalization has also displaced
the stores such people patronized—food and liquor shops, used clothing
stores, pawnshops. New shops and the firms in new office buildings displace the labor market. Unlike the old docks, railroad yards, and ware-
houses that used to abut the center, they do not recruit the homeless as
casual labor. The new downtown provides so much less living space for a
poor population that these men and women are literally homeless. High
property values and low vacancy rates decrease their chances of finding
even a temporary place to settle down, while the density of activity and

transportation downtown continually lure them to the center. In recent years the homeless population has been swelled by more women and by families with children that cannot make enough money to pay the rent. Ironically, they are driven out of most private-sector public spaces, especially in front of the tonier shops, and so they try to find shelter in the bus and subway stations, railroad terminals, and city streets.[25]

Just as middle-class consumers of the city demand more meaningful public space, so do homeless men and women seek public space as the last remaining shelter. Whether cities can provide public space for either group—in which proportion, and where—has become an index of public and private social power.

CITIES AND SOCIAL POWER

As the largest cities have begun to elect mayors from African-American and Latin communities, the cities themselves have become less prized. Public institutions are required to expand their functions to cover more human needs—adjudicating court cases, tending children all day, providing temporary shelter—while funding lags. Crime and drug sales plague many residents who cannot insulate themselves behind private security guards. From banker to mayor to drug gang, in the city there are many kinds of social power.

When we talk about cities in America today, we should differentiate between three "orders" of cities that create vastly different claims to social power. Within the global social order, the most power is concentrated in New York and Los Angeles, America's largest cities and largest financial and communications capitals. These cities are not fatally threatened by recent downturns in jobs and housing prices that are so inflated they forestall mobility. But their prosperity has left a hollow ring of outer boroughs or inner suburbs between downtown's expansion and more affluent suburban counties. In both cases, the "city" will only continue to grow as a result of regional growth; most older areas of the city house new immigrants who are saving to move out and an underemployed native population. Other cities may look like smaller versions of New York and Los Angeles. By contrast, they lack the base in transnational enterprises that gives these two cities global scope and scale as well as a fearsome glamor.

Aside from the two world cities, a more purely national order differentiates power according to cities' age and region of the country. Newer cities are mostly southwestern and southeastern. They have a "suburban" style of life, which is automobile-dependent, home-owning, private. They also have a base in newer manufacturing industries—mainly as a result of extensive military contracts—as well as regional and national services. Lacking a claim to the social power of global capitals, they none-theless provide the sort of middle-class life that people identify with the American Dream. And they may be the only cities in the country to do so.

Within cities, another order differentiates between the populist power of the neighborhoods and the financial power of the business center. Neighborhood residents hold the city's remaining manufacturing jobs, work in the civil service, and provide the major part of the work force in the private service economy. But because they cannot or will not move out of the city—for reasons of income and race—they bear the burden of the moral problems that no city government can solve. In the neigh-borhoods are the homeless shelters, the drug wars, the violence that rips through public schools. And in the neighborhoods we also find the fierce sense of territory that inspires racial terror. From these contradictions arises that which is known in American society as community, the city's only form of legitimate social power.

Since the urban reforms that began in the late 1960s, "community" has been a universal rallying cry for improving public services. The con-cept of community has also been a focus for organizing low-income men and women to demand access to political power. While community move-ments have made social power in the city more competitive than before, they have also provided a way to integrate unorganized groups into po-litical life.

Twenty years of experience indicate that the vehicles of community empowerment are flawed. Administrative decentralization, for example, has often suffered from too little funding controlled by too few people. Central bureaucracies, both federal and citywide, have been reluctant to give up control over hiring and budgets. Many civil servants, moreover, such as police and fire fighters, do not live in the cities where they are employed, either because they cannot afford high housing prices or they want better living conditions. Neither are coalitions that elect minority-group mayors effective tools for community empowerment. On the one hand, urban minorities are often divided along the racial and ethnic, as well as political, lines. Terms like the "black community" and "Latin com-munity" encompass a wide variety of competing local groups. On the other hand, the public goods and social conditions toward which they strive are not necessarily allocated by public command. Quality of life in the city is so dependent on income that it is essentially controlled by pri-vate decisions.

Despite its real limitations, the concept of community suggests how little even the poorest neighborhoods of a city conform to the stereotype of "social disorganization." [26] Non-nuclear families and the working poor make up a large portion of the urban population, but the areas where they live generate their own, fairly continuous structure of community organizations. Linked by individual activists, these organizations respond to both community issues and external conditions. The encouragement of City Hall (and formerly, the federal government) enables them to develop a fairly stable base that may remain outside the control of traditional urban institutions, especially political parties. At best, community organizations goad the city government into giving poor residents of the city a little more access to public goods—longer library hours, a drug treatment program, a slightly more responsive police department. At worst, they have no effect on housing, jobs, and income— the basic parameters of living conditions.

The structure of the whole society affects the issues that are considered urban problems. But while poverty, drug addiction, and decaying public infrastructure are national in scope, no national institution has the moral authority to compel their solution. Moreover, as long as cities have little autonomy in the face of global markets, their problems are defined in terms set by the private sector. Americans still visualize cities as the public center of their society. Yet it is a hollow center, more an image of power than a means of empowerment.

PART THREE

Institutional Adaptations

TWELVE

National News Culture and the Rise of the Informational Citizen

Michael Schudson

If being well informed means having at hand reliable information about the community and nation, the international world as it impinges on national interests, the natural world, and the world of the arts, then Americans have never before been so well informed nor so abundantly served by broadcasting, the press, and publishing.

If, however, being well informed means having a world view coherent enough to order the buzz of information around us, and having enough personal involvement with people, ideas, and issues beyond our private worlds to absorb and use information, then there is little reason for self-congratulation. This second sense is more nearly what we mean, or should mean, by "the well-informed citizen." The well-informed citizen is defined not by a consumer's familiarity with the contemporary catalog of available information but by a citizen's formed set of interests that make using the catalog something other than a random effort. The news media increasingly help provide the materials for the *informational* citizen, but they do not and cannot create the *informed* citizen. The informed citizen appears in a society in which being informed makes good sense, and that is a function not of individual character or news media performance, but of political culture, broadly defined.

Well-reported news, free from censorship, does not a democracy make. Full and accurate reporting of candidates' records and policy positions, even if we had that, would not a well-prepared voter create. What, then, is the impact of all the information around us? What sort of person does it help establish or, at least, set the conditions for? Who are we, these informational people, who daily digest political scandal here and earthquake there, a crime wave in our home town and a guerrilla movement in El Salvador, a ban on alcohol at the local beach and a surgeon general's report on passive smoking, a protest against local developers and a worried report on Third World debt? Are we disabled by media saturation? Distracted or deadened or at least thrown off stride by the avalanche of information?

I don't think that's what happens. People probably muddle through their lives as well today as people ever did (although that may not apply to the poorest residents of urban ghettos). Indeed, they may muddle along a little better, armed with the view that the world is subject to their control. Fundamental matters of fertility, contraception, sexual satisfaction, pain relief, and contact with other human beings across a distance are all more within human capacity and even individual control than ever before. At the same time, different groups in society feel newly entitled to control over their lives—notably blacks and women—and they have found broad political support for their sense of entitlement.

The growth of the media, the explosion of information, and the pounding headache of hype have not prevented this; on the contrary, they have helped it along. Most anxious and apocalyptic commentators on the media forget these and other fundamental realities. Without firmly planting their feet in sociological soil, they examine the media out of social context, picturing the media as self-contained technologies rather than porous social practices, and they often ask unreasonably that "art" or "truth" flow from the media spigot.

Often critics find major cause for alarm in a trend or development of the past year or five years or decade, although, in a somewhat larger compass, our media environment has not changed. The media in the United States, in 1990, as in 1960, are more completely controlled by private corporations than are the media in any other industrialized country in the world. The range of political opinion available in mainstream media in the United States is narrower than in much of Western Europe; this has been true not only for the last generation but for much of American history. At the same time, the freedom of the American media to investigate and to publish is more supported by institutional resources and more protected by constitutional safeguards than in any other country, both today and thirty years ago.

That said about fundamental continuities in the American media, changes in the past thirty years have significantly altered the ordinary person's experience of popular and public culture and have surely enlarged the role of the media, especially the news media. One sign of change is that the concept of "the media" itself has become inescapable. The term *the media* (meaning, especially, the news media), was not much used before the 1970s. It came into play, I think, in part because the term *the press* began to seem limited as a descriptor of both print and broadcast journalism (although the term survives in this usage). It gained wide exposure thanks to the Nixon administration's vendetta against "the media." Nixon inherited both the Vietnam War and Lyndon Johnson's "credibility gap." He and Vice-President Spiro Agnew declared war on the news media, arguing publicly and privately that the nation's leading news institutions were an independent source of political power managed by bleeding-heart liberals and dyed-in-the-wool Nixon-haters. This forceful attack helped create the beast it sought to describe. It certainly helped give the beast a name.

So, too, did Vietnam and Watergate and the events leading up to what Hedrick Smith has described as the "political earthquake" of 1974.[1] As Vietnam tore apart consensus between the executive and the Congress in the conduct of foreign policy, between hawks and doves within the Congress, between parents and children even in families where fathers were Cabinet officers or *New York Times* editors, the media scrambled to represent these divisions. When governing leaders spoke in a single voice, so did the press; when dissent sparked on the floor of the Senate, it fired the media. If the media followed rather than led the breakdown of consensus, they learned from the experience a new style of journalism. In covering Vietnam and Watergate, journalists did not abandon "objectivity" so much as recognize what a poor shadow of objective reporting they had been allegiant to for a generation. Journalism sought, sometimes awkwardly, sometimes irresponsibly, sometimes bravely and brilliantly, to invent the independence it had long claimed to exercise. This, too, helped establish "the media" as a distinct institution.

The present uneasy feeling of media omnipresence and information overload comes in part from this sharp, visible presence of the media as an institution. It comes also from the increasing nationalization of the news media and the identification of the nation itself as an "imagined community," to use Benedict Anderson's phrase, with the national news. It comes as well from other transformations in the character of mass-mediated information—the blurring of the line between news and entertainment, the melding of public and private, and the politicization of once private affairs, and the increasing efficiency of organizations that "target" messages to specialized audiences. All of this makes American citizens informational cousins, even if we are not a particularly close-knit family. These are the features of cultural transformation I want to discuss in the sections that follow.

NATIONALIZATION OF THE NEWS MEDIA, 1960–90

"Nationalization" did not happen all at once. In fact, Godfrey Hodgson has argued that the "nationalizing of the American consciousness" was the primary trend in the media in the late 1950s and early 1960s.[2] But in 1960 or even 1963, the machinery of nationalization was only partially in place, the political and social consequences of cultural nationalization still on the horizon of consciousness, the sense that citizens know too much about things they can do too little about not so keenly experienced.

A national television news system, present in the 1950s, took on new importance in the 1960s and later. The 30-minute format (instead of 15) became standard in 1963. In that same year, the Roper poll found, for the first time, more Americans claiming to rely on television than on newspapers as their primary source of news. To the three network evening news shows were added "60 Minutes" (in 1968) and its imitators, "20/20" (1978) and others. ABC began a late-night news program in 1979 called "America Held Hostage," a daily update of the Iranian hostage crisis. In 1980, its name changed to "Nightline" and it became a regular part of the broadcast news diet.

Only in the 1970s did news on television take on a central role in the thinking of the broadcasting corporations themselves as "60 Minutes" became the most highly rated program in the country and local news began to turn big profits. "60 Minutes" made television news interesting and profitable. This economic maturing of television news coincided with its political coming of age. When President Kennedy began holding live televised press conferences, television as a regular news source gained official imprimatur (the famous Murrow-on-McCarthy programs of the early 1950s were exceptional; television news was superficial, unvisual, and short). It was not until the Vietnam War that television news coverage took on a centrality, both for Washington elites and the public at large. Then the evening news became the symbolic center of the national agenda and the national consciousness. Political campaigners measured their success as much by seconds on the evening news as by polls; presidents—notably Johnson and Nixon—became obsessed with the television screen.

Within two decades of the time television network news became ringmaster of the American circus, network dominance was challenged. The networks in 1970 had no competition; only 10 percent of American homes had cable systems. By 1989 the figure was 53 percent. The networks' share of total television viewership has steadily declined, so much so that in 1990 the networks formed their own public relations firm to promote themselves collectively against cable (and other) competition.[3] In news gathering in recent years, new technologies have enabled local television stations to steal a march on the networks. The availability to local stations of vans equipped with satellite dishes, combined with the growing costs of syndicated news programs, has led to several satellite-connected consortiums of local stations that cover national news events on their own. The combined audience for the three evening network news programs has declined by nearly 25 percent since 1980.[4]

In 1979, the cable industry began C-SPAN as a public service gesture. C-SPAN's tiny audience is important and the presence of C-SPAN in the Congress has affected the conduct of public affairs. The House of Representatives was on C-SPAN from the beginning; the Senate joining in in 1986.[5] Cable News Network (CNN) began operations in 1980; it provided news around the clock and quickly established a reputation for responsible reporting. Also unknown in President Kennedy's day was television news on public television; in 1975, the Public Broadcasting Service brought the McNeil-Lehrer program to most communities.

As television news has expanded, radio news has had something of a renaissance. In 1970, noncommercial and educational radio licensees formed National Public Radio and a year later launched their first network news program, "All Things Considered." The NPR audience is relatively (seven million listeners) small but devoted;[6] among academics a reference to a recent "All Things Considered" interview is as likely to be common coin as reference to a current Hollywood hit.

News means money on radio as well as television. There had been some experiments with an all-news format in the 1950s, but only in 1964, when WINS in New York became an all-news station, did the phenomenon attract general attention. WCBS joined as a second all-news station in New York in 1967. Soon dozens of cities had all-news stations. "When you want water," said one station manager, "you turn on the faucet. When you want news, you turn us on."[7]

Equally important, "talk radio" became lively and popular. Larry King's nationally syndicated show made its debut on twenty-eight stations in 1978 but eventually served more than 350. CNN adapted it to television in 1985, and by 1990 the program was running nightly on both radio and television. There were interview programs before Larry King's, but his innovation (begun in Miami in 1960) was to add live call-ins to the interview format.[8] News, or "reality programming," has become a pervasive cultural experience.

In the 1990s, if I want to get a copy of the *New York Times* or the *Wall Street Journal* in my home town of San Diego, I need only open my front door and pick up my home-delivery copy on the driveway. As late as 1971, when Anthony Russo had strong incentive to read the *New York Times* because they were publishing the Pentagon Papers, which he had helped Daniel Ellsberg photocopy, there were only a few locations in Los Angeles where the paper could be found.[9] Overcoming the vast size of the country, satellite communication technology and computerized printing systems have made the regional and national newspaper a reality.

The *Wall Street Journal* has had a national presence for some time, but in the past generation it sharply increased its coverage as a general newspaper, rather than an exclusively business newsletter. It expanded to a

two-section format in 1980. The *Los Angeles Times,* when Otis Chandler
became publisher in 1960, had one foreign bureau and two reporters
in its Washington bureau. It was a provincial, conservative paper that,
within a decade, developed into a distinguished, professional newspaper.
The same thing happened at the *Washington Post.* When the late Howard
Simons joined the *Post* in the early 1960s, the paper had a single foreign
correspondent and a single business reporter. Not until it released the
Pentagon Papers in 1971, according to editor Ben Bradlee, did the *Post*
make "some kind of ultimate commitment to go super first class."[10]

Another indicator of nationalization is that elite newspaper news services began to compete with the standard Associated Press (AP) and
United Press International (UPI) services. The *Los Angeles Times–Washington Post* news service began in 1961 and grew to more than 350 clients
by 1980. The *New York Times* news service began during World War I, but
as late as 1960 had only 50 clients; by 1980 there were 500 clients. These
news services are not so much high-fiber substitutes for the traditional
wire services as they are dietary supplements, adding more detailed and
analytic news for the local subscriber. So while metropolitan daily newspapers have continued to die, new sources of national news have become
available. *Time* and *Newsweek* developed into professional publications,
and other magazines provided new sources of public affairs news and
comment, too, including the *Washington Post* national weekly edition
(1983) and several magazines that reached a mass market—notably *Roll-
ing Stone* and *Mother Jones.*

The largest and most prosperous newspapers exert regional influence
well beyond city limits. The *Los Angeles Times* challenges the *Orange
County Register* in Orange County, and still further south, its San Diego
County edition competes with the *San Diego Union* and *San Diego Tribune.*
In Santa Cruz, California, the local daily, the *Sentinel* (owned by Ottaway
Newspapers, a Dow-Jones company), is only one of several newspapers
available by home delivery: there are also the *New York Times,* the *San
Francisco Chronicle,* the *San Jose Mercury* (a Knight-Ridder paper), and the
Wall Street Journal.

All this needs emphasis when the most visible national newspaper is
the flashy and widely disparaged *USA Today.* Begun in 1982, it had a
circulation of more than 1.5 million by 1987. Printed in thirty-two different sites and produced by satellite transmission of copy, it is a technical achievement of considerable proportion. There is some question
about its journalistic achievement, though little dispute about its influence on the look and style of other newspapers in the country. It initiated widespread use of color, for example. Its almost pathological focus
on the weather has encouraged more comprehensive weather reporting
elsewhere.[11]

While an average citizen has access to more, better, more critical, and more diverse sources of national news today than a generation ago, control over news is paradoxically in the hands of fewer and fewer institutions, run more and more by accountants. The chain newspapers are not so much politically conservative as economically risk-averse, which generally comes to the same thing. (In 1986 there were 1,657 dailies, down only slightly from 1,763 in 1960—and the number of cities with a daily newspaper actually increased. But a mere fourteen corporations account for over half of daily newspaper circulation.) [12] While the quality of journalism may be more often increased than decreased in communities whose independent newspapers are bought out by chains, the chance for an independent-minded publisher or individual eccentric to run his or her own show is dying fast. There is a legitimate concern that chain ownership inevitably precludes diversity. The op-ed page, a development that became a standard practice in the 1970s to increase the diversity of opinion, increasingly seems the same from one newspaper to the next. In leading news institutions, the reliance on official government sources is overwhelming, the absence of left-wing critics or commentators consistent, and the inside-the-northeast-corridor orientation hard for a midwesterner, southerner, or westerner to ignore.

NATIONAL NEWS CULTURE

Accompanying the nationalization of news institutions is the nationalization of newsroom culture. The managers of small papers or television news shows around the country are aware, as never before, of what goes on on the networks, in *USA Today*, in the *New York Times*. So are their employees. One result has been the ability of blacks and women, and in some instances other minorities (Chicanos in Los Angeles, for example) to press their institutions for better treatment in the newsroom and more appropriate play in the news pages for the groups they identify with.[13] It may be hard to recall how recent these changes are. Before the 1960s, women journalists wrote about fashion and society—and rarely anything else. The National Press Club only admitted women in 1971. In 1966, the Chicago bureau chief for *Newsweek* could turn down a woman reporter from UPI for a job, explaining that "I need someone I can send anywhere, like to riots. And besides, what would you do if someone you were covering ducked into the men's room?"[14] That would be hard to get away with today.

The diversification of the newsroom may be less than it appears. In television news, women and minorities are most often seen on weekends, what has been known in the business as the "weekend ghetto." By the end of 1990, there were no women or minority anchors regularly assigned to any network evening news. Still, anecdotal evidence suggests that women (and to a lesser extent minorities) in the newsroom have made a real difference in what gets covered and what emphasis coverage receives. Women staff members at the *Los Angeles Times* spearheaded a major ten-part series on women in the work force in 1984; a woman editorial writer at the *Seattle Times* asserts that almost all the editorials done on subjects concerning children are done "because I'm here." [15]

Journalists at national news institutions are better educated than ever before, more likely than in the past to have come from relatively privileged backgrounds, and more likely to be paid relatively privileged wages. They are more and more likely to get their views from other journalists, not their own editors or publishers. They are likely to share in what Herb Gans calls a "Progressive" outlook—a belief in a two-party system, responsible capitalism, the virtues of small-town life, individualism, moderate measures under all circumstances, and some vague notion of the public interest.[16] The solidity of these values grows as more and more news is reported out of a single location—Washington, D.C. In Washington there is more of a social arena for journalistic culture than ever before. In 1961, there were some 1,500 journalists working in Washington—but more than 5,300 by 1987.[17] Journalists there can, and apparently do, talk mostly to one another.[18]

This is not to say that ours is now a seamless, coherent national journalistic culture. Look, for instance, at the growth of the Spanish-language media. In 1974, there were fifty-five Spanish-language radio stations; today there are 237. Twenty years ago, there were only a handful of television stations that broadcast Spanish-language programming. Today Univision, the largest Spanish-language television network, claims over 400 broadcast and cable affiliates. A new Spanish-language cable company, Galavision, began in 1989. Thirty-one television stations now are broadcast entirely in Spanish. These stations are concentrated in the "Hispanic Top Ten": Los Angeles, New York, San Francisco, Houston, Dallas, El Paso, Brownsville-McAllen, San Antonio, Miami, and Chicago.

Ethnic and linguistic diversity is well represented in the American media, both print and broadcast. So, too, are media flourishing that appeal to different religious groups, most visibly with the rise of the "televangelists." The technological capabilities that have made possible a dominant national news culture have also been a key resource for the growing power of more parochial but nonetheless nationally based "consumption communities." The nationalization of the news media has not meant the homogenization of media experience, but the creation of a new set of national arenas for a variety of distinctive subcultural tastes. For instance, thanks in part to computers and desktop publishing, there are (by rough estimate) some 100,000 newsletters in the country that circulate for free or as a part of an organization, association, or business. There is a newsletter industry, with its own trade associations; *Newsletters in Print* catalogs over 10,000 newsletters.[19] Pluralism is not without problems. Such cases as Ku Klux Klan use of easily accessible computer bulletin boards or unscrupulous evangelists on their own cable programs raise difficult issues. The new national media increase the visibility of pluralism more than they insist on homogenization.

In the world of information, the poor grow richer but the rich grow richer more rapidly (the "knowledge gap" hypothesis as communication researchers call it). The rich have more information and more incentive to get and use information efficiently. Take, for instance, the Republican National Committee's 1984 opposition research group that started collecting data and quotations on leading Democratic contenders early in the primaries. By the time the Democratic convention opened, the Republican computer had 75,000 items on Walter Mondale, including 45,000 quotes from all through his career. The data base was updated daily during the campaign. The materials were accessible through a computer reference dictionary, and computer links were made to 50 state party headquarters, 50 state campaign headquarters, and Republican spokesmen in all 208 broadcast rating markets. This was impressive. More impressive still was that similar systems were available to all Republican candidates for the House in 1986 through the Republican Information Network. If a candidate was running against a Democrat incumbent, he could instantly learn the incumbent's voting record back to 1974 on any issue. Now, this did not change the outcome of the 1984 election; and Republicans remained a minority in the House, even after 1986. But it gives a sense of the sophistication of the new information technologies for matters very close to the heart of the democratic process.[20]

Thanks to the campaign reform acts of the early 1970s, parties have taken to new forms of campaign fund raising, especially direct mail advertising. With computerized mailing lists and sophisticated targeting of zip code locations most likely to provide names of wealthy contributors, direct mail experts have transformed political fund raising. One senator (Tim Wirth, Democrat from Colorado) has 150,000 names in his computerized lists, divided into a thousand categories according to topic of interest, field, or occupation (117 names appear on the list of people interested in women's issues, 8 on the list of those interested in women in mining).[21] These lists are used for fund raising and self-promotion so that the right message can be addressed to the right people.

While the disproportionate weight of media and publicity lies, of course, with established powers, guerrilla media use has its brilliant practitioners. The first "Earth Day" (in 1970), a scheme of Wisconsin Senator Gaylord Nelson's to draw attention, especially through college teach-ins (an invention of the anti-war movement), to environmental issues, was a "patchwork of demonstrations and community activities," though a patchwork that attracted significant media attention and public interest. Planning for Earth Day 1990 was run by two different groups, one with 38 employees, and received backing from labor, business, and the media.[22] Weeks before Earth Day 1990, the *Los Angeles Times* was already covering not only Earth Day but the coverage of Earth Day. Like the 1988 election campaign, the media were as attracted to the story of media coverage as to the stories media coverage was covering.[23] News culture tends to consume itself.

THE NEWSIFICATION OF POPULAR CULTURE

An important corollary to the nationalization of news has been the nationalization of public problems and the nationalization of an audience for them. Most observers of the media have complained that serious news institutions have been turning news into entertainment, but the larger trend is that entertainment has turned into news. If "60 Minutes" exemplifies a trend to make news entertaining, the "Donahue" program is the model for making entertainment that feeds on the news.

"Donahue" was first syndicated out of Chicago in 1979; the "Oprah Winfrey Show" was syndicated in 1984, and in the last few years several other competitors have entered the fray. These programs are sometimes televised sideshows, parading the American psyche before us with an exaggerated, freakish self-consciousness. At the same time, cheaper than psychotherapy and more readily available than a close friend, they inform people about a wide range of social, psychological, medical, and occasionally (at least on "Donahue") political problems. The producers of "Donahue" conceive of their topics as "serious issues" or more precisely, "serious issues that are in the news." News culture becomes the central storehouse for the various national conversations in American society.[24]

Television unashamedly, in fact, proudly, runs dramatic programs, sit-coms, and soaps that borrow from contemporary controversies for plot material. This is not like the "spy" shows of the early 1960s that reflected a general Cold War ideology; these are programs whose makers frequently engage in careful research to model a plot episode after a recent news event or to mimic in a sit-com the arguments that rage around a contemporary social problem. This began with "All in the Family" in 1971. Over the course of just a few months, that new sit-com dealt with homosexuality, cohabitation, race and racism, women's rights, and miscarriage. By the end of the 1971–72 season, it was the top show in television, and producer Norman Lear developed enough clout to retain some independence from network censors. When a group called the Population Institute, a lobbying organization for promoting population control, set up a meeting in 1971 with television executives to encourage them to deal with population issues, Lear became personally interested in doing an episode that would deal with the population issue.[25] The "Maude has an abortion" episodes on "Maude" (a spin-off from "All in the Family") the next year were the highly controversial result. "M.A.S.H." dealt with the war in Vietnam (through displacement to Korea), and a whole array of made-for-television "problem" movies dealt with issues from child abuse to chemical pollution of the environment to wives murdering abusive husbands. "Lou Grant," a popular drama in the 1970s and early 1980s, was set in a metropolitan newsroom, and it borrowed directly from recent news events. *Mother Jones* took pride in telling its readers that the January 19, 1981, "Lou Grant" show on the United States dumping hazardous products in the Third World drew on a 1979 special issue of the magazine, thereby using television fiction to legitimate its own journalism.[26] In 1989, after a jury found for the defendants in a medical malpractice suit in Florida, the plaintiff's lawyer asked for a new trial because, he claimed, a recently aired "L.A. Law" episode in which the doctors won in a malpractice case was "propaganda" that probably influenced the jury.[27]

This newsification of popular culture is no doubt rooted in a long-standing Puritan temper that distrusts entertainment unless it is instructional. But the leakage of news into comedy and drama in the past decades has a more contemporary ideological source, too. Critics of popular culture argued convincingly from the 1960s on that entertainment is a form of instruction, whether it is meant to be or not. It was an old complaint that mass media portrayal of crime and violence encourages crime and violence, renewed in the 1960s with television as the target. It was more novel and more challenging to complain that the subordinate status of women and minorities in contemporary society was encouraged by mass media stereotyping. This criticism was effectively turned into politics by Action for Children's Television in its persistent attacks on children's television programming and by the Ford Foundation's support for Children's Television Workshop and "Sesame Street." "Sesame Street" may look almost painfully self-conscious about racial and sexual stereotyping and, critics charge, not nearly self-conscious enough in its submission to the rapid-fire pace and gleam of commercial broadcasting. But it provides parents a televisual haven of safety from the persistent violence, sexism, and racism of commercials and programming emanating from the commercial stations.

The cultural, rather than political, consequences of newsification may be the more important. We live with more vivid, dramatic knowledge of events around the world than ever before. We live our "real" lives bodily, in our homes and work places and on our streets. But at the same time we live alongside the hyper-reality on our television screens and radios and in our newspapers. Contemporary life becomes some kind of science fiction, two parallel worlds moving along in tandem, usually disconnected, only occasionally, and then perhaps jarringly, in touch.

TELEVISION IN THE MEDIA SYSTEM

To tell the story of dominant developments in the news media in the past generation as a story of nationalization, newsification, and the rising symbolic centrality of something called "news" differs substantially from some other popular accounts. Perhaps the most common story is that *television* is the simple one-word answer to the question What has happened to the media in the past 30 years? In this view, television has overwhelmed society, propelling the decline of literacy, the decline of seriousness, and the decline of political participation.

But consider what should be a simple instance: as television news has expanded and as the public's professed reliance on television news has increased, newspaper "penetration" has declined. Newspaper readership among young people is particularly low. What could be a simpler cause-and-effect relationship? Vulgar television does in virtuous newsprint. This has often been cited as incontrovertible evidence of the dangers of television. But in a comparison of 20 Western countries (and Japan) from 1964 to 1984, Leo Bogart found no overall relationship between the spread of television and newspaper penetration.[28] While the number of television receivers per capita and the total time spent viewing television are pretty much the same from one Western country to the next, newspaper circulation per 1,000 population differs dramatically from Japan (562 newspapers per 1,000) to Sweden (521) to the United Kingdom (414) to the United States (268) to Canada (220) to Italy (96). During this period, when television penetration increased everywhere, newspaper circulation per capita also increased in Japan and Sweden, declined imperceptibly in Canada (1 percent) and Italy (5 percent), and declined dramatically in the United States (16 percent) and Britain (21 percent). Television certainly is vital in American news today, yet its centrality can be (and usually is) exaggerated. American journalists underestimate how much time people spend reading newspapers and overestimate how much time they spend watching television news. They mistakenly believe that making print more like television, with shorter news items and more feature stories, will bring in more readers. In fact, in recent years, papers gaining circulation showed no markedly different editorial practices from those losing circulation. Distribution, not content, is the cause of a loss of readership.[29] That is, the main decline in newspaper circulation is in single-copy sales, rather than home delivery, in large metropolitan areas, and the problem seems to be not that people find television more satisfying, but that the suburbanization of American life, the decay of urban neighborhoods, and the unemployment, poor health, poor education, and disaffection of the urban poor make engagement in a community through the newspaper an irrelevancy. The other side of that coin, as Ben Bagdikian has observed, is also important: the economics of newspaper production has led competing papers in a city to fight for the same upscale consumers in order to attract the same advertisers. This process, leading to more and more monopoly newspaper cities, leads to news content less and less relevant to the blue-collar citizens who were once reliable newspaper subscribers. The newspaper, in short, in moving upscale, has significantly authored its own irrelevance.

Television is a centrally important medium in American culture, but it is not in and of itself either the sum of or an explanation for the changing informational environment of American citizens.

ARE THE NEWS MEDIA MOVING RIGHT OR LEFT?

Another story is that the main development in the news media has been a sharp move of news content to the right (a favorite theory on the left) or, alternatively, that the national news media have been captured by a corps of too well paid, too comfortable, too Eastern, too Ivy League, and too liberal journalists (a favorite, naturally, on the right).

In 1969 an economist with the Federal Reserve, Reed Irvine, created Accuracy in Media, an organization devoted to pointing out every actual, and imagined, left-wing bias in what Irvine calls "Big Media," meaning the networks, the few newspapers of national influence, the news magazines, and the wire services.[30] Today AIM reports a membership of more than 25,000, an annual budget of $1.5 million, a speakers bureau, a newsletter with a circulation over 30,000, a daily 3-minute radio program that appears on 200 stations nationally, and a weekly column that appears in some 100 newspapers. A variety of other right-wing critics of the media arose in the wake of AIM. For instance, Robert and Linda Lichter, conservative media scholars, founded the Center for Media and Public Affairs in 1986, which surveys media performance and analyzes media impact on public opinion. In 1986, Fairness and Accuracy in Reporting (FAIR), a left-wing counterpart to AIM, was established.

While the right-wing institutes pushed a view of the left-wing media, their very existence, coupled with the general rightward tilt of elite political thinking in the 1980s, helped promote the idea of a shift to the right in the press. FAIR went over the "Nightline" guest lists for 1985–

88 and found an overwhelming preponderance of government officials, almost all of them white and male. What else is new? FAIR observes the flourishing of political talk shows hosted by conservatives—William Buckley's "Firing Line" being the grandaddy, followed by John McLaughlin, Patrick Buchanan, Rowland Evans, and Robert Novak. No show at the time of FAIR's study was hosted by a liberal.[31]

If there was a shift to the right in the media in the 1980s, it may have had something to do with consternation in the business world in the 1970s over the media seeming to tilt against it. Mobil began taking out ads in the 1970s (and the new terms *advocacy advertising* and *advertorial* were coined) in the *New York Times*. In 1975 corporations spent $100 million in advocacy advertising, aiming as much as a third of their total advertising expenses toward people as "citizens" rather than as "consumers." Business groups began to seek ways to influence the news media by giving prizes for economic reporting, establishing business reporting training programs at universities, sponsoring arts and cultural programs on television, creating or supporting new neo-conservative think tanks, and holding roundtables with journalists and complaining loudly that they were being maligned by a "liberal" press.[32]

Perhaps the desire to influence the media had something to do with a loss of direct control over them, notably over television. In the 1950s, sponsors of television programs had significant influence over the content of programming, to the point of reviewing scripts before broadcast. But from the time of the "quiz show scandal" in 1959 (when it was revealed that quiz shows were "fixed") on, the networks took tighter control of the reins themselves. Moreover, as advertising time grew more and more expensive and competition for television time increased, the program with but a single sponsor disappeared from the screen. Between 1967 and 1981 the number of commercials on the networks per week increased from 1,856 to 4,079, while "spot" commercials increased from 2,413 to 5,300 as the standard length of the commercial declined from 60 seconds to 30 seconds.[33] It's no wonder that recently General Motors, among others, has asked for something new in advertising lingo—"pod protection." That is, GM wants to be the only automobile ad within a group of commercials (or "pod") aired consecutively within a single commercial break in a program.[34]

The decline of direct advertiser control over television was minor compared to the loss of business control over the political agenda. The sixties created the climate for a set of issues and institutions that cast a cold eye on business in the 1970s. The Congress, especially the Senate, was influenced beginning in the early 1960s by northern Democrats, who successfully challenged what had been a domain of conservative southern Democrats. This helped the passage of liberal policies in the late

1960s and 1970s, including the creation of new government agencies to monitor business activity—the Environmental Protection Agency (1970), the Equal Employment Opportunity Commission (1965), the Occupational Safety and Health Review Commission (1970), and the Consumer Products Safety Commission (1973), not to mention a newly militant Federal Trade Commission. The press, devoted as always to covering government, covered the new agencies and so shone a light on business that was necessarily more critical and concentrated than in the past.

Business antipathy to the media was also a response to the success of Ralph Nader, who helped invent a new public opposition to business. Nader used some old-fashioned media methods in his rise to prominence. He first published an article on automobile safety in *The Nation* in 1959. His book *Unsafe at Any Speed* propelled the 1966 legislation that made the federal government a guarantor of highway and automobile safety and led to the "recall" of automobiles with safety defects. In the following years, Nader established a fleet of public interest lobbying and research organizations both in Washington and around the country. The federal government, by establishing new agencies to protect occupational health and consumer safety, and private industry, by getting itself into and mishandling near-disasters (Three-Mile Island) and major disasters (Bhopal), did the rest. The Congress, while still the center of Washington legislative activity, was increasingly a consumer of policy initiatives, not only from the White House but from a mushrooming assortment of lobbyists.[35] While citizens groups and public interest groups remain a small fraction of the total lobbying effort in Washington, they nonetheless proliferated between 1960 and 1980.

So the media, following Washington, moved left in the 1970s; again following Washington and the coming to power of the Reagan administration, they moved right in the 1980s. Too many media critics, left and right, have overestimated the independence of the media and underplayed the power of media routines, repeatedly documented in studies by Edward Epstein, Herbert Gans, Todd Gitlin, Daniel Hallin, Stephen Hess, Michael Robinson, Leon Sigal, Gaye Tuchman, and others.[36] What changed from the 1960s to the 1970s to the 1980s was the political climate that gave differential legitimacy to different sources. The media, in the middle when a polyphony of voices are raining in, have few intellectual resources for independent judgment and no political portfolio for independent polemic.

The 1960s did change the internal culture of working journalists. Television news coverage of election campaigns is more negative than it used to be for both Republican and Democratic candidates.[37] Reporters, like patients seeking medical counsel, are more likely than they used to be to seek second opinions. Institutions well versed in giving second opinions have multiplied rapidly in and around Washington. There is a "social movement industry" now, as Mayer Zald and John McCarthy write, with more resources than ever before.[38] The result, in the national media, is a picture of the world not more left or more right but more muddled and multidimensional (and, if your tastes run to such terminology, more postmodern).

THE SURVIVAL—AND FLOURISHING—OF PRINT

It remains to say a word about the not negligible medium in which this chapter appears—the book. Little is more important in characterizing the changing contemporary culture than the fact that in 1960 only 41 percent of the adult population (aged 25 and over) had graduated from high school, while in 1988 it was 76 percent. In 1960, 7.7 percent of the adult population had four years or more of college, by 1988 this had jumped to 20.3 percent.[39] While most college education is largely technical or preprofessional, many institutions stress a "liberal education," and pockets of "liberal education" exist even in technically oriented schools, providing an opening for critical inquiry that high schools rarely afford. Literacy is not on its last legs. In fact, there are more books published by a greater variety of publishers and distributed through more bookstores today than ever before. Despite major mergers and acquisitions in the publishing business, the total number of publishers has increased—to say nothing of the "desktop publishing" that the personal computer has made possible. Where some 15,000 new books and new editions were published in 1960, there were 36,000 in 1970 and 56,000 in 1987.[40] In 1963, there were 993 book publishing establishments; 2,264 in 1987.[41]

Still, books reach the public through an increasingly concentrated distribution network. B. Dalton had more than 500 stores by 1980 and nearly 1,000 when it was bought by Barnes & Noble in 1987; Waldenbooks had more than 700 stores in 1980; 1,100 by 1987.[42] The ten largest bookstore chains accounted for 57 percent of all book sales, and B. Dalton and Waldenbooks exercise a significant impact on the industry as a whole.

Books as a category are up against heavy entertainment and leisure competition—not just television, but the new adaptations of the home television set. There are twice as many video rental outlets as bookstores.[43] But the uses of print literacy are still growing. Reports that ours is now a television culture are vastly exaggerated.

CONCLUSIONS

It is tempting to suggest that with the present flood of information and the hype that carries the informational load, our eyes glaze over more and more readily, that increasingly we surrender our critical powers or never assume them, accepting that "all politicians are crooks" or that "everything causes cancer." But people keep making sense of their own lives, despite all. People still get irritated, bored, incensed, and mobilized, despite all. We make a mistake if we judge the public mind by the menu for public consumption. There is a tendency to believe that if the television news sound bite has shortened from a minute to 10 seconds (and it has in the space of 20 years),[44] the public capacity for sustained attention has shrunk accordingly. But this does not square with the intensity of careerism in business, the growth of the two-income family, the vitality of the pro-life and pro-choice movements, the return of religious revivals, and even the upturn in S.A.T. scores.[45]

Then what does media saturation mean? Consider a fast food analogy. Most people I know eat more Big Macs than salmon dinners at fine restaurants. McDonald's is faster, cheaper, more predictable, easier to squeeze into the rest of life. This does not mean people prefer Big Macs to salmon. It does not mean, aside from economistic tautology, that they greatly "value" Big Macs. It does not mean that their palates are jaded. It means they have made some decisions about their priorities and, then and there, eating a good meal is lower on the list than quickly reducing hunger. I do not think the growing success of *USA Today* necessarily indicates anything different: it does not mean people judge McPaper the "best" meal or the only meal they seek; simply that they find in it what they need from a newspaper at a given moment, given the constraints of daily life. With world enough and time, or with an important local issue, or with a hot presidential race, their choices might be different. Their choices, in any event, at any given moment, include an array of other sources of information.

If we cannot infer individual tastes from public menus, can we nonetheless observe something about how available cultural repertoires limit or shape opportunities for consciousness? Yes, but carefully. The flourishing of McDonald's forces other restaurants to change and still others to close up. The prevalence of McDonald's tutors citizens, particularly the young, in what food is good, what food *is*, what a meal is supposed to feel like. This may not be the tutor we would most like to have for our children. At the same time, Americans eat less beef today than they did when McDonald's was a gleam in Ray Kroc's eye; McDonald's is not the only tutor in the culture. Nor is McDonald's itself untutored by larger social and cultural change; witness the availability of salads and the declaration that french fries will no longer be fried in animal fat. Again, judging American habits or structures from the most visible elements of public consumption is something to undertake only with great care.

American citizens have more information today than they had a generation ago. More credible information. More national sources of information. More authenticated conflicts of information and opinion, thanks to the proliferation of expert lobbying groups and the changing habits of the media to seek out a variety of sources. More information coming to the laity through the media rather than through expert intermediaries. If the *New England Journal of Medicine* publishes research of possible interest to the laity, it does not percolate down through family physicians, but goes straight to the newspaper, magazine, and broadcast science reporters, and gets picked up soon thereafter in women's and consumer magazines, too. At least with middle-class citizens who read the women's magazines or Jane Brody's column in the *New York Times* and are empowered by their education and social standing to instruct their friends and families and talk back to their doctors, this kind of information is useful and gets used.

I do not conclude from this that we have the right information at the right time or that available information is distributed equitably or that the informational citizen is well informed. Our increasingly dazzling library of information provides only an illusion of knowledge and a false promise of citizenly competence if the social order does not equip people to use it, if young people are cynical, if the poor have no hope, if the middle class is self-absorbed, and if forays into public life are discouraging and private pursuits altogether more rewarding than public enterprise.

THIRTEEN

Schools under Pressure

Caroline Hodges Persell

It is fashionable today to attack education in the United States. Conservatives and liberals alike agree that education is in trouble. They disagree about why and what should be done, but they agree that the educational system needs to be improved. I suggest that systemic shifts and demographic changes make the situation facing education more serious than in recent decades and exacerbate the challenges education faces. Chief among these is the challenge of social inequality. But there are other challenges facing education as well, namely those of pedagogy, personnel, national testing, and a shift in the purposes of education.

CHANGES IN THE SOCIAL CONTEXT OF EDUCATION

Education is a broader concept than schooling, and the social institution of education includes more than just what happens in schools. Education refers to both formal and informal ways that the older members of a society or group try to teach newer members the attitudes, behaviors, skills, beliefs, and roles considered necessary to become participating members in that group or society. Education occurs both informally and formally. Informal education occurs through child rearing by parents and other members of the family, through peer-group interactions, and through observation and imitation of behaviors seen in the neighborhood, on television, or elsewhere. Some of what is observed and imitated may not be intended to be learned. Formal education occurs in schools, where trained personnel try to transmit information, teach skills, and guide inquiry and learning. Formal education in the United States reaches increasing numbers of pupils, for growing numbers of years.

Systemic Shifts in Society

Two systemic shifts in society are creating a new crisis in education. The first is that our society is becoming a postindustrial one, as numerous others have noted already. As physical labor and manufacturing become less important, interpersonal services and symbol manipulation become more important. Dropping out of, or being excluded from, education increasingly means being shut out of the economic and cultural core of society. Education, both formal and informal, is particularly important for integrating people into a society where symbolic distinctions are increasingly prevalent. The second shift is the shrinking of the informal sphere of education, and the growing burden being placed on the formal system of education, without concomitant increases in time, staff, money, or innovation. The informal sphere is shrinking because of changes in other social institutions, namely the family and the economy. Children are spending much less time with their families than they did in the past. Many more mothers of even very young children are working full time. A projected 59 percent of the children born in 1983 (who are now in school) will live with only one parent before the age of eighteen, there are at least 4 million latchkey children in the United States of school age, and 20 percent of all children in the United States are being reared in poverty.[1]

As a result of changes in other institutions described in other chapters in this volume, parents can bring less time to the informal education of their children. There is no systemic acknowledgment of the need for, or support for, child care in the United States, unlike Canada and most Western European countries. This is in no way to blame single parents or working mothers, but to recognize the fact that the family's capacity to provide informal education has eroded.

The formal sector might be able to compensate for limitations in the informal sector if it were given more resources. Instead what we see is ever-growing demands being placed on formal education, with no significant increase in the resources needed to meet those demands. Schools are asked to offer all their usual instruction in literacy, numeracy, civil education, science education, language instruction, and reasoning skills, and they are charged with meeting each new challenge facing society, whether for driver's education, the teaching of moral values, technological "literacy," the provision of adequate nutrition, or the avoidance of drug and alcohol abuse, teen pregnancy, and AIDS. Not only is education called upon to solve these social problems, but problems such as these make the task of education more difficult. In addition, schools in the United States educate a larger percentage of youth for a longer period than any other society in the world. Thus the size and the expense of the system has continued to increase, simply because it is touching more lives.

Demographic Changes

Demographic changes intensify the crisis in education. The population to be educated is changing dramatically. No longer are the majority of school children from white middle-class families who live in suburban homes with white picket fences. At least ten states face the prospect of "minority majorities" in their public schools by 1995.[2] In 1987 the Los Angeles public schools were teaching children who spoke eighty-one languages other than English at home.[3] Such children pose major challenges for schools.

A second demographic change is the increase in disabled and handicapped youngsters. There are increasing numbers of teen parents and babies born to addicted parents. Twenty-five percent of babies get no prenatal care. All of these factors are related to increased numbers of disabled children, who may need different kinds of education. In short, massive systemic and demographic changes increase the demands and expectations placed on education, and they heighten the challenges facing education.

THE CHALLENGE OF SOCIAL INEQUALITY

Demographic diversity makes the realization of equal educational opportunity all the more important if society is to be perceived as just, legitimate, and reasonably cohesive. How can education mitigate inequality based on class or ethnicity when, in practice, education reinforces inequality by virtue of vast differences in public and private schools and extensive tracking in public schools? The United States, perhaps more than any other society, holds as a cherished ideology the concept of a fresh start for each new generation. Young people, the creed goes, should be given a fair chance to be all that they can be. For a nation of immigrants, two opportunities are essential—the opportunity to learn the language, the culture, and skills, and the opportunity to work. Other chapters in this book explore the availability of opportunities to work. Here we consider opportunities to learn.

Despite imagery to the contrary, American education is not a uniform system. Therefore, it is very important to understand the broad contours of American education and to discern how variations are related to social class and ethnicity and to educational consequences. The configurations of American education are remarkably related to class and ethnicity. In most schools, students' social class and backgrounds are likely to be similar because most people in the United States live in relatively homogeneous neighborhoods. Children who grow up in large cities or mixed suburbs are less likely to attend a local school with neighborhood children. Private schools flourish in such areas. If by chance students of different backgrounds do attend the same school, they are very likely to have different classmates and to experience different programs of study because of tracking. Distinctions between public and private schools and the practice of tracking have important educational as well as social consequences.

Public, Parochial, and Private Schools

A private school is one controlled and funded by nonstate sources. While 25 percent of all elementary and secondary schools are private schools, they educate only 12 percent of the student population.[4] This is because they are generally quite small; their average enrollment is 234, and 75 percent enroll fewer than 300 students. Only 7 percent enroll 600 students or more. They are thus much smaller than most public schools, which average 482 students. Many urban secondary schools are much larger, often enrolling several thousand students.

The most elite private schools are attended by children of the upper and upper middle classes. In the early 1980s, 90 percent of the fathers of elite boarding school students were executives or professionals, and nearly half had family incomes above $100,000 per year. Fewer than 20 percent of the parents were divorced. The ethnic composition of elite boarding schools has become more diverse in recent decades than in the past, although it is still considerably less diverse than the public school population. Four percent of students are black, 5 percent are Asian, 11 percent are Jewish, and 27 percent are Catholic.[5]

Despite their relatively small size, elite private schools have spacious and well-kept grounds, and extensive computer, laboratory, language, arts, and athletic facilities. The teachers have been educated in the liberal arts at selective colleges and are responsive to students and parents. Teachers generally do not have tenure or belong to unions, so they can be fired by the school head if they are considered unresponsive or incompetent. Although three-quarters of private school teachers nationally are women, at elite private boarding schools 60 percent are male, as are 61 percent of the students.[6] Nationally, 92 percent of private school teachers are white.[7] Classes are small, often having no more than fifteen students, and sometimes considerably fewer. Students are required to be prepared for class and to participate in class discussions, and they write a great deal. Virtually all students study a college preparatory curriculum, and considerable homework is assigned. Numerous advanced placement courses offer the possibility of college credit. There are also many opportunities for extracurricular activities, such as debate and drama clubs, publications, and music, and the chance to learn unusual sports that colleges value, such as crew, squash, and ice hockey. Students have both academic and personal advisors who monitor their progress, help them resolve problems, and try to see that they have a successful school experience.

In terms of the family backgrounds of children who attend them, other private schools and parochial schools are quite similar to each other, although the philosophy and organization of the schools may vary considerably. Parental education, especially the mother's education, is highly related to student aspirations, and mothers of parochial school students are comparable to public school mothers. In parochial schools, 6 percent of students are black and 10 percent are Hispanic. In other private schools, 2 percent are black and 8 percent are Hispanic.[8] Hence, the ethnic composition of these schools is less diverse than that of the public schools.

Like elite boarding schools, parochial and other private schools are almost exclusively academic, and their students take more credits in mathematics, English, foreign language, history, and science than do public school students. There is also little grade inflation. Parochial schools more closely resemble public schools than other private schools or elite schools in terms of the levels of student participation in extracurricular activities, with more students participating in the latter two types of schools.[9]

The costs at parochial schools are relatively low, especially compared to private schools, because the schools are subsidized by religious groups. These schools have relatively low teacher salaries and usually have no teachers' unions. Currently there are more lay teachers and fewer nuns, sisters, priests, and brothers as teachers than in the past.

Parents are generally involved in private schools, first by paying directly for them, and also in terms of attending parent conferences, school meetings, and doing volunteer work. They are often involved in fund raising and promotion for the schools.[10]

Although there is wide variation among public schools in the United States, they are usually quite large, and part of an even larger school system that is highly bureaucratic. They are usually comprehensive schools, which means that they offer varied courses of study, including academic, vocational, and general curricular tracks. James Coleman and Thomas Hoffer, authors of a recent book on public and private high schools, note that "two-thirds of the public schools, enrolling three-quarters of all public school students, are organized as comprehensive schools."[11]

In the early 1980s, the median income of parents of public school students was $18,700,[12] four to six thousand dollars less per year than that of parochial and other private school parents. The parents are much more likely to be working or lower class, with lower average levels of education, and they are more likely to be divorced. Among public school students in 1984, 16.2 percent were black, 9.1 percent were Hispanic, 2.5 percent were Asian or Pacific Islander, and .9 percent were Native American or Alaskan Natives.[13]

In 1986, 90 percent of public school teachers were white and 69 percent were female. The authority of professional educators is often buttressed by bureaucratic procedures and by unionization of teachers and administrators. In general, there is a higher ratio of administrators to teachers and students in public than in private schools, perhaps partly because of the numerous governmental requirements public schools have to meet.

Clearly there are differences in terms of who goes to different types of schools, and what they experience there. The question is, are there different consequences, and can any of those differences be attributed to school effects rather than to selectivity bias? There are a number of differences in outcomes, which we will consider briefly, before turning to the question of their causes.

A perfectly reasonable question is what proportion of the students drop out. Among public high school students, 24 percent drop out, compared to 12 percent of parochial and 13 percent of other private school students. In terms of achievement test scores, private and parochial school students score higher than public school students in every subject. When Coleman, Hoffer, and Kilgore introduced statistical controls for various relevant family background factors, they found that achievement differences between public and private sectors were reduced (more for private schools than for parochial schools), but that differences remain.[14] In other analyses, Catsambis found that most of the "school effect" of Catholic schools was due to curricular track placement and types of courses taken.[15]

A third differential outcome is college attendance. Private and parochial school graduates are much more likely to attend college than are public school seniors; 45 percent of public school students, compared to 76 percent of Catholic school students and 76 percent of other private school students, enrolled in college.[16] Part of this difference is due to differences in individual abilities and social backgrounds, part is due to curricular placement, and part is related to type of school attended (whether public, private, or parochial). Among elite boarding school graduates, virtually all (99 percent) attend college, a result that is related to parental and peer expectations, curricula, and highly organized efforts by college advisors in those schools.[17] Such graduates are also much more likely to attend high-status selective private colleges than are public high school graduates.[18]

A fourth consequence is seldom considered in discussions of American education. As Cookson notes:

> Schools not only impart to students skills, but they also confer social status. Status competition is an ever-present fact of social life, and the effects of having high-status educational credentials ripple through graduates' lives like waves emanating from a central source; in time, they touch every social and economic boundary. Much of what is currently being written about public and private schools shapes the issue in terms of "choice," a value-free term that implies that private schools are educational alternatives more or less available to all families. This is not true. Private schools, especially socially elite private schools, are similar to private clubs; admission is contingent not only on the ability of the client to pay but [on] his or her personal and social attributes. Educational choice is not a neutral, self-regulating mechanism that acts as a kind of invisible educational hand, sorting and selecting students according to their preferences. To make a meaningful choice one must have the resources to act.[19]

These resources are both financial and social. If private schools were to be supported by public funds, as Chubb and Moe urge,[20] Cookson suggests that such a policy would be likely to increase educational opportunities for already advantaged members of society, result in greater stratification of school children, promote the founding of more and weaker private schools, limit the autonomy of existing private schools, and promote further racial and ethnic segregation.[21]

Finally, graduates of private schools earn more than public school graduates, even when appropriate background characteristics are controlled.[22] Graduates of thirteen elite boarding schools comprise 10 percent of the members of the board of directors of large American business organizations, and 17 percent of those who sit on multiple boards of such corporations.[23]

Whether or not differences between types of schools are the decisive factors in these unequal social outcomes, there is clearly a pattern of cumulative advantage at work here. More privileged families—families that have ethnic, economic, occupational, and structural advantages—gravitate toward certain types of schools, where their children experience different educational programs. The combined effects of initial advantage and educational experience contribute to the more advantaged positions and incomes such children attain in their adult lives. In these ways, family, educational experiences, and resources combine to reproduce social inequalities from one generation to the next. One of the major challenges facing education is how to provide equal educational opportunities to children, regardless of their family backgrounds. The educational practice of curricular tracking in the public schools is one that needs to be reconsidered if educational inequalities are to be reduced.

Curricular Tracking

As we have seen, in private and parochial schools most students study an academic curriculum. This is not the case in public schools, however, where most students are tracked into different curricula. Tracking consists of two elements: sorting by ability and by curriculum. Ability grouping assigns students to learning groups based on their background and achievement in a subject area at any given moment. Their skills and knowledge are evaluated at relatively frequent intervals, and students showing gains can be shifted readily into another group. Students might be in different ability groups in different subjects. Ability grouping can occur while students share a common curriculum, with only the mix of student abilities being varied. All students are taught the same material, although they may be taught in different ways or at different speeds. Quite often, however, different ability groups are assigned to different courses of study, resulting in simultaneous grouping by curriculum and ability. Such placements tend to become self-perpetuating.[24]

One major result of tracking is the differential respect students receive from peers and teachers, with implications for both instruction and esteem. Curricular track placement has long-term consequences with regard to whether people go to college or not, and what type of college they attend.[25] Among public school graduates, 73 percent of academic track students attended college, compared to 30 percent of nonacademic track students.[26] Because where people attend college is related to their chances of graduating, and because college attendance and graduation are related to occupational prestige and income,[27] the issue of educational tracking has profound social implications. Many researchers recommend that tracking should be used much more carefully,[28] or abandoned completely.[29]

Desegregation, Bilingual Education, and Special Education

In addition to struggling with the issue of offering equal opportunity, education is confronted with meeting a number of social and political goals including desegregation, bilingualism, and special education. By putting responsibility for these issues onto education, our society may try to absolve other institutions from worrying about them. Systematic research has been done on desegregation. In the last decade "many education policy makers seem to have decided that high-quality education rather than equal educational opportunity should be the primary goal of public education."[30] However, desegregation and quality education need not be mutually exclusive goals. In fact, they may be mutually reinforcing. This is particularly likely if we accept Willis Hawley's definition of quality or effectiveness in education in terms of "(1) academic achievement in mathematics and language arts and (2) tolerance and understanding of people of different races and social backgrounds."[31] He concludes that desegregation improves the achievement of ethnic minorities and does not undermine the achievement of whites.[32]

Bilingual education has been less extensively researched than has desegregation. Bilingual education often results from court cases on behalf of non-English-speaking children who are alleged to be receiving unequal educational opportunities.[33] One short-term study found that students enrolled in bilingual programs did not achieve any better than their counterparts who were not enrolled in such programs.[34] Other research, however, which followed students enrolled in bilingual programs for at least four years, found that they made positive academic gains.[35] The issues surrounding bilingual education involve more than education; they include social and political issues that affect the rights of non-English-speaking persons in a predominantly English-speaking country. On the one hand, in an ever-shrinking international world, multiple linguistic traditions can enrich a society. On the other hand, lack of proficiency in the dominant language of a country can lead to linguistic ghettos, fragmentation, and distrust within a society. These issues need to be resolved at a societal level before the mission of bilingual education can be clarified.

About 10 to 12 percent of all students are currently classified as in need of special educational services.[36] As Public Law 94-142 was implemented, a new category of handicap, namely, "learning disability," was introduced. The term refers to students who display inadequate achievement in speech, language, spelling, writing, or arithmetic, as a result of cerebral dysfunction. By 1986–87, the number of students identified as learning disabled was 1,914,000, or 44 percent of all handicapped students.[37] Although couched as a psychological model to explain why children fail, many children who are classified as learning disabled do not match the theoretical model. "Learning disabled" is the latest in a long list of labels applied to children who are having trouble in school. Like all deficit theories, this one places the blame for failure squarely on the child's limitations and effectively diverts blame from curriculum or pedagogy. Both of these, however, should be considered candidates for explaining pupil failure. The concept of learning disability also has self-fulfilling potency; that is, if teachers believe that children cannot learn because of their disability, they will expect less of them, teach them less, and it is likely that the children will learn less.[38] Learning disability theory diverts attention from the issue of how children learn and what kinds of cognitive skills they have. Such diversions make it less likely that effective forms of teaching and learning will occur.

OTHER CHALLENGES FACING EDUCATION

Four other challenges facing education also warrant consideration: pedagogy, personnel, national testing and standards, and the purposes of education.

Pedagogy

The need for improved methods of teaching has already been mentioned. If tracking is going to be discontinued, if desegregation is to work, if children with special needs are to be effectively educated, new and better forms of pedagogy are required. At least three possibilities exist, and others might be found with further experimentation and research. The three are peer teaching and counseling, cooperative learning, and new technologies, specifically microcomputers.

In peer teaching and peer counseling programs, students who have been trained by teachers and counselors help and tutor other children. Already widely used in a variety of public and private schools, peer teaching has three major strengths. First, those doing the teaching learn more and consolidate their own knowledge and skills. Second, peer tutors are often able to communicate very effectively with students slightly younger than they are. Third, enlisting students in pursuit of the school's goals expands the resources of the schools, at no additional cost. Peer tutors can help teach academic skills, they can help mediate conflict, and provide drug education and AIDS awareness. A study of 143 adolescent drug prevention programs, for example, found that "peer programs are dramatically more effective than all other 'interventions.'"[39]

Cooperative learning is an instructional method whereby students of different abilities and achievements work together in small groups to achieve a group goal. It is a more effective pedagogy than traditional classroom methods, in terms of learning subject matter, increasing self-esteem, and improving race relations.[40] The learning groups usually have four members, one who is a high achiever, two who are average, and one who is below average. Each student is responsible not only for learning the material taught in class but also for helping the other members of the group learn it.[41] The benefits are that each individual's achievement brings glory to the group rather than depresses the group achievement, as happens in conventionally structured systems of classroom rewards. Such an arrangement motivates students to help each other to learn.

Robert Slavin, who has studied cooperative learning extensively, cautions that several conditions must be present if it is to be effective. As noted, there must be a group goal, but it must be of a particular type. It is not enough to have the group complete a single project because there the temptation is great simply to have the strongest students do the work. Rather, the group goal needs to be to prepare *each* member for success on an individual test or other appraisal. Therefore, group success needs to be measured in terms of the individual achievement of each member. When the above conditions are met, student achievement improves.[42]

Cooperative learning strategies have been used in both elementary and secondary schools, in urban, rural, and suburban schools in the United States, Canada, Israel, West Germany, and Nigeria, from grades 2 to 12, and in such subjects as mathematics, language arts, writing, reading, social studies, and science.[43] They have led to social growth and improved academic achievement.[44]

If education sometimes resists new ways of socially structuring learning, it has often looked to the latest in technological wizardry for quick cures. The dust still gathers on teaching machines, and audiovisual equipment lies broken or unused in many schools. The big question is whether personal computers (PCs) will go the same route as other promised technological fixes or whether they can improve teaching efficiency and effectiveness. If they can, several major stumbling blocks must first be overcome. These include shortages of computers in many schools, the need for suitable instructional software, and the need to provide teachers with time and training to use computers effectively in courses. These are issues that schools and communities need to address.

Personnel

The teaching force is aging and many experienced people are leaving the field. In the next decade, an estimated two million new teachers will be needed. This need will pose tremendous recruitment problems for school districts across the country. As many local and state governments face deficits and resistance to higher taxes, districts will need to marshal public support for higher teacher salaries and devise creative new strategies for attracting academically talented people to teaching. Only when teachers can have more influence on curriculum, choice of books, and pedagogy, is the occupation likely to attract highly able people.[45]

If teaching is to become an attractive occupation, it needs to be a well-paid career, with professional training, responsibility, accountability, and respect. If it were to change in those ways, it is quite likely that it could appeal to intelligent young men and women who want to work with young people. It is a career that provides flexibility for young adults who want to help raise their own children while pursuing a professional occupation. If certain features of teaching could be changed, namely pay and working conditions, it is possible that education's drawing power could increase.

Testing and Standards

One problem that efforts to mobilize support will face is a perception that public education is not doing a very good job. The bombshell report by the National Commission on Excellence in Education, *A Nation at Risk* (1983), reported that "international comparisons of student achievement, completed a decade ago, reveal that on nineteen academic tests American students were never first or second and, in comparison with other industrialized nations, were last seven times."[46] However, the data used to support this statement were gathered between 1964 and 1971. Furthermore, the comparisons were based on averages for different countries as reported by the International Assessment of Educational Achievement (IEA). The problem with using country averages is that the student bodies in different countries are not comparable.[47] For example, only 9 percent of eighteen- and nineteen-year-olds in other countries reached the last year of high school in the period studied, compared to about 75 percent of those in the United States.[48] Not surprisingly, the more academically select students in other countries did better than the average U.S. student. There is no adequate international study of the academic performance of comparable populations of students. As a result, we do not really know whether U.S. education is suffering internationally.

A Nation at Risk also argued that educational content has been watered down over time, suggesting that the growth of electives has diminished the academic focus of secondary schools, resulting in a "curricular smorgasbord."[49] This assertion depends on one analysis of high school transcripts from a 1964–69 sample and a second based on a 1975–81 sample. But these two samples are not comparable.[50] Even if the two samples could be compared, the evidence does not fully support the Commission's conclusions. While the second sample showed more students in the general track and big increases in the numbers of students taking such courses as driver's education and marriage training, students in both samples spent nearly the same amount of total time on academics (the first sample had 69 percent of their credits in academic subjects, while the second had 62 percent).[51] Other research based on representative samples indicates a modest decline in academic emphasis overall.[52]

Additional school practices were also cited as declining: amounts of homework required, disciplinary standards, and the standards required for high grades (so-called grade inflation).[53] It is hard to prove that such changes are the causes of lower academic performance. One often-cited indicator of lower performance is declining Scholastic Aptitude Test (SAT) scores. In its own analysis, the College Board (who makes the test) found that the decline was largely due to changes in the students taking the test. The College Board attributed the remainder of the decline to changing social conditions, such as increased television watching, student unrest, and other factors. Curricular differences among schools accounted for little of the difference in scores between schools.[54] While there appear to be some small declines in curricular content over time, and some small performance declines over time, no one has pinpointed the causes of the performance declines in terms of educational practices.

In more recent years there is some evidence of educational improvement. For example, there were fewer dropouts in 1985–88 than in 1978, and reading scores have increased in recent years.[55] However, these seemingly mixed and noncomparable results over time lead some to call for national educational testing.

Recent Gallup polls reveal that the majority of Americans favor national education standards, national tests, and a national curriculum, the strong tradition of local control over education notwithstanding.[56] The National Assessment of Educational Progress (NAEP) has done periodic studies to assess what American children know. A national test would set absolute standards of what children should know and would ascertain their mastery of that prescribed content. In this sense it is different from tests, such as the SAT, which grade students in relation to each other, that is, essentially on a curve. But the possibility of such a test raises a series of important questions. Would such a test be a politically attractive substitute for improving teacher pay and teaching methods? Who would decide what all children should know? How would that knowledge be tested? Standardized multiple-choice tests are not usually the best way to measure higher-order thinking and reasoning, which many educators consider an important educational goal. If such tests lead to tighter requirements for high school graduation, they could increase the number of students having difficulties, and the number who drop out earlier.[57] Debates over national testing are invariably linked with discussions of the goals of education.

The Goals of Education

Over time, American education appears to have shifted its primary purpose. In colonial times, education was designed to produce literacy so people could read the Bible. Reading and simple arithmetic were also helpful to people conducting their daily lives. Most people did not go beyond the eighth grade. With the giant waves of immigration in the nineteenth century, education took on the additional goal of preparing people for citizenship. There were literacy tests for voting in some states, and English tests for immigrants seeking naturalization. The importance of education for citizenship should not be forgotten. Every totalitarian regime that takes power tries immediately to seize control of the educational system. Education is considered a nerve center of political control.

An educated citizenry is an essential ingredient for a healthy democratic society.

In recent years, education has added the goal of preparation for a vocation or career. Education and the economy are increasingly closely coupled, at least for people who want to work in corporate or nonprofit bureaucracies.[58] Education is an increasingly important passkey to reasonably well paid and secure employment. The continuing importance of education for citizenship should not be overlooked, however, particularly in an era when the labor market is becoming increasingly polarized and pressures are on education to become increasingly tightly linked to the labor market. If education succumbs to this trend, it will relegate large numbers of lower-class and minority children to second-class citizenship and membership in a permanent underclass. As a recent report from the New World Foundation notes:

> Education for citizenship means that schools should provide children with the social and intellectual skills to function well as members of families and communities, as political participants, as adult learners, as self-directed individuals. It means educating children about the way the world works, and arming them to influence how it works. Citizenship requires basic skills, but it requires other forms of learning as well: critical thinking, social awareness, connection to community, shared values. The call is for educational values which recognize student needs as legitimate and which prepare students for multiple roles as adults, regardless of their labor-market destinies or economic status. The bottom line for democratic education is empowerment, not employment.[59]

DIRECTIONS FOR THE FUTURE

To address the current crisis in education, two major directions need to be pursued. First, the United States needs to change its political and social orientations. It needs to become willing to invest now for future benefits, and it needs to move from a "scrap heap" mentality to a reclamation stance toward difficult cases. Second, we need to structure innovation into education.

Investment now could pay big dividends for the future. One area of educational investment that has a proven track record is Head Start, the preschool program for four-year-olds.[60] Every dollar invested in quality preschool education yields $4.75 because of lower costs later on for special education, public assistance, and crime.[61] However, only 16 percent of the low-income children eligible for Head Start are now in it.[62] Liberals and conservatives both are coming to the view that Head Start is an essential but incomplete program.

As the United States struggles to change its stance toward natural resources and the environment, it might similarly change its attitude toward human resources. The country could move away from scrapping undeveloped human talent and toward developing and utilizing it. Much could be learned from the nation of Israel in this regard. There every child is needed and valued, partly because the country is in a virtual state of military seige. In the United States, the "birth dearth," which is following on the heels of the "baby boom," may produce labor shortages and may help to mobilize public support for salvaging human talent and developing it from a young age.

Part of developing youthful talent involves ameliorating the worst features of poverty. As long as hundreds of thousands, perhaps millions, of people are homeless, reaching the children and youth living under such conditions with the fact and the promise of education will be difficult, if not impossible. Twenty-five percent of pregnant women in the United States receive no prenatal care. One result is an infant mortality rate in the United States that places it nineteenth in the world, above Cuba and Bulgaria, but below Singapore, Hong Kong, and Spain.[63] A second result is a greater number of handicapped children. Of the 11 percent of school children who are classified as handicapped, one-third would have had a lesser handicap or none if their mothers had received prenatal care.[64] Handicapped children can cost the state as much as $100,000 per year to educate.[65] Prevention is cheaper for society in the long run than treatment after the fact.

Schools need to consider how to structure innovation into a bureaucratic system. Schools and teachers need to be given incentives and support to experiment with new pedagogies, such as peer teaching, cooperative learning, and new educational technologies.

Because so many children are being reared in poverty, so many are being raised by single parents, and the informal sphere of education is shrinking, the formal sphere of public education must take up the slack or our future will founder. Social justice is a noble reason for changing the level of investment and innovation we pour into education. The threat of international competition is a catchy, if somewhat irrelevant, rallying cry. But if those reasons fail to convince in this age of rational self-interest then good sense, social pragmatism, and even self-interest can be summoned to elicit support. Do we want to see our society become increasingly polarized, to the point where there is a permanently excluded underclass and an increasingly besieged dominant class? Given this prospect, Americans might try to think more rationally about several interrelated questions. What do they need and want from their schools? Can tracked public schools and socially segregated private schools accomplish the goals Americans have for education? Is the form and level of funding for education adequate to the tasks that it faces?

FOURTEEN

Doctor No Longer Knows Best

Changing American Attitudes toward Medicine and Health

Jonathan B. Imber

> *The physician, who killed me,*
> *Neither bled, purged, nor pilled me,*
> *Nor counted my pulse; but it comes to the same:*
> *In the height of my fever, I died of his name.*[1]
> —CALLICTER

> *The wounded surgeon plies the steel*
> *That questions the distempered part;*
> *Beneath the bleeding hands we feel*
> *The sharp compassion of the healer's art*
> *Resolving the enigma of the fever chart.*
> —T. S. ELIOT

In the 1970s, a debate was launched by numerous observers of medicine and medical practice about the fate of one of the most powerful institutions in modernity. Some referred to it as "The End of Medicine" debate because nothing less was at stake than the autonomy of physicians to determine how to practice medicine as they saw fit.[2] The challenges to this autonomy contrasted sharply to the image of doctors in the 1950s. During that time, with the medical profession at the seeming height of its scientific and professional powers, the comparison of doctors with gods may have been overstated in reality, but not in perception. The authority of medicine was secure.

Doctors were guardians of hope and progress that derived from medical innovations and "discoveries" (antisepsis, penicillin, insulin, X rays, etc.) and that vastly increased their power to diagnose, treat, and prevent disease. The search for new discoveries and cures, following upon a more systematic understanding of the etiology of disease, was uniquely medical and scientific in its social organization. The growth of the modern hospital and the increased resources devoted to laboratory research were hailed as evidence of true progress in the conquering of human disease and disability. Only recently, in the past quarter century, has the optimism of medical progress been challenged by forces within and beyond medicine.

The internal dynamics of medical authority are obviously tied to the external dynamics of medical power. Sociologists and social historians have argued, for example, that consistent with their aim to dominate professionally, doctors deliberately allied themselves with the state during the nineteenth century in order ostensibly to protect the public from the malpractices of quacks and legally to assure that the only medical practitioners would be those certified by university and governmental authorities.[3] These studies have confirmed that the maintenance of the physician's authority was deeply tied to the creation and preservation of medical organization. Further, the sociological understanding of medicine has placed a decided, and perhaps fateful, emphasis on the external power of doctors to map out their jurisdiction, to eliminate competition, and to use science and the state to consolidate their professional powers.[4]

Talcott Parsons' pioneering discussion of themes in the sociology of medicine in *The Social System* (1951) provides a classic example of the difference between the internal dynamics of medical authority and the external dynamics of medical power.[5] Parsons ably drew the line between these two dynamics by focusing on how the physician-patient relation was possible. What did this relation presuppose? What was expected of those who entered into it?

Parsons' formulation of the "sick role" captured all of the human tensions that were naturally a part of being ill and of treating illness. These tensions were diffused in a series of institutional expectations that enabled the patient and the practitioner to negotiate their way through the uncertainties that each had about the outcome of those negotiations. Parsons articulated a normative faith for medical practice whose tenets included specificity of function (specialization), affective neutrality (scientific objectivity), and suppression of the profit motive in the provision of treatment. Each of these tenets was a theoretical guide to how the doctor-patient relation was possible and why that relation was sociologically determined by the growth of scientific knowledge and technical expertise and by the dedication to a vocation. Both expertise and dedication reassured patients that the doctor acted first and foremost in the patient's best interest, based upon long training and a commitment that transcended monetary reward. The "sick role" was also a description of the expectations incumbent upon the patient, who, by entering into this inevitably asymmetrical relation, understood that caring and curing were not always synonymous. But "care" symbolized a fiduciary responsibility and communicative trust on the part of the physician against which any failure to "cure" had to be measured.

What may be most remarkable to someone arriving on the scene of contemporary medicine and the delivery of medical services in the last decade of the twentieth century in the United States is how far Parsons' normative description of medical practice is from the popular perception of physicians, who are seen as uncaring, uncommunicative, self-interested, and ambitious. One genre of medical autobiography in which this popular perception is also confirmed has been written by young physicians who passionately contend that the rites of passage to physicianhood, especially in the resident years, bring out the worst in doctors, forcing them into a structured indifference toward patients and a near-hostile contempt for attending physicians who oversee the residency programs. Of course, patients, and especially those with the least financial means, are said to suffer most.[6]

Critics of Parsons' "sick role" have argued that the ideal typical physician-patient relation cannot be judged apart from the diverse social contexts in which it is played out. Patients with acute symptoms amenable to specific therapies are significantly different from those whose symptoms are either nonspecific or chronic and less amenable to standard therapies. Doctors practicing alone with long-term, stable patient populations are not the same as doctors moving in and out of medical groups whose patient populations are constantly changing. In other words, Parsons' depiction was accurate insofar as an illness was assumed to be either temporary or controllable (for example, diabetes) and the doctor-patient relation was believed to be a personal, mutually informed encounter between people known to one another.

Parsons has also been chided for uncritically depicting a "middle-class" portrait of medical work. His depiction was more hopeful than class-determined. The "class" critique does not explain why the sovereign and charismatic image of doctoring has come under such fire during the past quarter century. More than a century ago, Marx and Engels recognized the historical transformation of the professions under the class domination of the bourgeoisie. The stripping of the halo from medicine, like the disenchantment of the world, is not so much a function of class conflict as a cultural struggle to determine the nature of individual and group authority at any time and place.[7]

Like Charles Horton Cooley's hopeful and resilient image of the "primary group"—a bulwark against the inevitable incursion of modern mass society—Parsons' physician-patient relation is no longer a bulwark against the omnipresence of illness and illness-causing agents that are said to pervade the workplace, food, and the environment in all societies. Something more substantial than middle-class values is at stake in understanding health and the expectations about it. Medical malpractice and the part played by the law in raising the ante on the decisions made by doctors are symptoms of a cultural transformation that goes well beyond the long-standing concerns about unequal access to medical services. Parsons spoke unwittingly and authoritatively for cultural assumptions that are no longer fully our own. New assumptions, to which the remainder of this chapter will be devoted, have taken hold, and they have led to a revaluing and devaluing of doctoring.

Three types of transformative cultural forces and movements in and around medicine have altered, perhaps permanently, the popular perception of doctoring and have led to new expectations about human health. The first type, and by far the oldest, is constituted in the forces of epidemiological thought and research that have largely shaped medical and public health understanding in their modern forms. The second type is the influence upon medicine of self-help movements, including the most challenging, feminism, and the most sublime, bioethics. The third is the environmental movements and other cultural/political movements, including parts of the public health movement, that have sought to redefine the relation between human beings and nature.

In the face of these forces and movements, the insulated character of medical "progress," the inner dynamics of which are celebrated in histories of scientific discovery, can no longer be maintained. On the contrary, the modern doctor as a figure of authority born of that progress has been challenged not only because the power granted by science is said to be insufficient or abused but also because that power is said to be impossible to control completely. The physician is the personification of a cultural struggle to define the limits of both scientific knowledge and professional power. A double meaning applies to all contemporary critiques of professional power. The jurisdictional meaning of that power is the operative one fully explored by sociology.[8] The cultural meaning of that power is less operative and more illuminative precisely in the sense that it reveals similar features of legitimation for all roles deemed authoritative, including those of parent, teacher, priest, and doctor. As that authority wanes—that is, as it is challenged as illegitimate power—something of the lasting meaning of physicianhood may still be visible to the naked eye insofar as it can see in superordinate/subordinate relations the moral nature and moral limits of human life.

THE FORCES OF EPIDEMIOLOGY

Epidemiology, the study of the incidence, distribution, and determinants of disease in a population, has been the dominant scientific influence in shaping the early and present character of public health policy. It has also deeply affected the way in which medical innovations and treatments are ascertained, administered, and withdrawn. Harm to individuals can be calculated and predicted statistically, given certain controls. The role that epidemiology has played in defining how harm is understood, both scientifically and commonsensically, has yet to be fully assessed. Probabilistic reasoning is not new.[9] But how it relates to an understanding of individual health and to the formulation of health policy is neither obvious nor settled, and it represents an intellectual force whose influence is systemic in all advanced societies.

Because it costs money to maintain health, actuarial studies of morbidity and mortality have been central guides in enabling the insurance industry to develop profitably in alliance with those delivering medical services during this century. Just as legal hegemony was sought by professionally minded practitioners in the nineteenth century, economic security has been assured in this century for both patients and physicians through a system of insurance that depends upon epidemiologically derived analyses of risk. Medical services and insurance coverage for them are interactive, and their escalating costs have been driven by the cultural and political belief that good health should be one of the essential benefits of living in modern society.

In the United States, the poor, the unemployed, and their children do not stand on equal footing with those able to obtain medical services by qualifying for private insurance. No other belief about social equality and equity raises more fundamental questions about justice for all than the belief that a right to medical services should be guaranteed to all. Inequity in services intensifies the conflict between aspiring rights and actual privileges. The economic privilege of health insurance determines not only the quality of medical services but their availability as well.[10] In this sense, Parsons articulated a norm of equity for the medical encounter that remains implicitly intact. No "sick role" can exist without a corresponding availability of medical services. The number of persons presently without health insurance is estimated to be close to forty million, or over 15 percent of the American population.

In light of the tremendous impact that the insurance industry has had on establishing the economic vitality of the profession and the financial security of the patient, it is important to consider how the idea of "risk" is used to determine what kinds of behavior are encouraged and discouraged in the name of good health and good medical practice. Obviously, age, gender, class, race, and ethnicity can be used to define categories of insurance risk in broad, probabilistic ways. The same is true for practitioners, except that one substitutes for class, race, and ethnicity, the categories of medical specialty, medical procedure, and region of the country. When viewed in terms of how to calculate the costs of doing business, the principles of epidemiology can be applied in ways that can selectively correlate certain behaviors with illness and certain medical practices with law suits. Cigaret smoking illustrates the first case and is taken up in this section; obstetrical care illustrates the second case and is taken up in the next section.

Thomas McKeown has argued that, in the advanced societies, diseases of affluence have replaced diseases of poverty as the primary focus for public health study and action.[11] Most diseases of poverty have been prevented by immunization, proper housing, sufficient food, clean water, sanitation, and other measures that for nearly three centuries have represented the minimal conditions for maintaining the public health. Most diseases of affluence, however, have been studied in terms of the behavior of individuals. The epidemiology of the past proved how diseases of poverty could be reduced or prevented by use of law and regulation, in the name of public welfare. The epidemiology of the future has set its sights on the control and transformation of individual behavior by use of similar strategies, in the name of public health.

As recently as forty years ago, doctors endorsed cigaret smoking as a benign, even stress-reducing, behavior. With the notable exception of the United States, the rest of the world continues to consume cigarets with an ardor that shows little sign of weakening in response to the new American—indeed, federal—moral stance toward smoking. The rise of modern epidemiological thinking about diseases of affluence owes much to the struggle over social policy toward smoking. Doctors, insurance companies, and consumers have been generally persuaded that statistical analyses of future risk can and should serve as the basis for the formulation of policy in matters pertaining to health and welfare.

American liberalism, as distinct from libertarianism, has long embraced the principle that the state should support efforts to protect citizens from undue risks, including those risks assumed by individuals voluntarily. In previous centuries, the public health was protected in the belief that risk—for example, of contagion—could be reduced by legally mandating who could leave or enter a home. The quarantine was a community- or state-enforced action that took for granted the legal and moral sufficiency of acting on the basis of probabilities to prevent the spread of disease. Harm averted was welfare maintained. The logical and historical extension of this policy has led to the largely noncontroversial requirements that children should be immunized against measles and other childhood diseases before being permitted to enter school.[12]

Far greater controversy remains over smoking because the "public" health is now defined by probability studies that identify individuals whose actions pose no immediate threat to their own or anyone else's life or health. Rather, these studies establish statistical links between certain behaviors and the future onset of disease. Epidemiological studies of smoking and disease have shown, within the canons of statistical reasoning, that the use of cigarets and any tobacco product will inevitably cause disease in a significant percentage of the people who use them. These studies confirm that hundreds of thousands of people suffer disease and death each year from smoking, and that nothing short of reducing the number of people who smoke will reduce the incidence of morbidity and mortality associated with the behavior. Yet probability theory allows that the diseases may or may not appear at some undetermined time in the future, and that they will certainly not appear in all persons regardless of how they behave.

The medical profession can play only a minor part in reducing probabilities of the onset of future disease, given the specialized, and thus more limited, skills at its command. Its power in regard to smoking is now mostly rhetorical—often called "preventive" medicine. Patients are persuaded that giving up smoking is the best bet against a whole host of afflictions that are associated with it. Beyond the capacities of trained doctors, a dogma of sorts is in the social process of creation. Because the more magical and immediate skills of doctors cannot fend off the ghosts of new probabilities, an ancient school of thought has reasserted itself, claiming that the best cure is self-discovered. But this new self-discovery is neither theocratic nor Socratic but rather sociocratic: it concerns less the meaning of individual mortality and more the fate of a society, indeed, of an entire planet.

The doctor is necessary, but no longer sufficient, for saving lives. A more ominous hope rises out of the epidemiological project, requiring the full backing of the state in all of its agencies of influence—legal, regulatory, and rhetorical. Contemporary society stands on the verge of a full-scale institutionalization of the belief that no perfection of the public welfare can be achieved without the elimination of most, if not all, of the diseases of affluence. A significant question, taken up later in this chapter, is whether affluence, in all its supposedly costly and wasteful forms, must be eliminated along with the diseases it causes. The new dogma of health as self-discovery encompasses the agony of lung cancer as well as the horror of nuclear war.

The Office of the Surgeon General has about it totalitarian designs of an entirely new sort, more cultural than political, and perhaps not fully recognizable for what they augur. The liberal impulse in its postmodern guise is a profoundly satisfying one and is undeniably rooted in a concept of health that has served to protect the public in positive and substantial ways. A new kind of cultural politics is emerging as insurance companies have recognized the financial implications of actuarial calculations based on studies of behaviors deemed risky by evidence gathered epidemiologically. Automobile insurers have operated on a similar principle for many years, charging higher rates on automobiles classified as

"sports cars" and driven by persons under a certain age. The principle
has found its way into newer, more controversial applications. Acquired
immune deficiency syndrome (AIDS), for example, has opened a new
chapter in the history of discriminatory insurance practices.[13]

Beyond the politics of epidemiology, a cultural transformation in the
meaning of health has made epidemiology the true policy science of modernity, for, in effect, no behavior is immune from being designated as
health promoting or health defeating, in a personal or social sense. The
modern dogma of health also contains its own lessons in new styles of
conformity, the most obvious one of which is exemplified in the learned
revulsion toward smoke, especially among born-again, reformed, ex-
smokers.

The argument about the cultural impact of epidemiology can now be
summarized. In an effort to map out the causal nature of disease, the
epidemiological study of behavior has superseded the epidemiological
study of disease organisms. The new vectors of disease are defined in
terms of specific human behaviors, for which individuals can be held accountable. The logic of this accountability invites the call for evermore
refined correlations that amount to a cultural recycling of older styles of
moral conformity that dictated, for example, what one should eat and
drink. The return of sumptuary norms in a culture of radical individualism is not likely to be recognized as totalitarian, but the establishment
of such norms is one of the most significant consequences of the institutionalization of an ethic of public health based on correlation studies. All
types of behavior and consumption are subject to this ethic, though, its
imposition will not succeed solely at the level of the individual. Instead,
by means of a dedicated force of governmental and voluntary regulators
of behavior and consumption, the institutional producers of bad health
will be monitored, transformed, and if necessary, eliminated.

The quest for better health promises a kind of certainty about well-
being that parodies the old-time religion of certainty about the next life.
The jargon of the authenticity of health owes an outstanding debt to science and epidemiology, which have brought probability and health policy together in ways that may render older styles of medical authority
obsolete. As the focus on health maintenance has changed, chronic disease has been identified as the central concern of future health policy.[14]
In the United States, as the majority of citizens continues to grow older,
the links between behavior and chronic illness are bound to be made
more publicly explicit and culturally compelling.

The place of the physician and of the physician-patient relation in the
new discourse on health is neither obvious nor secure. Asymmetry remains but is now mediated more than ever by a class-bound system of
medical insurance and by the sociocratically based mandates of epidemi-

ology. Health may not be the exclusive domain of medicine, but medicine is still held accountable for diagnosing and treating disease. The popular image of doctoring has been undermined not least of all by the overpowering nature of diagnosis. The demand for greater knowledge about how illness comes into being has led to the paradoxical result of greater uncertainty about what to do with this new knowledge. The paradox works against preserving any residues of charismatic authority in the physician. This authority was first revitalized by scientific understanding in the last century and is now being displaced by diagnostic and prognostic technologies that cannot possibly give reassurance in the same forms once entrusted to the deeply personal authority of the medical practitioner. The modern uncertainties about health have invited the present demands for reassurance that can be heard in various social and intellectual movements beyond medicine.

THE SELF-HELP MOVEMENTS

During the last twenty-five years, a variety of voluntary associations have appeared in American society in direct response to the idea that practitioners of conventional medicine should not be left to decide alone what is in the best interests of patients. Although "alternative" forms of medicine are sometimes heralded as successors to the institutionally dominant and conventional form, these alternatives have remained a luxury for people seeking some release from the scientific and cultural presuppositions of Western medicine. Homeopathy, chiropractic, and other competitors in the Western tradition have re-emerged in the late twentieth century with some measure of respectability because the conventional, allopathic market is secure.

Laetrile and faith healing can easily be tested within the scientific paradigm of medical practice, can be shown to be ineffective epidemiologically, and can be tolerated only insofar as the illnesses they are putatively treating are not amenable to standard therapies. Acupuncture and other imported medical practices from the East are also tolerated as first or last resorts, while all other resorts are defined and controlled by scientific medicine. Whether for cancer or backache, the modern patient seeks cure in an environment that offers numerous alternatives to the standard therapies. The meaning of "cure" is in flux and always has been, from the religious cure of souls to Freud's psychoanalysis. Conventional medicine still has social legitimacy because it has demonstrably succeeded where others have failed. The American expectation that no disease should be beyond cure has been reinforced by those successes even as new challenges appear on the horizon.

The movements that have been most influential in supporting and challenging professional dominance are indigenous to American society and the American present. Around each medical specialty, for example, various types of groups have arisen whose expressed aim is to represent the interests of those under the care of that specialty. The American Heart Association is an example of an early support movement for cardiology. Without undermining the authority of the cardiologist, the Association has utilized epidemiological data to demonstrate that the health of the human heart is linked to exercise, diet, and other behavioral factors. Controversy is growing about the ways in which the Association publicizes its claims about healthful behavior. Epidemiological studies are sometimes conflicting: how much exercise is "necessary" and what kinds of foods are "healthful" are questions not yet fully settled. In contrast, smoking is an old enemy, as is fatty food. The devils are clear, even if the angels are not, and cardiology owes a great deal to the publicity and research machines that have made heart disease the pre-eminent disease of affluence.[15]

Other medical specialties have their allied associations. The point here is that, working together, specialists and voluntary associations have been able to justify their mutual recognition and livelihood to a larger public, which has then been asked to donate money and effort to the cause of fighting disease. Marathons to raise money for particular diseases are part of the same social process. In some cases, where medicine has failed to provide satisfactory therapy, for whatever reason, an extraordinary number of self-help groups have responded, continuing the long-standing American tradition, noted by Tocqueville, of voluntary effort and association. Support groups for the deaf and blind have long histories, but an aging population produces degrees of loss of hearing and eyesight that are not the immediate concerns of practitioners who are trained to diagnose and treat disease rather than to respond to the consequences of aging on health and the provision of medical services. The demographic realities of an aging American population suggest that resources will naturally begin to shift away from specialized diagnoses and therapies of "cure" toward new responses of "care" if the medical profession intends to retain control over the largest and most affluent market of health consumers.

That shift has already begun, as is evident in the reluctance of pharmaceutical companies to devote extensive venture capital to the discovery of cures for "orphan" diseases, that is, diseases that afflict a statistically and politically insignificant number of individuals. Diagnosis, as already noted, has exceeded the ability to treat. Medical power creates new inequities and injustices because knowledge exceeds the resources to apply it. Organ transplantation is an especially poignant example in this regard. Scarcity of medical resources is paralleled by a "scarcity" of donors. In the search for new forms of medical treatment, new demands are being made on Americans to broaden their sensibilities about what altruism itself means. Bone marrow, kidneys, hearts, and livers have become elements of a moral calculus not yet fully developed. A lurching progress has ensued, leaving many people uncertain how to respond. Advice about how to establish priorities for the use of all these resources has come most clearly and often from two politically unrelated but sociologically influential movements, feminism and bioethics.

The impact of feminism on health issues has been most strongly felt in the medical specialty of obstetrics and gynecology. The abortion issue and the broad range of health issues related to women's reproductive lives have been central subjects of feminist concern and political action. At the same time, bioethics has sought to clarify the medical responsibilities over life and death in the hope of improving both medical practice and health policy. One of the earliest studies of bioethical significance by a leading figure in this movement was, not coincidentally, on abortion.[16] Feminism has been, in its most recent wave, a politically powerful "self-help" movement that has challenged the autonomy of medical judgment. Bioethics has also attempted to introduce its insights into medical practice in the form of "clinical ethics," though, unlike the feminist challenge, its intellectual perspective has been institutionalized in medical schools across the country. Coming from different sides of the physician-patient relation, these two movements reflect the diminishing importance of professional self-determination.

Epidemiologically, childbirth is safer for mother and child in the United States today than it was a century ago. Yet the medical profession, in particular obstetrics and gynecology, has been under sustained pressure to redefine the roles of physician and patient in this particular encounter. The professionalization of obstetrics during the last two hundred years marginalized other forms of birthing (for example, midwifery) in such a way that contemporary countermovements to obstetrical, professional dominance have sought a reinstatement of the values, if not of all the practices, that preceded professionalization.

Demarginalization and accommodation are two very different social processes, and "natural" childbirth belies a disingenuous affirmation of older values that would hardly be so popular if it were not for the fact that medicine waits in the wings on the chance (indeed, likelihood) that emergency measures have to be taken. The medical environment in which birth occurs has been transformed, but not because the physician has been somehow genuinely marginalized, and the midwife made central, to the event. The process might be thought of in bureaucratic terms as a decentralization of responsibility, in which patient, family, nurse, nurse-midwife, and physician communicate with one another, even though the physician hovers just out of sight, being on call to respond to any complications. Emergency imposes asymmetry with startling speed. Here is an example of too much caution and control giving way to a reinstatement of the nonmedical meanings of the event. If improvement has occurred, it has little or nothing to do with what counts as scientific or technical knowledge. On the contrary, the birth event can be demedicalized temporally only because the medical ability to respond to complications is so sophisticated. The impact of feminism in this regard has been socially, rather than scientifically, progressive.

Medical innovation in the treatment of women's health has resulted in a number of classic instances of iatrogenically induced harm. The oral anovulant contraceptive "pill" is a case study in the hidden history of medical experimentation on women's bodies.[17] Despite the fact that clinical studies for this drug were conducted, mass distribution produced a scientific awareness of its effects that could not have been obtained in any other way, or so it seems. The use of Diethylstilbestrol (DES) to prevent miscarriages represents another tragic instance of discovering the untoward effects of treatment long after mass distribution has occurred, in this case across generations.[18] The use of both these drugs implicates physicians, but not in any direct malpractice sense. Pharmaceutical firms have been held liable for the distribution of certain prescribed contraceptives, such as the Dalkon Shield, but these legal settlements cannot begin to address the underwriting process of clinical and epidemiological investigation that in the attempt to "control" human reproduction instead has sometimes harmed it.

Just as research on orphan drugs has been slowed, so, too, has research on and development of new forms of mass-distributed birth control. Epidemiology is a double-edged sword, revealing both how few may be helped by expensive treatments and how many may be harmed by inexpensive ones. Yet, primarily because of feminist activism, litigation (against manufacturers and distributors implicated in the mass-produced harm to women's reproduction) has slowed the search for the perfect, that is, harmless, form of birth control. Courts might someday limit the kinds of suits permitted for "statistical" victims of drugs that do not harm the vast majority of users. In such a world, all kinds of birth control innovations might appear in the medical marketplace. The acceptance of inevitable harms when weighed against disproportionately larger benefits would signify a cultural hypocrisy that is plausible if the consumers of these therapies believe, too, that the benefits outweigh the risks. "Informed consent" is the professional safeguard designed to protect everyone but the patient from what cannot be known until the risk is taken.

The reduction of risk can probably not be accomplished without harm to someone. William Ray Arney has described the negotiations between women and doctors over the birth event as a series of historical transformations in how the health of mother and child has been guaranteed.[19] Beyond the problems of professional management at the time of birth, a more fundamental transformation in knowledge about birth, from conception to "bonding," has provided obstetrical science with an exceedingly broad mandate to propose and demonstrate its guarantees. Like the epidemiological project, the obstetrical project has enormous implications for the cultural understanding of disease, well-being, and, most importantly, normalcy.

The evolution of the obstetrical project can be sketched as a series of attempts to monitor the outcome of birth. At the level of bodily function, women's bodies are personally and professionally monitored in order to maximize conception. The range of artificial maximizations include a variety of drug therapies and in vitro fertilization. Once conception is achieved, professional monitoring assumes an even greater role in identifying, analyzing, and judging the progress of fetal growth through ultrasound scanning, prenatal diagnosis (chorionic villus sampling and amniocentesis), a standard range of tests to determine the physical health of the fetus, and fetal surgery. These technological forms of professional monitoring have been given a substantial boost in their sophisticated uses by the science of genetics, which offers the ability to predict the lifelong fate of the fetus. The diagnostic strategy used to foretell the fate of the individual before birth coincides with the epidemiological strategy used to foretell the future of the individual after birth. Taken together, these two strategies further the social processes of rationalization, disenchantment, and attenuation of the meaning of individuality; leaving nothing to chance, the individual enters into the world and acts in the world entirely at the design of specific others.[20]

Once again, as in the case of health problems defined by epidemiology, the role of doctors in the obstetrical project is subordinated to the predictive role of knowledge. Against the backdrop of change in the asymmetrical character of the doctor-patient relation, a more substantial change in what is produced out of that relation has occurred. The liberal-feminist focus on interaction and communication has concealed what modern obstetrical science has sought to guarantee for sometime, in addition to the preservation of the lives and health of women. Professional dominance has shifted its focus to life before birth and, in the course of doing so, has made birthing more "natural" while offering, because of genetics, more ways to guarantee that what is born will be "normal," according to whatever sociocratic standard is imposed. The achievement of normalcy will emerge in the twenty-first century as the central goal of the obstetrical project, but notice will hardly be given to what appears to be little more than the end result of a series of tests to determine the "health" of the unborn, perhaps eventually in the form of a blood test administered to women who are no more than a few weeks pregnant.

If the state could be persuaded, the principles used to institutionalize a federal moral stance toward smoking could be, and no doubt will be, applied to bring the new science of the unborn to the conscious attention of health policymakers. Carrier screening, genetic screening, and post-natal screening are becoming effective agents of a new social control that discourages the birth or nurturing of any children whose "life chances" are sufficiently dim or who require extraordinary amounts of money to maintain. Advocates of this control endorse the strategy that "abnormal" individuality should be consciously and deliberately "prevented."

The politics of choice in the abortion issue have remained unconnected to the science of prevention that has focused a considerable amount of its attention on the status and health of the unborn.[21] After natural child-birth comes the normal child. The first client class of the obstetrical proj-ect has been wealthy, white, educated, and willing to comply to the man-dates of the Surgeon General. Here is a client class, fully insured, who embody the sociocratic ideology of normalcy—a demand for long life, if not immortality. This ideology has implications for the public under-standing of disability and the private and public responsibilities that are encouraged to accommodate all manner of human differences.

A few feminist intellectuals have recognized the dilemmas raised by the institutionalization of the obstetrical project.[22] The reshaping of ex-pectations about how human reproduction is accomplished (that is, in terms of perfectibility) has given medicine extraordinary power to shape future generations. The feminist challenge has been to question how that power is used and by whom. But it is probably already too late in the history of cultural individualism to disestablish the eugenics of choice as it has developed out of modern obstetrics. Some residual revulsion is still expressed about aborting females when males are desired, but the statis-tical significance of such desire, at least in the United States, is so small that the principle of choice is unlikely to be compromised. In other words, the confidential relation between doctor and patient is making over the world in an unprecedented way—quietly, effectively, and with consequences that are destined to exacerbate tensions between those who have bad luck and those who have medicine.

The doctor is no longer a univocal figure. Malpractice represents, of course, incompetence in doctors, but that is only its operative meaning. Its illuminative or cultural meaning points to an increased readiness to make accusations about who is responsible for bad luck when bad luck cannot be clearly distinguished from medical practice. The obstetrical project in its scientific turn toward "guaranteeing" the outcome of each pregnancy has invited deep suspicions on both sides of the physician-patient relation about how certain any guarantee can ever be. Genetic counseling, for example, is the vanguard therapy of twenty-first century obstetrical medicine. The doctor, in conjunction with genetic counselors, administers information about the probabilities of producing genetically ascribed illnesses in one's offspring. The choices thus far, given such information, have been limited. Such "information therapy" will eventually give way to the direct treatment of genetic disorders. Already "gene therapy" trials are being conducted on patients with disorders that have not responded to other forms of medical treatment. In this progress, probabilities give way to new certainties in the approaches to disease.

Yet uncertainty remains. The receding presence of the doctor who reassures in the old belief that no one can know anything for certain, at least not without fail, has left in its wake a kind of resignation that a doctor's competence is the only thing worth valuing. The pastoral role of the physician is undermined by the demand that the "right" doctor should always be the one whose competence results in the outcome one desires. "Defensive" medicine is thus the legal strategy to dissuade patients from doubting the competence, if not giving up the demand.

If feminism has challenged more than resolved the meaning of progress in late-twentieth-century medicine, bioethics has aimed to achieve in the name of the whole society the role of mediator and advisor to the medical profession and the government about possible resolutions. Bioethics has gained prestige and influence over the years in large part because it maps a terrain left virtually unexplored and thus undisturbed by earlier generations of philosophers and theologians. Throughout history, the religious and philosophical observers of medicine were not unaware of the misuses of doctoring. But they were confident that a "profession" of medicine retained its links to a culture of character and conduct that instructed, among other things, what could not be done in the name of medicine and remain medicine. Progress thus conformed to moral as well as technical limits of what constituted proper medical practice. The medical profession now regularly tests the limits of its inherited moral understandings of the uses of scientific and technical advance, and bioethics has captured the divided imagination of a culture that no longer easily recognizes how these limits function to protect both physician and patient. As the contemporary voice of reason, bioethics speaks ever more loudly and often about what those limits are and what the tests of them should be.[23]

Of course, a limit so recognized is bound to be tested, and this is why bioethics cannot address its complicity in the very challenge to those limits it supposedly sets out to establish. Not since the advent of psychoanalysis has an intellectual movement been so transformative in character and yet so decidedly in search of the truth. Unlike Freud's psychoanalytic movement, bioethics has deliberately sought to insinuate itself into forums whose goals are to clarify the relation between state and medicine in those cases where both face such dilemmas as abortion, euthanasia, or any other one that blurs the line between the technically possible and the morally dubious. In its didactic mode, bioethics is highly influential. Governmental commissions are the most well known and the most visible of these didactic forums, but hundreds of "seminars" and "workshops" contribute to the perception that bioethics has set its sights well beyond the sphere of intellectual and reflective debate. The pragmatism of bioethics makes every theoretical exercise an opportunity to settle, so it seems, once and for all, matters that have yet to yield fully to bureaucratic control.

Bioethics has not required highly trained experts to conduct its investigations. As an "applied" discipline, it has attracted numerous academics who have sought some greater say in what the public responses should be toward medical innovation. Like epidemiology, bioethics is dedicated to a kind of impartiality that lifts it above the fray of politics. It has superseded sociology which, for a time, offered its own empirically derived wisdom about the conduct of medicine and other major institutions. The only part of sociological investigation that remains influential is expressed methodologically in the framework of epidemiology.

Unlike the cultural impact of feminism, the bioethical challenge to medicine suggests a further inclination toward specialization in which the intellectual division of labor requires a kind of metadoctoring. The bioethicist is doctor to the public, "on call" much as the physician used to be, ready to answer questions from those who are curious and concerned and who are just as likely to be news reporters as patients. The persona of bioethicist is as much therapist as "philosopher king," offering to an anxious public a means to formulate *ways* to think about medicine and its moral dilemmas, but not necessarily *what* to think about them. Occasionally, bioethicists do call for global, rather than incremental, assessments of the progress of medicine.[24] Although bioethics has succeeded in dominating the present conversation about medical morality, feminism shows more what is at stake in that morality. Both movements will continue to influence how doctors themselves think about what they do.

ENVIRONMENTAL MOVEMENTS

Affluence in the advanced societies has brought with it an increased recognition and understanding of the effects of production and consumption on health. At times, depending on what aspect of environmentalism one is addressing, affluence and its effects on health and the environment are said to be tied to the forces of capitalist production and consumption. Environmental damage in socialist countries has alerted most observers to the possibility that industrialization and the demands of population size have contributed to problems of health and welfare in ways that cannot be ideologically assigned to one or another economic system.

The versions of apocalypse that environmentalism brings to the conference tables and the heads of state is not illusory. The idea of the greenhouse effect has recently developed into a kind of unifying theory that explains how the depletion of ozone in the atmosphere, the burning of fossil fuels, and the explosion of nuclear weapons each contributes to a scenario that would at best substantially reduce the standard of living or possibly destroy life as we know it. Ecosystems, food chains, and the politics of development are said to be intimately linked. If sufficient preoccupation with the kinds of food consumed did not already exist, environmentalists have added the sometimes terrifying claims that the ways in which foods are produced promote disease, in particular, cancer. The public scares about Alar on apples and the dozens of other less well publicized "contaminations" have affected consumer confidence in the name of health.[25]

The cataloguing of disease-causing substances diverts attention from the epidemiology of the behavioral causes of disease. Unlike those health movements more closely allied with medicine and devoted to reforming the individual, the environmental movements have consciously set their sights on regulating industry and government. The growing interest in regulating industry for public health reasons finds parallels in research conducted to determine the healthfulness of work environments themselves. Occupational health movements target the workplace as another environment that under certain conditions produces stress, reduces productivity, and eventually causes disease, including and especially heart disease.[26]

Similarly, environmental movements also prevail upon industry and government to preserve the natural environment and all that is in it besides what is created by human beings. Greenpeace opposes certain types of fishing methods and nuclear submarines; voluntary activists and state authorities together oppose nuclear power; celebrity opponents of all kinds of harmful things (including harm to animals) have popularized the environmental agenda. Just as medicine has responded to the demands of its consumers, so, too, have many manufacturers of foods and goods. The result is a kind of cultural conspiracy to reduce to zero the costs—in terms of disease and harm—of living well. Among those in search of health and active longevity are some who design to eliminate certain forms of manufacture and consumption altogether.

Since the creation of nuclear weapons, scientists have maintained an ambivalent relation toward those in political and military power who determine how many such weapons are produced and where they are located. The clock with hands close to midnight has come to symbolize both ambivalence and a distinct incapacity to do anything about resolving it.[27] The symbol of time, or not enough of it, shapes an ambivalence about mortality that is felt individually and collectively. The power of science is so great that no single person or state can be trusted to determine its ultimate and fatal uses. And so, given the increased and fearful recognition of what the world and planet would be like after a nuclear war, some physicians have led a small but noticeable movement to oppose the production of all nuclear weapons. Physicians for Social Responsibility devotes its resources to informing the public about the medical consequences of nuclear war. Their strategy, supported and endorsed by schools of public health across the country, has been to demonstrate why medicine in its presently organized form would be useless against the injuries, illnesses, and hopelessness resulting from wide-scale nuclear conflagration.

The everyday practice of medicine is, indeed, some distance from the strategies and goals of physicians who actively oppose nuclear war. The idea that the calling of medicine includes such strategies and goals is not entirely fantastic. Great physicians of the past have voiced their concerns about human suffering and war. What is different is that these strategies are construed as defining the very possibility for medicine and its practice. As in the case of bioethics, the preaching function is a powerful source of self-legitimation in the lives of those who seek ultimate cures for ultimate diseases. The more modest endeavors of practicing physicians may not be the subject of modern heroism, but they are fraught with the same anxieties and uncertainties that characterize the larger politics of environmentalism. The end of medicine, in this final twist, is not unlike its purported demise in the face of self-help movements. That those trained in medicine would actively lobby, however rhetorically, for their own irrelevance speaks to an extensive division of labor in the medical-industrial-public health complex.

With the rise of environmental movements, consumption has become a form of political behavior; the foods we eat, the products we use, the work we do, have all come under the increased scrutiny of the environmental agenda. Health is no longer the principal responsibility of medicine, and physicians actively working to eliminate nuclear weapons symbolize how encompassing the health agenda has become. Environmentalism, in its elective affinities with the rich and famous, has linked individual health with cosmic destiny. The famous voice, as distinct from the voice of institutional authority, speaks in a language that effortlessly inspires fear and trembling. Under different circumstances, for example in the confidential relation of physician and patient, such inspirational language might sound entirely inappropriate or unreasonable. The movie star reciting the latest update of politically correct habits of consumption, condemning this or that form of manufacture, and "speaking for" a safer world, is the "carrier" of the new power of environmentalism to make health a moral ideal and a political project. The greening of the world will, no doubt, list health as a high priority. Whether governments, industries, and individuals will actively conform to the future agendas of health and safety remains to be seen.

THE END OF MEDICINE?

This chapter has proposed to review those forces within and beyond medicine that have deeply altered the public image of doctoring in American society. If a severe shortage of physician authority exists in matters pertaining to the health and welfare of the nation, the causes are multifarious. First, modern attitudes toward health are impossible to understand without assessing the influence of epidemiology on the progress of medicine. Second, the same epidemiological methods applied to diagnosis and treatment are applicable to an understanding of health behavior and of the harmful effects of environmental contamination. The various movements that have taken shape in response to the voluminous knowledge about risk are central to the politics of all advanced societies. Their influence has yet to be fully gauged politically, but can be appraised culturally.

The class interests of the worried well will determine the future direction of the medical profession, but whether toward more care or more cure is far from settled. As the economic interests of the medical profession are subordinated to corporate, insurance, and governmental interests, a devaluation in the cultural meaning of doctoring will likely continue. The health maintenance organization will devote its resources to "preventive" rather than "defensive" medicine. Yet the worried well will not be fully appeased by either strategy so long as the public anxiety about individual and collective health is so strong. Unless the medical profession abandons its historic responsibility to heal, this anxiety will never disappear.

Since competing strategies for reducing such anxiety cannot be exclusively assigned to either the preventive or defensive side, the figure of the physician will not give up its authority entirely. It cannot. Even physicians who advocate euthanasia cannot abolish the authority invested in that figure of the healer for whom death is both enigmatic and inevitable. Death, as it can be understood in the vocation of medicine, can no more be actively sought than it can be denied by the use of technology to achieve immortality.[28] There are many kinds of death in life, and no government commission will eliminate the perfectly frightening fact that the pronouncement of death is not and cannot be fully in the hands of human beings. An acknowledgment of the limits of medicine is one key to its preservation and is found in the physician's ethic of responsibility to offer those calming hopes and finalities that make our lives together possible.

FIFTEEN

Unlikely Alliances

The Changing Contours of American Religious Faith

James Davison Hunter and John Steadman Rice

- On March 9, 1986, a coalition of members of the Presbyterian Church, the United Church of Christ, the Unitarian Universalist Association, the Reform and Conservative branch of Judaism, the Episcopal Church, the Methodist Church, and numerous other denominations, all committed to pro-choice policy, led a line of 100,000 marchers in Washington, D.C., in the National March for Women's Lives, the largest women's rights demonstration in American history.
- Four months later, on July 25, 1986, approximately thirty prominent leaders, representing a broad-based coalition of Mormons, conservative Protestants, Catholics, Jews, and Greek Orthodox, met at the residence of John Cardinal O'Connor, Archbishop of New York, to address the problem of child and adult pornography.
- At the Citicorp annual shareholders meeting in New York in April 1987, a group of ministers, priests, and rabbis, fully bedecked in clerical garments, stood outside the building singing songs and praying for the dead and detained in South Africa, in protest against the company's investment policies.
- In early May 1988, Operation Rescue brought orthodox activists of every religious stripe together at an abortion clinic in midtown Manhattan to protest the practice of abortion through civil disobedience. Eight hundred people were arrested that day, including four Orthodox rabbis, eleven Evangelical pastors, one Catholic bishop, two monsignors, and four nuns. Similar "rescues" were performed in Long Island, Philadelphia, and Atlanta.

This chapter draws on the book *Culture Wars: The Struggle to Define America,* by James Davison Hunter (forthcoming).

In a previous century and, indeed, earlier in the present century, events such as these would have been unthinkable. What, exactly, is going on when liberal Protestants, liberal Catholics, and Reform Jews speak out in one voice for progressive abortion legislation? Or when Evangelical Protestants, traditionalist Catholics, Orthodox Jews, and even Moonies become allies in the war against pornography?

Although these alliances are historically "unnatural," they have become increasingly commonplace in this last decade of the twentieth century. Indeed, on a broad spectrum of social issues, religious opinion now reflects not only divisions *within* each faith community but alliances *across* denominational lines. These vignettes point to a fundamental shift in American religious pluralism. Namely, the politically significant divisions in American religion are no longer those that divide Protestants and Catholics or Christians and Jews, but those that divide the "orthodox" and "progressive" within each religious tradition.

The divisions between orthodox and progressive within the various religious traditions in America did not just spontaneously emerge in the 1980s, but developed out of a series of events and circumstances that span the course of a century. The question is, then, how precisely did this realignment come to be?

EARLY FAULTLINES

The origins of the present realignment can be traced back at least to the late nineteenth century in a society at the threshold of world economic and political dominance. All three of the major religious traditions in America were struggling to cope with the intellectual and social dilemmas of contemporary life: labor and public health problems, increased crime, poverty and indigence, deep ethnic distrust, political instability, the weakening of the credibility of religious faith, and so on. Each denomination, of course, forged its own responses to these changes, but at a broader level, the breaks within each community were between those who longed to preserve the ancient truths and traditional way of life and those who aspired to forge new moral ideals appropriate to novel social circumstances. First, consider the emergence of the progressivist appeal.

In Protestantism, for example, the Social Gospel movement espoused active institutional measures of redress for these institutionally based *social* ills. Rejecting the individualistic view that sin and personal moral failure were to blame for human hardship, the Social Gospel traced many of the problems of modernity to the brutal power of contemporary social and economic institutions; and it was here, its advocates contended, that the modern church could most effectively serve the cause of Christianity.

By the 1890s an enormous literature advocating the tenets of the Social Gospel was being published and distributed. Prominent in this work was the manifesto, published in 1908, "The Social Creed of the Churches." Translating these tenets into a programmatic agenda were new organizations, such as the Brotherhood of the Kingdom, the Department of Church and Labor of the Presbyterian Church's Board of Home Missions, the Methodist Federation for Social Service, and the commission on the Church and Social Service.

Within Catholicism, liberal or progressivist initiatives came in the 1890s, primarily in the form of new attitudes and policies articulated by particular bishops in the American hierarchy. In part they were associated with the rights of labor, particularly in the support for the "Knights of Labor," a Catholic precursor to the labor union. In part, they were associated with the desire to cooperate with Protestants in the realm of education. But the movement that came to embody these progressive ideas more prominently than any other was the Americanist movement.

At the heart of the Americanist movement in the Catholic hierarchy was the desire to integrate the American Catholic Church into the mainstream of modern American society. To do this the Americanists sought to phase out what they considered inessential Romanist traditions and to present the Catholic faith positively to a Protestant society. To this end, they endeavored to eliminate the foreign cast of the church by Americanizing the immigrant population (through language and custom) as quickly as possible, to celebrate and promote the American principles of religious liberty and the separation of Church and State, and to participate in fostering American-style democracy globally. By the mid-1890s the Americanist movement acquired a more universal appeal through its espousal of progressive biblical, theological, and historical scholarship emanating from Europe. The coupling of these two was based on mutual affinities: the Americanists' praise of religious liberty complemented the European modernists' advocacy of subjectivity in theology; the former's praise of democracy and scientific progress fit well with the latter's program to reconcile the Church with the modern age.[1] The modernist movement within American Catholic scholarship was fairly small at the beginning of the twentieth century. Yet whether European or American, the progressive theology of modernism was associated with, and found support in, the Americanist movement, and the movement foreshadowed contemporary developments.

As with the Catholics, accommodation to American life and purpose was perhaps the dominant inspiration behind progressivist Jewish thought. To that end, the worship service was shortened, the vernacular was introduced, the use of the organ was sanctioned, and the segregation of men and women in all aspects of the worship service was ended. More important than these modifications, though, were the theological accommodations. In this there was a decisive move away from traditional belief and ritual observance toward ethical idealism.

These theological alterations first became crystallized in a series of resolutions drawn up in Philadelphia in 1869 and then, more formally, in the Pittsburgh Platform of 1885. In these documents, progressives maintained that a Rabbinical Judaism based on the Law and Tradition had forever lost its grip on the modern Jew. The only viable course, therefore, was to reinterpret the meaning of Judaism in light of new historical developments. As such the entire range of traditional rabbinic beliefs and practices were abandoned. The first to be rejected was the traditional conviction that the Torah, or Jewish law, was unalterable—that it was somehow sufficient for the religious needs of the Jewish people at all times and places. From this the doctrine of the bodily resurrection was declared to have "no religious foundation," as were the concepts of Gehenna and Eden (hell and paradise). Repudiated as well were the laws regulating dress, diet, and purification and the excessive ritualism of traditional worship. And not least, the messianic hope of a restored Jewish state under a son of David was also completely disavowed.

In its stead was the affirmation of the universalism of Hebraic ethical principles—that Judaism was the highest conception of the "God-idea." Having abandoned any conception of Jewish nationalism, the mission of Israel was now to bring the ethical ideals of the Jewish tradition to the rest of the world. Remarkable given the historical context in which it was made, the document even extended the hand of ecumenical cooperation to Christianity and Islam. As "daughter religions of Judaism" they were welcome as partners in Judaism's mission of spreading "monotheistic and moral truth." In large measure, the ethical truths they desired to proclaim could be translated into a language that harmonized with the Protestant Social Gospel. As stated in Principle I of the Pittsburgh manifesto, Reform Jews would commit themselves "to regulate the relations between rich and poor" and to help solve the "problem presented by the contrasts and evils of the present organization of society."

As if to leave absolutely no doubt about the rightness of their cause, the authors of the Pittsburgh Platform threw down the ultimate challenge to their nonprogressive rabbinical counterparts:

> We can see no good reason why we should ogle you, allow you to act as a brake to the wheel of progress, and confirm you in your pretensions. You do not represent the ideas and sentiments of the American Jews, [in] this phase upon which Judaism entered in this country, you are an anachronism, strangers in this country, and to your own brethren. You represent

yourselves, together with a past age and a foreign land. We must proceed without you to perform our duties to God, and our country, and our religion, for WE are the orthodox Jews in America.[2]

The boldness and enthusiasm (even if not the audacity) expressed by these Reform rabbis for their campaign of change in Judaism was remarkable, but it was not isolated. It was in large measure shared by progressives in both Protestantism and Catholicism as well.

The orthodox responses to these progressivist challenges varied within the main religious traditions, but the common thread among them was the conviction that such revisionism posed a serious threat to the sacred authority upon which each faith rested. Thus, the orthodox response within Protestantism called for a return to Scripture as the source of moral authority. By demonstrating that the Bible was the Word of God, inerrant in all of its teachings, they felt confident that they would have an adequate foundation to reject heresy and to prevent the ordinary churchgoer from straying into impiety and irreligion. Reflecting this spirit, throughout the late nineteenth and early twentieth century the defenders of Protestant tradition established a wealth of Bible colleges, such as the Moody Bible Institute (1886), the Bible Institute of Los Angeles (1913), St. Paul Bible College (1916), Faith Baptist Bible College (1921), Columbia Bible College (1923). (The Moody Bible Institute was originally founded for the purpose of urban ministry, but within ten to fifteen years it became caught up in the fundamentalist reaction.) Also created were a variety of Bible conferences—such as the Niagara Bible Conferences, the American Bible and Prophetic Conference, the Northfield Conferences, the Old Point Comfort Bible Conference, and the Seaside Bible Conference—devoted to the careful study and affirmation of scriptural principles.

In a similar vein, in Catholicism, the Americanist movement was seen as an unconscionable challenge to the authority of the Holy See. By the end of January 1899, Pope Leo XIII voiced his opinion in the form of an apostolic letter, *Testem Benevolentiae,* and though he was not totally condemnatory, his censure was still broad and effective. Through the eyes of the Vatican, the Americanist idea of presenting the truths of the Catholic Church "positively" in a Protestant context was seen as the watering down of doctrine, their praise of religious liberty was perceived as the praise of religious subjectivism, and their desire to accommodate the Church to American democratic institutions (the separation of Church and State) was viewed as a desire to surrender the temporal powers of the papacy—to introduce democracy into the Church.

The orthodox response in Judaism also asserted the inviolability of the tradition to which the present generation were heirs. All traditional

Jews interpreted the Pittsburgh statement as an insult and immediately proceeded to sever their relations with the Union of American Hebrew Congregations. Likewise, Hebrew Union College was declared unfit to educate the next generation of rabbis. However, the most orthodox and observant Jews found themselves a beleaguered and ghettoized minority, with few adherents and little resources. Of approximately two hundred major Jewish congregations in existence in the 1880s, only a dozen of these, representing between three and four thousand people, remained strictly Orthodox.[3] The larger portion of traditionalists pursued compromise. These traditionalists remained committed to traditional practices and teachings—to the foundation provided by biblical and Talmudic authority—but they were also committed to the political emancipation and westernization (and therefore, deghettoization) of Jewish experience. They recognized that this would entail modifications to orthodoxy, but they were persuaded that these changes should only be made according to Talmudic precedent and with the consent of the whole community of believers.[4] In 1886, one year after the publication of the Pittsburgh Platform, the Jewish Theological Seminary in New York was founded, and with it, the Conservative movement in American Judaism was formally launched. By 1901, with the founding of the Rabbinical Assembly of America (the national association of Conservative Rabbis), and 1913, with the establishment of the United Synagogue of America (a national union of the Conservative synagogues), the Conservative movement had become a more fully distinct and powerful force in American Judaism.

As these brief glimpses illustrate, pluralism has long been characteristic of both intra- and interdenominational religious life in American history. What is surprising about current developments, however, is that the divisions between orthodox and progressive within each tradition have, in large measure, come to outweigh or take precedence over those separating the major faiths. This historical realignment has taken place in conjunction with, and is evident in, other structural changes.

THE WANING OF DENOMINATIONAL LOYALTIES

However deep the internal disagreements were within each faith community between the 1880s and the 1960s, opposing factions always implicitly understood the limitations of their quarrel. As such, Protestants, Catholics, and Jews retained their theological and ideological distinctiveness.

A number of empirical studies of the post–World War II period confirmed the seemingly unchangeable nature of these denominational lines. Perhaps the most famous of these was the 1958 public opinion sur-

vey of the residents of the Detroit metropolitan area. The study, re-
vealingly entitled *The Religious Factor,* found that vast differences still
existed among Protestants, Catholics, and Jews, not only in terms of
their relative socioeconomic positions but in terms of their broader view
of the world. Religious tradition was the source of significant differences
in their general political orientation and commitment to civil liberties
(for example, freedom of speech and desegregation), not to mention the
differences in voting behavior and in attitudes toward the exercise of
governmental power (for example, in setting price controls, establishing
national health insurance and medical care, lessening unemployment,
and strengthening educational programs). The religious factor also had
a marked effect in shaping the public's views of morality (for example,
gambling, drinking, birth control, divorce, and Sunday business), and
the public's views on the role of the family. Finally, religious differences
had consequences for economic aspirations and attitudes toward work
(as seen in various views on installment buying, saving, the American
Dream, and the like).[5]

Yet within two decades, new evidence was showing a certain reversal
in these trends: people were becoming less and less concerned about denominational identity and loyalty.[6] Surveys of the period showed that the
majority of people of all faiths (up to 90 percent) favored increased cooperation among local churches in community projects, in promoting
racial tolerance, in sharing facilities, and even in worship.[7] The weakening of denominational boundaries extended to the relations among
denominations within the Protestant community as well. According to
Gallup surveys conducted from the mid-1970s to the mid-1980s, the
overwhelming majority of Protestants carried equally positive feelings
toward Protestants belonging to denominations other than their own.[8]

The waning of denominational loyalty was reflected in people's attitudes, but it was confirmed increasingly in their behavior. Since mid-
century, Americans of every faith community have become far more
prone to change denominational membership in the course of their
lives.[9] The evidence on interreligious marriages also suggests this pattern. For example, the proportion of Jews marrying non-Jews increased
from 3 percent in 1965 to 17 percent in 1983. The proportions of interreligious marriage between Catholics and Protestants and of different
denominations within Protestantism are considerably higher.

IDEOLOGICAL REALIGNMENT

As denominational affiliation has weakened, so too have the effects of
denominational identity on the way people actually view the world. The
1987 General Social Survey showed no significant differences among

Protestants, Catholics, and Jews on most issues, including capital punishment, the tolerance of communists, gun control, interracial marriage,
welfare, and defense spending. And there was no significant difference
between Protestants and Catholics on the abortion issue.[10] What is more,
the only significant differences among Protestant denominations exist
according to their general location on the ideological continuum between orthodoxy and progressivism.[11]

These ideological affinities across denominational lines are reflected
time and again. (It is important to recall, however, that public culture is
largely constituted by the activities and pronouncements of elites. The
key players, then, are not so much the "rank and file," the ordinary passive supporters of a cause, but the activists and leadership. The ideological constructions of elites are most consequential and, importantly, it is
here that ideological affinities are most clearly crystallized.) The 1987
Religion and Power Survey, for example, documented just this—that
two fairly distinct cultural orientations take shape across religious tradition on the basis of theological commitment.[12] The theologically orthodox of each faith and the theologically progressive of each faith divided
predictably on the issues of sexual morality, family life and family policy,
political party preference and ideology, political economy, and international affairs. (In the appendix to this chapter, the exact distribution
of opinions on these issues and their statistical significance are analyzed.)

Moreover, this same survey found that Protestants, Catholics, and
Jews on both ends of the new cultural axis generally agreed that America
bore tremendous responsibility in world affairs. Virtually all were prone
to agree that the United States is not "pretty much like other countries,"
but "has a special role to play in the world today."[13] So, too, leaders of
all faiths were strongly disposed to affirm that "the United States should
aspire to remain a world power" and not "a neutral country, like Switzerland or Sweden."[14] But orthodox and progressive factions sharply
disagreed as to how the United States should actually carry out that responsibility. When asked "How much confidence do you have in the ability of the United States to deal wisely with present world problems?" progressives in all three faiths were at least twice as likely as their more
orthodox counterparts to say "not very much" or "none at all."[15]

The same kind of division was exhibited between the orthodox and
the progressives when they were asked to make moral assessments of
America's place in the world order. The overwhelming majority of the
orthodox in Protestant (78 percent), Catholic (73 percent), and Jewish
(92 percent) leadership circles said, for example, that the United States
was, in general, "a force for good in the world." By contrast, the majority
of the progressives in Protestantism and Catholicism (51 percent and 56
percent respectively) said that the United States was either "neutral" or

"a force for ill." [16] The contrast was even more stark when respondents were asked to assess how America treats people in the Third World. Progressives, particularly in Protestantism (71 percent) and Catholicism (87 percent), were much more likely to agree that America "treats people in the Third World unfairly." The majority of the orthodox in each tradition claimed just the opposite. [17]

Opposing perspectives of America's moral status in world affairs became apparent when respondents were asked to compare the United States and the Soviet Union. A plurality of all religious leaders characterized the competition between the United States and the Soviet Union as a struggle in power politics, as opposed to a moral struggle, yet the more orthodox Catholics and Protestants were three times more likely (and orthodox Jews more than twice as likely) to say that it was a moral struggle. [18] Ideological disparities between orthodox and progressive respondents were even more dramatic, however, when they were asked which was the greater problem in the world today, repressive regimes aligned with the United States or Soviet expansion? The majority of progressives within Protestantism (61 percent), Catholicism (71 percent), and Judaism (57 percent) claimed it was the repressive regimes aligned with the United States; the majority of the orthodox in these three faiths (Protestants, 84 percent; Catholics, 64 percent; and Jews, 87 percent) identified Soviet expansion as the greater problem.

The results of a survey of the political opinion of Christian theologians conducted in 1982 reveal similar divisions in perspectives on domestic spending. [19] Nearly two-thirds (63 percent) of the progressives compared to less than one-fifth (19 percent) of the orthodox claimed that the government was spending too little on welfare. Eighty percent of the progressives said that the government was spending too little on national health, compared to just 52 percent of the Evangelicals. Likewise, nearly nine out of ten (89 percent) of the progressives agree that the government was spending too little on protecting the environment; just half (50 percent) of the orthodox Protestants felt the same way. Almost nine out of ten (87 percent) of the progressives complained that the government spent too little money on urban problems compared to 56 percent of the orthodox. And roughly six out of every ten of the progressives (59 percent) claimed that too little was spent on foreign aid; just one out of every four (24 percent) of the orthodox agreed.

In short, not only in surveys but in other recent empirical studies as well it is clear that the relative embrace of orthodoxy is the single most important factor in explaining variation in political values. [20] Indeed, it accounts for more variation within and across religious tradition than any other single factor, including social class background, race, ethnicity, gender, the size of the organization the person works in, and the degree of pietism each one individually lives by. Obviously, some words of caution are in order. The attempt to dichotomize these religious leaders according to either an orthodox or progressive theological inclination is admittedly forced. Dichotomies may be more prone to show up in organizations, but among individuals the distinctions would seem artificial and perhaps unfair. Among individuals intuition suggests a continuum, with orthodoxy and progressivism being the two extreme poles. Undoubtedly this is true. Even so, at least in the present situation there appears to be an increasing polarization among denominational and para-denominational organizations. What is more, there may be a tendency for the leadership to align themselves dichotomously as well. Would the differences between orthodox and progressive camps in each religious tradition have been as prominent if this were not the case? Though a dichotomy may not adequately reflect reality, as an analytical exercise it has still proven to be extremely instructive. The evidence pointing to a restructuring of ideological affinities within America's religious leadership would seem overwhelming.

The importance of these changes is nothing short of world-historical. For the full length of American history, from colonial times to the middle of the twentieth century, pluralism in American public culture existed primarily within the limits or boundaries of a biblical culture. As such, cultural diversity revolved principally around the cultural axes of doctrine and ecclesia. With the erosion of those boundaries, the primary axis defining religious and cultural pluralism in American life shifted and is continuing to shift.

A NEW ECUMENISM

Increasingly, these cosmological positions have come to be expressed institutionally and manifested in the form of alliances that reach *across* denominational lines. Because of the commonalities of vision and concern, the orthodox wings of Protestantism, Catholicism, and Judaism are forming associations with each other, as are the progressive wings of each faith, and each side does so in opposition to the influence the other seeks to exert in public culture. The vignettes recounted at the beginning of this chapter merely illustrate this development. The heart of the new cultural realignment, then, are the pragmatic alliances being formed across faith traditions, alliances that constitute an altogether new form of ecumenism.

The clearest ways in which this new ecumenism takes tangible expression is within the newly expanded structure of para-church organizations. Most obviously it is seen in the way these organizations relate to each other. In some instances groups will, as a matter of long-standing

policy, join together with other groups in pursuit of realizing a particular
policy objective. The Catholic League for Religious and Civil Rights provides a telling illustration of this dynamic on the side of orthodoxy.[21] The
Catholic League was established in 1973 by a Jesuit priest, as a Catholic counterpart to the Jewish Anti-Defamation League and the secular
American Civil Liberties Union, "to protect the religious rights and advance the just interests of Catholics in secular society."[22] While it claims
to be a nonpartisan organization, working to serve the needs of the whole
Catholic community, it tilts decisively toward the orthodox community
in Catholicism. In this, it openly supports the work of like-minded Protestants and Jews. Indeed, the League's first major legal case was the defense of Dr. Frank Bolles, a Protestant physician and right-to-life activist.
(Bolles had been charged by a Colorado district attorney for "harassing
and causing alarm" by mailing out antiabortion literature.) In the first
fifteen years of existence, the Catholic League also has publicly defended the rights of a Jew to wear his yarmulke while in uniform; it
supported Reverend Sun Myung Moon, the leader of the Unification
Church, in his tax-evasion case; it has publicly "defended the right of
parents [Protestant, Catholic, and Jewish] to give their children a God-
centered education"; and so on.

A similar dynamic operates on the progressive side of the cultural divide. The Religious Action Center of Reform Judaism, for example, officially serves as a government liaison between the Union of American Hebrew Congregations and the Central Conference of American Rabbis by
representing the positions of these groups to the federal government.
Beyond this, however, it cooperates with a wide variety of liberal Protestant and Catholic denominations and organizations on progressive policy concerns, issuing statements against the nuclear arms race, America's
involvement in Central America, and Supreme Court nominee Robert
Bork. In both cases, the alliances formed are built upon a perceived self-
interest. Both organizations tend to support groups and individuals of
other religious faiths when such support also advances their own particular objectives.

The pattern here is frequently repeated. The activists in these organizations communicate with each other and even draw direct support from
each other. For example, in a survey of forty-seven of these public affairs
organizations, the leadership of all of these groups claimed to be in communication with individuals or groups outside their own religious or
philosophical tradition, and most of these had engaged in active cooperation.[23] The public affairs office of the Orthodox Jewish organization, Agudath Israel, for example, regularly allies with Catholics on concerns over private education and with conservative Protestants on moral
issues. The overwhelming majority of these organizations were sup-

ported by grass-roots contributions and of these, all but one or two claimed to receive contributions from Protestants, Catholics, the Eastern Orthodox, and Jews. In the early 1980s, for example, 30 percent of the membership of the Moral Majority was Catholic. Finally, roughly half of these groups sought to make explicit and public their commitment to coalition formation (that is, the larger ecumenism) by deliberately including representation from the range of traditions on their organization's board of advisors or board of trustees. For example, the (orthodox) American Family Association—which is located in Tupelo, Mississippi, and led by Donald Wildmon as its executive director—advertises an advisory board that includes four Catholic Bishops and one Cardinal, three Eastern Orthodox Bishops, including the Primate of the Greek Orthodox Church, and dozens of Evangelical and Pentecostal leaders.

LEGITIMATING THE ALLIANCES

Although these coalitional organizations on both sides of the divide vary considerably in their size, scope of activity, and ability to actually unify member groups, their very presence on the political landscape aptly symbolizes the nature and direction of a major realignment in American public culture. And the degree to which the activists themselves recognize the historically unique positions that they have come to occupy with regard to this realignment is evident in the legitimations offered by both sides to account for their newly forged alliances. On both sides of the divide, the accounts are framed in terms of a pragmatism necessary to the survival of their respectively besieged ways of life. Speaking from the orthodox point of view, for example, Tim LaHaye has asserted the following:

> Protestants, Catholics and Jews do share two very basic beliefs: we all believe in God to Whom we must give account some day for the way we live our lives; we share a basic concern for the moral values that are found in the Old Testament. . . . I really believe that we are in a fierce battle for the very survival of our culture. . . . Obviously I am not suggesting joint evangelistic crusades with these religions; that would reflect an unacceptable theological compromise for all of us. [Nevertheless] . . . we can respect the people and realize that we have more in common with each other than we ever will with the secularizers of this country. It is time for all religiously committed citizens to unite against our common enemy.[24]

Of a very different generation, but from a like-minded perspective, Evangelical activist Franky Schaeffer observed that *"the time has come for those who remain to band together in an ecumenism of orthodoxy.* Unlike liberal ecumenicism which is bound together by unbelief, this ecumenicism is based upon what we *agree* to be the essence of the Christian faith, including an orthodoxy of belief in social concerns and priorities."[25]

Nor are these solely the sentiments of the Protestant fundamentalists.[26] As the director of the public affairs office of Agudath Israel argued, "Joint efforts with Catholics and Protestants do not mean that we Jews are endorsing their theology. We can overlook our religious differences because politically it makes sense."[27] So, too, a spokesman for the Catholic League maintained, "the issues are too important to have a denominational focus."[28]

The moral reasoning employed by both sides of the cultural divide to legitimate these alliances, then, is very similar. Although the alliances being formed are, as suggested above, historically "unnatural," they have become pragmatically necessary. In the end, they are justified by the simple dictum "an enemy of an enemy is a friend of mine."

RELIGIOUS REALIGNMENT AND SOCIAL SCIENCE

It is important to recognize that the lines separating orthodox and progressive are not, in reality, always sharp. There are some notable ideological cross-currents that flow against the larger cultural tendencies—the pro-life organization Feminists for Life, for example, or the left-wing Evangelicals for Social Action. Yet recognizing the existence of these counterintuitive phenomena does not negate the broader tendencies taking place within the realm of American public culture. The dominant impulse at the present time is toward the polarization of a religiously informed public culture into two relatively distinct moral and ideological camps.

Curiously, these developments have been almost completely ignored for nearly two decades. If anything, the social scientific establishment has seemingly documented what it has long (and incorrectly) assumed—that religious and cultural phenomena really are "epi-phenomenal" to the course and conduct of contemporary affairs. Attitudinal surveys and organizational studies, for example, have consistently shown that religious affiliation is insignificant (statistically and substantively) in explaining social and political reality. Social scientists will concede that the distinct traditions of creed, religious observance, and ecclesiastical politics are important sources of personal meaning and communal identity. Even so, the conceptual apparatus they employ and the evidence they marshal support the view that there is no longer a distinct Protestant position or Catholic position or Jewish position (or, for that matter, Mormon or Buddhist position) with regard to American public culture. The guiding assumption about the secularization of modern life has been substantiated.

The cultural realignments discussed here, however, suggest that the social scientific reports of the effective death of religion are, as were those of Mark Twain's demise, "greatly exaggerated." Indeed, events of the past two decades have clearly caught social scientists looking in the wrong places. The relationship between religion and public life has, if anything, become more significant, but it is because the contours of the religious organization and expression in America have fundamentally changed.

These changes, in turn, have and will continue to have a fundamental significance for American culture. The reason for this is clear: this realignment is not based on a facile division between "liberals" and "conservatives" in different faith communities. Political ideology is merely an artifact of a much deeper disagreement. Namely, what *unites* the orthodox and the progressive *across* tradition and *divides* the orthodox and progressive *within* tradition are different formulations of moral authority. Whereas the orthodox side of the cultural divide is guided by conceptions of a transcendent source of moral authority, the progressive formulation grants that authority to what could be called, "self-grounded rational discourse." These opposing conceptions of moral authority are at the heart of most of the political and ideological disagreements in American public discourse—including the debates over abortion, legitimate sexuality, the nature of the family, the moral content of education, Church/State law, the meaning of First Amendment free speech liberties, and on and on.

We are dealing with more than "religion," strictly defined. The politically consequential divisions in American culture are no longer ecclesiastical, as they once were; they are "cosmological." They no longer revolve around specific doctrinal issues or styles of religious practice and organization; they revolve around fundamental assumptions about value, purpose, truth, freedom, and collective identity. This realignment in American "religion" and the conflicts that are born from it, then, are neither narrow nor trivial, but are central to the restructuring of America itself.

Appendix to Chapter Fifteen

The survey part of the Religion and Power Project, funded by the Lilly Endowment, was conducted under the direction of the author by the Opinion Research Corporation of Princeton, New Jersey. A sample of roughly 1,300 religious leaders was drawn from the 1985 edition of *Who's Who in Religion*. After deaths and nonforwarded mail were discounted, a total of 791 individuals responded, representing a 61 percent response rate. Protestantism, Catholicism, and Judaism were dichotomized into *theologically* liberal and conservative camps, in line with the present argument. The divisions took the following form: conservative Protestants were operationalized as those who identified themselves as either an Evangelical or a Fundamentalist; liberal Protestants comprised the remainder. Conservative Catholics were defined as those who identified their theological inclinations on the conservative side (values 4, 5, 6, and 7) of a 7-point liberal/conservative, continuum, while liberal Catholics identified their theology on the liberal side of the continuum (values 1, 2, and 3). The Orthodox Jews identified themselves as such in the survey just as Conservative and Reform Jews identified themselves this way.

The results of this survey with respect to the issues discussed in this chapter are as follows:

Sexual Morality

The orthodox wings of Protestantism, Catholicism, and Judaism were significantly more likely to condemn premarital sexual relations and premarital cohabitation as "morally wrong" than each of their progressive counterparts. The question for this series of behaviors reads as follows: "Please indicate how you personally feel about each of the following. Do you believe each is morally wrong, morally acceptable, or not a moral issue." On premarital sexuality, the actual figures were as follows: Protestants—orthodox, 97 percent, and progressive, 59 percent; Catholics—orthodox, 97 percent, and progressive, 82 percent; Jews—orthodox, 72 percent, and progressive, 31 percent. Chi-square significant at the .000 level. On premarital cohabitation: Protestants—orthodox, 95 percent, and progressive, 58 percent; Catholics—orthodox, 93 percent, and progressive, 82 percent; Jews—orthodox, 74 percent, and progressive, 33 percent. Chi-square significant at the .000 level.

The orthodox were also between two and three times more likely than progressives to condemn the viewing of pornographic films as morally wrong. The pattern holds for Catholics, but not as dramatically as for Jews and Protestants. Catholics were a bit more uniform in their opinion here. The actual figures were as follows: Protestants—orthodox, 94 percent, and progressive, 47 percent; Catholics—orthodox, 87 percent, and progressive, 75 percent; Jews—orthodox, 64 percent, and progressive, 15 percent. Chi-square significant at the .000 level.

Family Life

When presented with the statement "It is much better for everyone involved if the man is the achiever outside the home and the woman takes care of the home and family," Evangelical Protestants were three times more likely to agree, conservative Catholics were twice as likely to agree, and orthodox Jews were nearly six times as likely to agree than their progressive counterparts. On this question the actual figures were as follows: Protestants—orthodox, 68 percent, and progressive, 23 percent; Catholics—orthodox, 57 percent, and progressive, 32 percent; Jews—orthodox, 45 percent, and progressive, 8 percent. Chi-square significant at the .000 level.

The pattern of response was similar when subjects were asked about authority in the home. The theologically orthodox of each faith were more apt to agree that "the husband should have the 'final say' in the family's decision making." The actual figures were as follows: Protestants—orthodox, 53 percent, and progressive, 10 percent; Catholics—orthodox, 27 percent, and progressive, 8 percent; Jews—orthodox, 13 percent, and progressive, 4 percent. Chi-square significant at the .000 level.

One of the more important tests of this authority concerns the decision to bear children: "Is it all right for a woman to refuse to have children, even against the desires of her husband to have children?" The majority of progressive leaders in Protestantism and Judaism agreed that it was all right, compared to minorities in the orthodox sides of these faiths. The figures for this item were as follows: Protestants—orthodox, 49 percent, and progressive, 70 percent; Catholics—orthodox, 27 percent, and progressive, 8 percent; Jews—orthodox, 23 percent, and progressive, 63 percent. Chi-square significant at the .000 level. Progressive Catholic leaders (18 percent) were more likely to agree than orthodox Catholic leaders (11 percent), and yet the majority of both camps disagreed with the statement.

Few in either the orthodox or progressive camps in Protestantism, Catholicism, and Judaism maintained an unqualified traditionalism in family affairs. For example, only a very small number held that a married woman should not work if she has a husband who can support her, and just as few in either camp would allow that "women should take care of running their home and leave the running of the country up to men." (The statement read "It is all right for a married woman to earn money in business or industry, even if she has a husband capable of supporting her." Among all groups the number disagreeing with this statement was under 5 percent. The same is true with the second statement, with the exception of conservative Protestant leaders, 18 percent of whom agreed that women should take care of running their home and leave the running of the country up to men.) Yet they disagreed sharply when responding to the question of priorities. More than eight out of ten of the orthodox leaders in these faiths agreed that "a woman should put her husband and children ahead of her career," compared to only four out of ten of the progressive Protestant and Jewish leaders and six out of ten of the liberal Catholic leaders. (The actual figures were as follows: Protestants—orthodox, 86 percent, and progressive, 40 percent; Catholics–orthodox, 83 percent, and progressive, 63 percent; Jews—orthodox, 80 percent, and progressive, 46 percent. Chi-square significant at the .000 level.) This general disposition extended to attitudes about the mother's relations with her children. Leaders on the progressive side of the theological continuum in all faiths were more inclined than their theologically conservative counterparts to agree that "a working mother can establish just as warm and secure a relationship with her children as a mother who does not work." Accordingly, they were disproportionately more likely (twice as likely if they were Protestants) to disagree that "a preschool child is likely to suffer if his or her mother works." (For the first question about mother-child relationships, the figures were: Protestants—orthodox, 57 percent, and progressive, 81 percent; Catholics— orthodox, 65 percent, and progressive, 77 percent; Jews—orthodox, 56 percent, and progressive, 82 percent. Chi-square significant at the .000 level. For the second question, the figures [disagreeing] were: Protestants—orthodox, 32 percent, and progressive, 65 percent; Catholics— orthodox, 41 percent, and progressive, 48 percent; Jews—orthodox, 46 percent, and progressive, 76 percent. Chi-square significant at the .000 level.)

Family Policy

Not surprisingly, this pattern was generally reflected in the opinion of these leaders when asked about three divisive public policy issues: support for the Equal Rights Amendment, the morality of abortion, and the morality of homosexuality. Roughly eight out of ten of the progressives in Protestantism (80 percent), Catholicism (78 percent), and Judaism (88 percent) favored the passage of the ERA compared to much smaller numbers on the orthodox side (Protestant, 31 percent: Catholic, 42 percent; Jewish, 54 percent). On abortion, progressives of all three faiths were significantly less likely to condemn abortion as morally wrong, particularly within Protestantism and Judaism. (The actual figures were as follows: Protestants—orthodox, 93 percent, and progressive, 41 percent; Catholics—orthodox, 100 percent, and progressive, 93 percent; Jews—orthodox, 40 percent, and progressive, 8 percent. Chi-square significant at the .000 level.) So, too, the orthodox and progressive wings of these faiths were deeply split over the issue of homosexuality and lesbianism; the former were between two and three times more likely to denounce the practice of homosexuality and lesbianism as morally wrong than the latter. Nine of ten Evangelicals, and eight of every ten Catholic and Jewish leaders condemned homosexuality as morally wrong, compared to fewer than five of every ten mainline Protestant and liberal Catholic leaders, and fewer than three of every ten of the liberal Jewish leaders. The actual figures on the question on homosexuality read as follows: Protestants—orthodox, 96 percent, and progressive, 45 percent; Catholics—orthodox, 81 percent, and progressive, 49 percent; Jews—orthodox, 80 percent, and progressive, 25 percent. Chi-square significant at the .000 level. The responses to the question on lesbianism were, within a percentage point, identical.

Political Party Preference

Once again, for reasons relating to the political and ethnic history of the Jewish community in America (for example, their longstanding political liberalism), the pattern is generally less distinct among Jewish elites than among Protestant or Catholic elites, but the divisions there are still quite remarkable. For example, the survey showed that by a margin of about 2 to 1 in the Protestant and Catholic leadership and 1.5 to 1 in the Jewish leadership, progressives identified themselves as Democrats. (On political party preference, the percentage of those who identified themselves as Democrats were: Protestants—orthodox, 25 percent, and progressive, 53 percent; Catholics—orthodox, 46 percent, and progressive, 77 percent; Jews—orthodox, 38 percent, and progressive, 57 percent. Chi-square significant at the .000 level.)

Ideology

Progressives in Protestantism were six times as likely, in Catholicism were seven and a half times as likely, and in Judaism were nearly twice as likely as their more orthodox counterparts to describe their political ideology as liberal or left-wing. (Those describing themselves as somewhat liberal, very liberal, or far left were as follows: Protestants—orthodox, 11 percent, and progressive, 60 percent; Catholics—orthodox, 12 percent, and progressive, 77 percent; Jews—orthodox, 36 percent, and progressive, 67 percent. Chi-square significant at the .000 level.)

Political Economy

There was basic agreement among all parties on the basic functions of the welfare state: that "the government has the responsibility to meet the basic needs of its citizens, even in the case of sickness, poverty, unemployment, and old age," and that "the government should have a high commitment to curbing the economic and environmental abuses of Big Business." At least eight out of ten of all religious leaders, regardless of theological orientation, agreed with these statements. (The only exception was the opinion of Evangelical leaders on the issue of governmental responsibility; 54 percent agreed.) While there is basic agreement all the way around, there still are differences in the intensity with which the various factions agree. Catholic and Protestant leaders on the progressive side were significantly more likely to "strongly agree" with these statements.

There was also a certain agreement that "the government should work to substantially reduce the income gap between the rich and the poor." The difference between liberal (76 percent) and conservative (43 percent) Protestants is 33 percentage points, and between liberal (78 percent) and conservative (59 percent) Jews, it is 19 percentage points. Among Catholics, however, there is only a 2 percentage point difference (92 percent to 90 percent).

Beyond this, however, the agreement came to an end. As one might predict, the more progressively oriented leaders in Catholicism and Protestantism were up to twice as likely as the orthodox to agree that "big business in America is generally unfair to working people." Though not as striking, the same general pattern held for Jews as well. (The actual figures were as follows: Protestants—orthodox, 27 percent, and progressive, 48 percent; Catholics—orthodox, 39 percent, and progressive, 69 percent; Jews—orthodox, 36 percent, and progressive, 42 percent. Chi-square significant at the .000 level.)

Similarly, progressives in each tradition were up to twice as inclined as their theologically orthodox counterparts to disagree with the statement "economic growth is a better way to improve the lot of the poor than the redistribution of existing wealth." (The actual figures of those disagree-ing with that statement were: Protestants—orthodox, 14 percent, and progressive, 44 percent; Catholics—orthodox, 23 percent, and progres-sive, 50 percent; Jews—orthodox, 24 percent, and progressive, 33 per-cent. Chi-square significant at the .000 level.) A similar statement was made about the application of this principle to the Third World: "Capi-talist development is more likely than socialist development to improve the material standard of living of people in the contemporary Third World." The ideological gap between the orthodox and progressive ranged between 24 percentage points (Catholic) and 34 percentage points (Protestant), with Jews in between, at 28 percentage points of difference.

When presented with the statement "The United States would be better off if it moved toward socialism," less than half of all the religio-cultural factions agreed, yet the pattern once again held true to form: progressives of all traditions were three or four times more likely to agree than their orthodox rivals. (The figures of those agreeing with that statement about socialism were: Protestants—orthodox, 7 percent, and progressive, 33 percent; Catholics—orthodox, 13 percent, and progres-sive, 46 percent; Jews—orthodox, 8 percent, and progressive, 25 per-cent. Chi-square significant at the .000 level.)

International Affairs

When asked whether they thought "U.S.-based multinational corpora-tions help or hurt poor countries in the Third World," the orthodox were substantially more prone to believe that they helped—at a ratio of 2 to 1 in Protestantism and 3 to 1 in Catholicism. (The percentages of those responding "helped" were: Protestants—orthodox, 76 percent, and progressive, 38 percent; Catholics—orthodox, 53 percent, and pro-gressive, 16 percent; Jews—orthodox, 76 percent, and progressive, 53 percent. Chi-square significant at the .000 level.)

On the political rather than economic side of this concern, the pattern again holds true. When asked whether they favored or opposed the U.S. policy of "selling arms and giving military aid to countries that are against the Soviet Union," the orthodox of these three faiths were more inclined to favor this action by dramatic margins. The differences between the orthodox and progressive in Protestantism were, respectively, 73 per-cent and 35 percent; within Catholicism, 52 percent and 22 percent; and within Judaism, 92 percent and 61 percent. Chi-square significant at the .000 level.

This was also the case when these leaders were pushed further on this issue, with the special case of the anti-Sandinista Contras of Nicaragua. Only in the case of Evangelicals did a decisive majority actually favor the policy, yet the ratio of those favoring to opposing the policy (according to theological disposition) within the other traditions was equally strong. (Those favoring the policy were as follows: Protestants—orthodox, 62 percent, and progressive, 14 percent; Catholics—orthodox, 39 percent, and progressive, 5 percent; Jews—orthodox, 45 percent, and progressive, 18 percent. Chi-square significant at the .000 level.) So, too, when asked about the relative "importance of Central American countries (like El Salvador and Nicaragua) to the defense interests of the United States," the orthodox were at a margin of nearly 2 to 1 in all traditions more likely to respond with "very or fairly important."

The now predictable configurations were generally borne out on numerous other issues:

a. Economic sanctions against South Africa for its policies of apartheid: The favorable responses were as follows: Protestants—orthodox, 52 percent, and progressive, 87 percent; Catholics—orthodox, 83 percent, and progressive, 90 percent; Jews—orthodox, 47 percent, and progressive, 78 percent. Chi-square significant at the .000 level.

b. The creation of a Palestinian homeland in Israel (even among Jews): The favorable responses were as follows: Protestants—orthodox, 42 percent, and progressive, 82 percent; Catholics—orthodox, 87 percent, and progressive, 85 percent; Jews—orthodox, 3 percent, and progressive, 20 percent. Chi-square significant at the .000 level.

c. Europe's neutrality in the East-West conflict: The favorable responses were: Protestants—orthodox, 26 percent, and progressive, 47 percent; Catholics—orthodox, 20 percent, and progressive, 46 percent; Jews—orthodox, 18 percent, and progressive, 27 percent. Religious leaders were also asked, as a corollary to this, whether they favored or opposed keeping American troops in Europe as part of the North Atlantic Treaty Organization (NATO) commitment. The differences were not so dramatic, but they were in line with predictions: Protestants—orthodox, 95 percent, and progressive, 80 percent; Catholics—orthodox, 84 percent, and progressive, 70 percent; Jews—orthodox, 95 percent, and progressive, 88 percent. Chi-square for both of these was significant at the .000 level.

d. The policy of a "freeze" in the construction and deployment of nuclear weapons: When asked about a nuclear freeze for both the United States and the Soviet Union, the differences flattened out considerably. When asked whether they favored the implementation of the policy by the United States even if the Soviet Union did not pursue it, striking divisions between the orthodox and progressive camps re-emerged. The actual figures of those favoring a freeze for both superpowers were: Protestants—orthodox, 78 percent, and progressive, 95 percent; Catholics—orthodox, 95 percent, and progressive, 98 percent; Jews—orthodox, 92 percent, and progressive, 90 percent. Favoring the policy for the United States alone (regardless of what the Soviet Union does), the split resurfaced. Those favoring: Protestants—orthodox, 16 percent, and progressive, 52 percent; Catholics—orthodox, 35 percent, and progressive, 70 percent; Jews—orthodox, 10 percent, and progressive, 29 percent. Chi-squares were all significant at the .000 level.

The question for this and other issues reviewed in this section of the appendix asked if the respondent favored or opposed the policy.

SIXTEEN

Pluralism and Disdain
American Culture Today

Gaye Tuchman

THE SHIFTING DEBATE OVER CULTURE

According to the critics of the 1950s, the stratification of American culture was relatively simple. The critics respected "high culture"—arts deemed to be of such lasting value that they supposedly spoke to people across the ages. They thought popular culture was ephemeral, sometimes dismissing it as "mass culture" or, even worse, as "kitsch." The choice of term to characterize popular culture revealed political attitudes. Critics who spoke of mass culture debated visions of an emergent mass society. According to some, each individual was an atom in a formless aggregate and so was potentially susceptible to recruitment by totalitarianism—either the fascism defeated in World War II or what was then seen as the threatening totalitarianism of the communist world. Others praised democratic institutions, especially American voluntary associations, which supposedly protected social and political stability. Yet another group decried kitsch to establish the "aristocracy of taste"—the superiority of their taste to that of other social groups. Those who defended the fare of popular culture were an embattled minority.

Since the 1950s, the nature of the debate about American culture has shifted. Now relativism reigns. Some critics doubt the validity of any criteria for assessing the worth of any cultural phenomenon. Others seek to demonstrate the innate connections between cultural phenomena and the material conditions of those who appreciate them. In both cases, though, critics fear that American culture has become hegemonic, an ideology of individualistic values imposed on consumers who unknowingly imbibe the basic notions of corporate capitalism with every viewing of "The Bill Cosby Show" or every rerun of "Family Ties."[1]

The views from the 1950s were simplistic; so are the views many propound today. American culture of the 1950s was not all "I Love Lucy," Bob Hope and Bing Crosby on the road, or souvenir salt shakers shaped like Florida flamingos. Nor was it simply abstract expressionism or seats at the symphony. Today some Americans continue to buy flamingo salt shakers or small silver-plated spoons emblazoned with the shield of Niagara Falls, some collect the 1950s salt shakers as now valuable artifacts of days gone by, while still others form reading groups—not to imbibe the Great Books program issued in the 1950s by the University of Chicago, but rather to ensure that they make time to read and so maintain their notion of themselves as readers.[2]

Recognizing the diversity found in the cultures of both the 1950s and the late 1980s raises important sociological issues. Is contemporary culture as diverse as the culture of the 1950s had been? If, as many claim, the commodification of culture has decreased diversity, how are we to understand such uniformity as exists. How does our society understand cultural pluralism and cultural divergence? Do we celebrate it? Or, as I will argue, does an embattled elite seek to reassert its distinction—even though that elite has lost much of its historic ability to define what constitutes high culture? For most Americans join Sesame Street's Cookie Monster as he explained his artistic taste in the Sesame Street special "Don't Eat the Pictures." Cookie Monster confronted a still life of a ham. Wanting to devour it, he exclaimed, "Me know what me like!" Secure in our knowledge that "we know what we like," many Americans feel disdain for others' preferences.[3]

Such issues as pluralism, disdain, and commodification matter. Historically, the structure of art worlds and art itself have been shaped by social structure. For instance, the rise of impressionism, including the size of most impressionist paintings, resulted from both the demise of the system of art academies serving aristocratic patrons with large-walled palaces and the advent of the gallery system, which specialized in paintings for the walls of the homes of the French bourgeoisie and haute bourgeoisie.[4] Conversely, one may infer characteristics of a society from its culture.[5] Huge tapestries, one might say, bespeak badly heated, gusty, stone-walled castles. The current state of American culture suggests the importance of corporate control to our society, a homogenization of values and increased uniformity—even though we know that the American class structure is essentially the same as it was at the turn of this century.[6]

American culture also affects the American economy. At least since World War II, American popular culture has had great power internationally. In recent years, the movie and television industries have been among the few American businesses to show a profit internationally; they have also exported our values around the world. Furthermore, since World War II, but less so in recent years, New York City has been the international center of the art world. The once-central international stature of abstract expressionism enabled elite Americans to see themselves as the culmination of the Western heritage, the heirs to the past and so the embodiment of the future. The American elite can no longer justify such a claim.

AMERICAN CULTURE IN THE FIFTIES

Demographically, the 1950s were an aberrant period in American history. In defense of the returning veterans who reclaimed many of the jobs held by women during the war, the middle classes espoused a fierce belief in familism, insisting that women belonged at home. For both women and men, the median age at marriage fell, only to begin a slow climb in the 1960s. The birthrate rose, producing that now middle-aged demographic blip still known as the postwar baby-boomers. Immediately after the war and for the first time since the 1890s, women's participation in the labor force decreased. In 1950, women's labor-force participation once again reached its 1940 peak, but its rate of growth slowed and did not return to pre–World War II levels until the 1960s. Canny members of the housing industry created suburbs where there had been still-fertile farms. Some of those homes were in tract developments. Sometimes, as was the case of the Levittowns, sarcastically mocked in *New Yorker* cartoons, whole suburbs seemed to pop up at once. For many of the people who moved into them, these ranch and neocolonial tracts represented the fulfillment of the American Dream: a house to own, a street for children to play on, a home for a wife to fashion as her husband took pride in what his labor had purchased for his family.[7]

George Gerbner once said that the family-centered suburban existence of some members of the middle class would not have been possible without technological change.[8] The state's failure to provide decent public transportation, the growth of highways, and the more widespread use of cars enabled men to commute to work and middle-class women to become their children's chauffeurs. Television gave families something to do in homes geographically removed from the city. Air-conditioning enabled them to stay inside even in summer, and so to eschew the on-going interactions that still characterize the rich street life of many ethnic neighborhoods in Manhattan. The isolation of some suburbs was so profound that in many northern New Jersey communities, such as the one in which I was reared, most high school students first traveled the scant fifteen miles to New York on a rented bus after their senior prom.

While the new suburbanites treasured their consumer goods, the sophisticated *New Yorker* cartoonists and writers were not the only ones to mock what, a decade later, Malvina Reynolds was to sing of as "little ticky-tacky boxes." Cosmopolitan cultural critics condemned suburbanites' cultural preferences as "ticky-tacky" too—tasteless kitsch, a degradation of Western culture. Lucille Ball, Sid Caesar, and Jerry Lewis were funny, but bereft of political significance, pale imitations of the slapstick of Charlie Chaplin whose *Modern Times* still provides a brilliant cinematic exposition of the ideas of Karl Marx. Seen as social commentary, as Chaplin must be viewed, these television shows seemed an affirmation of middle-class mores, whose propriety they supported by demonstrating the ludicrous results of challenging conventional norms. Bob Hope and *Time* and *Life* magazines all espoused blind patriotism. Norman Rockwell's covers for the *Saturday Evening Post* offended more than Hallmark cards' saccharine sentimentalism. In their freckle-faced realism and celebration of small-town life, they were also artistically anachronistic.[9] They were viewed as little more than outmoded genre paintings in an era when such soon-to-be-mainstream art critics as Clement Greenberg and Harold Rosenberg celebrated the exploration of the two-dimensional canvas, the painterly application of color, form, and line, and the perpetual invention of the tradition of the new.[10] Even worse, these working- and middle-class suburbanites refused to be guided by the cultural critics who could improve their taste. They refused to enjoy what these once politically left self-appointed guardians of Western culture deemed valuable, and so represented what the conservative Ortega y Gasset had viewed as the tyranny of the masses.

For many 1950s critics, including sociologists, that tyranny of bad taste had a political dimension. It transcended the notion of politics inherent in the public school system's celebration of the two-party system, Bob Hope's July 4th show for the troops in Korea, the cold warriors' detestation of both communism and fascism, and even Hollywood's imposition of blacklisting—a topic many once politically left critics did not want to discuss.[11] Rather, they debated the fundamental meanings implicit in the structure of American society. Most simply, they asked whether totalitarianism of the right or of the left could happen here. This question seemed particularly compelling because of the power attributed to the ever more popular electronic media, especially television. Increasingly omnipresent, television might sever the complex personal networks expressed through voluntary associations. In the early nineteenth century, in his classic *Democracy in America,* Alexis de Tocqueville had identified voluntary associations not only as characteristic of American life but as the backbone of American democracy. If television destroyed that backbone, if the media were to dominate political debate, would Americans become susceptible to the appeals of totalitarism?

In the 1950s, two classic sociological monographs provided reassurance that American political life would survive the allure of electronic popular culture. One was William Kornhauser's *The Politics of Mass Society;* the other, Elihu Katz and Paul Lazarsfeld's *Personal Influence.*[12] Both affirmed that although mass culture was indeed popular, the United States was not a mass society. As befitting the emergent respect for science of both American sociology and American society, both books argued from survey data analyzed with the most advanced statistical techniques of their day. But each book took a different tack.

Following Tocqueville, Kornhauser argued that voluntary associations serve two functions.[13] First, they buttress citizens from authoritarianism imposed by the government (as then the case of the Soviet Union). For, he claimed, through voluntary associations an active populace can exert pressure on government and make it serve their needs. Second, he explained, active voluntary associations protect government from totalitarian mass movements, such as Nazism. When they are able to express themselves through an intricate web of associational networks, citizens do not need to join mass movements to express their political desires. Thus, so long as government is responsive to the activity and lobbying of voluntary associations, it is protected from charismatic revolutionaries.

To prove that America was not (yet) a mass society, William Kornhauser asked how many Americans were involved in what sorts of voluntary associations and whether, compared to the recent past, participation rates were constant when one took social class into account. Social class matters because members of the middle class are more likely to vote and to be "joiners" than either the poor or members of the working class. Most simply, Kornhauser found that Americans belonged to churches, unions, political clubs, parent-teacher associations—the full spectrum of groups that together comprise civic associations. Middle-class people were indeed more likely to join groups and to volunteer their time than were working-class people, but then such had always been the case. For Kornhauser, then, the continuing American proclivity to join voluntary associations meant that democracy was alive and well in the United States. We were not a mass society.

The social movements of the 1960s undermined one of Kornhauser's primary assumptions—that public officials and administrators are responsive to relevant voluntary associations, including those most likely to join social movements. Sometimes the interests of voluntary associations conflict. Although officials in the South were responsive to White Citizens' Councils and perhaps even the average *white* voter, these officials failed to listen to dissent from voluntary associations *outside the mainstream* of American political life, such as the Southern Christian Leadership Conference. They responded violently to the challenge of the Civil Rights Movement. Although the chancellor of Kornhauser's own campus, the University of California at Berkeley, was probably being receptive to officials and trustees when he called in police to quell the student dissent that crystallized around the Free Speech Movement, he was not accurately gauging the views of the students and many of the faculty. But in the fifties, at least, Kornhauser's work provided reassurance about the stability of both the American political structure and middle-class culture.

So, too, Katz and Lazarsfeld's *Personal Influence* provided comfort: the American public was not to be swayed by its media.[14] In some ways, to write about *Personal Influence* as a book of the 1950s is to characterize the work inaccurately. Funded by Macfadden publications, Lazarsfeld and C. Wright Mills collected the data for the study in the early 1940s to expand an analysis of a key point in Lazarsfeld's earlier book with Bernard Berelson and Hazel Gaudet, *The People's Choice: How the Voter Makes Up His Mind in a Presidential Election.*[15] In *The People's Choice*, the authors discovered that voters paid more attention to the political views of members of their pertinent reference groups than to newspaper reports and editorials. I assume that Macfadden was interested in this finding because it might mean that advertising had a larger impact than was suggested by merely counting the number of people who had paid attention to a magazine advertisement. That possibility might enhance advertising revenue. And although *Personal Influence* is not crudely concerned with ads, Katz and Lazarsfeld do make that point.

Personal Influence is an analysis of the early 1940s snowball sample of women in Decatur, Illinois, who had been asked what or who had most recently influenced a decision to initiate a change in one of four areas. These were fashion (such as changing lipstick color), buying essential household items (such as changing brands of toothpaste or laundry detergent), selecting a movie to see, or voting. When a woman, say Mary Smith, indicated that her friend Ann Jones had recommended she change her lipstick color (a fashion decision), the interviewers checked whether Ann Jones recalled making that suggestion. If she did, Mary Smith's purchase was counted as an example of "personal influence."

Using these data, Katz and Lazarsfeld formulated a basic theorem known as the two-step flow of communication. It suggests that when an individual is interested in a topic, such as fashion, she will pay attention to ads and other sorts of information pertinent to that interest. Knowing of her interest and potential expertise, her friends will consult her or pay attention to her opinion when she offers it. Thus, the first step in the flow of communication goes from the media to an interested individual. The second step flows from that interested individual or opinion leader to the family members, friends, and colleagues who are *personally influenced* by their knowledge of her interests and expertise. Personal influence, Katz and Lazarsfeld conclude, has more impact on people's decisions than the direct message of the media; people are more likely to take recommendations of members of their reference groups than merely to concur with media messages.

Katz and Lazarsfeld were so wedded to their interpretation of their data that they overlooked changes introduced by television and even some alternative explanations. The data analyzed in *Personal Influence* are pre-television and so predate viewers' "para-social interaction" with television—the tendency of some viewers to talk back to their television sets and of other viewers to respond to television characters as though they were personally acquainted.[16] More important, Katz and Lazarsfeld never really come to grips with some of their findings. Some people do attend to ads. Their views about what is fashionable come from the media, and so the information they pass on through personal influence has itself been generated by the media. Indeed, many of my undergraduate students are happy to explain that they use "meta-media" (media about media), such as television ads for movies and television critics' reviews of movies, to decide what shows they will see. Similarly, others use newspapers, television, and magazines to choose other cultural fare—what play they will see, what books they will read, what video tapes they will rent, which computer program is most versatile.[17] The media may foster fads and fashions, including consumption of cultural fare and political attitudes.[18]

Analyses by then-left-wing prophets of doom have stood up better. Leo Lowenthal's 1944 essay "Biographies in Popular Magazines" is an apt example.[19] Written soon after Lowenthal immigrated to the United States, the study is a content analysis of biographies printed from 1901 through 1941 in *Collier's* and *The Saturday Evening Post*, two magazines aimed at the middle class. Lowenthal suggests that just as the American economy had shifted from the sphere of production to the sphere of consumption, so too, American heroes had shifted from heroes of production, such as banker J. P. Morgan, to heroes of consumption, such as Clark Gable. In the arts, according to Lowenthal's analysis, American heroes shifted from classical musicians to Hollywood stars. According to Lowenthal, the magazines presented figures from the world of leisure as "souls without history," individuals without individuality, "grotesques." Their biographies were "written—at least ideologically—for someone who the next day may try to emulate the man whom he has just envied." Emphasizing the consumer goods used by these "idols of the masses," these stories supposedly encouraged "the little man who has become expelled from the Horatio Alger dream, who despairs of penetrating the thicket of grand strategy in politics and business, to see his heroes as a lot of guys who like or dislike highballs, cigarettes, tomato juice, golf and social gatherings—just like himself. . . .

[The reader] knows how to converse in the sphere of consumption and here he can make no mistakes." [20]

Lowenthal patronized that "little man" and did not even speak of the "little woman." His tone captured many intellectuals' disdain for popular culture. But his study also captured a truth. American culture has changed as the American economy has been transformed. Since 1941, there has been a steady expansion of voyeurism about heroes of consumption, personified in such publications as *People,* such television staples as the "Johnny Carson Show," or such supposed innovations as the 1989–90 "Arsenio Hall Show," intended to appeal to the children of those watching Johnny Carson. Television "eats up" the lives of celebrities who, as Daniel Boorstin wrote, are known "for being celebrated." [21] Indeed today some popular-culture figures, such as Madonna, may try to make a "comeback" after being out of the public eye for a year or two. In the past, a year of two may not even have been enough time to disappear.

The apotheosis of this expansion of the consumption of others' lives occurred in the late 1960s during CBS's live coverage of the funeral of Robert F. Kennedy. Walter Cronkite commented from the studio; Daniel Schorr was stationed in front of New York's Saint Patrick's Cathedral to interview celebrities as they approached the church steps. The technology of live coverage was more primitive then than now. If Cronkite wanted to get Schorr's attention, he had to say so on the air; through his earphone, Schorr could hear Cronkite's words. At one point Cronkite informed Schorr that Coretta King's limousine was approaching and asked whether Schorr could get near enough to ask Mrs. King whether she had heard about the arrest a few hours earlier of James Earle Ray, the alleged assassin of her husband, Martin Luther King, Jr. Schorr did not interview Mrs. King. On the air, Cronkite hypothesized that there had been a break in communications between the studio and the Fifth Avenue spot where Schorr stood. I have no idea why Schorr did not ask Cronkite's question. But Cronkite's question was as tacky as the "ticky-tacky boxes" about which Malvina Reynolds sang, an escalation of the consumption of others' lives. Mrs. King's feelings about her husband's death as she went to yet another funeral were rightfully her own.

However, merely characterizing institutionalized prurience as tackiness begs the sociological issue. For Lowenthal's analysis neglected one aspect of the magazine biographies about the "idols of the masses." They were published for profit. The editors of the magazines Lowenthal studied either hoped to build a readership interested in the lives of others or to cultivate such readership as already existed. Sold as part of the magazines, these biographies were commodities. *People* magazine is a commodity. Similarly, when celebrities discuss aspects of their lives on the "Johnny Carson Show," they are transforming themselves into commodities. So, too, Cronkite's inquiry about Mrs. King's reaction to the arrest of James Earle Ray represents the commodification of her personal life. A network news special, especially "live coverage," may not make a profit. But news specials and respected news announcers build audiences faithful to a particular network. Asking a question to which viewers might have wanted an answer, Cronkite was potentially building "his" audience and so enhancing the economic viability of the "CBS Evening News." (My students assure me that had they been watching, they would have liked to have known what Mrs. King felt.) We are dealing with an escalation of commodification.

Although Lowenthal's analysis of American heroes still rings true, there is another truth as well. In the 1950s, even in the nation's largest cities, American culture was not uniform. The cultural fare favored in Manhattan, supposedly the seat of American high culture, provides an apt example. By and large, wealthier New Yorkers and suburbanites favored high culture, but their "tastes" were not identical. As Gans was to argue in an article anticipating both his own *Popular Culture and High Culture* and Bourdieu's *Distinction,* groups with different levels of education and income have different "taste."[22] A corporate lawyer might adorn the walls of "his" home with oil paintings; a college professor, with primitive artifacts.

Simply consider the plethora of art styles available in the 1950s. New York critics celebrated abstract expressionists; the Guggenheim Museum opened in a building whose architect, Frank Lloyd Wright, had found his style decades earlier and featured a permanent collection of pre–abstract expressionists. Impressionism flourished at the Museum of Modern Art and on the auction block, while Andrew Wyeth's realistic paintings began to command high prices. Despite the variety of art styles available, abstract expressionism held sway. When a New York museum bought a painting by a living artist, it was most likely to purchase the work of an abstract expressionist.

Broadway theater was more diversified. That prototypical American genre—musical comedy—flourished. To some, the names of Rodgers and Hammerstein were synonymous with a long run, to others, with sugary optimism. On Broadway, in the same decade, Arthur Miller challenged the Cold War with his acclaimed four-act play *The Crucible,* and Dore Schary celebrated Franklin Delano Roosevelt's courage in *Sunrise at Campobello.* Off-Broadway theaters thrived, too. Sometimes comedic, sometimes grim, off-Broadway plays received reviews in New York's major newspapers. Unaware of all this theatrical activity, many middle-income New Yorkers celebrated the Brooklyn Dodgers and enjoyed a "subway world series" before easy airplane travel enabled East Coast teams to head for the midwestern and western states. But some who used high culture, especially men, were also fans of local teams. Wall Street law firms bought box tickets to games to woo graduating lawyers to their organizations.

Outside of New York, people's cultural allegiances also varied. Although most of the high school students in New Jersey's industrial cities had never gone to New York, others traveled fifteen or more miles to visit museums, go to concerts, and attend Broadway, and even off-Broadway, plays. For a few, week-end visits to Greenwich Village were de rigeur. Their trips to the Village and thonged peasant sandals laced mid-calf enabled them to claim membership in a cultural elite. In a small town outside of Seattle, the high school friends of a colleague found yet another way to claim cultural superiority—to distinguish themselves from the other high school students who would attend local colleges, if they were to attend college at all. These teenagers, bound for such out-of-state private universities as Stanford, showed their sophistication by driving to Seattle to eat at a Chinese restaurant and take in a foreign movie with subtitles. In Iowa, particularly in the Mennonite country relatively near the urbane university in Iowa City, there were other high school students who did not know about the existence of subtitled movies, the Beatles, or even Elvis Presley, though some of the boys may have played fiddle in a local bluegrass band. (The girls may have been learning to quilt.)

Although the media may have promulgated a seemingly hegemonic message—buy, consume, fun in leisure hours compensates for alienated labor, ours is the best of all possible worlds—some people did not receive that message and others did not heed it. The dissent of the sixties did, after all, arise after television had firmly established its presence in American homes. By 1964, 93 percent of all American households had television sets. The furniture in most living rooms or family rooms was oriented toward the ubiquitous television, not the outmoded hearth. Even in the late eighties, when asked whom they most admired, a few Queens College students did not mention rock stars, movie stars, television stars, sports stars, high-living Donald Trump, or even the sainted Mother Teresa. They nominated their parents.

How, then, are we to understand American culture today? We must recognize the hegemonic power of the electronic media, the power of mass distributors and chain bookstores to make some books potential best-sellers and other books just so much waste paper,[23] the canny business acumen that turned an everyday item—blue jeans—into a fancy-pocketed status symbol.[24] But we must also come to terms with changes in the definition of high art, the declining popularity of network television, the plethora of musical styles that vie to be identified as popular, and the abundant messages about ourselves that we choose to construct as we select clothing in what sometimes seems the seamless web of similar stores in the similar shopping malls along the highways of the nation.

AMERICAN CULTURE TODAY

Pehaps the best way to start is to understand that there are many American cultures. To those viewing us from outside, we may seem one people with one culture. To those who travel across our country, we seem diverse indeed. To be sure, almost all Americans can identify Johnny Carson, though they are less likely to know the names of the anchormen on the network evening news. Yet, despite the best efforts of the clothing industry and the advertising industry, we dress in assorted ways. As Goffman explained so well, we understand the unspoken messages about self and society expressed in those variations. We also know how to read the variations in self-presentation offered by the celebrities who sell themselves as commodities.

The blatant commodification of all aspects of culture has robbed the traditional cultural elite of its ability to maintain hegemony. To be sure, cultural variations still exist; they vary by region, social class, race, ethnicity, gender, and training in the arts. But they have diminished in part because of the marketing techniques of the culture industry. From aesthetic preferences in art to dietary habits and preferences in home furnishing, cultural taste corresponds to the stratification of the culture industry. That is, the various business sectors selling culture attempt to define their market and then to reach it. Doing so, they express their own notions of the American stratification system. But some American industries are blurring class distinctions through their marketing techniques.

Consider the term *designer*. It connotes a specially fashioned elite item, perhaps a dress fashioned by a Parisian couturier. Applied to such everyday items as jeans, towels, sheets, and pots, the term transforms these mundane artifacts into status symbols that most Americans can afford. They make "downscale" items seem "upscale." Destroying the dichotomy "downscale/upscale," those who market "designer products" help Americans to believe that social distinctions have been obliterated in our society.

Social distinctions remain. In the 1960s, Bourdieu explained how the aesthetic tastes of French audiences correspond to their economic and cultural capital, including their jobs.[25] Many of Bourdieu's comments apply to American culture as well. Here, as in France, the more affluent and more educated are more likely to use "high culture." Consider some of the findings of a survey commissioned by the Ford Foundation in the early 1970s.[26] (It is important because it anticipated more recent sociological studies of cultural consumption that confirm and amplify its findings.) The 1970s study found that "the percentage of upper-income people . . . who attended a performance of a symphony last year was seven times as large as the percentage of low-income people who attended. . . . Comparable upper- to lower-income ratios [were] roughly 6 : 1 for opera, 5 : 1 for theater, 5 : 1 for musicals, and 4 : 1 for ballet. . . . A comparable relationship exist[ed] between attendance and education"— *although at any one performance, there may have been more lower- than higher-income people in the audience,* simply because there are more lower-income people.[27] To a lesser extent, the more affluent were also more likely to use the popular performing arts, namely jazz, rock, or folk music, and movies.

But even in the 1970s, there was not a unified cultural elite. The same people did not use the same performing arts. Of the 23 percent of informants in twelve cities who had been exposed to the theater, symphony, opera, or ballet in the previous year, most had gone to the theater. Only 1 percent of all informants had attended three out of the four sorts of performing arts about which they were queried.

This survey and later reports confirm that the audience for the arts is indeed stratified.[28] However, they also reveal, there is no *one* group that can be identified as *the* audience for high culture qua high culture. Furthermore, the studies affirm, the more affluent and more educated are not outside the mainstream of American cultural life. They use mass culture. As early as 1964, Wilensky found that the highly educated watched television shows supposedly designed for the lowest common denominator.[29]

Perhaps because *all* Americans have some exposure to the mass media, those who are also familiar with the fine arts and the literary canon use that familiarity as a badge of distinction. As DiMaggio put it, they use their knowledge as a commonly recognized "cultural currency."[30] "High culture tastes or 'cultural capital'," DiMaggio tells us, "assist in developing or reinforcing relations with high-status persons."[31] Most simply, the social elite uses its possession of cultural currency to recognize its own. Such symbols of group membership, DiMaggio adds, may be particularly important when the distinctions between sorts of culture—high culture versus popular culture versus folk culture—are eroding.

These distinctions are clearly eroding in many regions of the United States. In Mennonite Iowa, popular and folk culture now unhappily coexist. A county seat near Iowa City has two museums scarcely a hundred yards apart. One, a Mennonite museum, contains such items as family Bibles. The other, the county museum, includes in its displays a collection of such Americana as salt and pepper shakers. There was a county celebration the evening I saw these museums. Local residents performed musical selections on a flatbed truck for an audience of Mennonites in traditional garb and ex-Mennonites in contemporary dresses, slacks, and colorful knitted sweaters. All listened attentively to men, including boys in their late adolescence, play country music on their fiddles and guitars. But the more traditionally clad did not clap when the only females appeared: two young sisters, perhaps aged nine and twelve, dancing in leotards to amplified rock. (They were the daughters of the county doctor and so were exempt from local religious custom.) The Mennonites did not clap after the dancers had performed, but they did not leave during the performance. The music, like the museums and the audiences' clothing, were tautly juxtaposed.

Popular culture and high culture also tensely coexist among the social elite. They have done so at least since the baby-boomers were in high school. For instance, in the late 1950s and early 1960s even such liberal elite boarding schools as the coeducational Putney encouraged students to listen to classical music and forbade them to hear rock and roll. The rules were designed to ensure that these students would obtain a currency appropriate to their class—familiarity with high-culture music. Yet many Putney students went out of their way to listen to forbidden popular music. They wanted to participate in the musical life of "their" generation.[32]

And, in America, as in France, the most well educated probably have some of the same cultural proclivities as the less elite. In the 1960s, Bourdieu asked people with varying levels of education and class membership, what sort of picture a photographer would make of a variety of subjects, including a snake and a cabbage.[33] Bourdieu reported significant trends, as seen in table 16.1, collapsed from Bourdieu's more complex presentation. Those with the most educational capital were more likely than others to believe that almost any subject might make an interesting or beautiful photograph. But the differences within and between social classes and educational qualifications are not especially striking. Rather, the similarities are surprisingly strong given the fact that the 432 upper-class people with more education were significantly more likely to hold university degrees than the 335 middle-class people classified as having more education. In American terms, these populations were not distinct markets; one group did not express "upscale" tastes and the other "downscale" preferences.

No American sociologist has undertaken a detailed replication of Bourdieu's *Distinction*. But we do know that market segmentation seems to be decreasing. In music, as in bed linen, there is relatively little market segmentation. Although there are class and racial differences in musical taste, they are not sufficiently divergent to speak of segmentation of the

TABLE 16.1   Percentage of Respondents Reporting that a
Photograph of a Cabbage or Snake Might Be Either Interesting
or Beautiful, by Social Class and Educational Qualifications

	Cabbage	Snake	N
Lower Class:			
Little educational capital	13.5	48.0	143
More educational capital	22.0	50.0	18
Middle Class:			
Little educational capital	14.0	51.0	243
More educational capital	30.5	54.5	335
Upper Class:			
Little educational capital	16.0	50.0	25
More educational capital	34.5	66.0	432

SOURCE: Adapted from Pierre Bourdieu, *Distinction,* trans. Richard Nice (Cambridge: Harvard University Press, 1984), table 3, 37–38.

American music market.[34] So, too, there is less segmentation in the fine arts. We know that people of the upper-working, the upper-middle, and the lower-upper classes are all likely to hang a landscape in their living room—although the type of landscape they choose may vary considerably.[35] We know that in any one home, especially in wealthier homes, many sorts of culture coexist. In sum, we know that as all culture has become commodified, the boundaries between high culture and popular culture have eroded.

Because of cultural coexistence, today in the United States, cultural competence may require the ability to converse in the language of many cultures, as could the ex-Mennonites and Putney students. DiMaggio notes:

> Being a successful member of the middle class requires some mastery of prestigious status cultures; but is abetted by easy familiarity with cultures of occupation, of region, and of ethnicity as well . . . so middle-class adults learn how to "culture-switch" as they move from milieu to milieu. Such individuals command a variety of tastes . . . [and] deploy them selectively in different interactions and different contexts. (An upper-working-class father with a white-collar wife must know about sports and rock music at work, discuss politics and natural foods with his wife's friends, and instill an admiration of Brahms and Picasso in his daughter or son).[36]

Even such "professional readers" as professors of literature may "culture-switch." The book reviews many of these professors write for newspapers or middle-class magazines contain a different structure and frequently use a different mode of evaluation than their discussion of texts in professional publications.[37] In the former, they may summarize the plot and analyze the characters. In the latter, they eschew such mundane concerns, presuming instead that anyone who reads their criticism is necessarily familiar with the texts they discuss. In newspapers, they may seem sophisticated lay readers. In professional journals, they may "deconstruct." Other professional readers may pick apart their deconstructions according to the latest theoretical fad. Lay readers may also discard their newspaper reviews, placing a book in a context of meaning created out of their own experiences and personal concerns.[38]

Ultimately, culture-switching and cultural relativism challenge the authority some professional readers wish to maintain. In the nineteenth century, when literacy increased to the point that the ability to read books or even to write them was no longer a mark of distinction, the British cultural elite redefined the criteria for identifying a "good" novel. Those supposedly universal criteria helped elite men to praise the work of other men and to dismiss "women's novels."[39] In the 1980s, when roughly half the population being graduated from high school continued on to some sort of formal education, a self-appointed cultural elite identified either familiarity with the classical humanistic canon or the ability to speak in new theoretical tongues as marks of distinction. I read the seemingly deliberate obfuscation of literary deconstructionism as an affirmation of the cultural superiority of those familiar with the theory. Similarly, I read Allan Bloom's *Closing of the American Mind,* a defense of the value of a classic humanism, as a peroration against culture-switching and cultural relativism.[40] Some books are good; some are not. Supposedly the self-anointed cultural elite can tell the difference.

Although an elite claims distinction, it cannot halt the convergence of high culture and popular culture, for the state and other complex bureaucracies unwittingly encourage the commodification of high culture. At least, such appears to be the case with fine art.

Today art is defined as a commodity for investment, and the costs of mounting museum shows have escalated (as have costs in the performing arts). Because of escalating costs, corporations and government agencies are the most important groups maintaining art worlds.[41] Corporations invest in art that graces both lobby-galleries and the offices of the corporate elite. Corporations and government sponsor museum shows intended to "expose" as many people as possible to specific artists, styles, and even collectors. Supposedly, such exposure lifts the cultural horizons of those who view this art; it may make the fan of Keene's paintings of big-eyed children capable of appreciating more subtle art.

State and corporate funding of the arts has altered the definition of art. Even the wealthiest individuals are losing their historic ability to define genres and forms. As Crane explains, "The barriers between high culture and popular culture are declining . . . [because the] new pa-

trons—government agencies and corporations—. . . can better provide
the ever-increasing resources needed to support [arts] institutions. Maintaining these barriers is less advantageous to the new patrons."[42] A corporate or governmental sponsor's tendency to evaluate the success of a
museum show by learning how *many* people have seen it rather than
whether the *right* people have viewed it obviates the ability of wealthy
individuals to control high culture as the reserve of those endowed with
cultural capital.

During the Reagan administration, the National Endowment for the
Humanities decided to emphasize late-nineteenth-century humanistic
ideals. To say the least, late-nineteenth-century ideals are out of whack
with late-twentieth-century postmodernism. For a while the National Endowment for the Arts (NEA) stayed more in tune with contemporary
trends. But it ran up against right-wing Congressional pressure, as did
the congressionally funded Corcoran Gallery. In 1989, the Corcoran
cancelled a show by fine-arts photographer Robert Mapplethorpe, whose
work was deemed pornographic by the political right. In summer 1990,
the NEA refused to fund performance artists whose work it deemed
pornographic. These right-wing judgments directly opposed the evaluations of these photographs by critics, artists, and collectors.

Although the United States has a tradition of public art—nineteenth-
century sculpture in parks, national monuments on or near the Washington mall, murals by artists on the public payroll in post offices erected
during the 1930s—more public art was commissioned in the late 1970s
and 1980s than in the 1950s. Some recent public art has been controversial. Debates about sculpture, in particular, revealed the underlying conflicts between critics and brokers of popular culture. Balfe and Wyszomirski report that "there has been a record of particular difficulties
concerning local acceptance of corten steel works by any artist, especially
if these were installed in congested urban settings and/or away from
communities that were accustomed to dealing with abstraction (e.g., university campuses)."[43] A case in point is the fight over the artistic merit of
Richard Serra's sculpture "Tilted Arc," commissioned in 1979 by the
Arts-in-Architecture program of the General Service Administration
after a competition juried by elite critics chosen by the National Endowment for the Arts.[44] "Tilted Arc" was ultimately dismantled because it
displeased the regional head of the GSA appointed in 1984. That bu-
reaucrat's estimate of the sculpture's "worth" prevailed. In the 1950s,
New York critics had the cultural power to declare one work brilliant and
another unacceptable. In the 1980s, they did not.

Public sponsorship of art may validate art that is politically neutral
and artistically inoffensive. Such was the experience of artists hired
under the Comprehensive Employment Training Act (CETA) of the

1970s. According to Steven Dubin's study of the art supported by the Chicago CETA program, the need to justify expenditures to high-ups and to authorities in city agencies led bureaucrats to avoid politically or artistically venturesome work.[45] They favored art that used validated conventions. That tendency to fund artists working within approved conventions may hamper the emergence of new ideas. At least, so Howard Becker's work on the conventions of art worlds implies.[46]

Corporate and governmental sponsorship also matter in another way. Today many paintings and sculptures are huge. An individual collector may not be able to commission mammoth works. Or even if a collector has the resources to purchase such a very large work, it is unlikely that she or he will be able to display it properly. As then-four-year-old Ethan R. Tuchman exclaimed when first visiting Storm King, which displays gigantic sculptures on its many acres, "These statues are too big for a museum house." They would also overwhelm an investor's home or carefully landscaped property.

Finally, the fragmentation of the art world—the battle among artists, critics, collectors, museums, and bureaucratic sponsors about what constitutes art—has led to an uneasy pluralism. In New York's avant-garde art world today, a variety of styles compete for recognition.[47] New York is no longer the international home of contemporary art. A California "school" now shows in New York. West German paintings have received front-page coverage in the Sunday magazine of the *New York Times*. Minorities have formed their own artistic conventions. Sometimes, as in the case of Miriam Schapiro and other middle-class feminists, their work has converged with shifting avant-garde conventions and so they, too, jostle for recognition.[48]

Unable to accommodate many mammoth works in their homes, unable to determine which of the many competing styles will eventually be recognized as "important," those who invest in art have turned to the past. At Christie's and Sotheby's, works by the recognized masters of the late nineteenth century, early twentieth century, and even the mid-twentieth century are commanding record prices. When a Picasso sells for $40 million, as has already happened, the number of potential bidders is limited to perhaps five hundred capitalists. Museums no longer have sufficient acquisition budgets to bid at the auction block. One consequence is that museum-goers will not have access to some exceptional paintings and sculptures. Another is that when investors turn to the past, private support for contemporary art is fragmented. New York no longer boasts an art world; it has art world*s*. In "high-culture music," too, Gilmore finds, New York is the home to competing worlds.[49] This uneasy pluralism does not obliterate the treatment of art as a commodity. Rather it decreases the international significance of American art.

Emphasizing commodification, I have concentrated on the line between high culture and popular culture in the fine arts. But the fuzziness of the distinction now extends to classification of staples of 1950s "mass culture." "I Love Lucy" is now revered as a cultural classic. Alfred Hitchcock is no longer classified as a director of genre movies; today he is praised as an auteur of high art. The intermingling of high culture and popular culture extends to more contemporary popular culture as well. As DiMaggio asks, "When Frank Zappa's compositions are performed or recorded by symphony orchestras in the United States, England, and France . . . can boundaries [between types of culture] be more in question?"[50]

WHAT'S NEW?

Classificatory fuzziness and culture-switching are not new phenomena. Nor is cultural disdain. In the mid- and late nineteenth century, critics had trouble deciding where to draw the line between "popular novels" and "high-culture novels." High-culture authors read the Victorian equivalent of pulp fiction and were friends with the "sensation novelists" who wrote that fiction. Simultaneously, critic and poet Matthew Arnold denounced the taste of philistines and barbarians—religious moralists and middle-class readers—who rejected his notions of art.[51]

The cultural relativism with which eroding boundaries have been greeted is new. Sociological studies of the production of culture may feed this relativism.[52] In significant ways, Diana Crane's description of the contemporary New York avant-garde art scene is echoed in Todd Gitlin's analysis of the production of prime-time television shows. Each of these cultural milieux is market driven. To succeed financially, neither can offend its potential audience. When one understands some of the similarities in the institutional production of music, art, television, and the daily news, it becomes more difficult to condemn any of them as trash. The cultural analyst is, in a sense, in the position of a psychoanalyst who has come to understand how the warped personality of a client got that way. Understanding his past and seeing some of his virtues, it may be difficult to hate him.

Nonetheless, some cultural critics continue to hate. In *Inside Prime Time*, Todd Gitlin goes so far as to say that American viewers have received the shows they deserve.[53] Yet it is more difficult for contemporary critics to discount popular culture so completely. Gitlin's tone is not as sneering as Lowenthal's description of "the little man" who takes an interest in the consumer habits of the heroes of consumption. Nor is it as abstruse and biting as Marcuse's condemnation of popular culture in *One-Dimensional Society: Studies in the Ideology of Advanced Industrial Society*.[54]

But the reigning cultural relativism does pose important questions. From an elite point of view, we may ask: When critical approbation of neorealism leads others to acclaim Andrew Wyeth, can Norman Rockwell be far behind? Does cultural relativism and insistence on cultural pluralism "lower" artistic standards? From a political point of view, we may ask: Why should social commentators care if cultural standards decrease? After all, one might argue, cultural standards are not as pressing a public issue as, say, race and gender inequality.

But the debate about the relevance of standards obfuscates more sociologically relevant issues. What does the erosion of cultural boundaries and the commodification of all culture say about American society? It tells us that we may have become the mass society so feared in the 1950s. But the vision of a mass society projected by today's culture differs from the 1950s' nightmare. In the 1950s, critics feared both a society of amorphous individuals whose decreasing social ties might lead them to support totalitarian mass movements and a society whose government imposed its will without taking the desires of the people into account. Today we must contend with a vision of corporate and bureaucratic control—now being realized in the arts. And we must also confront increasing cultural homogenization. Perhaps today's uneasy cultural pluralism is a transitional phase representing passage from a segmented society to a society that celebrates sameness. For research indicates that all of the arts are most likely to flourish in cities blessed with diversity.[55]

However, there is an irony here. Those who express the most disdain toward pluralism, popular culture, and the erosion of boundaries between high culture and popular culture are the cultural elites. They are the groups battling to retain control of "*their*" art worlds. But elites will not be the biggest losers should current trends continue. Museums' decisions about what shows to mount may be influenced by corporations, but elites may still attend them. Corporations may underwrite symphonies, but the social elite may still have their names emblazoned on the backs of their seats in orchestral halls.

Ultimately, American society is the loser. When culture is determined from the top—when the state, bureaucracies, and corporations define our culture—it becomes more difficult for new forms of art to percolate up from the bottom, as did so much of what we celebrate as American: jazz, bluegrass, Stephen Foster's ballads, Walt Whitman's celebratory poetry, and even graffiti art.[56]

American ethnic and class relationships have frequently been turbulent. Yet should a society of sameness come about, Americans will have lost part of the heritage of a multiethnic society—the freedom to be different. To maintain that heritage, we must determine how we can have pluralism without disdain.

PART FOUR

——

Coming to Terms with Change

SEVENTEEN

Complexities of Conservatism
How Conservatives Understand the World

Rebecca Klatch

American society has undergone enormous social and political changes in the past three decades. The Civil Rights Movement, anti-war protest, and the student and feminist movements not only challenged the political realm but also provoked re-examination of cultural and social relations. Issues spawned by social movements of the 1960s instigated changed relations between white people and people of color, between women and men, and between children and parents. Old ways of doing things no longer seemed to work as traditional roles and mores came into question.

Yet just as suddenly, the mid-1970s to 1980s was marked by a shift in mood and conservative protest. In fact, the rise of the New Right must be seen in the context of this enormous social upheaval, as arising amidst the breakdown of traditions and the challenge to existing institutions.

All too often discussion of the New Right focuses solely on organizations or on the conservative leadership in Washington, D.C. Yet how are we to understand the grassroots embrace of conservativism? What do people at the local level have to say about their own involvement in these countermovements to the 1960s? When we take seriously the people involved in various aspects of the Right and listen to their concerns, we find people genuinely concerned about the direction of American society, expressing their fears and hopes about the future of the nation.[1]

Although today's conservative movement is a reaction to social, political, and economic changes of the 1960s, the New Right is historically based and continuous with past right-wing movements in the United States.[2] It is also essential to realize that while the New Right speaks a common language in responding to these recent changes in American society, beneath this seeming unity rests a multiplicity of meaning.

The phrase "the New Right" seems to imply a unified entity, homogenous in its beliefs and goals. Yet the New Right is *not* a monolithic group. It is not one cohesive movement that shares a single set of beliefs and values. Rather, the New Right is composed of a range of groups and individuals who hold diverse—and even opposing—views about human nature, the role of government, and the political world. There is, in fact, a fundamental division that I characterize as "the social conservative" and "the laissez-faire conservative" world views. These two ideologies are rooted in different theoretical traditions and are constructed around divergent values.

THE WORLDVIEWS OF SOCIAL AND LAISSEZ-FAIRE CONSERVATIVES

Every ideology has a central lens through which the world is viewed. This lens serves to filter and refract reality. Events and objects come into focus through this lens, forming images of meaning. Social conservatives view the world through the lens of religion, meaning specifically Christianity or the Judeo-Christian ethic. In looking at America, social conservatives see a country founded on religious beliefs and deeply rooted in religious tradition. They speak of the religiosity of the Founding Fathers. The Constitution is seen as a gift from God; even the Declaration of Independence is interpreted as a religious document. In this view, America is favored in God's plan. As Phyllis Schlafly commented, "The atomic bomb was a marvelous gift that was given to our country by a wise God."[3]

The family stands at the center of this world, representing the building block of society. The family's role as moral authority is essential; the family instills children with moral values and restrains the pursuit of self-interest. Implicit in this image of the family is the social conservative conception of human nature. Humans are creatures of unlimited appetites and instincts. Without restraint, the world would become a chaos of seething passions, overrun by narrow self-interest. Only the moral authority of the family or religion tames human passions, transforming self-interest into the larger good.

The ideal society, then, is one in which individuals are integrated into a moral community, bound together by faith, by common moral values, and by obedience to the dictates of the family and religion; it is a world in balance, based on a natural hierarchy of authority.

Laissez-faire conservatives, in contrast, view the world through the lens of liberty, particularly the economic liberty of the free market and the political liberty based on the minimal state. Laissez-faire belief is rooted in the classical liberalism associated with Adam Smith, John Locke, and John Stuart Mill. All of human history is seen as either the inhibition or progression of liberty. America is lauded as the cradle of liberty, created out of the spirit of self-reliance. The American Revolution is seen as a revolt against despotism, a milestone in the achievement of human liberty. The Declaration of Independence and the Constitution are revered as sacred symbols of limited government and individual rights.

The concept of liberty is inextricably bound to the concept of the individual. As the primary element of society, the individual is seen as an autonomous, rational, self-interested actor. Laissez-faire conservatives view humans as beings endowed with free will, initiative, and self-reliance. Left on their own, individuals will be creative and productive. The aim of the good society is to elevate the potential of humans by bringing this nature to fruition. This is best accomplished by protecting the economic liberty of the free market and the political liberty of the limited state.

In stark contrast, then, to the ideal world of social conservatism, in which moral authority restricts self-interest and thereby integrates individuals into a community, the laissez-faire ideal poses a society in which natural harmony exists through the very pursuit of self-interest. It is the marketplace, rather than God or moral authority, that creates social harmony out of individual interest.

Despite these disparate views of human nature and the ideal society, social and laissez-faire conservatives share a mutual dismay over the current spirit and direction of the nation. For social conservatives, the country has moved away from biblical principles and away from God; this threatens America's standing and particularly threatens the American family. While in the past the family has been stable and strong, "a haven in a heartless world," contemporary America is plagued by an attack on the family.

The pervasive image is of moral decay. References to moral decay permeate social conservative ideology, for the signs of decadence abound: sexual promiscuity, pornography, legalized abortion, and the disparagement of marriage, family, and motherhood. As one woman, active in the pro-family movement, put it:

> I think our society is in decay. Everyone is so concerned about themself, the me generation. I see people around here taking aerobics or so concerned about fertilizing their lawn. Meanwhile the whole world is crumbling. It's as if I had one son who was on drugs, one daughter pregnant, another son doing some kind of criminal activity, and I looked around and said, "Well, I think I'll go do some gardening." But this is the time to stay close to home, to protect the family in these times of trouble. There are too many humanists running around. All these people jogging and so concerned about *themselves*. . . . You have mothers who want to go out and have a career, children who know their parents don't have time for them so

they turn to other kids for advice, and husbands who think it's okay for them to have extracurricular activities. The family is falling apart.

Moral issues are not only the root of America's problems; they take precedence over all other issues. A national pro-family leader told me:

> From my perspective worrying only about economics and defense is sort of like building a house on a slippery mountainside with no foundation. Then along comes a rainstorm and it'll just wash the house right down the road. But if you had a foundation, you could get the whole thing anchored. . . . So I would say the biggest problems are moral. If the social order would get cleaned up, the economic problems could be resolved more readily. Because if people were in a more stable society, they wouldn't have the frantic thirst for more material goods that they have. And so if you had a stable social order, a lot of the other things would fall into place.

Thus, social conservatives look toward moral solutions, spiritual renewal, revival of prayer, repentance, and also toward concrete political involvement. Through political action they hope to push America back onto her righteous path. They see themselves as having a special mission: to restore America to health, to regenerate religious belief, and to renew faith, morality, and decency.

While laissez-faire conservatives also see a historical shift in the direction of the country, they view it in contrasting terms. It is the erosion of liberty, rather than moral decay, that is of utmost concern. In particular, America's departure from the traditions of self-reliance and the limited state threatens the individual's economic and political liberty. One local activist put it this way:

> The last twenty years have seen an increase in a general, liberal, progressive thought. Everyone is concerned about altruism, promoting those who can't help themselves. Meanwhile look what's happened—the talented, the gifted, are overlooked. . . . People today are no longer proud. We've learned to be ashamed of our talents. We hide what we've achieved. There's nothing wrong with achieving, with wanting to improve yourself. That's what this country was built on. That's how cities and towns were built.

Unlike the social conservative activist who reacts against the obsession with self, this activist expresses the opposite: she speaks against the altruism rampant in society. Her concern, above all, is with the obstacles to the spirit of human liberty, the stifling of individual initiative at the expense of productivity.

Thus, laissez-faire conservatives point to the economic realm, not to the moral realm, as the answer to America's problems. When asked to name the most important problem facing the nation, laissez-faire conservatives unanimously select issues regarding the economy—and secondarily, defense issues—as most essential. One activist responded to this question by saying:

> Definitely the economic issues [are most important]. Everything else is connected to the economic issues. Crime, for example—well, teenage unemployment. I think if they would lift the minimum wage for some jobs, they could train teenagers; they could give them jobs so they could earn a little money and meanwhile learn some skills. . . . The pocketbook is the main thing. . . . I think those people for the social or the moral issues are really a minority. That's not what most people are upset about. It's really the economic thing people want to change.

It is not the loosening of moral bonds, but restraints on the free market that are responsible for America's decline. Only economic recovery through a return to laissez-faire policies will assure the stability of society.

In short, while the social conservative activists use their influence to return the nation to its moral foundation, the laissez-faire conservative activists' efforts are directed toward returning America to her economic foundation. Laissez-faire conservatives believe that only protection of the free market, and a strengthening of individual initiative, self-reliance, and hard work will assure the future of the nation. It is not religious faith, but faith in the market that will solve America's problems. It is not the miracle of God, but the miracle of capitalism that will save America.

CONSERVATIVES' MOTIVES FOR ACTIVISM

It is important to acknowledge not only the philosophical differences between these two views of the world, but also the different motivational bases of New Right activism. While both groups are reacting to changes in American society, they do so from different vantage points. For example, the expansion of government during the 1960s and 1970s induced a common antipathy on the parts of both social and laissez-faire conservatives. Yet while activists in both groups mention "Big Government" as provoking their involvement, their impetus for action is rooted in separate realities. To illustrate, one social conservative woman discusses how government interference instigated her involvement. Describing busing as her "baptism" into conservatism, she explains:

> I had been a schoolteacher. And then I quit to raise my family. Then during all the busing time—about 1973—I began to get involved. My husband and I both saw what was happening in Massachusetts with the forced busing. You know, we're not against integration; I live in an integrated neighborhood in Dorchester. We're against the federal government forcing parents—telling them how to raise our children. . . . Now I see it as stopping government intervention in our lives. . . . You know, I was

brought up like everyone else, "mother and apple pie." It took awhile for me to see things [as a conservative]. We see ourselves as pro God, family, and the country. The issue that I see that connects these different causes is government intervention. The government should not have responsibility over our lives. . . . If an earthquake happens, that's God will. That we can't control. But the government has no right to tell someone what to do with their life.

The issue of control, and the boundaries between governmental authority and the authority of parents and God, is clearly of key concern.

In contrast, listen to the words of another activist who also names government interference as an important spark to her activism. She recounts a particular incident that had a radicalizing effect:

I remember one key event which had an impact on me. I was nineteen and dating a big black fellow from the Bronx. He designed missiles for the Vietnam War. No one thought anything of it then; it wasn't an issue. You have to remember, those were the Kennedy years. But there were some southerners who couldn't understand what a cute blonde thing was doing with a black man. They figured something was up. All we were really doing was sleeping together, the normal thing. One day two young guys came to see me to question me and they'd say things and I'd say, "How'd you know about that?" They told me, "We tapped your phone." Just like that! My jaw dropped down to the floor. That really hit me. Here I was only nineteen and realizing the government was invading my privacy.

While government authority is again of key concern, there is no mention of God, the Church, or parents. Not only is the meaning of government interference posed in a different way but the differences in these two activists' views are fundamentally in opposition. The laissez-faire conservative activist is horrified at government intrusion in the personal realm; the government illegitimately meddled with her right to privacy, to sleep with whomever she wants, "the normal thing." Both the life-style of this laissez-faire conservative activist and her perception of what constitutes government interference are at odds with the social conservative view, roted in religious belief, which argues that there is no such thing as moral neutrality regarding governmental action.

HOW CONSERVATIVES VIEW THE ROLE OF GOVERNMENT

The unifying cry, "get government off our backs," uttered by the New Right, in reality rests on different—and even opposing—notions of the legitimate role of government. Social conservative opposition to Big Government is rooted in the belief that government expansion inevitably usurps traditional authority. Thus, responsibilities traditionally designated to the family (for example, care for the aged, the religious upbringing of children) or to the church (for example, relief for the poor) increasingly are monopolized by the state. The public schools are a major battleground for the struggle between governmental and parental authority. Social conservative protest centers on such issues as who determines which schools children attend, who controls the curriculum, and what values are taught in the classroom.

The other reason social conservatives oppose Big Government is because they believe it promotes immorality. For example, government support and funding of organizations such as Planned Parenthood, the National Organization for Women, the National Welfare Rights Organization, the United Farmworkers, and the like, is interpreted as endorsement of secular humanism, a belief system in opposition to traditional values.

Big Government also promotes immorality through its own programs, in particular, through the welfare system and the tax system. George Gilder argues, for example, that welfare encourages immorality by "rewarding" illegitimacy. Equating the increase in government welfare with the rise in black illegitimacy rates, he argues that the government offers so many enticements to black teenagers that they cannot pass up the "good deal." Similarly, he maintains, the tax system promotes immorality by rewarding particular life-styles:

> The tax burden has shifted from single people and from groovy people without any children to a couple trying to raise the next generation of Americans. . . . But if you're willing to leave your children in a day care center and go out to work, the government will give you $800 right off the top, a pretty good deal. . . . So the government very much wants you to leave your kids in day care centers. But if you raise your children yourself, you have to pay through the nose. However, that's nothing. If you could really kick out your husband and go on welfare, the government will give you $18,000 in benefits every year.[1]

Such government efforts are seen as undermining the traditional family and endorsing alternative life-styles.

Social conservatives contrast this current of government with the legitimate role of government set forth by the Founding Fathers. One common refrain is that the United States is meant to be a republic and not a democracy. Democracy is equated with mob rule, in which masses of individuals, unrestrained, each pursues his or her own desires. For example, Senator Jeremiah Denton, speaking at Phyllis Schlafly's celebration of the defeat of the Equal Rights Amendment, characterized the democracy of Plato's *Republic* in the following way:

> It was a kind that was so democratic that the leaders were appointed by lot. They would rule according to the whims of the mob. And the animals

roamed in the streets because there was a complete feeling of liberty—you know, do your own thing and I'll do mine. There was a good deal of chaos. That form doesn't last very long and you work down into that form called despotism.

Here, liberty represents the unleashing of moral bonds, the anarchy of a society based on the precept "do your own thing," in which Man's primal instinctual nature results in chaos. This dreaded image of liberty unbound clearly parallels the ideal society of laissez-faire conservatism.

In many ways the 1960s epitomizes this social conservative vision of a society in chaos. Signs of moral decay pervaded the 1960s—captured in the images of the blue-jeaned, beaded and bearded long-haired youth, Timothy Leary and the LSD cult, Woodstock and communes, skinny-dipping and bra-less women, head shops and rock concerts and, ultimately, in the image of a burning American flag. Part of the fear evoked by this era is connected to the uprooting of traditional forms of authority, evidenced in the generation gap and the slogan "Don't trust anyone over thirty," by the embrace of Eastern religion, yoga, Hare Krishna, and occultism, and perhaps most radically designated by buttons declaring "God is dead" or "Question Authority." These images of the 1960s desecrated the sacred symbols of the social conservative world.

The 1960s is also seen as the era that initiated an attack on the American family. While the pill and the sexual revolution ate away at the traditional moral norms governing the family unit, the New Left, and later the feminist movement, launched an ideological attack on the family. The rising divorce rate and the increased number of working mothers were also perceived as eroding the moral bases of family life.

Further, the 1960s is associated with a new emphasis on self, the ushering in of the Me Decade of the 1970s. Social conservatives attribute this elevation of the self to the predominant ethic of the 1960s, "Do your own thing." The popularity of psychology, with stress on self-exploration, "I'm Okay, You're Okay," and the multitude of new therapies, also added fuel to the fire of "Me Firstism." The net result of these developments was the breeding of a culture of narcissism.

In contrast to the fears of the social conservatives, what laissez-faire conservatives fear, above all, is the loss of individual freedoms, the imposition of collectivism, and ultimately, the slavery of the totalitarian state. Thus, for laissez-faire conservatives the 1960s and 1970s ushered in an era of governmental growth, increased regulations, higher taxes, and, consequently, the loss of freedom. The image evoked from this era is of government dangerously expanding, becoming a vast bureaucracy, a modern leviathan. The soaring rise in government spending, the expansion of federal regulations, the growth of federal agencies and the enlargement of Congressional staffs are signs of the government stretching its tentacles, ever extending into new areas.

As with classical liberals, laissez-faire conservatives fear that any extension of government beyond limited functions will interfere with the unrestricted pursuit of self-interest and the functioning of the free market. Hence, the laissez-faire conception of the legitimate role of government is necessarily linked to belief in the limited role of government. External authority is suspect because it conflicts with individual autonomy and decision making.

Specifically, Big Government limits economic freedom through intervention in the free market. By bailing out large corporations in need of assistance, for example, government acts to protect particular actors in the marketplace, thereby upsetting the workings of the "invisible hand." Similarly, government regulations not only create impediments to free trade, but also stifle innovation, the vital spark to the entrepreneurial process.

Laissez-faire conservatives also oppose government expansion of the welfare system. Welfare represents the replacement of self-reliance, the robbing of initiative by giving services and goods away for free. As one local activist put it:

> People used to hate charity when I grew up. They'd be embarrassed to take handouts; they'd take pride in being self-sufficient. To take responsibility for oneself and to have opportunity without restrictions—that's what this country is about. Now, instead of relying on their own abilities and opportunity, people today expect the government to help them out. A whole generation has been raised to expect to hold out their hand and the government will put money in it.

Opposition to welfare is closely connected to opposition to high taxes. The tax system punishes savings and investment and thereby is a disincentive to output and production. Again, government interferes with market forces, crushing the incentive to work harder, to produce. Further, taxation of the productive American citizen combined with the plethora of welfare programs offered to the nonworking, nonproductive citizen, not only kills individual initiative in both but also moves government dangerously beyond the limited role intended by the Founding Fathers. This compulsory transfer of wealth places human liberty in jeopardy by fundamentally redefining the role of government. Such programs promote equality at the expense of freedom.

In short, while both social and laissez-faire conservatives oppose the tax and welfare systems, they do so for fundamentally different reasons. Social conservatives view these systems as promoting immoral life-styles that conflict with religious values and undermine traditional authority.

Laissez-faire conservatives, on the other hand, oppose state interference in the economic realm, which strangles individual initiative, thereby depriving the entire nation of greater wealth.

In addition to laissez-faire fears regarding government intrusion on economic liberty, equally abhorrent is intrusion on political liberty. Fear of government expansion, then, is also the fear of government as "morals police," as Big Brother. Laissez-faire conservatives oppose government interference in the private realm, whether it be in terms of abortion, school prayer, or pornography. As one activist put it:

> I don't want Big Brother in my house. I think we're headed towards "1984" fast enough without having him come in and say, "Hey, you can't determine what you're doing with your own body." Or "Hey, lady, get back there and do the dishes," or whatever. I don't want him in my home. That's what's important to me. I just don't want government involvement in my personal life. . . . I don't rush right out and get an abortion, but then I don't want the federal government telling me whether or not I can. I'm absolutely opposed to funding them. I don't think that the federal government should be funding anything now in terms of that. Just missiles.

Typically, this laissez-faire activist is pro-choice but against government-sponsored abortion. The government has no right to deny a woman's choice, or to support her decision with funding. In their adherence to maximum free choice for individuals and protection of civil liberties, laissez-faire conservatives consider such government interference illegitimate and dangerous. In fact, the libertarian dictum of total freedom of action, barring the use of force or fraud, parallels the very slogan of the 1960s that social conservatives condemn: "Do your own thing as long as it doesn't hurt anyone else."

Thus, the two worlds are in fundamental disagreement over the role of the state. While both social and laissez-faire conservatives criticize the existing state, essentially they call for its replacement by different kinds of state. Social conservatives attack the present state—government institutions, the schools, and so on—as representative of secular humanism. They wish to replace the values and interests now embodied in public institutions with their own set of beliefs and values. Rejecting any notion of moral neutrality, they are willing to use the state to achieve righteous ends, calling for the insertion of traditional values based on biblical principles. In particular, social conservatives rely on the state to legislate moral issues, for example, abortion and homosexuality.

Laissez-faire conservatives, on the contrary, reject any effort to introduce public authority into the private realm. They do not want to replace the values embedded in public institutions with some other set of values; rather, they wish to cut back or eliminate the public sector altogether. Extension of the state into the private realm violates the sacred tenets of laissez-faire conservative belief—limited government in both public and private spheres. For laissez-faire conservatives, then, the state itself is inherently evil, a threat to individual rights.

In sum, while social and laissez-faire conservatives share a mutual hostility toward federal power, they do so for different reasons. While social conservatives view Big Government as immoral and a threat to traditional authority, laissez-faire conservatives view Big Government as dangerous to the political and economic liberty of the individual. While both agree on the need to oppose Big Government, social conservatives seek to return the country to the authority of God, the Church, and parents. Laissez-faire conservatives, on the other hand, seek to return authority to the very hands of the individual, for each person to act in his or her own best interest in both the public and the private realm.

Thus, while the laissez-faire conservative dreams of a world in which individuals are freed from the external constraints of authority and thereby attain true self-determination, such a vision is anarchic to the social conservative. Social conservatives view such "pure liberty" as a "do your own thing" type of despotism that defies divine laws and results in social disintegration. In essence, the laissez-faire vision of liberty, based on voluntaristic action, clashes with the social conservative world of hierarchical authority, based on moral absolutes.

THE FUTURE OF THE NEW RIGHT

Finally, what is the likelihood of continued coalition between the two worlds of the New Right? Although social and laissez-faire conservatives have united to "get government off our backs" in three presidential elections, as we have seen they hold different—and even opposing—views of human nature, the ideal society, and the role of the state. If tension between the two worldviews should lead to conflict, what is the likely outcome? In terms of electoral politics, laissez-faire conservatives are currently in the stronger position. Gallup polls indicate that social issues have declined in general import among the public since the early 1970s.[5] Additionally, while there seems to be a conservative trend among the college-age generation,[6] it is not the social issues that they support.[7] As Martin Franks, executive director of the Democratic Congressional Campaign Committee, put it: "If there is anything that puts a shudder into young voters, it's the right wing's social agenda." In fact, Edward Rollins, the director of Reagan's 1984 re-election campaign, reported that most of the young voters Republicans had success with in 1984 were libertarian in orientation.[8] In addition, the baby-boom generation also tends to be economically conservative but liberal on the social issues.[9]

These factors indicate that should conflict erupt within the New Right, laissez-faire conservatives, who have a greater degree of support among the mass population, are likely to be the victors. However, while social conservatives have been relatively unsuccessful in promoting their social agenda through legislative means, the judiciary offers another possible avenue for social conservative victory. Because judicial appointments are made for life, they have more long-term impact than the election of officials. President Reagan made more lower-court appointments than any of his recent predecessors. In October of 1985, 30 percent of all U.S. District Court judges and 27 percent of all U.S. Court of Appeals judges were Reagan appointees.[10] Moreover, the appointment of Judge Anthony Scalia and the promotion of Justice Rehnquist to Chief Justice of the Supreme Court show promise for social conservatives.[11] The recent Supreme Court decision upholding Georgia's law prohibiting homosexual sodomy as well as the erosion of support for *Roe v. Wade* signify triumphs for the social conservative view of the state's role in legislating morality.

In short, while the two worlds of the New Right will continue to share a common opposition to the size of government and will continue to favor dismantling the welfare state, tax cutbacks, rearming America, and a foreign policy based on anticommunism, disputes over the *priorities* of the political agenda are bound to escalate in the coming years. Further, any measure of the relative success of social or laissez-faire conservatism must pay attention to shifts both in the legislative and the judicial realms.

But the future of the New Right does not simply depend on whether internal dissension results in divorce between the two worlds. The future of the New Right also depends on the response of those who fall outside its borders. For those who are concerned about America's shift to the right, it is essential to understand that the New Right speaks to real social problems and to see how the hopes and fears implicit in each world view tap into wider currents within American society.

Social conservatism speaks to problems and fears created by the enormous social upheaval of the past few decades. In her study of the right-to-life movement, Rosalind Petchesky warns that the pro-family movement should not be written off as religious fanaticism or as mere opportunism. The pro-family movement expresses fears resulting from teenagers' cultural independence from parents; it expresses parents' concerns about their children getting pregnant, having abortions, abusing drugs, or being sexual without a context of responsibility. Petchesky argues that neither the left nor the women's movement has offered a model for a better way for teenagers to live, and she urges the development of alternative visions that provide a sense of orientation in dealing with this disruption and insecurity.[12] Added to this, the pro-family movement speaks to fears regarding women's precarious position in society. During a time of increased divorce and the feminization of poverty, women seek to assuage their anxiety, to secure their place in the social structure. Social conservatives also react against the vision of a society steeped in self-interest. They criticize the hedonism and obsession with self of a society that has taken individualism to an extreme, in which self-fulfillment takes priority over responsibility to others.

These concerns over excessive materialism, over the instilling of values beyond self-interest, over the need for a larger community, are shared with those of other political persuasions. In *Habits of the Heart: Individualism and Commitment in American Life,* Robert Bellah and his colleagues report that while individualism remains a deeply held and precious tradition in America, excessive individualism has led to isolation and to a preoccupation with self and with private interests.[13] Whereas in the past people derived meaning from their connection to others—to parents and to children, to a religious community—and from participation in public life, today freedom is largely defined negatively; people define themselves through breaking from past connections.

During a time in which neither work nor public participation provides meaning, people look for meaning through "expressive individualism" of shared life-styles. "Freed" from all social ties, people choose others like themselves, forming life-style enclaves centered on a private life of consumption and leisure. Echoing Tocqueville, Bellah and his colleagues conclude that the antidote to excessive individualism is participation in public life and a reconnection of individuals to true communities, which, unlike life-style enclaves, are inclusive, celebrate the differences among individuals, and reconnect people to their past and to their future.

In contrast, the social conservative answer to cultural narcissism is moral absolutism—the firm and unquestioning assertion of biblical principles and traditional values. There is a certain irony to this moral absolutism. On the one hand, social conservatives have faith in divinely ordained laws, solid and eternal truths that form the moral code by which to live. On the other hand, they continually fear that, with even the smallest of questioning, the entire foundation of morality is likely to crumble. This fear of collapse results in antagonism toward critical thought.

Further, the moral absolutism that divides the world into two camps of right and wrong, Good and Evil, reduces society to irreconcilable conflict. There are no shades of grey. For, if moral absolutism leaves little room for different interpretations of the Bible, it leaves even less room for the existence of a plurality of cultural and moral codes. In American society, historically rooted in heterogeneous cultures of diverse traditions, such a stance is suicidal.

If the urge toward community is a central concern underlying social conservatism, the urge toward freedom is one of the central concerns of laissez-faire conservatism. Laissez-faire conservatives speak to the reality of living in a world that is increasingly so huge and technological that the individual is lost, submerged in the structure. The laissez-faire conservative response expresses fear that as bureaucracies grow bigger and bigger the individual will be abandoned by the wayside. Horrified by the curtailment of civil liberties, appalled by Big Brother's intrusion into the private realm, ultimately the laissez-faire conservative fears the imposition of the totalitarian state.

Again, the very real issues voiced by laissez-faire conservatives are shared by those outside its borders. Bellah and his colleagues find nostalgia for the small town common in discussions with Americans across the country, regardless of political ideology. They interpret this longing, as well as the opposition to Big Government, as the desire to replace large-scale organizations with face-to-face interaction.

The concern, as well, over protection of civil liberties and opposition to government involvement in the private realm are issues laissez-faire conservatives share with those of other political persuasions. In their study of American's attitudes toward civil liberties, Alida Brill and Herbert McClosky find that whether ideology is measured by membership in particular groups, by self-identification, or by use of a scale, the strongest support for civil liberties is found among liberals rather than among conservatives.[14]

But there are crucial differences between laissez-faire conservatives and liberals in response to the curtailment of liberty. While all concerned might agree with the call to protect individual rights and to uphold freedom of action, for laissez-faire conservatives this translates into support for a foreign policy based on anticommunism and military strength. Consequently, while laissez-faire conservatives advocate less government intervention and uphold individual self-determination, many also support paternalistic foreign policies that rely on Big Government and deny self-determination to people in other lands. They fear state expansion and cherish individual liberties in America, yet support authoritarian dictatorships abroad in which the state reigns through terror, curtailing even the most basic liberties.

A consistent state policy would come closer to the isolationist position promoted by a faction of the libertarians. Yet even the libertarian notion of liberty defines liberty negatively as the absence of coercion. As Stephen Newman points out, the sensitivity to external power and control embedded in this notion of liberty disappears at the entrance to the marketplace. There is no recognition, for instance, of the private power wielded by large corporations. Arguing that autonomy is limited to the extent that the alternatives among which we may choose are conceived by others, Newman calls for a return to classical citizenship in which individuals participate in the decisions that determine their lives.[15]

Bellah and his colleagues also conclude that prevention of public despotism must entail a strengthening of citizen influence rather than a knee-jerk reaction to "get government off our back" or to "decentralize our economy." Recognizing that in a large and complex society some degree of centralization is necessary, they recommend individual participation through associations and social movements aimed at humanizing rather than abolishing government. They, too, urge a renewal of citizenship, by which individuals make the state more responsive and responsible to the community.

Ironically, the fears expressed by each of the worlds of the New Right are actually being realized through the actions of the other. The social conservative fear of a world enveloped in self-interest is, in fact, the world promoted by laissez-faire conservatism. The laissez-faire world of autonomous actors is a world of anomic individualism. Driven by self-interest, it is a world without altruism, void of any notion of responsibility and care for others. A world of social atomism is a world without community. In the extreme, the libertarian ideal reduces the entire world to private interest. It rejects the world of public citizens for a world of individuals, each pursuing his or her own ends.

On the other hand, the laissez-faire conservative fear of a world in which the individual is constrained by external authority is the very world promoted by moral absolutism. In a world in which there is one true interpretation of the Bible, one cultural tradition, one correct way to live, the individual cannot act autonomously. There is no freedom in a world reduced to black and white.

Yet the underlying yearnings of the New Right tap into very real issues which speak to main currents in American life. Only to the extent that the issues raised by the right are recognized and addressed is it likely that the rightward tide will be turned. Only by attention to these fundamental issues and only through the renewal of citizenship, public debate, and reasoned critique can avenues of choice remain open and hope truly remain to protect individualism and to sustain community.

EIGHTEEN

The Return of Rambo
War and Culture in the Post-Vietnam Era

J. William Gibson

As the 1990s begin, the forty-five-year Cold War between the United States and the Soviet Union and their respective allies appears to have come to an end. The prospect of improved international relations among former foes and of reductions in nuclear and conventional arsenals means that the threat of World War III may be substantially reduced. As the fear of world war recedes, American society has the potential to develop a very different culture and politic by mobilizing the energies formerly directed toward preparation for war. Yet abandonment of war as a central social institution is by no means guaranteed. The United States approaches the end of the Cold War not as a victorious, satisfied world power now ready to lay down its arms, nor as a country that has finally learned that war does not pay. Instead we have spent the last decade trying—and at best, only partially succeeding—to come to terms with the first major military defeat in our history: Vietnam.

The U.S. defeat in the Vietnam War created serious, prolonged political and cultural crises. The fighting had involved tremendous military resources. Over 2.5 million men served in Vietnam; at the height of the war in 1968–69, the United States deployed more than 550,000 troops, a figure that excluded at least 100,000 to 300,000 more people, serving in logistic and training capacities outside Vietnam. Roughly 40 percent of all U.S. Army divisions, more than 50 percent of the Marine Corps divisions, one-third of U.S. naval forces, half of the Air Force fighter bombers, and between 25 and 50 percent of the B-52 bombers in the Strategic Air Command fought in the war. From 8 to 15 million tons of bombs were dropped on Southeast Asia (at minimum, four times the amount the United States dropped in World War II), along with another 15 million tons of artillery shells and other munitions.

Given their vast technological superiority over a largely peasant army from a poor agrarian society, U.S. political and military leaders thought they could "produce" victory by killing so many Vietnamese that the enemy could no longer replace casualties.[1] The failure of this approach—what I call "technowar"—raised questions about our method of warfare and the Pentagon's continual demands for vast economic resources to construct its capital-intensive, high-technology apparatus. Moreover, since military intervention had long been the ultimate threat behind much U.S. diplomacy, military defeat meant a loss of international political power as well.

Defeat also created a cultural crisis for America's national identity. According to historian Richard Slotkin, European settlers created a fundamental American myth he calls "regeneration through violence" during their wars against the Indians: American technological and logistic superiority in warfare became encoded as a sign of cultural and moral superiority. Thus, European and American civilization morally "deserved" to defeat Indian "savagery," and in turn, each victory by Anglo warriors "regenerated," or revitalized, the society as a whole.[2] The long history of U.S. victories, from the Indian wars through World War II, reinforced the centrality of wars and warriors as symbols of masculine virility and American virtue.

There was no victorious "regeneration through violence" to redeem the 58,000 Americans killed and the more than 300,000 Americans wounded in Vietnam. If the nation's long tradition of military victories had always been portrayed as divine omens of cultural and moral superiority, then defeat, by definition, cast doubt on the entire American social fabric. German social critic Walter Benjamin once observed that the terms "winning" and "losing" in war refer to more than just the war's outcome. Writing about Germany's defeat in World War I, Benjamin explained his thought that "losing" a war meant losing *possession* of it:

> What the loser loses is not simply war in and of itself, war in general: it is the most minute of its vicissitudes, the subtlest of its chess moves, the most peripheral of its actions. Our linguistic usage itself is a marker of the depth to which the texture of our being is penetrated by winning or losing a war; it makes our whole lives richer or poorer in representations, images, treasures. And we have lost one of the greatest wars in world history, a war intertwined with the whole material and spiritual substance of our people. The significance of that loss is immeasurable.[3]

Although the United States was not conquered, as was Germany in World War I, the dispossession of cultural tradition and institutional powers that accompanied defeat, and the subsequent struggles to "repossess" the war and determine its meaning, have formed a major dimension of American politics and culture. At issue is not just one war, Vietnam, but the entire cultural legacy of war as fundamental to the American experience, the role of becoming a warrior as a male gender ideal, and the political wisdom and morality of fighting new expeditionary wars in other Third World countries. How American society comes to view the Vietnam War thus has major repercussions for how it views its historical past, the kind of future world order it hopes to create, and America's place in that order.

REPRESSION OF THE VIETNAM WAR, 1972–79

To understand why the Vietnam War became a major topic for cultural and political debate in the 1980s, it is necessary to remember the *repression* of the war during the 1970s, its strange absence from public life. By the end of 1971, all of the major conventional army and marine ground-combat units, together with much of their helicopter and jet fighter-bomber air support, had been withdrawn from Southeast Asia, as part of Nixon's "Vietnamization" strategy. The U.S. military had no choice but to leave. Discipline in many combat units had vanished as more and more soldiers participated in "search and avoid" missions or, more seriously, committed mutinous "fragging" attacks against officers and sergeants.[4] This breakdown and revolt received some attention by both network television news and the print media.

In February 1971, the *New York Times* began publication of the Pentagon Papers, a secret study on the history of U.S. involvement in Vietnam. This revelation provided the public with several extraordinary accounts of deception by their leaders. Nineteen seventy-one was also the last year of major anti-war protests. This last round differed from earlier ones in that the Vietnam Veterans Against the War held shocking demonstrations in Washington, D.C. Although the VVAW's two "Winter Soldier" investigations into American war crimes failed to receive media attention, powerful pictures of veterans throwing their medals over the White House fence were shown on network television news.[5] All in all, 1971 was an extremely disturbing time. It looked as if the war was coming to a close and the United States had lost. For the next year, the war virtually disappeared from public view.

But it hadn't ended. U.S. material support, advisory efforts, and periodic intrusions of air power continued. Then in December 1972, the U.S. Air Force Strategic Air Command was ordered to bomb Haiphong and Hanoi. Before the American government would sign the Paris Peace Accords, the world had to be shown that the United States was still very powerful. The bombing allowed Secretary of State Henry Kissinger to declare that America had achieved "peace with honor"; then the treaty was signed, in January 1973, and American prisoners of war were returned home. The treaty signing and prisoner return created a second "ending" to the war, and the conflict again receded from the news.

When the communist forces launched a major offensive in the spring of 1975, again the American news media returned to Vietnam. New pictures and stories told of escalating chaos as South Vietnamese army divisions dissolved and former soldiers fled southward. Finally, on April 30, Ambassador Graham Martin ordered the final evacuation of U.S. personnel from Saigon. Television news showed footage of U.S. helicopters, that had been used to evacuate refugees, being pushed off aircraft carriers and sunk in the South China Sea. It was an image of total defeat.

Twice before the war had "ended," only to return in yet a more terrible form, like a recurrent nightmare from which there was no awakening. Consequently, the finality of the April debacle created a perverse kind of relief. President Ford delivered a eulogy on April 23, a week before the fall/liberation of Saigon:

> Today, America can regain the sense of pride that existed before Vietnam. But it cannot be achieved by refighting a war that is finished. . . . These events, tragic as they are, portend neither the end of the world nor of America's leadership in the world.[6]

Other U.S. political leaders and the press followed his lead. The Vietnam War had been a "tragedy" and a "disastrous mistake," but it was time to move on to better things. Neither the leadership nor the public was prepared to re-examine the war and determine who was responsible for the debacle, either in terms of decision makers or broader examinations of institutions and culture.

Communications scholar Harry W. Haines calls this repression "strategic forgetting," in that the collective amnesia helped stabilize the American political system.[7] And the system desperately needed stabilizing. President Richard Nixon was forced to resign from office under the threat of impeachment in August 1974. Scores of his administration officials had previously been indicted for crimes during the long Watergate crisis. Many people thought the government was corrupt beyond repair.

President Carter's election in 1976 did not bring a return to normalcy. The Organization of Petroleum Exporting Countries' (OPEC) second, longer oil embargo against the United States (the first took place while Nixon was still in office) resulted in Americans spending long hours in lines, waiting to buy gasoline at vastly inflated prices. It was a humbling experience, a symbol of American decline. To make matters worse, the embargo came at a time when the erosion of U.S. manufacturing strength was resulting in plant closures and increasing unemployment. Massive trade deficits, high U.S. budget deficits, high inflation, double-digit interest rates, and high unemployment combined to destroy the post– World War II pattern of continual economic growth. The American Dream of high wages, home ownership, abundant consumer goods, and increased educational and economic opportunities for one's children seemed to be fading away.

Foreign policy failures also heightened people's sense of living in an era when America was losing its empire and sliding from world power. The Soviet Union apparently did not fear American retaliation when it ordered its troops to invade Afghanistan in 1979. That same year, Sandinista revolutionaries overthrew Anastasio Somoza in Nicaragua, ending a dynasty that had begun when U.S. Marines appointed his father head of the National Guard in the early 1930s. In neighboring El Salvador, the Faribundo Martí National Liberation Front (formed after leftist political candidates were shot by the army during national elections) began protracted guerrilla war against the government, another U.S. ally. And in 1978, Muslim forces overthrew the Shah of Iran, whose father had been put in power by the Central Intelligence Agency in 1954. For over two years, U.S. embassy employees were held hostage in Iran, a national humiliation witnessed each night in the ABC News "Nightline" logo, "America Held Hostage." In April 1980, Delta Force commandos went to the rescue of those hostages, but their helicopters malfunctioned during the raid. The disaster made the feelings of national powerlessness worse.

With each new national trauma, the Vietnam War became more and more a symbolic harbinger of that decline: defeat in Southeast Asia had been America's first fall from grace, and now no one knew when the falling would stop or what the bottom might look like. All the old national mythologies seemed invalidated by these startling reversals, but to admit that the American system needed more than "tinkering" was deeply threatening. To open the Vietnam War up to serious examination meant that, potentially, *everything* else was open to the same scrutiny. The political elite, the news media, and certainly the majority of ordinary Americans were exhausted from all these conflicts and disillusionments; they wanted to avoid new national debates that might lead to yet further disruptions.

So, the Vietnam War was ignored. There were no films, no television shows, and no major academic conferences or other sustained public discussions about it. But the men who had fought were not so easily dismissed; their mere physical existence served as a reminder of what had happened in a war that few civilians wanted to remember. The veterans, of course, were human beings, all with different war experiences, who drew different conclusions from those experiences. But their humanity was lost in the nation's early effort to deny the war. Those who mentioned their veteran status frequently found that people backed away. In consequence, a great many veterans later told of how they had previously lived "in the closet," and either denied or did not tell other people that they were veterans.

When they were acknowledged, veterans found themselves cast as symbols of a war that many suspected had been morally wrong. They came to represent American guilt. People called them "baby killers," meaning they were the living embodiment of evil. U.S. air power, artillery, and ground troops did indeed kill thousands of civilian Vietnamese, as veterans' novels, memoirs, oral histories, and testimonies—like those offered at the Winter Soldier investigations—all indicated. However, most of their stories provided a context for understanding how all those civilians came to be killed and opened a view of the chain of responsibility that went far beyond the man with the gun.

But in the mid- and late 1970s, this kind of crude name-calling was not intended and not used to open up debate about the war. Instead, it rang with archaic echoes from the history of Western culture. During the Middle Ages, Jews had been called "baby killers" and had been tortured and killed for supposedly conducting human sacrifices with Gentile babies (a revision of the older Christian claim that the Jews, not the Romans, had killed Christ).[8] A more modern example was the image of the German "Hun," who bayoneted children, created by British propagandists in World War I.[9] "Baby killer" is a tried and true castigation that divided the "good" people who opposed the war from the "bad" people who went to Vietnam. It was a form of ritual excommunication that cast veterans outside of human society.

Another label used to categorize Vietnam veterans was "crazy." There is no doubt that many combat veterans were disturbed, first by their combat experiences and second by the stigmatization they suffered at home. Newspaper reports of former soldiers undergoing hallucinatory flashbacks, acting violently toward other people, and committing suicide appeared regularly in the 1970s. But rarely was there any accompanying explanation for their psychological problems and violent acts. The accusation of madness created its own suffocating silence: sane people do not have to listen seriously to what crazy people say—because they are crazy. The negative images used to stigmatize Vietnam veterans also silenced them, and that silence was an intrinsic part of the continuing social repression of the war during the 1970s.

THE VIETNAM WAR RESURFACES
IN LITERATURE AND FILM, 1977–80

The break from the repression of the war began in literature. In 1976, Ron Kovic published *Born on the Fourth of July*, the story of his life as a marine and his ordeal after the war as a paraplegic. Michael Herr, a writer for *Esquire,* released his collection of war essays, *Dispatches,* in 1977. Gloria Emerson, a former *New York Times* correspondent, saw her memoir and war analysis, *Winners and Losers,* in print in 1978. The critical and commercial successes of books like these had two important consequences. First, the New York publishing world began looking for more books on Vietnam. Second, Hollywood writers, directors, and producers, who are constantly searching the horizon for cultural trends, noticed the success of the books.

Five major films concerning the war or the predicament of veterans after the war appeared in the 1970s: *Taxi Driver* (1976), *The Deer Hunter* (1978), *Who'll Stop the Rain* (1978), *Coming Home* (1978), and *Apocalypse Now!* (1979). The 1970s films put the Vietnam war back into American culture. However, the images of war and the stories of war veterans that they gave viewers presented a very particular version of what the war meant. All five films shared four important characteristics.

First, the movies showed veterans returning to war. Travis Bickle, the character played by Robert De Niro in *Taxi Driver,* becomes an armed warrior again (whether in fact or in fantasy is ambiguous) in a desperate hope to win recognition and somehow change society. In *The Deer Hunter,* De Niro plays a man who returns to Vietnam to rescue his lost childhood friend, a soldier who never came home. In *Who'll Stop the Rain,* Nick Nolte plays a former marine and Michael Moriarty plays a war correspondent who fight the bad guys to make a heroin deal. Bruce Dern, playing a returning marine in *Coming Home,* pulls a Vietcong rifle on a paraplegic veteran, played by John Voigt, when he realizes that the man has had an affair with his wife. In *Apocalypse Now!,* Martin Sheen plays a veteran who goes back to Vietnam because he can no longer function in the United States.

Second, almost all veteran characters are shown either as mentally ill or walking a psychological tightrope. They perform superbly in battle, but that is obviously about all they are capable of doing. As human beings, they are damaged.

Third, there is no successful "regeneration through violence." The character played by De Niro in *The Deer Hunter* brings back his friend's body, not a living man. Although taxi driver Travis Bickle becomes a media hero (at least in fantasy), his second war effort does not make him sane. The man played by Nick Nolte saves his friend in *Who'll Stop the Rain,* but he is killed in the effort, and corrupt intelligence agents (who set up the "buy") get the heroin. In *Coming Home,* a returned veteran commits suicide by swimming out to sea and drowning after he realizes that he cannot win back his wife's love. And in *Apocalypse Now!* the character played by Martin Sheen kills the renegade Colonel Kurtz (Marlon Brando), not because he is following orders from higher command, but because Kurtz wants to die. The killing frees the veteran from his last connection to the military.

The fourth aspect these films share concerns their portrayal of the Vietnamese. None of them examines who the Vietnamese were or why they fought for thirty years, first against the French and later against the Americans. *Taxi Driver, Coming Home,* and *Who'll Stop the Rain* take place inside the United States. In *Apocalypse Now!,* Coppola presents the First Cavalry Division (Airmobile) attacking a bamboo village while wearing old western cavalry hats—the reference to the Indian wars is obvious. Michael Camino, director of *The Deer Hunter,* also cast the Vietnamese as "Indians." He portrays them as sadistic torturers, pure and simple.

PRIVATE HEALING WITHOUT PUBLIC PEACE: CULTURAL POLITICS OF POST-TRAUMATIC STRESS DISORDER

In 1980, the common belief that many veterans were "crazy" was changed. After years of lobbying efforts by veterans' groups and affiliated therapists, the American Psychiatric Association listed Post-Traumatic Stress Disorder (PTSD) as a medical diagnosis in the third edition of its official Diagnostic and Statistical Manual (DSM III). The manual defined PTSD as a reaction to a severe trauma "generally outside the range of usual human experience." Reaction to the trauma could appear in a wide range of symptoms:

> The characteristic symptoms include autonomic arousal, which is often manifest in panic attacks or startle reactions; a preoccupation with the traumatic event in the form of nightmares, flashbacks, or persistent thoughts about the trauma that intrude into everyday affairs; and a general dysphoria, a numbness that takes the meaning out of life and makes it hard to relate to other people. In [some] cases . . . the symptoms manifest themselves after a latency period of several years or . . . alternate with apparently asymptomatic periods that, on closer inspection, turned out to be periods of denial.[10]

Once PTSD became an official diagnosis, important symbolic and material resources became available to disturbed Vietnam veterans. Describing veterans' symptoms as disease partially eased the stigma that attached to men whose histories included anti-social actions, such as alcohol and drug abuse, wide mood swings, emotional withdrawal, and violence. What much of society had formerly seen as personal moral failures were reinterpreted as signs of PTSD, a kind of psychological suffering that could potentially be cured. Materially, the PTSD diagnosis helped secure continued political support for funding Vietnam Veterans Outreach Centers, which provided psychological and job counseling services, and it allowed some veterans to receive disability payments.

More money also became available for academic studies, and the strongest finding they turned up was that extensive combat experience often led to postwar psychological problems. Prewar differences in family stability, social class, and race proved to be much less important in the development of PTSD and Post Combat Violent Behavior (PCVB) than combat experience. Similarly, combat trauma caused veterans far more problems than hostile civilian attitudes.[11]

Early PTSD researchers also specifically connected the kinds of trauma veterans experienced to the American mode of warfare. Dr. Chaim F. Shatan, who cofounded the Vietnam Veterans Working Group in 1975, quotes one of his former soldier patients who knew something about the war was deeply wrong: "When I saw all the kids missing arms and legs in Saigon, I knew we shouldn't be there."[12]

Psychiatrist Robert Jay Lifton also showed the connection between the psychological problems experienced by veterans and the serious contradictions in the American war effort. He created the concept of the "counterfeit universe" to indicate the sense of fraud and betrayal many soldiers felt when they encountered the lies that permeated the U.S. military. False body counts, burned houses counted as "military structures destroyed," medals given to commanders for flying above the battlefield, and other routine practices embittered many soldiers. Lifton also heard repeated testimonies from guilt-ridden soldiers about how they had killed civilians and armed combatants who were only old men, women, and children. To help soldiers (and others) understand their guilt in context, Lifton conceptualized the American approach to war as creating "atrocity producing situations." When soldiers are sent to fight guerrillas who either live among the people or *are* the people, then atrocities occur regularly as part of the war's social dynamics. Moral responsibility for creating atrocity producing situations extends beyond the rank and file soldier.[13]

Since, from this perspective, the psychological disturbances experienced by veterans were caused by something larger than the individual, "curing" them would have to take the form of a *public* process in which collective responsibility for the Vietnam War was examined. Illuminating the contradictions between the goals of stopping what U.S. leaders called totalitarian communism and the reality of what this political stance and military strategy meant in terms of day-to-day warfare would be a crucial part of that process.

Instead of leading to the examination of collective responsibility, PTSD became a way to "repossess" the Vietnam War more comfortably. Chaim F. Shatan, who collaborated extensively with the DSM III task force, contended that the concept of PTSD that was officially adopted minimized the disorder's connection to war:

I would have preferred Postcombat Stress Disorder or, if we include survivors of other disasters, Postcatastrophic Stress Disorders. The words trauma, stress, and stressors are bloodless compared with disaster and catastrophe. While they satisfy nosologists, they also create confusion. The term "psychic trauma" was originally devised by Freud and his followers to describe "ordinary" psychic wounds, such as the loss of a parent or sibling, abandonment, the failure of a relationship, or the loss of one's station in life, not massive communal disaster.[14]

Through the diagnosis of PTSD, the veteran in essence was transformed into a patient for therapy and ritually reincorporated back into American society in exchange for depoliticizing his or her knowledge of the war. The potential political threat for destabilizing major power structures and creating opportunities for social change that is implicit in what I call the "warrior's knowledge" was thus neutralized.[15]

TO HEAL A NATION:
CREATION OF THE VIETNAM VETERANS MEMORIAL

In this therapeutic approach, the Vietnam War itself became a "wound" upon the nation's body that needed to be healed. In April 1979, Jan C. Scruggs founded the Vietnam Veterans Memorial Fund to privately raise money for a monument to honor American war dead. Scruggs had served in the infantry, and suffered hallucinatory flashbacks after seeing *The Deer Hunter*. His effort soon gained support among veterans and families of fallen soldiers. In January 1980, Congress passed a bill authorizing the Memorial, and later that year, President Jimmy Carter signed it into law, adding his own prologue:

A long and painful process has brought us to this moment today. Our nation, as you all know, was divided by this war. For too long, we tried to put that division behind us by forgetting the Vietnam War and, in the process, we ignored those who bravely answered their nation's call, adding to their pain the additional burden of our nation's own inner conflict.[16]

As Harry Haines points out, this prologue was an early indicator that the Memorial was intended to serve as a kind of therapy. Carter "names the Memorial as a sign of national expiation, a sign through which Vietnam veterans are purged of an unidentified 'inner conflict.'" After the Fund's success in getting public appropriations for construction, it then formed an eight-person jury to select a design. The judges issued instructions "that the memorial must include a list of names of the war dead, that it must relate sensitively to the Washington Monument, the Lincoln Memorial, and other major monuments, and that it should be 'reflective and contemplative in nature,' refraining from making any 'political statement regarding the war or its conduct.'"

The jury received 1421 entries and in May 1981 selected Maya Lin's design. At first, the Yale undergraduate's famous black wall received approval from the National Capitol Planning Commission, the Fine Arts Commission, and the Department of the Interior. But by the fall, a conservative critique of the Memorial design had become a powerful political force. Tom Carhart, a Vietnam veteran and lawyer at the Pentagon complained, "Are we to honor our dead and our sacrifices to America with a black hole? . . . Can America truly mean that we should feel honored by that black pit?"[17] James Webb, a Vietnam veteran, author of the novel *Fields of Fire* (1977), and a well-known Washington official, called the design a "wailing wall" for future anti-war protests. H. Ross Perot (who had financed the design competition) also disliked it, as did several congressmen. They all wanted an above-ground, white monument.

Secretary of the Interior James Watt subsequently refused to build the wall. Scruggs mobilized his allies among veterans and the armed services and fought back. Watt then ordered Scruggs to compromise. Frederick Hart's proposal for statues of three soldiers approaching the wall was accepted to give the Memorial a more traditional look.

In March 1982, construction began and the first of *three* dedication ceremonies was held. Virginia Governor Charles S. Robb, a former Marine officer and Lyndon Johnson's son-in-law, recalled that he never knew how to answer "why" his men had died when he wrote to their parents, "and this memorial doesn't attempt to say why, but it does say we cared and we remembered."[18] Attempts to understand why the war happened were thus displaced to therapeutically heal the "wounds" it inflicted.

Later in the fall, the wall was completed and dedicated during a four-day event entitled the "National Salute to Vietnam Veterans." Secretary of Defense Casper Weinberger used the occasion to generate public support for the Reagan administration's Cold War agenda. He affirmed the conservative analysis of the Vietnam War, namely that the U.S. military suffered from what the Joint Chiefs of Staff called "self-imposed restraints." The Secretary of Defense said that the United States would never again ask its men to "serve in a war that we did not intend to win."[19] National unity would require learning that lesson before fighting another war.

But the meaning of the Memorial was not completely determined by Weinberger's speech. Different cultural forces were set in motion by the way its design framed experiences for visitors. Communications scholar Sandra Foss theorizes that the Memorial's presence within the earth, together with its enveloping walls, creates a "feminine sensibility" resonant with Jung's "Mother archetype." Visitors are warmly embraced while the inscribed names of the war dead communicate tragedy.[20] Both Foss and novelist Bobbie Ann Mason believe that touching the wall creates a bond between the living and the dead. Vietnam War scholar (and veteran) Rick Berg concludes that this process takes Vietnam away from the state and instead locates the war "as an experiential and historical fact in the lives of . . . families."[21]

For Vietnam veterans, the Memorial created opportunities to break through what psychoanalyst Shatan calls "impacted grief" and mourn for their lost comrades. Armies do not encourage grieving; battle demands that soldiers keep fighting. Mourning is first blocked and then transformed into "ceremonial vengeance," the desire to make the enemy suffer.[22] Photographs of former soldiers crying became one of the most common representations of the Memorial, and thus of the Vietnam War.

In November 1984, the Reagan administration orchestrated the third ceremonial dedication to honor Hart's statues. A week-long series of televised events called "Salute II," and subtitled "American Veterans— One and All," was held. This dedication's political objective was to consecrate the Vietnam War as a "traditional" American war. President Reagan began his speech by saying that "this memorial is a symbol of both past and current sacrifice." He concluded:

> There has been much rethinking by those who did not serve, and those who did. . . . There has been much rethinking by those who had strong opinions on the war, and those who did not know which view was right. There's been rethinking on all sides, and this is good. And it's time we moved on, in unity and with resolve to always stand for freedom, as those who fought did, and to always try to protect and preserve the peace.[23]

By implication, both the civilian and Vietnam veteran anti-war movements were wrong to protest. Healing requires unity. Unity creates the resolve to "stand for freedom" and fight another war. The "price" of freedom is periodic sacrifice of the nation's youth. Consequently, the memorial is a "symbol of both past and current sacrifice." Reagan's attempt to recuperate the Vietnam War makes new wars necessary and desirable—*blood sacrifice can only be redeemed by more blood sacrifices.* Without new sacrifices, then all those who have died before will have died in vain.

This concept of blood sacrifice appeared in many other commentaries during the 1980s. Tom Carhart, the lawyer who called Maya Lin's design a "black hole," had submitted his own design in which an army officer held a dead soldier up to the sky, like an ancient offering to the gods. Christopher Buckley similarly argued in *Esquire* that those who avoided military service had "forfeited what might have been the ultimate opportunity, in increasingly self-obsessed times, of making the ultimate commitment [self-sacrifice] to something greater than ourselves: the survival of comrades."[24] Francis Ford Coppola's second Vietnam film, *Gardens of*

Stone (1987), focuses on ritual sacrifice. A noble young lieutenant is first trained by two veteran sergeants. He volunteers for Vietnam and is killed. The movie concludes with his burial at Arlington National Cemetery and the mourning of his symbolic fathers. They know that he died for them.

Some veterans foresaw that the Memorial would be used to promote the revitalization of war culture. Poet William D. Ehrhart made the connection in "The Invasion of Grenada": [25]

> I didn't want a monument,
> not even one as sober as that
> vast black wall of broken lives.
> I didn't want a postage stamp.
> I didn't want a road beside the Delaware
> River with a sign proclaiming:
> "Vietnam Veterans Memorial Highway."
>
> What I wanted was a simple recognition
> of the limits of our power as a nation
> to inflict our will on others.
> What I wanted was an understanding
> that the world is neither black-and-white
> nor ours.
>
> What I wanted
> was an end to monuments.

REGENERATION THROUGH VIOLENCE

In 1983, a new kind of Vietnam War film reached the American public. These films departed from those of the 1970s in one crucial respect—the warriors won their wars. *Uncommon Valor* showed a former U.S. commando team leader with private financing organize a rescue mission to retrieve members of his reconnaissance unit who had been captured years before and who remained POWs in Laos. He recruits his old crew for the project. Training shows the men becoming mentally and physically fit again. They transcend the egotism of civilian life and become a united team, complete with a purpose in life for which they are willing to die—and most of them do. The trade-off of killed rescuers for saved POWs is about one-to-one. [26]

Two years later, Sylvester Stallone's John Rambo, who in 1983 destroyed an Oregon town while experiencing a prolonged flashback in *Rambo: First Blood,* receives a presidential pardon to rescue POWs. Before accepting the offer, he asks "Do we get to win this time?" Having located the POWs, Rambo is then betrayed by his CIA case officer (who in turn takes orders from higher authority). No longer a subordinate member of the bureaucracy, Rambo's full power is unleashed. He brings the prisoners back by himself.

Almost immediately, Stallone-Rambo became an object of ridicule in the mainstream press. Everyone laughed at his corny dialogue, massive body-builder physique, and cartoon killing proficiency. But the ridicule obscured the huge success of these films and the important opening they made in the culture.

The ostensible motivation for the heroes of *Uncommon Valor* and *Rambo: First Blood, Part II* was getting POWs out of Southeast Asia, and it was true that this was still an issue. When the Paris Peace Accords were signed in 1973, more than 2000 American soldiers, primarily members of air crews shot down over Laos and Vietnam, were listed as missing-in-action (MIA). Their families faced highly secretive Defense and State department officials. Both the Carter administration and a Special Select Committee of the House of Representatives announced that they had not found credible evidence that Americans were still being held prisoner. Reagan administration officials later said that although they had no *proof* of live Americans, "the information available to us precludes ruling out that possibility." [27]

Despite these statements, belief in POWs persisted. Many Americans no longer trusted their government. Pictures of desperate Vietnamese boat people fleeing their country after the long (thirty years) revolutionary war and subsequent economic collapse reinforced the old concept of the barbarian enemy. Moreover, there is no doubt that the American POWs who returned in 1973 had been brutally tortured. This combination of popular distrust and belief in a savage enemy created the idea that living POWs had been abandoned by the U.S. government because they were politically inconvenient.

But these two films (and the clones, like Chuck Norris's *Missing in Action* series) had a deeper cultural significance, beyond the POW debate. They gave birth to a new incarnation of a fundamental cultural archetype in American mythology. The old American figure of the avenging warrior who saves a society that cannot save itself was resuscitated. Suddenly a vast cultural outpouring created new images and stories of American men (frequently Vietnam veterans) who are "reborn" as powerful warriors fighting either criminals inside the United States or guerrillas, terrorists, drug dealers, or KGB agents abroad, on a worldwide battleground.

This reworking of traditional war culture constituted what I call "paramilitary culture." The new warrior hero was only rarely portrayed as a member of a conventional military or law-enforcement unit. Instead, he fought alone or with a small, elite group of fellow warriors. By being outside the dominant power structure and bureaucracy, the new

paramilitary warrior could overcome legal and political restraints supposedly imposed by higher-ups on their subordinates, and thus achieve
new mythic victories to replace American defeat in Vietnam. Each victory regenerated society by infusing it with the warrior's strength and
virtue.

In the mid- to late 1980s this culture blossomed. Scores of warrior
films were released. From twenty to thirty men's "action" adventure pulp
novel series were published; each book featured from 20 to 120 graphically described killings (much like pornographically described sex). The
genre sold millions. *Soldier of Fortune* magazine and half a dozen imitators together fabricated a universe filled with visits to elite commando
units; battlefield reports from Nicaragua, Angola, and Afghanistan; old
war stories from Vietnam; and extensive testing of every possible small
arm, knife, and military accessory. Together they sold well over a million
copies a month. And the domestic weapons market changed. In 1989 the
Bureau of Alcohol, Tobacco, and Firearms estimated that Americans
had bought two to three million military "assault" rifles.

A central component of the paramilitary culture is the old war movie
tradition that only war can provide males the key ritual transition from
boyhood to manhood. The feminist movement seriously challenged traditional gender roles and declared that customary male privileges and
practices were no longer acceptable. Reaffirming the warrior role was a
response to that challenge as well as an attempt to recover from Vietnam. Even Oliver Stone's critical Vietnam film, *Platoon* (1987), shows a
conflicted young soldier emerge from battle as an adult. Only Stanley
Kubrick's *Full Metal Jacket* (1987) found no redemption in war; in his
film, both the military training experience and the permissive lawless-
ness of war infantilized men.

Paramilitary culture also stresses that soldiers and police are not the
only ones to do battle. The warrior role is an identity for all men, not just
an occupation for some. All men, be they bankers, professors, factory
workers, or postal clerks, can be warriors, always prepared for battle
against the enemies of society.

Most of all, paramilitary culture has provided men with a world view
that frames virtually all social conflicts between groups as potential life-
and-death confrontations. America became the imaginary war zone. Images of the enemy proliferated. Poor Mexicans who immigrated to the
United States became "illegal aliens" and were accused of being disease
ridden, drug dealing, and communist infested. New racist and neo-Nazi
groups surfaced, each filled with dreams of killing blacks and Jews and
federal officials of the "Zionist Occupational Government." Fears of "terrorist" attacks by foreign and domestic groups have prompted massive
escalations in police arsenals. Ordinary people across the country have

felt that "terrorists," foreign invaders, black gangs, economic collapse, nuclear war, or some other chaos-causing foe would soon appear. And many have *hoped* for this imaginary enemy to come, because then it could be slain or mastered. With the enemy's death, their fears would vanish and America would be restored.

Cultural regeneration through violence found a political partner in the Reagan administration. As a Hollywood actor, Reagan had starred mostly in secret agent, war, and western movies. As a politician, during his election campaign he promised to reject the "Vietnam syndrome" that had inhibited the Carter administration from military intervention. Once in office, he showed strong interest in war fantasies, such as Tom Clancy's novels about American and NATO victories in World War III battles, *The Hunt for Red October* (1984) and *Red Storm Rising* (1985). Extensive covert operations and military interventions by elite units became favored solutions to combat the spreading tentacles of what Reagan called the Soviets' "Evil Empire."

To be sure, not everyone supported Reagan. Tens of millions of people voted for his opponents in 1980 and 1984. Nor did every American deeply believe (or even casually fantasize) that either threatening to fight or actually fighting a new war would solve the country's domestic and international problems. Nor did the old anti-war movement of the 1960s completely disappear. Activists moved on to new issues, such as opposing intervention in Central America.

However, the cultural and political movements that embraced the warrior and war as sacred symbols of America achieved a crucial kind of hegemony in the 1980s. First, the desire for a victory to bring mythical redemption was strong enough that many people accepted the principle that "small" wars, air strikes, commando raids, and other "limited" military engagements were both politically and culturally good for the nation. In accepting this principle, the Vietnam War's major lesson was ignored, namely that war cannot be rationally managed and controlled. It is easy to underestimate enemies, particularly those from less technologically advanced societies. But when the "enemy" fights back as hard as possible, small wars can quickly escalate into big ones.

Second, the public desire for victory was also strong enough to avert massive public outrage and political crises when several of these new covert and overt military exercises failed. For example, after 241 marines were killed in Beruit in October 1983, a new sense of national power was generated days later by the invasion of Grenada. The drama of success in Grenada was far more palatable to most Americans than a sustained investigation and public discussion of what those marines were doing in Lebanon and how they had become such an accessible target.

In 1984, it looked as if this new interventionist foreign policy would be partially restrained. Congress passed the Boland Amendment, prohibiting military aid to the Nicaraguan Contras. In response, the White House's National Security Council and other intelligence operatives initiated covert fund raising operations (including the sale of 5000 TOW antitank missiles to Iran) to support them. Yet when these covert transactions became public in 1987, public reaction was firmly split, even though Iran was probably America's most hated enemy. While some people were angered and frightened by these illegal acts, many Americans saw Lieutenant Colonel Oliver North as a hero (like Rambo) who righteously overcame Congress's self-imposed restraints to do what was necessary to win. Consequently, "Irangate" did not cause a legitimation crisis for the Reagan administration. That same year the United States sent warships to the Red Sea to protect oil tankers. Subsequently, they sank some small Iranian gunboats, replacing the Iran-Contra affair with another victory.

The first significant threat to this mutually reinforcing cycle of political and cultural regeneration through violence came in the summer of 1989, when the reforms initiated by then Soviet president Gorbachev signalled that the post–World War II Communist order was undergoing serious changes. During the late summer and fall months, strong popular movements overthrew the Communist regimes of Eastern Europe. Important changes also took place in Central America during this same period. The Nicaraguan Contras began to fragment politically in the face of an impending peace settlement. In El Salvador, the Farabundo Martí National Liberation Front (FMLN) guerrilla offensive in December discredited U.S. claims that the insurgency had been defeated. Thus U.S. foreign policy in Central America was in crisis.

President George Bush, former director of the CIA under Gerald Ford and later Reagan's vice-president, and other seasoned U.S. leaders had spent their entire political careers fighting the Cold War. They were unable to respond quickly to the drastic internal changes in the Soviet Union and Eastern Europe. The U.S. leadership instead reaffirmed the old policy of fighting an enemy to illustrate American power. Drug lords became the new target.

The December 1989 invasion of Panama by U.S. forces achieved high acclaim after Manuel Noriega was forced to turn himself over to U.S. authorities for trial on drug trafficking charges in Florida. Lee Atwater, chairman of the Republican National Committee, said that with the invasion President Bush "knocked the question about being timid and a wimp out of the stadium."[28] Public opinion polls showed from 77 percent to over 80 percent of respondents in favor of the military action. Syndicated columnist David Broder concluded:

> The static on the left should not obscure the fact that Panama represents the best evidence yet that, 15 years after the Vietnam War ended, Ameri-

cans really have come together in recognition of the circumstances in which military intervention makes sense. The elements of agreement have been in place for some time. President Bush's contribution is to demonstrate that the new national consensus will survive when tested.[29]

President Bush certainly agreed with Mr. Atwater's and Mr. Broder's assessments that he had proven himself a warrior-leader and had a political and cultural consensus for more military expeditions abroad. In August 1990, he ordered over 200,000 U.S. soldiers to Saudi Arabia in response to Iraq's seizure that month of oil-rich Kuwait. Later that fall, Bush declared that he had "had enough" of Iraqi dictator Saddam Hussein and did not want to wait a year or more to see if the United Nations economic embargo of Iraq would cause it to give up its conquest. New orders were given to double U.S. forces to over 500,000 troops. Troops and aircraft from Great Britain, France, Italy, Egypt, Syria, and other Middle Eastern countries also moved into positions in Saudi Arabia. In mid November, the United Nations Security Council passed a resolution authorizing the use of force against Iraq if that nation did not leave Kuwait by January 15, 1991. In December the U.S. Congress passed a resolution authorizing President Bush to go to war. On January 16 at 7:00 P.M., American fighter-bombers bombed Baghdad; Cable Network News broadcast the bombing live. Within six weeks, the campaign was over, as allied troops retook Kuwait. What was striking about the very short war was not only its duration but also its resonance with the earlier war—Vietnam.

Two hours after the bombing began, President Bush addressed the American public on television. In that speech, he promised that the new Persian Gulf War would not be like the war in Vietnam. This time, he said, American forces "will not be asked to fight *with one hand tied behind their back.*"[30] Like Secretary of Defense Weinberger before him, President Bush also saw U.S. defeat in Vietnam as the result of self-imposed restraints rather than the efforts by Vietnamese who had been fighting for generations against various foreign occupations of their country. By unleashing the American military, victory was assured. As he said later in his January 30th State of the Union speech, the "dark chaos of dictators" would be vanquished and a "New World Order" would be established.[31]

Many other key features of the war culture that developed in the 1980s helped frame the ways the Persian Gulf War was described and pictured. Both President Bush and the reporters and experts interviewed on television news frequently talked about the struggle against "Saddam," a practice that transformed a war involving over a million troops into an imaginary duel between two lone paramilitary warriors. At the same time, the news media showed deep fascination with mod-

ern weapons systems. Most striking of all were the films taken from
video-guided air-to-surface missiles and "smart" bombs. Distant bunkers
appeared in the middle of the camera's cross-hairs and then got larger
and larger as the missile or bomb approached its target. Suddenly, like
magic, the bomb detonated and the target was destroyed. The image of
America successfully waging high-technology warfare against Iraq created a world that made "sense" at a very deep level to many people. The
issue at stake was good versus evil, and the problem evil posed *was being
solved* by technology. In this way Tom Clancy and the many other
"techno-thriller" novelists made their presence felt.

Across the land, both American flags and yellow ribbons appeared,
tied to homes, cars, and coat lapels. Each ribbon signified "support" for
U.S. soldiers in the Persian Gulf, but what this support meant was not
certain. Undoubtedly, many Americans learned from the agony of Vietnam veterans, and consequently wanted to make sure the troops knew
that people cared about them, regardless of the rightness or wrongness
of the war. However, the strong public support for fighting Iraq also indicated that many Americans viewed their displays of patriotic symbols
as essential actions needed to win victory.

Taken to the extreme, this view led to the development of racist para-
phernalia, such as T-shirts showing an Arab riding a camel with an F-15
bearing down on him, with the caption "I'd fly 10,000 miles to smoke a
camel." The fantasy of becoming personally empowered through vicari-
ously killing the enemy was, of course, one of the principal attractions
presented in post–Vietnam War movies, pulp novels, and paramilitary
magazines. With the camel jockey's death, everything would return to
"normal." "It's almost like the whole burden of Vietnam has been lifted
off everyone's shoulders," said Clayton Yeurter, Lee Atwater's successor
as chairman of the Republican National Committee. "Americans have
pride again."[32] Or as George Bush exclaimed after the defeat of Saddam Hussein, "By God, we've kicked the Vietnam syndrome once and
for all."[33]

CONCLUSION

Thus, although the end of the Cold War creates the possibility of a far
less dangerous, more peaceful world, the transformations in the Soviet
Union and Eastern Europe do not by themselves ensure that peace will
come. As Walter Benjamin indicated, since "our whole being is pene-
trated by winning or losing a war," then making war or peace is not
simply a matter of flipping a switch and choosing a foreign policy. America lost the Vietnam War, and much of its symbolic life—its heroes and
dreams, its movies and novels, its therapies and monuments—have all
tried to cope with this loss.

Defeat in Vietnam challenged the traditional national culture of re-generation through violence. Critical novels, oral histories, and films provided some sense that the conduct of the Vietnam War contradicted the professed American value of fighting for freedom. A significant part of the intelligentsia eventually came to think that the war was wrong, as did sections of the general public. However, the older mythology of war, with its twin promises to society that boys can achieve full manhood through the ordeal of combat and that their victories will renew the en-tire society, proved to be stronger.

Both the Vietnam Veterans Memorial and the therapy provided to PTSD victims have helped heal some of the pain felt by Vietnam vet-erans, their families, and the larger public. But these therapeutic forms developed as subordinate cultural constructs. Their limits for healing were determined by the repression of open debate on the war and the refusal to make peace and establish new relationships with the Republic of Vietnam and the Vietnamese people. Because of these limits, much of the healing effort was recuperated by the state as a way of restoring America's martial tradition.

This does not mean that American war culture, with the heroic war-rior as its national symbol, can never be overcome. But the strength of that culture and its mythic appeal as a path to personal and social em-powerment and adventure must be acknowledged. The "representa-tions, images, treasures" and excitements of a new peaceful world will require much more elaboration before they convince skeptics that peace offers more than more war and that the way of the warrior belongs to the past, not the future.

NINETEEN

Criminals' Passions and the Progressive's Dilemma

Jack Katz

INTRODUCTION

Progressives in the United States, defined here as those who are at once critical of business elites and supportive of policies that directly benefit the lower classes, now face street crime as a daunting political problem. Conservative politicians triumph in stirring up fears of street crime; they can maintain a broadly moralistic posture even as they discard particular leaders who have become tainted by scandal. But progressives, who occasionally have their own problems with corrupt leaders, have become virtually speechless on criminal violence. Progressives risk alienating important constituencies—especially supporters of civil liberties, minority groups, and socialists—if they rail against violent predatory crime; and they appear morally weak to many voters when they drop a posture of indignation and speak in positive tones on behalf of remedial programs.

The current quandary created for progressive politicians by criminal violence is not simply the result of right-wing campaign advertising tricks, as apologists too often believe; the current difficulty is deeply rooted in the structure of progressive thought. The makeup of progressive thought is itself a complex matter. Over this century, the American progressive agenda has not had a uniform or constant partisan character. Before World War I, "progressives" were often Republican; and Democrats, since World War II, have been deeply divided between progressive and conservative wings. But despite these partisan shifts, and underlying the complexities of support for specific policies, progressives have adopted several distinctive positions on crime.

Since 1950, three lines of initiative, corresponding to three independent intellectual sources, have shaped progressive policies toward violent criminals. In the 1950s, theories of *depth psychology* were invoked to depict violent criminals as emotionally disturbed and to reform criminal court procedures and penal institutional policies that had been characterized as insensitive, cruel, and ineffective in reducing crime. In the 1960s, *sociological* writings that attributed criminality to a contradiction between materialist culture and inadequate economic opportunities, were drawn on to develop various governmental programs in an effort called the War on Poverty. In the 1970s, progressive forces in the legal profession succeeded in implementing *norms of legality* in various American institutions, with significant if unforeseen consequences for the ability of government to implement progressive policies in criminally violent sectors of the population.

In the following pages, I will argue that the progressive's current dilemma with violent crime has been structured by: (1) an emergent awareness of the repressive consequences of reforms inspired by psychological theory; (2) the inadequacies of sociological theories of crime for appreciating the passions in criminal motivations; and (3) the success of efforts to institutionalize legality, which has placed deviant sectors of the population at a historically unprecedented remove from the conventionally respectable centers of American society. The result has been a thoroughgoing failure to develop policies that can grasp the realities of criminal violence, either intellectually or practically.

DEPTH PSYCHOLOGY AND CRIMINAL JUSTICE

Early in twentieth century, progressive forces operated through social networks that coordinated academic research and private philanthropic efforts. Progressives produced a large body of social research criticizing criminal justice institutions as insensitive to the urban poor, and they mounted recurrent waves of pressure demanding institutional reforms from state legislatures. Their most celebrated permanent success in the domain of criminal justice was the creation of specialized courts and confinement facilities for juveniles. Depicting a process in which the age-indiscriminate housing of offenders led to the socialization of youths into mature criminal life-styles, and calling for institutions responsive to the individual needs of youths, the progressives created a national climate of opinion in which resistance to the differentiation by criminal justice administration of adolescent and older offenders was regarded as barbaric and archaic. Beginning in Chicago in 1898, juvenile courts were soon established throughout the nation.[1]

Progressives originally appreciated juvenile delinquents, in a sociological perspective, as members of vulnerable social groups, namely as residents of impoverished, usually immigrant, urban neighborhoods. By the 1950s, progressive thought about juveniles had become dominated by psychological perspectives. Settlement-house and related local-action philanthropic agencies became self-consciously "professionalized," in

part through their increasing governance by psychological social workers. When publicity about "gang" violence in American cities created a
sense of crisis in the 1950s, the psychologically trained incumbents of the
old-line social agencies called for further differentiation in the treatment
of juvenile delinquents, not only by age category but by type of personality disorder.[2]

During the 1960s, progressive opinion on the juvenile court shifted in
a way that came to characterize disenchantment with a series of criminal
justice reforms that had been instituted to promote greater sensitivity to
individual needs. If the juvenile court system had minimized earlier problems of physical abuse and moral corruption of young by older offenders, critics pointed out that the juvenile justice system had also extended
the reach of state control, providing justification for state funding of
an increased confinement capacity and for confinement criteria, such as
being a "person in need of supervision," that were inherently vague and
administratively arbitrary. Juvenile court judges, operating in a special
adjudicatory environment, sought to distinguish "good kids" from "hard-
core offenders" within proceedings lasting a matter of minutes.[3] This
prototypically modern criminal justice institution hardly seemed to exercise power in an enlightened manner.

From the 1930s to the 1960s, the insanity defense had been treated
as a vehicle for bringing compassionate, progressive social science into
the criminal justice process. Legal academics demonstrated the sophistication of their scholarship by bringing psychological theory into their
teaching and treatises. When violent crimes drew extraordinary journalistic interest, psychological arguments were promulgated to the general public by writers intent on opposing capital punishment.[4] But discontent about discretionary power grew rapidly in the sixties, and an
early target of criticism was the realm of discretion authorized by psycho-
legal interpretations which held that impassioned violence reflected
insanity.

In the early 1960s, a criticism emerged that pointed to the ironically
repressive implications of the insanity defense.[5] In some jurisdictions,
the prosecution had been able to invoke the charges of insanity, over defense objections, in order to reduce its burden of proof. More generally,
a defendant who had been adjudged insane and unfit to stand trial, or
one who had escaped conviction on a successful insanity defense, faced a
liability to confinement beyond set statutory terms and might be placed
interminably under the administration of institutional psychological experts. In the 1970s, Western intellectuals found it increasingly difficult to
ignore disturbing resonances from revelations of the repressive use of
insanity issues in Soviet criminal processes.[6] Psychological science, previ-

ously thought to be a perspective of enlightened compassion working for the defense, now became seen as a tool of limitless state repression.

Progressives promoted the following debate over the proper content of an insanity defense: should the traditional standard, that exculpation depended on showing that the defendant did not know the difference between right and wrong, be replaced by a deeper psychological understanding that, even knowing the moral meaning of given behaviors, a person might be unable to control his or her actions because of an underlying mental disease or defect? The inclination of progressives to adopt psychological theories alleging that criminal conduct might be caused by "mental disease or defect" rather than by a person shaping his or her behavior according to a coherent, if idiosyncratic, frame of understanding, was intellectually as well as administratively problematic. Throughout the shift among progressives away from trust in psychological expertise and toward a suspicion of repressive state power, there was little effort to appreciate the details of the lived experience of criminal violence. Progressive thought was consistently unable to grasp the nonrational, moral, and sensual logic of impassioned personal violence.

Even though offenders may not formally think out the rationale of their behavior, their violence has a tripartite coherence.[7] First, impassioned attacks typically are righteous efforts to defend some version of the Good. A father who beats a five-week-old child to death may initially seem to have gone berserk, but the details of his mounting violence—the issuance of orders to stop crying, the shaping of violence into forms of discipline rather than into more expeditious methods of killing—commonly describe an effort not so much to kill as to restore respect according to the biblical injunction that parents be honored. Similarly, a spouse, in fatally attacking an adulterous mate, will not simply and temporarily go mad, but may become mad about defending the sanctity of the marital union. A fellow taking up a shotgun and leveling it at a driver who has blocked his driveway will understand himself to be standing up for the rights of property owners in general. Two fellows, enraged and in a violent struggle, will typically be refusing to accept insults that not only they, personally, but that any "real man" should refuse to tolerate. Far from giving way to dark or evil impulses, the attackers will understand themselves as trying to be Good in some sense that they, at the moment, feel is widely embraced by the community.

Second, the violence in righteous attacks is not simply a "release" or a resolution of frustrated emotions, but a positive, creative act. In essence, the attacker attempts to write the truth of the offense he has received in the body of the person attacked. The attack at once reconstructs and attempts to transcend the offense. This is sometimes evident in a struggle to turn the mouth into a compliant tool for delivering curses. Sometimes it is seen in the homologous relationship between the attacking acts and the background they respond to: he burned my school books in a trash can, I'll burn him in his bed; she insulted my taste in music, I'll smash her record player.

And third, the extremity of the act is felt and specifically desired by the offender, who acts out of a sense that he must take a last moral stand in defense of his respectability. Many of the paradoxes of impassioned homicide—that these serious acts occur so often during leisure times and in casual social settings, that they occur so rarely against superiors at work—make sense if we appreciate that enraged attacks, although emerging from humiliating situations, tend not to emerge when the humiliated person feels there is some other time and place where respect might be taken for granted.

Righteously impassioned violence is typically employed to coordinate an array of activities (insulting gestures and curses, pushes and shoves, attacks on inanimate objects, strategies to scar the victim's body, and so on). Such violence emerges from a logic that is profoundly moral and sensual, if not reflectively generated. These are not simply aberrations or "mental explosions"; righteously enraged violence emerges through universal interpersonal rather than unique psychopathological dynamics. Yet these acts are also products of idiosyncratic systems of brutal meaning, emerging over an extended period of time and through multiple attacks, through an elaborated, private semiotics of violence. And there lies at least a small promise for effective intervention.

Shortly after the attack, offenders often "wake up" to regret their new existence as criminal killers in a world that regards them not as protagonists in immortal dramas written in biblical terms, but as mortals caught in the prosaic workings of the criminal justice system. The most recent progressive policy response to impassioned domestic violence, supported now by some suggestive experimental evidence, encourages early and sustained intervention in domestic disputes by local criminal justice agencies. Such intervention appears promising in part because arrest, confinement, court appearances, and mandated counseling may together significantly undermine the moments in which transcendent myth governs experience.[8]

What lends a perhaps surprisingly progressive character to this new impetus toward police intervention into the most intimate regions of private life is its affiliation with the feminist and anti–child abuse social movements. But the state's social welfare bureaucracies do not operate in a manner indifferent to social class. Through the administration of income and housing assistance, foster care and adoption programs, drug treatment and public medical services, the state massively and thoroughly interrogates the private lives of the poor. (The middle class knows nothing comparable. The forms used by mortgage loan officers, for example, have no place to record suspicions of spouse and child abuse.) And so, over the course of a generation, the progressive perspective has moved from a posture of compassionate, deep psychological understanding of the offender toward a moral alliance with the victim in an outraged call to expand the state's punitive and constraining powers into the private lives of the lower classes.

SOCIOLOGICAL MATERIALISM AND CRIMINALS' PASSIONS

About fifty years ago, Robert K. Merton, in his paper "Social Structure and Anomie,"[9] formalized what became the dominant sociological version of the progressive view of crime causation, at least in journalism and in the public's understanding. Once counted as the most frequently cited professional article in the history of sociology, Merton's argument had both theoretical and political appeal.

Merton developed two now-familiar themes: deviance is the result of a commercial culture that stimulates desires, within a social structure that unequally distributes the opportunities to fulfill material goals. Published when the Depression was well advanced and the Democratic party was well entrenched in national office, the theory cast a chastising eye in familiar directions, appealing to widespread sentiments that structural problems could unjustly put masses of otherwise good people to desperate choices. The argument also appealed to culture critics who disdain the false gods of mass advertising.

While positing the emergence of an intermediate state of anomie from which various lines of deviant action might emerge, Merton's theory put materialistic motives and opportunities for material gains at the driving foundation of deviance. A brief review of some central patterns in youth crime and in predatory adult crime will indicate the massive irrelevance of this materialist version of progressive thought to the lived experience of deviance.

Delinquency

Merton's theory made its most rhetorically successful appearance in statements on youth crime, or "delinquency." Revised and applied specifically to juvenile delinquency by Richard Cloward and Lloyd Ohlin,[10] "opportunity theory" became part of the intellectual foundation of the Democratic administration's War on Poverty in the 1960s.[11] Three patterns indicate the broad inadequacies of this version of progressive thought in application to youth crime.

First, despite a popular tradition of locating in the lower class a distinctive culture of toughness, a fascination with aleatory risk taking, and the death defying pursuit of illicit action, mortality statistics on males aged fifteen to nineteen point to a quite different contemporary social reality. In the United States, the mortality rate for white males in late adolescence is not clearly lower than the rate for blacks; in some years it is slightly higher. Teenage white males die from motor vehicle accidents at about three times the rate for their black counterparts. Teenage black males die from "homicide and legal intervention" at almost five times the rate for their white counterparts. The white rate is not simply the product of the greater availability of cars to white adolescents; the adolescent white male rate of death from auto accidents is several times that of white female adolescents, just as the black male adolescent rate of death from "homicide and legal intervention" is several times that of the black female adolescent rate.[12] White male adolescent mortality seems related not simply to access to automobiles but to the way they are driven.

These mortality data indicate criminogenic forces that operate powerfully across the lines that progressive theory traditionally addresses: the fascination with tempting fate is common among young men, and is often combined with a widespread preoccupation with the cultures of alcohol and drug use. As with "gang" violence, youths' reckless driving typically emerges spontaneously and without connection to material, instrumental objectives. In the domain of fatal criminal activity by young males, social inequality appears to structure the form more clearly than the incidence of deviance. C. Wright Mills's old argument that social pathologists are biased to focus on deviance in urban, lower-class, ethnic minority settings is still worth heeding.[13]

The irrelevance of materialist causes and intentions explains the similarly general neglect by sociologists of relatively innocent forms of youthful criminal activity. Vandalism, for example, has rarely been studied. Vandals take material destruction, not acquisition, as their objective, except when they take an item as a souvenir of an adventure. "Joyriding" forms of auto theft are not typically instrumental efforts to remedy problems of access to transportation. Adolescents who shoplift often have the money to buy the stolen goods in their pockets, or they discard the booty soon after it has served its function as trophy. And young burglars often break and enter successfully and then wonder what they might reasonably do once inside. Some act out a version of the Goldilocks story, sitting here and there, messing up this or that room, perhaps taking a beer from the refrigerator. When caught, these amateur offenders frequently experience a metaphysical shock as they simultaneously realize, prospectively, the conventional criminal definition that their activity may be given; and retrospectively, that they had been operating in a world of myths.

None of the powerful attractions of these sneaky thrills has mattered much to social research and social theory. But precisely because these forms of deviance have cross-class appeal to amateurs, they can lead us to recognize motivational dynamics that social theory should grow to appreciate. In part, these forms of sneaky thrills are attractive as games: they have goal lines, tricky maneuvers to fake-out the opposition, and a concern to "get away with it" that justifies action, regardless of the value of the "it." In part, they are seductive plays with sexual metaphors of foreplay, penetration, and orgasmic climax. In part they are strategic interactions over social visibility in which the line between what others think and what one knows about oneself is put to the test.

And they all share as well the temptations of desecration. Vandalism pursues a pure fascination with defiling the sacred. Its outrageously senseless character, to victims, points toward its explanation. The common view misunderstands vandals as simply trying to destroy; but destruction appeals because it is a strategy to release positive powers. Across social and ethnic divisions, adolescents live in a world of material goods that, independent of their market value, serve, through orderliness and surface perfections, to provide a sense of cosmological coherence to adults.[14] Wherever things soiled and things out of place stir anxieties not rationally related to instrumental activities, there adolescents can find objects that are treated as possessing totemic power.

But it has been common to see only a negative force—"frustration" or "deprivation"—behind vandalism, just as it is common to see only "acting out" or "frustration" behind a child's knocking down of a pyramid of blocks. Yet the construction has a compelling majesty for the child; as parents celebrate it with mock expressions of awe, the whole obviously attains a spiritual presence that is infinitely greater than the sum of its parts. Drawn to the visible majesty that is obviously before him, the child seeks to touch the untouchable, acting more in the spirit of exploration than of malevolence. Observers who can see only "anger" and a "mess" speak more about the limits of their own theories than about the lived experience of youth.

More clearly than in any other area of criminal behavior, the traditional progressive view has dominated popular and academic understandings of street "gang" violence. Related to the great rhetorical appeal of "opportunity" theory and the call for expanded job opportunities to which opportunity theory predictably leads, has been the extraordinarily tired intellectual texture of the field. For a while in the 1960s, books on delinquency won awards from professional research societies without working their arguments through data of any sort, quantitative or qualitative.[15]

Part of the narrowness of traditional inquiry into group delinquency has been a neglect of comparative class analysis. At least since World War II, a series of forms of collective deviance have been embraced by middle-class youth: beats, hippies, punks. What makes a comparative examination important is not simply that it makes analysis more deeply sociological; it helps isolate the essential attractions of violence to ghetto youth gangs.

Middle-class and ghetto forms of collective youth deviance have been regularly and radically different along a series of dimensions. While members of ghetto fighting groups profess a proud affiliation with a local neighborhood and with identities as "homeboys," middle-class youths cover up their affluent and suburban origins in tawdry dress and in trips to city locations. While middle-class youth develop "gender blender" styles of deviance (jeans for everyone, makeup for males and females alike), ghetto gangs organize power around males and sustain emphatically dominant relations with female acquaintances and groups. Middle-class collective youth deviance movements identify with underclass and pariah groups, symbolically integrating diverse classes and ethnicities. Meanwhile ghetto gangs have a segregating thrust, dramatizing inherent, irremediable, deadly differences with just those others in society who are most like them in age, sex, geographic location, social class, and usually ethnicity. And middle-class forms of collective deviance typically take leftist overtones, often defining themselves as collective movements through historically decisive battles with police and the "Establishment." Ghetto gangs, on the contrary, are by and large fascistic. Even when they are being hunted by the police, they treat official authority as essentially outside their sovereign reality and employ various symbols of aristocratic, in-born rights of absolute authoritarian rule.

In crucial respects, the traditional progressive understanding of ghetto gang violence has it precisely backwards. Far from being a response to limited opportunities to enter the larger society, the gang encourages its members to look backward and downward; the gang has its attractions as a vehicle for demonstrating elite status by dominating others as aristocrats would dominate a lower caste. Thus Mexican-American barrio warriors do not emulate the advertised models of modern commercial affluence, they mimic the arrogant posture of premodern landed elites. And contemporary black gangs in Los Angeles continue to enact a fascination with the legacy of their southern rural heritage in which one group dominates another group on the bare basis of color (in this case, red and blue colored clothes).

The ghetto gang's principles of social organization and culture are those of childhood: stay close to home, relate primarily to members of the same sex, engage the myths and symbols of Knights and Lords and other fantastic premodern rulers. Ghetto violence is, then, not a cause of gang formation; the fabric of gang life has its own fascinations, and violence is valued, indeed treasured, as a way of transforming what might be seen as a "punk" affiliation with childhood ways into a heroic loyalty to the neighborhood or group.

The social divisions central to violent ghetto gangs are not between the ghetto and the affluent ethnic majority society; they are divisions within ghetto communities. The arrogant style of gang domination shows up vividly in juxtaposition to the humility of others in the gang's generational or neighborhood background, and not at all in anticipation of a dismal occupational fate within a long biographical view or a larger socioeconomic framework. What progressive commentators have not wanted to acknowledge is that America's distinctive, century-old youth gang problem is related neither to a more avidly commercial culture nor to a greater degree of rigidity in stratification in this country than in economically comparable Western societies. It is related to the distinctive external and internal migration patterns in U.S. history that have repeatedly brought in masses of ethnic minority, peasant-origin peoples who maintain traditions of deference toward authority and vivid concerns over respectability. Along with such strange bedfellows as the Ku Klux Klan and Hell's Angels, ghetto gangs are the form that the mass appeal of the fascistic spirit, which revels in lording nativist advantages over humbled ethnic minorities, has taken in our country.

With respect to the ghetto gang phenomenon, progressive theorists have been caught on the horns of an inescapable dilemma. They cannot confront the sensual and moral attractions that inspire gang members and then turn to present these youths as petitioners for leftist policies. And they cannot acknowledge the central contribution of rural-urban migration patterns in establishing the framework for gang formation without turning cruelly against morally compelling masses of optimistic newcomers.

Stickup

The contemporary social reality of robbery provides superficial support for ideas that offenders calculate crimes as instruments for obtaining material goals. Robbers, after all, typically demand money, and in interviews, robbers often say that they do it for the money. But:

- Robbers are often employed when they commit their offenses, and their jobs sometimes provide them with information, and with opportunities for emotional hostilities with superiors, that generate an insider's knowledge and resentments as resources for the offense. The instrumental, materialist perspective rebounds with an appreciation of the low pay and status of the jobs robbers generally hold.

But the progressive's perception of white-collar crime turns the debate around once again. If good jobs don't stifle criminal motives,
why assume that bad jobs breed them?

- A look at how little planning goes into the typical street robbery, and
the very limited rewards and high risks of capture the offense entails, suggests that the instrumental perspective is applicable only superficially, if at all.
- If there are instrumental, materialist reasons for robbery, it is striking that poor women can virtually never grasp them. And in places
where the ethnic comparison can be made clearly, as in Southern
California, poor black males commit robbery four to five times more
often than do poor Hispanic males. This disproportion is much
greater for robbery than it is for nonproperty violent offenses, such
as assault and homicide, or for nonviolent property offenses, such as
burglary.[16]
- The fact that robbers are typically well aware of alternative opportunities to make more money at less risk through other illegitimate
activities, in nonviolent property crime and in vice markets; and the
fact that many burglars, check forgers, pimps, and drug dealers ab-
jure robbery as a fool's game should persuade researchers to attend
to the special, nonmaterial attractions of robbery.
- If lack of legitimate opportunity motivates entry into and persistence with robbery, the progressive is well aware that, after the many
years in prison that virtually all persistent robbers will serve, legitimate job opportunities will not be any better. And yet, when the
ages of robbers are noted and compared to the number of people in
the population of the same ages, it appears that robbery peaks in the
early twenties and declines precipitously a few years later.
- And, what is perhaps most neglected about the social reality of robbery, early experiences with robbery often show that materialist motives are clearly secondary during the formative stages of the robber's criminal career. Robbery as a "professional" line of criminal
work typically grows out of adolescent years spent cultivating an
awesome presence as a badass. Teenage badasses will often go out of
their way to embed robbery in a transcendent immoral project.

A repeat offender's first robberies will often victimize peers and even
friends, and will not be limited to situated action, but will make robbery
an ongoing feature of his identity. A fearsome fellow may, for example,
ask a series of acquaintances for small "loans" that are, it is initially promised, to be paid back at some future date. When those dates come, and
when repayment dates are rescheduled again and again, the cynicism behind the debtor's excuses and promises, delivered with casually subtle in-

timidating undertones, will become increasingly transparent, with the result that both parties will realize retrospectively that the "loan" was the first stage in an artfully interminable robbery.

In recent years, the instrumental, materialist perspective has reached into the patterns of robber-victim interaction to find supporting evidence. Asked to generalize about the matter, robbers will typically say that they don't want to use violence and only do when a victim's resistance makes it necessary. A great variety of studies have seemed to show support in the form of high correlations between resistance by victims and their experience of suffering injuries in robberies. The ironically inverse relationship between the means of intimidation used by a robber and the probability of injury to victims seems to provide further support. Considering nonfatal injuries, robbers who use guns are less dangerous than those who use knives, who in turn are less dangerous than those who use clubs or strong-arm force, presumably because the more lethal the means of seeking compliance, the less likely one will be required to use it. Various demographic characteristics of offenders and victims— age, sex, number of co-offenders—significantly distinguish robberies from assaults and nonrobbery homicides, also indicating that a different, presumably more rational, framework governs robbery than governs impassioned violence.

But a more intimate view of the meaning of robbery within its full social and processual context undermines the persuasiveness of a rational, instrumental understanding of the robber's behavior. Correlation, we must always recall, does not establish causation; but more troubling is the distinct possibility that there is a causal relation between victims' resistance and robbers' use of force that runs in a direction opposite to the one that the rationalist view would presume. Resistance by victims may be their response to a robber they perceive as bent on gratuitous violence.

Moreover, even if victims resist and trigger the offender's violence, considering the nature of the resistance victims produce, they often do not provide very compelling reasons for a violent response. What is usually coded by researchers as "resistance" by victims is an array of behaviors, such as a slow pace in complying with the offender's demands, shouts for help, or attempts to escape, that do not threaten the offender physically and that increase the offender's risk of capture less than the offender's own violent response. Given the lack of planning typical of the robbery, the offender would often be much more rational to abandon the current victim and move on to the next criminal opportunity he encounters.

Most importantly, offenders have so many reasons to use violence in robberies that virtually all, and thus ultimately virtually none, of their brutality can be explained instrumentally. After taking all the betting money at a crap game held in a public housing project, robbers are well advised to fire a few warning shots because their victims are likely to have guns and to use them. When robbing a pimp or drug dealer whom they know, and who knows them, robbers are "rational" to defend themselves from subsequent attack by killing their victims. Because they often rob with others who are equally as or more fearsome than they, and because they cannot bring to legitimate forums their disputes over how to split the take, robbers send an instrumentally sensible message to their co-offenders when they viciously attack victims. And because they are frequently involved in vice activities that make them well-known carriers of large amounts of cash in their communities, robbers have additional reasons to display a random proclivity to "nonrational" violence.

Given the context of the typical robber's social life, gratuitous violence carries so many instrumental benefits that it may almost always be "rational." Most fundamentally, the uncertainties in robbery are so numerous and so inherent in the offense that offenders cannot rationally anticipate using violence rationally. They know that they cannot know if the victim will have the means and inclination to respond irrationally to their offer to forbear violence in exchange for money. They often suspect that even if they make their use of force precisely contingent on the victim's compliance, their co-offenders, who are often under the influence of intoxicating substances and who often boast badass reputations themselves, may not. At some point in their careers most offenders will realize that they do not know themselves well enough to know whether they will respond rationally to an unexpected occurrence within an offense. In the end, those who would persist in robbery know that to engage in this type of offense, they must steel themselves to it beyond rational calculation. And toward that end, gratuitous violence is an especially valuable self-portraying resource.

In referring to their offense as "stickup," robbers summarize the attraction in the offense that makes an instrumental understanding superficial. At once phallic and fiercely willful in its connotations, "stickup" is attractive almost exclusively to males and to males who are inclined to treat personal relationships as well as robbery scenes as spontaneously subject to violent domination by their will. "Stickup" promises to freeze the will of victims so that the offender can become the only being present with a purpose that must be respected. Within such an egocentric cosmological project, the robber need not have reasons for his behavior because he need not attend to the reasons of anyone else.

White-Collar Crime

Contemporary realities, broadcast so vividly and continuously that they can no longer be ignored, undermine social theories that would attribute deviant motives either to materialist culture or to inequalities in social

structure. White-collar crime generates waves of publicity far out of proportion to the little puddles of criminal cases that are officially filed
against political and business elites, and white-collar crime does not fit
neatly into the critique of commercial culture. The motivational dynamics behind great political scandals, such as the abuses of power in "Watergate" and "Irangate," are connected less clearly to material self-seeking
than to an image of national identity under attack and needing extraordinary measures of defense. When they are committed for economic
gain, white-collar crimes are incompatible with notions that deviant motives are bred in disadvantaged sections of society, and they are not
neatly limited to any particular national culture. International bribery
scandals have demonstrated that political corruption at the highest levels
effectively tempts royal families, socialist party officials, and bureaucrats
throughout the Third World. And the business forms of America's white-
collar crimes—from the price-fixing scandals of the 1950s, with their
anti–free market design, to inside traders operating on capitalism's heart
in the 1980s—show well-placed executives criminally financing conventional life-styles, and arbitragers taking in money in amounts so fabulous
that they far outpace the capacity of commercial culture to stimulate the
offenders' desires. The latter talk about money not necessarily as a means
to an advertised life-style, but in terms strikingly reminiscent of street
criminals, as a way of keeping score in a gamelike pursuit of high risk
"action."

In the light of white-collar crime, the progressive view of crime causation has been pushed back from explaining the emergence and incidence of deviant motives to the politically less inspiring claim that social
inequalities only shape the form or quality of deviance. But here, on the
qualitative turf of common crime, the traditional view of progressives is
even less convincing. In its lived details, street crime does not clearly
exhibit materialistic motives but, rather, hedonistic pursuits sometimes
united with gratuitous patterns of violence that border on the sadistic.

LEGALITY AND THE MARGINALIZATION OF DEVIANCE

Several indirectly connected, long-term patterns of social change that
have been promoted by American progressives have had the joint,
unintended consequence of increasing the social distance between the
criminally violent sectors of the population and the conventionally respectable centers of society. One broadly relevant pattern of development has been the long-term expansion of higher education from the
large-city-based, private universities that dominated academic research
earlier in the century to rural and small-city-based state universities that
became major research centers in sociology after World War II.

First-hand, qualitative, individual-case-based research on crime and deviance has typically been produced in research centers located in large cities, often through private universities that had no local public university competition and that were responsive to community concerns to address urban problems. The development of large public universities, historically justified in part as a way of opening opportunities to those not favored by family wealth, created major research centers that were commonly located at great distances from the high-crime urban areas. As national police case data, first produced in the 1930s, and national victim survey data, first produced in the 1970s, became increasingly available, researchers could participate in the development of empirical knowledge about crime without disadvantage due to their location, provided that their research was statistical, and especially if they pursued demographic and ecological questions.

In the 1960s and 1970s, American sociology received the products of a small number of intensive field studies, many of them on youth gangs, conducted by academically based researchers located in Boston, Chicago, Los Angeles, San Francisco, and Philadelphia. At the same time, American sociology and criminology journals received voluminous contributions in which academics, housed primarily in state university research centers located primarily outside of major cities, used statistical data bases to analyze demographic and ecological issues about crime. Graduate students who today are looking for a dissertation focus can find ready access, at any major research center, to nationally administered, computerized tapes containing police, victim, and census data. Similarly convenient access to sites for first-hand field research are not as widely distributed. Despite some crosscurrents (for example, the more recent growth of public universities in some urban centers; individually negotiated grants that enable the conduct of research away from an academic home base), the dominant trend is for academic social research on crime to be conducted at a greater social remove from the deviants studied, both in geographic terms and in terms of the methodology and types of data employed.[17]

But geographic and technological changes in the social institutional basis of academic research on deviance have played a relatively minor role in moving the lived experience of deviance to the obscured peripheries of American society. Of far greater importance has been the pursuit of legality through a variety of indirectly related social movements, movements that have promoted civil rights in racial relations and in prisons, and that have attacked political corruption and union racketeering. Without any ideological planning directing the pattern, progressive forces have been more or less consistently successful in infusing the rule of law, principally ideals of due process and equal protection, through American society; while progress in reducing substantive social inequalities has been stalled, abandoned, and reversed. One of the results of the uneven implementation of the progressive agenda has been the displacement of criminal violence to the margins of the American social structure.

One dimension of this change, the historical ironies of the Civil Rights Movement in separating an Afro-American underclass from white and black middle-class society, has now been frequently noted. By reducing racial barriers to education, employment, and housing, the Civil Rights Movement created pathways out of racially segregated southern communities, and out of northern urban ghettos, that were especially useful for upwardly mobile African-Americans.[18] As one experienced field-worker of American ghetto life has put it, the "old heads"—the locally respected, well-educated, professional and small-business elite of the black community—had become far more scarce in ghetto areas by the 1980s than they had been in the 1950s.[19] The American black ghetto, once a multiclass area containing the black bourgeoisie, the black working class, and the black urban poor, became increasingly dominated by a black "underclass." Young men who are tempted by life-styles characterized by criminal violence have always been concentrated in ethnically segregated, poor urban neighborhoods. But over the last twenty-five years, young African-American men attracted to a dangerous life-style of illicit "action" have had decreasing personal contacts with conventionally respectable black men, except in one area—through their frequent contacts with increasingly integrated police forces.

Related to the race relations side of the Civil Rights Movement, a number of ancillary movements brought legality into institutions that traditionally governed the relationship between the criminal population and the centers of societal authority. In prisons, Black Muslims, who combined freedom of expression and freedom of religion claims with complaints about racially motivated oppression, initially spurred the judicial reform of authority relations.[20] Once begun, prisoners' rights movements spread to represent white and Hispanic complainants, stimulated the formation of specialized legal action support groups, and became national. In the *Wolff* decision in the early 1970s, the U.S. Supreme Court made clear that the courts would broadly place procedural requirements on prison administrators' power to discipline inmates.[21] In several states, federal courts have taken control of prisons away from incumbent officials and have appointed monitors to supervise the reconstruction of everyday authority relations.

Currently, the impact of the prisoners' rights movement on prison social order is the subject of great methodological controversy. Conservative critics of activist judges have charged that judicial intervention has stimulated unprecedented waves of inmate violence directed against inmates and staff. They appear to have been right, but only in the short run. Judicial intervention typically meant the destruction of "tender" systems in which prison administrators delegated tasks of control, including the perception of deviance and the recommendation of disciplinary action, to inmate leaders. When judges became responsive to complaints about the discretionary exercise of disciplinary power, the *ultra vires* power of inmate leaders was replaced with formal systems in which correctional officers "write up" alleged infractions by inmates, who then have the opportunity to contest major charges before independent hearing officers. In several major prison systems, judicial intervention appears to have stimulated inmate violence by breaking the old system of prison authority and signalling to inmates that a judicial audience now existed for their protests. But in the longer run, sometimes after a full decade of administrative resistance to judicial control of prisons, the new, constitutionally sanctioned system of prison authority has taken hold and inmate violence has receded.[22]

Yet even with the decline of inmate violence, the "legalized repression" that now characterizes prison administration has two enduring consequences that progressives must find disturbing. One is a dramatic increase in caste-like segregation among inmate groups and between inmates and staff. Initially spurred by Black Muslims, who rode the Civil Rights Movement of the 1960s into federal courts, judicial intervention has authorized inmate associations and has undermined the ability of prison administration to select inmate leaders and shape the social structure of the inmate world,[23] with the result that U.S. prisons today are dominated to an unprecedented extent by fascist-styled gangs organized around a bizarre array of racist mythologies, from Black Muslims to Mexican Familias to Aryan Brotherhoods. We should not flinch from the historical paradox that the most highly rationalized, modern form of enlightened beneficence, as represented by progressive judges battling cruelty and arbitrary power in prisons over the last twenty-five years, has led to the most intense expressions of peer-directed racist hatreds among contemporary inmates, whose vengeful and creatively vicious acts of maiming and mutilation[24] are strangely reminiscent of the ancient and spectacular official brutality that the Enlightenment revolutions aimed to eradicate.

Second, and more subtly, the legalization of prison authority, which was finally achieved on a national scale during the 1980s, has reconstituted the control capacities of prisons, expanding enormously their organizational powers to incarcerate. Before the judicial revolution, correctional officers in many state systems were "good old boys" who, through patterns of violence, corruption, and limited educational achievement, maintained social ties with inmate leaders. Now, correctional officers are better educated, much more often female, preoccupied with the legalities of power (such as the proper form to "write up" inmate infractions), and increasingly professional in their career orientations. More socially distant from inmates in gender, education, and everyday culture, correctional staffs now equip prisons with a greatly enhanced organizational sophistication. It is not a coincidence that as prisons finally became "legalized" in their daily operations during the 1980s, the raw size of the inmate population doubled on a national scale (and in California, which has been a leader in the acceptance of legality in the prisons, the prison population quadrupled), even as crime rates ended the decade at a lower level than existed when it began. Without the professionalization and legalization of prison administration, this increase in incarcerative capacity would have been opposed by judges who, when confronted with resistant "good old boy" administrations, have in extreme instances ordered the release of inmates subject to arbitrary, discriminatory, and "cruel and unusual" treatment.

Legality, in the forms of judicial oversight, the reshaping of the exercise of authority to conform with published rule, and the introduction of intraorganizational procedures for questioning authority, has changed the relationship of deviant populations to the center of American society by dismantling traditional, subterranean social bridges between the conventional center and the deviant periphery. The attack on the corruption of prison authority was paralleled by interrelated attacks on corruption in urban political machines, in police departments, and in local criminal courts. Even before Watergate, an uncoordinated but national-scale legal campaign against local political corruption had begun, as federal law enforcement institutions became gradually more professionalized and, in the nonpartisan style of pre–World War I progressives, became mobilized to "clean" government.

The historical marking point of the modern onslaught against corrupt "machine" politicians was Robert Morgenthau's leadership of the New York U.S. Attorney's office in the 1960s against Carmine De Sapio and the vestiges of Tammany Hall politics. Before Watergate, in sporadic bursts of prosecutions in Los Angeles, New Jersey, and Maryland, and after Watergate in a national wave of political corruption cases affecting jurisdictions as diverse as Chicago and Oklahoma City, federal prosecutors targeted local political organizations whose members had profited financially by selling the powers of their offices to respectable businessmen and "connected" criminals alike.[25] Along with numerous other social trends that undermined political "machines," anticorruption prosecutions dismantled a complex network of ties between inner-city deviants and respectable government officials.

When urban political machines mobilized the vote in ethnic neighborhoods, neighborhood toughs, who traditionally hung out around social and athletic, especially boxing, clubs, were appreciated as politically valuable symbols of ethnic group pride and were at times literally as well as figuratively publicly embraced by ward bosses.[26] If intervention in the criminal justice system could not always be counted on for an efficacious "fix," many local criminals found that it made sense to keep "connected" lawyers on "retainer" and disposed to exercise "influence." A reader of the life histories of common criminals who operated in U.S. cities from the West through the East coasts will find matter-of-fact descriptions of corrupt influences on local criminal justice institutions continuing through the 1950s,[27] descriptions that have no parallel in the ethnographies and life histories that trace criminal careers within the last twenty years.

By the time in American history that African-Americans were able to be elected municipal leaders, the traditional infrastructure through which ethnic leaders reached and were reachable by residents in ethnic neighborhoods had been severely weakened by force of law. The dismantling of corrupt bridges to deviant inner-city populations is significant for progressive policies in at least two respects. The absence of subterranean connections in contemporary cities presents special difficulties for implementing remedial programs. A new educational, job opportunity, or drug rehabilitation program must now bootstrap its own social mechanisms for reaching its targets. On the other side, the increased social distance of predatory criminals from conventional social organization hardens the boundaries of their deviant life-styles and makes their motivations less ambiguously antisocial.

Consider the transformation in the role of the criminal hardman that was shaped by the legalization of labor relations through the structuring of a national legislative framework for administering labor relations, from the 1930s through the 1950s, and by "labor racketeering" prosecutions that began in the 1960s, scored major successes in the 1970s and 1980s, and are continuing to date. From the 1930s into the 1950s, there were hundreds of labor racketeering murders in New York City alone, and uncounted employment opportunities for strong-arm activities; in many cases the toughs conducting violent criminal activity on behalf of unions had acquired records for robbery and other forms of criminal violence in their youth.[28] For today's criminal hardman, political and labor organizations are as foreign as businessmen's clubs downtown; the life-styles of criminally violent young men now easily take them into illicit drug distribution networks at the street level, and virtually never connect them with the subtleties of the union's "business agent" role.

The moral universe in which the contemporary violent criminal typically operates has been isolated gradually but firmly by the broad institutionalization of legality throughout American society. Consider the implications of the transformation of local neighborhood commercial culture, from the days of the urban American Jewish ghetto, as documented by Louis Wirth early in this century, to the realities of the African-American ghetto today. In Wirth's ghetto, market transactions were routinely moralized; price, quality, and service were constantly subject to bargaining; fraud was an everyday risk; any transaction could provide evidence of one's acumen or prove one a fool.[29] The implementation of mass merchandising and consumer protection legislation has eradicated the routine moral dramas of negotiating consumer transactions. The poor still pay more, but they usually pay it up front; large-scale and legally reviewable marketing has made retail negotiations too costly and bothersome for most merchandisers. Today the predatory criminal, whose objectives are superficially material but whose motives are fundamentally centered on transcending humiliation and "taking" victims by making them fools, stands as a harsh, extreme, archaic representative of a lost moral world.

CONCLUSION

The challenges that criminals' passions represent for contemporary progressive thought reflect essentially two troublesome empirical patterns. First, while legality, or procedural justice, and substantive equality, or social class justice, have frequently been joined in progressive thought, legality has made a much steadier empirical advance in recent decades. Progressive thought has failed to adjust to this emergent disjuncture in its ideals. The increasing institutional commitment to legality in the United States has made it more difficult to reach populations of the criminally violent; in addition, legality increasingly confuses social class interpretations of crime by enhancing public awareness of white-collar crime. While progressives may take ideological comfort from the expanded prosecutions of conservative political and business elites for corruption and fraud, they cannot in the same breath blame socioeconomic conditions for deviant motives. If social class position shapes the form more clearly than it shapes the incidence of crime, reducing crime inequalities cannot as easily be promoted by a promise of improved collective moral character.

Second, and more disturbing, as political advertising effectively parades the details of criminal victimization before the public, the lived experience of contemporary street crime is dominated by moral and sensual dynamics, not material strivings.

If the lived experience of crime poses fundamental difficulties for progressive politicians, there are equally troublesome implications for modern social theory in general. My overall argument, that criminality is best explained by moral and sensual dynamics, will seem to some antiprogressive, in part because of the nature of its approach to social explanation. Crime is neither the product of extraordinary emotional pathology ("insanity" or "sickness") nor the instrumental execution of materialist plans. Its coherence is deep and detailed, but it is sensually embodied, not reflectively produced. But so is much of our routine, conventional, everyday behavior. When we write, walk, or talk, we do so interactively, anticipating how our lines of action will be seen and responded to by others, but we do not live our interactive awareness rationally; we do not produce our routine action reflectively. Rather we rely on rhythms and holistic senses of the projects we are engaged in, such that our writing is better grasped as a kind of prosaic drawing; our talking, as a usually banal singing; our walking, as a dancing that typically does not parade its aesthetic dimensions even as we rely fundamentally on them. Were we able to see the moral and sensual dimensions of everyday behavior more clearly, an analysis of the moral and sensual dynamics of crime would not stand out as damning. But we still teach a legacy of eighteenth- and nineteenth-century rationalism in our social theory classes; and our version of interactionist analysis overplays the role of reflection ("the looking-glass self") and thought, to the neglect of the embodiment of conduct (we read classic interactionist theory on "mind, self and society," but not on "body, self, and social interaction").

Considering the distinctive anxieties of twentieth-century life and the special horrors of its massive deaths, our clinging to centuries-old theoretical perspectives is a deep and pathetic intellectual failure. Existentialism and phenomenology, the philosophical movements that arose with the twentieth century's unprecedented, vicious chaos, remain outside the mainstream of empirical research and of American social thought. So do the central sticking points in American policy development on crime, where sensual and moral dynamics are as central as they are to crime causation.

If homicides commonly arise out of quickly developing passions, we should reduce the availability of guns so that enraged attackers might turn to less lethal instruments of violence. But guns remain symbols that are embraced with uniquely profound passions in America. The key research question about guns and American violence is not how much or whether removing guns will reduce violence, but why guns have acquired such strong moral and sensual meanings in the United States.[30]

And if robbery grows out of a fascination with dominating social interaction so that it provides signs of respect, we should acknowledge the special challenges of humiliation that are maintained within ethnically bounded, and particularly black, poverty communities. But policies of racial integration that would specifically address the unique roots of America's criminal violence evoke fears that repeatedly turn progressive political leaders to more broadly defined, and less specifically relevant, institutional solutions. Ironically working in the same direction, the recent rise of African-Americans to local political leadership positions, through electoral successes that are based on the size of segregated voting blocks, has itself contributed to the deterioration of the national commitment to integration.

And if robbery pays so poorly that a commitment to it can only be sustained when intermixed with more economically rewarding opportunities in gambling, prostitution, and illegal drug markets—vice worlds that, when combined with robbery, sustain the moral and sensual attractions to a way of life characterized by illicit action—then we should appreciate that our criminal legal framework, through making vice activities so remunerative, provides crucial support for the robber's career. But the sensualities of vice activities stir such powerfully moralized passions that we are barely able as a community to bring alternative regulatory frameworks into rational political discussion.

Dominated by a materialist, instrumental perspective on crime, progressive thought has mislead us because it has directed attention away from those distinctive features of American ethnic relations and moral culture that are most closely related to the exceptionally violent dimensions of the crime problem in the United States. The progressive's failures are mirrored rather than avoided by the Right. Indeed, no voice on the contemporary political scene speaks to the distinctively national character of America's criminal violence. In a notable way, both political sides share a materialist, instrumental perspective on crime causation, the one calling for more "opportunity," the other for higher "costs" to offset the "benefits" that criminals are presumed to calculate. If we would abandon the instrumental, materialist framework that supports tired remedial policies and turn research attentions to the moral and sensual dynamics that animate criminal violence, we might generate an empirically grounded progressive response to crime.

PART FIVE

Emerging America

TWENTY

Through the Prism of Time
Temporal Structures in Postindustrial America

Carmen Sirianni and Andrea Walsh

> *You have to give up something to be a success in business. There's not time for everything. Me . . . I have very little time for my spiritual life. I don't have a civic life. And I do very little with friendships—anything that doesn't have to do with business. I don't have time to cultivate relationships that aren't profitable.*
> —LORRAINE MECCA, successful businesswoman [1]

> *I felt like I was going under, and I couldn't do my job because I was pretty much in pieces. I was furious at my brother, who didn't help at all. My fifteen-year-old daughter is mad at me because I am so engaged with my mother. My son has stopped visiting me. And the friends who had been wonderful and supportive through the babies and the divorce just faded away now that I needed them most. I am alternately so sad about my mother's decline that I can't stop crying and so enraged that my life is being messed up that I want to dump her. I used to think that I was good at crises, but this just goes on and on, and I'm falling apart.*
> —JUANITA EUBANKS, forty-eight-year-old woman
> with a chronically ill mother [2]

THE FEMINIZATION OF THE TIME FAMINE

If the changes taking place in American society, no matter how significant, were played out against a background that itself did not change, they would not necessarily be destabilizing. But the fact is that at least one important dimension of the background—the temporal one—is changing simultaneously with events in the foreground. This chapter will deal with how Americans use and think about time. It will argue that transformations in the way time is experienced are stressful, but also capable of providing more equitable social arrangements.

Carmen Sirianni would like to thank the National Endowment for the Humanities for its support during his stay at the Institute for Advanced Study in Princeton, New Jersey, in 1985–86, where he began work on the issues discussed in this chapter, and to Michael Walzer and Joan Scott, who chaired the study groups to whom they were initially presented.

One way to obtain an introductory glance at the way in which time distributions are being altered is to begin with gender relations. Twenty years ago, economist Steffan Linder characterized the condition of advanced industrial societies in terms of a "time famine" and wondered how we might redirect the path of progress that has led to an affluence of goods (at least for the middle classes) at the cost of a pervasive scarcity of time for so many of the other worthwhile activities of life.[3] Lorraine Mecca's choices, illustrated above, were quite familiar to Linder. Engagement in community affairs, committed friendships, or spiritual life were simply too costly, relative to the lost earnings or forgone career opportunities. To be sure, in 1970 Linder would have recognized the dilemmas as those of professional and managerial *men*—although he would probably not have been surprised to find that greater gender equity at work would have the ironic effect of democratizing the sense of time scarcity as well.

Lorraine Mecca's choice to capitalize on as much of her time as possible, however, does not simply reflect gender equity, but disguises a deeper inequity, since the unpaid caring work of family and community life, the work of nurturing and repairing the moral fabric of society, must be done by others, and often at great cost to their own personal and professional lives. Today the Lorraine Meccas may be labeled as "career-primary" women, willing and able to devote their time single-mindedly to their jobs, just as men have been expected to do, while their sisters who choose to spend time raising children risk being placed on the "mommy track," with opportunities delayed if not decidedly derailed. Or, like Juanita Eubanks, a middle-aged black woman who struggled through divorce and single parenthood to remain full time in the labor market, they may find themselves on the "daughter track" because they refuse to turn a blind eye to the needs of their elderly parents or to attach a dollar value to time for care. If Juanita Eubanks unravels much further, she may lose her job or fall into the part-time ghetto with other mommy- and daughter-tracked care givers. Her time squeeze is thus also an equity crunch. In fact, it represents a moral crisis that strains family and friendship support networks to the breaking point. But the moral crisis is no less evident in the poverty of choice represented by Lorranie Mecca's decision to forgo community, friendship, and spirituality as activities whose opportunity costs are simply too great. On the one hand, the successful modern woman is expected to swallow the clock and imbibe the dictum that "time is money," and in this she is aided by an army of consultants and popular guides that instruct her in the "mastery and management of time"—though on can perhaps detect some regret in her voice. Juanita Eubanks, on the other hand, may be falling apart, but she chooses with a moral clarity that reflects an alternative sense of reciprocity over the course of time. She is sustained by the knowledge that she and her sister are providing the best care possible for her mother, and she notes with pride, "My mother will say, 'Lord, isn't it something: my baby's taking care of me just like I took care of her,' and we'll all laugh."

CHANGING CONTOURS OF TIME

The feminization of the time famine is only one indication of the fact that many of the ways in which we organize time are changing. There are new forms of time scarcity, even as new technologies appear to lessen the temporal burdens of toil. New forms of flexibility in working time (and space) enhance individual choice and equity for some, even as others experience these as more insidious forms of control and social marginalization. The rigid sequencing of life activities represented by the education-work-retirement lockstep that had evolved over the past century is beginning to loosen, as the boundaries between different life stages and activities become more blurred, fluid, and reversible. And the gendered distribution of time spent in paid work in the market and unpaid work in the home is undergoing its most significant challenge since the industrial revolution. Temporal rigidities in the organization of social life are relaxing, and this process presents us with genuine opportunities as well as distinct hazards. Time is increasingly becoming a contested terrain, and our very notions of individual autonomy, gender equity, democratic opportunity, and moral responsibility are likely to become ever more dependent on our capacity to develop a pluralist and democratic politics for reorganizing time in postindustrial society.

Rigid temporal norms, linear life course models, and gendered distributions of market and household labor time have been made increasingly problematic by a variety of developments in work, family, education, aging, technology, and ecology. Prominent among these, of course, is that the labor force participation rates of women, including women with young children, have been steadily increasing in the postwar period and are beginning to converge with those of men. No other factor seems as important as this in accounting for the sense of time famine in many families. Women who try to combine paid work with household responsibilities, and especially with raising children, are often confronted with a double burden, especially in the face of most men's resistance to sharing significantly in the housework and child care tasks.[4] Women's coping strategies incude cutting back on household labor time (for example, by lowering standards of cleanliness, hiring help, having fewer children, and scheduling more "quality time" with their children), and working part time and discontinuously in the labor market. Working women with children have thus, not surprisingly, been in the forefront of efforts to develop innovative working time policies, such as job sharing, flexible hours, and part-time career lines, with continued access to opportunity and equitable salaries and benefits, which we will discuss later in this chapter. Those women (and men) who have come to be most supportive of egalitarian and nontraditional family and sex role patterns show the strongest interest in flexible work options in daily as well as life course scheduling, and the greatest willingness to forgo earnings for increases in free time.

And yet, under present conditions, women who choose to reduce or interrupt the time they spend in the labor market face serious disadvantages in earnings and future opportunities, and often reproduce their unequal positions of power in the home relative to their husbands. There are a variety of reasons why temporal flexibility often compounds inequality, not the least of which is that the dominant model of a work career is a gendered one that favors men.[5] The male career model hoards the time of the individual, and requires that family and other commitments be cancelled, interrupted, or postponed, if need be. Competition is temporally tight and age-graded, and many of the most vigorous pressures and promotion stages occur during childbearing years, thus disadvantaging those who cut back on work in order to bear and care for children. Continuous and uninterrupted progress along a linear time line is the ideal of serious career pursuit. And willingness to devote surpluses of time above and beyond what is formally required serves as a sign of trustworthiness for organizations greedy for employees' commitment and often uncertain how to measure their real contributions. The time of wives, in this model, is directly and indirectly enlisted by their husbands and their employers (for example, typing manuscripts or hosting colleagues and business prospects). And wives' availability for housework and child care permits husbands to pursue their careers single-mindedly and respond unhindered to organizational demands that require unplanned late nights at the office or time away for business travel.

The institutional hegemony of this time-devouring linear career model is reinforced at a deeper symbolic and cultural level, where men imagine themselves conquering time heroically by rationalizing it, thereby transcending nature and repetition (often associated with female temporal rhythms of giving birth or caring for children and the home), and protecting themselves against vulnerability, limits, and even death. The rationalized view of time inherited from the Renaissance, which promised that those who knew how to exploit time would become "the master of all things," and which portrayed time as a strict father figure watching lest precious moments be wasted, or as an antagonist that men heroically battle, has embedded itself deeply into the male career model. Men in a variety of careers with excessive time demands often express a sense of heroic sacrifice and invulnerability, and even take pride in earning the "purple heart" in the face of professional and personal burnout. Some, like Seth Stein, a thirty-six-year-old litigation lawyer, interpret their addiction to work as a sacrifice to their families, even as they forfeit emotional bonds to their spouses and children in the process. Many men, to be sure, live up to the male career model only reluctantly, but even they are generally unwilling to express this reluctance publicly, lest they be considered unserious, even "wimps," by colleagues and employers. Bill Wallace, a thirty-six-year-old product manager in a high-tech firm, for instance, is aware that he is shortchanging his wife and ten-month-old son by working late nights and weekends, but says "it's just that the models of success in the company are people who do that." Bill and other reluctant men, however, asked that their real names not be published.[6]

This linear and time-devouring career model exercises hegemony insofar as it is accepted as defining the main legitimate route of access to high opportunity in the labor market, even by those who are unable (or unwilling) to live up to the terms it establishes, and who blame themselves for such failure, and insofar as those who reject the model have insufficient power to alter those terms. Paradoxically, the hegemony of this male model of structuring a career has been simultaneously reinforced and challenged by the recent democratization of access to jobs and education for women and others previously excluded. Greater access increases the competition for high-opportunity jobs, especially in the slack labor markets of the 1970s and 1980s, and thus, on the supply side, puts a greater premium on employees' utilizing steep levels of time commitment as a method of competing and signaling worthiness, and, on the demand side, strengthens the hand of employers to require such commitments. In this light, Lorraine Mecca's choice, and that of other reluctant women and men who buy into the model, becomes easier to understand. However, the greater numbers of women who pursue higher education and professional and managerial careers, or who are unwilling or unable to abandon the labor market completely to become full-time housewives and mothers, continue to challenge a career model requiring continuous and high levels of time commitment. And thus the agenda of the women's movement, as well as many women not formally aligned with feminist politics, includes at its center more flexible and diverse working time options and alternative rhythms for integrating work and family over the life course. As the baby-boomers give way to the baby-bust generation, and as labor shortages in the coming years make employers more dependent than ever on attracting and retaining professional and managerial women, the latter may have the opportunity to redefine the male model in a more profound way.

There are a variety of other factors as well that challenge rigid and linear forms of temporal organization. No longer, for instance, are education and work so strictly sequenced and separated. As a growing portion of youth go on to higher education, it becomes more common (especially for those from less privileged backgrounds) to combine education with paid work, and this is often facilitated by part-time and other flexible options. Industrial restructuring and technological change displace increasing numbers of people from their jobs and shorten the half-life of skills and credentials that once seemed as if they might serve for a lifetime of opportunity and security in the labor market. Skill renewal and retraining thus become increasingly necessary throughout the work career if the labor force is to adjust to change. The most optimal use of new technologies in postindustrial work settings requires opportunities for continuous learning, and often blurs the distinction between time working on the job and time learning off the job. Longer life spans make career changes in mid-life more feasible and often desirable, and many blue- and white-collar workers have come to view recurrent education and "second chances" as a right. For those in low-opportunity occupations, this can imply a "deferred right to education" and a rejection of the idea that failure to acquire appropriate training at the earliest possible stages of the life course should permanently disenfranchise the individual from further education and the opportunity it might bring. But even for those with some advanced schooling, recurrent education becomes an avenue to further mobility and career change. This is consonant with the more general value shifts that have occurred since the 1960s in virtually all industrial countries: a much greater stress on work as a source of self-realization, self-fulfillment, continued growth, and challenge, as well as for more individualized options and personal autonomy. The transition to adulthood has itself become more extended, diversified, and individualized over the past few decades, and psychology has become more oriented to personal development and human plasticity over the entire life span. Educational institutions have responded to these changes with a variety of adult education, "lifetime learning," and "flex degree" programs.

While the participation of women in the labor market has increased, thus challenging us to develop new ways of integrating paid work and family life, the total proportion of lifetime hours that the average male worker must spend at work has declined significantly since the industrial revolution. A male employee born in the mid–nineteenth century spent roughly 30 percent of his lifetime hours at work, while his grandson, born at the end of the century, spent 20 percent, and his grandson, in turn, born in the 1950s, will spend only 10 percent. These changes generate increasing opportunities and incentives for what Fred Best has called "flexible life planning," thus challenging temporally well defined and rigidly sequential stages in favor of more fluid, diverse, and reversible timing of major life activities.[7]

Similar developments are evident at the boundary between work and retirement. As life expectancy, and particularly healthy life expectancy, has steadily increased, more elders have become capable of continued work and resistant to forced retirement. Pensions and Social Security benefits are often inadequate, and inflation and economic uncertainty put a premium on maintaining links to paid work. Thus many people desire to continue working past official retirement ages, but prefer or require part-time or less than year-round jobs, or need retraining for jobs more suitable to their health status. Others respond to industrial restructuring by retiring early from their regular jobs. Retirement lifestyles continue to diversify, thus increasing the need to structure a new life-cycle period as a flexible and multi-option stage for older persons. As Malcolm Morrison has noted, this will require more flexible working time options and the right to phased and temporary retirement.[8]

Greater longevity among a growing proportion of eldery also increases needs for care giving, most of which are still served by female relatives outside of institutional settings. And as more women remain in the labor market, including those with elderly parents, flexible working time options become even more necessary to accommodate this. As Bernice Neugarten and Dail Neugarten have argued, "the old distinctions between life periods are blurring in today's society," and particularly as the boundary lines fade in the later years, our aging society is challenged with developing a *new definition of productivity and qualitative growth* that encompasses various kinds of volunteer, self-help, and caring work decoupled from the marketplace and paid labor time.[9] We are thus increasingly faced with the question of how to recognize and facilitate such work performed by the elderly themselves, and how to develop supports for their children and others who care for them when they cannot provide adequate care for each other. Can we find ways to help make Juanita Eubanks' choice to return care to her mother a less harried and morally rending one—and can we encourage her brother to likewise recognize such care as work worth doing and time worth giving? The male model of work is at issue as much here as it is in integrating child care with careers in the market.

The destandardization of working hours is also propelled by changes in technology and product markets. New information technologies lessen time and space constraints for production, communication and service.

Telecommuting increases the possibilities of work at home and blurs the boundary between the two. It can create problems for regulating working conditions for some, but also provide genuine opportunities for flexible work for others. More highly intensive capital investment and rapid upgrading of available technologies encourage employers to extend work into periods of the day and days of the week that were previously outside "normal" working hours in order to recoup investments more quickly. This can entail not only more shift work, but more innovative shift systems, part-time, and other flexible arrangements. And in the high-growth area of services, flexible and part-time schedules permit greater responsiveness to peak service times and the broadening of hours when service is available. New computer technologies also make it easier to process employee information, and thus reduce the costs and increase the benefits of hiring people on nonstandard schedules.

New technologies may also make the future of employment less certain, although little can be said definitively about the extent of technological unemployment in the coming decades. What can be said, however, is that the traditional response of labor movements to seek across-the-board reductions in the normal workweek has become increasingly problematic. Campaigns for workweek reductions in Europe in the 1970s and 1980s reveal this rather clearly. The thirty-five-hour or thirty-two-hour workweek may retain a certain symbolic value, especially among trade union leaders, but the individual life situations and preferences for work time among rank and file members have become highly diversified and pluralized, thus making a collective strategy based on across-the-board reductions quite problematic. Unemployment may continue to challenge the ways we distribute work and working time, but the models for redistributing these that we inherit from the past are no longer very compelling.[10]

We are also approaching ecological limits to quantitative growth models that have previously served to generate employment opportunities and to define the meanings of "the good life" in a consumer society. A pace of production, consumption, and disposal that exceeds nature's ability to recycle wastes and renew basic resources now appears profoundly problematic for the future of the planet. And the pace of social and economic life can also pose threats to our bodies and psyches directly. Modern industrial civilization has progressively separated human rhythms from those of nature, and the "nanosecond culture" of computer-based systems threatens to disjoin these even more radically.

Computer-related distress manifests itself in the temporal schizophrenia of many who move in and out of computer time. They become less tolerant of interruptions, less patient with those who cannot respond appropriately to the precision and speed of programs and fax machines, and less capable of slow reflection and genuine commemoration. We are bombarded with a quick succession of 15-second television commercials that attempt to define our needs, and political campaigns are increasingly determined by 30-second sound bites rather than extended discourse. As one Hollywood publicist has put it, "the fax has destroyed any sense of patience or grace that existed. People are so crazy now that they call to tell you that your fax line is busy." A variety of medical and psychological disorders are increasingly recognized as forms of "hurry sickness," often triggered by an exaggerated sense of urgency or time scarcity, and successful therapies, from biofeedback to meditation, aim to replace these with ways of experiencing time that are more focused on the present and less relentlessly flowing. The "time famine" of contemporary society, or what Barry Schwartz has called the "phobia of time waste and preoccupation with efficient scheduling," have become real concerns for broader sectors of the population, and increasingly call into question conceptions of the good life of affluence and achievement that are purchased by such an overriding sense of time scarcity.[11]

DILEMMAS OF TEMPORAL UTILIZATION

Part of the problem of the "time famine," as noted in a 1989 cover story in *Time* magazine, may be that Americans have been working more and playing less since the early 1970s. This is buttressed by Harris poll data showing that the average workweek has increased by 15 percent since 1973, and average leisure time has declined by 37 percent. But when all market and nonmarket working hours are considered (including housework, school, and commuting to work), Americans do not seem to have been working significantly longer hours over the past two decades. Some groups have clearly experienced a crunch, such as working women with children (and families with children generally), although, on average, women's increases in market labor (219 additional hours per year) have been almost completely offset by decreases in nonmarket labor (208 fewer hours per year).[12] The media attention to the experience of time scarcity, as Laura Leeta-Guy and Juliet Schor suggest, may be due to the life cycle experience of the baby-boom generation, which is now at that stage of life when work and family demands are greatest. And this may be compounded by the power and prominence of the professionals, managers, and self-employed business people among them, who have been increasing as a portion of the labor force, and whose working time demands are often the most difficult to contain.

But the problem of time scarcity and freedom over our time is more than a simple question of the quantity of hours we have available—or scheduled—for different activities. The very success of highly complex and productive societies leads to permanent quandaries about the scarcity of time and how we choose to organize it. The relative scarcity of time is a function not only of constraints but of the extent and variety of opportunities for spending our time. The clock and the schedule, which serve as means for rationalizing and calculating time, are thus not just *disciplinary* techniques, such as the bureaucratic employer uses over the worker, or the school over the student. They also can serve as *diversifying* techniques, enabling us to expand options and coordinate a broader range of choices. If we can count on the subway running on time, the day care center operating according to a predictable schedule, the published movie timetable being accurate, courses beginning and ending at specific hours, and friends and professional contacts who have internalized the discipline of the clock, we may be able to structure our day so that we can integrate a rich set of working, caring, cultural, and friendship activities. And if we also have a flexible working schedule—whose very flexibility often depends on ever more refined forms of calculability—our choices expand even further. But in the very process of expanding our choices, we experience a scarcity of time relative to the many things we could choose to do, and the schedules we must keep and the attention we must pay to the clock in order to do them.

As our options expand, in other words, the choice of how to time them itself becomes a greater burden, requiring greater time management skills to cope, and often making us feel as if we have even less time and less choice than we did before. Juanita Eubanks may have less time than her own mother did at a similar point in her life—or she may not, and nonetheless still feel the relative deprivation because she is now burdened by the choice of spending that caring time herself or institutionalizing her mother and feeling guilty, of giving up opportunity in the labor market that her own mother didn't have and feeling once again economically vulnerable, of negotiating with her brother and feeling exploited by the sexist assumptions of his behavior, which is no longer taken for granted, as it was a generation ago. Lorraine Mecca may not have less time for leisure than a full-time professional or business woman did a generation ago, especially if she has no children and hires housecleaning services. But the way opportunity has opened up for her now makes it appear that there can be no time for anything but business and that all other time must be calculated in terms of its profit yield and career payoff. And as she herself measures her career progress and her time against the traditional male model, other women who face more diverse options than they did in the past are haunted by the image of both Lorraine and her male counterparts: should they delay having children until their careers are well established? Should they work part-time while the children are young and risk being mommy-tracked because they appear less serious than Lorraine? Should they pursue a degree to improve their options when they do return to full-time work, and can they coordinate classes with child care schedules and part-time jobs? Should they struggle with their husbands to renegotiate the distribution of household and child care time and attention so that they are less disadvantaged at work and have more time to relax and take courses—or will such equity struggles simply increase their own psychic and temporal burdens?

As the options for working, building families, pursuing education, consuming culture, and enjoying leisure have become richer and more diverse, and as the life course has gradually become destandardized and more individualized over the past generation, the question of how we sequence our choices, ration our time, and distribute our efforts becomes ever more prominent. The condition of postmodernity, as Marlis Buchmann has noted, is one of proliferating action alternatives in a variety of spheres of life, which does not so much displace the autonomous self but makes its task of constructing a life through time and over time much more complex.[13] The baby-boom generation may be the focus of attention for today's time famine, not just because its cohorts are at that point in the life cycle when work and family demands are greatest but because they are the generation to have experienced the transition to less standardized life courses, more diverse options, more equitable gender values, and perhaps the greatest expectations for leisure, culture, and autonomy over their time than any generation before them. But it is not their experience alone that poses the challenge of how to develop coherent time policies for postindustrial America. Changes are occurring across a broad range of institutional spheres and affecting other generational cohorts as well. It is the experience of forty-eighty-year-old Juanita Eubanks and her eighty-one-year-old chronically ill mother that challenges us to develop alternative ways to sequence and distribute our paid work and unpaid caring time. It is the experience of George Jenkins, a displaced fifty-five-year-old steel worker who still has the health and skills for productive work, but will need to retrain; who, after fourteen months without a job, has begun to share housework more equally as his wife's income has become crucial; and who has come to appreciate spending time with his grandchildren in a way that he never had a chance to do with his own kids. It is the experience of Rodney James, a sixteen-year-old black boy who has dropped out of school "to help my mother out some" and get some experience "in the real world," but who expects to go on to college later on, though he can't say exactly when. It may even be the experience of Lorraine Mecca, who decides several years from now that her career is not that exciting after all, that her spiritual and civic life are too impoverished, or that she wishes to raise a family with someone she has fallen in love with. It is exactly these kinds of vicissitudes in contemporary life, often unanticipated, that lead women and men to revise the ways they think about distributing their time among different activities, altering their sequence, and revising the relative value they attach to them.[14]

THE POST–NEW DEAL POLITICS OF TIME

The question facing our society in the coming years is whether we can develop a coherent politics of time that progressively permits us to respond to these changes and opportunities in ways that enhance individual autonomy over the life course, that encourage diversity of choices and career patterns while enhancing gender equity, that value time for civic activity and caring work outside the marketplace, and that enable us to integrate our complex social lives with the rhythms of nature in a more ecologically balanced and less self-destructive fashion. If our political economy can be said to represent a moral economy of time that structures the way that we make and reflect on our commitments to each other, can we begin to rethink the temporal contours of our institutions and culture in a way that clarifies the moral implications of the options available? Some of our deepest values are at stake here: individual freedom and autonomy, diversity and equality, democracy and community, nurturance and stewardship of the earth. As Michael Young has recently argued, "a new approach to time could be the key to a new enlightenment."[15] The postindustrial and postmodern conditions we face would seem to require no less.

Some aspects of a new approach to time have begun to emerge over the past few decades, at least in outline form, and the challenge before us is whether we can progressively lend them coherence as both democratic vision and practical politics. Let us briefly consider what this might mean at several different levels: the workplace, the family, the state, and culture.

In the workplace, the elements of a new approach to time are manifest in the variety of innovative working time options that have emerged in the past two decades. These include job sharing between two people, voluntarily reduced hours that are adjusted periodically (often called V-time), flexitime programs that allow one to vary starting and quitting times and bank and borrow time across days and weeks, innovative shifts that provide larger blocks of time away from the job, part-time jobs where skill development and career progress remain available, temporary leaves for parenting and further education, and partial and reversible retirement policies. Job sharing, for instance, has proven workable in a great variety of settings, from the factory floor and secretarial office to professional, technical, and managerial positions. Consider the case of Donna Hellewell and Karen Whitehead, who share the senior personnel officer position in a bank. Like many other job sharers, they proposed this arrangement as a way to avoid burnout and to combine work and family without sacrificing career opportunities. The arrangement also allows them to benefit from each other's specific competence and insight. Many job sharers note the advantage of continual learning and cross-training that job sharing makes possible. One chemist, who wished to cut back her hours so that she could return to graduate school, worked out a sharing arrangement with another woman from the production floor, whom she trained as a technician—an arrangement that allowed both of them to upgrade their skills. Many people involved in job sharing have noted that it enables them to allocate their time better, and to reflect more carefully and critically on how they use that time, thus gaining a "renewed perspective" on their life and having "time to take a deep breath and know yourself again."

Joel Greifinger, a psychiatric social worker, has been on voluntary reduced work time for the past four years so that he could spend one and one-half days during the week with his young daughter. Along with other men and women on the negotiating team of their local of the Service Employees International Union, Greifinger has fought to strengthen the provisions permitting such flexible arrangements (including parental leave), with prorated pay, full benefit coverage, and the option to return to full-time work at a later date. Other SEIU locals have developed V-time programs as a way of responding to anticipated budget cuts and possible layoffs. Some male computer professionals have negotiated part-time and other flexible options so that they could be active in church activities or daily religious services or in local politics. With genuine options over time at the workplace, in other words, Lorraine Mecca's choice to forsake time for spirituality, civic involvement, family, and friends no longer appears so compelling and preordained.[16]

These and other options reveal great possibilities for organizing work time on a more autonomous basis, for better integrating work with family and other activities, and for enabling people to reflect more critically on their own moral economies of time in everyday life. Yet the question that must be resolved if these innovations are to yield their fullest potential is how to couple diversity with equity and democratic control. If this cannot be resolved, diverse options will tend to reinforce inequalities, especially between men and women, and to enhance the power of managers to schedule work in ways that disrupt their employees' lives and marginalize those who deviate from standard worktime and career models. For instance, the increasingly popular "mommy track" proposals for reduced and discontinuous working time, as put forth in the *Harvard Business Review* by Felice Schwartz, although intended to accommodate work and child care responsibilities for women, fail to challenge in clear and forthright fashion the gendered access and legitimacy of such options.[17] They are premised on distinguishing early those *women* who are career-primary (and hence deserve rapid access to opportunity) from those who will seek to combine career and family. We hear little about similar options being made available to men. Still privileged is the male model that presumes linear and continuous commitment and minimal contribution to housework and child care, rather than a career model genuinely premised on diversity and reversibility of choices. But if alternative options are to result in gender equity, Schwartz's critics have noted, they must be gender neutral, with the institutional and cultural supports within the workplace so that men are just as free as women to take advantage of them without unduly jeopardizing their future opportunities, and they must be premised on rights to reversibility rather than tracked predictability.

Furthermore, if equity is to be achieved along with increased autonomy over the management of time, employees must have some rights to participate in designing and overseeing work time options, whether this be through unions, professional associations, labor-management committees, or other means. More flexibility without more democracy at the workplace will simply leave many workers even more vulnerable to management control of their time and more liable to suffer lower wages and decreased benefits and career opportunities as a result of their deviation from standard temporal norms. They will remain deviants and second-class citizens at work, tracked and marginalized, as many women are today who try to combine less than full time work with family commitments.[18]

In addition to more diverse working time options provided on an equitable and democratic basis, the distribution of time between men and women within the household itself also must be open to renegotiation if systematic gender inequities are to be addressed. This is much easier to do when men no longer have the excuse that they simply can't arrange their working time and career trajectories differently, that is, when there are more gender-neutral working time options available. And it is much easier when comparable worth and other equity strategies decrease labor market segmentation and make women's pay and career opportunities more likely to be comparable to that of their husbands. The woman's bargaining power within the home is increased and the economic rationale underlying the (often automatic) choice to cut back on the wife's paid work rather than the husband's when child care and other responsibilities increase is removed. The capacity of such institutional changes in the workplace to trigger redistribution of time within the family should not be underestimated. But, as Arlie Hochschild and others have pointed out, the gender strategies of men who resist significant sharing of household work and real attention to the care of children and the temporal rhythms of children's development belie simple notions that gendered distributions of time within the home are simply rational accommodations to wage structures and time commitments in the labor market.[19] A new economy of time within the family would entail some profound changes in how men, in particular, value time for children. And it would require that men and women alike, especially those with greater opportunity in the labor market, reflect on how much they are willing to purchase child care and household services in the market as an alternative to spending the time on such tasks themselves.

It would be a great loss—indeed, the ultimate irony—if the revolution in gender roles results in ever greater invasion of the market and rational time calculation into the home, and if we cannot recover some of the time affluence here that we have otherwise lost. As anthropologist Peter Hammond has noted, "making an appointment is one way to relate to your child, but it's pretty dessicated. You've got to hang around with your kids." Yet hanging-around time and unstructured play time are often sacrificed to the complex schedule. "The very culture of children, of freedom and fantasy and kids teaching kids to play jacks, is collapsing under the weight of hectic family schedules."[20] Not all family life can be neatly parceled into "quality time" bundles. If we can gain greater autonomy over our working time and achieve greater gender equity at work and at home, should we not also be engaged in revaluing the daily rhythms of reproducing a household? Should we not also recognize that dusting our tsatskes can be a way of recovering our memories? And should we not be willing to take the time to teach these lessons to our children—and let them reteach us the rhythms of play?

Government can also perform an important role in shaping the contours of a democratic politics of time. Legislation can mandate *rights* to alternative working time options, as has already begun to happen for government workers at municipal, county, state, and federal levels across the country. The Federal Part-Time Career Employment Act of 1978, for instance, made reduced-time options available to all federal employees from GS-1 to GS-15, while guaranteeing their continued access to promotion opportunities, proportional salaries, and prorated benefits. And job sharing, voluntary reduced working time, and other options have been made available, often through collective bargaining, in many state and local government agencies. Part-time residency programs in hospitals receiving federal funds (as virtually all hospitals do) were also mandated by an act of Congress. And parental leave in private industry, as well, which would guarantee both parents rights to work leave upon the birth of a child *and* the right to return to the same or a comparable position upon return, is now on the agenda of Congress, as well as many states. Such legislated rights are common in Europe, where a further use of state policy for supporting innovative time policies is also evident, namely public funding for such leaves. In Sweden, for instance, both parents are entitled to a full leave of absence until a child is eighteen months old. Parents can work at 75 percent of normal working hours (for example, six-hour days) until the child is eight years old or has completed its first year of school. The parents can share between themselves, at their own discretion, up to 360 parental insurance benefit days (most of which are set at full salary). This coverage will probably be expanded in the near future so that it will finance up to a year or more of parental leave for each child a couple has. Flexible retirement policies also permit workers over fifty-eight years of age to reduce their hours to as few as seventeen and a half per week, with 65 percent compensation for the reduced hours, thus yielding a total after-tax income that is 80 to 90 percent of their full pay. Proposals for funding mid-life sabbaticals of one year are also being seriously debated, as are the much more radical proposals of the influential economist Gösta Rehn to rethink the entire social security system (including educational and parental leaves, retirement, and so forth) in terms of rights to reduce or discontinue working time and to withdraw accumulated funds throughout the entire life course.[21]

There exists, in short, a rich variety of innovative ways in which the state can facilitate greater personal control over time and encourage a moral economy of time responsive to peoples' nurturance and care needs and obligations outside the marketplace. Another option is the Service Credit Volunteer System, funded by government and foundation sources on an experimental basis in a number of states, which encourages voluntary service contributions among the elderly. Participants who help care for other elderly (for example, by shopping for them or helping with household repairs) can then draw upon time credits earned for care when they themselves need help. Such a system might relieve the burden of people like Juanita Eubanks, with her ailing mother, and help mend rather than rend the moral fabric that binds neighbors and friends in time of need.

Such approaches also avoid further bureaucratizing and professionalizing care giving functions. We can also imagine state support for the kinds of social service leaves developed by a few corporations, which fund time away from the job for employees to do drug and alcohol rehabilitation work, provide remedial education to inner-city youngsters, or, as in the case of one engineer, to develop the computer systems for a regional branch and then for the national Muscular Dystrophy Association offices. None of these programs is antithetical to good social services, and all, in fact, can be nicely complemented by them. Juanita Eubanks could benefit greatly from a home healthcare nurse who really takes the time to teach her about her mother's illness and the therapeutic techniques she might employ, just as she might benefit by a law that mandates employers to give leave time for the care of ill family members, or a social security system that compensates for lost wages if workers reduce their hours in order to care for infirm family members.

Rights to working time options, parental and educational leaves, retraining programs, flexible retirement policies, support for volunteer service outside the market—all of these are innovations the state can use to enhance individuals' control over their time. They also provide opportunities for more flexible life planning. All of these are ways in which we can help reinforce and reorient the moral foundations of our political economy of time and engender equity between men and women as well as reciprocity of care across the generations. Such policies are both an extension of and a break with the logic of welfare-state policies of the past.

On the one hand, government programs such as Social Security, unemployment insurance, and educational scholarship and loan programs have increased the capabilities of ever broader groups of people to *construct* and *revise* their occupational biographies and life plans more deliberately and with less vulnerability to the vicissitudes of the market and of human biology. The working-class youth who can delay entry into the labor market to seek further education, her parents who can plan their lives knowing that their own parents will receive Social Security and Medicare benefits as they age, and her grandparents who are able to retire before their health deteriorates without fear of being plunged into poverty or becoming an undue burden on their children, are all considerably freer to formulate life plans of their own than were the generations before them that lacked such institutional supports.

On the other hand, the extension of the state had, until recently, facilitated such security and predictability of life planning by institutionalizing and standardizing the life course—by establishing ages for mandatory school attendance and retirement, for example. Formal credentialing systems reinforced standard age-graded transitions from one status to another over the life course. Yet the other side of using formal and universal norms to govern life course transitions has been an ideology of democratic individualism, and under the impact of the changes described in the first part of this chapter, the very institutionalization of a more predictable life course has created the basis for more diverse and individualized plans and paths.[22] The progressive logic of this ideology goes something like this: if one has a right to seek an educational credential based on merit at age eighteen, why shouldn't one be able to do so, and with the same rights to scholarships and student loans, at age thirty-five? Or after one has raised children?

Innovative time policies further extend this logic of increasing diversity and plurality of choice over the life course. But instead of thinking of them piecemeal, each as a response to a specific issue (such as further education or child care, for example), we might now begin to think of them more coherently as a *politics of time* that can increase personal autonomy, enhance equity, revive civic participation, and facilitate care. We might begin to think of them as part of a democratic vision for organizing our time, as the elements of a postindustrial New Deal.

Institutional innovations such as these can facilitate new economies of time in our everyday lives, but not without complementary shifts in values and culture. This is perhaps clearest in the earlier discussion of child care activities, whose rhythms cannot always be synchronized with the clock, parceled into "quality time" bundles, or purchased with the dollar. If busy working parents are not able to find ways to revalue hanging-around time, they may manage to achieve greater gender equity and opportunity, but at the cost of rationalizing care and routinizing play—which would represent, we believe, an ironic form of cultural impoverishment.

The ways that we value time and invest it with meaning need to be as much a part of a political discourse on time as the ways in which we can institutionally restructure it. How might we revalue time for citizenship and participation in civic and political life, rather than capitulate to the logic that such time is simply too costly? How might we orient ourselves as well as our economic activities more toward the biological and physical clocks of nature, toward stewardship and greater harmony, rather than view our capacity to rationalize time as a form of conquest and domination, male heroism, and invulnerability? How might we begin to redefine affluence itself in terms of an abundance of time rather than of goods— time for friendship and kibbitzing, for play and nurturance, for prayer and meditation, for thinking and public discourse?

We have much to learn from preindustrial cultures that reject haste as a lack of decorum or as a sign of diabolical ambition, that have developed the fine arts of taking enough time and passing time without specific goals or the expensive input of goods, and that have developed rich techniques for "properly interpreting the day."[23] Each day is not the same, each minute is not reducible to the same measure.

And yet we can never recapture the temporal affluence of earlier times or completely harmonize our personal and social lives with those of nature. Our rationalizing techniques (clocks, schedules) and internal time disciplines have made it possible for us to engage in much more complex and diverse relationships in pluralist societies that are rich in possibilities for utilizing time. The old disciplines have served us poorly in some ways, no doubt, but they have also enhanced the richness of our lives in other ways that we are unlikely to want to give up. To establish time affluence, we would need new disciplines: the discipline to know when to "just say no" to more busyness, consumption, and "obituary-improving activity" (as Albert Hirschmann has called the source of much harriedness among the professional middle classes today).[24] We would need to learn how to manage our time in complex ways, even as we rediscover play or learn techniques, such as meditation and biofeedback, that expand our sense of time and permit us to step outside of clocks and schedules, of only temporarily. There is much in American cultural tradition, as well as in more recent countercultural and New Age movements, that provides a basis for reinvesting time with new meanings and new forms.[25]

For those whose "time poverty" is determined by their economic poverty, of course, there can be no substitute for jobs with good pay, entitlement to vacations, and freedom from the myriad social welfare bureaucracies whose schedules and queues are imposed on dependent clients. But those who are free from these kinds of constraints can only regain some forms of time affluence by achieving greater autonomy over their time. The time affluence of preindustrial cultures was, in many ways, imposed by the relative poverty and limited diversity of life opportunities. The time affluence of postindustrial and postmodern societies can only be achieved by expanding options, which entails—paradoxically—enhancing our capacities to manage our time in complex and rationalized ways, even as we revalue the nonrational. There is an irreducible dialectical tension here, to be sure, but hardly a vicious circle that traps us in ever greater time scarcity.

If we can legitimate a broad range of choice over how we organize our time, we can open up to much greater individual, interpersonal, and public reflection on the values that underlie the choices that we make. The self-management of time, which is entailed by some of the institutional innovations outlined earlier, can become the basis for a self-conscious moral pedagogy about the ways in which we choose—or refuse and excuse—to apportion our time. Many people who opt for working time alternatives express their reasons in just such moral terms. Self-managing our time might thus become a process of permanent moral education about the value we place on the different kinds of time that we can spend together—as producers and consumers of goods and culture, as citizens of communities and members of churches, as friends and family who nurture each other over the life course. The self-management of time, in short, might serve as the basis for an integrative process of critical reflection and public discourse about the kind of people we wish to become and the kind of society we choose to sustain.

TWENTY-ONE

Contentless Consensus
The Political Discourse of a Segmented Society

Richard Madsen

Flo Harris, like so many Americans these days, is outraged because so many people in her community seem unconcerned about the public interest. Her ire is focused especially on the local businessmen in her community—retailers, real estate agents, and building contractors—whom she sees as working to turn her semirural surroundings into a dense conglomeration of housing tracts. They are doing this in the name of exercising their "property rights." As Flo describes it, "To them it's their sacred right under the Constitution to be able to do whatever they want with their property. Property is a very important right. But it shouldn't just be the only thing." People should be able to use their property to make a reasonable profit for themselves, but they should not do so at the expense of the quality of life that makes their community a good community. "Human greed," says Flo, "is limitless," and because of this, she believes that it is important for people to "get together and organize for their rights," and in the process to establish "the regulations, the government protections, that enable people to get together in an orderly way." Those who proclaim their "property rights" in order to justify the destruction of the peace and quiet, the clean air, and the beautiful scenery of her community represent the private interests of people who value only money rather than the public interests of people who "value the American Dream—government *of* the people."[1]

Gloria Harper, who lives just a few miles away from Flo, sees the situation very differently, however. She sees Flo Harris as the leader of a group of selfish environmentalists who don't care about the over-all good of the community. "They're anti-business. They're anti-this, anti-that, anti, anti. I think it's because of megalomania, myself." Gloria sees Flo Harris and her associates as destroying the homogeneity of the community. "What I would like to see in this community is a homogeneous community—people not taking potshots at each other anymore. Like Flo Harris—if someone takes a position on property rights that she doesn't agree with, she doesn't accept that. It's just from the realtors and developers, she says. She won't compromise. I'm getting disgusted at all this. There's such a rift in our community. A rift so deep that it will never be healed." Gloria firmly believes that she is working "for the greater public good. What I'm doing is very noble for me." "I do what I do," she says, "because somebody's got to look out for individual rights. Our rights have been eroded away—especially the right to own property. It's a right given to us under the Constitution and I don't think the framers of the Constitution would be happy at all if they saw what was taking place today."

Such charges and countercharges are common at all levels of American politics. Whether cast about, as in this case, at the local level over concrete issues, like land development, or beamed across the airwaves in the rhetoric of the opposing candidates of our national political parties, American political discourse oscillates continually between the claim that one's own side represents the public good and one's opponent's side the private interests of the selfish and greedy. What is remarkable, however, is the *ease* with which either side in our public debates can claim that it represents the public interest and its opponents, private interests. If the same words can so easily be used to express the claims of fundamentally opposite positions, is not the language of American politics so flexible as to be almost formless? And if our basic vocabulary of politics is so immune to any kind of firm definition, is not moral argument in politics ultimately meaningless? Are not the key terms used to construct statements of moral principles in politics—terms like "public interest" and "individual rights"—simply building blocks for ideology in the crudest sense, simply a mask for particular kinds of self-interest? Is the moral vacuousness of our political language simply a sign that, as Alasdair MacIntyre has put it, politics is merely "civil war carried on by other means"?[2]

Flo Harris and Gloria Harper certainly would not see it that way. Like most Americans arguing about political issues, not only citizens at the grass-roots level but also politicians on the national scene, they couch their arguments in resonant moral terms and seem to sincerely convince themselves, if not their opponents, that they are standing up for principles that are noble and intrinsically good. It is simply not acceptable for American politicians to admit that they are standing up only for their own self-interests or even for the special interests of the group or class to which they belong. Foreign observers of America are often bemused by this constant recourse to moral principle.[3] Why then do Americans find it so natural to use such lofty moral language in their political discourse, and why does it seem so easy for them to convince themselves that they are standing for the public interest, even when their version of the public interest corresponds so obviously to their own self-interests?

In an attempt to answer such questions, I wish to explore the different meanings that such key terms as "individual rights" and "the public good" have in the language of grass-roots political activists like Flo Harris and Gloria Harper, and to examine the social processes that give birth to those meanings.

When people like Flo and Gloria talk about such matters as individual rights and the public good, they are not engaging in abstract academic discussions (neither of them has, in fact, completed college). But they are giving voice to particular concerns arising out of the specific communities in which they live their lives. The first step toward understanding what they are saying is to describe those communities.

A CONTESTED PARADISE

There is both an objective and a subjective dimension to those communities. Objectively, they are defined by the particular geography and demography of the place where Flo and Gloria live. That suburban area fits many of the popular, idyllic images of Southern California. Rocky, chaparral-covered hills roll toward magnificent sandstone cliffs overlooking the Pacific Ocean. The climate is beneficent, with sea-breeze cooled summers and mild winters. Stately palm trees, shaggy eucalyptus, and masses of brilliantly colored flowers line the streets and gardens of the suburb's ninety-eight square miles. The area has been called the "Flower Capital of the United States" because it is the location of the largest fields of commercially grown flowers in the country.

The place fits many of the popular negative images of Southern California as well. In 1970, no more than 26,000 people lived in the area; by 1984, there were 55,000 residents, with projected increases of about 1800 a year. Once-empty hillsides are now paved with concrete and crisscrossed with tract homes. Beaches that were once almost deserted are now jammed with swimmers, surfers, and sunbathers. Traffic jams have begun to clog the freeways during rush hours, and air pollution is becoming a problem. Still, the area is not yet as heavily developed or as crowded and polluted as the suburbs immediately around Los Angeles. The worry of community activists like Flo Harris, however, is that if development continues at its present pace the area will become "like another Los Angeles"—the ultimate disaster in their view.

Together with the influx of population has come an explosion in property values. Houses that sold for $30,000 in 1970 are worth over $300,000 today. This extraordinary inflation has made the area into a kind of sociological fault line: socioeconomic strata no longer lie neatly on top of one another, but are jumbled together in intricate patterns. Blue-collar workers and small shopkeepers who bought houses in the area two decades ago sometimes live side by side with successful professionals and corporate executives who have only recently bought their way into the California Dream. This jumble of socioeconomic strata has been the locus for the different moral commitments that have defined the subjective dimensions of the communities within which Flo Harris and Gloria Harper live their lives.

Gloria Harper's closest commitments are to people who consider themselves to be old-time residents of the area where she lives. In this part of Southern California, however, an "old-time resident" is not necessarily someone whose family has lived in the locality for generations. To have lived in the area for more than thirty years—since before the recent building boom—qualifies one as an old-time resident.

Gloria, who came as a young child with her mother several years after World War II, has in fact a longer history in the area than most of those who consider themselves "old timers." Married in the mid-1960s, she was occupied pretty much as a housewife until 1975, when there came a turning point in her life. It was then that her mother got a notice from the county advising her of a new land-use plan that would affect the disposition of the one-acre parcel of property in back of her house. Until then the land had been zoned for dense housing, over thirteen dwellings per acre; but the new rules would only three dwellings per acre. Gloria and her mother were outraged. "People like my mother, who weren't planning for the immediate future to put up any sort of house anyway, were now going to be discriminated against. . . . Now if [my mother] had got the idea of putting up a kind of duplex or other buildings on her property—this was not going to be possible. People who had put these things up before had already had them up and would have made their profit. This was totally unfair. I was really furious."

Gloria began to attend county planning committee meetings and to testify that the new zoning regulations were grossly unfair to old people who had lived on their land for years and hadn't gotten around to subdividing their property and building on it. In the ten years since then, she has become one of the most active members in her community in local politics, constantly pushing a "simple position": "Individuals have rights, rights to their private property. These rights are given to them by the Constitution and these rights are being infringed upon."

It is tempting to argue that Gloria's passionate defense of "property rights" is simply what Bennett Berger has termed "ideological work," that is, a rationalization for her economic self-interests.[4] But Gloria's ideological commitments seem more complicated than that. Her rhetoric does indeed conveniently legitimize her mother's desire to make a profit from her surplus landholding, and it also legitimizes the real estate business that her husband operates as a sideline to his primary occupation as an engineer. Yet even some of Gloria's allies in the local "property rights" movement acknowledge that her ideological commitment is more than just a rationalization of her interests in assuring the profitability of her family's property. As one local businessman allied with Gloria put it, "She represents a point of view that drives her. She's a very bright person, but I don't know what the hell motivates her." This man, who has extensive economic interests that would be harmed by local restrictions on land development, was in effect admitting that much of his ideological stance was a rationalization for his economic interests; but Gloria, he thought, did not have enough such interests to explain her level of commitment to property rights. What, then, motivated her? Something less than commitment to an abstract principle, but something more than merely an economic interest. Gloria seems driven by an interest in affirming the goodness of a particular kind of community life. She speaks a great deal about following the example of her mother, who since her arrival in the 1940s put an enormous amount of effort into making the area into a "real neat community," especially through serving on boards that improved the roads and established the water delivery and sewage systems for the area. The investment of such an amount of work in the community makes her mother entitled, Gloria believes, to the modest economic rewards that could have come from selling her piece of property for a profit. Gloria sees herself as following in her mother's footsteps, working hard for the community in the expectation of getting something back. When laws get passed denying the opportunity for such hard work to reap rewards, an injustice has been done. The validity of finding self-fulfillment through a certain kind of participation in the community has been undercut. It is this way of enhancing the self through a particular kind of participation in community that Gloria is interested in defending.

Economic interests are of course part of this more general interest in maintaining a certain form of community life, but in Gloria's case, they seem to be only a relatively small part, smaller certainly than that of most of the more prosperous businessmen who make up the backbone of the property rights movement in Gloria's area. Yet, if one listens carefully to such local businessmen, one finds that even for them, their property rights ideology is based on more than economic interests. Take for example the story of Frank Stansky, a local entrepreneur who has been one of Gloria's allies.

Like Gloria and most of the other members of the property rights group, Frank came to the area soon after World War II. He came as a teenager, with his parents. Eventually, he took up the trade of electrician, and in the sixties, joined up with his brother to form a small construction company. But by the early seventies, as he recalls, "all the fun had gone out of building. There were too many regulations." This was the result of an influx of "new people and new ideas." "The attitude of these new people toward building was 'Stop that building!'" Frank was initially ambivalent about the efforts of the newcomers to slow down the pace of development. "I was against tract development myself. Tracts came in and then left, using up the sewer capacity, and so forth. So I was sympathetic with the people who wanted to stop big development. But it became apparent that the people couldn't stop the big developers without stopping the small developers, too. I realized this around 1972. I made a phone call to the county telling them I wanted to do a lot split. And the person asked me on the phone, 'Are you a developer?' I said, 'Well, I guess so.' I hadn't thought of myself as a developer before. But according to their logic I was a developer and I had to be restricted like the other developers from doing lot splits and so forth."

The threat confronting Frank and Gloria because of the new restrictions on housing development advocated by the newcomers to the area was not merely economic; it was a threat to a whole way of achieving meaning in life through commitments to a particular kind of community. This comes across very clearly and poignantly in Frank's story of the consequences of the new land use regulations for him. "It used to cost you thirty-five dollars to do a lot split and you could do it in thirty days. Then things began to get so bad that it could cost you a thousand dollars and take a year and you might never be able to get it done." As a result of the costs of these new regulations, Frank was forced out of business. One of the net results of the slowdown of growth in the area, however, was that the value of land skyrocketed, and Frank, who had bought a number of parcels of land with a view to developing them, "got rich because of it."

Frank has indeed reached a comfortable level of middle-class prosperity. He drives a large new car and lives in a spacious home in an expensive part of the suburb. He is far better off than his father (who worked as a policeman on skid row in Seattle) was at his age. "So," as he puts it, "I should be the last to complain. If it was simply a matter of making money, I wouldn't have anything to complain about at all." But money, and the things that money can buy, are not, he thinks, satisfactory ends in themselves. Money is valuable as a sign of, and a reward for, work well done. "A year ago," Frank said, "somebody called me an activist. I thought that was funny. I thought activist was a bad word. But maybe that's what I am now—a *working* activist. The other activists [on the other side] aren't working activists. A lot of them are women or students or professors. They are people who have plenty of time and can go to meetings and organize things and keep people like myself, who are working people, from having our voice heard."

By what logic can Frank refuse to recognize that the energetic efforts that students or professors or housewives put into lobbying for protection of the local environment constitute a kind of work? Real work, he assumes, is the investment of one's time and resources into the economic development of the community. People who do real work produce things, like houses, that other people in the community would want to buy, and in the process of doing so, they create jobs for others. His opponents, he says, "treat money as something to be stored." They treat money this way, he believes, because of stinginess, a basic defect in their moral character. To confirm his judgment, he points to their attitude toward local charities. "In the Kiwanis Club we had a project to help repair the high school stadium stands. I got on the phone and called people throughout the community to help donate some money for this. But the people on the other side . . . didn't want to do anything about it, wouldn't donate."

Frank thus sees himself as a generous man, whose generosity is exercised primarily in the work of investing capital and effort into the improvement of the community, even though this work is obviously done for profit. He would probably have enthusiastically approved of the assertion of George Gilder, the social theoretician highly favored by the Reagan White House, that such capitalist investment is really a kind of altruism: "Capitalist production entails faith—in one's neighbors, in one's society, and in the compensatory logic of the cosmos. Search and you shall find, give and you shall be given unto, supply creates its own demand."[5]

In Frank's view, the essentially altruistic nature of his work as a local businessman has been supplemented and verified by his contributions to local charity through such "service clubs" as the Kiwanis: "In high school, I was influenced by an old physics teacher I had, Mr. Smith. He felt that you should give 10 percent of your earnings back to the community. He told us that in class one day. That stuck with me. It's important."

From Frank's point of view, he has been unjustly harmed by his opponents, not because they have made him lose money—they haven't—but because they have made his money lose meaning. They have diminished his ability to see himself as earning money in exchange for investing his land, labor, and capital in construction work for the good of the community. They are doing this because they are selfish; and in being selfish, they have ironically lost themselves, because they have given up their individuality. There was a time, Frank says, when "individuality was a big concept." But his opponents don't act as individuals. "They all work together, have the same party line. They are a special interest group." And what they want is "a type of socialism." "There are principles involved here," says Frank, "the principle of freedom—the basic commodity that we have in this country."

I interviewed in depth (three to ten hours apiece) eight other people in Southern California who were allied with Frank Stansky and Gloria Harper. They all spoke in similar terms of individual freedom, capitalist enterprise as an investment in the development of the community, and personalized charity as a sign that their commitment to the community was genuine. And they all criticized their opponents in similar terms, as selfish elitists who formed special interest groups and were willing to give up their freedom for the sake of a kind of socialism. A dozen other small businessmen whom I interviewed in a suburb of Boston also spoke in much the same way.

Their opponents, the advocates of "slow growth," like Flo Harris, speak a very different kind of moral language rooted in a different subjectively experienced community. Theirs is a community formed not through investing in the economic and commercial development of an area, but through commitments to building a home for their families in cooperation with like-minded neighbors. Most of the active slow-growth advocates came to the area around the same time, in the early 1970s, to escape the congestion of cities. When asked why they came, they typically reply that they did it for the sake of their children: they wanted a good, decent, quiet, peaceful place for their children to grow up in, and they couldn't find this in the city.

The life of Flo Harris is a very good example of this quest to establish roots in a community through building a home for one's family. She and her husband came to the area with their teenage children around 1970 after her husband had retired from an inner-city police department. After living for a while in a house trailer, they bought some land and began building their present house. They did much of the construction themselves. Their house is a large, rambling structure with an expansive living room that looks out through huge picture windows onto a beautiful mountainous vista. In the back of the house there is a pen for a goat and a corral for several horses. Flo and her family have poured years of their life into the construction of that dwelling to make it a home that now embodies much of the history of sacrifice and joy and hope that ties their family together. Many of their closest allies in the slow-growth movement have also built their houses with their own hands, expanding and improving their dwellings over countless evenings and weekends in projects often taking up to a decade of hard work. And many of those who did not do the actual construction themselves nevertheless played a large part in designing the houses to their own specifications.

These homebuilders come from a wide variety of social backgrounds.

Some, like Flo and her family, are from blue-collar or low-status white-collar occupations—policemen, electricians, school teachers. Others are professionals—architects, engineers, university professors. Their political affiliations range from far right (one family allied with Flo belongs to the John Birch Society) to moderate Republican (which is what Flo would consider herself to be) to left-liberal (typically, the professionals fit this category) to "New Age" anarchists (like several artists associated with the slow-growth movement). What brings them together is not only their sharing of similar individual experiences—the experience of making a home through one's own arduous effort—but also their sharing of ten years or so of common effort in encouraging one another in their home-building and in protecting one another's projects from forces that would destroy them.

The main force that would destroy their projects is the dynamics of the free market. In the 1970s, as they were building their homes, the market value of real estate in Southern California skyrocketed, leading to massive investments by large development companies. As this happened, the houses of people like Flo Harris have appreciated enormously in monetary value, but have started to lose those less tangible qualities that made them ideal homes for their residents. It is not simply a matter of quiet roads being turned into noisy thoroughfares or fresh air becoming contaminated by smog. Even more important to Flo and her friends is the destruction of the social environment that they sought in the area. The kind of family that would move to a sparsely inhabited area and spend years constructing a house with their own hands feels threatened by the influx of the kind of people who can afford the new tract houses—affluent young professionals who speculate in real estate or live as sojourners in heavily mortgaged dwellings as they contemplate another move up and away on the ladder of corporate success. As Tom Sutherland, one of Flo's close supporters, put it: "What's important to us is the sky, the quiet, and the space. It makes for a particular type of personality—calm, slow paced. But there's this new type of personality moving in—go, go, go, nervous personality, fast, fast paced."

Thus Flo and her fellow homebuilders slowly came to realize that their individual efforts to create decent homes for their families could only be realized if they worked together politically. They did this by forming "town councils" composed of different kinds of fellow citizens who shared their common predicament. In the town councils they discussed what would be done to maintain the integrity of their homes and the wholesomeness of the physical and social environment in which their homes were located. Some of them learned the arcane language of government planning documents. Some of them fought back almost overwhelming feelings of shyness to make speeches at public hearings. Most sacrificed hundreds of hours of free time to attend public hearings on growth plans for the area and to draft letters petitioning their elected officials to slow down local growth. A few, like Flo Harris, even ran for election to local government planning boards, school boards, and land and water use boards. And as time went on, they sponsored festivals and picnics and parties to share the joys and sorrows of their victories and defeats and to celebrate their sense of community.

They were not, of course, all of one mind. They disagreed with one another on many issues not connected with their concern for slow economic growth. Some, for example, zealously espoused traditional family values were antihomosexual, "pro-life," and so forth. Others were liberally tolerant of "alternative life-styles." But they usually managed to keep such differences of opinion out of their common political discussions, relegating them to the realm of private life. They also had differing opinions about the extent to which different forms of economic growth should take place, the degree of compromise that was possible with their opponents, the kinds of land use regulations that should be enforced. These issues were debated in their gatherings, sometimes acrimoniously; but participants in the process tended to view these debates optimistically, as a natural part of a highly valued democratic process—citizens arguing, on the whole civilly, with fellow citizens over common concerns for the public good. Through their public debates, they were, as Flo Harris put it, pursuing "the American Dream—government of the people. It's a dream. A lot of it isn't true. But . . . you *can* make it work."

The chief obstacle to making it work was, again in Flo's words, the power of money. "Money is such a powerful force nowadays that if people don't value things other than money, then money is the only thing that anybody cares about, and then you can buy politicians—you can buy politics. So people who really want to help their community have to value the American Dream, can't just value money." To be a true citizen of a good community, one had to shape one's social world through face-to-face discussion and debate rather than through investments of cash in an impersonal market.

"Property rights" advocates like Gloria Harper and Frank Stansky claim that the ideology of Flo and her allies in the slow-growth movement is simply a mask for selfishness. One member of the property rights movement speaks of people like Flo as being like people "who had gotten into a lifeboat and then wanted to pull up the ladder so no one else could get in." Flo would counter that she is dedicating an enormous amount of energy to preserving something greater than herself, a community that is a "gem, the last vestige of rural community," a place where "people have lived all their lives, where they knew each other, where they have animals, where there are buildings that had meaning because they had lasted so long and so many things had been associated with them." Her opponents say that people like her are advocating socialism. Flo, a registered Republican, says that she is simply trying to preserve government by the people. "I will try to keep going in this work as long as I see it as being of some use. As long as I see people getting involved in committees . . . and becoming interested in making some headway in improving the community. That's all there is left, you know. If you don't have people like this you don't have a government of the people. It's hard to get people involved. People don't want to get involved in local politics. Because it's dirty and scummy, people don't want to get involved. But if you leave it to [the businessmen advocating property rights] they will take the whole pie. The people have to get involved, have to be encouraged not to become apathetic."

Flo's words are an eloquent expression of the bonds of solidarity that bind together a group of self-sufficient families into a community of friends who cooperate together to preserve and enhance the quality of the homes they have built for themselves. But such words make no sense to people who consider themselves to be part of a community primarily based on exchanges of investment and profit among independent producers and consumers. In the Southern California suburb where Flo and Gloria live, the opponents in local land use disputes subjectively belong to different communities, while objectively sharing the same living space. This is what gives their moral language its peculiar ambiguity. When they talk about doing things for the good of *the* community, they are talking both about the objective social space that they share and about the moral commitments that constitute their different subjectively experienced communities. What to people who consider themselves to belong to one community appears to be a spacious rationalization for self-interest and even a denial of the basic values on which this country is based is felt by people who consider themselves to belong to the other community to be a genuine expression of moral commitment and a reaffirmation of the basic principles of the American tradition.

To understand the controversies about the balance between "individual rights" and the "public good" that Flo and Gloria and their respective allies are engaged in, we must, then, further consider the different ways they give meaning to the term "community."

"COMMUNITY" AS A CONTESTABLE MORAL NOTION

"Community," says Marra James, an environmental activist allied with Flo Harris, "is a very special word. It means people interacting and working together. Many people feel empty and don't know why they feel empty. The reason is we are all social animals and we must live and interact and work together in community to become fulfilled." Most of the political activists I interviewed, on both sides of the land use controversies in Southern California, would have agreed with her statement, which not only expresses the general moral aspirations carried by the idea of community but also illustrates the difficulties of specifying the implications of those aspirations in practice.

First of all, in the everyday speech of those I interviewed, community was a kind of "very special word" that always meant something good. When people want to denigrate some group, they do not call it a community, they call it a clique or a special interest group or a crowd or perhaps (but in America not often) a class. Or they just talk of it as an agglomeration of people who belong to a particular type. For instance, those of my interviewees who thought that homosexuality was a moral abomination never spoke of the "gay community"—that would dignify homosexuals too much—but only of "homosexuals" or "perverts." To speak of a group as a community is to imply that its members are brought together by some genuine, if imperfectly realized, moral aspirations. To be a member of a community means to fulfill the social dimensions of one's humanity through interaction with others. Belonging to a community does not, though, entail the sacrifice of one's self for the good of the group. Some of those I talked with spoke of their opponents as having made such an oblation. Gloria Harper, for example, said of one of the slow-growth advocates, "whenever she stands up, she represents another organization. She represents this group, that group, and so on, and so on. At first I couldn't figure out how that could be possible, what motivated that woman, where she was coming from. But then one day my husband . . . told me. That sort of thing comes right from the little book of Mao—the communist cell system." If one submerges one's personality in a group, then that makes one part of an un-American activity. In a true community, one retains one's individuality even as one fulfills it through generous interaction with others.

Yet to be a member of a community means that one has made an effort to overcome one's selfishness. To be greedy is to deny one's responsibilities toward community. All of those whom I interviewed agreed that individuals who pursued self-interest or personal ego gratification at the expense of community responsibilities would not only be morally reprehensible, but also lonely and empty. Thus Gloria Harper criticizes her opponents for "megalomania" and accuses them of "being unwilling to care at all for the over-all good of the community," and of trying to block anything that is "against their own immediate interests." And she insists that one of the primary qualifications for doing the kind of work she does is to have "a *true* concern for your community." Similarly, Flo Harris insists that she is working so hard as a local activist because she cares for her community and wants to enhance the quality of her community, all the while accusing her opponents of acting for selfish interests.

Thus when Americans talk in ordinary language about community, they name an experience through which the self achieves its ultimate interests, finds its ultimate fulfillment through combatting selfishness, overcoming solipsism, and entering into respectful interaction with others. The way they talk assumes that a genuine commitment to community always involves a balance between the interests of the individual and the interests of social groups, so that to be legitimately a member of a community an individual must resist the twin temptations of submerging oneself in the group and of denying one's responsibilities toward the group.

Yet when one moves down from this level of generality, it is very difficult to give the term "community" any specific content. What are legitimate self-interests and how are they to be balanced with responsibilities toward the community? When has one given up one's individuality by submerging oneself in the group? When has one indulged one's selfishness by denying one's responsibilities toward others? Different people develop different answers to such questions. These answers are not totally arbitrary, however. They depend on what individuals affirm to be the primary terms of relationship linking themselves with communities. Thus Gloria Harper and the other property rights activists I interviewed saw the basis of their relationship to their community to be their willingness to invest time, energy, and capital into the area where they live in such a way that it would benefit not only themselves but, ultimately, all of those in the area who enter into economic relations with them. As they see it, they can be considered genuinely community-minded, despite their pursuit of profit, because their pursuit of profit is balanced by a genuine care for the community (expressed through doing work on the community's behalf that is not directly remunerated) and because they are committed to refrain from pursuing their short-term profit in such a way as to harm their community. Flo Harris and her fellow slow-growth advocates see the basis of their relationship to their community to be the devotion of time and energy to supporting one another in the preservation of the kind of living environment that they individually desire. The kind of energetic, entrepreneurial effort that is defined by the business community as hard work, deserving of a financial reward, is defined by the home builders as greed for profit. The kind of passionate activism that is defined by the home builders as an admirable defense of the quality of the environment is seen by the business community as a selfish obstruction of economic growth.

Yet, although definitions of the terms of relationship between the self and community are subjective and particular, they are couched in objective, universal terms. Gloria Harper criticizes Flo Harris and her associates for disrupting the harmony of *the* community; Flo criticizes Gloria and her associates for destroying *the* community out of greed for money. Opponents in local political debates consider everyone in their area to belong to one community, even though one side believes that the other side fails to live up to its responsibilities to the community. Why do they think that?

The answer takes us to the central myth upon which American culture is founded, the myth that society is ultimately the product of autonomously choosing individuals. If this is so, then communities that are not formed as the result of such voluntary consent are not legitimate. If one lives one's intellectual, emotional, and moral life under the spell of this myth, then it will not seem paradoxical that political opponents like Gloria Harper and Flo Harris each proclaim a relativistic morality with universal intentions. They each stand up for a type of morality that sees the individual's true self-interest being fulfilled only through commitment to a community. They each proclaim that individual rights have to be understood in the context of corresponding responsibilities to community. But like the religious believer in the Protestant tradition—who in theory decides on his or her own, without the mediation of a church, to make an act of faith in God, and only then enters into a fellowship with other believers who have independently made the same faith commitment—the American political activist thinks of him- or herself as deciding on his or her own what it means to balance the interests of the self with commitment to community, and then enters into communal relationships with others on those individually chosen terms.

And just as the Protestant believes that the God he or she has found through faith is the one true God, so does the American who has made a moral commitment to community believe that his or her community is the only legitimate community that a right thinking, independent person could want to belong to. Herve Varenne has elegantly analyzed this American cultural imperative to affirm the universal validity of the community one happens to belong to:

> When I was invited to a party of John's group, I was often told that "everybody" had been invited. This could mean all the members of the core group or all the members of the larger group. The word was used by many people on different occasions to refer to the same sort of very small unit. Its use was particularly striking in the context of discussions of ideological questions. . . . Any position had to be legitimized by reference to the fact that "everybody" held it to be valid, not only the actual group in which the position was uttered but any intelligent, sincere person. . . . And in cases where it was known that only a minority accepted the idea or the form of

behavior—drug taking, for example—the argument easily became that "everybody" would accept it "if they knew what it is really about.". . .
. . .

At the most microlevels, to refer to half a dozen people as "everybody" or as representing everybody, mediates the group in its aloneness with the rest of society by denying the relevance, if not the existence, of alternatives: outside of everybody there is nobody.[6]

When the opponents in the land use debates that I have described in this chapter condemn each other for representing greedy private interest, they are each making universal certain moral standards that make sense only in the context of the particular commitments that they have chosen as the basis of their own lives in the community. By making such particular standards universal, they are in effect intending to include within their own subjectively conceived community all those who objectively live within a certain physical area. And those neighbors who do not identify themselves with that particular conception of community are then criticized for failure to care about the public good that "everybody" is presumed to participate in. Thus each subjectively conceived community constitutes its own way of redeeming self-interest by active concern for others; the ways are incompatible; but members of each community see their way as the only way, the way for everybody. Their arguments about morality follow the same logical form: it is a corollary to the American myth that morally legitimate communities are the sum of the autonomous individuals who have freely chosen to be part of them. The content of their arguments is different, however, and comes from the obscure, unchosen social facts that the American myth of voluntarism denies.

Those obscure, unchosen facts are, of course, the realities that the social scientist tries to study: the weight of peer-group pressure, the opportunity structure of the market, the pressure of subconscious psychological urges. The American language of moral choice, rooted in the myth that we are a people who realize our sociability only in the process of "making something of ourselves," is not able to account for these intractible social facts. A psychologist might argue with some plausibility that Gloria Harper's passionate defense of property rights is driven by her emotional closeness to her mother, which makes her extraordinarily sensitive to any land use regulations that would harm her mother's interests. But it is important for Gloria that she be regarded as acting out of her own personal conviction, not simply fulfilling her mother's hopes. She is against slow-growth, as she sees it, not simply because it is contrary to her mother's interests, but because it violates a universal principle, it is against the interests of all good people everywhere. A sociologist might argue with some plausibility that Gloria got involved with her present community of freinds and allies because they were the group whose economic interests most fully corresonded with her own. But Gloria would argue that she chose to associate with them because they stood for all that was good and decent about the American way of free enterprise. Similarly, a political scientist might argue with some plausibility that Flo Harris is involved in the slow-growth movement because, given her economic resources, that movement offers her the best hope for maximizing the value of her property. But she would argue that she is simply standing up for that is good and wholesome about "the American Dream—government *of* the people."

One cannot argue that, when they make their moral statements, Flo and Gloria and their allies bracket the sociological, economic, and psychological factors behind their professions of universal principle simply because they lack a formal higher education or are unsophisticated. Even were one to assume (in my view, falsely) that they lack sophistication, one would still have to account for the fact that sophisticated politicians, who are, presumably, aware of many of the explanations proffered by various social scientists for their political commitments, often bracket such explanations when as politicians they make statements of moral principle. Such considerations are simply not relevant in American moral-political discourse.

They are relevant, of course, in societies like rural China, where one can consciously take a moral stand not because it is right in principle for everyone, but because it is right for a member of one's particular family or for the network of intertwined families that constitutes one's native place.[7] In many Euorpean societies (Italy, France) politicians can explicitly admit that they are taking a stand because it is good for their particular social class, not because it is good for all people everywhere.[8] American politicians characteristically stake out political positions that spring from the interests of their particular regions or of the particular social strata that constitute their constituencies. But they feel compelled to justify their particular positions by high-minded assertions that they are acting out of universal principles for the public good. The high-mindedness is made possible by the sociological blindness of the moral language central to American culture.

CAUSES, CONSEQUENCES, AND CHALLENGES

The cultural roots of this American habit of speaking of diverse particular interests as if they were universal goods extend back as far as the origins of the American republic, and are embedded in the liberal individualism that has dominated American political discourse since the founding of the nation.

From the beginning, in the minds of its founders, the United States of

America was based not upon common values given but upon individual choices taken. As Thomas L. Pangle puts it, "The Declaration by which Americans made themselves independent marked the birth of the first nation in history explicitly grounded not on tradition, or loyalty to tradition, but on appeal to abstract and philosophical principles of political right. As Tom Paine put it in the *Rights of Man,* 'the Independence of America was accompanied by a Revolution in the principles and practice of Governments. . . . Government founded on a moral theory . . . on the indefeasible hereditary Rights of Man, is now revolving from west to east.'"[9]

According to this culturally hegemonic view of the moral foundations of the American republic, the national community is first and foremost a collection of autonomous individuals. The basis of their autonomy is their inalienable right to pursue happiness by acquiring property. By freely engaging in social contracts, such individuals create the United States of America.

But how can an orderly society arise out of the voluntary decisions of millions of different, self-interested individuals? This is possible, according to John Locke, whose philosophy decisively influenced the American founders and continues to form the core of our political thought, because there is a natural harmony of interests among individuals. The participants in the political debates that I have described do indeed seem to stake their claims on this supposed natural harmony of interests. Thus they can assume that in pursuing what subjectively seems good to them and to other individuals like them, they are not just helping themselves, but benefiting everybody—they are contributing to the larger public good.[10]

But under the circumstances of late-twentieth-century America, the notion of a natural harmony of interests seems less plausible. In a society as diverse as ours has become, different kinds of people, shaped by different social experiences, think about their interests in very different ways. Those on both sides of the disputes described above, for instance, share a consensus that their basic interests lie in acquiring and preserving private property. But to an important degree, it is a contentless consensus, a matter of form rather than substance, because they understand the nature and purpose of property in different ways.

Gloria Harper, Frank Stansky, and those who agree with them, see their property primarily as a commodity. To own land and buildings means for them to be free to buy and sell and do whatever they want with them in accordance with the logic of the free market. Asked if there should be laws that would regulate the use of the land so that houses would be built upon that land only in such a way as to benefit the interests of the community as a whole, Gloria says flatly, "That's just socialism." Flo Harris, on the other hand, declares that "the right to own property is a very important thing. But it shouldn't be the only thing." She by no means considers herself a socialist. She has voted Republican most of her life and believes strongly in the importance of maintaining the integrity of the free market. But for those with her social background and in her social circumstances, the value of the piece of land that is her property lies in its ability to be enjoyed with her family in peace and quiet after a hard day's work at the office. The noise and crowding caused by uncontrolled housing development would destroy the value of her property for her (even though it might increase its price). Thus, she does not consider land to be a commodity in the same way as, say, goods in a department store are. Land is special because the disposition of it gives a fundamental shape and texture to a community's life, with the result that political discussion by all the members of a community, not just the impersonal dynamics of the marketplace, should determine its disposition. Private property for her is valued as a means to a different kind of community life than for Gloria or Frank. Because they understand the value of the right to property in different ways, neither side can coherently argue with the other about how to link their private interests in acquiring property with a commitment to the public good.

So they do not really speak to each other. Perhaps it has always been thus for those who have understood themselves solely according to the logic of Lockean individualism. "What has held Americans together," writes the historian Robert Wiebe, "is their capacity for living apart." [11] According to Wiebe, American society has never been tied together by any over-arching consensus of beliefs or values or theories of social order; rather it is broken into innumerable segments—"primary circles of identity, values, associations, goals"—that have nonetheless managed to coexist more or less peacefully (compared with other societies). [12] Their success in peaceful coexistence has been tied to their success in insulating themselves from one another. In earlier periods of American history, this insulation was made possible by the abundance of American society.

Abundance produced "a general dispersal. First it diffused power. Many centers of economic activity so complicated the process of dominating a broad domain that even ambitious people tended to make the most of their own bailiwicks. . . . American abundance also diffused attention. The many points of attraction, each with an impressive promise, each with its own peculiarities, subdivided society into innumerable interests that took their differences for granted and found their common concerns only under duress. In its normal state America was a scattering of visions and energies, a society of mutual preoccupations where even sustained dialogues were rare. Finally, abundance diffused economic re-wards—not equitably, but widely."[13] In an abundant society, based on a dynamic, constantly growing economy, members of each segment could focus their energies mostly inward on the task of acquiring their own share of the abundance. They would not worry much that the success of other segments would undermine their own chances of success—success understood in terms of the common values of their segment. They could adopt toward other segments an attitude of benign neglect.

But by the late twentieth century, the abundance that had enabled the various segments of American society to insulate themselves from one another has been disappearing. The conflicts in the Southern California suburb I have described are a result of this disappearance. For instance, the amount of land available for housing in the coastal areas of Southern California is limited, even as increasing numbers of Americans have de-veloped aspirations for life in the Sun Belt. Moreover, as new people crowd into the area, the resultant pollution and congestion make the area lose the attractiveness it once had. Thus, land use battles in South-ern California are increasingly becoming zero-sum competitions for the people committed to living there. Such problems are cropping up in other realms of our society as the limits to economic growth are reached, and may reach crisis proportions if economic growth with severe infla-tion can only be sustained by widening the gap between rich and poor and cutting back in social welfare programs for the poor.

How can Americans continue to insulate themselves from one an-other under these circumstances? The insulation strategy pursued by the opponents in our Southern California land use dispute seems typi-cal: while seeming to talk to one another, they are really directing their attention away from one another to the state. They are not really con-cerned with convincing one another about the rightness of their cause, but with gaining the attention of helpful patrons in the government. It is, after all, various county, state, and federal government agencies that will ultimately decide whether a regulatory climate will be created to favor rapid real estate development or to control growth for the sake of various social and ecological concerns. To influence this regulatory pro-cess, local interest groups must speak loudly and in universal terms. They must make a case to the relevant government agencies that they represent not just a particular interest but the general interest, which all government agencies—even those that work at cross-purposes—are con-stitutionally supposed to uphold.

In late-twentieth-century America, then, a civic politics is giving way to a claimant politics. A civic politics is one in which citizens try to govern themselves by becoming informed about public affairs, seriously debating common issues, and choosing representatives who will articulate their interests in public assemblies. There are many indicators of a declining interest in this kind of politics—declining voter turnouts, declining participation in political parties, declining interest in "hard" news about public issues. At the same time, there are increasing indications of a general awareness that particular local needs require solutions at national levels. And thus in the past two decades there has been an astonishing increase in all kinds of lobbying activities. Ronald Jepperson and David Kamens have called this newly predominant political activity as indicative of a "claimant political culture." The American citizen less seriously seeks to govern himself or herself through the art of association— that is, through debate, negotiation, and compromise with fellow citizens. American citizens of all types now increasingly seek to satisfy themselves through the arts of acquiring favorable attention from the state. They do not need to develop a political discourse that makes sense to one another, just one that elicits a response from the government.[14]

Insofar as democracy entails engaging in honest, civil debate with different people representing different interests within the same community, the move toward a claimant politics represents a move away from the necessary conditions of a genuine democracy. American citizens seem to sense this. Even as they develop greater sophistication in methods of packaging in universalistic language their particular claims on the state, they seem to be losing confidence in their political institutions and manifesting increasing levels of cynicism about their government.[15]

The reclamation of a civic, democratic politics will entail parallel changes in two realms, political culture and political structure. We need to revivify those "second languages" of American culture that have historically enabled Americans to understand themselves not simply as self-determining individuals but as persons constituted by their social relations. Such languages enable them to understand how their individual rights are grounded and fulfilled in their responsibilities toward one another as members of a community. As my colleagues and I argued in *Habits of the Heart,* the primary American languages of community are those of biblical religion and civic republicanism.[16]

We also need to restructure institutions of government. Citizens like Gloria Harper and Flo Harris will never be able to speak to rather than past each other if they cannot really make decisions together about matters they share in common. For them to really engage one another as citizens, rather than as rival claimants to government largess, some political power would have to be decentralized.[17] To the degree that citizens in a locality might really have a significant degree of power to determine for themselves what kind of balance should be struck between economic

growth, protection of the environment, and respect for the legitimate social needs of one another—to the degree that such decisions might partially be taken out of the hands of huge banks and land development
corporations and distant, impersonal government bureaucracies—then
different citizens would be encouraged to pay one another the respect of
truly grappling together in the painful, yet humanly fulfilling, process of
searching for a common good.

TWENTY-TWO

Out of the Frying Pan, into . . . What?

Alan Wolfe

THE DECENTERING OF AMERICA?

Ever since the first Europeans landed on this side of the Atlantic, a significant number of theories have been advanced to explain Americans, both to themselves and to others.[1] These theories have varied from an emphasis on the character of the Puritans, to the effects of equality, to the impact of frontier, to the consequences of immigration, to the importance of consensus and stability. But however different in content, in form these theories shared one thing in common. All of them were "centered": they assumed that America could be explained by one crucial development, around which everything else could be organized.

Such centered theories have played an especially important role in the social and historical sciences. Under the influence of Talcott Parsons in sociology, equilibrium models of society were assumed to have the greatest validity in the 1950s. The notion of an equilibrium, borrowed from the marginal utility school of economics, was a perfect metaphor for a centered society. Even if things were not in harmony at any one moment, the model suggested, there was always a harmony toward which they were aiming. This way of thinking about a center was especially appealing because it was never subject to disconfirmation: equilibria, like tea leaves, could always be read, and, like any good reading of tea leaves, could usually be read with a slant pleasing to the listener.

Because of their optimistic assumptions about the future, consensus theories did not survive the controversies of the 1960s. When dissent and anger were turned against established institutions, conflict replaced consensus as the dominant imagery for a theory of American society. But as the end of ideology went out and Marxism came in, not as much changed as expected. For the Marxist model of society was also centered, even if

This chapter reflects the views of the editor alone. The views expressed here have not been endorsed by—or even necessarily discussed with—the other contributors to this volume.

in a plural rather than a singular way. Marxists emphasized the centrality of class against the integrationist inclinations of Parsonianism, and, in so doing, added a dollop of real life to sociology. Yet a class-based model still assumed that the world out there could be mapped in a one-to-one relationship between reality and its representations. The sociology of Erik Olin Wright, for example, which was inspired by a political vision quite at odds with Parsons, nonetheless resembled Parsons in being equally as cartographic in its imagery of the real world.[2] Doubts in the Marxist camp were as rare as doubts in the Parsons camp that there was a theory out there that possessed a center around which empirical explanations could be organized. Some Marxist theories even used words such as "center" and "core" as a way of describing the locus of a capitalist world system, contrasting the center to the "periphery" and "semiperiphery" elsewhere.[3]

From the empirical material assembled in this book, there is cause to question any theory that seeks to account for the changes in American life by describing those changes as a shift from one form of centered experience to another. Consider the work that Judith Stacey has done on family and class. Pamela Gama and Dotty Lewison, two women whose lives Stacey came to know in intimate detail, live in what Stacey calls "recombinant" families that bear little resemblance to anything we, or they, grew up thinking families ought to be. There is, Stacey concludes, no longer one model of the family—usually called the "Ozzie and Harriet" model—after which all others ought to pattern themselves. That point has been made very often, so often, in fact, that some have challenged its correctness.[4] But what makes Stacey's research on this subject so fascinating is the way she links the changing American family to changing stereotypes about class. The "postmodern" family, we learn from ethnography—and, one is tempted to say, only from ethnography—is not something dreamed up by the quiche and Muscadet crowd for an episode of "thirtysomething." It is also part of the lived reality of people who inhabit trailer camps and like to be tattooed. Social class can no longer be counted on to organize automatically our understanding of how people think and act in the everyday world. With respect to the relationship between class and family life, in other words, we are, in Stacey's accounting, witnessing the decentering of some of our most important institutions.

The same goes for numerous other aspects of American society that have been discussed in this book. It was once assumed that America was a European country, an assumption that not only provided direction for the country's foreign policy but also supplied the criteria for deciding which literature non-European Americans would learn, what historical traditions they would study, and what value system they would possess. No one who teaches in a major American city can accept that assumption so easily nowadays. What is striking about the new America is not just the diversity of immigration—that has always been the case—but the lack of agreement on a model of behavior that new immigrants ought to emulate. It is only with the most recent immigration that bilingualism, for example, has been generally accepted—a sure sign of the increasing inability of language to mean the same thing to every person.[5] Yet even as Americans have come to recognize the presence of so many Spanish-speaking people among them, they are now faced, as Rubén Rumbaut shows, by a wave of immigrants from parts of the world where no European language is spoken at all. Not new in quantity, recent immigration to the United States, for these reasons, is new in quality.

It may, consequently, no longer make much sense to use the term "American society" to describe anything meaningful about the United States. A resident of this country living in Manhattan may have a good deal in common with a Parisian, while a resident of Queens would feel fairly close to someone living in Terre Haute.[6] People living on one side of the Berkeley hills often drive cars, buy food, arrange their furniture, select what they put on their walls, and teach their children values quite differently from people who live ten miles away on the other side of the Berkeley hills. Advertisers recognize these new realities when they aim their products at "niche" markets; as opposed to the days when everyone ate corn flakes, Wheaties, or Rice Crispies, there is now a breakfast cereal for every taste.[7] (And, indeed, corn flakes and Rice Crispies have been repackaged to match new niches.) Political fund raisers know the same phenomenon: they tailor their mailings, with the aid of computers, to exactly the right ethnic group, income level, religious denomination, or zip code most likely to respond to their appeal. The media have chipped in as well; not only do advocacy groups try to shape programming to reflect the values of their particular subgroup, but cable television makes it possible to target audiences for pornography as easily as for God.[8] In their living patterns, Americans increasingly inhabit neither a rural world, thought by Thomas Jefferson to be the best guarantor of virtue, nor an urban world resembling Theodore Dreiser's Chicago or Henry Roth's New York; they live instead in some new kind of spread-out semi-cities that, in resembling neither of the old models, demand that people organize their social relations more or less from scratch. Our economy is based neither on agriculture nor on heavy industry, but on a mix of production and service-oriented industries. One political party dominates the executive and the other Congress; neither, however, can be said to govern. We are simultaneously sure that our way of life has triumphed over communism and unsure of what our way of life is.

Academics, especially those who make the study of American society their terrain, ought to be especially sensitive to the lack of a center in American life because the academic world itself has become so decentralized. New York City no longer dominates the world of ideas, as even New York intellectuals, seduced by the attractiveness of tenure and academic salaries, consider living elsewhere.[9] But the universities to which they move are themselves no longer characterized by centered status rankings. There was a time—one that corresponded almost exactly to the period in which Talcott Parsons and Robert K. Merton defined so much of sociology that even their opponents acknowledged their importance—when Harvard and Columbia dominated the field of sociology. Other schools, such as the University of California at Berkeley, rose during the 1960s to challenge that hegemony, but as any sociologist knows, in the 1980s there is no one place that defines the field and attracts the best students and researchers. We have many different kinds of sociology and many different kinds of sociologists. Some observers lament this, just as some lament the lack of sufficient *Gemeinschaft* or the decline of American power in the world or any one or another of transformations in the nature of a center. But to many sociologists—since, in any centered model of reality, more will always be excluded than included—it is rather pleasing to be opened up not only to multiple realities but to multiple ways to study reality. In any case, America and the study of America have both seemingly lost their core: subject and object are mixed up in increasingly complex ways, making it all the more difficult to find a satisfying way to live as well as to find a satisfying way to study, and come to terms with, the ways others live. America as a whole has seemingly become "decentered" in a way not dissimilar from what thinkers like Jacques Derrida mean—or seem to mean—by that term.

RECENTERED REACTIONS

If it is true that America is moving away from any model of society based on the assumption of a central core of values—or economic activity, social organization, moral standards, or ethnic composition—ought we to conclude that those who look at the world through the eyes of postmodernism would have the most to say about our condition? It is becoming increasingly common in many academic fields to argue that our understanding of the world, as well as the world itself, is organized by concepts that reflect not some ultimate truth, but instead the relative power of local and contingent interests.[10] Surely a number of American institutions seem to demonstrate the power of such a way of thinking, which is why the concept of postmodernism is attractive to some of the contributors to this book. Besides Stacey, Katherine Newman writes eloquently about how, for the downwardly mobile, the world no longer seems to have a center at all, while Sharon Zukin demonstrates the hollowing out of the "center city." Moreover, the loss of American hegemony in the world economy, described by Fred Block, and the failure of America to come to terms with the experience of Vietnam—the subject of William Gibson's chapter—all contribute to a sense that the world is spinning out of control. The revolution in epistemology associated with postmodernist and poststructuralist ways of thinking has had a much larger impact on literature, philosophy, history, and even law than it has had on sociology. Sociology may well be next.

Despite the initial evidence in favor of a postmodern perspective, however, there is also evidence—again, from the chapters contained in this book—that although many Americans feel that the world around them is losing its center, they also hope to create a new one—to reconstruct, not to deconstruct, their institutions. To take that most contested of terrains, the family, it is one thing to discover that the 1950s model of a "traditional" family, in which the man went out to work and the woman stayed home to raise the children, is no longer especially relevant for most Americans. But it is quite another to suggest that families themselves are a dead institution. What comes across strikingly in the work conducted by Kathleen Gerson and reported in this volume is the way in which both men and women understand differing moral imperatives and try to find balances between them. Although there are, of course, exceptions—women who want to stay home and be domestic and men who are completely absorbed in their work and ignore their families—most people find neither the workplace nor the home the single focus for what they ought to do. Typical in this respect are those women interviewed by Gerson who do not reject but redefine the notion of having children. When someone says to Gerson, "I want [equal] participation, and without it I don't want children," she is expressing anything but the idea that the institution of families with children ought to be bypassed. Instead, she is trying to find a new basis upon which a more just and perhaps even emotionally satisfying family can be created.

A similar attitude of ambivalence emerges with respect to changes in how and where Americans live. To be sure, Zukin is correct in her portrayal of how America's urban centers not only have failed to preserve their vitality but are increasingly coming to resemble each other in their problems. New York and Los Angeles, both characterized by increasing poverty and increasing wealth—the one as unimaginable as the other—appear to us as postmodern nightmares, organized, if organized at all, by rules that no one understands. (Bart Landry's chapter on the enduring dilemmas of race in America also demonstrates how, for large numbers of black Americans, the center has literally fallen out of their lives.) Yet as Zukin also points out, and as Claude Fischer emphasizes in his chapter, Americans have long possessed a deep ambivalence about the places in which they live. Although longing for "more" community and lamenting the uprooting and alienating tendencies in American urban life, many people would not have it any other way. Who can blame them? Although their desires for stability and neighborly friendliness are no doubt genuine, the newly created living arrangements they show a fantastic knack for developing do allow greater choice for most people and also create new, redefined ways of linking individuals together. Such ways may not correspond to our nostalgic views of "community," but they hardly involve a rejection of the concept, as Fischer emphasizes in this book. Our cities are fragmented and disjunctured, yet, somehow people still live and work in them (or around them). We are not so much at the end of urbanization as part of a process in which the meaning of "city" and "community" are being constantly redefined.

A similar sense of ambivalence also applies to our politics. Every thirty or thirty-six years, Americans realign their politics by shifting from one coalition to another.[11] The failure of a realignment to occur in the 1970s, and the incomplete realignment associated with the Reagan and Bush victories in the 1980s and 1990s, raise the possibility of what has been called a "dealignment" of American politics.[12] We have experienced quite a few of the symptoms of dealignment, including difficulty in passing legislation, establishing goals for public policy, and holding parties and legislators responsible for their behavior. It has been suggested that such traditionally democratic ways of establishing mandates as elections or public opinion polls are increasingly losing their relevance.[13] Yet for all the political instability, some constants remain. As David Halle and Frank Romo show, blue-collar workers demonstrate distinct political behavior, if measured more by their likelihood not to vote than by whom they do vote for. In life-style and at the workplace, as well as in voting behavior, class is not completely dead as an explanatory factor in American life.

The ambivalence of blue-collar workers—unsure whether they are Democrats but unwilling to shift to the Republicans—is part of a larger tentative search for new sources of consensus rather than either dogmatic certainty or complete political cynicism. Surely one place where we would expect to find certainty is among those who identify strongly with one or the other political extremes in American life. Yet Rebecca Klatch's work on the political views of conservatives does not present a picture of monolithic conservatism prepared for deadly battle with the forces of liberalism and secular humanism—a picture one gets if one simply reads newsletters or listens to spokespeople for conservative organizations. Rather, we witness people caught between traditionalism and modernity, convinced that they are conservative, but uncertain about what kinds of conservatives they are. Dispute over the issue of abortion, surely the most divisive issue in American politics in the 1990s, provides further illustration of the uncertainty that often lies beneath the views that individuals express to pollsters (or convey to their leaders). Yet ethnographic work undertaken by anthropologist Faye Ginsburg in the city of Fargo, North Dakota, discovered that women on either side of the issue were not very different from each other.[14] There is far more ambiguity in American politics than initially meets the eye, even on matters that tend to be associated with firmly held beliefs. Like Flo Harris and Gloria Harper, whose opposing views Richard Madsen explores in this book, Americans want to protect their private interests but at the same time universalize them in the language of American life. That the resulting consensus is often, in Madsen's term, "contentless" supports both the view that there is no longer any consensus, but also the view that people seem to want to find one.

The social institutions and practices of American society, while no longer operating by principles inherited from the 1950s, are also not as anarchic as they may at first appear to be. Our schools, it would seem, satisfy no one; there are critics who find them far too decentered to teach basic cultural values, at either the elementary or university level, while other critics still find them too Eurocentric and unresponsive to diversity.[15] Yet despite increasing private school enrollment, and despite experiments with vouchers, schools, as Caroline Persell points out in her chapter, still *matter* to both liberals and conservatives. That we continue to fight so much over what ought to be taught within them suggests that we still view them as places in which values and standards are taught. People may not like what schools teach, but they are hardly prepared, as some urged in the spirit of the 1960s, to do without.[16]

Much the same kind of ambivalence surrounds patterns of institutional life in areas involving doctors and patients, criminals and victims, preachers and the faithful, culture givers and culture consumers, and other subjects that are discussed in this book. It is my impression that James Hunter and John Rice's findings with respect to religion may be relevant to all of them: the fact of new patterns of faith does not necessarily mean that faith itself is no longer important to people. When Hunter and Rice conclude that sociologists, in being so quick to predict the demise of religion, simply looked in the wrong place, they are saying something of importance to analysts of all social institutions. Just as the distinction between high and low church is dissolving, moreover, so is the distinction between high and low culture. The cultural mandarins of the 1950s were, as Gaye Tuchman argues, restrictive in their definition of what constituted a proper cultural artifact. When they now lament the decline of standards associated with the popularization of high art, they, too, may be looking in the wrong place. More people have access to more cultural goods than ever before—just as, according to Michael Schudson, more people have access to more media. Neither theories of culture that emphasize the inherent value of elite forms nor those that stress the democratic vibrancy of popular forms capture this blend of experiences—which means that it may be our theories that ought to change.

It is therefore, finally, our theories about the social world that require a special sensitivity to ambivalence. Of all the authors in this book, Jack Katz makes this argument most strongly. Both liberal and conservative theories on one important American experience, crime, simply do not account, given their materialist bias, for the thing itself. But Katz is not alone. Ruth Milkman, for example, finds that neither those who find an ingenious capitalist plot in the reconstruction of industry nor those who welcome a "post-Fordist" regime of flexible accumulation offer relevant insights for understanding the world of work. Milkman shows how both management and labor have fought change—sometimes successfully, sometimes not. Weak unions and incompetent managers add up to a picture, once more, of ambivalent patterns, caught between nostalgia for the past and fear of the future. Complex realities require complex understandings.

About the only conclusion that can be reached with any certainty from the observations included in this book is that in the absence of models that define what is expected of them—both older models that no longer seem valid as well as ones so new they have not yet been formed—Americans will increasingly have to define for themselves the rules by which they will structure their lives. What this means concretely is that things once taken for granted will increasingly be subject to complex and difficult negotiations. The chapter by Carmen Sirianni and Andrea Walsh is illustrative of these negotiations. Time, they argue, has moved from background to foreground; instead of the distribution of time being accomplished as a product of natural cycles, individuals both in families and firms increasingly view the time distribution and allocation as political decisions, not as givens. That same negotiability appears again and again in American life—for example, in the breakdown of the model of medical authority analyzed by Jonathan Imber, and in the increasingly negotiated world called childhood analyzed by Gary Alan Fine and Jay Mechling. The number of contested terrains in American life seems inexhaustible.

It is precisely because we do not yet know whether any new patterns of normality will emerge from these negotiations, or whether they will continue indefinitely, that it would be incorrect to invest too much in the concept of postmodernism. For a way of thinking that emphasizes openness and diversity, postmodernists are often closed on the question of postmodernity itself. To adopt such a perspective is to already answer the question of what will emerge in America: nothing will, or at least nothing that resembles a stable reordering of practices and institutions.

Moreover, to the degree that postmodernist thinkers have a pretty good idea of how they think the world works (or doesn't work), irrespective of the way people actually think it does or should, adopting such a point of view in the absence of an ethnographic inquiry seems, like both the theory of mass society and the Marxist theory of false consciousness, one other way of putting theory before data. If the viewpoint of real people is to be taken into account, if our understanding of what is taking place and what will emerge is to be evidence-driven, then postmodernism fails to help us. (That so many postmodernists do not believe in an autonomous self or subject—and only an autonomous self is worth studying ethnographically—does not help much either.) [17]

Perhaps the best way of characterizing the evidence collected in this book is to say that large numbers of Americans—regardless of social class, location, or cultural life-style—increasingly recognize that their institutions no longer work by the models they have been given to believe were, at some point in the past, "normal." At the same time, however, they are split in their responses. Some want to go back to what they believe to have been a golden age, even while recognizing that they cannot. Others luxuriate in the freedom that their liberation from earlier constraint has brought them, celebrating their new life-styles while remaining suspicious toward any efforts to reimpose what they believe to be Puritanical and obsolete moral rules. The majority, in all likelihood, belong to neither position. Uncertain to the core, they appreciate the changes they have seen, even while expressing some worries about where those changes might lead. Whether left or right, traditional or modern, secular or religious, the one thing that ties so many Americans together is their common refuge in ambivalence. Their lives have been neither decentered nor recentered; they have changed, and the struggle to define what those changes are, and what they will continue to be, lies at the heart of the America that is emerging.

FACING THE FUTURE

If this interpretation of what the sociologists have found who have looked into so many corners of American life is correct, it seems in accord with common sense. Decentering involves powerful feelings of freedom, but, at the same time, scary visions of chaos. It can hardly be surprising that many people experience with some relief the collapse of traditional standards around such issues as the family, abortion, strict work rules, role-specific institutions, discipline, hierarchy, and other features of a more centered world. It would be impossible to exaggerate the sense of freedom and the capacity to experience oneself as a self-choosing moral agent when one is allowed, by law or custom, to make a decision that was once reserved only for a priestly elect. Yet it would be also impossible to exaggerate some of the fears that are also associated with such changes, not only from opponents of such developments as working women, childhood discretion, or patient rights, but also from people determined to exercise their new freedoms but filled with doubts about their capacities and what the consequences of their new freedom might mean in terms of new responsibilities. To want to do away with the old standards, even while hoping that out of ferment will emerge new and more flexible standards, is anything but an unthoughtful response to a society in transition.

Because of the ambivalence and uncertainties recounted here, it would be futile, as well as false, to conclude with either an optimistic or a pessimistic note about the future: both those who find the world falling apart as well as those who find much of value in it will be comforted (and dismayed) by what we have reported here. But that, in a sense, is the point. There may well be too many voices in American life speaking in tones of certainty. Politicians, for one group, seem to speak with more authority the more they do not understand the world around them. There are lessons for both liberals and conservatives in listening to the people for whom they would make policy. Conservatives want parental consent before teenagers are allowed to have abortions, for example, a point of view that assumes the existence of parents available to give consent. Anyone sensitive to the dynamics of family life as lived, rather than as preached, might recognize the folly of such a course. But liberals are not all that different in assuming that something like crime could be solved by doing something about poverty; those, like Jack Katz, who listen to the criminals, have a different story to tell.

Intellectuals and academics have also been known to speak with unwarranted certainty from time to time. If, indeed, American institutions and practices are undoing a process of reestablishing themselves on a new basis, the need is clear for renewal of efforts to empirically study the institutions described in the introduction to this book. That our theories of how the world works ought at all times to be driven by a concern with empirical realities seems a truism for the social sciences. That this truism is, if possible, even more true when those institutions are undergoing the kinds of stress and reordering of moral claims described here ought also to be emphasized. A healthy respect for people—for the dilemmas they face; the ingenuity they show in resolving them; the sometimes awkward, sometimes flawed, but just as often idealistic and brave manner in which they face a bewildering world—has to be accompanied by a healthy skepticism toward overdetermined theories about the way the world works. The last thing the social sciences need at this moment is ambitious and systematic theorizing about the whole of society. We ought to understand the forms that institutions and practices are going to take before pronouncing them explained and categorized.

As people learn to live with, to use Judith Stacey's term, brave new families—let alone brave new communities, jobs, and schools—they will need help. They would be wrong if they turned to people who practice sociology to tell them what to do; our job is not to provide moral advice. We have more serious moral business at hand: to use the skills we develop through our methods to describe as accurately as we can the ways in which people live. If, in bringing clarity to the world, we can bring clarity to those who live in the world as well, we will have done our job. Our obligation is to listen to the people who are our subjects, think about what they tell us, and then tell them what we have learned.

This book is intended for readers who care about what has been happening to them, their families, their communities, and their society at a time when nothing is working the way they were led to believe things would work. It contains two messages: One is that they are correct if they perceive that the older moral models are of little help. The other is that they are wrong if they think that the result must be either a return to traditional standards or complete moral anarchy. What actually happens is, in many ways, up to them. We hope, in reporting on our conversations with them, our interpretations of their history, and our examination of the structure and function of their institutions, to help them make up their minds.

NOTES

PREFACE

1. Needless to say, sociologists doing research in the 1950s were making comparisons with a past as well. Too often that past, usually pre-Depression America, was also viewed as good old days, when examples of a *Gemeinschaft*, or folk society, could still be found, when life seemed much more stable and society more cohesive than they were in the 1950s. Robert and Helen Lynds's classic community study, *Middletown* (New York: Harcourt Brace, 1929), and its graphic description of the condition of the working class in mid-1920s Middletown should persuade anyone that those days were not good even for most whites. As for blacks, their deprivation seems to have made them too invisible to be studied during the 1920s.

2. I do not now remember how we described the economic conditions of the 1950s, but the word *affluence* did not become popular until after the publication (by Houghton Mifflin) of John Kenneth Galbraith's *Affluent Society,* and that took place only in 1958.

3. The same question can be raised about the 1960s, given the assassinations of several major American leaders and the violence in Vietnam as well as America's ghettos, even though many liberal and radical intellectuals view the decade as one of liberating and therefore positive social and cultural change. Everyone has the right to his or her own perception of every decade, but serious differences in perception add to the disadvantages of using decade as an analytic concept.

INTRODUCTION

1. Michel Crozier comes close to fitting this description. See *The Trouble with America: Why the System Is Breaking Down* (Berkeley and Los Angeles: University of California Press, 1984).

2. For greater documentation of these changes, see Alejandro Portes and Rubén Rumbaut, *Immigrant America: A Portrait* (Berkeley and Los Angeles: University of California Press, 1990).

3. A collection of essays exploring these changes at length is Gary Gerstle and Steve Fraser, *The Rise and Fall of the New Deal Order, 1930–1950* (Princeton, N.J.: Princeton University Press, 1989). For a good overview, see Ruy A. Teixeira, "Things Fall Apart: Americans and Their Political Institutions," in *Change in Societal Institutions,* ed. Maureen T. Hallinan, David M. Klein, and Jennifer Glass (New York: Plenum, 1990), 239–55.

4. For an analysis of how the rhetoric of American politics has changed under the impact of electronic technologies, see Kathleen Hall Jamieson, *Eloquence in an Electronic Age: The Transformation of Political Speechmaking* (New York: Oxford University Press, 1988).

5. This, of course, is one of the major themes of Robert N. Bellah and others, *Habits of the Heart: Individualism and Commitment in American Life* (Berkeley and Los Angeles: University of California Press, 1985).

6. For statistics of the changing income distribution in the United States in recent years, see Frank Levy, *Dollars and Dreams: The Changing American Income Distribution* (New York: Norton, 1988). What the figures mean in human terms is explored in Barbara Ehrenreich's *Fear of Falling: The Inner Life of the Middle Class* (New York: Pantheon, 1989).

7. Katherine S. Newman, *Falling from Grace: The Experience of Downward Mobility in the American Middle Class* (New York: Free Press, 1988).

8. An overview of the general changes in American industrial relations can be found in Thomas A. Kochan, Harry C. Katz, and Robert B. McKersie, *The Transformation of American Industrial Relations* (New York: Basic Books, 1986).

9. One of the best treatments of the changes in union life in the postwar period is Gordon L. Clark, *Unions and Communities under Siege: American Communities and the Crisis of Organized Labor* (Cambridge: Cambridge University Press, 1989). See also Michael Goldfield, *The Decline of Organized Labor in the United States* (Chicago: University of Chicago Press, 1987).

10. A study of the ideology of the American family in the 1950s is Elaine Tyler May's *Homeward Bound: American Families in the Cold War Era* (New York: Basic Books, 1986).

11. Arlie Russell Hochschild and Anne Machung, *The Second Shift: Working Parents and the Revolution at Home* (New York: Penguin, 1989).

12. Some of the debates spawned by these developments are explored in Edward F. Zigler and Meryl Frank, eds., *The Parental Leave Crisis: Toward a National Policy* (New Haven, Conn.: Yale University Press, 1988).

13. One sociologist who is worried about the possible consequences of the decline of the nuclear family, and who has written extensively about it, is David Popenoe (see *Disturbing the Nest: Family Change and Decline in Modern Societies* (Hawthorne, N.Y.: de Gruyter, 1988). The chapters in this book by Judith Stacey and Kathleen Gerson present a perspective quite distinct from Popenoe's.

14. See Marie Winn, *Children without Childhood* (New York: Pantheon, 1983).

15. For an ethnographic treatment of how peer group subcultures emerge among American youth, see Gary Schwartz, *Beyond Conformity and Rebellion: Youth and Authority in America* (Chicago: University of Chicago Press, 1987).

16. Constance Perin, *Everything in Its Place: Social Order and Land Use in America* (Princeton, N.J.: Princeton University Press, 1977) and *Belonging in America: Reading between the Lines* (Madison: University of Wisconsin Press, 1988).

17. These changes are explored in Walter Russell Mead, *Mortal Splendor: The American Empire in Transition* (Boston: Houghton Mifflin, 1987).

18. An in-depth review of some of the changes facing African-Americans in the United States in the 1980s is Gerald David Jaynes and Robin M. Williams, Jr., eds., *A Common Destiny: Blacks and American Society* (Washington, D.C.: National Academy Press, 1989). For a sensitive treatment of what these changes mean to both black and white Americans, see Bob Blauner, *Black Lives, White Lives: Three Decades of Race Relations in America* (Berkeley and Los Angeles: University of California Press, 1989).

19. That these technological changes have not necessarily given women greater free time is the theme of Ruth Schwartz Cowan's *More Work for Mother: The Ironies of Household Technology from the Open Hearth to the Microwave* (New York: Basic Books, 1985).

20. The ways in which computers will alter how Americans understand themselves are explored by Sherry Turkle in *The Second Self: Computers and the Human Spirit* (New York: Touchstone, 1985). On the impact of computers on the workplace, see Shoshana Zuboff, *In the Age of the Smart Machine: The Future of Work and Power* (New York: Basic Books, 1985).

21. For an ethnographic portrayal of how the elderly view themselves, see Sharon B. Kaufman, *The Ageless Self: Sources of Meaning in Late Life* (Madison: University of Wisconsin Press, 1986).

22. For historical material on the actual shape and dimension of American social institutions in this period, see Robert H. Bremmer and Gary Reichard, eds., *Reshaping America: Society and Institutions, 1945–1969* (Columbus: Ohio State University Press, 1982). Studies of the cultural dynamics of the period are included in Lary May, ed., *Recasting America: Culture and Politics in the Age of Cold War* (Chicago: University of Chicago Press, 1989).

23. Robin Williams, Jr.'s *American Society: A Sociological Interpretation* (New York: Knopf, 1951) is the best account.

24. Though British, the works of R. D. Laing and of David Cooper remain the best illustrations of this tendency; see, for example, David Graham Cooper, *The Death of the Family* (New York: Pantheon, 1971). A less extreme American example of the "second generation" study of institutions is Jerome H. Skolnick and Elliott Curry's *Crisis in American Institutions* (Boston: Little, Brown, 1970).

25. James G. March and Johan P. Olson, *Rediscovering Institutions: The Organizational Basis of Politics* (New York: Free Press, 1989).

26. Jon Elster, *The Cement of Society: A Study of Social Order* (Cambridge: Cambridge University Press, 1989), 248. Elster does go on to admit the existence of "clusters of individuals who interact more strongly with each other than with people in other clusters," thus making the study of institutions possible.

27. The work of Oliver Williamson is the most relevant. See, for example, *The Economic Institutions of Capitalism: Firms, Markets, and Rational Contracting*

(New York: Free Press, 1985). Another interesting work is Andrew Schotter, *The Economic Theory of Social Institutions* (Cambridge: Cambridge University Press, 1980).

28. See Samuel Weber, *Institutions and Interpretation* (Minneapolis: University of Minnesota Press, 1987); and E. J. Burt and Janie Vanpee, eds., *Reading the Archive: On Texts and Institutions, Yale French Studies* 77 (1990), entire issue.

29. For a recent example of this concern, see Margaret Weir, Ann Shola Orloff, and Theda Skocpol, eds., *The Politics of Social Policy in the United States* (Princeton, N.J.: Princeton University Press, 1988).

30. For examples of an institutional turn in sociology, see Hallinan, Klein, and Glass, eds., *Change in Societal Institutions* and Michael Hechter, Karl-Dieter Opp, and Richard Wippler, eds., *Social Institutions: Their Emergence, Maintenance, and Effects* (New York: de Gruyter, 1990).

31. For examples of sociologists interested in neo-institutionalism from an organizational perspective, see W. Richard Scott, "The Adolescence of Institutional Theory," *Administrative Science Quarterly* 32 (December 1987): 493–511; and the literature cited therein; Lynne G. Zucker, ed., *Institutional Patterns and Organizations: Culture and Environment* (Cambridge, Mass.: Ballinger, 1988); Marshall W. Meyer and Lynne G. Zucker, *Permanently Failing Organization* (Newbury Park, Calif.: Sage, 1989); and Paul J. Dimaggio, ed., *Nonprofit Enterprise in the Arts* (New York: Oxford University Press, 1986).

32. One of the best examples of this tendency from an earlier period is *Sociology Today: Problems and Prospects*, 2 vols., ed. Robert K. Merton, Leonard Broom, and Leonard S. Cottrell, Jr. (New York: Harper & Row, 1959).

33. Besides other works cited in this chapter, I would also cite as representative examples of this concern the following: Robert Wuthnow, *The Restructuring of American Religion* (Princeton, N.J.: Princeton University Press, 1988); Paul Starr, *The Social Transformation of American Medicine: The Rise of a Sovereign Profession and the Making of a Vast Industry* (New York: Basic Books, 1982); Barbara Katz Rothman, *Recreating Motherhood: Ideology and Technology in a Patriarchal Society* (New York: Norton, 1989); Andrew Scull, *Social Order/Mental Order: Anglo-American Psychiatry in Historical Perspective* (Berkeley and Los Angeles: University of California Press, 1989); Viviana Zelizer, *Pricing the Priceless Child: The Changing Social Value of Children* (New York: Basic Books, 1985); Mark Baldassere, *Trouble in Paradise: The Suburban Transformation in America* (New York: Columbia University Press, 1986); Roger Waldinger, *Through the Eye of the Needle: Immigrants and Entrepreneurs in New York's Garment Trades* (New York: New York University Press, 1986); Jonathan Rieder, *Canarsie: The Italians and Jews of Brooklyn against Liberalism* (Cambridge: Harvard University Press, 1985); Eviatar Zerubavel, *Hidden Rhythms: Schedules and Calendars in Social Life* (Chicago: University of Chicago Press, 1981); Murray Melbin, *Night as Frontier: Colonizing the World after Dark* (New York: Free Press, 1987); Carole Joffe, *The Regulation of Sexuality: Experiences of Family Planning Workers* (Philadelphia: Temple University Press, 1986); and Nicole Woolsey Biggard, *Charismatic Capitalism: Direct Selling Organizations in America* (Chicago: University of Chicago Press, 1989). There are, no doubt, many relevant works I have neglected to mention.

34. For the reflections of Riesman—and many other sociologists born two decades before those assembled in this book—see Bennett M. Berger, ed., *Authors of Their Own Lives: Intellectual Autobiographies by Twenty American Sociologists* (Berkeley and Los Angeles: University of California Press, 1990).

CHAPTER ONE

1. Writing the majority opinion in the New York ruling, Judge Vito Titone elaborated four judicial criteria for determining what constitutes a family: (1) "exclusivity and longevity of a relationship"; (2) the "level of emotional and financial commitment"; (3) how a couple has "conducted their everyday lives and held themselves out to society"; (4) the "reliance placed upon one another for daily family services" (Philip S. Gutis, "Court Widens Family Definition," *New York Times* [July 7, 1989], A1, A13).

2. Kathy Bodovitz, "Referendum Petitions Block S. F. Domestic Partners Law," *San Francisco Chronicle* (July 7, 1989), A1, A20; and Don Lattin, "How Religious Groups Stopped Partners Law," *San Francisco Chronicle* (July 10, 1989), A1, A20.

3. For pessimistic assessments of family decline, see Christopher Lasch, *Haven in a Heartless World* (New York: Basic Books, 1977); Kingsley Davis, "The Meaning and Significance of Marriage in Contemporary Society," in *Contemporary Marriage: Comparative Perspectives on a Changing Institution*, eds. Kingsley Davis and Amyra Grossbard-Schectman (New York: Russell Sage Foundation, 1985); and Peter Berger and Brigitte Berger, *The War over the Family* (Garden City, N.Y.: Anchor Press/Doubleday, 1983). For optimistic appraisals of "the family," see Mary Jo Bane, *Here to Stay: American Families in the Twentieth Century* (New York: Basic Books, 1976); Theodore Caplow, Howard Bahr, Bruce Chadwick, Reuben Hill, and Margaret Holmes Williamson, *Middletown Families: Fifty Years of Change and Continuity* (Toronto: Bantam Books, 1983); and Randall Collins, *Sociology of Marriage and the Family: Gender, Love, and Property* (Chicago: Nelson-Hall, 1985). More centrist, but still somewhat anxious, evaluations of the state of "the family" include Alan Wolfe, *Whose Keeper? Social Science and Moral Obligation* (Berkeley: University of California Press, 1989); Robert Bellah, Richard Madsen, William M. Sullivan, Ann Swidler, and Steven M. Tipton, *Habits of the Heart* (Berkeley: University of California Press, 1985); and Andrew Cherlin, "Marriage, Divorce, Remarriage: From the 1950s to the 1980s," (paper presented at the annual meeting of the American Sociological Association, San Francisco, August 11, 1989).

4. Linda Gordon, *Heroes of Their Own Lives* (New York: Viking, 1988), 3.

5. Kathleen Gerson, *Hard Choices: How Women Decide about Work, Career, and Motherhood* (Berkeley: University of California Press, 1985), 237.

6. Andrew Cherlin, *The Changing American Family and Public Policy* (Washington, D.C.: Urban Institute Press, 1988), 5; and Susan Householder Van Horn, *Women, Work, and Fertility 1900–1986* (New York: New York University Press, 1988), 152. Of course, far more than 7 percent of American families pass through a life cycle stage in which they practice the "modern" pattern, but the sharp con-

trast in the demographic snapshots of the two periods reflects the steady decline in both the duration of that stage and the proportion of Americans who experience it at all.

7. For data and analyses on the steady rise of divorce rates, see Carl Degler, *At Odds: Women and the Family in America from the Revolution to the Present* (Oxford: Oxford University Press, 1980), 165–77; Davis, "Wives and Work"; Stone, "The Road to Polygamy"; and Sar Levitan, Richard Belous, and Frank Gallo, *What's Happening to the American Family? Tensions, Hopes, Realities,* rev. ed. (Baltimore: Johns Hopkins University Press, 1988). The first "modern" American divorce case, which included "alienation of affection" as one of its complaints, occurred in 1776. See Sara M. Evans, *Born for Liberty: A History of Women in America* (New York: Free Press, 1989), 42.

8. The memorable opening line of Leo Tolstoy's *Anna Karenina* (trans. David Margarshack): "All happy families are like one another; each unhappy family is unhappy in its own way." (New York: New American Library, 1961).

9. Clive Dilnot, "What Is the Post-Modern?" *Art History* 9 (June 1986): 245–63.

10. Dilnot, "What Is the Post-Modern?" 245, 249.

11. The postmodern condition emerges, Jean-Francois Lyotard argues, when legitimation through grand historical narratives has broken down. See *The Postmodern Condition: A Report on Knowledge,* trans. Geoff Bennington and Brian Massumi (Manchester: Manchester University Press, 1984). Here I sidestep the debate over whether the postmodern represents a clear break with the modern, or whether, as Nancy Scheper-Hughes argued (during a conference on anthropology and modernity held at the University of California at Berkeley in April 1989), it is simply "capitalism on speed." Frances E. Mascia-Lees, Patricia Sharpe, and Colleen Ballerino Cohen, "The Postmodernist Turn in Anthropology: Cautions from a Feminist Perspective," *Signs* 15 (Autumn 1989): 7–33, discuss feminist concerns that the rejection of grand narratives coincides with new attempts by women and other subordinated groups to write their own. For additional useful discussions of feminism, modernism, and postmodernism, see Janet Wolff, *Feminine Sentences: Essays on Women and Culture* (Berkeley and Los Angeles: University of California Press, 1990).

12. The frequency and irregularity of mortality in the premodern period and the economic interdependence of women and men fostered high remarriage rates and the complex kinship relationships these generate. There were also significant regional differences in premodern family patterns. For excellent overviews of the diversity of premodern family patterns, see Stephanie Coontz, *The Social Origins of Private Life: A History of American Families 1600–1900* (London: Verso, 1988); and Steven Mintz and Susan Kellogg, *Domestic Revolutions: A Social History of American Family Life* (New York: Free Press, 1988).

13. Alice Kessler-Harris and Karen Sacks consider it doubtful that a majority of working-class men ever earned a family wage. See "The Demise of Domesticity," in *Women, Households and the Economy,* ed. Lourdes Beneria and Catharine R. Stimpson (New Brunswick, N.J.: Rutgers University Press, 1987), 65–84.

14. Janet Flammang, "Female Officials in the Feminist Capital: The Case of Santa Clara County," *Western Political Quarterly* 38 (March 1985): 94–118; Flam-

mang, "Women Made a Difference: Comparable Worth in San Jose," in *The Women's Movements of the United States and Western Europe,* ed. Ira Katznelson and Carole Mueller (Philadelphia: Temple University Press, 1987), 290–309; Linda Blum, *Re-Evaluating Women's Work: The Significance of the Comparable Worth Movement* (Berkeley and Los Angeles: University of California Press, forthcoming). Ironically the San Jose comparable worth strike was called when the feminist mayor and the city council, on which women held the majority of seats, failed to meet the city employees' demand to proceed on a proposed job study prerequisite to evaluating pay equity.

15. For data on divorce rates and household composition for Santa Clara County, in comparison with California and the United States as a whole, see U.S. Bureau of the Census, *Census of Population* for 1960, 1970, and 1980. During the 1970s the county recorded 660 abortions for every 1000 live births, compared with a statewide average of 489.5 and a ratio of less than 400 for the nation. See U.S. Bureau of the Census, *Statistical Abstract of the United States, 1981* (Washington, D.C.: Government Printing Office, 1981).

16. Jean Holland, *The Silicon Syndrome: A Survival Handbook for Couples* (Palo Alto, Calif.: Coastlight Press, 1983).

17. Michael S. Malone, "Family in Crisis," *Santa Clara Magazine* (Spring 1989): 15.

18. For literature describing working-class families as favoring "traditional" gender arrangements, see Mirra Komarovsky, with Jane H. Philips, *Blue-Collar Marriage* (New York: Summit Books, 1962); Lillian Rubin, *Worlds of Pain: Life in the Working-Class Family* (New York: Basic Books, 1976); Van Horn, *Women, Work, and Fertility;* Caplow et al., *Middletown Families;* and Robert Coles and Jane Hallowell Coles, *Women of Crisis: Lives of Struggle and Hope* (New York: Delacorte Press, 1978). Barbara Ehrenreich argues that the media constructed this stereotype of the blue-collar working class after they "discovered" this class in 1969. See *Fear of Falling: The Inner Life of the Middle Class* (New York: Pantheon, 1989). I return to this issue a little later in this discussion.

19. Judith Stacey, *Brave New Families: Stories of Domestic Upheaval in Late Twentieth-Century America* (New York: Basic Books, 1990).

20. Judith Stacey and Susan Elizabeth Gerard, "We Are Not Doormats: The Influence of Feminism on Contemporary Evangelicalism in the United States," in *Negotiating Gender in American Culture,* ed. Faye Ginsburg and Anna Tsing (Boston: Beacon Press, 1990).

21. There is a great deal of empirical and theoretical support for this view, from feminist psychoanalytic analyses of mothering to time-budget studies of the domestic division of labor. For a direct discussion of women and "the work of kinship," see Micaela di Leonardo, *The Varieties of Ethnic Experience: Kinship, Class, and Gender among California Italian-Americans* (Ithaca, N.Y.: Cornell University Press, 1984), 194–205. For an in-depth treatment of domestic labor, see Arlie Russell Hochschild, with Anne Machung, *The Second Shift: Working Parents and the Revolution at Home* (New York: Penguin, 1989).

22. For fuller discussions of this masculinity crisis see Kathleen Gerson's chapter in this volume and Lynne Segal, *Slow Motion: Changing Masculinities, Changing Men* (London: Virago, 1990).

23. Lynne Segal arrives at a similar conclusion in *Slow Motion,* chapter 2. Patricia Zavella's research on the division of household labor among "Hispano" couples provides additional support for this view. See her paper "Sun Belt Hispanics on the Line," presented at the History and Theory Conference, University of California, Irvine, April 1, 1989. A more comprehensive treatment of issues affecting Anglo and Hispanic households will appear in Louise Lamphere, Felipe Gonzales, Patricia Zavella, and Peter Evans, *Working Mothers and Sun Belt Industrialization,* a booklength work in progress.

24. Segal's summary of research on changes in the domestic division of labor supports this view. See *Slow Motion,* chapter 2. And while Arlie Hochschild's recent study of domestic labor emphasizes men's resistance to assuming a fair share of the burden, it also demonstrates that this has become a widely contested issue. See *The Second Shift.*

25. Colleen Leahy Johnson, *Ex-Familia: Grandparents, Parents and Children Adjust to Divorce* (New Brunswick, N.J.: Rutgers University Press, 1988).

26. On extended, cooperative kin ties among the poor, see Michael Young and Peter Willmott, *Family and Kinship in East London* (Middlesex, England: Penguin, 1962); David M. Schneider and Raymond T. Smith, *Class Differences and Sex Roles in American Kinship and Family Structure* (Englewood Cliffs, N.J.: Prentice-Hall, 1973); and Carole Stack, *All Our Kin: Strategies for Survival in a Black Community* (New York: Harper & Row, 1974). David Halle, *America's Working Man* (Chicago: University of Chicago Press, 1984), 279, takes as a premise the existence of extensive kin ties among blue-collar workers.

27. Stack, *All Our Kin;* Young and Willmott, *Family and Kinship.*

28. Allan Schnaiberg and Sheldon Goldenberg, "From Empty Nest to Crowded Nest: The Dynamics of Incompletely Launched Young Adults," *Social Problems* 36, no. 3 (June 1989): 251–69.

29. On premodern family patterns, see Coontz, *Social Origins of Private Life,* and Mintz and Kellogg, *Domestic Revolutions.*

30. Martha May, "Bread before Roses: American Workingmen, Labor Unions and the Family Wage," in *Women, Work and Protest: A Century of U.S. Women's Labor History,* ed. Ruth Milkman (Boston: Routledge & Kegan Paul, 1985), 1–21. May argues that the demand for a family wage was primarily a class-based demand made by labor unions on behalf of working-class men and their wives in the nineteenth century, but it was achieved in the twentieth century through a cross-class gender alliance between capitalists and unionized men. This analysis helps to resolve a theoretical and political debate among feminist and socialist-labor historians concerning the class and gender character of the family wage struggle. Heidi Hartmann, "Capitalism, Patriarchy, and Job Segregation by Sex," in *Capitalist Patriarchy and the Case for Socialist-Feminism,* ed. Zillah Eisenstein (New York: Monthly Review Press, 1979), 206–32, criticized the sexist character of the struggle, while Jane Humphries, "The Working-Class Family, Women's Liberation and Class Struggle: The Case of Nineteenth-Century British History," *Review of Radical Political Economics* 9 (Fall 1977): 25–41, defended the struggle as a form of class and family resistance.

31. After a sharp postwar spurt, divorce rates stabilized only temporarily during the 1950s, and above prewar levels. Levitan et al., *What's Happening to the*

American Family? Tensions, Hopes, Realities, rev. ed. (Baltimore, Md.: Johns Hopkins University Press, 1988), 27. The proportion of women entering college climbed slowly throughout the 1950s, before escalating sharply since the mid-1960s: in 1950, 12 percent of women aged 24–29 had completed one year of college; this figure rose to 22 percent in 1965 and reached 43 percent by 1984. Steven D. McLaughlin, Barbara D. Melber, John O. G. Billy, Denise M. Zimmerle, Linda D. Winges, and Terry R. Johnson, *The Changing Lives of American Women* (Chapel Hill: University of North Carolina Press, 1988), 33–34. Van Horn (*Women, Work, and Fertility,* 194) makes the interesting, provocative argument that a disjuncture between the limited kinds of jobs available to women and the increasing numbers of educated women seeking jobs during the 1960s helped to regenerate feminism. For additional discussions of the rising numbers of working wives, see Kingsley Davis, "Wives and Work: A Theory of the Sex-Role Revolution and Its Consequences," in *Feminism, Children, and the New Families,* ed. Sanford Dornbusch and Myra Strober (New York: The Guilford Press, 1988), 67–86; Gerson, *Hard Choices;* Degler, *At Odds,* chapter 17; Elaine Tyler May, *Homeward Bound: American Families in the Cold War Era* (New York: Basic Books, 1988); and Evans, *Born for Liberty,* chapter 11.

32. See Evans, *Born for Liberty,* 253–54; Van Horn, *Women, Work, and Fertility,* chapter 12; and Kessler-Harris and Sacks, "Demise of Domesticity."

33. Larry Bumpass and James Sweet in "Preliminary Evidence on Cohabitation" (National Survey of Families and Households Working Paper No. 2, Center for Demography and Ecology, University of Wisconsin-Madison, September 1988), report higher education rates among those with high school education than among those with college education, and higher divorce rates among those who cohabit prior to marriage. For differential divorce rates by income and race, see also, Van Horn, *Women, Work, and Fertility;* Levitan et al., *What's Happening to the American Family?;* and Henry A. Walker, "Black-White Differences in Marriage and Family Patterns," in Dornbusch and Strober, *Feminism, Children, and the New Families.* A classic ethnography of matrilineal support systems among working-class people is Young and Willmott, *Family and Kinship.* See also, Schneider and Smith, *Class Differences and Sex Roles.* Stack's *All Our Kin* is the classic ethnographic portrayal of matrifocal cooperative kin networks among poor African-Americans. However, Gordon (*Heroes of Their Own Lives*) cautions against the tendency to exaggerate and romanticize the existence of extended kinship support systems among the very poor.

34. For data and discussions of noneconomic motives for paid employment among blue-collar women, see Mary Lindenstein Walshok, "Occupational Values and Family Roles," in *Working Women and Families,* ed. Karen Wolk Feinstein (Newbury Park, Calif.: Sage, 1979), 63–83; Gerson, *Hard Choices;* and Kessler-Harris and Sacks, "Demise of Domesticity." Even Komarovsky's early, classic study *Blue-Collar Marriage* discusses the growth of noneconomic motives for employment among the wives of blue-collar men.

35. See Jessie Bernard, *The Future of Marriage* (New York: Bantam Books, 1973), 53, for her famous pronouncement that being a housewife makes many women sick.

36. For example, Barbara Ehrenreich suggests that "the working class, from

the moment of its discovery" by the professional middle class in 1969, "was conceived in masculine terms" (*Fear of Falling*, 108). See also Joan Acker, "Women and Social Stratification: A Case of Intellectual Sexism," *American Journal of Sociology* 78, no. 4 (1973): 936–45.

37. This was one of the understated findings of a study that attempted to operationalize Marxist categories of class. See Eric Olin Wright, Cynthia Costello, David Hacker, and Joey Sprague, "The American Class Structure," *American Sociological Review* 47, no. 6 (December 1982): 709–26.

38. Ehrenreich, *Fear of Falling*, 101.

39. Ibid., 115.

40. Ibid., 223. In December 1989, *Time* magazine ran a cover story on the future of feminism that drew quick, angry rebuttals from many feminists, a response I find out of proportion to the substance or the data in the story. A survey of 1000 women, conducted in 1989 by Yankelovich Clancy Shulman for *Time/CNN*, found a smaller proportion of the women sampled—33 percent—choosing to identify themselves as "feminists." However, 77 percent of the women surveyed claimed that the women's movement has made life better, 94 percent said the movement helped women become more independent, and 82 percent said it was still improving the lives of American women. Addressing a perceived discrepancy among these data, Claudia Wallis, the story's author, opined that "in many ways, feminism is a victim of its own resounding achievements" (p. 82). See "Onward, Women!" *Time* (December 4, 1989): 80–89.

41. For example, Daniel Bell, *The End of Ideology: On the Exhaustion of Political Ideas in the Fifties* (New York: Free Press, 1962); and Seymour Martin Lipset, *Political Man* (Garden City, N.Y.: Doubleday, 1963).

42. Employing conservative measurement techniques designed to understate the extent of income loss, a recent study of changes in family income found that 40 percent of American families have lost income since 1979, and another 20 percent have maintained stable incomes only because working wives' earnings compensated for falling wages of husbands. See Stephen Rose and David Fasenfest, "Family Incomes in the 1980s: New Pressure on Wives, Husbands, and Young Adults," Working Paper No. 103 (Washington, D.C.: Economic Policy Institute, November 1988). See also Katherine S. Newman's chapter in this volume and her *Falling from Grace: The Experience of Downward Mobility in the American Middle Class* (New York: Free Press, 1988); Bennett Harrison and Barry Bluestone, *The Great U-Turn* (New York: Basic Books, 1988); Sara Kuhn and Barry Bluestone, "Economic Restructuring and Female Labor: The Impact of Industrial Change on Women," in *Women, Households, and the Economy*, ed. Beneria and Stimpson, 3–32; Joan Smith, "Marginalized Labor Forces During the Reagan Recovery" (paper presented to Society for the Study of Social Problems, Berkeley, California, August 19, 1989); and Alan Wolfe, *Whose Keeper?* Moreover, income measures grossly understate the extent of economic inequality in this society. A recent study of the distribution of wealth, commissioned by the Census Bureau, surveyed assets as well as income and found grave disparities. For example, the median net worth of the top 1 percent of American households was twenty-two times greater than the median net worth of the remaining 99 percent. See David R. Francis, "Study Finds Steep Inequality in Wealth," *San Francisco Chronicle* (March 30, 1990), A19.

43. William Wilson, *The Truly Disadvantaged*, and J. Smith, "Marginalized Labor Forces." One consequence of this is an increasing divergence in the family patterns of whites and African-Americans as marriage rates, in particular, plummet among the latter. See Andrew Cherlin, "Marriage, Divorce, Remarriage, 1950–1980s" (paper presented at American Sociological Association Meetings, San Francisco, August 11, 1989, 17–18). Francis reports that the median net worth of whites is 11.7 times that of African-Americans ("Study Finds Steep Inequality in Wealth").

44. Vlae Kershner, "The Payoff for Educated Workers," *San Francisco Chronicle* (December 26, 1989), A2.

45. J. Smith, "Marginalized Labor Forces," 1. See also, *The Forgotten Half: Pathways to Success for America's Youth and Young Families.* (Washington, D.C.: William T. Grant Foundation Commission on Work, Family, and Citizenship, November 1988).

46. J. Smith, "Marginalized Labor Forces," 1; Levitan et al., *What's Happening to the American Family?* 117. Rose and Fasenfast report a 17 percent decline in absolute earnings between 1979 and 1986 for men with high school educational levels or less ("Family Incomes in the 1980s," 11). Kershner reports that workers with five or more years of college gained 11 percent income between 1980 and 1987, while workers with high school diplomas broke even, and those with less education lost at least 5 percent of their earnings ("Payoff for Educated Workers"). See also, Smith, *The Forgotten Half*, and Harrison and Bluestone, *Great U-Turn.* As the size of the standing army has decreased, military recruiters can be much more selective. For example, the U.S. Army Corps now takes very few recruits who do not have a high school diploma. The sudden collapse of the Cold War is likely to exaggerate this trend.

47. Ehrenreich, *Fear of Falling*, 205.

48. Quoted in Wolfe, *Whose Keeper?* p. 65.

49. Eric Olin Wright and Bill Martin, "The Transformation of the American Class Structure, 1960–1980," *American Journal of Sociology* 93, no. 1 (1987): 1–29; Kuhn and Bluestone, "Economic Restructuring and Female Labor"; Kershner, "Payoff for Educated Workers."

50. Ehrenreich, *Fear of Falling*, 202; Rose and Fasenfest, "Family Incomes in the 1980s," 8. The gap between single-parent and married-couple households is even more dramatic when assets are surveyed. The recent Census Bureau study found the net financial assets of households headed by married couples to be nine times greater than those of households headed by unmarried people. (Francis, "Study Finds Steep Inequality in Wealth.")

51. Ehrenreich, *Fear of Falling*, 206. For supportive data, see Wright and Martin, "Transformation of Class Structure."

52. J. Smith, "Marginalized Labor"; Kuhn and Bluestone, "Economic Restructuring and Female Labor"; Kessler-Harris and Sacks, "Demise of Domesticity."

53. The controversial *Time* cover story on the future of feminism, for example, reports a 1989 survey by Robert Half International in which 56 percent of men polled said they would forfeit one-fourth of their salaries "to have more family or personal time," and 45 percent "said they would probably refuse a promotion that involved sacrificing hours with their family." See Zavella, "Sun Belt Hispanics on the Line," for a discussion of the active participation in child care

and housework by Hispanic husbands of women who are "mainstay providers" for their households. And see Gerson's chapter in this volume, and Segal, *Slow Motion*, chapters 2 and 10, for fuller discussions of men's changing family lives.

54. Cherlin, "Marriage, Divorce, Remarriage," 17.

55. Between 1960 and 1980, there was a 43 percent decline among men between the ages of twenty and forty-nine. Frank F. Furstenberg, Jr., in "Good Dads, Bad Dads: Two Faces of Fatherhood," in *The Changing American Family and Public Policy*, ed. Andrew J. Cherlin (Washington, D.C.: Urban Institute Press, 1988), 201, offers an intelligent, historically situated analysis of the contradictory evidence on contemporary fatherhood.

56. The 90 percent datum is reported in Andrew Cherlin's introduction to his edited collection, *The Changing American Family and Public Policy* (Washington, D.C.: Urban Institute Press, 1988), 8. See Nancy D. Polikoff, "Gender and Child-Custody Determinations: Exploding the Myths," in *Families, Politics, and Public Policy: A Feminist Dialogue on Women and the State*, ed. Irene Diamond (New York: Longman, 1983), for a careful refutation of the widespread view that women retain an unfair advantage over men in child-custody decisions by divorce courts.

57. Emily Abel, "Adult Daughters and Care for the Elderly," *Feminist Studies* 12, no. 3 (Fall 1986): 479–97.

58. Particularly histrionic, but not unique, is the rhetoric in a promotional letter I received in 1990 for a new journal, *The Family in America*, which promises to cover such issues as "Vanishing Moms" and "Day Care: Thalidomide of the 90s."

59. See, for example, Lasch, *Haven in a Heartless World;* Davis, "The Meaning and Significance of Marriage"; and Berger and Berger, *The War over the Family*. Recently, Alan Wolfe attempted to formulate a centrist position in the debate over contemporary family change that would resist nostalgia for patriarchal family forms while recognizing the destructive effects of state and market intrusions on "the family" (*Whose Keeper?*). He, too, worries about women's increasing involvement in the market and neglects to question men's inadequate involvement in domesticity.

60. Lisa Belkin, "Bars to Equality of Sexes Seen as Eroding, Slowly," *New York Times* (August 20, 1989), A1, A16. The *Time/CNN* survey data found even greater support for the women's movement (see note 40). Claudia Wallis, "Onward, Women!" *Time* (December 1989): 82. Similarly, Furstenberg reports a variety of surveys indicating steady increases in preferences for more egalitarian marriages. "Good Dads, Bad Dads," 207–8.

61. Zavella, "Sun Belt Hispanics on the Line," finds a similar discrepancy between "traditionalist" ideology and reformist practice among Chicanas who serve as primary wage earners in their households.

62. According to Joan Smith, low-income African-American families provide the sole exception to this generalization because the majority contain only one possible wage earner ("Marginalized Labor Forces," 1). For additional data, see Myra Strober, "Two-Earner Families," in *Feminism, Children, and the New Families*, ed. Dornbusch and Strober, 161–90.

63. According to Myra Strober, in 1985, 42 percent of households were of this type ("Two-Earner Families," 161). However, Census Bureau data for 1988 report that only 27 percent of all households included two parents living with

children (quoted in Philip S. Gutis, "What Makes a Family? Traditional Limits Are Challenged," *New York Times* [August 31, 1989], B1).

64. Larry Bumpass and Teresa Castro, "Trends in Marital Disruption," Working Paper No. 87-20 (Madison: Center for Demography and Ecology, University of Wisconsin, June 1987), 28.

65. As one of the journalists who reported the results of the *New York Times* survey given earlier concluded, "Despite much talk about the decline of feminism and the women's movement, American women very much want a movement working on their behalf as they try to win equal treatment in the workplace and to balance the demands of work and family" (E. J. Dionne, Jr., "Struggle for Work and Family Fueling Women's Movement," *New York Times* [August 22, 1989], A1, A14). The *Time/CNN* survey data cited in note 40 provide strong support for this claim, as do survey data reported by Furstenberg. For example: "From 1974 to 1985, women significantly increased (from 46 to 57 percent) their preference for a marriage in which husband and wife shared responsibility for work, household duties, and child care more equitably" ("Good Dads, Bad Dads," 208).

66. Study by Albert Solnit quoted in "Most Regard Family Highly," *New York Times* (October 10, 1989), A18. Andrew Cherlin also reports increasing marital satisfaction rates, despite popular concerns over family decline ("Economic Interdependence and Family Ties" [paper presented at American Sociological Association, San Francisco, September 9, 1982]).

67. Wolfe, *Whose Keeper?* 211.

68. Freud's famous goal for psychoanalysis was to convert "hysterical misery into common unhappiness" (Sigmund Freud with Joseph Breuer, *Studies in Hysteria* [1895], in the standard edition of the *Complete Works of Sigmund Freud*, vol. 2, ed. and trans. James Strachey [London: Hogarth Press, 1954], 305).

CHAPTER TWO

1. For a summary of the demographic changes in American family structure and the position of women since World War II, see Kathleen Gerson, "Changing Family Structure and the Position of Women: A Review of the Trends," *Journal of the American Planning Association* 49 (Spring 1983): 138–48.

2. This debate is closely linked to the "decline of community" argument, which has been recently revitalized by the popular success of books such as *Habits of the Heart* by Robert Bellah and his colleagues. This perspective argues that close-knit bonds of moral reciprocity have declined, leaving even middle-class Americans bereft of a language of commitment in which to create their moral discourse. The argument was foreshadowed by the publication of Christopher Lasch's critique of the modern family in *Haven in a Heartless World*. See Robert N. Bellah and others, *Habits of the Heart: Individualism and Commitment in American Life* (Berkeley and Los Angeles: University of California Press, 1985), and Christopher Lasch, *Haven in a Heartless World: The Family Besieged* (New York: Basic Books, 1977).

3. For a refreshing analysis of how changes in gender relations have improved, not detracted from, the quality of interpersonal bonds—at least for some

couples—see Francesca Cancian, *Love in America: Gender and Self-Development* (Cambridge: Cambridge University Press, 1987). Cancian argues that egalitarian interdependence has become a third alternative to extreme individualism and unequal commitment in sexual, marital, and other intimate relationships.

4. Indeed, it is misleading to refer to "the family," since no one family form currently predominates. Instead, people coming of age today live in a diverse range of household types and family forms, and are likely to change their family circumstances over the course of their lives. For descriptions and analyses of the "patchwork quilt" of current family forms, see, among others, Andrew Cherlin, *Marriage, Divorce, Remarriage* (Cambridge: Harvard University Press, 1981), and James A. Sweet and Larry L. Bumpass, *American Families and Households* (New York: Russell Sage Foundation, 1987).

5. See, for example, Barbara Ehrenreich, *The Hearts of Men: American Dreams and the Flight from Commitment* (Garden City, N.Y.: Anchor, 1983); and Lenore Weitzman, *The Divorce Revolution: The Unexpected Social and Economic Consequences for Women and Children in America* (New York: Free Press, 1985).

6. See Judith Stacey's chapter in this volume for further discussion of the contours of continuity and change in what she aptly calls the "postmodern family."

7. If, as Webster's dictionary states, "tradition" means "cultural continuity in social attitudes and institutions," then there is no historically stable pattern that warrants the label "traditional family." Family structure has always changed in response to changing social-historical conditions. The male breadwinner–female homemaker household that is often referred to as traditional is actually a relatively recent, comparatively short-lived historical pattern. For an up-to-date overview of historical changes in American family patterns, see Steven Mintz and Susan Kellogg, *Domestic Revolutions: A Social History of American Family Life* (New York: Free Press, 1988).

8. Although children are profoundly affected by these dilemmas and conflicts, they will be considered only indirectly in this chapter, which focuses on the resolutions developed by adult women and men. For a closer look at the lives of children, see Gary Alan Fine and Jay Mechling's chapter in this volume. For now, suffice it to say that children will be the greatest beneficiaries of social policies that provide satisfying resolutions to the conflicts adults face between employment and parenthood.

9. Despite areas of notable change, gender inequality in wages and occupational sex segregation have persisted to a significant extent. See, for example, Paula England and George Farkas, *Households, Employment, and Gender: A Social and Demographic View* (New York: Aldine, 1986); Sara M. Evans and Barbara J. Nelson, *Wage Justice: Comparable Worth and the Paradox of Technocratic Reform* (Chicago: University of Chicago Press, 1989); and Barbara Reskin, *Sex Segregation in the Workplace* (Washington, D.C.: National Academy Press, 1984). Time-use studies conducted over the last several decades show mixed results concerning changes in the gender division of household labor. Although men, on average, appear to be spending more time performing housework than they were several decades ago, the gap between women's and men's time spent in housework remains substantial. While there are important substantive differences between

housework and child care, few surveys have disentangled these two dimensions of domestic labor. For summaries of the literature on the gender division of household labor, see Sarah F. Berk, *The Gender Factory: The Apportionment of Work in American Households* (New York: Plenum Press, 1985); Arlie Hochschild with Anne Machung, *The Second Shift: Working Parents and the Revolution at Home* (New York: Viking, 1989); Joan Huber and Glenna Spitze, *Sex Stratification: Children, Housework, Jobs* (New York: Academic Press, 1983); Joseph H. Pleck, *Working Wives/Working Husbands* (Newbury Park, Calif.: Sage, 1985); and John P. Robinson, "Who's Doing the Housework?" *American Demographics* 10 (December 1988): 24–28, 63.

10. Government and employer responses to the widespread changes in family structure and women's employment patterns are notable primarily by their absence. The good news is that the number of companies offering some form of child care assistance has grown from 2500 in 1986 to 5400 in 1990. The bad news is that we still lack national family and child care policies as well as widespread commitment among employers to provide supports for working parents as a right and not just a privilege. See Carol Lawson, "Hope for the Working Parent," *New York Times* (March 15, 1990), C1.

A widely publicized approach, dubbed "The Mommy Track" by journalists, was proposed by Felice N. Schwartz in an article entitled "Management Women and the New Facts of Life" (*Harvard Business Review* [January–February 1989]: 65–76). This proposal provides a remarkably regressive response to new family dilemmas. By relegating mothers, and mothers only, to a second tier in the managerial structure of organizations, it provides an old solution to a new problem. It relieves employers of the responsibility to address the twin dilemmas of gender inequality and work-family conflicts; it reinforces an unequal division of labor between women and men; it forces women to continue to make wrenching decisions between employment commitment and motherhood; and it maintains the historic obstacles to male parental involvement.

11. Both studies are based on in-depth life-history interviews with a carefully chosen sample of adult men and women. Each study focuses on comparisons of diverse patterns within each gender group—including comparisons between "traditional" and emerging patterns of family commitment. The first study examines the process by which women coming of age during this period of rapid social change have made choices between work and family commitments over the course of their adult lives. See Appendix 1 in Kathleen Gerson, *Hard Choices: How Women Decide about Work, Career, and Motherhood* (Berkeley and Los Angeles: University of California Press, 1985), for a full description of the study's sample and methodology. The second study analyzes men's changing commitments to family life and especially changes in the structure of male parental involvement. These findings will be fully presented in my forthcoming book, tentatively entitled *The Uncertain Revolution: Men's Changing Commitments to Family and Work* (New York: Basic Books, in progress).

Cynthia F. Epstein, in *Deceptive Distinctions: Sex, Gender, and the Social Order* (New Haven, Conn.: Yale University Press, 1988), and R. W. Connell, in *Gender and Power* (Stanford, Calif.: Stanford University Press, 1987), both argue persuasively for analyses that move beyond the assumption of "dichotomous distinctions" to explore the socially constructed, historically variable "varieties of masculinities and femininities."

12. The proportion of employed women who work year-round, full time, and who define employment in terms of career commitment is considerably smaller than the total percentage of women in the paid labor force. Although about two-thirds of mothers with children under six are now in the paid labor force, about one-third of this group is employed part-time. In terms of their family priorities, women with intermittent or part-time employment may have more in common with nonemployed women than with women committed to full-time, long-term careers. Both nonemployed and part-time employed women represent the persistence of older patterns amid the nevertheless indisputable trend toward increasing labor force attachment among women as a whole.

13. Drawing a distinction between "domestic" and "nondomestic" orientations necessarily oversimplifies a complex array of world views and behavioral strategies among women. While wide variation surely exists within each of these groupings, they nevertheless represent useful categories for understanding women's political outlooks and personal choices. See Kristin Luker, *Abortion and the Politics of Motherhood* (Berkeley and Los Angeles: University of California Press, 1984), for an insightful analysis of how the abortion debate has been fueled by the emergence of two opposing groups of women.

14. In confronting a gap between what they want and what they feel they should want, these women must also engage in what Hochschild calls "emotion work" in order to create some cohesion between what they are doing and what they feel they should be doing. See Arlie R. Hochschild, *The Managed Heart: Commercialization of Human Feeling* (Berkeley and Los Angeles: University of California Press, 1983).

15. Recent estimates from the Census Bureau suggest that about 15 percent of baby-boom women will remain permanently childless. This figure is below earlier estimates, but still above the childlessness rates of earlier generations of American women. See Felicity Barringer, "U.S. Birth Level Nears Four Million Mark," *New York Times* (October 31, 1989), A18.

16. The recent increase in the number of births does not represent an increase in the number of children per woman. Instead, as baby-boom women move through their childbearing years, more women are having children, but not a lot of them. Even as the number of births has risen in recent years, the average number of children per woman of childbearing age has remained below the replacement rate of 2.2 children per woman (ibid.).

17. A vivid example of this "cultural contradiction" in women's status is the current move to require poor mothers to work at a paid job in order to qualify for welfare while politicians and journalists simultaneously lament the increasing numbers of latchkey children among the middle and working classes. Clearly, the dilemmas women face span the class structure, affecting both domestic and work-committed women in the middle, working, and poorest classes.

18. See Ehrenreich, *The Hearts of Men,* for a discussion of the growth of the first group and Weitzman, *The Divorce Revolution,* for an analysis of the rise of the second. For insightful discussions of the emerging range of patterns among contemporary American men, see Frank F. Furstenberg, Jr., "Good Dads, Bad

Dads, Bad Dads: Two Faces of Fatherhood," in *The Changing American Family and Public Policy,* ed. Andrew J. Cherlin (Washington, D.C.: Urban Institute Press, 1988), 193–218; and Joseph H. Pleck, "The Contemporary Man," in *Men's Lives,* ed. Michael Kimmel and Michael A. Messner (New York: Macmillan, 1989), 591–97.

19. In addition to Pleck, *Working Wives,* see also William R. Beer, *Househusbands: Men and Housework in American Families* (South Hadley, Mass.: J. F. Bergin, 1983), and Kyle Pruitt, *The Nurturing Father: Journey toward the Complete Man* (New York: Warner Books, 1987).

20. For an analysis of the differences between women's and men's work-family choices, see William T. Bielby and Denise D. Bielby, "Family Ties:.Balancing Commitments to Work and Family in Dual Earner Households," *American Sociological Review* 54, no. 5 (October 1989): 776–89. For data on the decline of the male "living wage," see, for example, Frank Levy, *Dollars and Dreams: The Changing American Income Distribution* (New York: Russell Sage Foundation, 1987).

21. The argument that women will lose from equality was used by female opponents of the Equal Rights Amendment in their successful campaign to block its ratification. For penetrating analyses of the social and political bases of antifeminism among women, see Dierdre English, "The Fear that Feminism Will Free Men First," in *Powers of Desire: The Politics of Sexuality,* ed. Ann Snitow, Christine Stansell, and Sharon Thompson (New York: Monthly Review Press, 1983); Rebecca E. Klatch, *Women of the New Right* (Philadelphia: Temple University Press, 1987), and her chapter in this collection; Ethel Klein, *Gender Politics* (Cambridge: Harvard University Press, 1984); and Jane J. Mansbridge, *Why We Lost the ERA* (Chicago: University of Chicago Press, 1986).

22. See Rosanna Hertz, *More Equal than Others: Women and Men in Dual-Career Marriages* (Berkeley and Los Angeles: University of California Press, 1986), for an insightful analysis of the dynamics of dual-career corporate couples. Scott Coltrane shows significant parental involvement among a sample of fathers in dual-career partnerships (see "Household Labor and the Routine Production of Gender," *Social Problems* 36 [December 1989]: 473–90). John P. Robinson reports a modest rise since 1965 in the average amount of time all men spend doing housework, but this average masks important differences among men and does not include measures of child-rearing involvement ("Who's Doing the Housework?").

23. Although one-parent families headed by men remain rare, the percentage of male custodial households has grown from 1.9 percent in 1970 to 3.1 percent in 1989. See "Households Still Shrinking, but Rate Is Slower," *New York Times* (December 10, 1989), A47. The percentage of joint custody arrangements among divorced couples is growing at a much faster pace than male custody alone, but the exact statistical breakdowns are difficult to ascertain.

24. There is a "damned if you do and damned if you don't" aspect to everyone's choices. Working mothers are castigated for harming their children; childless women are accused of being selfish and unfulfilled; and homemakers are considered uninteresting. Similarly, involved fathers who withdraw from work are considered "wimps"; childless men are seen as irresponsible; and men who are primary breadwinners are "male chauvinists."

CHAPTER THREE

1. Peter Berger, "Sociology and Freedom," *The American Sociologist* 6 (February 1971): 3–4.

2. For example, John Boswell, *The Kindness of Strangers* (New York: Pantheon, 1989); Joseph F. Kett, *Rites of Passage* (New York: Basic Books, 1977); Philippe Ariès, *Centuries of Childhood* (New York: Knopf, 1962).

3. Gary Alan Fine and Kent Sandstrom, *Knowing Children: Participant Observation with Minors* (Newbury Park, Calif.: Sage, 1988).

4. For the notion of an oppositional culture, see Raymond Williams, "Base and Superstructure in Marxist Cultural Theory," in *Problems in Materialism and Culture: Selected Essays by Raymond Williams* (London: Verso, 1973), 31–49.

5. For "biformaties," see Michael Kammen, *People of Paradox: An Inquiry Concerning the Origins of American Civilization* (New York: Vintage, 1972). "Dualisms" are explored in Robert Lynd, *Knowledge for What? The Place of Social Science in American Culture* (Princeton, N.J.: Princeton University Press, 1939). The logic of "contradictions" is emphasized by Karen Horney in *The Neurotic Personality of Our Time* (New York: Norton, 1936) and by Daniel Bell in *The Cultural Contradictions of Capitalism* (New York: Basic Books, 1976).

6. The definition of a suburb is a difficult issue and, as a result, figures on suburban populations are not easy to come by. These percentages are derived from the population of metropolitan areas, excluding the central city; see Andrew Hacker, ed., *U/S: A Statistical Portrait of the American People* (New York: Viking, 1983), 27.

7. U.S. Bureau of the Census, *Statistical Abstract of the United States: 1941* (Washington, D.C.: Government Printing Office, 1942), 80; U.S. Bureau of the Census, *Statistical Abstract of the United States: 1987* (Washington, D.C.: Government Printing Office, 1989), 627.

8. On earlier forms of play, see Steven Zeitlin and Amanda Dargan, *City Play* (New Brunswick, N.J.: Rutgers University Press, 1990).

9. For example, Neil Postman, *The Disappearance of Childhood* (New York: Delacorte Press, 1982); Marie Winn, *Children without Childhood* (New York: Pantheon, 1983).

10. Brian Sutton-Smith, *Toys as Culture* (New York: Gardner Press, 1986), 37.

11. Ibid., 37–39.

12. J. A. Puffer, *The Boy and His Gang* (Boston: Houghton Mifflin, 1912).

13. Frederick Thrasher, *The Gang* (Chicago: University of Chicago Press, 1927).

14. Anthony D. Pelligrini, "Elementary School Children's Rough-and-Tumble Play and Social Components," *Developmental Psychology* 24 (November 1988): 802–6; S. R. St. J. Neil, "Aggressive and Non-aggressive Fighting in Twelve-to-Thirteen-Year-Old Pre-Adolescent Boys," *Journal of Child Psychology and Psychiatry* 17 (July 1976): 213–20.

15. Barry Glassner, "Kid Society," *Urban Education* 11 (April 1976): 5–22.

16. On case law, see Allan Korpela, "Tort Liability of Public Schools and Institutions of Higher Learning for Injuries Resulting from Lack or Insufficiency

of Supervision," in 38 ALR 3rd (1970), 879–80. For liability, see Jennifer Turner-Egner, "Liability of North Carolina Schools for Injuries During Nonschool Hours," *School Law Bulletin* 19 (Winter 1988): 7–19.

17. Spencer Cahill, "Childhood and Public Life: Reaffirming Biographical Divisions" (paper presented at the annual meeting of the American Sociological Association, Atlanta, Ga., August 1988).

18. L. W. Bowden, "How to Define Neighborhood," *Professional Geographer* 24 (August 1972): 227–28.

19. Data compiled from U.S. Department of Transportation, *Drivers Licenses 1963* (Washington, D.C.: Government Printing Office, 1964); U.S. Department of Transportation, *Drivers Licenses 1987* (Washington, D.C.: Government Printing Office, 1989). Nineteen sixty-three is the earliest year for which data are available, but records from 1945 would no doubt demonstrate a much more dramatic increase.

20. Gary Alan Fine, "Small Groups and Culture Creation," *American Sociological Review* 44 (October 1979): 736.

21. See for example, Richard Ruopp, Jeffrey Travers, Frederic Glantz, and Craig Coelen, *Children at the Center* (Cambridge, Mass.: Abt Associates, 1979); Spencer E. Cahill and Donileen R. Loseke, "Disciplining the Littlest Ones: Popular Day Care Discourse in Postwar America," (unpublished manuscript, 1990).

22. Gary Alan Fine and Sherryl Kleinman, "Rethinking Subculture," *American Journal of Sociology* 85 (July 1979): 1–20.

23. John P. Diggins, *The Proud Decades: America in War and Peace, 1941–1960* (New York: Norton, 1988).

24. Carol Stearns and Peter Stearns, *Anger: The Struggle for Emotional Control in America's History* (Chicago: University of Chicago Press, 1986).

25. See, for example, Beatrice Gross and Ronald Gross, eds., *The Children's Rights Movement* (New York: Anchor, 1977).

26. Alasdair MacIntyre, *After Virtue*, 2nd ed. (Notre Dame, Ind.: University of Notre Dame Press, 1984), 69.

27. For historical background, see Viviana Zelizer, *Pricing the Priceless Child: The Changing Social Value of Children* (New York: Basic Books, 1985).

28. Letty Cottin Pogrebin, "Do Americans Hate Children?" *Ms.* (November 1983): 47–50.

29. A similar transformation of informal social control into legal entanglements is evident in changing orientations toward adolescent sexual assault. Behaviors, such as fondling and ogling, that in the past might have been handled among peers or informally between the parents involved are now being brought into court. In this transition period, the victim (the teenage girl) may become the target of intense hostility for transforming naughty behavior into criminal behavior: for making a "federal case" out of these sexual assaults. See Doug Grow, "Suicide Ended Kathi's 'Fight for Dignity,'" *Star/Tribune* (St. Paul, Minn.) (July 5, 1987), 1A, 10A, 11A; Doug Grow, "Inver Grove Incident Highlights Attitudes on Sexual Harassment," *Star/Tribune* (December 20, 1987), 1A, 8A, 9A.

30. Pat Doyle, "School Faces Dilemma over Disruptive First-Grader," *Star/Tribune* (December 3, 1989), 1A, 18A.

31. Peter Asch and David T. Levy, statement prepared for presentation to the House Public Works and Transportation Committee, Subcommittee on Investigation and Oversight, September 18, 1986, p. 208.

32. Joel Best, *Threatened Children: Rhetoric and Concern about Child-Victims* (Chicago: University of Chicago Press, 1990); Neil Spitzer, "The Children's Crusade," *Atlantic* (June 1986): 18–22.

33. Joel Best and G. T. Horiuchi, "The Razor Blade in the Apple: The Social Construction of Urban Legends," *Social Problems* 32 (June 1985): 488–99.

34. The parallel move for older children in the 1980s has been the establishment of alcohol-free, supervised, all-night "grad night" parties to prevent drinking and driving, as well as sexual activity.

35. Gregory P. Stone, "Halloween and the Mass Child," *American Quarterly* 11 (Fall 1959): 372–79.

36. Best, *Threatened Children*, 22–64; Spitzer, "Children's Crusade."

37. Among the groups and singers so linked are Judas Priest, Ozzy Osbourne, and Iron Maiden. See Stephen Markson, "Rock 'n' Roll and the Politics of Cultural Prohibition" (paper presented to the American Sociological Association Annual Meeting, San Francisco, California, August 1989).

38. Stephen J. Pfohl, "The 'Discovery' of Child Abuse," *Social Problems* 24 (February 1977): 310–23.

39. William Kessen, "The American Child and Other Cultural Inventions," *American Psychologist* 34 (October 1979): 815–20.

40. Zelizer, *Pricing the Priceless Child*.

41. Elaine May, *Homeward Bound* (New York: Basic Books, 1988), 135–61.

42. An exception to this projection outside the family is the problem of incest and sexual abuse within the family. In these cases, a parent reluctantly comes to the conclusion that even the partner cannot be trusted.

43. Richard Gelles, *Family Violence* (Newbury Park, Calif.: Sage, 1979); Howard Erlanger, "Social Class and Corporal Punishment in Childrearing," *American Sociological Review* 39 (February 1974): 68–85.

44. It is said that there are only two ways to exert moral suasion over a child—through bribery and blackmail, and most parents employ both.

45. Elizabeth Walker Mechling and Jay Mechling, "Sweet Talk: The Moral Rhetoric against Sugar," *Central States Speech Journal* 34 (Spring 1983): 19–32.

46. If the central, broadly defined motif of the 1950s was how to raise a child and maintain a family, the motif of the 1960s was the flexing of adolescent political, cultural, and social muscle. The 1970s were justifiably called the "Me Decade" because young adults generally had too much money and insufficient responsibilities. The themes of the 1980s are the twin themes of the young middle age: parental concerns and economic security. Postwar American culture is in many ways a response to the demographics of the baby-boom generation, and the symbolic meaning that this demographic bulge has. This, too, is part of the *symbolic demography* of which we write.

47. Harry Stack Sullivan, *The Interpersonal Theory of Psychiatry* (New York: Norton, 1953), 227.

48. William Wells Newell, *Games and Songs of American Children* (New York:

Dover, 1983 [1963]); Peter Opie and Iona Opie, *The Lore and Language of School-children* (New York: Oxford University Press, 1959); Gary Alan Fine, "Children and Their Culture: Exploring Newell's Paradox," *Western Folklore* 39 (July 1980): 170–83; Jay Mechling, "Children's Folklore," in *Folk Groups and Folklore Genres,* ed. Elliott Oring (Logan: Utah State University Press, 1986); Simon J. Bronner, *American Children's Folklore* (Little Rock, Ark.: August House, 1989).

49. Fine, "Children and Their Culture."

50. Mechling, "Children's Folklore," 97–103; Brian Sutton-Smith, *A History of Children's Play* (Philadelphia: University of Pennsylvania Press, 1981).

51. Gary Alan Fine, "Good Children and Dirty Play," *Play & Culture* 1 (1988): 43–56.

CHAPTER FOUR

1. The rent-control and no-growth struggles of the 1970s and 1980s exemplify the increasing interest of the Left in the locality as a focus of action, with perhaps Santa Monica, California, as a model case. The 1960s and early 1970s gave us the "community control" movements associated with Lyndon Johnson's War on Poverty. Conservatives have always stressed the primacy of the locality. Neo-conservatives have further legitimated this view by borrowing from Tocqueville, calling the neighborhood one of the "mediating" institutions that make democracy possible in mass society (as in Peter Berger and R. J. Neuhaus, *To Empower People: The Role of Mediating Structures in Public Policy* [Washington, D.C.: American Enterprise Institute, 1977]).

2. The notable exceptions to many of these descriptions are the early Puritan villages, which only goes to show how atypical they were, their ideological legacy notwithstanding.

3. Rupert Wilkinson organizes his summary of the literature on American character around the "magnetic tension between individualism and community" (*The Pursuit of American Character* [New York: Harper & Row, 1988], 71).

4. The tension between individualism and community appears, among other places, in our contradictory images of city and country. For the most part, the city represents individual freedom, to the point of license, and the country represents communal fellowship, perhaps even to the point of oppression. (In some expressions, however, the city is a beehive of conformity, and the country, virgin land for individuality.) Most Americans prefer the small town, at least ideologically. For a comprehensive study of how Americans think of places, see David Hummon, *Commonplaces: Community Ideology and Identity in American Culture* (Albany: State University of New York Press, 1990).

Nineteenth-century Christian reformers instantiated these beliefs when they tried to create functional substitutes for small towns in the big cities (see, for example, Paul Boyer, *Urban Masses and Moral Order in America, 1820–1920,* [Cambridge, Mass.: Harvard University Press, 1978]). And twentieth-century sociologists who pursued the causes of deviance in the anomie of city neighborhoods formalized these beliefs (a paradigmatic example is Harvey W. Zorbaugh, *The Gold Coast and the Slum* [Chicago: University of Chicago Press, 1929]).

5. See David Hummon, *Commonplaces*. On the quest for local community, see, for example, Robert Hine, *Community on the American Frontier* (Norman: University of Oklahoma Press, 1980).

6. One should not exaggerate the stability of these old-world communities. There was considerable migration in Western Europe. Also, famine, plague, and other horsemen of the apocalypse often disrupted village life.

7. See, for examples, Laurence Wylie, *Village in the Vaucluse*, (New York: Harper & Row, 1964); George Foster, "Interpersonal Relations in Peasant Society," *Human Organization* 63 (Winter 1961): 174–84.

8. This pattern is the sort of thing treated by Robert N. Bellah and his colleagues in *Habits of the Heart* (Berkeley and Los Angeles: University of California Press, 1985).

9. Morris Janowitz, *The Community Press in an Urban Setting,* 2nd ed. (Chicago: University of Chicago Press, 1967).

10. The exceptions are largely "intentional communities," such as those of the Puritans or Amish, and transplanted European villages, such as some Scandinavian settlements in the Plains states.

11. For overviews, see Richard Lingeman, *Small Town America* (New York: Putnam, 1980); Hine, *Community on the American Frontier.*

12. This generalization should not hide the great variations among Americans in their orientations to locality, but rather highlight American tendencies. See Hummon, *Commonplaces.*

13. For example, Daniel J. Boorstin, *The Americans: The Democratic Experience* (New York: Vintage, 1973); Joshua Meyerowitz, *No Sense of Place: The Impact of Electronic Media on Social Behavior* (New York: Oxford University Press, 1985); Robert Wiebe, *The Segmented Society: An Introduction to the Meaning of America* (New York: Oxford University Press, 1975). See Thomas Bender, *Community and Social Change in America* (New Brunswick, N.J.: Rutgers University Press, 1978), for a commentary on these views.

14. One more direct study examined the extent to which real estate ads mentioned location as an attraction, comparing 1929 to 1979 Seattle. There was no change. Avery Guest, Barrett A. Lee, and Lynn Staeheli, "Changing Locality Identification in the Metropolis," *American Sociological Review* 47 (August 1982): 543–49.

15. See, for example, Stephen Thernstrom, *The Other Bostonians: Poverty and Progress in the American Metropolis 1880–1970* (Cambridge: Harvard University Press, 1973), 221–32, for a literature review; James P. Allen, "Changes in the American Propensity to Migrate," *Annals of the Association of American Geographers* 67 (December 1977): 577–87; and Donald H. Parkerson, "How Mobile Were Nineteenth-Century Americans?" *Historical Methods* 15 (Summer 1982): 99–109.

16. This settling-down is striking not only as a violation of expectations (why we have such expectations calls for another essay entirely), but also because it contradicts other changes that should have accelerated mobility, such as the dramatic increases in college attendance, divorce, retirement pensions, growth of the Sun Belt, and publicity about other places to live. Perhaps the best explanations are economic—that a mature and wealthy economy provides sufficient jobs to reduce the number of job-related dislocations—and technological—that the

abilities to commute and travel widely reduce the need to move for a job or for other reasons. See Larry H. Long and Celia Boertlein, *The Geographical Mobility of Americans,* Current Population Reports, Special Studies, Ser. P-23, No. 64 (Washington, D.C.: Government Printing Office, 1976), 27–58. They also look at such change data by age and education. The figure is drawn from Larry H. Long, *Migration and Residential Mobility in the United States* (New York: Russell Sage Foundation, 1988), 51; and U.S. Bureau of the Census, *Geographic Mobility: March 1986 to March 1987,* Current Population Reports, Series P-20, No. 430, (Washington, D.C.: Government Printing Office, 1989), 2.

17. Long and Boertlein, *Geographical Mobility;* Long, *Migration and Residential Mobility,* 253–82.

18. See reviews in Suzanne Keller, *The Urban Neighborhood,* (New York: Random House, 1968), and Claude S. Fischer, *The Urban Experience,* 2nd ed. (San Diego: Harcourt Brace Jovanovich, 1984), chapter 5. More recent studies include Robert J. Sampson, "Friendship Networks and Community Attachment in Mass Society: A Multilevel Systemic Model," *American Sociological Review* 53 (October 1988): 766–79; and Charles E. Connerly, "The Community Question: An Extension of Wellman and Leighton," *Urban Affairs Quarterly* 20 (June 1985): 537–56.

19. Housing style is hard to separate, in America, from home ownership (discussed below), but the detached house does seem to encourage neighboring, at least. See Carol J. Silverman, "Neighboring and Urbanism: Commonality versus Friendship," *Urban Affairs Quarterly* 22 (December 1986): 312–28; as well as Keller, *Urban Neighborhood;* and Fischer, *Urban Experience,* chapter 5. The issue of suburban government is more complex. On the one hand, participation in these polities tends to be low; they often have "caretaker" governments. On the other, when an issue threatens the typical consensus, these are strongly defensive and mobilized polities. See Fischer, *Urban Experience,* chapter 9; and "The City and Political Psychology," *American Political Science Review* 69 (1975): 559–71.

20. A national inquiry resulted in *Report of the Country Life Commission,* 60th Congress, 2d Session, Senate Document 705 (Washington, D.C.: Government Printing Office, 1909); see also O. F. Larson and T. F. Jones, "The Unpublished Data from Roosevelt's Commission on Country Life," *Agricultural History* 50 (October 1976): 583–99.

21. See Stanley Lieberson, *A Piece of the Pie: Black and White Immigrants Since 1880* (Berkeley and Los Angeles: University of California Press, 1980); Olivier Zunz, *The Changing Face of Inequality,* (Chicago: University of Chicago Press, 1982); Kathleen Neils Conzen, "Immigrants, Immigrant Neighborhoods, and Ethnic Identity: Historical Issues," *Journal of American History* 66 (December 1979): 601–15; Avery Guest, "Urban History, Population Densities, and Higher Status Residential Location," *Economic Geography* 48 (October 1972): 375–87.

22. See, for example, Susan K. Lewis, "Spatial Context in Network Building: Does Place Matter?" (paper presented to the American Sociological Association, Atlanta, August 1988); Silverman, "Neighboring and Urbanism"; Keller, *Urban Neighborhood;* and Fischer, *Urban Experience.*

23. On the long-term pattern, see Lieberson, *Piece of the Pie.* For recent data, see, for example, Douglas S. Massey and Nancy A. Denton, "Trends in the Resi-

dential Segregation of Blacks, Hispanics, and Asians: 1970–1980," *American Sociological Review* 52 (December 1987): 802–25; and Denton, "Suburbanization and Segregation in U.S. Metropolitan Areas," *American Journal of Sociology* 94 (November 1988): 592–626. On the cost blacks pay for this homogeneity, see, for example, Douglas S. Massey, Gretchen A. Condran, and Nancy A. Denton, "The Effect of Residential Segregation on Social and Economic Well-Being" *Social Forces* 66 (September 1987): 29–56. On concentrations of the poor, see Douglas S. Massey and Mitchell L. Eggers, "The Ecology of Inequality: Minorities and the Concentration of Poverty, 1970–1980," *American Journal of Sociology* 95 (March 1990): 1153–89.

24. Albert Chevan, "The Growth of Home Ownership: 1940–1980," *Demography* 26 (May 1989), 255.

25. See, for example, Edward Clark Clifford, Jr., *The American Family Home, 1800–1900* (Chapel Hill: University of North Carolina Press, 1986); David P. Handlin, *The American Home: Architecture and Society, 1815–1915* (Boston: Little, Brown, 1979); Claire Cooper, "The House as a Symbol of the Self," Working Paper No. 120 (Berkeley: Institute for Urban and Regional Development, University of California, 1971).

26. See Chevan, "Growth of Home Ownership"; Daniel D. Luria, "Wealth, Capital, and Power: The Social Meaning of Home Ownership," *Journal of Interdisciplinary History* 7 (Autumn 1976): 261–82; Margaret Marsh, "From Separation to Togetherness: The Social Construction of Domestic Space in American Suburbs, 1840–1915," *Journal of American History* 76 (September 1989): 506–27.

27. *New York Times* (February 28, 1985), 17. Three-fourths of *renters* interviewed in 1982 in suburban Orange County, California, still hoped to own their own homes (Mark Baldassare, *Trouble in Paradise: The Suburban Transformation in America* [Berkeley and Los Angeles: University of California Press, 1986], 64).

28. See, for example, Constance Perin, *Everything in Its Place: Social Order and Land Use in America* (Princeton, N.J.: Princeton University Press, 1977); and William Michelson, *Environmental Choice, Human Behavior, and Residential Satisfaction* (New York: Oxford University Press, 1977).

29. In one report it dropped from a peak of 66 percent of the population living in owner-occupied housing in 1980–82 to 64 percent in 1988; "Home Ownership Found to Decline," *New York Times* (October 7, 1989), 1; and U.S. Bureau of the Census, *Census and You* (Washington, D.C.: U.S. Government Printing Office, 1989).

30. One indicator of affordability is the ratio of the median sales price for a new single-family house to median family income (John S. Adams, *Housing America in the 1980s* [New York: Russell Sage Foundation, 1987], 83). The ratios are shown in the accompanying table.

	1965	1970	1975	1980	1985
Two-Earner Couples	2.3	2.7	2.3	2.4	2.3
Single-Earner Couples	3.0	3.5	3.1	3.4	3.4

Data drawn from Adams, *Housing America,* and U.S. Bureau of the Census, *Statistical Abstract of the United States: 1988* (Washington, D.C.: Government Printing Office, 1987), 430, 685. The data suggest that, for two-earner couples, affordability has remained essentially level since 1965, but that for single-earner households, housing prices have escalated. These numbers do not, of course, factor in fluctuations in interest rates, taxes, or utility costs, or regional differences.

31. Chevan, "Growth of Home Ownership"; "Home Ownership," *New York Times;* Adams, *Housing America.*

32. U.S. Bureau of the Census, *Historical Statistics of the United States, Colonial Times to 1970* (Washington, D.C.: Government Printing Office, 1975), 639, 683.

33. David Popenoe, *Private Pleasure, Public Plight: American Metropolitan Community Life in Comparative Perspective* (New Brunswick, N.J.: Transaction, 1985).

34. The qualifier "most" is important. For certain people, particularly poor children, changes in urban land use—further dilapidation and business development of the inner city—and the recent drop in subsidized housing construction have narrowed housing options, as is evidenced by increased homelessness.

35. See, for example, S. W. Greenberg, "Industrial Location and Ethnic Residential Pattern in an Industrial City: Philadelphia, 1880," and S. N. Burstein, "Immigrants and Residential Mobility," both in *Philadelphia,* ed. Theodore Hershberg (New York: Oxford University Press, 1981), 204–32 and 174–203; and Kenneth T. Jackson, "Urban Deconcentration in the Nineteenth Century," in *The New Urban History,* ed. Leo F. Schnore (Princeton, N.J.: Princeton University Press, 1975), 110–44.

36. U.S. Bureau of the Census, *Historical Statistics,* 133; idem., *Statistical Abstract: 1988,* 374.

37. See, for example, Keller, *Urban Neighborhood.*

38. U.S. Bureau of the Census, *Historical Statistics,* 41; idem, *Statistical Abstract: 1988,* 43. Most dramatically, elderly women increasingly lived alone. In 1900, 16 percent of noninstitutionalized elderly widows lived alone; in 1980, 67 percent did. See Tim B. Heaton and Caroline Hoppe, "Widowed and Married: Comparative Change in Living Arrangements, 1900 and 1980," *Social Science History* 11 (Fall 1987): 261–80; Frances E. Kobrin, "The Fall in Household Size and the Rise of the Primary Individual in the United States," in *The American Family in Social-Historical Perspective,* 2nd ed., ed. M. Gordon (New York: St. Martin's Press, 1978), 69–81.

39. Some types of Americans, however, do depend on the neighborhood for their social networks: the poor, the elderly, and children, for example. See Claude S. Fischer, *To Dwell among Friends: Personal Networks in Town and City* (Chicago: University of Chicago Press, 1982), chapter 13; the work of Barry Wellman, including "The Community Question: The Intimate Networks of East Yorkers," *American Journal of Sociology* 84 (March 1979): 1201–31; and Eugene Litwak and A. Szelenyi, "Primary Group Structures and Their Functions: Kin, Neighbors, and Friends," *American Sociological Review* 34 (August 1969): 465–81. Other recent studies include Connerly, "The Community Question"; Sampson, "Friendship Networks"; and Susan D. Greenbaum and Paul E. Greenbaum, "The Ecology of Social Networks in Four Urban Neighborhoods," *Social Networks* 7 (March

1985): 47–76. For reviews, see Keller, *Urban Neighborhood;* and Fischer, *Urban Experience,* chapter 5.

40. Barrett A. Lee, R. S. Oropesa, Barbara J. Metch, and Avery M. Guest, "Testing the Decline-of-Community Thesis: Neighborhood Organizations in Seattle, 1929 and 1979," *American Journal of Sociology* 89 (March 1984): 1161–88.

41. S. Dinitz, F. Banks, and B. Pasmanick, "Mate Selection and Social Class: Changes During the Past Quarter Century," *Marriage and Family Living* 22 (November 1960): 348–51, versus Norman T. Moline, "Mobility and the Small Town, 1900–1930: Transportation Change in Oregon, Illinois" Research Paper No. 132 (Chicago: Department of Geography, University of Chicago, 1971), 120–21; see also Claude S. Fischer, *Person-to-Person: The Telephone, Community, and Modernity, 1880–1940* (Berkeley and Los Angeles: University of California Press, forthcoming).

42. The quotation comes from Carolyn Marvin, *When Old Technologies Were New: Thinking about Electric Communication in the Late Nineteenth Century* (New York: Oxford University Press, 1988), 66. For academic analyses of the "placeless realm," see, for example, Melvin M. Webber, "The Urban Place and the Nonplace Urban Realm," in *Explorations into Urban Structure,* ed. Melvin M. Webber et al. (Philadelphia: University of Pennsylvania Press, 1964), 79–153; and Ronald Abler, "Effect of Space-Adjusting Technologies on the Human Geography of the Future," in *Human Geography in a Shrinking World,* ed. R. Abler, D. Janelle, A. Philbrick, and J. Sommer (Belmont, Calif.: Duxbury Press, 1975), 35–56. For a literary treatment, see Stephen Kern, *The Culture of Time and Space, 1880–1918* (Cambridge: Harvard University Press, 1983). The "annihilation of space" was a phrase American Telephone and Telegraph used in its advertisements.

43. One skeptical note was sounded by Malcolm M. Willey and Stuart A. Rice, *Communication Agencies and Social Life* (New York: McGraw-Hill, 1933). Willey and Rice, who argued that the telephone and automobile augmented *local* interaction more than they did distant ties.

44. By one estimate, "in 1902, local governments paid for 51.3 percent of all government services and delivered 64.0 percent. Today [1989], they pay for 14.1 percent and deliver 22.0 percent." See G. Ross Stephens, "Federal Institutional Centralization as a Response to Crisis: 1902–1988" (paper presented to the Southern Political Science Association, Memphis, Tenn., November 1989), 10; and idem, "State Centralization and the Erosion of Local Autonomy," *Journal of Politics* 36 (February 1974): 44–76.

45. According to Stephens ("State Centralization"), local governments received 51 percent of their revenues from their own sources in 1902 but only 18 percent in 1970.

46. On voter interest in levels of government, see Robert L. Morlan, "Municipal versus National Election Voter Turnout: Europe and the United States," *Political Science Quarterly* 99 (Fall 1984): 457–70; and Sidney Verba and Norman H. Nie, *Participation in America* (New York: Harper & Row, 1972).

47. In 1902, localities raised for themselves $41 per capita; in 1970, they raised—adjusted for inflation—$268 per capita (calculated from U.S. Bureau of the Census, *Historical Statistics,* 1133). Local governments increased their take, in terms of Gross National Product, from under 4 percent in 1902 to over 5 percent

in the 1980s. This pales beside the states' increase from 1 to 12 percent and the federal government's from 2 to 25 percent, but nevertheless represents real expansion (Stephens, "Federal Institutional Centralization," appendix table 6).

48. See Joseph L. Tropea, "Rational Capitalism and Municipal Government: The Progressive Era," *Social Science History* 13 (Summer 1989): 137–58; Joel Tarr, "The Evolution of the Urban Infrastructure in the Nineteenth and Twentieth Centuries," in *Perspectives on Urban Infrastructure,* National Academy of Sciences (Washington, D.C.: National Academy Press, 1984), 4–66.

49. Eric Schmitt, "Home Rule Gradually Slipping in New York Area," *New York Times* (August 10, 1988), A15.

50. Between 1947 and 1985, federal civilian employment grew from about 2.0 million to 3.0 million (51 percent). Municipal employees—*not* including employees of school districts—expanded from 1.2 to about 2.5 million (105 percent). (State employees grew fastest, from under one to nearly four million, 338 percent.) U.S. Bureau of the Census, *Historical Statistics,* 1100; idem, *Statistical Abstract: 1988,* 282. Between 1950 and 1985, local expenditures, including those for education, grew slightly faster than all federal expenditures, including those for defense (*Historical Statistics,* 1123–34; *Statistical Abstract: 1988,* 247, 294).

51. The proportion of urban Americans who resided in "places" whose populations were under 50,000 dropped as low as 38 percent in 1930 but grew to a majority of 51 percent by 1970 (U.S. Bureau of the Census, *Historical Statistics,* 11). The trend, by another measure, continued. In 1970, 47 percent of urban Americans lived in "cities" of under 50,000, and by 1986, the percentage was 49 (idem, *Statistical Abstract: 1988,* 32).

52. See John R. Logan and Harvey L. Molotch, *Urban Fortunes: The Political Economy of Place* (Berkeley and Los Angeles: University of California Press, 1987), especially chapter 5; Alan K. Campbell and Judith A. Dollenmayer, "Governance in a Metropolitan Society," in *Metropolitan America in Contemporary Perspective,* ed. Amos Hawley and Vincent P. Rock (New York: Sage, 1975), 355–96; Mark Schneider and John R. Logan, "The Fiscal Implications of Class Segregation: Inequalities in the Distribution of Public Goods and Services in Suburban Municipalities," *Urban Affairs Quarterly* 17 (September 1981): 23–36; and Scott Greer, *Metropolitics* (New York: Wiley, 1963).

53. On suburban politics, see, for example, F. M. Wirt, B. Walter, and E. F. Rabinovitz, *On the City's Rim: Politics and Policy in Suburbia* (Lexington, Mass.: Heath, 1972); Scott Greer and Ann L. Greer, "Suburban Politics," in *The Changing Face of the Suburbs,* ed. Barry Schwartz (Chicago: University of Chicago Press, 1976), 203–20; Fischer, *Urban Experience,* 283–85. One common kind of resistance is to metropolitanwide government. See, for example, Campbell and Dollenmayer, "Governance"; and Mark Baldassare, "Citizen Support for Regional Government in the New Suburbia," *Urban Affairs Quarterly* 24 (March 1989): 460–69.

54. The consumer language is borrowed from economists who have described this governmental fragmentation as an ideal marketplace where buyers can choose their preferred basket of services at their optimal price from a number of sellers (that is, townships). On the fiscal disparities among suburban municipalities, see Logan and Molotch, *Urban Fortunes;* also Kenneth T. Jackson,

Crabgrass Frontier (New York: Oxford University Press, 1985). For a recent study of how this fragmentation sustains school segregation, see David R. James, "City Limits on Racial Equality: The Effects of City-Suburb Boundaries on Public School Desegregation, 1968–1976," *American Sociological Review*, 54 (December 1989): 963–85.

55. On the history of neighborhood mobilization, see, for example, Zane L. Miller, "The Role and Concept of Neighborhood in American Cities," in *Community Organization for Urban Social Change: A Historical Perspective*, ed. R. Fisher and P. Romanofsky (Westport, Conn.: Greenwood, 1981), 3–32; Joseph L. Arnold, "The Neighborhood and City Hall: The Origin of Neighborhood Associations in Baltimore, 1880–1911," *Journal of Urban History* 6 (November 1979): 3–30; Patricia Mooney Melvin, "Changing Contexts: Neighborhood Definitions and Urban Organization," *American Quarterly* 37 (Summer 1985): 357–68; Ira Katznelson, *City Trenches* (New York: Pantheon, 1981); Manuel Castells, *The City and the Grassroots* (Berkeley and Los Angeles: University of California Press, 1983); and Harry C. Boyte, *The Backyard Revolution: Understanding the New Citizen Movement* (Philadelphia: Temple University Press, 1981).

56. Peter Rossi, "Community Social Indicators," in *The Human Meaning of Social Change,* ed. Angus Campbell and Philip E. Converse (New York: Russell Sage Foundation, 1972), 87.

57. In 1986, the median purchase price of an existing single-family house was, for example, $168,000 in the San Francisco Bay Area versus $82,000 in the similarly sized Detroit area, a ratio of 2 : 1. The ratio had been 1.8 : 1 in 1980 (U.S. Bureau of the Census, *Statistical Abstract: 1980,* 459). Within metropolitan areas, variations can be at least as great. One analysis compared identical new houses in three suburban San Francisco counties and found contrasts greater than 2 : 1 depending on specific location (Herbert Smokin Associates, Palo Alto, in *San Francisco Examiner* [March 25, 1990], F18).

58. This issue was raised by David Hummon.

59. See, for example, Carol J. Silverman and Stephen E. Barton, "Private Property and Private Government: Tensions between Individualism and Community in Condominiums," Working Paper No. 451 (Berkeley: Institute of Urban and Regional Development, University of California, 1986).

60. This issue was raised by Alan Wolfe.

61. Per capita, federal employment did *not* grow in the last forty years (Stephens, "Federal Institutional Centralization," 4).

62. Bender, *Community and Social Change,* chapter 5.

CHAPTER FIVE

1. Fred Block, *The Origins of International Economic Disorder: A Study of United States International Monetary Policy from World War II to the Present* (Berkeley and Los Angeles: University of California Press, 1977). In 1950, per capita Gross National Product (GNP) for the United States was $2,536, as compared to $1,000 for West Germany and $382 for Japan (Paul Kennedy, *The Rise and Fall of the Great Powers* [New York: Vintage Books, 1989], 369).

2. Imports of Third World countries, including Taiwan and South Korea, loom largest in the category of nondurable manufactured goods such as clothing and shoes. See Fred Block, "Rethinking the Political Economy of the Welfare State," in Fred Block, Richard A. Cloward, Barbara Ehrenreich, and Frances Fox Piven, *The Mean Season: The Attack on the Welfare State* (New York: Pantheon, 1987), 109–60. The core of the U.S. trade problem remains its bilateral deficits with Japan and Western Europe.

3. Defense spending was 6.6 percent of the 1985 GNP in the United States, 3.2 percent in West Germany, and 1 percent in Japan. Michael L. Dertouzos, Richard K. Lester, and Robert M. Solow, *Made in America: Regaining the Productive Edge* (Cambridge, Mass.: MIT Press, 1989), 114.

4. This argument has been developed particularly by Seymour Melman, *Profits without Production* (Philadelphia: University of Pennsylvania Press, 1987).

5. Melman, *Profits without Production*, reports that in 1976 research and development spending devoted to military purposes was estimated to be 31 percent in the United States, 8 percent in West Germany, and 1 percent in Japan (p. 158). Moreover, by 1977, Japan had 50 scientists and engineers serving civilian industry for every 10,000 people in the labor force; West Germany had 40; and the United States had only 38 (p. 171).

6. These competitive practices are described in Dertouzos et al., *Made in America*, chapter 9.

7. Ibid., chapter 7; Robert E. Cole, *Work, Mobility, and Participation: A Comparative Study of American and Japanese Industry* (Berkeley and Los Angeles: University of California Press, 1979); Charles F. Sabel and Michael J. Piore, *The Second Industrial Divide: Possibilities for Prosperity* (New York: Basic Books, 1984); Joachim Bergmann and Tokunaga Shigeyoshi, eds., *Economic and Social Aspects of Industrial Relations: A Comparison of the German and Japanese Systems* (Frankfurt: Campus Verlag, 1987).

8. Jocelyn F. Gutchess, *Employment Security in Action: Strategies that Work* (New York: Pergamon Press, 1985).

9. Thomas Kochan, Harry C. Katz, and Robert B. McKersie, *The Transformation of American Industrial Relations* (New York: Basic Books, 1986).

10. John Zysman, *Governments, Markets, and Growth: Financial Systems and the Politics of Industrial Change* (Ithaca, N.Y.: Cornell University Press, 1983), especially 245–51, 260–65. See also Dertouzos et al., *Made in America*, 61–63.

11. It is difficult to compare poverty rates across countries because of conceptual problems and issues of available data, so these figures are simply approximations. The poverty rates for children for West Germany and the United States are taken from a comparative study using data from 1979–81 (Timothy Smeeding, Barbara Boyle Torrey, and Martin Rein, "Patterns of Income and Poverty: The Economic Status of Children and the Elderly in Eight Countries," in *The Vulnerable*, ed. John L. Palmer, Timothy Smeeding, and Barbara Boyle Torrey [Washington: Urban Institute, 1988], 89–119). In this study, poverty is defined as a disposable income of less than half the national median adjusted income. The data on Japan are from 1985; the cutoff is equivalent to two-thirds of the U.S. poverty line (Samuel H. Preston and Shigemi Kono, "Trends in Well-being

of Children and the Elderly in Japan," in *The Vulnerable*, ed. Palmer et al., 277–307).

12. Richard Lynn, *Educational Achievement in Japan: Lessons for the West* (Armonk, N.Y.: M. E. Sharpe, 1988), 4–17. One study reported that the average Japanese student performed better than 98 percent of American high school students. See also Dertouzos et al., *Made in America*, 84–86.

13. Cynthia Hearn Dorfman, ed., *U.S. Study of Education in Japan* (Washington, D.C.: Government Printing Office, 1987), 7.

14. Dertouzos et al., *Made in America*, 87. Japan also has an extensive apprenticeship system.

15. According to OECD data, household savings rates for 1985–87 averaged 15.8 percent in Japan, 12 percent in West Germany, and 6.1 percent in the United States. Organization for Economic Cooperation and Development, *National Accounts*, vol. II (Paris: OECD, 1989). As we will see, serious questions have been raised about the validity of these figures.

16. George N. Hatsopoulos, Paul R. Krugman, and Lawrence H. Summers, "U.S. Competitiveness: Beyond the Trade Deficit," *Science* (July 15, 1988): 299–307.

17. Recent work has stressed the rhetorical nature of economic arguments. See Donald McCloskey, *The Rhetoric of Economics* (Madison: University of Wisconsin Press, 1986).

18. For an excellent discussion of the Federal budget deficit that addresses this metaphor directly, see Robert Heilbroner and Peter Bernstein, *The Debt and the Deficit* (New York: Norton, 1989).

19. White House Conference on Productivity, *Report on Productivity Growth* (Washington, D.C.: Government Printing Office, 1984).

20. Fred Block, *Postindustrial Possibilities: A Critique of Economic Discourse* (Berkeley and Los Angeles: University of California Press, 1990), chapter 5.

21. This evidence is reviewed in Block, *Postindustrial Possibilities*, chapter 4.

22. Barbara Ehrenreich, *Fear of Falling: The Inner Life of the Middle Class* (New York: Pantheon, 1989).

23. These arguments are developed at greater length in Fred Block, "Bad Data Drive Out Good: The Decline of Personal Savings Reexamined," *Journal of Post Keynesian Economics* 13, no. 1 (Fall 1990): 3–19.

24. Thomas M. Holloway, "Present NIPA Savings Measures: Their Characteristics and Limitations," in *The Measurement of Saving, Investment, and Wealth*, ed. Robert E. Lipsey and Helen Stone Tice (Chicago: University of Chicago Press, 1989), 21–100.

25. Fumio Hayashi, "Why Is Japan's Saving Rate So Apparently High?" *NBER Macroeconomic Annual* 1 (1986): 147–210. In a more recent study, Hayashi finds that there are only small differences (3 percent of Net National Product or less) between the national savings rates of the United States and Japan over the period 1978–1984. Fumio Hayashi, "Is Japan's Saving Rate High?" *Federal Reserve Bank of Minneapolis Quarterly Review* 13, no. 2 (Spring 1989): 3–9.

26. Ibid., 6.

27. Data on saving for housing and land in Japan are provided in Charles

Yuji Horioka, "Saving for Housing Purchase in Japan," *Journal of the Japanese and International Economies* 2, no. 3 (September 1988): 351–84. While Horioka does not believe that high land prices can explain high rates of personal savings in Japan, his data suggest otherwise.

28. Robert A. Blecker, *Are Americans on a Consumption Binge? The Evidence Reconsidered* (Washington, D.C.: Economic Policy Institute, 1990).

29. Connie Bruck, *The Predators' Ball: The Junk Bond Raiders and the Man Who Staked Them* (New York: Simon & Schuster, 1988), 272.

30. Block, *Postindustrial Possibilities*, 175–77.

31. Some ideas along these lines are elaborated in Block, *Postindustrial Possibilities*, chapter 7.

CHAPTER SIX

1. Barry Bluestone and Bennett Harrison coined this phrase in their book *The Deindustrialization of America* (New York: Basic Books, 1982). While I rely heavily on their perspective in this chapter, it is only fair to note that their thesis has its critics. For a review of the doubters see Katherine S. Newman, *Falling from Grace: The Experience of Downward Mobility in the American Middle Class* (New York: Free Press, 1988), 257–58.

2. Daniel Bell analyzed the importance of this transformation in his book *The Coming of Post-Industrial Society* (New York: Basic Books, 1973). The term "post-industrial" generally connotes the industries outside of goods-manufacturing, in which an increasing proportion of the American work force is employed. The consequences of this change in employment distribution, particularly a skewing of the wage structure toward low-income service jobs, is discussed at a later point in this chapter.

3. See Katherine Gerson's chapter in this volume for a discussion of working mothers.

4. Osha G. Davidson, *Broken Heartland: The Rise of America's Rural Ghetto* (New York: Free Press, 1990).

5. Bluestone and Harrison, *Deindustrialization*, 6. Emphasis mine.

6. Bluestone and Harrison, *Deindustrialization*, 10. Of course, many new jobs were created during the same decade. Hence Bluestone and Harrison argue that the net loss was a bit over one million jobs. Nonetheless, the job losers were not necessarily the same people as the new-job gainers, as persistently high rates of unemployment throughout the 1980s suggests. The focus of deindustrialization, then, is on the displacement that individuals and communities endure as a result of plant closures or relocations, all the while acknowledging that employment booms (of questionable benefit in terms of income) are occurring in other places.

7. Bennett Harrison and Barry Bluestone, *The Great U-Turn* (New York: Basic Books, 1988), 114–15.

8. Harrison and Bluestone point out that much of this loss was due to the elimination of more than 1.2 million jobs in durable-goods manufacturing. But $3.1 million was "salvaged" by forcing average real wages down (*The Great U-Turn*, 115–16).

9. Bluestone and Harrison, *Deindustrialization*. See also Terry Buss and F. Stevens Redburn, *Mass Unemployment: Plant Closings and Community Mental Health* (Albany, N.Y.: State University of New York Press, 1983).

10. L. Mishel and Julian Simon, *The State of Working America* (Washington, D.C.: Economic Policy Institute, 1988).

11. Newman, *Falling from Grace*, 31; See also Barry Bluestone and Bennett Harrison, "The Great American Job Machine: The Proliferation of Low-Wage Employment in the U.S. Economy" (study prepared for the Joint Economic Committee, U.S. Congress, December 1986).

12. Janet Norwood, the commissioner of the Bureau of Labor Statistics, is one of many who have critiqued virtually all the conclusions reached by Bluestone and Harrison about the proliferation of low-wage jobs. Norwood believes that Bluestone and Harrison have chosen too short a measurement period following the steep recession of 1980–81. She argues that after enough years of sustained recovery, these problems will disappear, since they were artifacts of the measurement period. There is reason to doubt this argument, if only because measurements of income inequality, wage stagnation, and job displacement more than six or seven years into the recovery period seem to show patterns similar to those identified by Bluestone and Harrison. See Janet Norwood, "The Job Machine Has Not Broken Down," *New York Times* (February 22, 1987), D5.

13. Harrison and Bluestone, *The Great U-Turn*, 127.

14. Mishel and Simon, *State of Working America*, p. iii.

15. Ibid., 23.

16. Peter Kilborn, "For Many Women, One Job Just Isn't Enough," *New York Times* (February 15, 1990), 1.

17. William Julius Wilson argues that an even more serious source of "havenots" involves inner-city men who depended on the manufacturing industries to gain entry to the formal labor market. Deindustrialization has meant a closing off of those very opportunities and, in Wilson's view, the creation of a growing urban underclass. See William Julius Wilson, *The Truly Disadvantaged* (Chicago: University of Chicago Press, 1987).

18. For a fascinating, if depressing, insight into the relationship between deindustrialization and homelessness, see Kim Hopper et al., "Economies of Makeshift: Deindustrialization and Homelessness in New York City," *Urban Anthropology* 14 (1985): 183–236.

19. Robert Jakall's insightful portrait of bureaucratic infighting in American corporations, *Moral Mazes* (New York: Oxford University Press, 1984), is a perfect manual for the rules of the game in the volatile financial service industries. For an analysis of what happens to white-collar management when the denouement finally arrives, see Newman, *Falling from Grace*.

20. CBS television news report, February 28, 1990.

21. In *Falling from Grace*, I discuss the meaning of plant shutdowns as moral commentaries on the state of American ideals of tradition and loyalty.

22. William Julius Wilson's much-discussed treatment of this issue appears in his book, *The Truly Disadvantaged*.

23. For the best discussion of the "mismatched" hypothesis, see John Kasarda,

"Jobs, Migration, and Emerging Urban Mismatches," in *Urban Change and Poverty*, ed. Michael McGeary and Laurence Lynn (Washington, D.C.: National Academy Press, 1988), 148–98.

24. This finding is reported in Frank Levy's important volume, *Dollars and Dreams: The Changing American Income Distribution* (New York: Russell Sage Foundation, 1987).

25. Susan Rose and David Fasenfest, *Family Incomes in the 1980s: New Pressure on Wives, Husbands, and Young Adults* (Washington, D.C.: Economic Policy Institute, 1988).

26. Harrison and Bluestone, *The Great U-Turn*, 130.

27. The declining-middle thesis as first offered by Robert Kuttner, "The Declining Middle," *Atlantic* (July 1983): 60. This thesis has many adherents, among them MIT economist Lester Thurow. But it also has its critics; among them is Frank Levy, who claims that, overall, the distribution has changed very little between 1947 and 1984 (*Dollars and Dreams*, 295). Much of the time the disagreement between economists depends on the time period they are measuring. Looked at from the vantage point of the "egalitarian" sixties and seventies, when income equality declined, the disappearance of the middle class is striking in the 1980s data. Examined from the bad old days of the immediate postwar period, when inequality was high to begin with, the present era doesn't look so bad.

28. Cited in Harrison and Bluestone, *The Great U-Turn*, 132.

29. David Halle has shown that blue-collar workers who are home owners consider themselves to be middle class, even though on the job they think of themselves as "working men." Home ownership is a major cultural symbol of arrival in the middle class and, to a degree, transcends occupation as a source of identity. See David Halle, *America's Working Man* (Chicago: University of Chicago Press, 1984), and the chapter by Halle and Frank Romo in this volume.

30. See Frank Levy's *Dollars and Dreams* (especially chapter 1) for an extensive treatment of the uneven impact of the post–1973 slowdown in income growth.

31. Newman, *Falling from Grace*, 78.

32. Barbara Ehrenreich takes a closer look at the pressures on baby-boomers in her book *Fear of Falling: The Inner Life of the Middle Class* (New York: Panthcon, 1989).

33. See Richard Sennett and Jonathan Cobb, *The Hidden Injuries of Class* (New York: Vintage, 1973), for an account of the idea of sacrifice among blue-collar workers. These authors show convincingly that low-level manual workers create an honorable identity out of an occupational category that is disrespected by "arguing" that they are sacrificing for their children.

34. This is, of course, a fictitious name for the community I studied. Since all the good fictitious names have already been used (Middletown, Plainville, etc.), I chose "Doeville" to signify the typical resident as John or Jane Doe.

35. "Average" is a tricky term here. It is no doubt the case that Doeville parents were on the high end of the middle-income spectrum, even in the 1950s. They were part of the new middle class. But they were not, and certainly did not think of themselves as, an elite. Only at the highest end of the community's scale would one have found the upper middle class.

CHAPTER SEVEN

1. "U.A.W.: World's Largest Union Is Facing Troubled Times," *Life*, 19 (September 10, 1945): 103–11.

2. Figures on 1945 unionization levels are from Michael Goldfield, *The Decline of Organized Labor in the United States* (Chicago: University of Chicago Press, 1987), 10; and US. Bureau of Labor Statistics, *Extent of Collective Bargaining and Union Recognition, 1945*, Bulletin No. 865 (Washington, D.C.: Government Printing Office, 1946), 1; the quote is from Nelson Lichtenstein, "From Corporatism to Collective Bargaining: Organized Labor and the Eclipse of Social Democracy in the Postwar Era," in *The Rise and Fall of the New Deal Order, 1930–1980*, ed. Steve Fraser and Gary Gerstle (Princeton, N.J.: Princeton University Press, 1989), 126.

3. See Goldfield, *Decline of Organized Labor;* Richard B. Freeman, "Contraction and Expansion: The Divergence of Private Sector and Public Sector Unionism in the United States," *Journal of Economic Perspectives* 2 (Spring 1988): 63–88; and Seymour Martin Lipset, "Labor Unions in the Public Mind," in *Unions in Transition: Entering the Second Century*, ed. Seymour Martin Lipset (San Francisco: Institute for Contemporary Studies, 1986), 287–321.

4. These figures are for private sector manufacturing wage and salary workers as a proportion of all employed civilian wage and salary workers, and are computed from U.S. Bureau of Labor Statistics, *Labor Force Statistics Derived from the Current Population Survey, 1948–87*, Bulletin No. 2307 (Washington, D.C.: Government Printing Office, 1988), 383, 386.

5. Figures for 1989 are from U.S. Bureau of Labor Statistics, *Employment and Earnings* 37 (January 1990): 231–32. Enumeration methods are different from those used in 1945 (see note 2 for sources for 1945 data), so that the figures are not strictly comparable; yet there can be no doubt as to the magnitude and direction of the change.

6. Employment in the motor vehicle and equipment industry (SIC 371) fell 194,600 between December 1978 and February 1988. See U.S. Bureau of Labor Statistics, *Employment and Earnings*, various issues.

7. Stephen Herzenberg, "Whither Social Unionism: Labor-Management Relations in the U.S. and Canadian Auto Industries," forthcoming in *Canadian and American Labor Respond: Economic Restructuring and Union Strategies*, ed. Jane Jenson; and *The Harbour Report: A Decade Later: Competitive Assessment of the North American Automotive Industry, 1979–1989* (Rochester, Mich.: Harbour & Associates, 1990), 244–46.

8. See Charles F. Sabel, *Work and Politics: The Division of Labor in Industry* (New York: Cambridge University Press, 1982), and Michael J. Piore and Charles F. Sabel, *The Second Industrial Divide: Possibilities for Prosperity* (New York: Basic Books, 1984).

9. The best account is Stephen Meyer III, *The Five-Dollar Day: Labor Management and Social Control in the Ford Motor Company, 1908–1921* (Albany: State University of New York Press, 1981). See also Joyce Shaw Peterson, *American Automobile Workers, 1900–1933* (Albany: State University of New York Press, 1987)

and David Gartman, *Auto Slavery: The Labor Process in the American Automobile Industry, 1897–1950* (New Brunswick, N.J.: Rutgers University Press, 1986).

10. See Carl Gersuny and Gladis Kaufman, "Seniority and the Moral Economy of U.S. Automobile Workers, 1934–1946," *Journal of Social History* 18 (Spring 1985): 463–75; Nelson Lichtenstein, "The Union's Early Days: Shop Stewards and Seniority Rights," in *Choosing Sides: Unions and the Team Concept,* ed. Mike Parker and Jane Slaughter (Boston: South End Press, 1988), 65–73; Piore and Sabel, *Second Industrial Divide,* 114–15.

11. See Irving Howe and B. J. Widick, *The U.A.W. and Walter Reuther* (New York: Random House, 1949); Nelson Lichtenstein, *Labor's War at Home: The CIO in World War II* (New York: Cambridge University Press, 1982); Howell Harris, *The Right to Manage: Industrial Relations Policies of American Business in the 1940s* (Madison: University of Wisconsin Press, 1982).

12. Women were better represented among workers in the auto parts industry, where wages were considerably lower. Blacks, on the other hand, remained largely excluded from the elite skilled trades workforce. For a historical account of the crystallization of postwar employment patterns in the auto industry by gender and race, see Ruth Milkman, *Gender at Work: The Dynamics of Job Segregation by Sex during World War II* (Urbana: University of Illinois Press, 1987). The best analysis of the history of blacks in the auto industry is August Meier and Elliott Rudwick, *Black Detroit and the Rise of the UAW* (New York: Oxford University Press, 1979). The 1987 Linden data were supplied by local management.

13. *1987 Agreement between Chevrolet—Pontiac—GM of Canada, Linden Plant, General Motors Corporation and Local No. 595, United Auto Workers, Region 9* (privately published), 37–42.

14. Computed from data supplied by local management at Linden.

15. Author's field interviews with GM workers in Linden, New Jersey. See also Eli Chinoy, *Automobile Workers and the American Dream* (New York: Random House, 1955).

16. See Emma Rothschild, *Paradise Lost: The Decline of the Auto-Industrial Age* (New York: Random House, 1973); Alan Wolfe, *America's Impasse: The Rise and Fall of the Politics of Growth* (New York: Pantheon Books, 1981).

17. Maryann Keller, *Rude Awakening: The Rise, Fall and Struggle for Recovery of General Motors* (New York: William Morrow, 1989), 204.

18. See Harry C. Katz, *Shifting Gears: Changing Labor Relations in the U.S. Automobile Industry* (Cambridge, Mass.: MIT Press, 1985).

19. Shoshana Zuboff, *In the Age of the Smart Machine: The Future of Work and Power* (New York: Basic Books, 1988), 395.

20. Larry Hirschhorn, *Beyond Mechanization: Work and Technology in a Postindustrial Age* (Cambridge, Mass.: MIT Press, 1984), 97.

21. Data supplied by local management. The finding that Linden is the most efficient GM plant in the United States is from *The Harbour Report,* 139.

22. Employment data supplied by local management. Other studies of auto assembly plant modernizations have found similar increases in the ratio of skilled trades to production workers. See for example Steven M. Miller and Susan R. Bereiter, "Modernizing to Computer-Integrated Production Technologies in a

Vehicle Assembly Plant: Lessons for Analysts and Managers of Technological Change" (paper presented at the National Bureau of Economic Research Conference on Productivity Growth in the United States and Japan," Cambridge, Mass., August 1985); See also Ulrich Jürgens, Thomas Malsch, and Knuth Dohse, *Modern Times in the Automobile Factory: Strategies for Modernizing Production: A Comparison of Companies and Countries* (forthcoming from Cambridge University Press, 1990); and Paul Windolf, "Industrial Robots in the West German Automobile Industry," *Politics and Society* 14 (1985): 459–95.

23. Harley Shaiken reports some evidence of this as well in his *Work Transformed: Automation and Labor in the Computer Age* (New York: Holt, Rinehart & Winston, 1984), 185–86.

24. This figure is from a survey conducted by the author and Cydney Pullman of fifty-two skilled trades workers at Linden.

25. This quote and those that follow are from interviews with Linden workers.

26. The complete list of skills we asked the skilled trades workers about was, in addition to the four mentioned in the text: "knowing about tools and machines, judgment, ability to communicate clearly, concentration, creativity, speed, knowledge of math, and physical strength." For production workers we used the same list with one exception: "creativity" was replaced with "knowing how your department works." In the case of the skilled trades, where the sample was relatively small (N = 52) the upgrading results were statistically significant for "memory," "accuracy/precision," "problem solving," "ability to communicate clearly," and "concentration." For the production workers' sample (N = 217), deskilling results were significant in all cases *except* "speed," "problem solving," "reading/spelling," and "knowledge of math." For a fuller account and analysis of the survey data summarized here, see Ruth Milkman and Cydney Pullman, "Technological Change in an Auto Assembly Plant: The Impact on Workers' Tasks and Skills," *Work and Occupations* 18, no. 2 (May 1991): forthcoming.

27. The term "flexible Taylorism" is from Christian Berggren, "'New Production Concepts' in Final Assembly—The Swedish Experience," in *The Transformation of Work?* ed. Stephen Wood (London: Unwin Hyman, 1989), 171–203. The term *Toyotism* is from Knuth Dohse, Ulrich Jürgens, and Thomas Malsch, "From 'Fordism' to 'Toyotism'? The Social Organization of the Labor Process in the Japanese Automobile Industry," *Politics and Society* 14 (1985): 115–46.

28. Keller quoted in Amal Nag, "Tricky Technology: Auto Makers Discover 'Factory of the Future' Is Headache Just Now," *Wall Street Journal* (May 13, 1986), 1. See also "General Motors: What Went Wrong," *Business Week* (March 16, 1987): 102–10; and Robert S. Harvey, "Misfiring with High Technology," *Metalworking News* (May 4, 1987): 30–31.

29. See Harris, *The Right to Manage;* Katz, *Shifting Gears;* and Thomas A. Kochan, Harry C. Katz, and Robert B. McKersie, *The Transformation of American Industrial Relations* (New York: Basic Books, 1986).

30. See Kochan et al., *Transformation;* Piore and Sabel, *Second Industrial Divide;* and Charles C. Heckscher, *The New Unionism: Employee Involvement in the Changing Corporation* (New York: Basic Books, 1988).

31. See Kochan et al., *Transformation,* 42–44; Parker and Slaughter, *Choosing Sides.*

32. See John F. Krafcik, "A New Diet for U.S. Manufacturing," *Technology Review* 92 (January 1989): 29–36.

33. Parker and Slaughter, *Choosing Sides*, 19.

34. Parker and Slaughter, *Choosing Sides*, 111. Lowell Turner points this out as well in his "Three Plants, Three Futures," *Technology Review* 92 (January 1989): 39–45.

35. The data on job classification are computed from rosters supplied by local management. Other information is from the author's fieldwork. The quotes in the paragraphs that follow are from interviews with Linden workers.

36. Horton quoted in Peter Downs, "Wentzville: Strangest Job Training Ever," in Parker and Slaughter, *Choosing Sides*, 190; Maurin quoted in *Choosing Sides*, 130.

37. Foote quoted in Richard Feldman and Michael Betzold, *End of the Line: Autoworkers and the American Dream* (New York: Weidenfeld & Nicolson, 1988), 178–79.

38. Turner makes this point in "Three Plants, Three Futures," 41.

39. See Clair Brown and Michael Reich, "When Does Cooperation Work? A Look at NUMMI and GM-Van Nuys," *California Management Review* 31 (Summer 1989): 26–44; Turner, "Three Plants, Three Futures"; Work in America Institute, Inc., "UAW-GM Joint Activities at the Plant Level," April 19, 1989, photocopy. On executive bonuses, see for example, "GM Chairman Got $1.9 Million in '85 in Salary, Bonuses," *Wall Street Journal* (April 21, 1986), 7; a year later GM ended the bonus program, partly in response to criticism from the union: see "GM's Goodbye to the Bonus," *New York Times* (April 17, 1987), D1.

40. Harry C. Katz, Thomas A. Kochan, and Jeffrey H. Keefe, "Industrial Relations and Productivity in the U.S. Automobile Industry," *Brookings Papers on Economic Activity* 3 (1987): 685–715.

41. See Turner, "Three Plants, Three Futures."

42. See Sabel, *Work and Politics;* Piore and Sabel, *Second Industrial Divide.* For a critical overview of the literature on post-Fordism, see Stephen Wood, "The Transformation of Work?" in *The Transformation of Work?* ed. Wood, 1–43.

43. Piore and Sabel, *Second Industrial Divide*, 261, 307; and in regard to the U.A.W., 244.

44. Harry Braverman, *Labor and Monopoly Capital* (New York: Monthly Review Press, 1974); Shaiken, *Work Transformed;* David F. Noble, *Forces of Production* (New York: Knopf, 1984).

45. Shaiken, *Work Transformed,* xiv. See also Barbara Garson, *The Electronic Sweatshop* (New York: Simon & Schuster, 1988).

46. See Guillermo J. Grenier, *Inhuman Relations: Quality Circles and Anti-Unionism in American Industry* (Philadelphia: Temple University Press, 1988); Parker and Slaughter, *Choosing Sides.*

47. For case studies from the auto industry supporting the deskilling thesis see Shaiken, *Work Transformed;* Harley Shaiken, Sarah Kuhn, and Stephen Herzenberg, "The Effects of Programmable Automation on the Work Environment: A Case Study of an Auto Assembly Plant," *Computerized Manufacturing Automation: Employment, Education and the Workplace* (Washington, D.C.: U.S. Congressional Office of Technology Assessment, June 1984), 293–357. Studies

supporting the upgrading thesis include: Kan Chen, Joe G. Eisley, Jeffrey K. Liker, Jack Rothman, and Robert J. Thomas, "Human Resource Development and New Technology in the Automobile Industry: A Case Study of Ford Motor Company's Dearborn Engine Plant," (Paris: Center for Educational Research and Innovation, Organisation for Economic Cooperation and Development, 1984, photocopy); and Miller and Bereiter, "Modernizing to Computer-Integrated Production."

48. Kenneth Spenner, "The Upgrading and Downgrading of Occupations: Issues, Evidence, and Implications for Education," *Review of Educational Research* 55 (Summer 1985): 146.

CHAPTER EIGHT

1. Werner Sombart provided an early example of both these approaches in the *same* book in his classic study, published in 1906, of why the American labor movement did not support Socialist parties in large numbers. Through most of the book Sombart listed many reasons why the American working class was integrated into society (and therefore not attracted to Socialism). Yet at the end he suggests that in the future all these reasons will wane, so that the model of the radical working class will soon become applicable to the American working class. See Werner Sombart, *Why Is There No Socialism in the United States?* trans. P. Hocking and C. Husbands (New York: International Arts and Sciences Press, 1976 [1906]).

2. For the view that the Western working class in general was integrated and quiescent in this period see Ralph Dahrendorf, *Class and Conflict in Industrial Society* (London: Routledge & Kegan Paul, 1959). For the use of the phrase "the American worker" to refer to the extreme case of this integration see Serge Mallet, *La Nouvelle Classe Ouvriere* (Paris: Editions du Seuil, 1969).

3. See, for example, Bennett Berger, *Working-Class Suburb: A Study of Auto Workers in Suburbia* (Berkeley and Los Angeles: University of California Press, 1968); Richard Hamilton, *Class and Politics in the United States* (New York: Wiley, 1972); and Lillian Rubin, *Worlds of Pain: Life in the Working-Class Family* (New York: Basic Books, 1976).

4. See, for example, Erik Olin Wright, "The Conceptual Status of Class Structure in Class Analysis," in *Bringing Class Back In*, ed. Scott McNall, Rhonda Levine, and Rick Fantasia (Boulder, Colo.: Westview Press, 1991); and Erik Olin Wright et al., "Rethinking Once Again the Concept of Class Structure," in *The Debate on Classes* (London: Verso, 1989).

5. The source for the data from 1900 to 1970 is U.S. Bureau of the Census, *Historical Statistics of the United States, Colonial Times to 1970*, Part 1, "Detailed Occupation of the Economically Active Population: 1900–1970" (Washington, D.C.: Government Printing Office, 1975). The sources for 1980 and 1989 are U.S. Bureau of Labor Statistics, *Employment and Earnings* (January 1981 and January 1990). All the data refer to the civilian labor force. "Blue-collar" in figures 8.1 and 8.2 refers to the data categories "precision production, craft, and repair occupations" and "operators, fabricators, and (nonfarm) laborers."

A data series extending over this length of time should be treated with caution. Note, for example, that prior to 1940 the data include workers ten years old and over; from 1940 to 1960, workers fourteen years old and over; and from 1970, workers sixteen years old and over. Definitions of clerical and sales workers in these statistical series are especially changeable over time, which makes defining the "lower-white-collar" sector especially hard. For the period 1900–1970, the lower-white-collar sector (as defined in figure 1) consists of two categories: "clerical and kindred workers" and "salesmen and bond salesmen." For the period after 1970, the lower-white-collar sector consists of the categories "administrative support, including clerical," "sales representatives, finance and business services," "sales representatives, commodities, except retail," "sales workers, retail, and personal services," and "sales-related occupations."

6. Thus, in the 1988 NES sample, men constituted 76 percent of all the blue-collar workers, and 94 percent of the skilled blue-collar workers. On the gender composition of the blue-collar labor force in the 1960s and 1970s, see Donald Treiman and Kermit Terrell, "Women, Work and Wages: Trends in the Female Occupational Structure since 1940," in *Social Indicator Models*, ed. Kenneth Land and Seymour Spilerman (New York: Russell Sage Foundation, 1974); and Valerie Kincade Oppenheimer, *The Female Labor Force in the United States: Demographic and Economic Factors Governing Its Growth and Changing Composition* (Berkeley, Calif.: Institute of International Studies, 1970).

7. In 1900 the proportion of blue-collar workers in the labor force was 23.4 percent, lower than now; in 1940 it was 30.4 percent, only a little higher than now.

The data presented in these paragraphs on blue-collar jobs are not, in fact, inconsistent with the data presented by Barry Bluestone and Bennett Harrison in their widely read *The Deindustrialization of America: Plant Closings, Community Abandonment, and the Dismantling of Business Industry* (New York: Basic Books, 1982). This is because the main data on aggregate employment over time that Bluestone and Harrison present (which lump together employment in factories, stores, and insurance companies) show that for the period 1969–76 there was a net *gain* of 8.6 million jobs (see Bluestone and Harrison, p. 30). On the other hand, the authors' central thesis –that there has been a major loss of industrial competitiveness in the global marketplace on the part of U.S. corporations operating from the United States—is undoubtedly true.

8. More specifically, "less-skilled blue-collar workers" here refers to blue-collar workers as defined in note 5, minus the category "precision production, craft, and repair occupations."

9. The overall estimates were calculated including Jewish respondents; however, owing to insufficient numbers, estimates of the Jewish blue-collar vote are unreliable and were therefore not graphed. (In the 1988 NES, 1 percent of the blue-collar workers were Jewish, 23 percent Catholic, and 77 percent Protestant.)

10. The NES data tend to overestimate voting rates. This is because the data are based on postelection surveys, and there is some tendency for respondents who did not vote to say they did. This tendency will not, of course, conceal the main trends in voting and nonvoting over time. For an argument that, despite a tendency to inflate turnout, the NES surveys provide the best data set for study-

ing trends in turnout, see Paul Abramson and John Aldrich, "The Decline of Electoral Participation in America," *America Political Science Review* 76 (September 1982): 502–21.

11. Twenty-one percent when controls are added for other factors, as in figure 8.15.

12. There is by now a large literature on the causes of the decline in voting rates in the last thirty years. Among the most plausible explanations are the reduction of the voting age in 1971 from twenty-one to eighteen (thus increasing the number of likely nonvoters, since young eligible voters are less likely to vote than others), the fading of political party loyalties, and a growth in the number of people who believe government is not responsive to them. For these perspectives, see Raymond Wolfinger and Steven Rosenstone, *Who Votes?* (New Haven, Conn.: Yale University Press, 1980); Richard Boyd, "Decline of U.S. Voter Turnout: Structural Explanations," *American Politics Quarterly* 9 (April 1981): 133–59; Paul Abramson, *Political Attitudes in America: Formation and Change* (San Francisco: W. H. Freeman, 1983); Paul Abramson, John Aldrich, and David Rhode, *Change and Continuity in the 1984 Elections*, rev. ed. (Washington, D.C.: Congressional Quarterly Press, 1987). For the argument that continuing barriers to registration have an important effect on the voting rate, see Francis Fox Piven and Richard Cloward, *Why Americans Don't Vote* (New York: Pantheon, 1988).

13. Although this belief does not vary by occupational group, it does vary by family income, union membership, and religion. Thus in a multinomial logistic regression analysis controlling for family income, age, education, region, union membership, religion, race, gender, and occupation, with the question "for whose benefit is the government run" as the dependent variable, we found for 1984 that the most significant determinants ($p = .05$ or less) were family income, union membership, and religion. People with lower family income, membership in a union, or Protestant or Jewish religious affiliation (in contrast to Catholic) were all more likely to believe that the government was run for the benefit of a few big interests.

14. See Craig Reinarman, *American States of the Mind: Beliefs and Behavior among Private and Public Workers* (New Haven, Conn.: Yale University Press, 1987); Jonathan Rieder, *Canarsie: The Jews and Italians of Brooklyn against Liberalism* (Cambridge: Harvard University Press, 1985); and David Halle, *America's Working Man* (Chicago: University of Chicago Press, 1984).

Although, typically, big corporations are seen as the major group controlling political and economic power, workers may add other groups as secondary members of the power structure (for instance, unions), or as beneficiaries of the power structure (for instance, public employees or organized minorities).

15. See Erik Olin Wright, *Classes* (London: Verso, 1985), 262.

16. In an influential study published in 1962, Robert Lane examined in detail the political and social beliefs of fifteen ordinary Americans—ten with blue-collar occupations and five with modest white-collar occupations such as supply clerk or bookkeeper. See Robert Lane, *Political Ideology* (New York: Free Press, 1967). In discussing the beliefs of his sample as to who runs America, he identified a minority of four whose views he dubbed "cabalism." Cabalism involved many

of the ideas just discussed—the belief that the government is run for the benefit of a small, influential group, often dominated by big business, who conduct their affairs behind the scenes away from the scrutiny of the public. (Of these four, some espoused farfetched views such as that a Jewish conspiracy underlay power in America. But others in the group believed simply that behind-the-scenes-big-business runs America.) Lane considered "cabalism" to be so farfetched that it must result from a personality defect—a weak control of ego on the part of those who held it. However, the survey and ethnographic data presented here suggest that, on the contrary, this set of beliefs pervades the outlooks of many blue-collar and other Americans.

17. For example, Herbert McClosky, in an article intended to stress the wide disagreements among Americans that national survey data revealed, commented that the question of freedom was an exception. All sections of the electorate "respond so overwhelmingly to abstract statements about freedom that one is tempted to conclude that for these values, at least, a farreaching consensus has been achieved." See Herbert McClosky, "Consensus and Ideology in American Politics," *American Political Science Review* 58 (June 1964): 361–82.

18. Werner Sombart, *Why Is There No Socialism in the United States?* 76. The 1975 figures are from an AFL-CIO survey of its members and are cited in Dolores Hayden, "What Would a Nonsexist City Be Like? Speculations on Housing, Urban Design, and Human Work," *Signs* 5 (Spring 1980): 170–87. See also Gwendolyn Wright, *Building the Dream* (New York: Pantheon, 1980).

19. By the early 1980s, and after a long period of rapid inflation in housing prices, purchasing a first home had become so expensive that the percentage of American families owning homes fell (between 1980 and 1986) from 66 percent to 63 percent. It was the first time this percentage had fallen since the end of World War II. See Alan Wolfe, *Whose Keeper? Social Science and Moral Obligation* (Berkeley and Los Angeles: University of California Press, 1989), 18. However, the recent leveling off, and even decline, in some regions, in the prices of houses may halt this decline in home ownership.

20. Home ownership and the ability to move to the suburbs and choose from at least some locations there is an important component of what Herbert Gans has referred to as "middle American individualism"—the desire (on the part of most Americans, but not necessarily the poor or the rich and upper-middle-class) to avoid obligatory membership in and commitments to institutions and organizations, in order to have the maximum choice about how to live, choice that in fact overwhelmingly prefers life in a "microsociety" of family and friends. See Herbert Gans, *Middle American Individualism* (New York: Free Press, 1988).

21. For this definition see Kenneth Jackson, *Crabgrass Frontier: The Suburbanization of America* (New York: Oxford University Press, 1985), chapter 1.

22. Eric Hobsbawm, "Labour in the Great City," *New Left Review* 166 (1988).

23. On these public transport developments see Kenneth Jackson, *Crabgrass Frontier.*

24. For the argument that, because of constraints imposed by public transport, especially the streetcar, skilled blue-collar workers in Boston in the late nineteenth and early twentieth centuries tended to live together in the inner sub-

urbs even though their incomes enabled them to buy houses in the outer suburbs where the middle class lived, see Sam Bass Warner, *Streetcar Suburbs* (Cambridge, Mass.: Harvard University Press, 1962).

25. These figures are based on detailed study of two areas—the post–World War II suburban areas developed on Long Island, and four counties of northeast New Jersey (Union, Middlesex, Monmouth, and Ocean counties).

26. See Herbert Gans, *The Levittowners*, (New York: Vintage Books, 1967), 22–23. As Eric Hobsbawm commented, "Migration to suburbs and satellite communities . . . for an increasing number of workers has snapped the links between day and night, or between the places where people live and those where they work, with substantial effects on the potential of labour organization, which is always strongest where work and residence belong together" (see "Labour in the Great City").

27. These figures on education levels come from the NES 1988 data.

28. Another occupational feature that might affect the leisure lives of blue-collar workers is that they typically have "jobs," not careers; their work is mostly dull, with limited chances for promotion. As a result, work is not a central interest. Thus many workers compensate for the dullness of their jobs by seeking leisure that is varied and exciting. This contrasts with the intrusion of work into leisure that is a recurrent theme in the lives of those upper-white-collar people with careers. The latter may become so absorbed in work that it displaces much of their leisure time; or they may mix work and leisure to the detriment of the latter (for instance, in the "social entertaining" of the business executive). The absence of an absorbing job protects the leisure lives of blue-collar workers from these consequences. Yet, as with the impact on leisure of their typically modest levels of education, the impact that having a "job" rather than a career has on leisure should not be exaggerated. For one thing, dull jobs with few prospects for promotion are not limited to blue-collar workers. Many lower-white-collar workers (clerical workers and secretaries) and numbers of people in upper-white-collar occupations, such as teaching, accounting, and managing at lower and middle levels, find their jobs of limited interest and have risen as high at work as they are likely to.

29. Besides the chapters in this volume by Stacey, Gerson, and Fine and Mechling, see *Families at Work*, ed. Naomi Gerstel and Harriet Engel Gross (Philadelphia: Temple University Press, 1987).

30. See Mirra Komarovsky, *Blue-Collar Marriage* (New York: Vintage, 1967); Theodore Caplow, Howard Bahr, Bruce Chadwick, Reuben Hill, and Margaret Williamson, *Middletown Families* (Minneapolis: University of Minneapolis Press, 1982); Gerald Handel and Lee Rainwater, "Persistence and Change in Working-Class Life-Style" and "Changing Family Roles in the Working Class," in *Blue-Collar World*, ed. Arthur Shostak and William Gomberg (Englewood Cliffs, N.J.: Prentice-Hall, 1964).

31. At the extremes of the class structure, the situations of wives are likely to vary. The best-educated wives can obtain upper-white-collar jobs, and the wives with wealthier spouses may not need to work at all. By contrast, women at the other extreme who are impoverished (especially single mothers with poor job prospects) face a set of problems in their family lives that are qualitatively more

severe than most. Still, in the middle are a large number of women who share many similar circumstances in their family lives.

32. For data showing the concentration among blue-collar workers of physical injuries incurred on the job and requiring amputation, see David McCaffey, "Work-Related Amputations by Type and Prevalence," *Monthly Labor Review* 104 (March 1981): 35–40.

33. Consider the relation between blue-collar and lower-white-collar work. Lower-white-collar work is not typically dirty or dangerous and does not involve heavy physical labor. Yet clerical and secretarial work is often as obviously repetitive and therefore dull as blue-collar work. It usually involves close supervision and surveillance. And it may offer limited chances of upward mobility, though probably not always as limited as most blue-collar jobs offer.

34. Eric Hobsbawm, "Farewell to the Labor Movement?" in *Politics for a Rational Left* (New York: Verso, 1989), 159–65.

35. See Samuel Lubell, *The Future While It Happened* (New York: Norton, 1973), 52, 95, 102; Herbert Gans, *Levittowners*, 105; Gavin Mackenzie, *The Aristocracy of Labor* (Cambridge: Cambridge University Press, 1973), 101; Robert Lane, *Political Ideology*, 66, 75, 357, 394; Studs Terkel, *Working* (New York: Pantheon, 1972), 189, 206–19, 552–58; John Leggett, *Working-Class Consciousness in Detroit* (New York: Oxford University Press, 1968), appendix A; and Jonathan Rieder, *Canarsie*.

36. For a brief discussion of the concept of the working woman, see Halle, *America's Working Man*, 214–18.

37. In his study of middle-income Italians and Jews in Canarsie, Brooklyn, Jonathan Rieder records this image of being middle class and referring to a lifestyle outside the workplace, and based on income level, a life-style that respondents saw themselves as either living or, more commonly, as falling short of. Consider the following comment by a resident: "Canarsie is up against the wall. That's what the lower-middle and middle classes feel pressing on them. It's all in danger: the house you always wanted is in danger, the neighborhood is in danger. It's all slipping away" (Jonathen Rieder, *Canarsie*, 98). On the importance for class consciousness of life outside the workplace, see also Ira Katznelson, *City Trenches* (New York: Pantheon, 1981).

38. For this technique, see James Grizzle, "Analysis of Categorical Data by Linear Models," *Biometrics* 25 (1969): 489–504; Michael Swafford, "Three Parametric Techniques for Contingency Table Analysis: A Nontechnical Commentary," *American Sociological Review* 45 (August 1980): 664–90; and G. S. Maddala, *Limited-Dependent and Qualitative Variables in Econometrics* (Cambridge: Cambridge University Press, 1983).

39. See Swafford, "Three Parametric Techniques," for more on this point.

CHAPTER NINE

1. Gerald David Jaynes and Robin M. Williams, Jr., eds., *A Common Destiny: Blacks and American Society* (Washington, D.C.: National Academy Press, 1989), 155.

2. Ibid., 11.

3. See, for example, Reynolds Farley and Walter R. Allen, *The Color Line and the Quality of Life in America* (New York: Russell Sage Foundation, 1987).

4. Bart Landry, *The New Black Middle Class* (Berkeley and Los Angeles: University of California Press, 1987).

5. Jaynes and Williams, *A Common Destiny*, 4.

6. Walter L. Updegrave, "Race and Money," *Money* (December 1989): 152–72.

7. Jaynes and Williams, *A Common Destiny*, 13.

8. Gordon Allport, *The Nature of Prejudice*, abr. ed. (Garden City, N.Y.: Anchor, 1958); W. Lloyd Warner and Paul S. Lunt, *The Social Life of a Modern Community* (New Haven, Conn.: Yale University Press, 1941).

9. On social Darwinism, see Stanford M. Lyman, *The Black American in Sociological Thought: A Failure of Perspective* (New York: Capricorn Books, 1972).

10. See, for example, Douglas S. Massey and Nancy A. Denton, "Trends in Residential Segregation of Blacks, Hispanics and Asians: 1970–1980," *American Sociological Review* 52 (6) (December 1987): 802–25; Gary Orfield, *Public School Desegregation in the United States, 1968–1980* (Washington, D.C.: Joint Center for Political Studies, 1983).

11. Nathan Glazer, "Blacks and Ethnic Groups: The Difference, and the Political Difference It Makes," *Social Problems* 18 (Spring 1971): 444–61.

12. Thomas Sowell, *Ethnic America: A History* (New York: Basic Books, 1981).

13. Edna Bonacich, "A Theory of Ethnic Antagonism: The Split Labor Market," *American Sociological Review* 37 (October 1972): 547–55; and Bonacich "Advanced Capitalism and Black/White Relations in the United States: A Split Labor Market Interpretation," *American Sociological Review* 41 (February 1976): 34–51.

14. William Julius Wilson, *The Truly Disadvantaged: The Inner City, the Underclass and Public Policy* (Chicago: University of Chicago Press, 1987).

15. Earl Raab and Seymour Martin Lipset, "The Prejudicial Society," in *American Race Relations Today: Studies of the Problems Beyond Desegregation*, ed. Earl Raab (Garden City, N.Y., Anchor, 1962), 30.

16. Lewis L. Knowles and Kenneth Prewitt, eds., *Institutional Racism in America* (Englewood Cliffs, N.J.: Prentice-Hall, 1969).

17. Stanley Lieberson, *A Piece of the Pie: Blacks and White Immigrants Since 1880* (Berkeley and Los Angeles: University of California Press, 1980); Stephan Thernstrom, *The Other Bostonians: Poverty and Progress in the American Metropolis 1880–1970* (Cambridge: Harvard University Press, 1973). The courts have recognized the phenomenon of "institutional racism" by declaring illegal occupational screening tests that disproportionally screen out blacks or females because of culturally biased questions with no relevance to job performance. The class and race biases of standardized tests used to screen applicants in academic settings have also come to be recognized.

18. Peter M. Blau and Otis Dudley Duncan, *The American Occupational Structure* (New York: Wiley, 1967).

19. Jeannie Oakes, *Keeping Track: How Schools Structure Inequality* (New Haven, Conn.: Yale University Press, 1985).

20. Updegrave, "Race and Money," 162.

21. Christopher Jencks, *Inequality: An Assessment of Family and Schooling in America* (New York: Harper & Row, 1972).

22. Stephen Steinberg, *The Ethnic Myth* (Boston: Beacon, 1981), 83.

23. Ibid., 154.

24. Ibid., 95.

25. Ivan Light and Edna Bonacich, *Immigrant Entrepreneurs: Koreans in Los Angeles, 1965–1982* (Berkeley and Los Angeles: University of California Press, 1988).

26. Steinberg, *Ethnic Myth*, 98.

27. John W. Blassingame, *Black New Orleans* (Chicago: University of Chicago Press, 1973).

28. Herbert G. Gutman, *The Black Family in Slavery and Freedom 1750–1925* (New York: Vintage, 1976).

29. Jacqueline Jones, *Labor of Love, Labor of Sorrow: Black Women, Work and the Family from Slavery to the Present* (New York: Vintage, 1985).

30. Ibid., 110.

31. Ibid., 137–38.

32. David M. Katzman, *Before the Ghetto: Black Detroit in the Nineteenth Century* (Urbana: University of Illinois Press, 1975), 104–5.

33. Ibid., 121–22.

34. Cited in Jones, *Labor of Love*, 154.

35. Bart Landry, "The Economic Position of Black Americans," in *American Minorities and Economic Opportunity*, ed. H. Roy Kaplan (Ithaca, Ill.: Peacock, 1977), 58.

36. St. Clair Drake and Horace R. Cayton, *Black Metropolis: A Study of Negro Life in a Northern City* (New York: Harper & Row, 1945), vol. 1, xlvi–xlvii.

37. Landry, *New Black Middle Class*, 47–48.

38. Lieberson, *A Piece of the Pie, passim.*

39. Bart Landry, "Race and Class: A New Paradigm" (paper presented at the 59th annual meeting of the Eastern Sociological Society, Baltimore, Md., 1989).

40. George M. Frederickson, *The Black Image in the White Mind: The Debate on Afro-American Character and Destiny, 1817–1914* (Middletown, Conn.: Wesleyan University Press, 1971), 49.

41. Cited in George M. Frederickson, *The Arrogance of Race* (Middletown, Conn.: Wesleyan University Press, 1988), 23.

42. Frederickson, *Black Image*, 52.

43. Frederickson, *Arrogance of Race*, 3.

44. Cited in Gutman, *Black Family*, 548.

45. Ibid., 471.

46. Steinberg, *Ethnic Myth*, 181.

47. Ibid., 176.

48. Ibid., 177.

49. Ibid.

50. Ibid., 179. Italics my own.

51. Jaynes and Williams, *Common Destiny*, 117.

52. Updegrave, "Race and Money," 154.

53. Jaynes and Williams, *Common Destiny*, 378.

54. Updegrave, "Race and Money," 168.

55. Gary Orfield, *Turning a Blind Eye: The Reagan Administration and Abandon-*

ment of Civil Rights Enforcement in Higher Education (Washington, D.C.: Joint Center Press, forthcoming).

56. Cited in Updegrave, "Race and Money," 162.

57. Jaynes and Williams, *Common Destiny*, 6.

58. Updegrave, "Race and Money," 156.

59. Landry, *New Black Middle Class*, 216–20.

60. Updegrave, "Race and Money," 159.

61. Jaynes and Williams, *Common Destiny*, 155.

62. Lynne Duke, "Whites' Racial Stereotypes Persist," *Washington Post* (January 9, 1991), A1, A4.

63. Leon F. Bouvier and Robert W. Gardner, *Immigration to the U.S.: The Unfinished Story* (Washington, D.C.: Population Reference Bureau, 1986).

64. *Washington Post* (August 11, 1990), E1.

65. *Washington Post* (August 10, 1990), A21.

CHAPTER TEN

1. Oscar Handlin, *The Uprooted*, 2nd ed. (Boston: Little, Brown, 1973 [1951]), 274–75.

2. Alejandro Portes and Rubén G. Rumbaut, *Immigrant America: A Portrait* (Berkeley and Los Angeles: University of California Press, 1990). The argument elaborated in this book provides the point of departure for this chapter.

3. See Portes and Rumbaut, *Immigrant America*, chapter 1; Stephen Steinberg, *The Ethnic Myth: Race, Ethnicity, and Class in America*, 2nd ed. (Boston: Beacon Press, 1989); "Immigrants: Special Issue," *Time* (July 8, 1985); Annelise Orleck, "The Soviet Jews: Life in Brighton Beach, Brooklyn," in *New Immigrants in New York*, ed. Nancy Foner (New York: Columbia University Press, 1987), 279; Thomas B. Rosenstiel, "L.A. Papers Speak a New Language," *Los Angeles Times* (November 9, 1987), A1; William Broyles, Jr., "The Promise of America," *U.S. News & World Report* (July 7, 1986): 25–31; Peter I. Rose, "Asian Americans: From Pariahs to Paragons," in *Clamor at the Gates: The New American Immigration*, ed. Nathan Glazer (San Francisco: Institute for Contemporary Studies, 1985), 182; "Ex-Pasadena Resident Earns Seventh Degree," *Houston Chronicle* (November 17, 1988), 26A; "Those Asian-American Whiz Kids," *Time* (August 31, 1987): 42–47; William A. Henry III, "Beyond the Melting Pot," *Time* (April 9, 1990): 29; Lawrence H. Fuchs, "Strangers and Members: The American Approach," *Brandeis Review* 6, no. 2 (Winter 1987): 3; *New York Times* (June 23, 1983), quoted in Ishmael Reed, "What's American about America? Toward Claiming Our Multicultural Heritage," *Utne Reader* (March-April 1989): 100.

4. Aristide R. Zolberg, "The Next Waves: Migration Theory for a Changing World," *International Migration Review* 23, no. 3 (Fall 1989): 403–30; Alejandro Portes and József Borocz, "Contemporary Immigration: Theoretical Perspectives on Its Determinants and Modes of Incorporation," *International Migration Review* 23, no. 3 (Fall 1989): 606–30. See also Aristide R. Zolberg, Astri Suhrke, and Sergio Aguayo, *Escape from Violence: Conflict and the Refugee Crisis in the Developing World* (New York: Oxford University Press, 1989); and the papers collected

in Mary M. Kritz, ed., *U.S. Immigration and Refugee Policy: Global and Domestic Issues* (Lexington, Mass.: Lexington Books, 1983).

5. Mary M. Kritz, "The Global Picture of Contemporary Immigration Patterns," in *Pacific Bridges: The New Immigration from Asia and the Pacific Islands,* ed. James T. Fawcett and Benjamin V. Cariño (Staten Island, N.Y.: Center for Migration Studies, 1987), 29–51.

6. Michael J. Piore, *Birds of Passage: Migrant Labor and Industrial Societies* (Cambridge: Cambridge University Press, 1979), 149–54; Maxine Seller, *To Seek America: A History of Ethnic Life in the United States* (Englewood Cliffs, N.J.: Jerome S. Ozer, 1977), 104–6; Alejandro Portes and Robert L. Bach, *Latin Journey: Cuban and Mexican Immigrants in the United States* (Berkeley and Los Angeles: University of California Press, 1985), chapter 2; Leonard Dinnerstein, Roger L. Nichols, and David M. Reimers, *Natives and Strangers: Blacks, Indians, and Immigrants in America,* 2nd ed. (New York: Oxford University Press, 1990), chapter 5.

7. For an analysis of changing immigrant sex ratios in recent decades, see Marion F. Houstoun, Roger G. Kramer, and Joan M. Barrett, "Female Predominance in Immigration to the United States Since 1930: A First Look," *International Migration Review* 18, no. 4 (Winter 1984): 908–59. On the development of migration networks, see also John Bodnar, *The Transplanted: A History of Immigrants in Urban America* (Bloomington: Indiana University Press, 1987); Robert R. Alvarez, Jr., *Familia: Migration and Adaptation in Baja and Alta California, 1800– 1975* (Berkeley and Los Angeles: University of California Press, 1987); Douglas Massey, Rafael Alarcón, Jorge Durand, and Humberto González, *Return to Aztlán: The Social Process of International Migration from Western Mexico* (Berkeley and Los Angeles: University of California Press, 1987); Sherri Grasmuck and Patricia Pessar, *Between Two Islands: Dominican International Migration* (Berkeley and Los Angeles: University of California Press, 1991).

8. The Immigration and Naturalization Service (INS) reported that a total of 3,038,825 illegal immigrants applied for legalization under IRCA by the 1989 deadline. These include immigrants who had resided in the United States since January 1, 1982, or who had been employed in seasonal agricultural work during 1985–86 ("Special Agricultural Workers"). Note that the annual INS data in tables 10.1, 10.2, and 10.3 refer to the years in which those immigrants were admitted to permanent resident status, which are not necessarily their years of arrival in the United States. Especially for refugees and others who are exempt from numerical quotas, but also for persons who entered with nonimmigrant visas (such as students) and later applied for permanent residency, there may be a time lag of a few years between their actual arrival and their formal adjustment to immigrant status. For that matter, many of the IRCA applicants (who will be counted in the INS legal admissions totals for 1989 and subsequent years, as their status is adjusted) probably arrived in the United States during the 1970s.

9. See Leon F. Bouvier and Robert W. Gardner, "Immigration to the U.S.: The Unfinished Story," *Population Bulletin* 41, no. 4 (November 1986).

10. David M. Reimers, *Still the Golden Door: The Third World Comes to America* (New York: Columbia University Press, 1985), 76; Thomas Kessner and Betty Boyd Caroli, *Today's Immigrants* (New York: Oxford University Press, 1982), 12–13.

11. U.S. Immigration and Naturalization Service, *Statistical Yearbook, 1988* (Washington, D.C.: Government Printing Office, 1989), xviii.

12. Calculated from annual data reported in U.S. Immigration and Naturalization Service, *Statistical Yearbooks*, 1978–89, and *Annual Reports*, 1970–77. For recent analyses of "chain migration" processes in U.S. immigration, see the papers collected in *International Migration Review* 23, no. 4 (Winter 1989); and Guillermina Jasso and Mark R. Rosenzweig, "Family Reunification and the Immigration Multiplier: U.S. Immigration Law, Origin-Country Conditions, and the Reproduction of Immigrants," *Demography* 23, no. 3 (August 1986): 291–311. For trends in refugee ceilings and admissions, see *Refugee Reports* 10, no. 12 (December 29, 1989): 6–9.

13. David W. Haines, ed., *Refugees in the United States* (Westport, Conn.: Greenwood Press, 1985); Silvia Pedraza-Bailey, *Political and Economic Migrants in America: Cubans and Mexicans* (Austin: University of Texas Press, 1985); Rubén G. Rumbaut, "The Structure of Refuge: Southeast Asian Refugees in the United States, 1975–1985," *International Journal of Comparative Public Policy* 1 (1989): 97–129; Rubén G. Rumbaut, "The Agony of Exile," in *Refugee Children: Theory, Research, and Services*, ed. Frederick L. Ahearn, Jr., and Jean L. Athey (Baltimore: Johns Hopkins University Press, 1991).

14. See Karen Tumulty, "When Irish Eyes Are Hiding . . . ," *Los Angeles Times* (January 29, 1989), A1; Portes and Rumbaut, *Immigrant America*, 230; Dinnerstein, Nichols, and Reimers, *Natives and Strangers*, 274–77.

15. The number of Border Patrol apprehensions of persons illegally crossing the U.S.-Mexico border surpassed one million during "Operation Wetback" in 1954, decreased to a low of 45,000 in 1959, and thereafter increased steadily each year until it reached a historical high of 1.8 million arrests in 1986, the year IRCA was passed; apprehensions then declined until 1989, when they suddenly increased again. In San Diego, where more arrests are recorded than anywhere else along the border, apprehensions totaled 215,860 during the six-month period of October 1989 to March 1990—an increase of over 50 percent from the 141,611 arrests made during the corresponding period a year before. Borderwide, total apprehensions increased by over one-third, from 341,675 to 472,121, for the same period. Illegal crossings follow a seasonal pattern; they are typically lowest during the fall and winter months, then rise sharply after Easter and during the summer months. See Patrick McDonnell, "Illegal Border Crossings Rise After 3-Year Fall," *Los Angeles Times* (April 22, 1990), A1; U.S. Immigration and Naturalization Service, *Statistical Yearbook*, 1989, xxxviii–xxxix, 109. See also Wayne A. Cornelius, "Mexican Immigration in California Today" (keynote presentation to the UCLA conference "California Immigrants in World Perspective," Los Angeles, April 26, 1990); Frank D. Bean, George Vernez, and Charles B. Keely, *Opening and Closing the Doors: Evaluating Immigration Reform and Control* (Washington, D.C.: Urban Institute Press, 1989).

16. Leonel Castillo, "Current Policies and the Effects of the Immigration Reform and Control Act on 'Extra-Legal' Refugees" (keynote presentation at the World Federation for Mental Health Conference on Immigrants and Refugees, Houston, March 24, 1990).

17. U.S. Immigration and Naturalization Service, *Statistical Yearbook,* 1989, 44; "Immigration Statistics: Fiscal Year 1989," *Advance Report* (April 1990).

18. By 1990 the Filipinos had passed the Chinese to become the largest Asian-origin population in the United States; they had already surpassed Japanese-Americans in 1980. See Leon F. Bouvier and Anthony J. Agresta, "The Future Asian Population of the United States," in *Pacific Bridges,* ed. Fawcett and Cariño, 291–92.

19. See Neal Harlow, *California Conquered: The Annexation of a Mexican Province, 1846–1850* (Berkeley and Los Angeles: University of California Press, 1982); Alvarez, *Familia;* Massey, Alarcón, Durand, and González, *Return to Aztlán.*

20. See Stanley Karnow, *In Our Image: America's Empire in the Philippines* (New York: Random House, 1989); Benjamin V. Cariño, "The Philippines and Southeast Asia: Historical Roots and Contemporary Linkages," in *Pacific Bridges,* ed. Fawcett and Cariño, 305–26; Antonio J. A. Pido, *The Philipinos in America: Macro/Micro Dimensions of Immigration and Integration* (Staten Island, N.Y.: Center for Migration Studies, 1986).

21. Reimers, *Still the Golden Door,* 29. It is more than an ironic coincidence that in Battery Park at the tip of Manhattan, just across New York Harbor from Ellis Island and the Statue of Liberty, a visitor will find a war memorial as well as several monuments memorializing the immigrant in American history, including the old Castle Garden depot through which most immigrants were processed until Ellis Island opened in 1892. One of these monuments—a few yards away from the Emma Lazarus memorial and her paean to "The New Colossus"—was erected on the "Admiral George Dewey Promenade" to commemorate the seventy-fifth anniversary of the battle of Manila Bay in 1898, which began the American colonization of the Philippines. The visitor cannot help but be struck by the "monumental" connection here, especially in light of the fact that Filipinos constitute the largest Asian-origin immigrant population in the United States today. It is curious that, except for refugee movements, the literature on recent immigration has paid scant attention to the role of the American military state and of politico-military relationships.

22. See Rubén G. Rumbaut and John R. Weeks, "Infant Health among Indochinese Refugees: Patterns of Infant Mortality, Birthweight and Prenatal Care in Comparative Perspective," *Research in the Sociology of Health Care* 8 (1989): 137–96.

23. See Ronald Takaki, *Strangers from a Different Shore: A History of Asian Americans* (Boston: Little, Brown, 1989); Ivan Light and Edna Bonacich, *Immigrant Entrepreneurs: Koreans in Los Angeles, 1965–1982* (Berkeley and Los Angeles: University of California Press, 1988); Illsoo Kim, "Korea and East Asia: Premigration Factors and U.S. Immigration Policy," in *Pacific Bridges,* ed. Fawcett and Cariño, 327–46; Stanley Karnow, *Vietnam: A History* (New York: Viking, 1983); Urmil Minocha, "South Asian Immigrants: Trends and Impacts on the Sending and Receiving Countries," in *Pacific Bridges,* ed. Fawcett and Cariño, 347–74; Grasmuck and Pessar, *Between Two Islands.*

24. Kim, "Korea and East Asia," 329.

25. See also Portes and Rumbaut, *Immigrant America,* chapter 7; Portes and

Borocz, "Contemporary Immigration"; Christopher Mitchell, "International Migration, International Relations and Foreign Policy," *International Migration Review* 23, no. 3 (Fall 1989): 681–708.

26. Data on international economic rankings are 1985 estimates for 211 countries compiled by *The Economist* and published in *The World in Figures* (London: Hodder and Stoughton, 1987). The fact that the United States was deeply involved in Indochina but not in Afghanistan or Ethiopia helps explain why Indochinese refugees were resettled in large numbers but Afghans and Ethiopians were not; see Astri Suhrke and Frank Klink, "Contrasting Patterns of Asian Refugee Movements: The Vietnamese and Afghan Syndromes," in *Pacific Bridges*, ed. Fawcett and Cariño, 85–104.

27. Alfonso Mejia, Helena Pizurki, and Erica Royston, *Foreign Medical Graduates: The Case of the United States* (Lexington, Mass.: Lexington Books, 1980); Rosemary Stevens, Louis W. Goodman, and Stephen S. Mick, *The Alien Doctors: Foreign Medical Graduates in American Hospitals* (New York: Wiley, 1978).

28. For a detailed analysis of the social process of foreign medical graduate (FMG) immigration to the United States, see Stevens, Goodman, and Mick, *The Alien Doctors*. For data on sending countries' proportions of FMGs, see Mejia, Pizurki, and Royston, *Foreign Medical Graduates*, 145–49. On the dramatic migration of Thai physicians, see Reimers, *Still the Golden Door*, 101. See also Charles Marwick, "Foreign Medical Graduates in U.S. Postdoctoral Programs: Concern Rises as Total Declines," *Journal of the American Medical Association* 257, no. 19 (May 15, 1987): 2535–37; "U.S. MD Glut Limits Demand for FMG Physicians," *Hospitals* 62, no. 3 (February 5, 1988): 67–69.

29. Robert Gillette, "Threat to Security Cited in Rise of Foreign Engineers," *Los Angeles Times* (January 20, 1988), A1; "Wanted: Fresh, Homegrown Talent," *Time* (January 11, 1988): 65; "Those Asian-American Whiz Kids," *Time* (August 31, 1987): 42–47; "Elegiacal: It Spells Success for Bee Champ," *Los Angeles Times* (June 3, 1988), A1; "2 in New York Are Top Science Winners," *New York Times* (March 1, 1988), A1; Portes and Rumbaut, *Immigrant America*, chapter 6.

30. See Rumbaut, "The Structure of Refuge"; Sonni Efron, "Sweatshops Expanding into Orange County," *Los Angeles Times* (November 26, 1989), A1. For a comparative analysis of "Asian" and "Jewish" cultural stereotypes of successful minority groups, see Steinberg, *The Ethnic Myth*, 263–302. For studies of the development of informal sectors in immigrant communities in New York, Miami, and Southern California, see Alejandro Portes, Manuel Castells, and Lauren A. Benton, eds., *The Informal Economy: Studies in Advanced and Less-Developed Countries* (Baltimore, Md.: Johns Hopkins University Press, 1989).

31. See Joan Moore and Harry Pachon, *Hispanics in the United States* (Englewood Cliffs, N.J.: Prentice-Hall, 1985); James D. Cockcroft, *Outlaws in the Promised Land: Mexican Immigrant Workers and America's Future* (New York: Grove Press, 1986); Joseph P. Fitzpatrick, *Puerto Rican Americans: The Meaning of Migration to the Mainland*, 2nd ed. (Englewood Cliffs, N.J.: Prentice-Hall, 1987); George J. Borjas and Marta Tienda, eds., *Hispanics in the U.S. Economy* (Orlando, Fla.: Academic Press, 1985). For two comparative studies of the effects of different social class origins and contexts of reception on the incorporation of Cu-

bans and Mexicans in the United States, see Portes and Bach, *Latin Journey*, and Pedraza-Bailey, *Political and Economic Migrants in America*.

32. Portes and Rumbaut, *Immigrant America*, 11–14, 247. See also Ted Conover, *Coyotes: A Journey through the Secret World of America's Illegal Aliens* (New York: Vintage Books, 1987); Grasmuck and Pessar, *Between Two Islands;* Jake C. Miller, *The Plight of Haitian Refugees* (New York: Praeger, 1984). Information on fees paid by Vietnamese "boat people" was obtained through personal interviews with refugees in San Diego, California. Interestingly, exchange arrangements via family branches similar to those reported by the Vietnamese have been developed by Soviet Jewish émigrés who are forbidden to take anything of value with them when they leave the U.S.S.R.; see Orleck, "The Soviet Jews," in *New Immigrants in New York*, ed. Foner, 289.

33. See Portes and Rumbaut, *Immigrant America*, chapters 2–4.

34. Ibid., chapter 2; see also Foner, *New Immigrants in New York*.

35. Gillette, "Threat to Security Cited in Rise of Foreign Engineers."

36. See Stevens, Goodman, and Mick, *The Alien Doctors;* it remains the most comprehensive available study of FMGs in the United States. See also Reimers, *Still the Golden Door*, 101; "FMG Residents Expensive to Replace," *Hospitals* 62, no. 10 (May 20, 1988): 77.

37. The most comprehensive analysis to date is Julian L. Simon, *The Economic Consequences of Immigration* (Cambridge, Mass.: Basil Blackwell, 1989). See also Portes and Rumbaut, *Immigrant America*, 235–39; George J. Borjas, *Friends or Strangers: The Impact of Immigrants on the U.S. Economy* (New York: Basic Books, 1990); and Borjas, "Economic Theory and International Migration," *International Migration Review* 23, no. 3 (Fall 1989): 437–85; Frank D. Bean, B. Lindsay Lowell, and Lowell J. Taylor, "Undocumented Mexican Immigrants and the Earnings of Other Workers in the United States," *Demography* 25, no. 1 (February 1988): 35–52; Borjas and Tienda, eds., *Hispanics in the U.S. Economy;* Adriana Marshall, "New Immigrants in New York's Economy," in *New Immigrants in New York*, ed. Foner, 79–101; Thomas Muller and Thomas J. Espenshade, *The Fourth Wave: California's Newest Immigrants* (Washington, D.C.: Urban Institute, 1985).

38. For specific findings see Simon, *The Economic Consequences of Immigration.* See also Ellen Seghal, "Foreign Born in the U.S. Labor Market: The Results of a Special Survey," *Monthly Labor Review* (July 1985): 18–24. As noted earlier, immigrants (but not refugees) granted permanent resident status are legally restricted from receiving welfare assistance such as AFDC and SSI during their first three years in the United States. In addition, a 1989 government survey of a sample of 5000 IRCA applicants in California, where over half of the undocumented population is concentrated, found that over 90 percent of the pre-1982 immigrants and 94 percent of the "special agricultural workers" had never collected food stamps or any other type of welfare assistance; see Maria Newman, "Immigrant Poll Debunks Some Myths," *Los Angeles Times* (March 21, 1990), A1.

39. Light and Bonacich, *Immigrant Entrepreneurs*, 3–4. A similar propensity for self-employment has been reported for Korean immigrants in New York City; see Ilsoo Kim, "The Koreans: Small Business in an Urban Frontier," in *New Immigrants in New York*, ed. Foner, 219–42. For an analysis based on 1980 census

data of the higher rates of self-employment among the foreign-born compared to the native-born, see Ivan Light and Angel A. Sanchez, "Immigrant Entrepreneurs in 272 SMSAs," *Sociological Perspectives* 30, no. 4 (October 1987): 373–99.

40. Alejandro Portes and Leif Jensen, "The Enclave and the Entrants: Patterns of Ethnic Enterprise in Miami Before and After Mariel," *American Sociological Review* 54 (December 1989): 929–49; Portes and Bach, *Latin Journey,* chapter 6; Alejandro Portes and Alex Stepick, "Unwelcome Immigrants: The Labor Market Experiences of 1980 (Mariel) Cuban and Haitian Refugees in South Florida," *American Sociological Review* 50 (August 1985): 493–514; Alejandro Portes, "The Social Origins of the Cuban Enclave Economy of Miami," *Sociological Perspectives* 30, no. 4 (October 1987): 340–72; Lisandro Pérez, "Immigrant Economic Adjustment and Family Organization: The Cuban Success Story Reexamined," *International Migration Review* 20, no. 1 (Spring 1986): 4–20.

41. Takaki, *Strangers from a Different Shore,* 425–26. For an analysis of different patterns of Chinese enterprise in New York City between the pre–1965 Lo Wa Kiu ("old overseas Chinese") and the post–1965 San Yi Man ("new immigrants"), see Bernard Wong, "The Chinese: New Immigrants in New York's Chinatown," in *New Immigrants in New York,* ed. Foner, 243–71.

42. Cornelius, "Mexican Immigrants in California Today"; Portes, Castells, and Benton, *The Informal Economy;* Light and Bonacich, *Immigrant Entrepreneurs.* For local coverage of recent events, see John M. Glionna, "Attacks on Migrants Heighten Tension," *Los Angeles Times* (January 6, 1990), B1; Bruce Kelley, "El Mosco," *Los Angeles Times Magazine* 6, no. 11 (March 18, 1990): 11–43; Efron, "Sweatshops Expanding into Orange County"; Sam Fulwood III, "'86 Immigration Law Causes Job Bias, Study Says," *Los Angeles Times* (March 30, 1990), A1. The GAO report is based on a 1989 study of 360 major employers in Chicago and San Diego, done by the Urban Institute.

43. Rumbaut, "The Structure of Refuge." See also the studies collected in David W. Haines, ed., *Refugees as Immigrants: Cambodians, Laotians, and Vietnamese in America* (Totowa, N.J.: Rowman & Littlefield, 1989); David S. North, *Refugee Earnings and Utilization of Financial Assistance Programs* (Washington, D.C.: New TransCentury Foundation, 1984); Robert L. Bach, Rita Carroll-Seguin, and David Howell, *State-Sponsored Immigrants: Southeast Asian Refugees and the Use of Public Assistance* (Washington, D.C.: Office of Refugee Resettlement, 1986); Nathan Caplan, John K. Whitmore, and Marcella H. Choy, *The Boat People and Achievement in America* (Ann Arbor: University of Michigan Press, 1989), 52–65; Rubén G. Rumbaut and John R. Weeks, "Fertility and Adaptation: Indochinese Refugees in the United States," *International Migration Review* 20, no. 2 (Summer 1986): 428–66; Rubén G. Rumbaut, Leo R. Chávez, Robert Moser, Sheila Pickwell, and Samuel Wishik, "The Politics of Migrant Health Care: A Comparative Study of Mexican Immigrants and Indochinese Refugees," *Research in the Sociology of Health Care* 7 (1988): 148–202.

44. Detailed information on Limited English Proficient and Fluent English Proficient enrollments by language groups, grade levels, and school districts is published semestrally by the California State Department of Education (Sacramento); see State of California Educational Demographics Unit, "Language Census Report for California Public Schools" (1989), and State of California Bi-

lingual Education Office, "Data/BICAL Reports" (1989–90 and previous years). See also Rubén G. Rumbaut, *Immigrant Students in California Public Schools: A Summary of Current Knowledge*, CDS Report No. 11 (Baltimore: Center for Research on Effective Schooling for Disadvantaged Students, Johns Hopkins University, 1990); and Laurie Olsen, *Crossing the Schoolhouse Border: Immigrant Students and the California Public Schools* (San Francisco: California Tomorrow, 1988). The number of LEP students in public schools nationwide was estimated at between 3.5 and 5.5 million by the mid-1980s; see Joan M. First and John W. Carrera, *New Voices: Immigrant Students in U.S. Public Schools* (Boston: National Coalition of Advocates for Students, 1988), 42–49.

45. For a comprehensive review of the literature, see Kenji Hakuta, *Mirror of Language: The Debate on Bilingualism* (New York: Basic Books, 1986).

46. Rubén G. Rumbaut and Kenji Ima, "Determinants of Educational Attainment among Indochinese Refugees and Other Immigrant Students" (paper presented at the annual meeting of the American Sociological Association, Atlanta, August 25, 1988); Portes and Rumbaut, *Immigrant America*, chapter 6.

47. Marcelo M. Suárez-Orozco, *Central American Refugees and U.S. High Schools: A Psychosocial Study of Motivation and Achievement* (Stanford, Calif.: Stanford University Press, 1989); Caplan, Whitmore, and Choy, *The Boat People and Achievement in America;* Margaret A. Gibson, *Accommodation without Assimilation: Sikh Immigrants in an American High School* (Ithaca, N.Y.: Cornell University Press, 1989); María Eugenia Matute-Bianchi, "Ethnic Identity and Patterns of School Success and Failure among Mexican-Descent and Japanese-American Students in a California High School," *American Journal of Education* 95, no. 1 (November 1986): 233–55; Sylvia A. Valverde, "A Comparative Study of Hispanic High School Dropouts and Graduates: Why Do Some Leave School Early and Some Finish?" *Education and Urban Society* 19, no. 3 (May 1987): 320–29.

48. Portes and Rumbaut, *Immigrant America*, chapter 6; Calvin Veltman, *Language Shift in the United States* (Berlin: Mouton, 1983); David E. López, "Chicano Language Loyalty in an Urban Setting," *Sociology and Social Research* 62 (1978): 267–78.

49. Portes and Rumbaut, *Immigrant America*, chapter 6.

50. As if to underscore the point, shortly after this chapter was written the Iraqi invasion of Kuwait in August 1990 triggered massive refugee flows into Jordan and elsewhere. In addition, the deployment of several hundred thousand American troops to Saudi Arabia raised the ironic prospect of significant future Arab migration to the United States. Concomitantly, the spread of ethnic separatist movements throughout many Soviet republics and the deepening economic crisis in the Soviet Union augured the possibility of large-scale population movements into bordering European countries—which may in turn create new and sudden pressures for resettlement in the United States. The landmark Immigration Act of 1990, signed into law by President Bush in November, became the most sweeping revision of the nation's immigration laws in sixty-six years: it will increase the number of legal immigrants by 40 percent (to approximately 700,000 annually), not including refugees (for whom the 1991 ceiling was boosted to 131,000) nor unauthorized immigration. Who had clearly anticipated these eventualities, or that they may yet combine with present trends in surpris-

ing ways to inaugurate a decade of ethnic diversification unprecedented in American history? (For a thoughtful analysis of the new legislation, see Gary E. Rubin and Judith Golub, *The Immigration Act of 1990* [New York: American Jewish Committee, December 1990].)

CHAPTER ELEVEN

1. Edward M. Meyers, *Rebuilding America's Cities: A Policy Analysis of the U.S. Conference of Mayors* (Cambridge, Mass.: Ballinger, 1986), 3.

2. On suburban and exurban residential patterns, see Robert Fishman, *Bourgeois Utopias* (New York: Basic Books, 1987); Kenneth T. Jackson, *Crabgrass Frontier* (New York: Oxford University Press, 1985); William H. Frey and Alden Speare, Jr., *Regional and Metropolitan Growth and Decline in the United States* (New York: Russell Sage Foundation, 1988). For businesses, see David C. Perry, "The Politics of Dependency in Deindustrializing America: The Case of Buffalo, New York," in *The Capitalist City*, eds. Michael Peter Smith and Joe R. Feagin (New York: Basil Blackwell, 1987), 113–37; Richard Child Hill, "Uneven Development in Metropolitan Detroit"; Joe T. Darden, Richard Child Hill, June Thomas, and Richard Thomas, *Detroit: Race and Uneven Development* (Philadelphia: Temple University Press, 1987), chapter 2; Staughton Lynd, *The Fight against Shutdowns: Youngstown's Steel Mill Closings* (San Pedro, Calif.: Singlejack Books, 1982); Ann Markusen, Peter Hall, and Amy Glasmeir, *High-Tech America* (Newton, Mass.: Allyn & Bacon, 1986); Barry Bluestone and Bennett Harrison, *The Deindustrialization of America: Plant Closings, Community Abandonment, and the Dismantling of Business Industry* (New York: Basic Books, 1982).

3. On the change from industrial to service-sector cities, see Thierry J. Noyelle and T. M. Stanback, Jr., *The Economic Transformation of American Cities* (Totowa, N.J.: Rowman & Allenheld, 1983).

4. This factor was first emphasized by Sidney M. Robbins and Nestor E. Terleckyj in *Money Metropolis: A Locational Study of Financial Activities in the New York Region* (Cambridge: Harvard University Press, 1960).

5. See the interesting view from the employers' side in *Meeting the Challenge: Maintaining and Enhancing New York City as the World Financial Capital*, A Report by the Financial Services Task Force of the New York City Partnership, June 1989.

6. John D. Kasarda, "Urban Change and Minority Opportunities," in *The New Urban Reality*, ed. Paul E. Peterson (Washington, D.C.: The Brookings Institution, 1985), 33–68; and "Economic Restructuring and America's Urban Dilemma," in *The Metropolis Era*, vol. 1, ed. Mattei Dogan and John D. Kasarda (Newbury Park, Calif.: Sage, 1988), 56–84.

7. Roger Waldinfer and Thomas Bailey, "The Continuing Significance of Race: Racial Conflict and Racial Discrimination in Construction," unpublished manuscript, August 1990; George R. Vickers and Sharon Zukin, with David Radick, "'Hedging Solutions': An Exploratory Study of a New York Securities Industry Firm" (paper presented at Eastern Sociological Society annual meeting, March 1988).

8. Douglas S. Massey, "The Ecology of Inequality: Minorities and the Con-

centration of Poverty, 1970–1980," *American Journal of Sociology* 95 (March 1990): 1153–88.

9. Tom Wolfe suggested the pathological though not the structural side of this consumption gap in his novel *Bonfire of the Vanities*. On New York, see Saskia Sassen, "Growth and Informalization at the Core," in *The Capitalist City*, ed. Smith and Feagin (1987), 138–54; and "New Trends in the Sociospatial Organization of the New York City Economy," in *Economic Restructuring and Political Response*, ed. Robert A. Beauregard, Urban Affairs Annual Reviews, vol. 34 (Newbury Park, Calif.: Sage, 1989), 69–114; on Los Angeles, see Mike Davis, *Prisoners of the American Dream* (London: Verso, 1986), chapter 5. Compare Bennett Harrison and Barry Bluestone, *The Great U-Turn* (New York: Basic Books, 1989).

10. Helen Thorpe, "In NY, How Many Make How Much?" *New York Observer* (December 4, 1989), 1.

11. Peter Marcuse, "'Dual City': A Muddy Metaphor for a Quartered City," *International Journal of Urban and Regional Research* 13 (December 1989): 697–708.

12. Brian J. L. Berry, "Islands of Renewal in Seas of Decay," in *The New Urban Reality*, ed. Peterson, 69–96.

13. George Sternlieb and James W. Hughes, "New York City," in *The Metropolis Era*, vol. 2, 48, ed. Dogan and Kasarda.

14. See Gregory D. Squires, ed., *Unequal Partnerships: The Political Economy of Urban Redevelopment in Postwar America* (New Brunswick, N.J.: Rutgers University Press, 1989). For a jaundiced view of the development process in Chicago, see Gerald D. Suttles, *The Man-Made City: The Land-Use Confidence Game in Chicago* (Chicago: University of Chicago Press, 1990).

15. See Mark Gottdiener, ed., *Cities in Stress*, Urban Affairs Annual Reviews, vol. 30 (Newbury Park, Calif.: Sage, 1986); Martin Shefter, *Political Crisis/Fiscal Crisis* (New York: Basic Books, 1987).

16. For contrasting but still critical views, see William H. Whyte, *City* (New York: Doubleday, 1988), and Rosalyn Deutsche, "Uneven Development: Public Art in New York City," *October* 47 (Winter 1988): 3–52. Exceptions include public art used to complement public or quasi-public cultural institutions, such as the Walker Art Center in Minneapolis.

17. A 1987 survey of cities with over 5000 and counties with more than 25,000 residents indicated that 80 percent of respondents had already used or planned to use some form of privatization of services to cut costs. (The response rate was only 19 percent.) Irwin T. David, "Privatization in America," *The Municipal Yearbook 1988* (Washington, D.C.: International City Management Association, 1988), A43–55.

18. The best example is described by James Fallows, who tried to find a working public telephone on the street in New York while people drove by talking on car phones. "Wake up, America," *New York Review of Books* (March 1, 1990): 18.

19. See Sharon Zukin, *Landscapes of Power: From Detroit to Disney World* (Berkeley and Los Angeles: University of California Press, 1991), chapters 3, 7. For a mainly uncritical view of downtown expansion and revival in recent years, see Bernard J. Frieden and Lynne B. Sagalyn, *Downtown, Inc.* (Cambridge, Mass.: MIT Press, 1989).

20. See Neil Smith and Peter Williams, eds., *Gentrification of the City* (Boston: Allen and Unwin, 1986), and Sharon Zukin, "Gentrification: Culture and Capital in the Urban Core," *Annual Review of Sociology* 13 (1987): 129–47. For racial aspects of these changes, see Elijah Anderson, *Streetwise: Race, Class, and Change in Urban Community* (Chicago: University of Chicago Press, 1990).

21. Sarah Bonnemaison, "City Policies and Cyclical Events," *Design Quarterly* 147 (1990): 29–31.

22. See Sharon Zukin, *Loft Living: Culture and Capital in Urban Change*, 2nd ed. (New Brunswick, N.J.: Rutgers University Press, 1989).

23. See the somewhat different reading of these spaces in Fredric Jameson, "Postmodernism, or the Cultural Logic of Late Capitalism," *New Left Review* 146 (July-August 1984): 53–92.

24. See Zukin, *Landscapes of Power*, chapter 8; compare David Harvey, *The Condition of Postmodernity* (Oxford: Basil Blackwell, 1989), chapter 4, "free-market populism" at p. 77. On the significance of image, fantasy, and consumption to the political economy of an entire region, see Mike Davis, *City of Quartz: Excavating the Future in Los Angeles* (London and New York: Verso, 1990).

25. Peter H. Rossi, *Down and Out in America* (Chicago: University of Chicago Press, 1989). Even publicly owned public spaces deter appropriation by the homeless. Far from the encouragement of shantytowns that occurred during the Great Depression, city parks today are policed so that the homeless cannot live semipermanently in them. The notorious late-1980s riots at Tompkins Square Park in New York City featured an incendiary mix of downtown urban types, that is, young anti-Establishment musicians, middle- and working-class neighborhood home owners, the police, and the homeless.

26. For a prominent misguided use of the term, see William J. Wilson, *The Truly Disadvantaged* (Chicago: University of Chicago Press, 1987).

CHAPTER TWELVE

1. Hedrick Smith, *The Power Game* (New York: Ballantine, 1988), 20.

2. Godfrey Hodgson, *America in Our Time* (Garden City, N.Y.: Doubleday, 1976), 152.

3. Kenneth C. Clark, "Networks Form Group to Pitch Themselves," *San Diego Union* (April 7, 1990), E11.

4. *Newsweek* (October 17, 1988): 94.

5. Alan Green, *Gavel to Gavel: A Guide to the Television Proceedings of Congress* (Washington, D.C.: Benton Foundation, 1986).

6. Marc Fisher, "All Things Reconsidered," *Washington Post National Weekly Edition* (October 30–November 5, 1989), 6.

7. David Shaw, *Journalism Today* (New York: Harper's College Press, 1977), 195.

8. Larry King, "Talk Radio: An Interview with Larry King," *Gannett Center Journal* 3 (Spring 1989): 17–24.

9. Sanford J. Ungar, *The Papers and the Papers* (New York: Columbia University Press, 1989), 107.

10. Quoted in Ellis Cose, *The Press* (New York: William Morrow, 1989), 58.

11. Peter Prichard, *The Making of McPaper: The Inside Story of USA Today* (Kansas City: Andrews, McMeel, and Parker, 1987), 311.

12. John C. Busterna, "Trends in Daily Newspaper Ownership," *Journalism Quarterly* 65 (Winter 1988): 833; and Ben Bagdikian, *The Media Monopoly* (Boston: Beacon Press, 1989).

13. Kay Mills, *A Place in the News: From the Women's Pages to the Front Page* (New York: Dodd, Mead, 1989), 149.

14. Mills, *A Place in the News*, 1. See also Marlene Sanders and Marcia Rock, *Waiting for Prime Time: The Women of Television News* (Urbana: University of Illinois Press, 1988).

15. Mills, *A Place in the News*, 247, 251.

16. Herbert J. Gans, *Deciding What's News: A Study of CBS Evening News, NBC Nightly News, Newsweek and Time* (New York: Vintage, 1979), 42–52.

17. Hedrick Smith, *Power Game*, 29.

18. Stephen Hess, *The Washington Reporters* (Washington, D.C.: Brookings Institution, 1981), 13.

19. Brigitte Darnay, ed., *Newsletters in Print*, 4th ed. (Detroit: Gale Research, 1988).

20. Jeffrey Abramson, F. Christopher Arterton, and Gary Orren, *The Electronic Commonwealth* (New York: Basic Books, 1988), 92–93.

21. Hedrick Smith, *Power Game*, 149.

22. Barnaby F. Feder, "The Business of Earth Day," *New York Times* (November 12, 1989), F4.

23. Connie Koenenn and Bob Sipchen, "Too Hip for Her Own Good?" *Los Angeles Times* (March 30, 1990), E1. See also, on media metacoverage, Todd Gitlin, "Blips, Bites, and Savvy Talk," *Dissent* (Winter 1990): 18–26.

24. From an interview conducted by America Rodriguez as part of a research project with Helene Keyssar. I am grateful to America Rodriguez for research assistance on this chapter.

25. Kathryn C. Montgomery, *Target: Prime Time* (New York: Oxford, 1989), 31.

26. Adam Hochschild, "And That's The Way It Was . . ." *Mother Jones* (May 1981): 5.

27. "Trial Losers Blame Verdict on 'L.A. Law' Episode," *San Diego Union* (December 25, 1989), A5. See also Alan Waldman, "Hear Ye, Hear Ye! 'L.A. Law's' in Session," *TV Guide* 38 (March 10, 1990): 7.

28. Leo Bogart, *Press and Public*, 2nd ed. (Hillsdale, N.J.: Lawrence Erlbaum, 1989), 337.

29. Bogart, *Press and Public*, 339. See also James Curran, "The Impact of TV on the Audience for National Newspapers, 1945–68," in *Media Sociology: A Reader*, ed. Jeremy Tunstall (Urbana: University of Illinois Press, 1970), 104–31, for a detailed argument that newspaper consumption rose substantially during the first decades of the growth of television in Britain.

30. Reed Irvine, *Media Mischief and Misdeeds* (Chicago: Regnery Gateway, 1984), 9.

31. "Are You on the Nightline Guest List?" *Extra!* (January/February 1989), 2–15.

32. Peter Dreier, "Capitalists vs. the Media: An Analysis of an Ideological Mobilization among Business Leaders," *Media, Culture and Society* 4 (April 1982), 111–32.

33. Leo Bogart, "The Case of the 30-Second Commercial," *Journal of Advertis-

ing Research 23 (February/March 1983): 11–18. In 1965, 77 percent of network commercials were a minute long and there were no thirty-second commercials; by 1970 25 percent of commercials were thirty seconds long, 95 percent by 1980. In the last few years, commercials have grown shorter still; in 1988 37 percent of all network commercials were fifteen seconds long, compared to 5 percent in 1984, while the share allocated to the thirty-second commercial has dropped from 89 percent to 60 percent. See *Television and Video Almanac 1989* (New York: Quigley Publishing, 1989), 23A. As Bogart shows, advertisers should not be pleased. In 1965, 20 percent of viewers could identify either the brand or at least the product line of the "last" commercial they saw before receiving a phone call from a market researcher; in 1981 only 9 percent could do the same.

34. Raymond Serafin, "Why GM Wants 'Pod Protection,'" *Advertising Age* (December 4, 1989): 25.

35. Key Lehman Schlozman and John T. Tierney, *Organized Interests and American Democracy* (New York: Harper & Row, 1986). On corporate lobbying, see David Vogel, *Fluctuating Fortunes* (New York: Basic Books, 1989).

36. This body of work is reviewed in Michael Schudson, "The Sociology of News Production," *Media, Culture and Society* 11 (1989), 263–82; and also in Gaye Tuchman, "Mass Media Institutions," in *Handbook of Sociology*, ed. Neil Smelser (Newbury Park, Calif.: Sage, 1988), 601–26.

37. Daniel Hallin, "Sound Bite News," in *Blurring the Lines*, ed. Gary Orren (New York: Free Press, forthcoming).

38. Mayer N. Zald and John D. McCarthy, *Social Movements in an Organizational Society* (New Brunswick, N.J.: Transaction Books, 1987).

39. U.S. Bureau of the Census, *Statistical Abstract of the United States 1990* (Washington, D.C.: U.S. Government Printing Office, 1990), 133.

40. Ibid., 227.

41. Ibid.

42. Lewis Coser, Charles Kadushin, and Walter Powell, *Books: The Culture and Commerce of Publishing* (New York: Basic Books, 1982), 349, and Robert Baensch, "Consolidation in Publishing and Allied Industries," *Book Research Quarterly* 4 (Winter 1988), 10.

43. Baensch, "Consolidation in Publishing," 13.

44. Daniel Hallin, "Whose Campaign Is It Anyway?" Columbia Journalism Review (November–December 1990); and Kiku Adatto, "Sound Bite Democracy: Network Evening News Presidential Campaign Coverage, 1968 and 1988," Research Paper R-2 (Cambridge, Mass.: Joan Shorenstein Barone Center, John F. Kennedy School of Government, Harvard University, 1990).

45. Lawrence C. Stedman and Carl F. Kaestle, "The Test Score Decline Is Over: Now What?" *Phi Delta Kappan* (November 1985): 204.

CHAPTER THIRTEEN

1. Harold L. Hodgkinson, "All One System: Demographics of Education—Kindergarten through Graduate School," in *Education and Society: A Reader*, ed. Kevin J. Dougherty and Floyd M. Hammack (San Diego: Harcourt Brace Jovanovich, 1990), 326, 327; U.S. Bureau of the Census, *Statistical Abstract of the United States: 1989* (Washington, D.C.: Government Printing Office), 454.

2. Hodgkinson, "All One System," 329.

3. Rubén G. Rumbaut, "Immigrant Students in California Public Schools: A Summary of Current Knowledge" (unpublished paper, San Diego State University, 1989), 9.

4. There are about 28,000 elementary and secondary schools in the United States, enrolling 5.6 million students (Center for Education Statistics, *Private Schools and Private School Teachers: Final Report of the 1985–86 Private School Study* [Washington, D.C.: Government Printing Office, 1987], 8).

5. Peter W. Cookson, Jr., and Caroline Hodges Persell, *Preparing for Power: America's Elite Boarding Schools* (New York: Basic Books, 1985), 60, 67–68.

6. National Center for Education Statistics, *Private Schools and Private School Teachers,* 55. Cookson and Persell, *Preparing for Power,* 1985, 68.

7. National Center for Education Statistics, *Private Schools and Private School Teachers,* 55.

8. James S. Coleman and Thomas Hoffer, *Public and Private High Schools* (New York: Basic Books, 1987), 30, 31.

9. Ibid., 51.

10. Peter W. Cookson, Jr., "The United States of America: Contours of Continuity and Controversy in Private Schools," in *Private Schools in Ten Countries: Policy and Practice,* ed. Geoffrey Walford (London: Routledge & Kegan Paul, 1989), 57–84.

11. Coleman and Hoffer, *Public and Private High Schools,* 43.

12. Ibid., 30.

13. National Center for Education Statistics, *Digest of Educational Statistics 1988* (Washington, D.C.: Government Printing Office, 1988), 54.

14. James S. Coleman, Thomas Hoffer, and Sally Kilgore, *High School Achievement* (New York: Basic Books, 1982), 124–25, 148, 178.

15. Sophia Catsambis, "Catholic School Effects and the Persistence of Gender Differences in Education" (paper presented at the annual meeting of the American Sociological Association, San Francisco, August 9–13, 1989).

16. Barbara Falsey and Barbara Heyns, "The College Channel: Private and Public Schools Reconsidered," *Sociology of Education* 57 (April 1984): 115.

17. Caroline Hodges Persell and Peter W. Cookson, Jr., "Chartering and Bartering: Elite Education and Social Reproduction," *Social Problems* 33 (December 1985): 114–29.

18. Caroline Hodges Persell, Sophia Catsambis, and Peter W. Cookson, Jr., "Gender, School Type, and Selective College Attendance: Comparing Status Attainment and Status Allocation Theories of Stratification" (paper presented at the annual meeting of the American Sociological Society, San Francisco, August 9–13, 1989).

19. Cookson, "The United States: Contours," 20–21.

20. John E. Chubb and Terry M. Moe, *Politics, Markets, and America's Schools* (Washington, D.C.: The Brookings Institution, 1990).

21. Peter W. Cookson, Jr., "Private Schooling and Equity: Dilemmas of Choice," *Education and Urban Society* (February 1991): (forthcoming).

22. Lionel S. Lewis and Richard A. Wanner, "Private Schooling and the Status Attainment Process," *Sociology of Education* 52 (April 1979): 99–112.

23. Michael Useem, *The Inner Circle: Large Corporations and the Rise of Business*

Political Activity in the U.S. and the U.K. (New York: Oxford University Press, 1984); Michael Useem and Jerome Karabel, "Educational Pathways to Top Corporate Management," *American Sociological Review* 51 (April 1986): 184–200.

24. Karl Alexander and Martha Cook, "Curriculum and Coursework," *American Sociological Review* 47 (October 1982): 626–40; Rebecca Barr and Robert Dreeben, *How Schools Work* (Chicago: University of Chicago Press, 1983), chapter 4; Robert Dreeben and Adam Gamoran, "Race, Instruction, and Learning," *American Sociological Review* 51 (October 1986): 660–69; Donna Eder, "Ability Grouping as a Self-Fulfilling Prophecy," *Sociology of Education* 54 (July 1981): 151–62; Warren G. Findley and Miriam M. Bryan, *Ability Grouping: 1970-I, Common Practices in the Use of Tests for Grouping Students in Public Schools* (Athens, Ga.: University of Georgia Center for Educational Improvement, 1970, ED 048381); Jerome Freiberg, *The Effects of Ability Grouping on Interactions in the Classroom* (ED 053194, 1970); John I. Goodlad, *A Place Called School* (New York: McGraw-Hill, 1984), 159–60; Linda Grant and James Rothenberg, "The Social Enhancement of Ability Differences," *Elementary School Journal* 87 (Spring 1986): 28–49; Maureen T. Hallinan, "Ability Grouping and Student Learning," in *The Social Organization of Schools: New Conceptualizations of the Learning Process*, ed. Maureen T. Hallinan (New York: Plenum, 1987), 41–69; Maureen T. Hallinan, "Summary and Implications," in *The Social Context of Instruction*, ed. Penelope Peterson, Louise Cherry Wilkinson, and Maureen T. Hallinan (New York: Academic Press, 1984), 229–40; Ron Haskins, Tedra Walden, and Craig Ramey, "Teacher and Student Behavior in High- and Low-Ability Groups," *Journal of Educational Psychology* 75 (December 1983): 865–76; Barbara Heyns, "Social Selection and Stratification within Schools," *American Journal of Sociology* 79 (May 1974): 1434–51; James D. Jones, Beth E. Vanfossen, and Joan Z. Spade, "Curriculum Placement: Individual and School Effects Using the High School and Beyond Data" (paper presented at the annual meeting of the American Sociological Association, Washington, D.C., August 26–30, 1985); Jeannie Oakes, *Keeping Track: How Schools Structure Inequality* (New Haven, Conn.: Yale University Press, 1985); Caroline Hodges Persell, *Education and Inequality: The Roots and Results of Stratification in America's Schools* (New York: Free Press, 1977), chapter 6; Ray C. Rist, "Student Social Class and Teacher Expectations: The Self-Fulfilling Prophecy in Ghetto Education," *Harvard Educational Review* 40 (August 1970): 411–51; James E. Rosenbaum, *Making Inequality* (New York: Wiley-Interscience, 1976); James E. Rosenbaum, "Social Implications of Educational Grouping," in *Review of Research in Education* 8, ed. David Berliner (Washington, D.C.: American Educational Research Association, 1980), 361–401; James E. Rosenbaum, "Track Misperceptions and Frustrated College Plans," *Sociology of Education* 53 (April 1980): 74–88; Brian Rowan and Andrew Miracle, "Systems of Ability Grouping and the Stratification of Achievement in Elementary School," *Sociology of Education* 56 (July 1983): 133–44; Frances Schwartz, "Supporting or Subverting Learning: Peer Group Patterns in Four Tracked Schools," *Anthropology and Education Quarterly* 12 (Summer 1981): 99–121.

25. Karl L. Alexander, Martha Cook, and Edward L. McDill, "Curriculum Tracking and Educational Stratification: Some Further Evidence," *American Sociological Review* 43 (February 1978): 47–66; Karl L. Alexander and Bruce K.

Eckland, "Contextual Effects in the High School Attainment Process," *American Sociological Review* 40 (June 1975): 402–16; Falsey and Heyns, "The College Channel"; Abraham Jaffe and Walter Adams, *Academic and Socioeconomic Factors Related to Entrance and Retention at Two- and Four-Year Colleges in the Late 1960s* (New York: Columbia University Bureau of Applied Social Research, 1970); Rosenbaum, "Track Misperceptions and Frustrated College Plans," 74–88; James D. Jones, Joan N. Spade, and Beth E. Vanfossen, "Curriculum Tracking and Status Maintenance," *Sociology of Education* 60 (April 1987): 104–22.

26. Falsey and Heyns, "College Channel," 115.

27. Duane Alwin, "College Effects on Educational and Occupational Attainments," *American Sociological Review* 39 (April 1974): 210–32; Peter Blau and Otis D. Duncan, *The American Occupational Structure* (New York: Wiley, 1967), 169; David L. Featherman and Robert M. Hauser, *Opportunity and Chance* (New York: Academic Press, 1978), 259; Christopher Jencks, Susan Bartlett, Mary Corcoran, James Crouse, David Eaglesfield, Gregory Jackson, Kent McClelland, Peter Mueser, Michael Olneck, Joseph Schwartz, Sherry Ward, and Jill Williams, *Who Gets Ahead?* (New York: Basic Books, 1979), 168–69, 178–79; David Kamens, "Colleges and Elite Formation: The Case of Prestigious American Colleges," *Sociology of Education* 47 (Summer 1974): 354–78; Jerome Karabel and Katherine McClelland, "Occupational Advantages and the Impact of College Rank on Labor Market Outcomes," *Sociological Inquiry* 57 (Fall 1978): 323–47; J. N. Morgan and G. J. Duncan, "College Quality and Earnings," in *Research in Human Capital and Development,* ed. I. Sirageldin (Greenwich, Conn.: JAI Press), 1979; Vincent Tinto, "College Origin and Patterns of Status Attainment," *Sociology of Work and Occupations* 7 (November 1980): 457–86.

28. Hallinan, "Summary and Implications," 229–40.

29. Oakes, *Keeping Track;* Edward B. Fiske, "More and More Educators Agree that Grouping Students by Ability Is Misguided," *New York Times* (January 6, 1990), B6.

30. Willis D. Hawley, "Achieving Quality Integrated Education—With or Without Federal Help," in *Education and Society,* eds. Dougherty and Hammack, 471.

31. Ibid., 473. Hawley is an authoritative source on this subject because his conclusions are based on his review and synthesis of more than 1200 books, articles, reports, and commentaries on the effects of desegregation (see Willis D. Hawley, *Strategies for Effective Desegregation: Lessons from Research* [Lexington, Mass.: Lexington Books, 1983]); surveys of numerous educators (see William T. Trent, "Expert Opinion on School Desegregation: Findings from the Interviews," in *Assessment of Current Knowledge about the Effectiveness of School Desegregation Strategies,* vol. 5, ed. Willis D. Hawley [Nashville, Tenn.: Vanderbilt University, Institute for Public Policy Studies, Center for Education and Human Development Policy, April 1981]); and the results of interviews with 135 local and national desegregation experts (ibid.).

32. Robert L. Crain and Rita E. Mahard, "Some Policy Implications of the Desegregation/Minority Achievement Literature," in *Assessment of Current Knowledge,* vol. 5, ed. Hawley.

33. Dougherty and Hammack, *Education and Society,* 464.

34. Malcolm Danoff, *Evaluation of the Impact of ESEA Title VII Spanish/English Bilingual Education Programs* (Palo Alto, Calif.: American Institutes for Research, 1978), 1–19.

35. Wallace E. Lambert and Richard Tucker, *Bilingual Education of Children: The St. Lambert Experiment* (Rowley, Mass.: Newbury House, 1972); William Mackey and Von Nieda Beebe, *Bilingual Schools for a Bicultural Community: Miami's Adaptation to the Cuban Refugees* (Rowley, Mass.: Newbury House, 1977); and Bernard Spolsky, "Bilingual Education in the United States," in *Georgetown University Round Table on Languages and Linguistics: International Dimensions of Bilingual Education*, ed. James E. Alatis (Washington, D.C.: Georgetown University Press, 1978).

36. Alan Gartner and Dorothy Kerzner Lipsky, "Beyond Special Education: Toward a Quality System for All Students," *Harvard Educational Review* 57 (November 1987): 367–95.

37. National Center for Education Statistics, *Digest of Education Statistics 1988*, 57.

38. For more on the generation, expression, and consequences of teacher expectations, see Persell, *Education and Inequality*, chapters 7 and 8.

39. Nancy Tobler, "Meta-analysis of 143 Adolescent Drug Prevention Programs: Quantitative Outcome Results of Program Participants Compared to a Control or Comparison Group," *Journal of Drug Issues* 16 (Fall 1986): 537–67, cited in Frank Riessman, "Transforming the Schools: A New Paradigm," *Social Policy* 19 (Summer 1988): 2–4.

40. Riessman, "Transforming the Schools," 3.

41. Robert E. Slavin, "Cooperative Learning and the Cooperative School," *Educational Leadership* (November 1987): 7–13.

42. Of thirty-eight studies lasting at least four weeks, thirty-three found significantly greater achievement for students in cooperatively taught classes, while five found no significant difference (ibid., 10; and Robert E. Slavin, "Cooperative Learning: A Best-Evidence Synthesis," in *School and Classroom Organization*, ed. Robert E. Slavin [Hillsdale, N.J.: Erlbaum, 1988]).

43. Idem, "Cooperative Learning and the Cooperative School," 10.

44. Shalom Sharan, "Cooperative Learning in Small Groups," *Review of Educational Research* 50 (Summer 1980): 241–71; Slavin, "Cooperative Learning and the Cooperative School," 7–13; Robert Slavin, "Cooperative Learning," *Review of Educational Research* 50 (Summer 1980): 315–42; Robert Slavin, "Synthesis of Research on Grouping in Elementary and Secondary Schools," *Educational Leadership* 46 (September 1988): 67–77.

45. Carnegie Forum on Education and the Economy, *A Nation Prepared: Teachers for the Twenty-first Century* (Princeton, N.J.: Carnegie Forum on Education and the Economy, 1986); Charles W. Case, Judith Lanier, and Cecil G. Miskel, "The Holmes Group Report: Impetus for Gaining Professional Status for Teachers," *Journal of Teacher Education* 37 (July–August 1986): 36–43; Linda Darling-Hammond, *Beyond the Commission Reports: The Coming Crisis in Teaching* (Santa Monica, Calif.: Rand, 1984); Holmes Group, *Tomorrow's Teachers: A Report of the Holmes Group* (East Lansing, Mich.: Holmes Group, 1986); Theodore Sizer, *Horace's Compromise: The Dilemma of the American High School* (Boston: Houghton Mifflin, 1985).

46. National Commission on Excellence in Education, *A Nation at Risk: The Imperative for Educational Reform* (Washington, D.C.: Government Printing Office, 1983), 8.

47. In the United States the averages were based on both college- and non-college-bound students in all kinds of high schools, whereas in most other countries they were based on a small select group of students attending only academic schools. (Lawrence C. Stedman and Marshall S. Smith, "Recent Reform Proposals for American Education," in Dougherty and Hammack, *Education and Society*, 649).

48. L. C. Comber and John P. Keeves, *Science Education in Nineteen Countries* (New York: Wiley, 1973), 159.

49. National Commission on Education, *A Nation at Risk*, 18.

50. The earlier sample contained only twenty-seven high schools, with few Southern schools included and no schools from cities with populations over one million. The second sample was a national sampling of households.

51. Steadman and Smith, "Recent Reform Proposals," 647.

52. Ibid.

53. Ibid., 648.

54. Ibid., 648–49.

55. Dropout rates in 1985–88 were 4.4 percent, down about 2 percent from 1978 (U.S. Department of Education, *News* [September 14, 1989], 2). The percent of seventeen-year-old students reading at the intermediate level increased from 80 percent in 1970–71 to 83.6 percent in 1983–84 (National Center for Education Statistics, *Digest of Education Statistics 1988* [Washington, D.C.: Government Printing Office, 1988], 103).

56. Susan Chira, "Support Grows for National Education Standards," *New York Times* (December 26, 1989), A1, B10.

57. Gary Natriello, Edward L. McDill, and Aaron M. Pallas, "School Reform and Potential Dropouts," in Dougherty and Hammack, *Education and Society*, 668–75.

58. Some argue that cognitive skills and human capital are increasingly important for participating in an increasingly complex economy; others argue that noncognitive traits such as docility, deference to authority, and personality are the consequences of education that employers truly value.

59. Ann Bastian, Norman Fruchter, Marilyn Gittell, Colin Greer, and Kenneth Haskins, "The Mission of Schooling: Quality and Equality," *Christianity and Crisis*, 18 (March 1985): 90.

60. David Weikart and Lawrence J. Schweinhart, *Changed Lives: The Effects of the Perry Preschool Program on Youths through Age 19* (Ypsilanti, Mich.: High Scope, 1984).

61. Children's Defense Fund, *A Call for Action* (Washington, D.C.: Children's Defense Fund, 1988).

62. Fred M. Hechinger, "A Consensus Emerges: The Future Depends on Improving Early Education," *New York Times* (February 15, 1989).

63. Children's Defense Fund, *A Call for Action*.

64. Harold L. Hodgkinson, *The Same Client: The Demographics of Education and Service Delivery Systems* (Washington, D.C.: IEL, 1989).

65. Albert Shanker, "It's More than Fixing Schools," *New York Times* (December 31, 1989), E7.

CHAPTER FOURTEEN

1. This epigram is attributed to Callicter and Nicarchus (who may have lived at the time of Nero). The translation, by H. Wellesley, appears in John Booth, ed., *Epigrams, Ancient and Modern* (London: Longmans, Green, 1865), 3. For the original Greek, see Hermann Beckby, ed., *Anthologia Graeca* (Munich: Ernst Heimeran, 1957), xi. 118, p. 604. A more literal translation might be: "Phidon didn't give me a clyster or lay hands on me, but when I had a fever, I thought of his name and died." My thanks to Mary R. Lefkowitz and Sir Hugh Lloyd-Jones.

2. Ivan Illich's *Medical Nemesis: The Expropriation of Health* (London: Calder and Boyars, 1974) initiated the public debate about the end of medicine and was followed by at least two interesting reflections along the same line. See Rick J. Carlson, *The End of Medicine* (New York: Wiley, 1975); and David F. Horrobin, *Medical Hubris: A Reply to Ivan Illich* (St. Albans, Vt.: Eden Press, 1977). The works of demographers and epidemiologists not only have anticipated these kinds of criticisms of medicine, they have provided the kinds of data that are now dominant in the public debate about the role of medicine. See below, note 10.

3. See the following representative works: James C. Mohr, *Abortion in America: The Origins and Evolution of National Policy* (New York: Oxford University Press, 1978); Paul Starr, *The Social Transformation of American Medicine* (New York: Basic Books, 1982); Kenneth M. Ludmerer, *Learning to Heal: The Development of American Medical Education* (New York: Basic Books, 1985); and Charles E. Rosenberg, *The Care of Strangers: The Rise of America's Hospital System* (New York: Basic Books, 1987).

4. Studies by sociologists of the external or professional legitimation of medicine should be noted. See, in particular, Eliot Freidson, *Professional Powers: A Study of the Institutionalization of Formal Knowledge* (Chicago: University of Chicago Press, 1986).

5. See Talcott Parsons, "Social Structure and Dynamic Process: The Case of Modern Medical Practice," in *The Social System* (New York: Free Press, 1951), 428–79. Parsons further developed his perspectives on the physician-patient relation in response to his critics. See "The Sick Role and the Role of the Physician Reconsidered," *Milbank Memorial Fund Quarterly/Health and Society* (Summer 1975), 257–78.

6. For a sociological study concluding with a similar diagnosis, see Terry Mizrahi, *Getting Rid of Patients: Contradictions in the Socialization of Physicians* (New Brunswick, N.J.: Rutgers University Press, 1986).

7. "The bourgeoisie has stripped of its halo every occupation hitherto honoured and looked up to with reverent awe. It has converted the physician, the lawyer, the priest, the poet, the man of science, into its paid wage-labourers" (Karl Marx and Friedrich Engels, *The Communist Manifesto* [New York: Penguin Books, 1967], 82).

8. See Andrew Abbott, *The System of Professions: An Essay on the Division of Expert Labor* (Chicago: University of Chicago Press, 1988).

9. See James H. Cassedy, *American Medicine and Statistical Thinking, 1800–1860* (Cambridge: Harvard University Press, 1984); and Stephen M. Stigler, *The History of Statistics: The Measurement of Uncertainty before 1900* (Cambridge: Harvard University Press, 1986).

10. Daniel M. Fox has written illuminating historical accounts of the numerous tensions between health care provision and its reimbursement. See "The New Discontinuity in Health Policy," in *America in Theory*, ed. Leslie Berlowitz, Denis Donoghue, and Louis Menand (New York: Oxford University Press, 1988), 163–77.

11. See Thomas McKeown, *The Role of Medicine: Dream Mirage or Nemesis?* (Princeton, N.J.: Princeton University Press, 1979).

12. If controversy about immunization does arise from time to time, it concerns the inevitable harm that results from efforts, including misguided ones, to protect the public from disease. The case of swine flu is one of the most recent examples. See Diana B. Dutton, with contributions by Thomas A. Preston and Nancy E. Pfund, *Worse than the Disease: Pitfalls of Medical Progress* (Cambridge: Cambridge University Press, 1988), chapter 5.

13. Deborah A. Stone has carefully traced the links between epidemiological reasoning and modern insurance practices. See "At Risk in the Welfare State," in *Social Research* 56 (Autumn 1989), 591–633; and "AIDS and the Moral Economy of Insurance," *The American Prospect* (Spring 1990): 62–73.

14. See Russell C. Maulitz, ed. *Unnatural Causes: The Three Leading Killer Diseases in America* (New Brunswick, N.J.: Rutgers University Press, 1989); and Daniel M. Fox, "Policy and Epidemiology: Financing Health Services for the Chronically Ill and Disabled, 1930–1990," *The Milbank Quarterly* 67, Supp. 2, Pt. 2 (1989): 257–87.

15. For a recent and controversial exposé of American cardiology, see Thomas J. Moore, *Heart Failure: A Critical Inquiry into American Medicine and the Revolution in Heart Care* (New York: Random House, 1989).

16. See Daniel Callahan, *Abortion: Law, Choice and Morality* (New York: Macmillan, 1970).

17. See Donald H. Merkin, *Pregnancy as a Disease: The Pill in Society* (Port Washington, N.Y.: Kennikat Press, 1976).

18. See Helen B. Holmes, Betty B. Hoskins, and Michael Gross, eds., *The Custom-Made Child? Women-Centered Perspectives*, Part I, "Diethylstilbestrol: An Interdisciplinary Analysis" (Clifton, N.J.: Humana Press, 1981), 21–61; Roberta J. Apfel and Susan M. Fisher, *To Do No Harm: DES and the Dilemmas of Modern Medicine* (New Haven, Conn.: Yale University Press, 1985); and Dutton, *Worse than the Disease*, chapter 3.

19. See William Ray Arney, *Power and the Profession of Obstetrics* (Chicago: University of Chicago Press, 1982). And see William Ray Arney and Bernard J. Bergen, *Medicine and the Management of Living: Taming the Last Great Beast* (Chicago: University of Chicago Press, 1984). I am indebted to the analyses and insights of these two books in the present chapter.

20. The improved forms of knowledge of genetics and epidemiology offer a way of reinventing the *conscience collective*. The rationalization of the world may produce powerful forms of solidarity in the name of health and well-being.

21. See, for example, Clifford Grobstein, *Science and the Unborn: Choosing Human Futures* (New York: Basic Books, 1988).

22. See Ann Oakley, *The Captured Womb: A History of the Medical Care of Pregnant Women* (New York: Basil Blackwell, 1984); Rita Arditti, Renate Duelli Klein, and Shelley Minden, eds., *Test-Tube Women: What Future for Motherhood?* (London: Pandora Press, 1984); Michelle Stanworth, ed., *Reproductive Technologies: Gender, Motherhood, and Medicine* (Cambridge, England: Polity Press, 1987); Patricia Spallone and Deborah Lynn Steinberg, eds., *Made to Order: The Myth of Reproductive and Genetic Progress* (New York: Pergamon Press, 1987); Patricia Spallone, *Beyond Conception: The New Politics of Reproduction* (Granby, Mass.: Bergin and Garvey, 1989); and Kathryn E. Moss, "New Reproductive Technologies: Concerns of Feminists and Researchers," *Affilia* 3, no. 4 (Winter 1988): 38–50.

23. At present, little research on bioethics as a social movement exists. One of the pioneering investigations of its latent agenda is by Renée C. Fox and Judith P. Swazey, "Medical Morality Is Not Bioethics—Medical Ethics in China and the United States," *Perspectives in Biology and Medicine* 27, no. 3 (Spring 1984): 336–60.

24. Two works by Daniel Callahan are indicative of the desire to speak more forcefully in the public policy arena about bioethical issues. See *Setting Limits: Medical Goals in an Aging Society* (New York: Simon & Schuster, 1987); and *What Kind of Life: The Limits of Medical Progress* (New York: Simon & Schuster, 1990).

25. See Edith Efron, *The Apocalyptics: Cancer and the Big Lie* (New York: Simon & Schuster, 1984).

26. See Robert Karasek and Tores Theorell, *Healthy Work: Stress, Productivity, and the Reconstruction of Working Life* (New York: Basic Books, 1990).

27. See Philip Rieff, "The Case of Dr. Oppenheimer," in *The Feeling Intellect: Selected Writings,* ed. and introd. Jonathan B. Imber (Chicago: University of Chicago Press, 1990), 202–22.

28. Leon R. Kass has written forcefully and gracefully on the physician's dilemma and obligation in face of the modern fulfillment of all possibilities, including ending life when one chooses and using technology to live beyond one's natural years. See *Toward a More Natural Science: Biology and Human Affairs* (New York: Free Press, 1985); "Mortality," in *Powers that Make Us Human: The Foundations of Medical Ethics,* ed. Kenneth Vaux (Urbana: University of Illinois Press), 7–27; "Why Doctors Must Not Kill," *The Public Interest* (Winter, 1989): 25–46; and "Death with Dignity and the Sanctity of Life," *Commentary* 89, no. 3 (March 1990): 33–43.

CHAPTER FIFTEEN

1. Gerald P. Fogarty, *The Vatican and the American Hierarchy* (Stuttgart, Germany: Hiersemann, 1982), 144.

2. This passage was quoted from John A. Hardon, *American Judaism* (Chicago: Loyola University Press, 1971), 104.

3. See Nathan Glazer, *American Judaism* (Chicago: University of Chicago Press, 1972), 38.

4. A good brief summary of the Conservative movement can be found in Bernard Martin, "Conservative Judaism and Reconstructionism," in *Movements and Issues in American Judaism*, ed. Bernard Martin (Westport, Conn.: Greenwood Press, 1978), 103–57. A more expanded history can be found in Marshall Sklare, *Conservative Judaism: An American Religious Movement* (New York: Schocken Books, 1972).

5. Roughly five years later, Rodney Stark and Charles Glock collected and analyzed both national and regional data and discovered similar denominational differences in religious commitment. Religious knowledge, belief, experience, religious commitment, and devotion all varied considerably depending upon denominational affiliation. See Rodney Stark and Charles Glock, *American Piety: The Nature of Religious Commitment* (Berkeley and Los Angeles: University of California Press, 1968).

6. The most comprehensive review of this evidence can be found in Robert Wuthnow, *The Restructuring of American Religion: Society and Faith Since World War II* (Princeton, N.J.: Princeton University Press, 1988), chapter 5. What I review here only samples from this literature.

7. Ibid., 92.

8. Indeed, negative feelings toward Episcopalians, Lutherans, Methodists, Presbyterians, and Baptists were almost nonexistent, and negative opinions of the more sectarian denominations, such as the Mormons and the Pentecostals, were only slightly more visible (up to one-fifth of the population held such views). See Wuthnow, *Restructuring of American Religion*, 91–92.

9. A Gallup poll in 1955 showed, for example, that only 1 of every 25 adults (or 4 percent) no longer adhered to the faith of his or her childhood. Almost thirty years later, 1 of every 3 adults belonged to a faith other than the one in which he or she had been reared. Among Presbyterians, Methodists, and Episcopalians, the ratios were even higher. Interestingly, these patterns even hold for Jews and Catholics, roughly 1 out of 6 of whom had switched to another faith. These figures are reported in Wuthnow, *Restructuring of American Religion*, 88.

10. From the author's reanalysis of the General Social Survey. The question about abortion was the most sweeping, approval or disapproval of abortion "under any circumstances."

11. The Baptists were, as expected, significantly more conservative politically than the Unitarians, Episcopalians, and the United Church of Christ. But again, I would argue that this is a function of the theological and political demography of the membership of these denominations.

12. The survey was part of the Religion and Power Project funded by the Lilly Endowment. For details, see the appendix to this chapter.

13. The question read, "Do you think the United States has a special role to play in the world today or is it pretty much like other countries?" Nine out of 10

of the religious leaders in all categories chose the former, with the exception of the liberal Protestants, 8 out of 10 of whom chose it.

14. The question read, "Do you think the United States should aspire to remain a world power or should it aspire to become a neutral country like Switzerland or Sweden?" Between 86 percent and 100 percent of all religious elites chose the former.

15. The actual percentages of those saying "not very much" or "none at all" were as follows: Protestants—orthodox, 21 percent, and progressive, 50 percent; Catholics—orthodox, 25 percent, and progressive, 60 percent; Jews—orthodox, 21 percent, and progressive, 45 percent. The chi-square was significant at the 0.000 level.

16. The majority of liberal Jews (71 percent) also agreed that the United States was "a force for good," but the gap between progressive and orthodox was still 21 percentage points.

17. The question actually read, "As a nation, do you think we treat people in the Third World fairly or unfairly." The actual percentages of those saying that America treats the Third World unfairly were as follows: Protestants—orthodox, 27 percent, and progressive, 71 percent; Catholics—orthodox, 50 percent, and progressive, 87 percent; Jews—orthodox, 19 percent, and progressive, 39 percent. The chi-square for this comparison was significant at the 0.000 level.

18. The question read, "How would you characterize the competition between the United States and the Soviet Union? Is it fundamentally a struggle in power politics or is it fundamentally a moral struggle?" The actual percentages of those saying that it was a moral struggle, were as follows: Protestants—orthodox, 43 percent, and progressive, 14 percent; Catholics—orthodox, 39 percent, and progressive, 14 percent; Jews—orthodox, 46 percent, and progressive, 21 percent. The chi-square for this comparison was significant at the 0.000 level.

19. Catholics were included in this survey, but were not easily divisible into orthodox and progressive camps. For this reason, the results for Evangelical and Liberal Protestants are reported.

20. A reanalysis of the 1982 Roper Survey of Theologians (Protestant and Catholic) showed that in analyses of variation of opinion on such issues as the spending priorities of the government, the evaluation of business practices, defense policy, moral behaviors (from homosexuality to abortion), and nuclear policy, belief orthodoxy, on average, accounted for 45 percent of the variation across tradition and for an average of 33 percent of the variation within traditions. See J. D. Hunter, James Tucker, and Steven Finkel, "Religious Elites and Political Values," unpublished manuscript, University of Virginia.

21. In addition to information provided by the Catholic League, I was greatly assisted by a scholarly treatment of the League by Joseph Varacalli, "To Empower Catholics: The Catholic League for Religious and Civil Rights as a Mediating Structure," *The Nassau Review*, 5, no. 4 (1988): 45–61.

22. *Hard Questions for the Catholic League* (Milwaukee, Wis.: Catholic League for Religious and Civil Rights, 1982), 2.

23. This survey was conducted by the author during the first two weeks of October, 1986. The organizations, listed here, were drawn from the *Encyclopedia of Associations:* The Catholic League for Religious and Civil Rights; Liberty Fed-

eration; The Roundtable; Morality in Media; Eagle Forum; Prison Fellowship; the National Right-to-Life Committee; The American Catholic Conference; The American Catholic Committee; The American Coalition for Traditional Values; Christian Voice; The American Society for the Defense of Tradition, Family, and Property; Coalitions for America; Christian Citizen's Crusade; Conservative Caucus; The Foundation for Religious Action in the Social and Civil Order; The Jewish Right; The National Pro-Family Coalition; The National Traditionalist Caucus; The Order of the Cross Society; Parents Alliance to Protect Our Children; The Ethics and Public Policy Center; The Institute for Religion and Democracy; Religious Heritage of America; Rock Is Stoning Kids; Students for America; United Parents Under God; American Life Lobby; Christian Action Council; Human Life International; Association for Public Justice; Voice of Liberty Association; Methodists for Life; Catholics United for Life; Human Life Center; Pro-Family Forum; Center on Religion and Society; American Pro-Life Council; the National Federation for Decency; Americans for Life; Concerned Women for America; Fund for an American Renaissance; We the People; The Ad hoc Committee for the Defense of Life; The National League of Catholic Laymen; The American Council for Coordinated Action; and The Black Silent Majority. In all but a few cases, I conducted a telephone interview with a representative of each organization. In some instances, though, the description of the organization in the *Encyclopedia of Associations* made interviewing unnecessary.

24. Tim LaHaye, *The Race for the 21st Century* (Nashville, Tenn.: Thomas Nelson Publishers, 1986), 109.

25. Franky Schaeffer, *Bad News for Modern Man* (Westchester, Ill.: Crossway Books, 1984). The emphasis is in the original.

26. At the very least, conservative Catholics and Jews are reconsidering their traditional posture toward Evangelicals—asking hypothetically, as one featured article in *The Jewish News* (in 1986) did, "Have we been misreading Jerry Falwell?" The general conclusion was, yes, the Jewish community has overreacted and Falwell may be a genuine ally of the Jews.

27. Telephone interview with Rabbi Kanett, of Agudath Israel, Washington, D.C., October 13, 1988.

28. Telephone interview with John Pantuso of the Catholic League, October 13, 1988.

CHAPTER SIXTEEN

1. See, for examples, the essays in Todd Gitlin, ed., *Watching Television* (New York: Pantheon, 1986).

2. Elizabeth Long, "Women, Reading, and Cultural Authority," *American Quarterly* 38 (Fall 1986): 591–611.

3. While walking with a prominent New York art critic through a room of modern art at the Metropolitan Museum of Modern Art, I encountered an example of this mutual disdain. Two upper-middle-class matrons agreed that a classic painting by Mondrian should not be in the museum because, one explained, it reminded her of her new placemats. The critic looked down on these

women because they did not know enough about the history of art to realize how Mondrian's work had influenced modern design. Yet, despite their disdain for the museum's acquisition, these women were engaging in class-appropriate behavior—a visit to a museum. The staff of "Sesame Street" may have intended Cookie Monster's comment ("Me no like art, but me know what me like") as a satire on such judgments. The art critic did not find the muppet's comment at all funny.

4. Harrison C. White and Cynthia A. White, *Canvasses and Careers* (New York: Wiley, 1965); compare Albert Boime, *The Academy and French Painting in the Nineteenth Century* (London: Phaidon, 1971).

5. See, for example, Leo Lowenthal, *Literature and the Image of Man* (Boston: Beacon, 1957), and Elizabeth Long, *The American Dream and the Popular Novel* (Boston: Routledge & Kegan Paul, 1985); Herbert Gans, "American Popular Culture and High Culture in a Changing Class Structure," pp. 17–37 in *Prospects: An Annual of American Cultural Studies* 10, ed. Jack Salzman (New York: Cambridge University Press, 1985).

6. Dennis Gilbert and Joseph A. Kahl, *The American Class Structure*, 3rd ed. (Chicago: Dorsey Press, 1987). However, today's "underclass" is probably less likely to escape poverty than was the underclass of yesteryear. For a different view of class, see Katherine S. Newman's chapter in this volume. At issue is whether one should compare the class structure today to that of the 1950s or to an earlier period. If one takes the 1950s as a base, middle-income groups have declined, while the wealthy have grown wealthier and the poor, poorer. But the distribution of Americans in social classes today resembles that of the Great Depression.

7. See Herbert Gans, *The Levittowners* (New York: Pantheon, 1967).

8. Personal communication.

9. Herbert Gans discusses small-town life as an American value in *Deciding What's News* (New York: Pantheon, 1979).

10. Harold Rosenberg, *Tradition of the New* (New York: Horizon, 1959).

11. Victor Navasky, *Naming Names* (New York: Viking, 1980).

12. William Kornhauser, *The Politics of Mass Society* (Glencoe, Ill.: Free Press, 1959); Elihu Katz and Paul F. Lazarsfeld, *Personal Influence* (Glencoe, Ill.: Free Press, 1955).

13. Kornhauser, *Politics of Mass Society.*

14. Katz and Lazarsfeld, *Personal Influence.*

15. Paul F. Lazarsfeld, Bernard Berelson, and Hazel Gaudet, *The People's Choice: How the Voter Makes Up His Mind in a Presidential Election* (New York: Duell, Sloan and Pearce, 1944).

16. Donald Horton and Richard Wohl, "Mass Communications and Parasocial Interaction," *Psychiatry* 19 (August 1956): 215–29.

17. For another critique, see Todd Gitlin, "Media Sociology," *Theory and Society* 6 (September 1978): 205–53.

18. The most recent research indicates that the media may set aspects of the political agenda, influence the decisions of the political elite, affect the course of social movements, and change individuals' political opinions and actions about topics salient to their identities. I review this research in "Mass Media Institu-

tions" in *Handbook of Sociology,* ed. Neil Smelser (Newbury Park, Calif.: Sage, 1988), 601–26.

19. Paul Lazarsfeld and Frank Stanton, *Radio Research 1942–1943* (New York: Duell, Sloan and Pearce, 1944), 507–48.

20. Ibid., 547.

21. Daniel Boorstin, *The Image* (New York: Atheneum, 1962).

22. Herbert Gans, "Popular Culture in America: Social Problem or Social Asset," in *Social Problems: A Modern Approach,* ed. Howard Becker (New York: Wiley, 1966); Herbert Gans, *Popular Culture and High Culture* (New York: Basic Books, 1974); Pierre Bourdieu, *Distinction,* trans. Richard Nice (Cambridge: Harvard University Press, 1984).

23. See Lewis A. Coser, Charles Kadushin, and Walter Powell, *Books* (New York: Basic Books, 1982); Walter Powell, *Getting into Print* (Chicago: University of Chicago Press, 1985); Gaye Tuchman, with Nina Fortin, *Edging Women Out* (New Haven, Conn.: Yale University Press, 1989).

24. Stuart Ewen and Elizabeth Ewen, *Channels of Desire* (New York: McGraw-Hill, 1982).

25. Bourdieu, *Distinction.*

26. Ford Foundation, *The Finances of the Performing Arts,* 2 vols. (New York: Ford Foundation, 1974).

27. Ibid., vol. 2, p. 13. For instance, 86 percent of the audience for theater earned less than $25,000 a year; 67 percent of the theater audience had not been graduated from college; 82 percent of the audience for ballet earned less than $25,000 per year, and 67 percent had not been graduated from college.

28. For example, Paul DiMaggio and Michael Useem, "Social Class and Arts Consumption," *Theory and Society* 5 (March 1978): 141–63, ed. Richard Peterson; *Patterns of Cultural Choice,* special edition of the *American Behavioral Scientist* 26 (1983): 422–552. I am also indebted to Paul DiMaggio for a very helpful reading of an earlier draft of this paper.

29. Harold Wilensky, "Mass Society and Mass Culture," *American Sociological Review* 29 (February 1964): 173–97.

30. Paul DiMaggio, "Classification in Art," *American Sociological Review* 52 (August 1987): 440–55.

31. Ibid., 443.

32. Personal discussion with ex-Putney students. Paul DiMaggio (personal communication, March 4, 1990) reminded me that upper-class familiarity with popular music dates back as far as the turn of the century.

33. Bourdieu, *Distinction.* I am indebted to David Halle's reinterpretation of Bourdieu in David Halle, "Class and Culture in Modern America: The Vision of the Landscape in the Residences of Contemporary Americans," *Prospects* 14 (1989): 373–406.

34. Paul DiMaggio and Francie Ostrower, "Participation in the Arts by Black and White Americans," *Social Forces* 68 (March 1990): 753–78.

35. Halle, "Class and Culture."

36. DiMaggio, "Classification of Art," 445.

37. Marjorie DeVault, "Novel Readings: The Social Organization of Interpretation," *American Journal of Sociology* 95 (January 1990): 887–921.

38. Ibid., and Long, "Women, Reading, and Cultural Authority."

39. Tuchman, with Fortin, *Edging Women Out.*

40. Allan Bloom, *The Closing of the American Mind* (New York: Simon & Schuster, 1987).

41. Diana Crane, *The Transformation of the Avant-garde* (Chicago: University of Chicago Press, 1987).

42. Ibid., 124.

43. Judith H. Balfe and Margaret J. Wyszomirski, "Public Art and Public Policy," *The Journal of Arts Management and Law* 15 (Winter 1986): 5–31.

44. Ibid.

45. Steven Dubin, *Bureaucratizing the Muse* (Chicago: University of Chicago Press, 1987).

46. Howard Becker, *Art Worlds* (Berkeley and Los Angeles: University of California Press, 1982).

47. Crane, *Transformation.*

48. Ibid.

49. Samuel Gilmore, "Collaboration and Convention: A Comparison of Repertory, Academic, and Avant-garde Concert Works" (Ph.D. diss., Northwestern University, 1984).

50. DiMaggio, "Classification of Art," 452, fn.

51. See discussion in Tuchman, with Fortin, *Edging Women Out.*

52. For an introduction to this approach, see Richard Peterson, *The Production of Culture* (Newbury Park, Calif.: Sage, 1976); Howard Becker, *Art Worlds;* Janet Wolff, *The Social Production of Art* (New York: St. Martin's Press, 1981).

53. Todd Gitlin, *Inside Prime Time* (New York: Pantheon, 1983).

54. Herbert Marcuse, *One-Dimensional Society: Studies in the Ideology of Advanced Industrial Society* (Boston: Beacon Press, 1964).

55. Judith Blau, Peter Blau, and David Golden, "Social Inequality and the Arts," *American Journal of Sociology* 91 (1985): 309–31.

56. See Richard Lachmann, "Graffiti as Career and Ideology," *American Journal of Sociology* 94 (1988): 229–50.

CHAPTER SEVENTEEN

1. For a full examination of the methodology and findings of the study discussed in this chapter, see Rebecca Klatch, *Women of the New Right* (Philadelphia: Temple University Press, 1987).

2. See, for example, Seymour Martin Lipset and Earl Raab, *The Politics of Unreason: Right-Wing Extremism in America, 1790–1970* (New York: Harper & Row, 1970).

3. Phyllis Schlafly, quoted in Carol Felsenthal, *Phyllis Schlafly: The Sweetheart of the Silent Majority* (Chicago: Regnery Gateway, 1981), 50.

4. George Gilder, speech presented at the Over the Rainbow celebration, Washington, D.C., July 1, 1982.

5. See Jerome L. Himmelstein and James A. McRae, Jr., "Social Conservatism, New Republicans, and the 1980 Election," *Public Opinion Quarterly* 48 (Fall 1984): 592–605.

6. For example, 58 percent of young voters aged eighteen to twenty-nine supported Reagan in 1984. See *New York Times*/CBS Poll in the *New York Times* (November 8, 1984), A19. Also see Neil Miller, "Is There a New Generation Gap?" *St. Louis Post-Dispatch* (October 28, 1984); and "The Conservative Student," *Newsweek on Campus* (March 1985): 6–14.

7. One Reagan campaign official acknowledged that in October of 1984 when television ads castigated Republicans as the party of the Moral Majority, Reagan support among eighteen- to twenty-four-year-old voters plummeted twenty points in five days. See Kevin Phillips, "Hubris on the Right," *New York Times Magazine* (May 12, 1985), 48.

8. Both Franks and Rollins reported in Phil Gailey, "Evangelism and a Fight with Peril to Both Sides," *New York Times* (March 17, 1986), A66.

9. Sara Rimer, "Experts Study the Habits of Genus Baby Boomer," *New York Times* (April 21, 1986), B6. Also see Steven Roberts, "Making Mark on Politics, 'Baby Boomers' Appear to Rally around Reagan," *New York Times* (November 5, 1984), B18.

10. "Reagan Justice," *Newsweek*, June 30, 1986, p. 14. Also see *Facts on File: World News Digest* 45, no. 2344 (October 25, 1985): 803.

11. Both Franks and Rollins cited in Phil Gailey, "Evangelism and a Fight with Peril to Both Sides."

12. Rosalind Pollack Petchesky, *Abortion and Woman's Choice: The State, Sexuality, and Reproductive Freedom* (Boston: Northeastern University Press, 1984).

13. Robert N. Bellah and others, *Habits of the Heart: Individualism and Commitment in American Life* (Berkeley and Los Angeles: University of California Press, 1985).

14. Alida Brill and Herbert McClosky, *Dimensions of Tolerance: What Americans Believe about Civil Liberties* (New York: Russell Sage Foundation, 1983).

15. Stephen L. Newman, *Liberalism at Wits' End: The Libertarian Revolt against the Modern State* (Ithaca, N.Y.: Cornell University Press, 1984).

CHAPTER EIGHTEEN

1. James William Gibson, *The Perfect War: Technowar in Vietnam* (New York: Vintage, 1988).

2. Richard Slotkin, *Regeneration through Violence: The Mythology of the American Frontier, 1600–1860* (Middletown, Conn.: Wesleyan University Press, 1973). Also see his sequel, *The Fatal Environment: The Myth of the Frontier in the Age of Industrialization, 1800–1890* (New York: Athenaeum, 1985).

3. Quoted by Klaus Theweleit, in *Male Bodies: Psychoanalyzing the White Terror*, Vol. 2 of *Male Fantasies*, trans. Erica Carter and Chris Turner, in collaboration with Stephen Conway (Minneapolis: University of Minnesota Press, 1989), 355–57.

4. Gibson, *The Perfect War*, 207–24.

5. Vietnam Veterans Against the War (VVAW) took the name "Winter Soldier" from George Washington's speech to his troops at Valley Forge in which he contrasted the "sunshine patriots," who left the Continental Army, and the "Winter Soldiers," who stayed the course. VVAW held two major public hearings

in 1971 on war crimes. A film documentary of the Detroit hearings made the college film circuit, but did not receive much off-campus exposure. In May, VVAW joined forces with Congressman Ronald Dellums, who sponsored a Congressional hearing by his subcommittee. See Citizens Commission of Inquiry, ed., *The Dellums Committee Hearings on War Crimes in Vietnam: An Inquiry into Command Responsibility in Southeast Asia* (New York: Vintage Books, 1972).

6. Quoted by Stanley Karnow in *Vietnam: A History* (New York: Penguin Books, 1984), 623.

7. Harry W. Haines, "What Kind of War? An Analysis of the Vietnam Veterans Memorial," *Critical Studies in Mass Communication,* no. 1 (1986): 2.

8. Hyam Maccoby, *The Sacred Executioner: Human Sacrifice and the Legacy of Guilt* (London: Thames and Hudson, 1982).

9. Sam Keene, *Faces of the Enemy: Reflections of the Hostile Imagination* (New York: Harper & Row, 1986).

10. Cited by Ghislaine Boulanger, Charles Kadushin, David M. Rindskopf, and Martha Ann Carey, "Post Traumatic Stress Disorder: A Valid Diagnosis?" in *The Vietnam Veteran Redefined: Fact and Fiction,* ed. Boulanger and Kadushin (New York: Erlbaum, 1986), 25.

11. See the collection of studies in *The Vietnam Veteran Redefined,* ed. Boulanger and Kadushin.

12. Ibid., 175.

13. Robert Jay Lifton, *Home from the War* (New York: Simon & Schuster, 1973).

14. Chaim F. Shatan, "Afterword—Who Can Take Away the Grief of a Wound?" in *The Vietnam Veteran Redefined,* ed. Boulanger and Kadushin, 176.

15. Gibson, *The Perfect War,* 461–76.

16. Jimmy Carter, *Public Papers of the Presidents of the United States: Jimmy Carter 1980–81,* vol. 2 (Washington, D.C.: U.S. Government Printing Office), 1268.

17. Quoted by P. McCombs in "Reconciliation: Ground Broken for Shrine to Vietnam War Veterans," *Washington Post* (March 27, 1982), 14.

18. Haines, "What Kind of War?" 5.

19. The Public Broadcasting Service's *Frontline* documentary series, June 21, 1983.

20. Sandra Foss, "Ambiguity as Persuasion: The Vietnam Veterans Memorial," *Communications Quarterly* 34 (1986).

21. Bobbie Ann Mason, *In Country* (New York: Harper & Row, 1985).

22. Chaim F. Shatan, "Happiness Is a Warm Gun—Militarized Mourning and Ceremonial Vengeance: Toward a Psychological Theory of Combat and Manhood in America, Part III," *Vietnam Generation* 3–4 (Summer–Fall 1989): 127–51.

23. Quoted by Ben A. Franklin in "President Accepts Vietnam Memorial: Crowd of Veterans and Others Hear His Call for Healing," *New York Times* (November 12, 1984), 1, 10.

24. Christopher Buckley, "Viet Guilt: Were the Real Prisoners of War the Young Americans Who Never Left Home?" *Esquire,* September 1983, 72.

25. "The Invasion of Grenada" is reprinted from William D. Ehrhart's *To*

Those Who Have Gone Home Tired: New and Selected Poems (New York: Thunder's Mouth Press, 1984), 71, by permission of author.

26. *Uncommon Valor* was not the first rescue movie. Director Ted Post had long wanted to do a picture about U.S. advisors to Vietnam in the early 1960s. However, to get funding for *Go Tell the Spartans* (1978), he had to direct a B-grade action adventure film, *Good Guys Wear Black* (1978), about a prisoner rescue mission. The film starred Chuck Norris in his first role outside of martial arts films.

27. Quoted by Joseph J. Zasloff in "Bartering Recognition for Putative POWs?" *Los Angeles Times Book Review* (January 14, 1990), 4.

28. Quoted by Jack Nelson, "For Bush, Panama Seen as Major 'Political Bonanza,'" *Los Angeles Times* (January 6, 1990), 21.

29. David Broder, "New Consensus Survives a Test," *Los Angeles Times* (January 14, 1990) (metro section), 5.

30. "Transcript of the Comments by Bush on the Air Strikes Against the Iraqis," *New York Times* (January 17, 1991), A14.

31. "Text of President Bush's State of the Union Message to Nation," *New York Times* (January 30, 1991), A14.

32. Quoted by Bruce Anderson, *Anderson Valley Advertiser* (February 20, 1991), 7.

33. Maureen Dowd, "A Different Bush Conforms to a Nation's Mood," *New York Times* (March 2, 1991), A7.

CHAPTER NINETEEN

1. Anthony M. Platt, *The Child Savers: The Invention of Delinquency* (Chicago: University of Chicago Press, 1977).

2. New York City Youth Board, *Reaching the Fighting Gang* (New York: Youth Board, 1960).

3. Robert M. Emerson, *Judging Delinquents: Context and Process in Juvenile Court* (Chicago: Aldine, 1969).

4. Psychiatrists and liberal legal academics entered public debates over crime and punishment in the 1950s and 1960s by pressing for changes in the criteria for applying the insanity defense in capital cases. Perhaps the most famous instance was the case that Truman Capote made into an immensely successful "nonfiction novel," *In Cold Blood* (New York: Random House, 1965).

5. Joseph Goldstein and Jay Katz, "Abolish 'The Insanity Defense'—Why Not?" *Yale Law Journal* 72 (1963): 853.

6. See, for example, Zhores A. Medvedev and Roy A. Medvedev, *A Question of Madness* (New York: Norton, 1979).

7. The following paragraphs summarize Chapter 1, "Righteous Slaughter," in Jack Katz, *Seductions of Crime* (New York: Basic Books, 1988).

8. Compare Richard A. Berk and Phyllis Newton, "Does Arrest Really Deter Wife Battery? An Effort to Replicate the Findings of the Minneapolis Spouse Abuse Experiment," *American Sociological Review* 50 (April 1985): 253.

9. Robert K. Merton, "Social Structure and Anomie," in his *Social Theory and Social Structure* (New York: Free Press, 1968 [1938]).

10. Richard A. Cloward and Lloyd E. Ohlin, *Delinquency and Opportunity: A Theory of Delinquent Gangs* (Glencoe, Ill.: Free Press, 1960).

11. Daniel P. Moynihan, *Maximum Feasible Misunderstanding: Community Action in the War on Poverty* (New York: Free Press, 1969).

12. Katz, *Seductions of Crime*, chapter 4, note 9.

13. C. Wright Mills, "The Professional Ideology of Social Pathologists," *American Journal of Sociology* 49 (September 1943): 165–80. For a rare hint that the lower- or working-class youth and middle-class youth may differ not so much in their pursuit of action as in its social visibility, see Herbert J. Gans, *The Urban Villagers* (New York: Free Press, 1962), 66 (comparing the visibility of street-corner life with the cover provided by the closed doors of the fraternity).

14. Compare Mary Douglas, *Purity and Danger: An Analysis of the Concepts of Pollution and Taboo* (London: Routledge & Kegan Paul, 1976).

15. Twenty-five years later, the body of "gang" theories that flourished in the sixties takes the appearance of an extreme phase of academic sophistry. With only rare consideration for grounding analysis in any recognizable data, theorists spun out intricate variations on such questions as the relationship between the pressures experienced by gang kids, the normative direction of their delinquent activities, and the gap between aspiration and legitimate opportunity in the larger society. For American society, the central significance of the academic debates was not in the elaborate distinctions made in book-length expositions of theory, but in the scholarly legitimizing of the simple social theory that stressed a clash between materialistic culture and inequalities in mobility opportunities, and that appeared in newspaper columns, in political speeches, and in government programs. My reference to "opportunity theory" is to this gross progressive perspective on lower-class deviance, not to the subtleties of any particular academic text.

16. Katz, *Seductions of Crime*, 240.

17. Tempted by massive statistical data bases that are provided, ready-made, by the state, academic researchers increasingly take the bait and focus their efforts on the handful of background conditions that such data happen to cover. By itself not publishing much of the data it collects, the state, which sympathetically allows researchers access to electronic data files, effectively controls a vast portion of formally independent intellectual energies. Faced with, on the one hand, the awful but inevitable risk of coming up with nothing new in a qualitative field study and, on the other, the certainty of "making a contribution" by exploring a virgin portion of an electronic data set, few Ph.D. students can resist the seduction. The niggardly resource commitments of governmental units to analyze and publish the data they collect has drawn academics to become out-of-house bureaucrats, promulgating state-created versions of social reality, rather than independent investigators of social phenomena (and this applies not simply in the area of crime but also to the study of ethnic groups, social mobility, etc.).

18. William Julius Wilson, *The Declining Significance of Race*, 2nd ed. (Chicago: University of Chicago Press, 1980), 129.

19. See Elijah Anderson, *Streetwise: Race and Class in an Urban Community* (Chicago: University of Chicago Press, 1990).

20. James Jacobs, *Stateville* (Chicago: University of Chicago Press, 1977).

21. *Wolff v. McDonnell*, 418 U.S. 539 (1974).

22. Malcolm M. Feeley and Roger A. Hanson, "The Impact of Jail and Prison Conditions Litigation: A Review Essay," and *passim*, in *Courts, Corrections and the Constitution*, ed. John J. DiIulio, Jr. (New York: Oxford University Press, 1989). The old sociological image of the prison as an informal society bound through the corruption of staff by inmate elites has long been discarded. See John Irwin, *Prisons in Turmoil* (Boston: Little, Brown, 1980).

23. Compare John J. DiIulio, Jr. *Governing Prisons: A Comparative Study of Correctional Management* (New York: Free Press, 1987).

24. See, for example, W. G. Stone, as told to G. Hirliman, *The Hate Factory: The Story of the New Mexico Penitentiary Riot* (Agoura, Calif.: Paisano Publications, 1982).

25. Jack Katz, "The Social Movement against White-Collar Crime," in *Criminal Justice Yearbook, II,* ed. Sheldon Messinger and Egon Bittner (Newbury Park, Calif.: Sage, 1980), 161–84.

26. See, for example, Warren Moscow, *The Last of the Big-Time Bosses: The Life and Times of Carmine De Sapio and the Rise and Fall of Tammany Hall* (New York: Stein and Day, 1971), and Steven P. Erie, *Rainbow's End: Irish-Americans and the Dilemmas of Urban Machine Politics, 1840–1985* (Berkeley and Los Angeles: University of California Press, 1988).

27. See, for example, Harry King and William Chambliss, *Box Man: A Professional Thief's Journey* (New York: Harper & Row, 1972).

28. See Alan Block, *East Side–West Side: Organizing Crime in New York, 1930–1950* (Cardiff, Wales: University College Cardiff Press, 1980).

29. Louis Wirth, *The Ghetto* (Chicago: University of Chicago Press, 1956).

30. The reason may have implications so sad that we would rather not appreciate them. Guns lost their popular charm and their potential to become icons in Europe when international wars brought home a level of destruction that the United States has never known. Elias remarks that the common celebratory practice of shooting off guns ended in Europe after the First World War. Norbert Elias, *The Loneliness of the Dying* (New York: Basil Blackwell, 1985). In various ways, the exceptional level of domestic criminal violence in the United States may be the trade-off for the exceptional immunity from international violence that the United States has enjoyed over the last two hundred years.

CHAPTER TWENTY

1. Suzanne Gordon, "Prisoners of Work: What Ever Happened to Leisure?" *Boston Globe Magazine* (August 20, 1989), 16–17, 39 ff.

2. Tamar Lewin, "Ailing Parent: Women's Burden Grows," *New York Times* (November 14, 1989), A1, B12.

3. Steffan Linder, *The Harried Leisure Class* (New York: Columbia University Press, 1970).

4. Arlie Russell Hochschild with Anne Machung, *The Second Shift: Working Parents and the Revolution at Home* (New York: Viking, 1989).

5. Hanna Papanek, "Men, Women, and Work: Reflections on the Two-Person Career," *American Journal of Sociology* 78, no. 4 (1973): 852–72; Arlie Hochschild, "Inside the Clockwork of Male Careers," in *Women and the Power to Change*, ed. Florence Howe (New York: McGraw Hill, 1975), 47–80.

6. Gordon, "Prisoners of Work"; and Hochschild and Machung, *The Second Shift*, 110 ff.; Gideon Kunda, *Engineering Culture* (Philadelphia: Temple University Press, 1991); and Lane Gerber, *Married to Their Careers* (London: Tavistock, 1983), 59, 66 ff.

7. Fred Best, *Flexible Life Scheduling* (New York: Praeger, 1980); Marlis Buchmann, *The Script of Life in Modern Society* (Chicago: University of Chicago Press, 1989).

8. Malcolm Morrison, "Work and Retirement in the Aging Society," *Daedalus*, no. 115 (Winter 1986): 272; "Flexible Distribution of Work and Leisure: Potentials for the Aging," in *Aging and Income*, ed. B. Herzog (New York: Human Sciences Press, 1978), 95–127; and Hilda Kahne, *Reconceiving Part-Time Work: New Perspectives for Older Workers and Women* (Totowa, N.J.: Rowman and Allenheld, 1985).

9. Bernice Neugarten and Dail Neugarten, "Age in the Aging Society," *Daedalus*, no. 115 (Winter 1986): 33, 46.

10. Karl Hinrichs, William Roche, and Carmen Sirianni, eds., *Working Time in Transition* (Philadelphia: Temple University Press, 1991).

11. Jeremy Rifkin, *Time Wars* (New York: Holt, Rinehart & Winston, 1987); Michael Young, *The Metronomic Society* (Cambridge: Harvard University Press, 1988); Barry Schwartz, *Queuing and Waiting* (Chicago: University of Chicago Press, 1975), 2; and "Fast Times," on "48 Hours" (CBS Television, March 8, 1990). Also see Eviatar Zerubavel, *Hidden Rhythms* (Chicago: Chicago University Press, 1981), for the best general sociological introduction to time.

12. Laura Leeta-Guy and Juliet Schor, "Is There a Time Squeeze? Estimates of Market and Non-Market Hours in the United States, 1969–1987" (unpublished paper, Department of Economics, Harvard University, November 1989). See also Lou Harris, "Americans Working More; Playing Less," *The Harris Survey*, no. 105 (1985); and Nancy Gibbs, "The Rat Race: How America Has Run Out of Time," *Time* (April 24, 1989): 58–67.

13. Buchmann, *Script of Life*, 70–76.

14. Kathleen Gerson, *Hard Choices* (Berkeley and Los Angeles: University of California Press, 1984), and her chapter in this volume; also see the case of Kathryn Colby, in Rand Jack and Dana Crowley Jack, *Moral Vision and Professional Decisions* (Cambridge: Cambridge University Press, 1989), chapter 5.

15. Young, *Metronomic Society*, 261.

16. Interviews conducted by Carmen Sirianni and Alise Young, March 1988; Gretl Meier, *Job Sharing* (Kalamazoo, Mich.: Upjohn Institute, 1978); Barney Olmsted and Suzanne Smith, *The Job Sharing Handbook* (New York: Penguin, 1983); Kathy English, *Options at Work: Case Study Series*, vol. 1 (1988–1989).

17. Felice Schwartz, "Management Women and the New Facts of Life," *Har-*

vard Business Review (January–February 1989): 65–76; also see Margaret Hennig's response in the May–June issue, and Vicki Smith, Kathleen Gerson, Carmen Sirianni, and Peter Stein, "Can Sociologists Contribute to the 'Mommy Track' Debate?" (panel discussion at the Eastern Sociological Society annual meeting, Boston, May 24, 1990).

18. Eileen Applebaum, "Restructuring Work: Temporary, Part-Time and At-Home Employment," in *Computer Chips and Paper Clips*, vol. 2, ed. Heidi Hartmenn (Washington, D.C.: National Academy Press, 1987).

19. In addition to Hochschild, with Machung, *The Second Shift*, see Sara Fenstermaker Berk, *The Gender Factory* (New York: Plenum, 1985), and Joseph Pleck, *Working Wives, Working Husbands* (Newbury Park, Calif.: Sage 1985).

20. Nancy Gibbs, "The Rat Race," 61; and Peter Hammond, quoted in Gibbs.

21. See Ulla Weigelt, "On the Road to a Society of Free Choice: Working Time Policy in Sweden," in *Working Time in Transition*, ed. Hinrichs, Roche, and Sirianni; and Sirianni's elaboration of the Rehn model in "The Self-Management of Time in Postindustrial Society" in the same volume.

22. Buchmann, *Script of Life;* and Martin Kohli, "The World We Forgot: An Historical Review of the Life Course," in *Later Life: The Social Psychology of Aging,* ed. Victor Marshall (Newbury Park, Calif.: Sage, 1985), 271–303.

23. Clifford Geertz, "Person, Time and Conduct in Bali," in *The Interpretation of Cultures* (New York: Basic Books, 1973), 360–411; Pierre Bourdieu, "The Attitude of the Algerian Peasant Towards Time," in *Mediterranean Countrymen,* ed. J. Pitt-Rivers (Paris: Mouton, 1963), 55–62.

24. Albert Hirschmann, "An Alternative Explanation of Contemporary Harriedness," *Quarterly Journal of Economics* 87 (November 1973): 634–37.

25. Benjamin Hunnicut, *Work without End* (Philadelphia: Temple University Press, 1988).

CHAPTER TWENTY-ONE

1. This chapter is based on ethnographic fieldwork carried out near San Diego in the early 1980s for the book *Habits of the Heart: Individualism and Commitment in American Life* (Berkeley and Los Angeles: University of California Press, 1985), jointly authored by Robert N. Bellah, Richard Madsen, William M. Sullivan, Ann Swidler, and Stephen M. Tipton. Very little of the material quoted here was used directly in *Habits*. The research included a series of in-depth interviews with twenty-seven local activists allied on both sides of local political conflicts over land regulations. From two to twelve hours of interviewing was done with each person. Detailed notes were taken of each interview, and, with the aid of the notes, a near-verbatim transcript of each interview was written up soon after the conversation. I have changed the names of those whom I interviewed.

2. Alasdair MacIntyre, *After Virtue* (Notre Dame, Ind.: Notre Dame Press, 1981), 236.

3. Personal observation by my sociologist friend from the University of Bologna, Paolo Mancini.

4. Bennett Berger, *The Survival of a Counterculture* (Berkeley and Los Angeles: University of California Press, 1982).

5. George Gilder, *Wealth and Poverty* (New York: Basic Books, 1982).

6. Herve Varenne, *Americans Together: Structured Diversity in a Midwestern Town* (New York: Teachers College Press, 1977), 92, 95.

7. See Richard Madsen, *Morality and Power in a Chinese Village* (Berkeley and Los Angeles: University of California Press, 1984).

8. Paolo Mancini, personal communication.

9. Thomas L. Pangle, *The Spirit of Modern Republicanism: The Moral Vision of the American Founders and the Philosophy of Locke* (Chicago: University of Chicago Press, 1988), 278.

10. Robert N. Bellah, Richard Madsen, William M. Sullivan, Ann Swidler, and Steven M. Tipton, *The Good Society* (New York: Knopf, 1991), chapters 2, 3.

11. Robert H. Wiebe, *The Segmented Society: An Introduction to the Meaning of America* (New York: Oxford University Press, 1975), 46.

12. Ibid., x.

13. Ibid., 39.

14. Ronald L. Jepperson and David H. Kamens, "The Expanding State and the U.S. 'Civic Culture': The Changing Character of Political Participation and Legitimation in the Postwar U.S. Polity" (Paper delivered at the annual meeting of the American Political Science Association, 1985).

15. Survey data on this "confidence gap" are summarized in Jepperson and Kamens, "The Expanding State," 7–9.

16. Bellah et al., *Habits of the Heart*, 275–96.

17. The concept of "subsidiarity" from Catholic social philosophy may provide a focus for a fruitful discussion about what kinds of social activities need to become more decentralized and what kinds more centralized. See Bellah et al., *The Good Society*.

CHAPTER TWENTY-TWO

1. A very recent effort, which seeks theory to explain how Americans think about theory, is Leslie Berlowitz, Dennis Donoghue, and Louis Menand, eds., *America in Theory* (New York: Oxford University Press, 1988).

2. See, for example, Erik Olin Wright, *Classes* (London: Verso, 1985).

3. See Immanuel Wallerstein, *The Modern World System: Capitalist Agriculture and the Origins of the European World-Economy in the Sixteenth Century* (New York: Academic Press, 1974). Ironically, the same language has been used by sociologists of a more conservative bent than Wallerstein. See Edward Shils, *Center and Periphery: Essays in Macrosociology* (Chicago: University of Chicago Press, 1975).

4. It has been particularly challenged by David Blankenhorn of the Institute for American Values. See for example, David Blankenhorn, "The Relationship of Public Policy to Family Well-Being," *American Family*, 11 (August 1988): 1–3.

5. There is anything but complete consensus on this issue. Groups such as U.S. English have challenged the notion that there ought to be more than one recognized language for official and public purposes.

6. Or Clermont-Ferrand. See Michele Lamont, "The Refined, the Virtuous, and the Prosperous: Exploring Boundaries in the French and American Upper-Middle Class" (paper presented at the 85th annual meeting of the American Sociological Association, Washington, D.C., August 1990).

7. See Michael J. Weiss, *The Clustering of America* (New York: Harper & Row, 1988). How food manufacturers recognized new markets for health-conscious consumers is the subject of Warren Belasco, *Appetite for Change: How the Counterculture Took On the Food Industry, 1966–1988* (New York: Pantheon, 1990).

8. On advocacy groups, see Kathryn C. Montgomery, *Target: Prime Time: Advocacy Groups and the Struggle over Entertainment Television* (New York: Oxford University Press, 1989). On the way television reflects in its programming cultural changes in the society, see Ella Taylor, *Prime-Time Families: Television and Culture in Postwar America* (Berkeley and Los Angeles: University of California Press, 1989).

9. Russell Jacoby, *The Last Intellectuals: American Culture in the Age of Academe* (New York: Basic Books, 1987).

10. Representative examples of this way of thinking include, for the question of aesthetic standards, Barbara Herrnstein Smith, *Contingencies of Value: Alternative Perspectives for Critical Theory* (Cambridge: Harvard University Press, 1988), and, for law, Stanley Fish, *Doing What Comes Naturally: Change, Rhetoric, and the Practice of Theory in Literary and Legal Studies* (Durham, N.C.: Duke University Press, 1989). An effort to examine the relevance of postmodernism to such matters as economic organization and urban life, themes very relevant to this book, is David Harvey, *The Condition of Postmodernity: An Inquiry into the Origins of Cultural Change* (New York: Basil Blackwell, 1989).

11. Walter Dean Burnham, *Critical Elections and the Mainsprings of American Politics* (New York: Norton, 1970).

12. Walter Dean Burnham, *The Current Crisis in American Politics* (New York: Oxford University Press, 1982).

13. Benjamin Ginsberg, *The Captive Public: How Mass Opinion Promotes State Power* (New York: Basic Books, 1986); Benjamin Ginsberg and Alan Stone, eds., *Do Elections Matter?* (Armonk, N.Y.: M. E. Sharpe, 1986); Benjamin Ginsberg and Martin Shefter, *Politics by Other Means: The Declining Importance of Elections* (New York: Basic Books, 1990); and Robert M. Entman, *Democracy without Citizens: Media and the Decay of American Politics* (New York: Oxford University Press, 1989).

14. Faye Ginsburg, *Contested Lives: The Abortion Debate in an American Community* (Berkeley and Los Angeles: University of California Press, 1989).

15. The former position, of course, is represented by E. D. Hirsch, Jr., *Cultural Literacy: What Every American Needs to Know* (Boston: Houghton Mifflin, 1987) and Allen Bloom, *The Closing of the American Mind: How Higher Education Has Failed Democracy and Impoverished the Souls of Today's Students* (New York: Simon & Schuster, 1987). (In listing these two books together, I do not mean to imply that the viewpoint of both authors is the same.) In contrast, in 1989 New York State Commissioner of Education Thomas Sobel released a draft report of a document called "A Curriculum of Inclusion," developed by his Task Force on Minorities, which argued that students in New York had been insufficiently exposed to the contributions of minorities and non-Europeans.

16. For example, Ivan Illich, *Deschooling Society* (New York: Harper & Row, 1971).

17. For an analysis of the impoverished theory of the human self in postmodern thought, see Luc Ferry and Alain Renault, *French Philosophy of the Sixties: An Essay on Antihumanism,* trans. Mary H. S. Cattani (Amherst: University of Massachusetts Press, 1990).

ABOUT THE CONTRIBUTORS

Fred Block teaches in the Department of Sociology at the University of California, Davis. His most recent books are *Postindustrial Possibilities: A Critique of Economic Discourse* (1990) and *Revising State Theory: Essays in Politics and Postindustrialism* (1987).

Gary Alan Fine is professor of sociology at the University of Georgia. He is the author of *With the Boys: Little League Baseball and Preadolescent Culture* (1987), which won the Opie Prize of the American Folklore Society, and *Shared Fantasy: Role-Playing Games as Social Worlds* (1983). His current research project is an in-depth study of the world of high school debate, focusing on socialization of argumentation and public discourse. Professor Fine has served as the chair of the American Sociological Association's Section on the Sociology of Culture.

Claude S. Fischer's books include *The Urban Experience* (1976, 1984), *Networks and Places: Social Relations in the Urban Setting* (1977), and *To Dwell among Friends: Personal Networks in Town and City* (1982). Currently a professor of sociology at the University of California, Berkeley, he is completing a book entitled *Person-to-Person: The Telephone, Community, and Modernity, 1880–1940*.

Herbert J. Gans is the Robert S. Lynd Professor of Sociology at Columbia University. Gans is the author of many books, including *The Urban Villagers* (1962, 1982), *The Levittowners* (1967, 1982), *People and Plans* (1968), *More Equality* (1963), *Popular Culture and High Culture* (1974), *Deciding What's News* (1979), *Middle American Individualism* (1988), and *People, Plans, and Policies* (1991). He has also been president of the Eastern Sociological Society and the American Sociological Association and has been elected to the American Academy of Arts and Sciences.

Kathleen Gerson is associate professor of sociology at New York University. She holds a Ph.D. degree from the University of California, Berkeley. Her writings include the book *Hard Choices: How Women Decide about Work, Career, and Motherhood* (1985) and numerous articles on gender, the family, and social change. She is currently completing a book, tentatively titled *The Uncertain Revolution,* on the transformation of men's family and work commitments in late twentieth-century America.

J. William Gibson is the author of *The Perfect War: The War We Couldn't Lose and How We Did* (1986) and coeditor of *Making War/Making Peace: The Social Foundations of Violent Conflict* (1990). His latest book, *Warrior Dreams: Para-Military Culture is Post-Vietnam America,* is forthcoming from Hill and Wang. Gibson teaches sociology at California State University, Long Beach.

David Halle teaches sociology at the State University of New York, Stony Brook, and at the University of California, Los Angeles. He is the author of *America's Working Man* (1984), an ethnographic study of working-class men in the oil refinery sections of Elizabeth, New Jersey. He is completing a book about culture and social class in a variety of neighborhoods in the New York area.

James Davison Hunter is professor of sociology and religious studies at the University of Virginia. Among his books are *American Evangelicalism* (1983), *Evangelicalism: The Coming Generation* (1987), *Making Sense of Modern Times* (1986), and *Culture Wars: The Struggle to Define America* (1991). He is also working, with Robert Coles, on a study of moral education in American life.

Jonathan B. Imber is Whitehead Associate Professor of Sociology at Wellesley College. The author of numerous articles and reviews in medical sociology, he is the author of *Abortion and the Private Practice of Medicine* (1986) and the editor of *The Feeling Intellect: Selected Writings of Philip Rieff* (1990).

Jack Katz teaches sociology at the University of California, Los Angeles, and is the author of *Poor People's Lawyers in Transition* (1982) and *Seductions of Crime* (1988).

Rebecca Klatch is assistant professor of sociology at the University of California, Santa Cruz. Her book *Women and the New Right* (1987) won the Victoria Schuck Award from the American Political Science Association. She is currently working on a book comparing left-wing and right-wing activists of the 1960s.

Bart Landry is associate professor of sociology at the University of Maryland, College Park, and the author of *The New Black Middle Class* (1987).

Richard Madsen is professor of sociology at the University of California, San Diego. He is the author or coauthor of several books on Chinese and American culture, including *Morality and Power in a Chinese Village* (1984) and (with Robert Bellah, William Sullivan, Ann Swidler, and Steven Tipton) *The Good Society* (1991).

Jay Mechling is professor of American studies at the University of California, Davis. He edited the annual bibliographic essay issue of the *American Quarterly* from 1974 through 1979 and edited *Western Folklore*, the journal of the California Folklore Society, from 1984 through 1988. He has authored or coauthored more than fifty essays and articles in books, journals, and encyclopedias.

Ruth Milkman teaches sociology at the University of California, Los Angeles, and writes frequently on workplace issues. She is the editor of *Women, Work, and Protest: A Century of Women's Labor History* (1985) and the author of *Gender at Work: The Dynamics of Job Segregation by Sex During World War II* (1987), which was awarded the Joan Kelly Prize in Women's History by the American Historical Association.

Katherine S. Newman teaches anthropology at Columbia University. Her book *Falling from Grace* (1988) is a study of middle-class downward mobility in the United States. She has also written *Law and Economic Organization* (1983).

Caroline Hodges Persell is the chair of the Department of Sociology at New York University. She is coauthor, with Peter Cookson, of *Preparing for Power* (1985), and has also written *Quality, Careers and Training in Educational and Social Research* (1976), *Education and Inequality* (1977), and *Understanding Society: An Introduction to Sociology*, 3rd ed. (1990).

John Steadman Rice is assistant professor of sociology at Boston University. He is a published poet, and he is currently working on a book about the co-dependency movement and therapeutic culture.

Frank Romo teaches sociology at the State University of New York, Stony Brook, and is a visiting scholar at the Russell Sage Foundation. Romo is currently finishing a book that is an ethnographic study of a mental institution, *Moral Dynamics: Social Networks, Conflict, and Coalition Formation in a Mental Institution*. He is also conducting a study of industrial growth and decline in New York State over the past twenty-five years.

Rubén G. Rumbaut teaches sociology at San Diego State University. He is the coauthor, with Alejandro Portes, of *Immigrant America: A Portrait* (1990). He is currently finishing a book, with Kenji Ima, called *Between Two Worlds: Southeast Asian Refugee Youth in America*, and co-editing a volume of essays, with Silvia Pedraza-Bailey, on *The American Mosaic: Race,*

Ethnicity and Immigration, Past and Present. His future projects include a comparative study of second-generation immigrant youth in San Diego and Miami.

Michael Schudson is professor in the Department of Communication and the Department of Sociology at the University of California, San Diego. He is the author of *Discovering the News* (1978) and *Advertising, the Uneasy Persuasion* (1984) and is the co-editor of *Reading the News* (1986) and *Rethinking Popular Culture* (1991).

Carmen Sirianni teaches sociology at Brandeis University. He is the author of *Workers Control and Socialist Democracy* (1982) and the forthcoming *Participation and Society.* He has also edited, with Frank Fischer, *Critical Studies in Organization and Bureaucracy,* (1984); with James F. Cronin, *Work Community and Power* (1983); *Worker Participation and the Politics of Reform* (1987); and, with Karl Hinrichs and William Roche, *Working Time in Transition* (1990). Sirianni cochairs the Study Group on Industry and Industrial Relations at the Minda de Gunzberg Center for European Studies at Harvard University, and co-edits the series *Labor and Social Change*, with Paula Rayman, published by Temple University Press.

Judith Stacey teaches sociology and women's studies at the University of California, Davis. She is the author of *Patriarchy and Socialist Revolution in China* (1983), which won the 1985 Jessie Barnard Award of the American Sociological Association and of *Brave New Families: Stories of Domestic Upheaval in Late Twentieth-Century America* (1990).

Gaye Tuchman teaches sociology at the University of Connecticut. She is the author of *Making News* (1978) and, with Nina Fortin, *Edging Women Out* (1989). She is editor of *The TV Establishment* (1974) and co-editor, with Arlene Kaplan Daniels and James Benet, of *Hearth and Home* (1978).

Andrea Walsh teaches sociology in the Social Studies Program at Harvard University. She is the author of *Women's Film and Female Experience: 1940–1950* (1950), and is the editor of the spring 1989 issue of *Qualitative Sociology*, "Sociology of the Screen." She is currently doing research on the representation of older Americans in popular film, and has recently completed an edited anthology, with Lynne Layton, *Women and Popular Culture.*

Alan Wolfe is the Michael E. Gellert Professor of Sociology and Political Science and dean of the Graduate Faculty at the New School for Social Research. Among his books are *The Seamy Side of Democracy* (1973), *The Limits of Legitimacy* (1977), *America's Impasse* (1981), and *Whose Keeper?* (1989), which was co-winner of the C. Wright Mills Award of the Society for the Study of Social Problems. He is at work on a book about the interpreting self and the meaningful society.

Sharon Zukin is professor of sociology at Brooklyn College and the Graduate Center of the City University of New York. Author of *Loft Living: Culture and Capital in Urban Change* (1982) and *Landscapes of Power: From Detroit to Disney World* (1991), she spent the 1989–90 academic year at the Russell Sage Foundation working on a study of blacks and Jews in New York.

INDEX

Compositor:	G&S Typesetters, Inc.
Text:	10/12 Baskerville
Display:	Baskerville
Printer:	Maple-Vail Book Manufacturing Group
Binder:	Maple-Vail Book Manufacturing Group